Texas Government & Politics
in the New Millennium
Third Edition

Texas Government & Politics in the New Millennium
Third Edition

VIRGINIA STOWITTS-TRAINA

Abigail Press   Wheaton, IL 60189

Design and Production: Abigail Press
Typesetting: Abigail Press
Typeface: AGaramond
Cover Art: Sam Tolia

Texas Government & Politics in the New Millennium
Third Edition, 2019
Printed in the United States of America
Translation rights reserved by the authors
ISBN 1-890919-96-9   978-1-890919-96-2

Contents in Brief

Table of Contents

PART II—THE FOUNDATIONS OF GOVERNMENT

CHAPTER ELEVEN
TEXAS CIVIL LIBERTIES & CIVIL RIGHTS

CHAPTER TWELVE
SOCIAL SERVICE PUBLIC POLICY ISSUES

MAPS, ILLUSTRATIONS, TABLES AND FIGURE

MAPS

ILLUSTRATIONS

TABLES

FIGURE

An Historical and Cultural Overview of Texas

Mission San Jose, 1927

Texas has always been defined as much by its myths as by its past. Perhaps more than any other state, Texas can claim a vibrant popular history, one that is familiar not only to natives of the state but to many people far beyond its borders. At the core of this popular history are such events as the revolution against Mexico, Indian wars, the cattle drives and the open range, and the oil-boom-episodes that are often cited as evidence of the state's unique frontier heritage and the spirit of individualism that it purportedly engendered. Yet these images are so deeply ingrained in the popular consciousness that they often tend to obscure other facets of the historical record. To regard Texas history as the narrative of Anglo males engaged in the process of triumphant conquest over alien enemies and a hostile environment is to provide an unbalanced and distorted view of the state's past. . . . The past can be seen from multiple perspectives, each valid in its own way, but necessarily incomplete. Only by adopting a more inclusionary approach can historians hope to present a reasonable complete version of the past.[1]

The political and social culture, as well as the economic state of modern-day Texas, has been to a large degree shared by its unique and colorful history. Unlike her sister states, Texas was governed and settled under six governing bodies, including a ten-year period as an independent nation. French and Spanish explorers set foot on Texas soil long before colonists arrived on the eastern shores of what was to become the United States. "When the Pilgrims landed at Plymouth Rock, Texas had already known the European and African for more than nine-tenths of a century."[2] Anglo-American migration began the wave of "colonists" to Texas. A large percentage of the arrivals came from the lower southern states, which introduced Texas to slavery, one political party affiliation, political conservatism, and governance by or with the consent of elites. Another large percentage of Texans are descendants of Spanish and Mexican settlers who resided in Texas long before the Anglo Americans crossed the boundary line. The European migrants included German, Swedish, Polish, Irish, English, Spanish, and numerous other nationalities who left their native lands to seek a better life. From different cultures, nationalities, and ways of life, they all had one thing in common, surviving the harshness of the frontier. Calling it the **frontier thesis**, noted historian Frederick Jackson Turner believed that the "Western American frontier functioned as a great lever of persons and a blender of cultures. On the frontier, people had to adapt to harsh conditions, confronting them by devising and sharing solutions to the problems they faced. People borrowed freely from the various cultures there and, in the process, developed a new American culture that contained significant contributions from the various participating cultures and society but was distinctly different from any of them."[3]

Native American Tribes in Texas

Of course, the first residents of Texas (or Tejas) were the Native American peoples. When the first European explorer put his foot on Texas soil, approximately thirty to forty thousand Indians inhabited the region. The major tribes included the Caddo, located in the eastern and northeastern sections of the state. Well advanced in agricultural skills, the Caddo were the most culturally advanced tribe in the region. "If the Comanches might be liken to the Asiatic Huns, the Caddos might crudely be called the Romans of Texas."[4] Predominately agriculturalists, they were considered to be the most advanced among the various tribes.

> Adopting a settlement pattern not unlike that found in much of East Texas to this day, the Caddos lived on scattered farmsteads, in small hamlets, and in a few larger towns. They built permanent, beehive-shaped residences of cane covered with grasses. A complete dwelling averaged forty to fifty feet in height and sixty feet in width, and its construction required the joint efforts of everyone in the community. Elevated beds lined the walls, mats covered the well-swept floor, and a fire always burned in the center. The Caddos used chipped-stone tools to clear trees and brush and to turn the soil. As in the building of the houses, the entire community planted crops, beginning with the fields of the elite and continuing down to those of ordinary members of the community.[5]

They also dabbled in trading with French and Spanish merchants and hunters. The Caddo tribes formed leagues

Indian Tribes of Texas

among their approximately two dozen tribes, to include the **Kadohadacho** and **Hasinai confederacies**. Under this arrangement the tribal chieftains selected a head chief who ruled over matters in common with the tribes while the individual tribes remained self-governing autonomous bodies. The Caddos are credited with giving Texas its name. "The Hasinai confederation called each other **Tayshas**, a term that meant 'allies' or 'friends.' When the Spanish came, the Hasinai let these wanderers know that they too were **Tayshas**, which the Spanish wrote as **Tejas**, latter to be transformed into Texas."[6]

South Texas was home to approximately two hundred small bands and tribes known collectively by their common language, **Coahuiltecan**. "While their exact number, location, and affiliation may never be known precisely, it appears that in south Texas there were four or five groups of tribes each composed of an ill-known number of bands. In some cases bands seem to have been independent, autonomous units, lacking any formal political connections with other groups; in other instances they were at least temporarily united under tribal leaders."[7] Now extinct, the various **Coahuiltecan** bands were inland groups while the **Karankawan** bands lived on the shores of the Texas coastline. Inland groups usually lived along the banks of rivers and streams. For example, the **Payayas** settled along the banks of the San Pedro Springs located in San Antonio, the **Aranamas** between the San Antonio and Guadalupe Rivers, the **Orejons** near the lower Neuces River, and the **Pachal** near the junction of the Frio and Neuces Rivers. Naming their village Yanaguana (place of spring waters), the Payaya Indians were the first Native Americans to be converted to Christianity by the Spanish

missionaries in San Antonio.[8] The **Capoques** who settled along the shores of Galveston Bay, the **Korenkake**, **Clamcoets** and **Carancaguacas** of Matagorda Bay and the **Kopano** of St. Joseph Island were among the largest of the Karankawan bands.

For Native American tribes, survival depended on their abilities to adjust to the harshness of the land dominated by the constantly changing whims of Mother Nature. "Few areas in North America were more difficult for hunters and gatherers to exploit or yielded more stubbornly its niggardly harvest than the brush and cactus country of South Texas. But the Coahuiltecans made an admirable adjustment to the restrictions and privations of their land with but crude and primitive tools and exploitative techniques. Their success, in the last analysis, was compounded of a willingness to utilize virtually everything in their environment that the human organism could digest, which in turn depended upon an intimate knowledge of their land—what each plant was good for, when fruits in certain places would be ripe, where elusive game could be taken."[9] Due to the harshness of the terrain, farming was, for all practical purposes, out of the question. Consequently, tribesmen were hunters and foragers, seeking small game and searching for nuts and fruits to supplement their diets. The Karankawan's survival was dependent upon the Gulf of Mexico's bountiful offerings of oysters, scallops, fish, porpoises, turtles, and an occasional alligator.

The buffalo-hunting tribes roamed the southern plains of central and northwest Texas. The Spanish introduced the Plains Indian to the horse. "The red man and the mustang formed an immediate partnership . . . and this union shook the life of the Great Plains, human and subhuman, like an earthquake."[10] The predominate tribes included the **Comanches**, **Lipan Apaches**, **Tonkawas**, and the **Kiowas**. A member of Philip Nolan's filibustering expedition into Texas in 1800 noted that "these red men have no towns, but roam over these immense plains, carrying with them their tents and clothing made of buffalo-skins. They raise no corn, but depend alone on the chase. Once a year they meet with their head chief on the Salt fork of the Colorado river, where he causes all the fire to be extinguished, and then makes new fire for the new year; and the bands also severely change their hunting-grounds."[11] Eventually it was the demise of the massive buffalo herds that drove the Plains Indians to the brink of starvation, desperation, and near extinction. The Apaches and Comanches were the most inhospitable of the tribes striking fear into the Anglo settlers in both Texas and the Southwest.

The **Jumanos** were a branch of the Pueblo Indians of New Mexico and Arizona. Whereas the Pueblos were sedentary agriculturalists, the Jumanos were initially nomadic tribes roaming the trans-Pecos area from present-day El Paso to the Rio Grande Valley region. Eventually, the Jumanos built villages similar to traditional Pueblo dwellings. The tribe was able to survive by combining farming with buffalo hunting.

Traditionally, Indians are usually portrayed in history books as hostile peoples bent on eliminating Anglo-American settlers. However, not all Indian tribes were hostile or naturally violent. The majority of the Spanish explorers found most tribes to be friendly. Initially, the Spanish "treated the Texas Indian as if he did not exist and for nearly two centuries neither used nor abused him."[12] The authors of *Texas: The Lone Star State* contend that the Indian, more often than the settler, determined the status of their relationship:

> If the natives were friendly, explorers and settlers found their way in the new country with ease; if they were docile, it was easy to exploit or at least to ignore their rights. If the natives were organized in weak and fragmentary alliances, settlers quickly drove them away; but if they were powerful and warlike, they retarded the advance of intruders for decades and even for centuries. Furthermore, native warriors largely determined the type of warfare that was carried out. The Caddo of the timber, the Comanche of the plain, and the Apache of the mountain all had different tactics, and the European and African Americans had to meet them in a fashion suited to the condition that prevailed.[13]

Texas had a so-called "Indian problem" in West Texas with the Comanches and Apaches until the late 1880s, ending with the capture of Geronimo, a great warrior and chief.

The Spanish Arrive in Texas

The Spanish were the first to discover Texas. In 1519 Alonso Álvarez de Pineda landed his four small ships and three hundred crew members at the mouth of the Rio Grande. Spending forty days on the Texas coast, the crew repaired their ships and explored the coastal area. Several minor expeditions followed. The most significant intrusion occurred in 1528. The Spanish government commissioned Pánfilo de Narvaez to embark from Cuba to the Texas coast to establish a colony. His crew of four hundred included **Álvar Núñez Cabeza de Vaca,** the

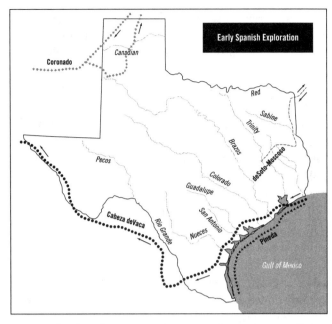

proposed colony's treasurer. In route, the entire expedition was shipwrecked. Several of the survivors, including de Vaca, washed up onto the sands of the Gulf Coast. As they began to explore their new surroundings, de Vaca and his comrades were among the first Europeans to encounter the Native American tribes of Texas. In his journal, de Vaca noted that the Indians were just as curious and suspicious of the Spanish as the Spanish were of them. As one of the crew members was leaving an Indian village,

> three Indians with bows and arrows followed and were calling to him, while, he, in the same way, was beckoning them on. Thus he arrived where we were, the natives remaining a little way back, seated on the shore. Half an hour after, they were supported by one hundred other Indian bowmen, who if they were not large, our fears made giants of them. . . . We endeavored the best we could to encourage them and secure their favor. We gave them beads and hawkbells, and each of them gave me an arrow, which is a pledge of friendship. They told us by signs that they would return in the morning and bring us something to eat, as at that time they had nothing. At sunrise the next day, the time the Indians appointed, they came according to their promise, and brought us a large quantity of fish with certain roots, some a little larger than walnuts, others a trifle smaller, the part got from under the water and with much labor. In the evening they returned and brought us more fish and roots. They sent their women and children to look at us, who went back rich with the hawkbells and the beads given to them and they came afterwards on the other days, returning as before.[14]

The survivors spent nearly eight years trying to find their way back to Mexico City. De Vaca and three others were the only ones to reach Mexico successfully. The adventures of the shipwrecked crew provided the Spanish with firsthand knowledge of the region. Published in 1542, de Vaca's documentary of his travels titled *La Relacion* (The Account), makes him the first to officially write about Texas. In particular, de Vaca heard about the tale of the **Seven Cities of Cibola**, where vast hordes of gold and silver were stored. The legend holds that these extremely wealthy cities were "settled by seven Portuguese bishops fleeing Muslim invaders in the eighth century."[15] The existence of the cities was confirmed by Fray Marcos who claimed to have seen one of them from a far distance. Of course, these tales were of great interest to the Spanish government in Mexico. Viceroy Antonio de Mendoza commissioned **Francisco Vásquez de Coronado** to find the cities and claim their treasures.

The expedition composed of 370 Spaniards and a large number of Indians departed in 1540 on foot and searched in vain for the fabled gold and silver. Along the way the Spaniards encountered a Plains Indian they nicknamed the "Turk" who vowed to show then the way to the golden cities. Reaching as far as present-day Kansas, members of the Coronado expedition became the first Europeans to see the majesty of the Grand Canyon. For the majority of their travels, however, they found nothing but rugged plains, disease, harsh weather conditions, and hostile Indians. Upon his return, Coronado issued a very dismal and discouraging report that reached the desk of Spain's King Charles I. The explorer wrote:

> For since I reached the province of Cibola, to which the viceroy of New Spain sent me in the name of Your Majesty, seeing that there were none of the things there of which Friar Fray Marcos told, I have managed to explore this country for 200 leagues and more around Cibola . . . It would not be possible to establish a settlement here, for besides being 400 leagues from the North sea and more than 200 from South sea, with which it is impossible to have any sort of communication, the country is so cold, as I have written to Your Majesty, that apparently the winter could not possibly be spent here, because there is no wood, nor cloth with which to protect the men, except the skins which the natives wear and some small amount of cotton cloaks.[16]

The Spanish government's days of the glory of conquest were diminishing. Confronted by the burden of maintaining an extensive empire, Spain found an obvious solution: abandon the idea of colonizing Texas and focus elsewhere in areas partially colonized and already tapped for natural resources, gold, and silver. In 1573, the King issued an order declaring that Spain's intentions in the New World including Texas, should focus more on the pacification of the Native American tribes rather than conquest. "For nearly 135 years after the conclusion of Vásquez de Coronado's expedition, Spanish authorities ignored the province of Texas. Content merely to claim the region as part of Spain's far-flung empire, they kept Texas outside the zone of immediate concern, the central corridor, which abounded with mines, ranches, presidios, towns and capital cities."[17] Despite the King's edit, the path taken by the Coronado expedition encouraged miners, ranchers, farmers, missionaries, adventurers, frontiersmen and soldiers to venture into areas beyond the Rio Grande River. "By 1598, for instance, Juan de Onate performed the requisite act of possession at El Paso de Norte as a preliminary step in his permanent occupation of New Mexico."[18] De Onate's efforts brought approximately "four hundred soldiers, missionaries, and settlers, including 270 women and children and more than seven thousand head of livestock" to El Paso.[19] Other settlements arose in Nuevo Leon and Coahuila. It is believed that the Spanish and not the English can lay claim to the nation's annual Thanksgiving traditions for on April 20, 1598, the residents of El Paso de Norte gathered to give their thanks, marking the first recorded formal Thanksgiving celebration in the Americas, twenty-three years before the Pilgrims landed at Plymouth Rock.

The French Presence

Texas counts the yellow and gold fleur-de-lis French flag as one of the six flags that flew over Texas. The French never really governed Texas nor did they make an earnest attempt at a permanent settlement. Their stay in Texas was short-lived yet long enough to wake up the Spanish to take some action to secure Texas before someone else's flag claimed the land. The French were already busy exploring the length of the Mississippi River, and had established valuable trading arrangements with various Indian tribes, including tribes located in east Texas. The major intrusion of the French into Texas occurred when Canadian trader and French explorer René Robert Cavelier, **Sieur de La Salle** crossed into Texas and explored as far as the Rio Grande. Without consulting Spanish authorities, La Salle claimed this vast territory for the King of France. Returning to France, La Salle

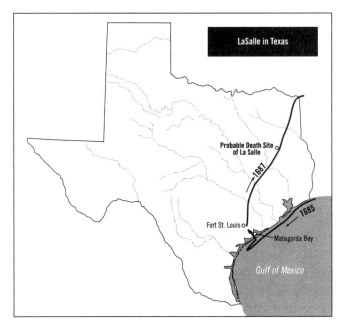

received the blessing of Louis XIV to establish a colony at the mouth of the Mississippi.

On paper, La Salle's accomplishments as an explorer and trader were impressive. Having already spent over twelve years exploring the Mississippi, Illinois, and Ohio Rivers and other areas of North America, La Salle was instrumental in establishing the shipping trade in the Great Lakes region. "Almost alone among the French in the New World, La Salle sought to understand Indian languages and cultures. Within three years of his arrival in Canada, he could speak at least eight Indian languages—an invaluable asset as he pushed into terra incognita."[20] The monarchy was impressed by La Salle's plan to "enter the Mississippi, push 180 miles upriver, build a fort, recruit 15,000 Indian allies, and strike against the Spanish forts and silver mines in northern Mexico."[21]

La Salle's expedition party consisting of four well-manned and heavily armed ships carrying approximately 200 potential colonists left France on August 1, 1684, with the anticipation of establishing a permanent foothold for the French at the southern mouth of the Mississippi River. However, La Salle's excursion would prove to be a devastating disappointment. Either from purposeful intent or lack of proper navigation, La Salle ended up at Matagorda Bay, Texas, on January 6, 1685, approximately 400 miles west of the Mississippi River. After building a crude stockade for his colonists (christened Fort St. Louis) on the banks of Gorcitas Creek, La Salle took a portion of his crew on a six-month exploring excursion. He left behind approximately 180 French men, women and children. Unfortunately, La Salle also left the colonists with dwindling food supplies and few weapons or tools

to defend themselves against hostile Indians. The priest at the fort wrote that "he [La Salle] was pleas'd to Honour me with the command, during his Absence, and left me an Inventory of all that was in our Habitation, consisting of Eight Pieces of Cannon, two Hundred Firelocks, as many Cutlaces, a Hundred Barrels of Powder, three Thousand Weight of Ball, about three Hundred Weight of other Lead, some Bars of iron, twenty Packs of Iron to make nails, and some Iron Work and Tools, as Hatchets and the like."[22] Upon his return, La Salle was dealt another severe setback. Holding in its cargo bay the remainder of the scarce supplies, the *Aimable* hit a sandbar and sank. "At this point a less stubborn commander might have given up the whole project. La Salle dispatched Beaujeu [one of his commanders] and the *Joly*, along with the crew of the *Aimable*, back to France. This left him with one ship, some 200 hapless colonists and few supplies, surrounded by hostile Indians. The next months read as a litany of failure and death. Settlers perished from illness and overwork, from eating prickly pear pads and from Karankawa arrows. . . . By July, 1685, half of the ill-fated colony was dead."[23] In 1686, the *Belle* was shipwrecked. This vessel was "La Salle's last chance. He could never have succeeded on the Texas coast without her. His whole enterprise depended on finding the Mississippi and settling the colony there. Without the *Belle*, that was no longer possible."[24] In total, his valiant attempt to establish a colony was an absolute disaster. La Salle decided to leave with the available able-bodied men, go eastward toward the Mississippi, and eventually, return to Canada to get help. La Salle never made it; he was killed by his own men. In 1688, the Karankawa attacked the fort, killed all but three of the remaining children, and left St. Louis a pile of rubble. In 1689, the remains of the colony were discovered by Spanish Governor Alonso de Leon of Cochuila. If La Salle accomplished anything in Texas, it was to shock the Spanish into action to put the territory permanently and securely under the Spanish flag. "Texas constituted a neglected frontier area that Spain vigorously defended in periods of crisis and ignored during interludes of peace."[25] French presence in Texas did indeed constitute a genuine crisis!

The Spanish Mission System

Concerned that another French intrusion was highly possible, the Spanish government decided to take immediate steps to establish permanent settlements. To attract colonists, the Spanish governor painted an extremely deceptive rosy picture of life in Texas. In his report to the

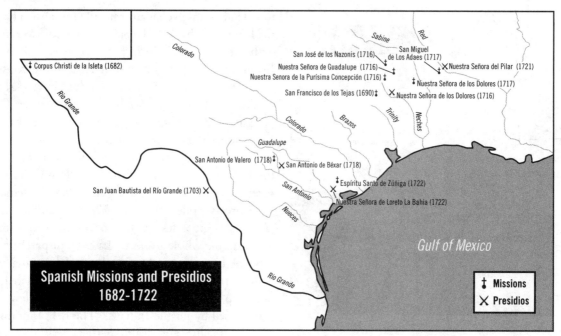

Spanish Missions and Presidios
1682-1722

‡ Missions
✕ Presidios

royal court in Spain, the governor housed in Mexico City, stated that in east Texas the "land was fertile; the climate salubrious; and the people were more highly civilized than most primitive groups."[26] This glowing report moved the Spanish government to bring the mission system to Texas. "The purpose of the mission was threefold: First, to convert the natives to Christianity [Catholicism]; second, to teach them the habits and customs of Spanish life and make them acceptable and self-sustaining subjects of the king; and third, to extend the influences of Spain and to hold the territory in its vicinity against all intruders."[27] The mission system was a unique partnership between the Spanish government and the Catholic Church. The Church would recruit and train the missionaries as well as maintain the missions. In turn, the Spanish government would pay the missionaries and cover the initial costs of establishing the missions.

The first Spanish mission in Texas was **Corpus Christi de la Iseta** built in 1682 near the present-day city of El Paso. In 1690, Father Massanet (who had originally accompanied de Leon) and de Leon himself left Mexico for east Texas. Their efforts produced the first Spanish mission in east Texas known as **San Francisco de las Tejas**, located in present-day Houston County. The Spanish soon learned from the Indians that the best locations for their missions were near or on the banks of major rivers. By the end of 1722, the Spanish had constructed nine missions in East Texas primarily near the Neches, Sabine and Trinity Rivers. However, the Spanish government soon realized that the cost of building new missions was prohibitive especially with the realization that the Native American tribes in the eastern part of the region were not enthralled

with mission life. Eventually, the Spanish government opted to selectively close and relocate missions to other areas of the region. Four of these missions were relocated to the south-central region near the banks of the San Antonio River. Originally built in Nacogdoches County in 1716, Mission Nuestra Senora de la Purisima Concepcion de Acuna commonly known as Mission Concepcion was relocated to San Antonio in 1731. In 1835, this mission was the site of the Battle of Concepcion, a minor clash between the regular Mexican army and Texas revolutionary forces. Relocated in 1731 to the banks of the San Antonio River, present-day **Mission Espada**, formally named Mission San Francisco de la Espada, is actually the original Mission San Francisco de Los Tejas. Originally built in 1716 once again, near Nacogdoches, **San Jose de los Nazonis** or more commonly known as **Mission San Juan de Capisrano** is located with the other missions along the banks of the San Antonio River. Celebrated as the 'Queen of the Missions', the proper name of **Mission San Jose** is Mission San Jose y San Miguel de Aguayo. Built in 1721, this mission is well known for its ornately carved Rose Window. The oldest mission in San Antonio is **Mission San Antonio de Valero**, commonly known as the **Alamo**.* This mission was originally established in 1700 as Mission San Francisco Solano near present-day El Paso by Father Antonio Olivares. It was closed in 1716 and moved to San Antonio.

*In 2015, all five of these missions were granted UNESCO status as World Heritage sites, guaranteeing them permanent preservation. With the exception of the Alamo regular church services are held in the mission chapels.

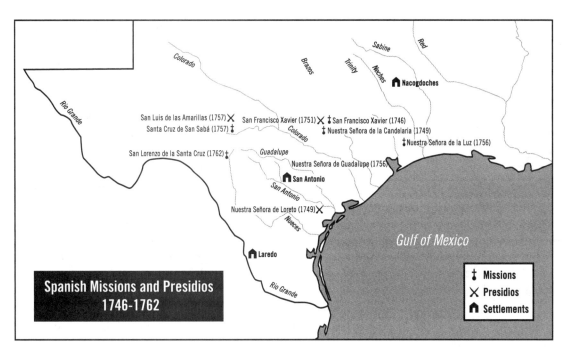

Spanish Missions and Presidios 1746-1762

‡ Missions
✕ Presidios
🏠 Settlements

Gulf of Mexico

Each mission consisted of a granary, textile shop, blacksmith, tannery, Indian and missionary housing, irrigated farms, a ranch, and, of course, the church. In 1785, Fray Jose Francisco Lopez was sent by the Spanish government to assess the progress of the missions. His very detailed report provides valuable information about each mission. At Mission San Francisco de la Espada, he noted that:

> The site of this mission is on the west banks of the river [San Antonio River], one half league from that of San Juan de Capistrano, one and a half leagues from San Jose, two and a half from Concepción. It lies between three and a fourth and four leagues down the river from San Antonio and the Royal Presidio, on a plain that is on the watershed, and is thickly covered with woods. The mission is square in shape and is surrounded by a stone and mud wall. Contiguous to these walls are the houses, mostly of stone and mud, where the Indians live. The missionary's house, the church, and the sacristy, which adjoin each other, take up half of the west side. They are of stone and lime and have sufficient room for all purposes. The church and the sacristy, on account of their superior construction and their ornaments and furnishings, are valued at three or four thousand pesos. On the south side stands the granary, which is of stone and mud, but which has enough room to meet its requirements. This mission, like the others, was very populous, but, . . . its population has fallen very much, as will be shown by the list of persons now living in it:

Married couples, 14, from 40 to 80 years of age . . 28
Widowers and widows, from 40 to 80 years of age..13
Bachelors and children, from 1 to 15 years of age.. 16
Total number of persons   57

These are descendents of the Pacao nation (which was fairly numerous when the mission was founded for its benefit, their language being the one most commonly used) and the Barrados Marahuitos.[28]

Basically, the missions were self-contained cities. The daily routine life within the missionary walls underscored that "the essence of the mission system was discipline: religious, social and moral. Days were structured, beginning with morning mass, singing and religious instruction. Men worked in the fields, gardens and shops and on ranches, some as many as 30 miles removed from the mission. Women learned to cook, sew and make pottery. Most clothing was made in mission workshops. Other supplies, including shoes, hats and necklaces, arrived once or twice each year from Mexico via [mule] train."[29]

The initial missionaries were members of the Franciscan Order, founded by St. Francis of Assisi, and traditionally followed the wishes of its founder to spread the word of God to all people, particularly the poor. The Franciscans chose plain, austere clothing rather than the ornate apparel of the other Orders. In the frontier regions of Texas, the Franciscan friars stood out among others in their plain bluish-gray cowls and habits, tied only with a plain white rope. Because horses were a materialistic taboo, the Franciscans used the mule or the donkey as their mode of transportation.

The process of converting the Indians to Christianity was a serious business. The Order established a series of colleges in Spain, beginning with the Apostolic College of Santa Cruz de Queretaro, to train missionaries. From a religious perspective, the initial step was to build the mission itself. The conversion process was a series of steps beginning with the formation of the congregation and ending with the pre-parish level. The whole process was to be completed in twenty years. "For the Indian converts who witnessed the secularization of a mission, the designation of parish denoted a change of their social status from wards of the state to *gente de razon* (rational beings) with law-living habits and civil responsibilities."[30] The Spanish government liked the Church's encouragement of civil responsibilities, especially to those reluctant to accept Spanish governing institutions and their laws. The mission system was viewed as "the most expeditious means of achieving the civilization of many tribes and peoples, who, influenced by the proximity of the settlements, or attracted by reasonable and polite dealings with the Spaniards, might without much difficulty, abandon their wild habits, become included to a more sociable life, and accept the catechism and Christian instruction."[31] The mission system relied heavily on a military presence commonly known as the **presidio**. Every mission was supposed to be protected by a garrison of well-trained soldiers. For example, the founding of Mission San Antonio de Valero was followed four days later by the opening of the Presidio San Antonio de Béxar. A properly staffed presidio meant, in many instances, a fairly successful mission effort. "These two institutions, representing the dual relationship of state and church, became the genesis of a modern metropolis—and a lasting tribute to the foresight and tenacity of a Franciscan missionary."[32] It was hoped that once the Indians were pacified by the missionaries and peace was guaranteed by the presence of a garrison of soldiers, settlers would come to Texas to build their ranchos and villas around the missions.

However, something went terribly wrong. The anticipated hordes of settlers never appeared. Only a few civilians made the treacherous journey from Spain to Texas. Perhaps the most successful colonization effort was the founding of present-day San Antonio. Located along the banks of the San Antonio River, "the first civil settlement in Texas was established in 1718. It consisted of 10 families under the protection of a military guard and was called Villa de Bexar."[33] In 1731, the population was augmented with the arrival of fifty-five colonists from the Canary Islands, known as the **Isleños**. Fearing further French intrusion into Texas, Florida, and in some areas of Louisiana, Philip V's government openly recruited volunteers from the Canary Islands to make the long ocean voyage across the Atlantic to form permanent settlements in Spanish-held territories. To entice them to come to Texas, the Council of the Indies showered them with incentives and privileges:

> Each of the Isleño founders . . . received a promotion in rank of nobility, carrying with it the title of **hidalgo**. Only the hidalgos had the right to hold places on the town council and to serve in other town offices, including sheriff (*alguacil*) and official secretary (*escribano de cabildo*). In addition, only these town officers could elect local alcaldes to administer justice . . . the Isleños received daily allowances during their first year in Texas, and they were provided with the seeds necessary for raising their first crop. Each family also received a quantity of sheep, goats, cattle and horses. In addition to the already cleared agricultural land given to them, Captain Almazan distributed among the Isleños other arable land as well as town lots on or near the main plaza of the new town.[34]

As evidenced throughout the Spanish Americas, the Spanish introduced their traditional social order upon their colonial possessions. One's place on the social ladder was dependent upon one's bloodlines and birthplace. The upper echelon was reserved for individuals born in Spain from the nobility—the **peninsulars**. Directly below them were the **criollos**, individuals of Spanish ancestry born in the New World. The Isleños, criollos, and the peninsulars were the landed aristocracy in the Spanish Americas. The **mestizo**, a person of mixed Spanish and Indian ancestry constituted the second social caste. The lowest rung of the ladder was reserved for the **casta**, a person of mixed Spanish, Indian and African ancestry, and Indians. A person from Mexico or of Mexican ancestry was known as a **Mexican**, and a Mexican residing in Texas was a **Tejano**. "By 1800 one can distinguish in San Antonio two broad social groups. One group was formed by the mass of the population, made up of poor late arrivals, Hispanicized Indians, and poor relations. Above them stood the better-off members of the community, most of who were descendants of the Islanders and original settlers, but also including merchants and a few other later arrivals who climbed to success. From this second group were drawn the ranchers, large-scale farmers, merchants, and politically active townsmen."[35] A census taken by the Spanish government in 1783 indicates that only 955 men, 777 women, 1,017 children and 36 slaves resided within the entire boundary of Texas.[36] However, the majority of the citizens hailed from Mexico, not Spain. Beginning with the abandonment of Mission Francisco de las Tejas, mission after mission closed its doors from east Texas to just north of San Antonio.

The mission system was at best, marginally successful in only a few instances. The system failed due to three basic problems. First:

> They [the Spanish] never did accomplish a lasting conversion of the Indians, who came and went almost at will. They [the Indians] would flirt with Christianity in the autumn, when cold weather was coming on and food and shelter through the winter were items for consideration. But with the first leafing out of the mesquites and huisaches, the Indians would drop their Christianity and take to the wilderness again.[37]

Marginal success was seen in San Antonio. "There was some success with the Coahuiltecans, who led such miserable lives that missions had something to offer them—although it seems to have been more material than spiritual."[38]

Second, the Spanish government did not devote all of its energies in support of the mission system. Too often the troops sent to Texas were ill-trained and substantially deficient in force to adequately protect the Franciscan friars or settlers from hostile Indians. The missionaries themselves lamented that "not only is the enemy not punished, repressed and taught a lesson, as in the past, but we behold, O Sorrow! These very troops so poorly governed that they turn in large part against us; and, leaving immune the former enemies, they even add to the damages caused by them [the Apaches], killing and destroying our cattle in one endless slaughter. While pretending to protect us, these troops only serve to inflict terrible punishment and reprisals upon us on the least provocation. . ."[39] Fearing that the military commitment was too costly, Philip V demanded that "the number of soldiers be reduced by more than half, a signal to the Indians that the Spanish were going to be less forthright in the colonization and defense of their Texas empire."[40]

Third, the biggest obstacle to a successful mission system was the Spanish government and its inability to exert any meaningful influence over Texas. The Spanish colonial governing system was very complicated. At home, the Spanish monarch did not exercise divine right authority instead he relied upon a cumbersome bureaucratic system of councils. The Council of the Indies was in charge of the American colonial activities. The Council had the authority to appoint all civil and ecclesiastic officials as well as approval of all legislation pertaining to the Americas.

In turn, the colonies including Mexico and Texas were governed by **viceroys**. Royal appointees, the viceroys exercised limited authority. Serving a five-year term of office, a viceroy was "always Spanish born, he received a high salary and usually came from the upper nobility, frequently the second son of an important family. Most of the viceroys turned out to be reasonably competent. Usually their appointments came as the result of court influence or as a reward for success in other royal activities, especially wars."[41] Within the colonies, the viceroys appointed various assorted governing officials. In 1720, the viceroy of both Coahuila [Mexico] and Texas was the Marqués of Valero who named the Marqués of San Miguel de Aguayo as governor for both provinces. The governor oversaw local governing units. Serving as the capital of the province of Texas, San Antonio de Bejar [later renamed Bexar] had "for its local government, a municipal council of two **alcades** [mayors], an attorney, all three elected, and six aldermen [councilmen]. La Bahía [Goliad] and Nacogdoches are commanded by lieutenants of the governor, assigned and replaced at his will; and the missions are governed by a corporal. In each town a company of cavalry is stationed."[42]

The vast distance between the Spanish court and the viceroys became too cumbersome for effective government. Spain refused to allow the viceroys to govern independently of the Spanish government. As Mexico was debating whether to launch a revolution against the Spanish government, in 1813, the few residents of Texas wrote a constitution demanding that they too should be separated from Spain. Texans justified their request by pointing out that

> a long series of occurrences, originating in the weakness and corruption of the Spanish rulers, has converted that monarchy into the theatre of

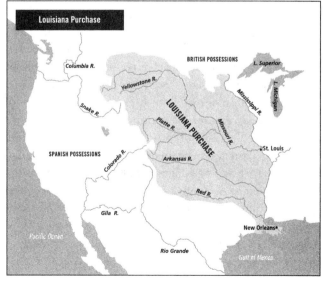

sanguinary war between two contending powers, itself destined the prize of the victor; a king in the power and subject to the authority of one of them, the miserable wreck of its government in the possession of the other, it appears to have most the substance and almost the form of sovereignty. Unable to defend itself on the Peninsula, much less to protect its distant colonies; those colonies are abandoned to the caprice of wicked men, whilst there exists no power to which they may be made responsible for the abuse of their authority, or for the consequence of the rapacity.[43]

The Spanish government simply could not govern the territory nor could they properly fulfill their obligations to the Catholic Church to protect the missionaries assigned to Texas. The combination of the harsh reality of the Texas climate and the elements, along with an Indian population less than thrilled with Christianity, and an underfunded and undermanned military effort coupled with a corrupt and ill-suited governing system on the part of the Spanish government, doomed the mission system in Texas.

The Empresario System

While the Spanish government was busy deciding what to do about Texas, the French government sold its territory of Louisiana to the United States in 1803. Settlers flocked into the Louisiana Territory, and on more than one occasion, crossed over into Spanish Texas. "A census of Nacogdoches in 1804 listed among the population sixty-eight foreigners, of whom fifty had lived in the area more than three years, thirteen of the fifty being originally or currently still Americans."[44] As early as 1812, the United States government desired to seize the Texas territory from Spain by openly backing a rebel force led by Jose Bernardo Gutierrez de Lara and Augustus Magee. Magee recruited a sizeable force under the banner of the Republican Army of the North. On March 29, 1813, Magee's 'army' successfully defeated the Spanish in the Battle of Rosillo, just outside San Antonio. Executing the Spanish governor along with a handful of prisoners drew the ire of the Spanish government. The Spanish Royal Army responded by decisively defeating Magee's 1,400 strong 'army' at the Battle of Medina on August 15, 1813. Other unsuccessful filibuster attempts were made by soldiers-of-fortune James Long and Philip Nolan. These military excursions into Spanish-held territory forced the Spanish government to take action to secure their North American holdings.

The Spanish government was caught in a quandary. Lacking the proper resources, officials realized they could not settle the area themselves. However, they were not willing to turn Texas over to the hordes of Anglo Americans just waiting for the opportunity to cross over that border. Whether settled by the Spanish or Anglo Americans, Spain did not have the will or the means to provide the proper infrastructure or the military man-power required to properly govern and protect a large settlement population. The dilemma was how to moderate immigration into Texas and, at the same time, secure colonists' safety without a costly commitment on the part of the Spanish government. The solution emerged with the **empresario system** whereby the Spanish government would give a large tract of land to a particular individual who, in turn, would offer parcels of it to settlers. Under both Spanish and Mexican rule, empresarios were "qualified personally to receive five leagues and five labors [for a total of 23,027.5 acres] for each 100 families they settled in Texas."[45] In return, the empresario, and not the Spanish government, would provide needed services including protection from hostile Indians.

On January 17, 1821, the Spanish government issued its first empresario land grant to Moses Austin, a land developer originally from Missouri. Austin agreed to bring three hundred families into Texas in exchange for a large tract of land, but he died before he could meet his contractual obligations. Subsequently, the task fell to his son, Stephen F. Austin. The situation was further complicated by Mexico gaining its independence from Spain on September 27, 1821. The renegotiated contract indicated that Austin's "acreage should be located on the coastal plain between the San Antonio and Brazos Rivers, that Mexico would grant 640 acres to each head of a family, 320 acres for his wife, 320 acres for each child, 80 acres for each slave. Essentially the land would be free, though Austin would collect 12.5 cents on the acre for his services."[46] In return, Austin had to supervise the colony, provide needed protection, and guarantee the good behavior of his colonists. Austin applied for additional land grants to bring in another nine hundred families. In recruiting his settlers, Austin set high standards:

> No one will be received as a Settler, or even be permitted to remain in the country [Texas] longer than is absolutely necessary to prepare for a removal who does not produce the most unequivocal and satisfactory evidence of unblemished character, good Morals, Sobriety, and industrious habits, and he must also have sufficient property to begin with either as a farmer or mechanic besides paying

for his land—no frontiersman who has no other occupation than that of a hunter will be received—no drunkard, nor Gambler, nor profane swearer, no idler, nor any man against when there is even probable grounds of suspicion that he is a bad man, or even has been considered a bad or disorderly man will be received.[47]

Once admitted into his settlement, Austin vowed that "those who are rejected on the grounds of bad character will be immediately ordered out of the country and if the order is not obeyed, they will be sent off under guard and their property seized and sold to pay the expense, and should forcible resistance be made by them, the guard will be ordered to fire on and kill them."[48] Unlike most empresarios, Austin dedicated the rest of his life to the development of Texas. Austin revealed his love of this rugged region and his own determination to settle it properly when he wrote: "I have been accused of having magnificent schemes for Texas, and I confess that I have had them. . . . It [Texas] is depopulated; I wish to people it. The population that is there is backward; I wish it to be advanced and improved by the introduction of industrious farmers, liberal republicans."[49]

Now a sovereign independent nation, the **Imperial Colonization Law** (1823) embodied Mexico's concept of the empresario program. Articles V and VII stipulated that "the measurement of the land shall be the following—the **vara**, at three geometrical feet; a straight line of five thousand varas shall be a **league**; a **square**, each of whose sides shall be one league; shall be called a **sitio**; . . . five sitios shall compose one **hacienda** . . . one **labor** shall be one thousand varas on each side."[50] The empresario was entitled to "three haciendas and two labors, for each two hundred families so introduced by him, but he will lose the right of property of said lands, should he not have populated and cultivated them in twelve years from the date of the concession. The premium cannot exceed nine haciendas, six labors, whatever may be the number of families he introduces."[51] Mexican officials also offered settlers another incentive—a tax abatement! As stated in the 1823 law, "during the first six years from the date of the concession, the colonists shall not pay tithes [taxes], duties on their produce, nor any contribution under whatever name it may be called. The next six years from the same date, they shall pay half tithes, and the half of the contributions, whether direct or indirect, that are paid by the other citizens of the empire. After this time, they shall in all things relating to taxes and contributions, be placed on the same footing with the other citizens."[52]

Since the majority of the immigrants were from the lower southern states, the Mexican government recognized that planters would, of course, bring their slaves with them. Consequently, the Mexican government allowed slavery in Texas. However, the Colonization Law stipulated that "there can be no sale or purchase which may be introduced into the empire. The children of slaves born in the empire shall be free at fourteen years of age."[53]

Green De Witt was granted an empresario agreement to bring 400 Catholic families into Texas. His grant specified that the "empresario shall not introduce into his colony criminals, vagrants, or persons of bad morals, and is such be found there he shall cause them to leave the republic, by force of arms if necessary."[54] The Mexican government also demanded that Green's empresario duties include the following:

He shall organize, in accordance with the law, the national militia, and he shall be commanding officer of it until other arrangements shall be made. When he shall have introduced at least one hundred families he must advise the government, in order that a commander may be sent to put the colonists in possession of their lands according to law, and to establish towns, for which he shall carry competent instructions. Official correspondence with the government or with state authorities, legal instruments, and other public documents must be written in Spanish, and when towns shall be formed, it shall be the duty of the empresario to establish schools in that language. It shall also be his duty to erect churches in the new towns; to provide them with ornaments, sacred vessels, and other adornments dedicated to divine worship; and to apply in due time for the priests needed for the administration of spiritual instruction. In all matters not here referred to he shall be governed by the constitution, the general laws of the nation, and the special laws of the state which he adopts as his own . . .[55]

In 1825, Haden Edwards received a grant to bring 800 families into an area near Nacogdoches, the oldest city in Texas. "Between 1821 and 1835, a total of forty-one empresario contracts were signed, permitting some 13,000 families to come to Texas."[56]

Rightfully named the "Father of Texas," Austin, his fellow empresarios, and the Mexican government accomplished what the Spanish tried in vain to do—colonize and settle Texas. "By 1836, the population of Texas stood at 35,000 to 50,000 people, living primarily in East Texas and along the upper Gulf Coast."[57] This census, however, revealed some ominous trends for the Mexican government by reporting that "about 10 percent [of the population] were black [African American], 7 percent Mexican and 28 percent Indian. The remaining 55 to 60 percent were Anglo-American."[58]

The Texas Revolution

The long lasting Texas myth begins with the Texas Revolution, as "patriots" such as Davy Crockett, James Bowie, William Barrett Travis, and Sam Houston become larger than life. The exploits of the Texas heroes have been portrayed in books, television productions, and movies. The chapel of Mission San Antonio de Valero is the famous Alamo that has become the symbol of Texas freedom and fierce rugged determination. The legend holds that the ghosts of the martyred defenders of the Alamo roam its sacred halls at night with Davy Crockett occasionally appearing to straighten a leaning painting. The Texas Revolution made Sam Houston a national hero to the point that he was a serious contender for the United States presidency. The myth, however, has been allowed to overshadow the reality of the events leading up to and during the Texas Revolution.

First, it is so easy to see the entire revolution as just two major encounters with the Mexican army—the Alamo and the ending battle at San Jacinto. It was a short revolution lasting only seven months. But in that time frame, there were numerous military skirmishes and battles that nearly destroyed that frontier spirit Texans are so prideful of. Second, while it was indeed a heroic standoff between the Texans and the Mexican army, the preeminent heroes of both the Alamo and the Texas Revolution were no candidates for sainthood. A wanted man, Bowie was a land speculator and slave trader. Hailed from Tennessee, Davy Crockett came to Texas after losing a bid for political office. The revolution's commander, Sam Houston had a notorious temper and fondness for the bottle. William Travis, the commander of the Alamo, deserted his pregnant wife and young child, leaving her saddled with a mountain of debt. Third, the myth portrays the entire revolution as a "them versus us" battle between Anglo Americans and Mexicans with each group clearly on different sides of the issues. Many Mexicans or Tejanos fought by Travis, Bowie and Crockett and suffered the same fate from the Mexican army. A room in the Alamo displays the various flags of the countries and states of origins of those who died in the battle for Texas freedom. Nestled among those flags is the Mexican flag. Texans should not forget that it was Colonel Juan Seguín who formed the Second Company of Texas Volunteers who fought at San Jacinto. Nor should we overlook that at the Consultation at San Felipe held on November 7, 1835, Tejanos were at the table in support of severing ties with Mexico. The official declaration of Texas independence signed four months later at the provisional capitol of Washington-on-the-Brazos bears the signatures of Jose Antonio Navarro and Fransicso Ruiz, both Texans born of Mexican/Spanish heritage.

The separation of Texas from Mexico was inevitable. Both sides misunderstood each other and made mistakes that could not be righted to bind them together. Initially, Anglo-American settlers in Texas were pleased with the laissez-faire attitude of the Mexican government. Few restrictions were placed upon them, and violators were rarely punished, if at all. Taxes were the exception rather than the rule. The Mexican government did stipulate that new settlers pledge their loyalty to the Mexican government. Technically, a man living in Texas gave up his rights to be an American citizen since he was now residing in Mexico. All settlers were required to join the Catholic faith, the national religion of Mexico. Neither the Mexican government nor the Anglo Americans took the religious oath seriously. "And the nice thing about being a non-Catholic in Texas was that the Mexican priesthood was understaffed and haphazard. Priests came around once every three to four years, sanctified the unions of act, baptized and legitimatized the issues of such unions, and then disappeared for another several years. They were hardly a factor in anyone's religious life."[59] Also, the Mexican government could have started a big ruckus over slavery and the continual flow of slaves into Texas. In 1829, the Mexican government proclaimed the emancipation of all slaves and prohibited it in all of its lands. Southern slave owners already in Texas protested this action; subsequently, the Mexican government acquiesced, exempting Texas from the anti-slavery requirement. The initial practices of the Mexican government suited the Anglo-American settler. The frontiersman carried the traditional American conservative position on the proper role of government. Basically, "on the one hand, the American frontiersman thought government should leave him alone and not interfere in his actions; on the other, he believed his government should stand ready to lend a hand if the load proved too heavy."[60] This is the same philosophy pervading the conservative political thought for the majority of today's Texans.

The lax policies of the Mexican government did not last for long. Fearful of the continuous flow of Anglo Americans into Mexico, the government issued a series of restrictive measures collectively known as the **Law of April 6, 1830**. The Mexican government abruptly forbade further American immigration into Texas. Slave owners were advised that future importation of slaves was prohibited. Trade with the United States was forbidden, with any items imported into Texas subjected to custom duties. Enforcement was ensured with the addition of Mexican investigators or custom agents, and the strengthening of Mexican garrisons stationed in Texas. To offset the growing Anglo-American population, the Mexican government passed a series of laws encouraging Mexican nationals to settle in Texas. Although the ban on American immigration was lifted in 1834, the seeds of discontent and revolution had been sown.

The deterioration of relations between the Mexican government and her colonists was enhanced by cultural differences, mistrust, and suspicion on the part of both parties. "At the bottom of the Texas trouble one fact remained: the Americans could not understand why the Mexicans feared them or why they would not let the Anglos have their own way in a land they so obviously dominated. And for their part, the Mexicans came to completely mistrust the Americans and failed to share their feelings of Anglo righteousness. In the end a kind of racial as well as political repugnance developed."[61] Under Spanish rule, and "before the arrival of the Anglo-Americans, these descendants of Indian, Canary Islander, Spanish and other European bloodlines had enjoyed an isolated and insulated existence."[62] Basically, Mexicans and Tejanos felt that their way of life was under siege. Initially, Mexican authorities believed that Anglo Americans should at least be thankful for the generosity and kindness extended to them by the Mexican government. Through empresario grants and cheap land prices, the Mexican government practically gave away millions of acres of very fertile land conducive to the agricultural and ranching needs of Anglo- American settlers without asking too much in return. Mexican citizens began to see Texas becoming more of an extension of the United States than as a providence of Mexico. "Spanish was eventually replaced by English as the lingua franca (common language) of Texas, a cash economy replaced a barter economy, and the Anglo-Americans eventually imposed a judicial system that was foreign to the Tejanos and often did not recognize traditional claims of land ownership."[63] In 1828, Manuel Mier y Teran wrote a letter to the president of Mexico expressing his concerns about the eroding relationship between the people of Mexico and Anglo-American settlers:

As one covers the distance from Bejar to this town [Nacogdoches], he will note that Mexican influence is proportionately diminished until on arriving in this place he will see that it is almost nothing.

And indeed, whence could such influence come? Hardly from superior numbers in population, since the ratio of Mexicans to foreigners is one to ten; certainly not from the superior character of the Mexican population, for exactly the opposite is true, the Mexicans of this town comprising what in all countries is called the lowest class—the very poor and very ignorant. The naturalized North Americans in the town maintain an English school, and send their children north for further education; the poor Mexicans not only do not have sufficient means to establish schools, but there are not of the type that any thought for the improvement of its public institutions or the betterment of its degraded condition. Neither are there civil authorities or magistrates; one insignificant little man—who is called an *alcalde*. . . . It would cause you the same chagrin that it has caused me to see the opinion that is held of our nation by these foreign colonists, since, with the exception of some few who have journeyed to our capital [sic], they know no other Mexicans than the inhabitants about here. . . . Thus I tell myself that it could not be otherwise than that from such a state of affairs should arise an antagonism between Mexicans and foreigners, which is not the least of the smoldering fires which I have discovered. Therefore, I am warning you to take timely measures. Texas could throw the whole nation into revolution.[64]

The first signs of revolt occurred near the Louisiana border when Benjamin Edwards, brother of empresario Haden Edwards, attempted to cut a deal with the Cherokee Indians to join forces to overthrow the Mexican government in Texas. If successful, the revolt would have severed a portion of Texas from Mexico to be hailed as the Republic of Fredonia. Joined by Stephen F. Austin, Mexican troops squashed the rebellion as Edwards fled back to the United States. A potentially more productive action was developing at the same time as prominent leaders such as Austin decided to meet to devise a plan for a peaceful solution or, if all else failed, a plan for war. The initial meeting of the Convention was held at San Felipe on October 1, 1832. The delegates selected Stephen F. Austin as their president. The attendees focused primarily on petitioning the Mexican government to reverse the prohibition against Anglo-American immigration. The Convention delegates petitioned for a three-year tariff exemption and mandated that custom agents must be chosen by local authorities and not by the Mexican government. Their requests, however, were never entertained by the Mexican government since authorities considered the entire "convention" to be a violation of the Mexican Constitution. Steadfastly, the delegates decided to meet the following year at San Felipe.

At this gathering Stephen F. Austin systemically laid out the major complaints against the Mexican government. Austin emphasized that it was the immigrants and not the Mexican government that ultimately settled and secured Texas for Mexico. While acknowledging the initial kindness of the Mexican government, Austin praised the immigrants who had "faithfully performed their duty as Mexican citizens, and fulfilled the intention and spirit of colonization laws, by settling the country, defending it from hostile Indians, or other enemies, and developing its resources, thus giving value and character to a large section of the Mexican territory which was before wild and almost unknown."[65] In return for their sacrifices, Austin emphasized that "the people of Texas ought therefore to rely with confidence on the government for protection, and to expect that an adequate remedy will be applied to the many evils that are afflicting them."[66] The long list of complaints included the inability of the Mexican military to adequately protect settlers from Indian raids, the ineptness of the Mexican bureaucracy, the distance between local governments and Mexico City, and the general lack of efficient and effective government. Basically, Austin called for the Mexican government to repeal the Law of April 6, 1830, and end the corruption of the alcaldes. In particular, Austin strongly objected to Mexico's system of justice by pointing out that "it has become proverbial in Texas that an appeal to Saltillo [the headquarters for the Supreme Tribunal of the State] is a payment of a debt. It amounts to a total denial of justice especially to the poor, and this is the frail tenure by which the most important rights of the people of Texas are suspended."[67] Convention attendees drafted a response to the Mexican government outlining their concerns, recommending remedies, and, if all else failed, their proposal to form a separate state under the Mexican flag. The document states "that the union which was established between Coahuila and Texas . . . may be dissolved, abrogated, and perpetually cease; and that the inhabitants of Texas may be authorized to institute and establish a separate statement, which will be in accordance with the federal constitution [of Mexico] . . . and that the state so constituted shall be received and incorporated into the great confederation of Mexico, on terms of equality with the other states of the union."[68] The delegates also drafted a proposed constitution for the new state of Texas. Despite these two conventions, many Texans were still deeply divided as to the proper course of action. "Roughly the country people constituted a peace element, and the town dwellers, with many new immigrants from the United States who had arrived too late to receive bonafide land titles, made up the war group."[69] Contemplating a peaceful solution, Austin was chosen to deliver the documents to Mexico City. The Mexican government, however, showed their displeasure with both the Convention and its recommendations by arresting and charging Austin with treason. He spent nearly two years in a Mexican prison.

The initial battle of the Texas Revolution was fought over the ownership of one small cannon. Colonel Domingo de Ugartechea, the Mexican military commander stationed in San Antonio, sent five men to Gonzales to retrieve a six-pounder cannon, loaned to the townspeople five years earlier to handle an Indian problem. Seeing this as an act of punishment and retaliation, the alcalde of Gonzales hid the cannon. Returning to San Antonio empty-handed, Ugartechea regrouped and sent a force of one hundred to seize the weapon. On October 2, 1835, the defiant Texans attached a sign to the cannon with the inscription "Come and Get It" and fired it on the surprised Mexican soldiers, killing one. This action officially launched the Texas Revolution. With their first military victory behind them, a force of 300 volunteers under the leadership of Ben Milam headed for San Antonio. "The four-day battle was the longest and most evenly balanced of the war, but finally the Texans—minus Milam, who was killed by a bullet through the brain—succeeded in expelling the Mexican forces."[70] The victorious Texans convinced General Martin Perfecto Cós to gather up his men and head back to Mexico!

In many respects one wonders how Texas survived and actually won its independence. The action in Gonzales threw the Texans into a confusing tailspin. Obviously, they lacked an organized leadership, a government, and, most importantly, an army with someone to lead it. Several of the delegates to the original conventions met once again on November 7, 1835. They renamed themselves the Consultation. With the understanding that Mexico would probably take punitive actions against them, the delegates opted to create an interim Permanent Council charged with creating a provisional government for Texas. Realizing they could not defeat the Mexican military by themselves, the Council sent Thomas McKinney to Washington, D.C., to ask for money and manpower. The Consultation voted initially to avoid complete separation from Mexico by declaring their loyalty to the Mexican Constitution of 1824 and proposing a separate state of Texas within the Mexican Republic. Falling short of a direct declaration of war, the Consultation drafted the "Texas Declaration of Causes for Taking Up Arms Against Santa Anna," the current president of Mexico. Prominent settler Henry Smith was elected provisional governor, and Sam Houston was designated as commander of the military. Having completed their tasks, the delegates decided to reconvene at Washington-on-the-Brazos on March 1. The provisional government was unfortunately a very weak one and left Texans wondering who was actually in charge of both the government and a revolution. Meanwhile, Sam Houston had problems of his own. The Texas army was far from a unified group; small armies were sprouting up all over the place operating under their own elected commanders, including many who lacked military experience, like Stephen F. Austin. Usually, "generals have to fret over how to make their men fight. Houston had the opposite problem: how to keep his men *from* fighting. His predicament wasn't helped by the squabbling that continued to afflict the provisional government."[71] Furthermore, Houston knew that turning a band of independent sharp shooting frontiersmen into a fine turned army would not happen overnight. What Houston needed was time.

While the Texans were trying to figure out who was actually in charge, the Mexican political scene changed rapidly. Before he became president, Santa Anna openly endorsed the liberal Mexican Constitution of 1824. Once he assumed the office, he replaced it with a centralist document, resigned the presidency, and became commander of the Mexican army. Bent on stopping the antics of the rebellious Anglo-Americans, Santa Anna, the self-proclaimed Napoleon of the West, marched across the Rio Grande. Before assuming the presidency, Santa Anna was already hailed as a military genius, the liberator of Veracruz, and a war hero from the battlefields of Veracruz and Tampico. While most Texans know him as the mastermind behind the Mexican victory at the Alamo, few can recall that at one time, he was the most powerful *caudillo* (military dictator) of his time. Despite periodic defeats that caused him public scorn, he was president of Mexico six times: 1836, 1839, 1841-1843, 1843-1844, 1846-1847, and 1853-1855. He preferred the battlefield to the presidential mansion. His military skills were commendable and formidable. "If not the most brilliant of military strategists in history, Santa Anna was perhaps the most vain. The general's uniform contained enough silver on the epaulets and frogging for an entire set of dinner spoons; he rode on a saddle with gold-plated trim; and at this side, hung a seven-thousand-dollar sword."[72] Sam Houston had cause for alarm. "Military experts have long praised Santa Anna as a master of logistics, a man who could take troops into forbidding country in the north of Mexico and the south of Texas in the middle of winter and somehow live off a land with nothing to give. Determined

Sam Houston

not to be outdone by aberrant Texans, Santa Anna came with the single purpose of exterminating the gringos . . . ."[73]

Santa Anna encountered the gringo rebels in San Antonio at the Alamo. The siege and eventual fall of the Alamo thirteen days later has been portrayed as an heroic standoff by a small band of brave Americans against the overwhelming manpower of the Mexican army. However noble and brave their actions were, the rationality of the deed is questionable. "Why a force of 187 men, which the Alamo subsequently came to number, would give everything to stop a force of 5,000 men who were bound to win defies logic. Why Santa Anna, with all of his generalship, would tie up 5,000 men for two weeks when all he had to do was march around the Alamo, leaving a small holding force behind, and catch the Texans deeper into the interior also is difficult to discern."[74] Experts believe the Alamo was indefensible in the first place. The Alamo "lacked proper parapets to shelter the troops holding the walls, had not bastions to permit flanking fire to enfilade attacking enemy troops, and had a wholly impossible trace, the outer perimeter actually being too long not only for the number of men available, but also given the amount of space which it enclosed."[75] Houston believed defense of the Alamo was hopeless. On more than one occasion, he ordered the Alamo to be blown up and the soldiers attached to the Alamo reassigned to the main force of the Texas army. Ironically, Houston ordered Bowie to carry out his orders. In a letter to provisional Governor Henry Smith, Houston stated that "if you should think well of it, I will remove all the cannon and other munitions of war to Gonzales and Copano, blow up the Alamo and abandon the place."[76] But petty jealousies intervened as the commander of the Alamo's forces, William Barrett Travis, determined to prove that he was a better military expert than Houston, decided to stay and take on the 5000-man army of Santa Anna. Bowie sided with Travis, responding back to Smith that "the salvation of Texas depends in great measure in keeping Bejar [Bexar] out of the hands of the enemy. . . These citizens deserve our protection, and the public demands our lives rather than to evacuate this post to the enemy."[77]

The siege began on February 23, 1836. Finally, realizing he was grossly undermanned, Travis sent courier after courier to Houston requesting additional troops. Travis's famous "victory or death" speech only brought a handful of desperately needed men to the gates of the fortress. Camped in Goliad, Colonel James Fannin could not decide whether to make the march to San Antonio or stay in Goliad. A message delivered by one of Fannin's couriers on March 1, 1836, informed Col. Travis that "Colonel Fannin with 300 men and 4 artillery pieces has been en [in] route to Bejar [Bexar] for three days now. Tonight we are waiting for some reinforcements from Washington [a settlement in Texas], Bastrop, Brazoria and San Felipe, numbering 300, and not a minute will be lost in providing you assistance."[78] Travis rightfully informed the defenders that help was on the way. But Fannin's men and artillery pieces never arrived! Houston absolutely refused all of Travis's requests. Playing the "El Deguello" for "take no prisoners," the Mexican army launched its final deadly assault. All 187 of the Alamo defenders died on March 6, 1836, while Santa Anna lost between three to six hundred men. It now appeared that Santa Anna was unstoppable. However, just like his hero Napoleon Bonaparte, he too met his Waterloo. After his victory at the Alamo, Santa Anna made his fatal strategic blunder by dividing his powerful army into a three-column advance moving in different directions to conquer city after city. Santa Anna left Houston for himself.

The fallen heroes at the Alamo did not know that on March 2, the Consultation convened in Washington-on-the-Brazos and officially declared its independence from Mexico. The document rehashes the various faults of the Mexican government and also echoes the sentiments of James Madison, Thomas Jefferson, George Washington, Alexander Hamilton and John Locke's theory of the social contract that the Framers used to justify their decision to severe their relationship with England:

When in consequence of such acts of malfeasance and abduction on the part of the government, anarchy prevails, and civil society is dissolved into its original elements, in such a crisis, the first law of nature, the right of self-preservation, the inherent and inalienable right of the people to appeal to first principles, and to take their political affairs into their own hands in extreme cases, enjoins it as a right towards themselves, and a sacred obligation to their posterity, to abolish such government, and create another in its stead, calculated to rescue them from impending dangers, and to secure their welfare and happiness.[79]

After drafting a constitution, the delegates named David Burnet provisional president and Sam Houston as the only commander-in-chief of the army. March 2 is officially celebrated as Texas Independence Day.

The next major defeat for the Texans happened at Goliad, where James Fannin was positioned with 350 desperately needed troops. On several occasions Fannin was ordered to leave and combine his troops with the major forces. Fannin would give the orders to march one day and cancel them the next. When he finally decided to leave Goliad, he marched his troops right into the middle of the Mexican army. Fannin surrendered with a promise from the Mexican commanders of "parole and transportation to New Orleans."[80] On Santa Anna's orders, all 350 were "released," only to be executed in the back as they ran. "The men were taken out in four divisions, and under different pretexts; such as, making room in the Fort for the reception of Santa Anna, going out to slaughter beef, and being marched off to Copano to be sent home. In about an hour, the closing scene of this base and treacherous tragedy was acted in the Fort; and the cold-blooded murder of all the wounded, who were unable to march out, was its infernal catastrophe."[81] Col. Fannin was the last to be executed. The massacre would have been worse if not for the efforts of Senora Francisca Alverez, the common-law wife of one of Santa Anna's captains. Called the Florence Nightingale of the Texas Revolution, she "persuaded soldiers to free about 20 of the men, and after the Goliad Massacre, she helped some 40 other soldiers escape in Victoria and the nearby port of Copano."[82] The Texas army continued to suffer defeat after defeat at San Patricio, Agua Dulce, Refugio, and Victoria.

The frightening brutality of the advancing Mexican army coupled with the reality that the Texas army was incapable of mounting a single victory began to take its toll on both the Anglo Americans and Mexican Nationals supporting the Texan cause for independence. Settlers were now refugees fleeing their homelands as they rushed towards the Louisiana border. "Loading their wagons, oxcarts, or sleds, or taking such simple belongings as could be carried on horseback or even on foot, the people set out in a desperate rush to keep ahead of the Mexican army. Streams were swollen, ferries became jammed, epidemics prevailed, and the misery and suffering were indescribable."[83] Known as the **Runaway Scrape**, thousands fled in sheer panic and unorganized confusion. Even the provisional government fled from Washington-on-the-Brazos to Harrisburg.

The dismal military situation prompted Sam Houston to retreat to the northeastern part of Texas. At best the Texas army consisted of only seven to eight hundred men and two major artillery pieces known as the **Twin Sisters**. Houston decided that his only option was to stage a forced retreat. Oddly enough, Santa Anna followed as Houston moved his army closer and closer to the Louisiana border. As the Texans retreated, Houston ordered a "scorched earth" strategy, burning everything behind them. Subsequently, Santa Anna's plan to follow Houston cut off the Mexican army from their supply lines and the burning fields and houses denied the tired and hungry soldiers shelter and food. Some branded Houston's retreat as a cowardly act. President David Burnet angrily condemned Houston's actions. "The enemy are laughing you to scorn,' he wrote, 'You must fight them. You must retreat no farther. The country expects you to fight. The salvation of the country depends on you doing so."[84]

On April 20, 1836, General Sam Houston, with his growing army of approximately nine hundred, took a position near the junction of the San Jacinto River and the Buffalo Bayou. Houston's scouts had been keeping track of Santa Anna's forces, which now numbered about sixteen hundred with the addition of General Cos's five hundred men. To the Texans surprise, Santa Anna was so close that they could view the Mexican army's camp. Santa Anna, however, committed a fatal military mistake. "Although Santa Anna had the Texans boxed in, he too was shut off on three sides, with the enemy less than a mile in front and already poised for an attack. The San Jacinto River on Santa Anna's right and swampy terrain behind him would make a disciplined retreat impossible."[85] And, Santa Anna decided to give his troops the day off to rest.

Seizing the opportunity, Houston called his forces to the attack. Yelling the battle cries of "Remember the Alamo and Goliad," the Texas army with the Twin Sisters firing away, charged the ill-prepared Mexican army. "The Mexicans, raked with grapeshot, horseshoes, and musketry, fell in heaps; some dropped their weapons in panic and fled to the rear, disorganizing units still being formed . . . Mexicans fought screaming Texans, flailing away in hand-to-hand combat . . . ."[86] The battle was over in just eighteen minutes! Santa Anna's losses included 630 dead, 208 wounded, and 730 captured, whereas the Texans counted 8 dead and 24 wounded, including Houston.[87] The majority of the Mexican command staff including Santa Anna were among the captured.

The Republic of Texas

The elation and surprise over the victory at San Jacinto was short-lived as the victors began to face reality. The Texans had "no assurance that they could hold Texas against the reinvasion by a determined Mexican army. They had no political parties, no viable government, no taxing authority, and no money."[88] The economy was at a standstill. The damage to property and crops was devastating since two marching armies and fleeing settlers had trampled and burned the countryside. To survive, Texas immediately needed strong leaders who would provide the people with a sense of direction and security.

Still a prisoner, Santa Anna's life was spared. The general wanted to negotiate a deal. At first, he told his captors to ransom him off to the Mexican government, but authorities in Mexico did not feel that Santa Anna was that valuable. Santa Anna eventually secured his release by tentatively agreeing to the **Treaty of Velasco**. This document called for the recognition of Texas's independence and the withdrawal of Mexican forces to south of the Rio Grande. The treaty proved to be invalid because Santa Anna had been disposed from power prior to his return to Mexico. To drive home the point, Mexican troops continued to attack settlers, and bribed several Indian tribes to raid ranches and farms.

Elections were held in 1836, with Sam Houston elected as president and Maribeau Lamar winning the vice president's job. The ballot included a referendum on the possibility of statehood for Texas. The results showed that "Texans had long favored joining the union, voting 3,277 to 91 in favor of it."[89] The newly formed government drafted a constitution establishing the Republic of Texas. With few exceptions, the Constitution of the Republic of Texas is an exact copy of the United States Constitution from the Preamble, to establishing three branches of government, separating governing authority among the branches, instituting a system of checks and balances, and the enumeration of protected civil rights and liberties. Since most Texans favored annexation, President Houston sent an emissary to Washington to negotiate statehood.

The timing could not have been worse. Although President Andrew Jackson favored annexation, statehood for Texas received major opposition in Congress. Texas would have entered the union as a slave state, upsetting the delicate balance between free and slave states. Statehood was rejected; however, the United States did recognize the independence of Texas.

The struggling Republic encouraged settlers to the area by offering generous land grants to both Americans and Europeans. From 1836 to 1842, "the republic granted 36,876,492 acres in headright certificates to reward those who had aided in the struggle for independence or to encourage immigration."[90] To promote immigration from European countries, Congress passed colonization laws creating a contract system similar to the empresario agreements. The proprietor was given a specified allocation of land, known as a colony. It was the proprietor's responsibility to settle the area. The most lucrative contracts were issued to W. S. Peters and Associates, who later changed its name to the Texas Emigration and Land Company. The majority of the newcomers were immigrants from Germany, Poland, Czechoslovakia, and Eastern European countries. The German Hill Country, around the Austin and Kerrville areas, became the home for the majority of German immigrants. The cities of Castroville, Fredericksburg, New Braunfels, Sisterdale, Boerne, and Comfort were initially immigrant colonies under this system.

The floundering Republic of Texas was always just one step away from disaster. Although the government did have the power to tax, revenues could not keep up with expenses. "At times the poverty of the government was embarrassing. For a period, Secretary of Treasury Henry Smith could not attend to his duties because he had no stationery and no funds with which to buy any. Houston could secure supplies for the army only by pledging his personal credit."[91] Basically, "Texans of the Republic bit off more than they could chew. The plantation system was never able to extend beyond the southeastern part of Texas. Texans were unable to settle, much less defend, their western frontier. Texas was so poor by the time it finally entered the Union that the federal government took no significant land for itself, as was the rule, but left the lands for debt-ridden Texas to sell."[92]

By 1845, the question of statehood seemed more favorable. The United States was caught up in the spirit of **Manifest Destiny**. President John Tyler favored annexation and sought United States Senate approval of a treaty making Texas a state. The Senate, however, failed to approve the treaty for a variety of reasons, including the pending threat of war with Mexico over Texas. James K. Polk, another supporter of annexation, had been elected to the presidency in 1844. Before Polk took office, Tyler signed a congressional joint resolution making Texas a state. The terms of the agreement were "(1) Texas to be assured a republican form of government and statehood to be effected by July 1, 1846; (2) all outstanding boundary questions to be adjusted to the satisfaction of the United States; (3) the state of Texas to retain title to its own public lands and apply the income from their sale to satisfy the republic's indebtedness; (4) with the consent of Texas, new states, not to exceed four in number, might be created out of the original territory, provided slavery was outlawed in such new states as might be organized north of the extended Missouri Compromise line."[93] In June, the Texas Congress met in special session to approve the annexation agreement and to draft a new state constitution. The Congress approved the annexation offer on July 4, 1845. Despite those who believe that Texas was illegally annexed, the final paragraph of the annexation document reads:

> Now in order to manifest the assent of the people of this Republic as required in the above-recited portions of the said resolutions; we, the deputies of the people of Texas in Convention, assembled, in their name, and by their authority, do ordain and declare, that we assent to, and accept the proposals, conditions, and guarantees contained in the first and second sections of the resolution of the Congress of the United States aforesaid.[94]

While most Texans were jubilant about joining the union, some, including Maribeau Lamar, did not want to see the end of the Republic. In Lamar's Inaugural Address delivered on December 10, 1838, the newly sworn-in president of the Republic of Texas told the audience that "there is, however, one question of the highest national concernment, on which I feel it a privilege and a duty to address myself to the great body of people themselves. I mean the annexation of our country to the American union. Notwithstanding the almost undivided voice measure . . . I have never been able myself to perceive the policy of the desired connexion [sic], or discover in it any advantage either civil, political or commercial, which could possibly result to Texas."[95] Even as the final documents were being drawn, debated, and ultimately signed, Lamar held steadfast to his belief that annexation would be the ruin of Texas. According to Lamar, "as only one of twenty-eight states, the sovereign Republic of Texas would be 'reduced to the level of an unfelt fraction of a giant power,' would

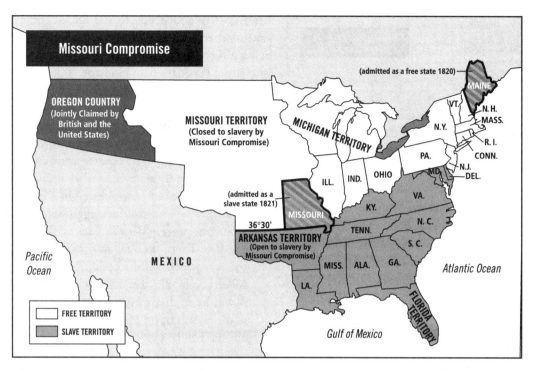

become a tributary vassal 'pouring her abundant treasures into the lap of another people than her own,' and as 'the cornucopia of the world' would give the United States far greater wealth than it would be able to extract as a state."[96] A special election was held on October 13, 1845, with Texans approving annexation by a 4,254 to 267 margin and a new constitution by a vote of 4,174 to 312.[97] On December 29, 1845, President Polk signed the act, making Texas the 28th state in the union. On February 16, 1846, the flag of the Republic was replaced at the state capitol by the United States stars and stripes. Anson Jones, the last president of the Republic, officially relinquished his position to J. P. Henderson, the first governor of the State of Texas. As he departed his office, Jones commented that:

> The lone star of Texas, which ten years since arose amid clouds over fields of carnage, and obscurely shone for a while, has culminated, and, following an inscrutable destiny, has passed on and become fixed forever in that glorious constellation which all freemen and lovers of freedom in the world must reverence and adore-the American union . . . Blending its rays with its sister stars, long may it continue to shine, and may a gracious Heaven smile upon this consummation of the wishes of the two Republics, now joined together in one. 'May the Union be perpetual, and may it be the means of conferring benefits and blessings upon the people of all the States' is my ardent prayer."[98]

War with Mexico

Upon hearing of Texas's statehood, the Mexican government officially severed its already strained diplomatic ties with the United States. No one in Washington, D.C., was surprised by their actions. The tensions between the two had been brewing since the beginning of the Texas Revolution. Despite Sam Houston's victory at San Jacinto, an unofficial state of war continued between Mexico and the Republic of Texas. Both sides were equally to blame. The Mexican government tried unsuccessfully to retake Texas by using paramilitary agents to infiltrate the struggling Republic's government offices. Although Texas claimed the Rio Grande as its border with Mexico, the Mexican government continued to see the Nueces River as the dividing line. The territory between the two rivers became a "no man's land" as the Mexican government encouraged the various Indian tribes to launch periodic raids against the settlers located on the eastern side of the Nueces while offering them a safe haven on the other side of the river.

Republic President Maribeau B. Lamar even tried unsuccessfully to purchase the disputed territory from the Mexican government. Failing on the diplomatic front, Lamar opted for an alternative plan. In 1841, he ordered a raiding party into the Mexican-held Santa Fe region. "Lamar posited that if Texas were to incorporate New Mexico. (He just assumed that the New Mexicans would prefer to live under the Texas Republic than under the sovereignty of Mexico.) the acquisition would enhance

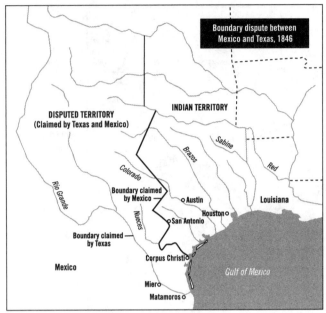

Boundary dispute between Mexico and Texas, 1846

DISPUTED TERRITORY
(Claimed by Texas and Mexico)

INDIAN TERRITORY

Sabine

Brazos

Colorado

Red

Rio Grande

Boundary claimed
by Mexico —

Austin

Louisiana

Houston

Nueces

San Antonio

Boundary claimed —
by Texas

Corpus Christi

Mexico

Gulf of Mexico

Miero

Matamoros

Texas's destiny in several ways. First, it could help the nation share in the trade between Santa Fe and Missouri (such commerce had begun in the 1820s), collecting specie at customhouses that would aid the struggling economy. Second, it would give Texas persuasive leverage in its position in the middle of the continent. Lastly, it might even be a stepping stone for further expansion towards the Pacific. Among this train of thought, if Texas were to annex California, it would enjoy strategic and commercial benefits on two oceans."[99] Lamar, however, acted without approval of his Congress. The raid was a disaster, resulting in the capture and imprisonment of Texans in Mexican jails. The political fallout for Lamar was irreversible. Lamar was officially sanctioned by his own Congress. If not for the reality that his term of office was nearly over, Lamar would have been impeached. Poor decision making on Lamar's part definitely played a role in the successful return of Sam Houston to the presidency of the Republic.

On March 15, 1842, Mexican General Rafael Vasquez briefly captured San Antonio. President Sam Houston decided to retaliate by recapturing San Antonio and driving the Mexican army back across the Rio Grande. Led by Brigadier General Alexander Somerville, the Texas army began its march on Mexico. Somerville, however, was discharged of his duties by his own men. The remaining troops fell under the command of Col. William Fisher, who subsequently surrendered to General Ampudia at Mier. Back in power once again, Santa Anna decided a unique punishment for his Texan prisoners. His staff mixed seventeen black beans with white beans in a jar. Each prisoner would decide his own fate: draw a white bean and live or a black bean and die by firing squad. The survivors were confined to jails in Mexico City. The Black

Bean Lottery added fuel to the fire as Texans waited for statehood in hopes of bringing the wrath of the United States military might upon Mexico. On March 28, 1842, a very angry President Sam Houston issued his own diatribe and threats against Santa Anna:

> We have desired peace. You have annoyed our frontier; you have harassed our citizens; you have incarcerated our traders after your commissioners had been kindly received, and your citizens allowed the privilege of commerce in Texas without molestation. You continue aggression; you will not accord us peace. *We will have it.* You threaten to conquer Texas; we will war with Mexico. . . . In the war which will be conducted by Texas against Mexico, our incentive will not be a love of conquest; it will be to disarm tyranny of its power. We will make no war upon Mexicans or their religion. Our efforts shall be made in behalf of the liberties of the people; and directed against the authorities of the country, against your principles.[100]

The last attempt by Mexico to reclaim Texas involved President Santa Anna calling upon Brig. Gen. Adrian Woll, a French mercenary serving in the Mexican army, to cross into Texas with approximately 1,500 infantry and cavalry troops, a small group of Cherokee warriors, and two cannons. The Texans gathered their own army composed primarily of volunteers from surrounding settlements. Under the command of Capt. Matthew Caldwell, they marched to Salado Creek, just outside of San Antonio. Meanwhile, President Sam Houston called upon the Texas Rangers under the command of Maj. John Coffee "Jack" Hayes to join the fray. The Texans won the day with only twelve wounded and the Mexican forces losing approximately 60 dead and 200 wounded.[101]

Washington was also preparing for military confrontation with Mexico over Texas even before the official annexation documents were signed. During the summer of 1845, General Zachary Taylor was ordered to establish a military post at the Nueces River near Corpus Christi with the understanding that no forces were to cross into the disputed territory between the Nueces River and the Rio Grande. Once the troops were established, President Polk decided to try the diplomatic approach by sending John Slidell to Mexico City to negotiate the purchase of California. Reaching his destination by December 1845, Slidell was informed by Mexican authorities that "Texas was the only quest in dispute and, that friendly relations could not be reestablished til Texas had been restored to Mexico."[102] Obviously, diplomacy failed. On February 3,

1946, Taylor was ordered to march to the Rio Grande but not to initiate an attack against Mexico without an official declaration of war.

With only the Rio Grande separating American and Mexican forces, the Mexican commander issued an ultimatum to Taylor on April 12, 1846, to pull his troops back from the river or face the consequences. The Mexican government officially declared war on April 23. The first official battle occurred on May 8, 1846, at Palo Alto (not far from Brownsville), resulting in the deaths of nine U.S. and approximately two hundred Mexican soldiers.[103] The United States Congress issued its own declaration of war on May 13, 1846. The war was a short one, with American forces ending the hostilities by invading Mexico City on September 14, 1847. Officially the causes of the war were "the annexation of Texas, the desire of the United States to acquire part or all of California, the failure of the Mexican government to settle claims by citizens of the United States, the instability of the Mexican government, and the location of the western boundary."[104] The war officially ended with the signing of the **Treaty of Guadalupe Hidalgo** on February 2, 1848. Mexico officially recognized the independence and statehood of Texas and acknowledged the Rio Grande as the boundary line separating the two nations. For $15 million, Mexico ceded the provinces of New Mexico and the remainder of upper California to the United States.

The war did produce a Texas legend—the Texas Rangers. The Texas Rangers were formed by Stephen F. Austin in 1821. "A corps of Texas Rangers was created before Thanksgiving 1835 complete with officers and one-year enlistments. Privates earned $1.25 a day."[105] Their primary duties included fighting Indians since the Republic of Texas did not have an official army to patrol the area. Taylor needed scouts to enter the Mexican side of the border prior to the official declaration of war. The Texas Rangers fulfilled that task handily. The fighting tactics of the Rangers were not fully appreciated by Taylor, but they became heroes. The Rangers were a "mishmash group insofar as military spit-and-polish was concerned. But they could fight; oh, how they could fight."[106] With their Colt revolvers in hand, the Rangers attacked both Mexican soldiers and, unfortunately, civilians, much to the disdain of the American commander.

The New Settlers of Texas

The Anglo Americans that crossed the border into the Mexican territory of Texas were far from a culturally homogeneous group. Primarily of British ancestry, many were an admixture of Scottish, Irish, German, French, and Scandinavian bloodlines. "The Texian victors of 1836 lived in Finnish log cabins, fought with German long rifles, drank Scottish whiskey, adhered to British dissenter Protestantism, and introduced the language and common law of the English."[107] Regardless of their bloodlines, they all were expatriates drawn by the promises of cheap land and abundant natural resources, and guided by the desire to start a new life for themselves and their families. Texas myth builders would have one to believe that Texas drew only the undesirables who were just one step ahead of the sheriff or the noose. In reality, "the people of Texas [were] unpretending farmers and planters from the middle walks of life, [and] all they desired on earth was the privilege of cultivating in peace those fertile lands which they had so dearly earned by the perils and privations consequent upon the colonizing of a wilderness."[108]

The first wave of Anglo Americans hailed from the southern states. The myth of the South portrays a region solidly behind the plantation culture and the slave system. In reality, there were two sub-cultural groups, referred to as **upper** and **lower south**. Their different agricultural needs mandated different settlement patterns. "In Texas, by 1850, a Texarkana-to-San Antonio line separated the domain of the planter, or lower southerner, to the east of the line, from the western interior stronghold of the yeoman or upper southerner."[109] In colonial America, the plantation system, which began on the shores of the Atlantic Ocean, gradually developed inward as growers realized that cotton production robs the soil of its nutrients, gradually eroding the productivity of the crop. The only options were to continue to see the profitability of one's cotton crop decline or move to untapped agricultural lands. The rich soil of East Texas was definitely suitable for cotton. The plantation class of the old South brought with them to Texas their beliefs of elitism, slavery, states' rights, conservative political philosophy, and one-party factionalism. As their numbers grew, it was the slaveholders who "dominated economic, political, and social life in antebellum Texas. They produced 90 percent of the state's cotton, dominated office holding at all levels of government, and by virtue of their wealth occupied the top rungs of the social ladder. Not surprisingly under these circumstances, most articulate Texans such as newspaper editors and ministers defended slavery with every manageable argument, and the vast majority of the state's people either supported or quietly acquiesced in the institution."[110]

In contrast, settlers from the upper southern states were predominately small-acre family farmers who did not need to own large numbers of slaves. Agriculturally diversified, they were not dependent upon cotton and its requirement for rich soils. Upper southern migrants moved into the northern area of East Texas. Fiercely and boastfully self-sufficient, these settlers were strong believers in the Protestant work ethic and relied heavily upon individual initiative. Leery of the encroachment of government, they firmly believed in states' rights and the old adage "the best government is the one that governs the least." The second major wave of Anglo-American settlers to Texas came from the mid-western and northern sections of the United States. The Panhandle region is indicative of Yankee migration, particularly wheat farmers from Kansas and Nebraska. It was and still is a socially and politically conservative region.

In the early 1800s, continental Europe and the British Isles were confronted with a series of economic disasters and famines, coupled with heightened political tensions. Against this backdrop, Europeans began to look to the United States and Texas as their only hope to a better life. Relatives and friends who had already made the long journey across the Atlantic wrote of what they had found in the "new world." For example, a letter written by German immigrant Fredrich Dirks in 1832, described Texas as "a land with winterless Italian climate, abundant game and fish, immense free land grants, gold and silver to be had nearby, low taxes, and huge privately owned herds of livestock, a land where only three month's labor was necessary each year to make a living."[111] This embellished and exaggerated description drew many Europeans to Texas.

The first to arrive were the Irish. Using an empresario land grant, Irish settlers founded the coastal bend colonies of San Patricio and Refugio. "Many residents spoke Gaelic and worked together to build homes that merged the architecture of Ireland with German and Spanish designs. Each dwelling was a collective effort. Friends helped friends erect the old-world homes, with walls of caliche and limestone so soft, they say the rock could be carved with a knife. . . . When the last stone was in place, the settlers put on a Gaelic celebration of music and dancing called a ceilidh, pronounced 'key=lee.'"[112] This "Irish Zone" served the Mexican government's desire to create a buffer zone between Anglo-American settlers and Tejano colonies. Remaining a cohesive group, the Irish introduced **cluster migration** as a means of fostering integration into a new environment. "Newly arrived settlers typically came to the mother colony, lived there while acquiring capital and experience, and then moved out to form daughter colonies nearby."[113] By clustering together, each group was able to maintain the uniqueness of its culture, while at the same time seeking to conform to the Texas frontier lifestyle.

The largest contingent of European settlers to Texas came from Germany. Settling in the counties of Austin, Colorado, Comal, De Witt, Fayette, Gillespie, Guadalupe, Kendall, Medina, and Washington, the German community founded the cities of New Braunfels, Fredericksburg, Kerrville, and Seguin. Clusters of German immigrants also settled in the established urban areas of Houston, Galveston and San Antonio. Henri Castro received a land grant and brought several thousand Alsatians to form the city of Castroville. German immigration to Texas continued despite the Texas Revolution, the Mexican War, and the American Civil War. "Toward the close of the major period of immigration in 1887, the 130,000 Germans in Texas constituted the second largest ethnic group in the state, after the African Americans, and made up over well half of the European element. A century later, over 750,000 Texans claimed to be wholly of German origin, and an additional almost one-and-one-half million persons listed partial German ancestry."[114] The foundations of the German community were a firm belief in the strength of the extended family, a sense of community togetherness, and a firm belief in self-sufficiency and the Protestant work-ethic.

In the 1850s, a second wave of European migration came to Texas from the Slavic or Eastern European countries. The history of both Poland and the former nation of Czechoslovakia is one of weak and easily conquered lands ruled by foreigners. "Denied the rights to pursue their own language, religion and traditions, Eastern Europeans flocked to the United States and Texas to find political, religious, and personal freedoms. These immigrants to Texas did not fit the image of a poor poverty-stricken immigrant landing in America with all of his worldly possession in one small suitcase. 'Peasant' might best be described as members of the farming class. They were landowners, taxpayers, and far higher in social status than the landless laborers they employed."[115] The first group of Czechoslovakians came through Galveston and migrated northwest, where they founded the first Czech settlement in Texas at Cat Spring. The oldest Polish settlement in the United States is Panna Maria, Texas. Located in Karnes County, Panna Maria (Virgin Mary in Polish) was founded by Franciscan priest Leopold Moczygemba in 1854. The cities of Bandera and St. Hedwig were initially founded by Polish immigrants. Swedish immigrants came to Texas in the middle 1840s and settled in Travis and Williamson counties. Wharton County was the site of a Danish colony called Davevang, founded in 1894.

Whether hailing from the United States or Denmark, all immigrants to Texas faced the hardships of the frontier. The conquest of the frontier mandated that the survivors of this experience emerge with a pervading sense of self-sufficiency, survival of the fittest or **Social Darwinism**, and a firm belief in individual achievements. The modern version of the frontier life has been romanticized as an adventure whereby settlers in covered wagons come into a virgin territory teeming with the abundance of nature and hopefully gold. Once the land is staked out, the family successfully turns a wilderness into a productive farm or ranch. In reality, life on the frontier was anything but romantic. Originally coming from Germany to New York City, Caroline von Hinueber's family decided to move to Texas. She described her journey and, subsequently, her early years in Texas:

> We set sail for Texas in the schooner *Saltillo*, [with] Capitan Haskins. . . . The boat was jammed with passengers and their luggage so that you could hardly find a place on the floor to lie down at night. I firmly believe that a strong wind would have drowned us all. . . . We landed at Harrisburg [Texas], which consisted at that time of about five or six long houses, on the 3d of April, 1831. Captain Harris had a sawmill, and there was a store or two, I believe. Here we remained five weeks, while Fordtran went ahead of us and entered a league, where now stands the town of Industry . . . After we lived at Fortran's place for six months, we moved into our house. This was a miserable little hut, covered with straw and having six sides, which were made out of moss. The roof was by no means waterproof, and we often held an umbrella over our bed when it rained at night, while the cows came and ate the moss. Of course, we suffered a great deal in the winter. My father had tried to build a chimney and fireplace out of logs and clay, but we were afraid to light a fire because of the extreme combustibility of our dwelling. So we had to shiver. . . . We had no money. When we could buy things, my first calico dress cost 50 cents per yard. No one can imagine what a degree of want there was of the merest necessities of life, and it is difficult for me now to understand how we managed to live and get along under the circumstances. Yet we did so in some way.[116]

In order to survive, one had to be self sufficient, totally committed to conquering both the land and the elements of Mother Nature, and, above all, be a jack of all trades. With few exceptions, everything had to be made by hand from candles to furniture. Everything found or produced on the land had a purpose, nothing was wasted:

Candles or lard-burning lamps supplied light. Ash hoppers and pork fat supplied materials for soap; corn was ground in steel hand mills; and cotton was carded, spun, and woven into cloth. Within less than five years one Texan recorded in his diary that he made a wheel, a coffin, a reel, a churn, a cradle, a bucket, a pump auger, an ox yoke, and a pair of shoes, in addition to working at the loom, hewing puncheons, and graining deerskins.[117]

It was not an easy life for anyone. Many settlers gave up, opting to return to their roots east of the Mississippi River. For those who remained, the experiences of life on the frontier bonded them together. Regardless of one's background, ancestry, or economic status, the Anglo-American settlers in Texas found common ground among themselves. An observer noted:

> There are no poor people here, and none rich; that is, none who have much money. The poor and the rich, to use the correlatives, where distinction, there is none, get the same quantity of land on arrival, and if they do not continue equal, it is for want of good management on the one part, or superior industry and sagacity on the other. . . They are bound together, by a common interest, by sameness of purpose, and hopes. As far as I could learn, they have no envying, no jealousies, no bickering, through politics or fanaticism. There is neither masonry, anti-masonry, nullification nor court intrigues. The common concerns of life are sufficiently exciting to keep the spirits buoyant, and prevent everything like ennui. Artificial wants are entirely forgotten, in the view of the real ones, and self, eternal self, does not alone fill up the round of life. . . They discover in themselves, powers they did not suspect themselves of possessing.[118]

Today, the unique combination of rugged individualism and a sense of community found in early Texas left its mark on the philosophical positions Texans take on both politics and the pressing public policy issues confronting modern Texas.

Secession and Civil War

The struggle between the North and the South became an issue in Texas immediately following statehood. Supporters for the southern cause included plantation owners. "Ninety percent of Texas's white population had come from the

Old South or had been born of southern parents. Their mores were southern, and their political opinions were southern."[119]   For the most part, the plantation system revolved around the use of slave labor. The southern planters were fighting for their economic survival as well as the preservation of their social order. Support for slavery was not just among slave owners. Many non-slaveholders supported slavery because "it provided not only a system of controlled labor but also a means for social domination of black [African-American] people, whom most whites in the nineteenth century considered to be inferior."[120] Following South Carolina's lead, Texas became the seventh state to secede from the Union. On February 1, 1861, the Texas Legislature approved the Ordinance of Secession. The rationale for leaving the Union that so many Texans fought and died to achieve was clearly stated in the Ordinance:

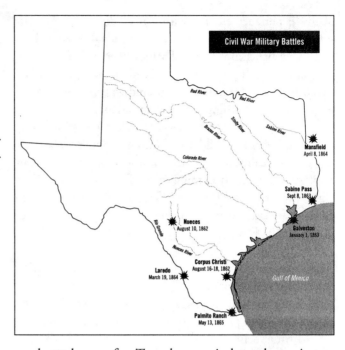

Civil War Military Battles

> Whereas, the Federal Government has failed to accomplish the purposes of the compact of union between the States, in giving protection either to the persons of our people upon an exposed frontier, or to the property of our citizens; and, whereas, the action of the Northern States of the Union is violative of the compact between the States and the guarantees of the Federal Constitution, and whereas, the recent developments of Federal affairs make it evident that the power of the Federal Government is sought to be made a weapon with which to strike down the interest and prosperity of the people of Texas and her sister slaveholding States, instead of permitting it to be, as was intended our shield against outrage and aggression . . .[121]

Those supporting the Confederate cause included both slave and non-slave owners who truly believed that the federal government was becoming too intrusive into the internal affairs of the states. They firmly supported the contention that the political climate in Washington, D.C., embraced the economic, social and political needs of the northern states to the detriment of the interests of the southern states. Texans, like most pro-Confederate Southerners, wanted to determine for themselves the merits of the slave system.

One of the prevailing myths of the Civil War was the belief that all Southerners openly embraced the institution of slavery. Not every landowner in the South owned slaves nor did every Southerner support the use of slave labor. The plantation system established in the lower sector of East Texas did depend upon the use of slave labor. In pre-civil war Texas, the slave population increased dramatically. "Estimated at 5,000 in 1836, slave numbers grew at an

accelerated pace after Texas became independent. A state census in 1847 counted 38,753, or approximately 27 percent of the total population, indicated a sharp rise in the numbers during the republic. The number of slaves grew even more rapidly after annexation, with the 1850 count of 58,161 reflecting a slave population growth of about 50 percent in the first three years of statehood. The census of 1860 showed 182,566 slaves and 430,891 white persons, the proportion of slaves in the total population amounting to about 30 percent. Since 1850, the slave population had increased 214 percent and the white population, 180 percent.[122] Another myth was that individual slaveholders in Texas owned hundreds of slaves. In fact, "only 2,163 of these [plantation owners] owned 20 or more slaves; 54 owned 100 or more. More than half of the slaveholders owned 5 or fewer. About 10 percent of all farmers operated on a scale large enough to necessitate hiring an overseer."[123] Although the number of slaves increased, the number of families owning slaves actually decreased. In the upper section of East Texas, the majority of the agricultural units were smaller holdings owned by non-slave owners who depended upon family members to tile the fields.

Of course, not all Texans were in favor of the southern call to arms. In particular, the German settlement communities were very anti-slavery, believing that enslavement was evil and should be abolished. In 1861, members of the German communities in Gillespie, Kerr and Kendall counties formed the Union Loyal League, a united protest against succession, the war, and conscription into the Confederate Army. "Sixty-five Union sympathizers, all Germans, left Kerr County for Mexico. Kerr and its contiguous counties were placed under martial law, and a party took out after the disaffected Germans. Over half were killed before they could reach Mexico."[124] The anti-war effort erupted in the northern portion of the state with the formation of the Peace Party in 1862. "The aims of its members were to avoid the draft, to provide a spy system for the northern army, to desert during battle, if drafted, and to prepare the way for an invasion of North Texas by federal troops."[125] Infiltrated by pro-Confederate sympathizers, members of the group were eventually arrested, tried, and convicted for crimes against the Confederacy.

The most visible and perhaps vocal spokesperson of the anti-Confederate movement was Sam Houston. Once the specially-called convention approved secession on March 5, 1861, all of the incumbent state executive officers had to take an oath of loyalty to the Confederacy. Governor Houston refused and was swiftly replaced by his Lieutenant Governor Edward Clark. Although President Lincoln offered Houston federal military assistance to keep Texas in the union, Houston refused, opting instead to simply leave Austin. He was not going to "deluge the capitol of Texas with the blood of Texans, merely to keep one poor old man in a position a few days longer, in a position that belongs to the people [of Texas]."[126] On March 31, Houston addressed an audience at Brenham, outlining his objections to rushing to join the Confederacy:

They [the secessionists] tell us that the Confederate Government will thus be permanently established without bloodshed. They might with equal truth declare that the fountains of the great deep blue seas can be broken up without disturbing their surface waters, as to tell us that the best Government that ever existed for men can be broken up without bloodshed. The secession leaders also tell us if war should come that European nations will speedily come to our relief, and aid us to win our independence because cotton is King and European commerce and civilization can not long exist without cotton, therefore, they must help us and maintain and perpetuate our Confederate Government. Gentlemen who use such false and misleading statements forget or else are ignorant of the facts that commerce and civilization existed a long period of time before cotton was generally known and used. They also forget or else are ignorant of the fact that the best sentiment in Europe is opposed to our system of slavery. They also tell us if war comes that the superior courage of our people with their experience of the use of firearms, will enable us to triumph in battle over ten times

our number of northern forces. Never was a more false or absurd statement ever made by designing demagogues. . . . For this reason I predict that the civil war which is now near at hand will be stubborn and of long duration. We are sadly divided among ourselves, while the North and West are united. Not only will we have to contend against a united and harmonious North, but we will also have to battle against tens of thousands of our own people, who will never desert the Stars and Stripes nor surrender the union of states for a Southern Confederacy of states, whose principles of secession must inevitably lead to discord, conspiracy and revolution, and at last anarchy and utter ruin. When the tug of war comes, it will indeed be the Greek meeting the Greek.[127]

Although not a primary battle area, Texas did play an important role during the war and sent a large contingent of soldiers to aid the cause of the Confederacy. Despite the capture of Galveston by Union forces in October 1862, Confederate troops in Texas continued to smuggle supplies through Mexico to the front lines. On January 1, 1863, Confederate General John B. Magruder recaptured Galveston. Terry's Texas Rangers, led by Benjamin Franklin Terry, a sugar planter from the Fort Bend area, fought with distinction on the battlefields of Kentucky and Tennessee. The majority of the Texas soldiers saw action in Mississippi and Virginia. "The census of 1860 revealed 92,145 white males in Texas from the ages of eighteen to forty-five, and probably at least two-thirds or more than 60,000, put on some kind of uniform."[128] Although the adverse impact of the war was clearly evident in the Deep South, Texas did not suffer the same fate. Of particular note, the last battle of the Civil War was fought in Texas on May 13, 1865, one month after Lee's surrender at Appomattox. The Confederates were victorious that day at Palmito Ranch near Brownsville, but as they began to round up their Union prisoners, the Confederates were informed that the war had indeed ended.

Reconstruction

To a large extent, the pervading political philosophies and attitudes Texans have towards government today are attributable to the impact of Reconstruction. President Abraham Lincoln envisioned returning the southern states back to the federal union without undue punishment. With his assassination and the rise of Radical Republicanism in Washington, D.C., the tone of Reconstruction changed. President Andrew Johnson appointed A. J. Hamilton as the interim governor of Texas and General Gordon Granger as commander of federal troops stationed in the state. The first item of business was to order freedom for all of the state's slaves. On June 1865, Granger declared "the absolute and equal rights of property between master and slaves."[129] Granger also issued a warning to the now former African-American slaves that they should "remain in their present homes and work for wages. They are informed that they will not be allowed to collect at military posts, and that they will not be supported in idleness, either there or elsewhere."[130] Each former confederate state was to officially nullify secession, abolish slavery, repudiate the Confederate debt, and write new state constitutions. Texas fulfilled those requirements by the summer of 1866. President Johnson proclaimed that the insurrection in Texas had ended, and Texas could re-enter the union, beginning with the election of senators and representatives to the United States Congress.

However, Texas, like most of her former Confederate sister states, fulfilled Washington's requirements to gain readmission with very little intention of implementing them. Throughout the South, state by state abolished slavery only to pass a series of laws commonly called the **Black Codes** or **Jim Crow Laws** designed to keep former slaves in a state of peonage. In Texas, African Americans were denied the right to vote, hold office, or testify against a white person in court. African-American laborers could not have visitors during working hours. There were laws requiring former slaves to be obedient and respectful to whites, even to the point of designating what side of the street African Americans could walk on. The Radical Republican majority in the United States Congress reacted to these tactics by taking over the Reconstruction program and initiating impeachment charges against President Johnson. Over his veto, Radical Republicans passed a series of Reconstruction acts that placed the southern states under military rule; required their legislative houses to ratify and actively implement the Thirteenth, Fourteenth and Fifteenth Amendments to the United States Constitution before being readmitted into the union; and denied voting rights and election opportunities to former Confederate officers, holders of property valued over $20,000 and those who refused to take a loyalty oath to the federal government. Making matters worse, the Texas military district, which also included Louisiana, was under the supervision of General William T. Sherman, well known for his burning of Atlanta, Georgia, and his march to the sea.

The Civil War and Reconstruction changed Texas society. "Thus the number of planters among the wealthy Texans with $100,000 or more of property had fallen from 65 percent in 1860 to 17 percent in 1870. Merchants among the wealthy had increased, however, from 16 percent in 1860 to 40 percent in 1870."[131] This change in the elite structure throughout the South was hastened by the arrival of the **carpetbaggers**. Carrying suitcases made from carpet, Northerners flooded into the southern states following the war. Carpetbaggers were able to buy plantations and business properties easily. Since plantation owners had cotton but no federally-issued greenbacks, the carpetbaggers merely paid off outstanding property taxes and acquired rich lands for very cheap prices. The carpetbagger and his southern ally, the **scalawag**, were simply not accepted into traditional Southern society. The tactics of the carpetbaggers in Texas were aided with the election of E. J. Davis to the governorship. Davis controlled the governing process through the Constitution of 1869. This document gave Davis sweeping appointive powers, the right to declare martial law, and unchallengeable mechanisms to increase taxes. The details of the Davis regime will be discussed in the chapter on state constitutions. The Davis era was well known for its overspending and repressive nature.

Granted the right to vote, former slaves initially affiliated themselves with the Republican Party while southern whites remained loyal to the Democratic Party. The more militant southern whites decided to retaliate against federal actions by forming groups to stop any social, economic, and political gains within the African-American community. Across the South, Ku Klux Klan members dressed in their white-hooded costumes, harassed, scared, and oftentimes lynched African Americans. In Texas, the Klan cause was carried out by ex-Confederate officers under the banner of the Knights of the Rising Sun. Across the South, Klan organizations held elaborate initiation ceremonies with each potential member taking an official oath "to maintain and defend the social and political superiority of the White race on this Continent; always and in all places to observe a marked distinction between the White and African races; to vote for none but White men for any office of honor, profit or test; to devote my intelligence, energy and influence to instill these principles in the minds and hearts of others; and to protect and defend persons of the White race, in their lives, rights, and property, against the encroachments and aggressions of persons of an inferior race."[132]

By 1873, the majority of former Confederates had regained their voting privileges. They subsequently elected Democrat Richard Coke as governor, defeating E. J. Davis. Davis refused to accept the election results and had his self-appointed court nullify the election. Locking himself in his capitol office and surrounding himself with state troopers, Davis refused to leave. On January 13, 1874, members of the newly elected Democrat-controlled legislature crawled into the second story window of the state capitol and declared Coke the governor of Texas. Davis departed. Texas was officially readmitted into the union, thus ending Reconstruction in Texas.

The Cowboy Era

The Texas cowboy is legendary, becoming the most dominate feature of the Texas image. Tall, brave, fighting the elements and intruders, ruggedly and stubbornly independent, the cowboy symbolizes the "typical Texan," a man with complete freedom under a clear starry night. However, there is a difference between legend and reality:

> He [the cowboy] didn't amount to much as an individual. He never made much money, just what today would be called minimum wage. He was usually small and wiry. He had little education. And he occupied the center ring in the American historical circus for only twenty-five years.[133]

The cowboy era began with the cattle drives to the railheads of Kansas and Missouri. After the Civil War, Texans had little money; but, they had vast numbers of roaming longhorns. The northern states had money but not enough beef to meet the needs of its people. It was a gold mine on hooves! "Beeves that sold for $3 or $4 a head in Texas might bring $30 to $40 in the upper Mississippi Valley."[134] Due to the chronic shortage of railroads, the only way to connect the cattle with the money was to drive them over hundreds of miles to the markets of Sedalia, Missouri, and Abilene and Dodge City, Kansas. The famous **Chisholm Trail** extended from south Texas through Austin, Lampassas, and Fort Worth to its final destination, Caldwell, Kansas. Other trails included the Goodnight-Loving starting its path from Fort Concho, to Cheyenne, Wyoming, the Western Trail from Bandera to Ogallala, Nebraska, and the Sedalia and Baxter Springs Trail, which began in Brownsville and subsequently after crossing the Red River split into two trails with one ending in Baxter Springs, Kansas, and the other in Sedalia, Missouri. "While no accurate account of the number of cattle driven over the trail exists, the 1880 census estimates that the drive to Abilene, 1867-1871, totaled 1,460,000; to Wichita and nearby deports, 1872-1875, 1,072,000; to Dodge City—'the Bibulous Babylon of the Plains'—and

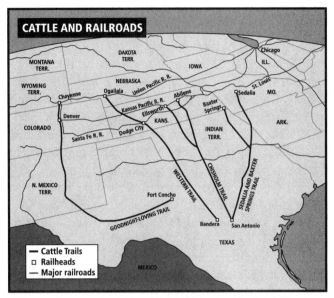

Ellsworth, 1876-1879, 1,046,732; to Dodge City and Caldwell, 1880, 382,000. Estimates for the whole period to 1890 run as high as 10,000,000 head."[135]

The era of the cattle drive was short-lived. "During the mid-1880's, the cattle boom waned. By this time, the long drives were proving less than cost effective; cattle lost weight on the trail and thus did not command a handsome price upon arrival to the railheads, the cost of provisioning the cowboys on the trail kept rising, and Kansas began to enact laws that prevented Texas cattle from passing through their state—because, they too, hoped to deter the spread of ticks that caused Texas fever. Furthermore, the long drives had upset the land's ecological balance; the range could only support so many cattle, but ranchers continually overstocked it. Yearly, the pastures grew thinner and quantities of good grass dwindled."[136] In addition, the hottest new invention of the era was barbed wire. In 1876, John Ware Gates and Pete McManus, barbed wire salesmen from the Illinois-based Washburn-Moen Co., conducted a demonstration of their product in San Antonio at the Menger Hotel. They built a corral of barbed wire that successfully enclosed a small herd of cattle. Subsequently, orders poured in for the wire, and the era of the open range ended. Unfortunately, many trail herders simply refused to seek permission to take their herds across someone else's property and opted simply to cut down the fences. Local ranchers had another problem to deal with—cattle wrestling. For example, "in Karnes County by 1886, local ranchers had banded together and paid a $2-per-mile fee to help maintain their fences from being cut."[137] In 1884, the Texas Legislature passed laws prohibiting fence cutting with a penalty of one to five years in prison. And of course, the rapid growth of the railroad also contributed to the demise of the cattle drive.

The miraculous rise of Richard King from a modest riverboat captain to the largest landholder in the state is legendary. Twenty-three year-old King first came to Texas in 1847 during the Mexican War offering his riverboat to help transport troops and supplies to the war front. After the war, King used the profits earned from his partnership in two steamboat companies to purchase ranch land. "Before the age of 30, King again in partnership purchased a 15,500-acre land grant for $300. Located approximately 40 miles southwest of Corpus Christi, the land, the Rincon de Santa Gertrudis grant, became the foundation of the fabled King Ranch."[138] During the Civil War, King received a contract with the Confederacy to ship cotton to Europe as well as to supply Confederate forces with much needed ammunition, food, and medical supplies. After the War, King joined his fellow ranchers in driving beef to northern markets. At the time of his death in 1885, "King's legacy included 614,000 acres, a $500,000 debt and these final instructions for his attorney, 'Tell him, tell him, to keep buying. And tell him not to let a foot of dear old Santa Gertrudis get away from us.'"[139] His survivors took his words to heart and over the years, built a multi-billion dollar business worthy of a cattle baron. Today, the family business, King Ranch, Inc., has increased its holdings to "11.5 million acres, including 825,000 on the King Ranch, and other ranches in Australia, Cuba and Brazil. With current estimated annual sales of $300 million, King Ranch Inc., is highly diversified, with income derived from oil, cattle, citrus, sugarcane and St. Augustine grass sod. . . . At 1,289 square miles, the ranch covers more territory than Rhode Island. Its fencing, laid out in a straight line, would stretch from ranch headquarters all the way to Boston, more than 2,000 miles. It would take a cowboy a full week of riding on horseback, night and day, to ride the perimeter of the ranch."[140]

The Progressive Era

Although Texas remained predominately in the hands of the Democratic Party, the political agendas of the **Greenbacks**, the **Populists**, and the **Farmers Alliance** ushered in a series of reforms and laws collectively known as the Progressive Era. A national movement, "the progressives got their name from the fact that they believed in the doctrine of progress—that governing institutions could be improved by bringing science to bear on public problems."[141] Reform in the Democratic Party was long overdue as the party was traditionally dominated by conservatives favoring the interests of wealthy landowners. The Republican Party held its traditional strongholds

in the German Hill Country, portions of east Texas and the Gulf Coast, and until the 1932 presidential election, the African-American community. The primary issues for conservatives, whether Democrat or Republican, were finally ending the Indian "problem" in Texas, maintaining law and order, and promoting improvements in transportation and communication. Conservatives were and still are traditionally opposed to any form of business regulation, taxes, and government-sponsored social programs.

The primary spokesperson for the political, economic and social reforms advocated by the Progressives was James Hogg, who was elected attorney general in 1886 and subsequently governor in 1890. Hogg strongly opposed the abusive practices of the railroads and insurance companies operating in Texas. He advanced an amendment to the state constitution creating the Railroad Commission to oversee the state's railroad operations. Today, the Texas Railroad Commission is the most powerful of the state's regulatory agencies. Hogg championed the **Sherman Anti-Trust Law** and vigorously challenged unfair business practices in Texas. In a speech delivered in 1905, Hogg provided insight into his political viewpoints:

> I should like to see: Rotation in office permanently established; nepotism forbidden; equality of taxation a fact; organized lobbying in Austin suppressed; the free-pass system honestly, effectively abolished; oil pipe lines placed under the commission's control; insolvent corporations put out of business; all bonds and stocks of every class of transportation limited by law; corporate control of Texas made impossible; and public records disclose every official act and be open to all, to the end that everyone in Texas shall know that, in Texas, public office is the center of public conscience, and that no graft, no crime, no public wrong, shall ever strain or corrupt our state.[142]

Unfortunately, Texas is still dealing with these unsolved issues.

The Progressive Era in Texas did produce some sweeping, innovative legislation, often enacted before the national government took action. In 1903, the Texas Legislature passed a law prohibiting child labor in certain dangerous occupations, thirteen years before the national child labor laws were passed. In 1905, it passed the **Terrell Election Law,** establishing the primary election as the tool for political parties to select candidates for general elections. The **Robertson Insurance Law** was passed in 1907, requiring that insurance companies keep 75 percent of their reserves in Texas. In 1918, Texas became one of the first states to ratify the **Nineteenth Amendment** to the United States Constitution, granting women the right to vote. Other reforms included state funding to provide free textbooks in the public schools, establishment of state-supported colleges and universities, and the creation of a state park system.

World War I

World War I brought to Texas one of its primary economic resources—military bases. Texas maintains numerous military installations, training centers, and strategic facilities for the United States Armed Forces. Shot in San Antonio, the first "talkie" motion picture *Wings* told the story of the development of the air force at Randolph Air Force Base.

However, the war ushered in anti-German sentiments aimed primarily at the German Hill Country. The Texas Legislature enacted a bill making it a crime for anyone to speak out against the United States' war efforts. Governor Hobby even line-item vetoed the appropriations for the German Department at the University of Texas. African-American soldiers merited worse treatment. Striking out against discriminatory actions, African-American soldiers participated in a deadly riot in Houston. Those designated as the "responsible parties" were executed. The nationwide anti-German sentiments revived the KKK in the 1920s. The Klan had a national membership of nearly five million by 1925.[143] Its membership roster included United States Senators, state governors, and county and city officials. "The motivation behind the Klan in Texas was more the imposition of moral conformity than racism and nativism."[144] Advocating that the state government was too lax in law enforcement, the Klan became the self-proclaimed protector of morality by harassing newspapers deemed too liberal, targeting unfaithful wives and husbands, and so forth. In Texas, Klan membership was openly accepted. Active Klan member Earle Mayfield was elected to the United States Senate, and Judge Felix Robertson ran an unsuccessful campaign against Democrat Miriam Ferguson for governor.

While American soldiers were fighting in the trenches of France, a 10,000 maned American military force under the direction of Brig. Gen. John J. Pershing crossed over the Mexican border headed for Chihuahua in pursuit of once Mexican revolutionary hero and now deemed outlaw, Gen. Francisco "Pancho" Villa (whose real name was Doroteo Arango). Villa's army had crossed into United States territory and attacked Columbus, New Mexico

on March 9, 1916. Pershing's military exploits were unsuccessful in capturing Villa. By January 1917, President Woodrow Wilson ordered the pullout of American forces from Mexico. Originally coming from China to work for the Southern Pacific Railroad, several hundred Chinese were caught in the middle of the conflict. The Chinese were fearful of the Mexican government particularly after in Torreon, Coahuila, "more than 300 Chinese residents were massacred in May, 1911."[145] The Chinese decided that their best option was to support the Americans. The Chinese "cooked for American troops, did their laundry, and provided them with pies, candy, tobacco, matches and fruit, which comprised all of the luxuries known to the men during this campaign in a poverty-stricken country."[146] For their support, Pershing defied a series of anti-Chinese immigration laws by bringing approximately 500 Chinese men to Fort Sam Houston. They subsequently applied for citizenship after Congress repealed the Chinese Exclusion Act in 1943 and settled in San Antonio.

The Depression Years

The Great Depression of 1929 brought economic hardships to Texas. "An unemployment census taken in 1933 showed that 105,045 families, representing 7.1 percent of the population were on relief. The next year there were 246,819 relief cases, representing one million people, or about 13 percent of the population."[147] Soup kitchens and bread lines were seen in every major city. States and cities were not prepared to handle an ever-growing number of homeless people. Available shelter spaces filled quickly as people sought shelter in abandoned buildings, discarded boxes, and caves. The unemployment picture grew bleaker as prices for commodities fell, forcing employers to lay off more people. In Texas, "cotton, which had sold for 18 cents a pound in 1928, dropped to 5 cents in 1932. East Texas oil, which was selling for 60 cents a barrel in 1930, fell to 5 cents a barrel; steak sold for 18 cents per pound; milk sometimes cost as little as 4 or 5 cents a quart; and hamburgers went for a nickel."[148] Business and industry was at a standstill in Texas, while agriculture was producing very little to meet the demand for food.

Relief from the Depression in Texas came, in part, with the discovery in 1930 of a large oil deposit in Kilgore. The greed factor soon took over; overproduction drove down the price of crude oil to ten cents per barrel. The major argument over who could drill in this area was between the major oil producers, such as Humble Oil (Exxon), Mobil, and Texaco, and the independent oilmen. Governor Sterling Ross finally ordered the Kilgore field closed and declared martial law. The "wildcat" era of oil subsided considerably when the governor gave the Railroad Commission the tasks of regulating production and issuing drilling permits.

The Politics of Oil

In Texas, oil and politics are at times, one and the same. For example, in the 1950s, Texans were fighting for their oil rights. The State of Texas declared three leagues or thirty miles of offshore territory for itself. The offshore lands were and still are oil-rich, and Texas wanted to profit from those deposits. The United States government deemed otherwise. Both Democrats Governor Allen Shivers and Attorney General Price Daniel took a political route to fight for the offshore deposits, known as the **Tidelands**. They began to sharply criticize the incumbent Democratic administration of President Harry Truman, who was not a candidate in the 1952 presidential election. Shivers and Daniel attracted the attention of Republican presidential candidate Dwight D. Eisenhower. In exchange for their support of Eisenhower's candidacy and working for him to gain an electoral win in Texas, Eisenhower agreed to grant the ownership of the Tidelands and its thirty mile offshore limits to Texas. For the first time since the Civil War, Texans voted in large numbers for a Republican presidential candidate. Eisenhower won Texas, and Texas won the Tidelands.

Modern Texas Politics: Ups and Downs

In the 1970s, Texas faced its biggest political scandal since the Post-Reconstruction government of E. J. Davis. In 1968, Governor John Connally(D) decided not to seek re-election. Preston Smith, his Democrat lieutenant governor, ran and won the election. Ben Barnes(D) was elected lieutenant governor and Gus Mutscher(D) speaker of the Texas House. All were re-elected in 1970. The problems began with a federal investigation of the Sharpstown Bank owned by a wealthy heavy supporter of the Democrat Party, Frank Sharp. He pressured and bribed Smith, Mutscher, and Barnes into passing state legislation prohibiting federal agents from auditing his bank. In 1971, the Federal Securities and Exchange Commission filed a civil suit against two dozen defendants including Texas Attorney General Waggoner Carr(D), Barnes, Mutscher and Sharp. Smith and Mutscher were accused of accepting bribes and inside business information from Sharp in return for the favorable legislation. Mutscher and his legislative assistant

were convicted, received four-year sentences in federal prison, and were eventually pardoned. The political careers of Barnes and Smith were ruined. Frank Sharp, the originator of the scandal, received a three-year probated sentence and a $5,000 fine.

In 1972, Dolph Briscoe won a tough Democrat primary against the second woman ever to run for the governorship—"Sissy" Francis Farenthold, a former state legislator and American Civil Liberties Union lawyer. It was a classic race between a traditional conservative millionaire rancher and oilman against a liberal Democrat woman. Although she lost her race, she opened the door for women seeking higher elective offices. In 1967, African-American Barbara Jordan began her career in politics. A native of Houston, Jordan overcame her family's poverty to become both the first African-American candidate and woman from Texas to take a seat in the United States Congress. Mentioned as a possible presidential and senatorial candidate as well as a future appointee to the Supreme Court, Jordan's political career was shortened due to multiple sclerosis. She died in 1996. Entering the political arena in 1972, Ann Richards's first elective office was a commissioner position in Travis County. She used this as her stepping stone to successful campaigns for state treasurer in 1982 and 1986. In 1990, she launched her bid for the governorship. Beating Republican opponent Clayton Williams, she became the state's second female governor. Richards quickly rose to national preeminence in the Democratic Party and at one time, was on the "short list" for the vice presidency. In 1994, she ran for an unsuccessful reelection bid for the governorship against Republican candidate George W. Bush, the man she famously criticized at the 1992 Democratic National Convention as being "born with a silver spoon in his month." Richards died in 2006 after a battle with esophageal cancer.

The political career of Lyndon Baines Johnson propelled him into the White House under tragic circumstances—the assassination of President John Kennedy. Johnson is very much a part of Texas myth and folklore. While people chuckled at his antics with the Washington elite, Johnson was the leader who drove through a very testy Senate the first two civil rights bills since Reconstruction. Johnson embraced both the liberal and conservative sides of a true Texas Democrat. "Johnson is a liberal to the extent that he wants the government to meet the human needs of the people. He is a conservative to the extent that he doesn't want to wipe out the Federal Treasury with more programs than the government can afford."[149] During his presidency, he crafted the War on Poverty program designed to possibly cure the suffering caused by economic deprivation. His tenure in the White House was cut short by the nation's unpopular involvement in Vietnam.

In January 1999, United States Congressman Henry B. Gonzales retired after serving nearly thirty-seven years as a representative from Texas. Son of Mexican immigrants, Gonzales began his political career by becoming a member of the San Antonio City Council in 1953. In 1956, he was elected to the Texas Senate where he served until his election to the United States Congress in 1961, making him the first Hispanic from Texas to be elected to Congress. Gonzales once commented: "Obviously what I've done and said has touched chords in the United States and Texas. But I am not an orthodox politician, and I've never intended to be one. I discovered legislative advocacy when I was on the San Antonio City Council. Without realizing it, I'd say what I thought, and it would cause a stir. In politics you're going to be criticized and you're going to be praised. I don't worry about when the praise will stop."[150] Congressman Gonzales died on November 28, 2000.

Other notables include the late John Tower, the first Republican elected to a Senate seat from Texas since Reconstruction; Lloyd Bentsen(D), former United States Senator, vice presidential candidate and presidential cabinet member; Phil Gramm former Republican senator; Kay Bailey Hutchison(R) first woman from Texas elected to the United States Senate; George H.W. Bush(R), former congressman, vice president and subsequently president; George W. Bush(R), governor and two-term president and Rick Perry(R), the first Republican governor to be elected to three four-year terms of office. Opting not to run for a fourth term, Rick Perry launched a very unsuccessful bid for the 2016 Republican presidential nomination along with Republican Texas Senator Ted Cruz. Losing out to Donald Trump, Perry is currently serving in Trump's cabinet as the Secretary of Energy. In January 2019, Gregory Wayne "Greg" Abbott was sworn in for his second term of office as the state's 48th governor. The state's only paraplegic governor, Abbott was only the second Republican to serve as Attorney General since Reconstruction. His legal career includes his appointment by Governor George W. Bush to the Texas Supreme Court. Former mayor of San Antonio and Secretary of Housing and Urban Development during the Obama administration, Julian Castro has officially launched his 2020 bid to become the Democratic Party's presidential candidate.

Conclusions

This brief historical picture of Texas points to many unique political attributes that are "typically" Texan and southern. Texas is politically a conservative state. At times, Texans are progressive, but not always. The role of government is viewed with suspicion. The current state constitution restricts the roles of both the legislature and the governor, creating a weak state government often unable to respond to the needs of its citizens. But every governmental reaction has some historical significance. It is all interwoven—government, history, culture, politics, and public policy.

Chapter Notes

[1]*Major Problems in Texas History*, Sam W. Haynes and Cary D. Wintz, eds., (New York, New York: Hougton Mifflin Co., 2002), 1-2.

[2]Joe B. Frantz, *Texas: A History*, 2nd ed., (New York, New York: Norton, 1984), 3.

[3]S. Dale McLemore and Harriet D. Romo, *Racial and Ethnic Relations in America,* 7th ed., (New York, New York: Pearson Education, Inc., 2005), 39.

[4]W. W. Newcomb, Jr., *The Indians of Texas: From Prehistoric to Modern Times,* 11th ed., (Austin, Texas: The University of Texas Press, 1995), 23.

[5]Randolph B. Campbell, *Gone to Texas: A History of the Lone Star State*, (New York, New York: Oxford University Press, 2003), 13.

[6]Frantz, *Texas: A History*, 10.

[7]Newcomb, 30—31.

[8]Jason Buch, "Immigration History Runs Dee Here," *San Antonio Express-News*, (Sunday, June, 25, 2017), A18.

[9]Newcomb, 56.

[10]Ibid., 85.

[11]"Philip Nolan's Filibustering Expedition-1800-1801," *Documents of Texas History*, 2nd ed., Ernest Wallace, David M. Vigness and George B. Ward, eds., (Austin, Texas: State House Press, 1994), 35.

[12]Frantz, *Texas: A History*, 13.

[13]Rupert N. Richardson, Adrian Anderson, Cary D.Wintz, and Ernest Wallace, *Texas: The Lone Star State*, 9th ed., (Upper Saddle River, New Jersey: Prentice Hall, 2005), 16.

[14]"The First Europeans in Texas-1528-1536," *Documents of Texas History*, 2nd ed., Ernest Wallace, David M. Vigness and George B. Ward, eds., (Austin, Texas: State House Press, 1994), 1.

[15]Campbell, *Gone to Texas: A History of the Lone Star State*, 31-32.

[16]"The Coronado Expedition: 1540-1541-Coronado's Report to the King," *Documents of Texas History*, 2nd ed., Ernest Wallace, David M. Vigness and George B. Ward, eds., (Austin, Texas: State House Press, 1994), 7-8.

[17]Felix D. Almaraz, "Spain's Cultural Legacy in Texas," *The Texas Heritage*, Ben Procter and Archie P. McDonald, eds., 1st ed., (Illinois: Forum, 1980), 9.

[18]Ibid., 7.

[19]Felix D. Almaraz, "Spain's Cultural Legacy in Texas," *The Texas Heritage*, Ben Proctor and Archie McDonald, eds., 4th ed., (Wheeling, Illinois: Harlan Davidson, Inc., 2003, 25.

[20]David Roberts, "Sieur de La Salle's Fateful Landfall," *Smithsonian*, Vol. 28, No. 1, April, 1997, 44.

[21]Ibid., 41.

[22]"La Salle in Texas-1685-1687," *Documents of Texas History*, 2nd ed., Ernest Wallace, David M. Vigness and George B. Ward, eds., (Austin, Texas: State House Press, 1994), 9.

[23]Roberts, "Sieur de La Salle's Fateful Landfall," 46.

[24]Ibid., 48.

[25]Almaraz, "Spain's Cultural Legacy in Texas," 14.

[26]Rupert N. Richardson, Ernest Wallace and Adrian Anderson, *Texas: The Lone Star State*, 4th ed., (Englewood Cliffs, New Jersey: Prentice Hall, 1981), 20.

[27]Richardson, etal., 9th ed., 32.

[28]"The Texas Missions: 1785," *Documents of Texas History*, 2nd ed., Ernest Wallace, David M. Vigness and George B. Ward, eds., (Austin, Texas: State House Press, 1994), 31.

[29]Harry Shattuck, "The Mission Trail," *The Houston Chronicle* (September 24, 1995) 4H.

[30]Almaraz, "Spain's Cultural Legacy in Texas," 9.

[31]"The Texas Missions: 1785," *Documents of Texas History*, 31.

[32]Almaraz, "Spain's Cultural Legacy in Texas," 11.

[33]Richardson, etal., 9th ed., 35.

[34]Jesus F. De La Teja, "The Making of a Tejano Community," *Major Problems in Texas History*, Sam W. Haynes and Cary D. Wintz, eds., (New York, New York: Houghton Mifflin Co., 2002), 74.

[35]Ibid., 72.

[36]"A Census of Spanish Texas—December 31, 1783," *Documents of Texas History*, 2nd ed., Ernest Wallace, David M. Vigness and George B. Ward, eds., (Austin, Texas: State House Press, 1994), 28.

[37]Frantz, *Texas: A History*, 32.

[38]Campbell, *Gone to Texas: A History of the Lone Star State,* 60.

[39]"The Texas Missions—1785," *Documents of Texas History*, 33.

[40]Frantz, *Texas: A History*, 31.

[41]John V. Lombardi, "Colonial Latin America," *Latin America: Perspectives on a Region*, 1st ed., Jack W. Hopkins, ed., (New York, New York: Holmes & Meier Publishers, Inc., 1987), 74.

[42]"The Government of Texas—November 7, 1811," *Documents of Texas History*, 2nd ed., Ernest Wallace, David M. Vigness and George B. Ward, eds., (Austin, Texas: State House Press, 1994), 39.

[43]"Texas's First Declaration of Independence and First Constitution—April 16 and 17, 1813," *Documents of Texas History*, 2nd ed., Ernest Wallace, David M. Vigness and George B. Ward, eds., (Austin, Texas: State House Press, 1994), 39.

[44]David M. Vigness, "The Coming of the Anglo-Americans," *The Texas Heritage*, 1st ed., Ben Procter and Archie McDonald, eds., (Illinois: Forum, 1980), 23.

[45]Campbell, *Gone to Texas: A History of the Lone Star State*, 61.

[46]Frantz, *Texas: A History*, 51.

[47]"Stephen F. Austin Seeks Settlers of 'Unblemished Character,' 1823," *Major Problems in Texas History*, Sam W. Haynes and Cary D. Wintz, eds., (New York, New York: Houghton Mifflin Co., 2002), 82.

[48]Ibid.

[49]Victoria Loe, "The Forgotten Father," *Dallas Morning News*, October 31, 1993, A25.

[50]"The Mexican Colonization Laws—The Imperial Colonization Law," *Documents of Texas History*, 2nd ed., Ernest Wallace, David M. Vigness and George B. Ward, eds., (Austin, Texas: State House Press, 1994), 47.

[51]Ibid.

[52]Ibid.

[53]Ibid., 48.

[54]"De Witt's Empresario Contract—April 15, 1825," *Documents of Texas History*, 2nd ed., Ernest Wallace, David M. Vigness and George B. Ward, eds., (Austin, Texas: State House Press, 1994), 59.

[55]Ibid.

[56]Robert A. Calvert, Arnoldo De Leon and Gregg Cantrell, *The History of Texas*, 3rd ed., (Wheeling, Illinois: Harlan Davidson, Inc., 2002), 61.

[57]Neal Tannahill, *Texas Government: Policy and Politics*, 4th ed., (New York, New Yor: HarperCollins, 1993), 15.

[58]Frantz, *Texas: A History*, 59.

[59]Ibid.

[60]Archie Mc Donald, "Texas Independence," *The Texas Heritage*, Ben Procter and Archie McDonald, eds., 1st ed., (Illinois: Forum, 1980), 37.

[61]Ibid., 42.

[62]John MacCormack, "Tejanos' Fortunes Fell in 19th Century," *San Antonio Express-News*, (Friday, November 17, 2017), A12.

[63]Ibid.

[64]"Manual Mier v Teran's Letter to President Guadalupe Victoria: June 10, 1828," *Documents of Texas History*, 2nd ed., Ernest Wallace, David M. Vigness and George B. Ward, eds., (Austin, Texas: State House Press, 1994), 65.

[65]"The Convention of 1833," *Documents of Texas History*, 2nd ed., Ernest Wallace, David M. Vigness and George B. Ward, eds., (Austin, Texas: State House Press, 1994), 74.

[66]Ibid.

[67]Ibid., 75.

[68]"The Memorial to Congress Requesting Separate Statehood—1833," *Documents of Texas History*, 2nd ed., Ernest Wallace, David M. Vigness and George B. Ward, eds., (Austin, Texas: State House Press, 1994), 76.

[69]McDonald, "Texas Independence," 45.

[70]H. W. Brands, "The Alamo Should Never Have Happened," *Texas Monthly*, March, 2003, 91.

[71]Ibid., 138.

[72]Holly Beachley Brear,"Creating the Myth of the Alamo," *Major Problems in Mexican American History*, Zaragosa Vargas, ed., (New York, New York: Houghton Mifflin Co., 1999), 115.

[73]Frantz, *Texas: A History*, 63.

[74]Ibid., 64.

[75]Albert A. Nofi, *The Alamo and the Texas War for Independence, September 30, 1835-April 21, 1836, Heroes, Myths and History,* (Pennsylvania: Combined Books, 1992), 67.

[76]Scott Huddleston, "Church at Shrine Long a Survivor," *San Antonio Express-News*, (Friday, July 7, 2017), A8.

[77]Ibid.

[78]Robert Kolarik, "An Answer from Goliad," *San Antonio Express-News*, (Saturday, March 3, 2018), A8.

[79]"The Texas Declaration of Independence—March 1, 1836," *Documents of Texas History*, 2nd ed., Ernest Wallace, David M. Vigness and George B. Ward, eds., (Austin, Texas: State House Press, 1994), 98.

[80]John Hoyt Williams, *Sam Houston: A Biography of the Father of Texas*, (New York, New York: Simon and Schuster, 1993), 137.

[81]"The Goliad Campaign and Massacre-March, 1836," *Documents of Texas History*, 2nd ed., Ernest Wallace, David M. Vigness and George B. Ward, eds., (Austin, Texas: State House Press, 1994), 110.

[82]Karen Adler, "A Heroine Unveiled," *San Antonio Express-News* (March 29, 2004), 1B.

[83]Richardson, et al., 9th ed., 106.

[84]Ibid.

[85]Calvert, etal., 83.

[86]Williams, 154.

[87]Ibid., 154-155.

[88]Frantz, *Texas: A History*, 73.

[89]_____, "Army Came Here Just Before Statehood," *San Antonio Express-News*, (Thursday, July 5, 2018), A10.

[90]Richardson, et al., 9th ed., 132.

[91]Ibid., 120.

[92]Kent Biffle, "Ist Republic Ended Up in Quite a State," *Dallas Morning News,* (Sunday, May 11, 1997), 38A.

[93]Stanley Siegel, "The Lone Star Republic," *The Texas Heritage*, 1st ed., Ben Procter and Archie P. McDonald, eds., (IL: Forum, 1980), 61.

[94]"The Annexation Offer Accepted—July 4, 1845," *Documents of Texas History*, 2nd ed., Ernest Wallace, David M. Vigness and George B. Ward, eds., (Austin, Texas: State House Press, 1994), 148.

[95]"President Lamar's Policies—Lamar's Inaugural Address-December 10, 1838," *Documents of Texas History*, 2nd ed., Ernest Wallace, David M. Vigness and George B. Ward, eds., (Austin, Texas: State House Press, 1994), 125.

[96]Frantz, *Texas: A History*, 88.

[97]Campbell, *Gone to Texas: A History of the Lone Star State*, 186.

[98]"The Republic of Texas Is No More—February 19, 1846," *Documents of Texas History*, 2nd ed., Ernest Wallace, David M. Vigness and George B. Ward, eds., (Austin, Texas: State House Press, 1994), 160.

[99]Calvert, etal., 3rd ed., 107.

[100]"Sam Houston Threatens Reprisals Against Mexico, March 21, 1842," *Major Problems in Texas History*, Sam W. Haynes and Cary D. Wintz, eds., (New York, New York: Houghton Mifflin Co., 2002), 160.

[101]_____, "Salado Creek Fight Upended Invasion," *San Antonio Express-News*, (September 18, 2018), A10.

[102]Richardson, et al., 9th ed., 144.

[103]Mariano Castillo, "Bloody Day Memorialized," *San Antonio Express-News* (Sunday, January 25, 2004), 7B.

[104]Richardson, et al., 9th ed., 144.

[105]_____, "Hays Fought Like His Comanche Foes," *San Antonio Express-News*, (Thursday, July 20, 2017), A9.

[106]Frantz, *Texas: A History*, 90-91.

[107]Terry G. Jordan, "A Century and Half of Ethnic Change in Texas, 1836-1986," *Texas Vistas: Selections from the Southwestern Historical Quarterly*, Ralph A. Wooster and Robert A. Calvert, eds., (Austin, Texas: The University of Texas at Austin, 1987), 321.

[108]March E. Nackman, "The Roots of Exceptionalism," *Major Problems in Texas History*, Sam W. Haynes and Cary D. Wintz, eds., (New York, New York: Houghton Mifflin Co., 2002), 7.

[109]Jordan, "A Century and Half of Ethnic Change in Texas, 1836-1986," 321.

[110]Randolph B. Campbell, "An Empire for Slavery," *Major Problems in Texas History*, Sam W. Haynes and Cary D. Wintz, eds., (New York, New York: Houghton Mifflin Co., 2002), 226.

[111]Jordan, "A Century and Half of Ethnic Change in Texas, 1836-1986," 336.

[112]Vincent T. Davis, "Irish Settled Land North of the Alamo," *San Antonio Express-News*, (July, 2017), A9.

[113]Jordan, "A Century and Half of Ethnic Change in Texas, 1836-1986," 336.

[114]Ibid., 342.

[115]Lindsay T. Baker, *The Polish Texans*, (San Antonio, Texas: University of Texas Institute of Texan Cultures at San Antonio, 1981), 11.

[116]"Caroline von Hineuber Describes the Hardships of Life in Austin's Colony, 1832," *Major Problems in Texas History*, Sam W. Haynes and Cary D. Wintz, eds., (New York, New York: Houghton Mifflin Co., 2002), 88-89.

[117]Richardson, et al., 9th ed., 174.

[118]"Life in Colonial Texas: December, 1831," *Documents of Texas History*, 2nd ed., Ernest Wallace, David M. Vigness and George B. Ward, eds., (Austin, Texas: State House Press, 1994), 71-72.

[119]Frantz, *Texas: A History*, 101.

[120]Alwyn Barr, "Revolutionary Changes in Civil War Texas," *The Texas Heritage*, 1st ed., Ben Procter and Archie P. McDonald, eds., (Illinois: Forum, 1980), 82.

[121]"Texas Secedes from the Union-February 1-2, 1861," *Documents of Texas History*, 2nd ed., Ernest Wallace, David M. Vigness and George B. Ward, eds., (Austin, Texas: State House Press, 1994), 194.

[122]Richardson, et al., 9th ed., 157.

[123]Ibid., 158.

[124]Frantz, *Texas: A History*, 112.

[125]Richardson, et al., 9th ed., 207.

[126]Campbell, *Gone to Texas: A History of the Lone Star State*, 244.

[127]"Sam Houston Opposes Secession," *Major Problems in Texas History*, Sam W. Haynes and Cary D. Wintz, eds., (New York, New York: Houghton Mifflin Co., 2002), 217.

[128]Frantz, *Texas: A History*, 108.

[129]Anne Gingus, "Independence Day," *Texas Monthly*, June, 2001, 64.

[130]"Granger's Proclamation Abolishing Slavery in Texas-June 19, 1865," *Documents of Texas History*, 2nd ed., Ernest Wallace, David M. Vigness and George B. Ward, eds., (Austin, Texas: State House Press, 1994), 201.

[131]Alwyn Barr, "Revolutionary Changes in Civil War Texas," *The Texas Heritage*, 1st ed., Ben Procter and Archie P. McDonald, eds., (Illinois: Forum, 1980), 87.

[132]"The Ritual of a Secret Society—June 4, 1868," *Documents of Texas History*, 2nd ed., Ernest Wallace, David M. Vigness and George B. Ward, eds., (Austin, Texas: State House Press, 1994), 208.

[133]Joe B. Frantz, "The Cowboy and the Cattle Industry," *The Texas Heritage*, 1st ed., Ben Procter and Archie P. McDonald, eds., (Illinois: Forum, 1980), 109.

[134]Calvert, et al., 3rd ed., 183.

[135]Frantz, *Texas: A History*, 132.

[136]Calvert, et al., 3rd ed., 186.

[137]_____, "Barbed-Wire Demo Redefined the West," *San Antonio Express-News*, (Monday, July 2, 2018), A7.

[138]Kit Myers, "The King of Ranches," *San Antonio Express-News* (Tuesday, November 30, 1999), 3M.

[139]Ibid.

[140]Ibid.

[141]*The HarperCollins Dictionary of American Government and Politics*, Jay M. Shafritz, eds., (New York, New York: HarperCollins Publishers, Inc., 1992), 469.

[142]Frantz, *Texas: A History*, 154.

[143]Calvert, et al., 3rd ed., 311.

[144]Ibid.

[145]Carmina Danini, "The Pershing Chinese in S.A.: In 1917, Alamo City Had Texas' Biggest Chinese Community," *San Antonio Express-News*, (Monday, June 8, 2015), A4.

[146]Ibid.

[147]Richardson, et al., 9th ed., 360-361.

[148]Ibid., 361.

[149]Leslie Carpenter, "Profile of a President," *San Antonio Express-News* (Sunday, February 9, 1964), 4.

[150]Leslie Hicks, "HBG's Classic Quest," *San Antonio Express-News* (Sunday, June 10, 1990), 1D.

Chapter 2

Interest Groups and Texas Politics

A striking feature of American politics is the extent to which political parties are supplemented by private associations formed to influence public policy. These organizations, commonly called pressure groups, promote their interests by attempting to influence government rather than by nominating candidates and seeking responsibility for the management of government. The political interests of agriculture, for example, may be advanced through lobbying and propaganda activities of pressure groups, such as the American Farm Bureau Federation. Such groups, while they may call themselves nonpolitical, are engaged in politics; in the main theirs is a politics of policy. They are concerned with what government does either to help or to harm their membership. . . They supplement the party system and the formal instruments of government by serving as spokesmen for the special interests within society.[1]

During the 2009 Texas Legislative session, Rep. Jose Menendez (D) from San Antonio and others either introduced or openly supported bills legalizing gaming casinos at race tracks as well as building resort casinos in major metropolitan cities and on Native American reservations. Other pieces of legislation called for installing video slot machines at horse and dog tracks. Traditionally, it has been the conservative position of the Baptist and Methodist religious groups to block any legislation dealing with gambling. The only way Paramutual betting passed in the first place was the threat that if it did not pass, the only option left to bring additional revenue into the state's coffer was a statewide income tax! At the State House hearings, those testifying in favor of the proposals were representatives from the horse industry, horse and dog track officials, land developers, and, of course, Las Vegas casino and gaming owners, in particular Sheldon Adelson, chairman and CEO of the Las Vegas Sands Corp. They stressed that gaming casinos would not only help the horse racing industry but bring much needed revenue to the state capitol. After his testimony, Adelson made a visit to the governor's office to convince a reluctant Governor Perry not to veto any gaming and casino legislation that could appear on his desk. The opposition camp included the Baptist Christian Life Commission who stressed that gaming casinos rarely bring in that "pot of gold" advocates promise. In the long run, all of the gaming legislation failed to make it to the governor's desk. The prospects of gaming casinos, professional horse racing, and other games of chance have been proposed without much success in every legislative session since 2009. Were legislators just independently presenting an alternative revenue source to address the state's deficit or were the gaming interests pushing the buttons of lawmakers to bring their agenda to fruition?

During the 2010 governor's race, challenger Bill White (D) openly accused incumbent Governor Rick Perry of brazenly appointing individuals to high level state positions who had made substantial contributions to his campaign. Was Governor Perry using his constitutional appointment powers to reward those who had paved his path to the governor's mansion or did his appointees have the qualifications to serve on these high profile boards and commissions despite the fact that they supported his reelection bid? In one campaign statement, White raised the issue far too often heard from challengers vying against incumbent officeholders: "You think in a state of some 24 million people that it's a coincidence that the very most qualified people to serve on boards and commissions would belong to one party and would be disproportionately his [Perry's] donors."[2] In every campaign across this nation, candidate after candidate vows they will not accept money from special interests nor, if elected, would they be swayed by persistent lobbyists hired by high profile interest groups. During the 2010 campaign, a candidate for the Texas House of Representatives ran an ad featuring the scenario of a lobbyist handing a bundle of money to his incumbent opponent on the floor of the House with the tag line that votes are for sale in Austin. Yet, every candidate openly seeks the endorsement of and money from interest groups particularly those that rate favorably with the electorate. For example, John Q. Public may not know much about a particular candidate's qualifications for office or his/her position on the issues. However, if that candidate is endorsed by the local Police Officers Association, John Q. Public knows that, at least, this candidate is supportive of law enforcement and is tough on crime. The Perry team made the headlines when the powerful Texas Realtors Association with its approximately 85,000 members endorsed his reelection bid. Calling them "kindred spirits," Perry praised the state's realtors by pointing out that "you [the realtors] help your clients find a place to live, find the dream home of their lives, help them relocate from one of those states with high taxes and high regulations to the great state of Texas."[3]

This chapter examines the oftentimes controversial role interest groups play in both the electoral process and eventually the development of public policy initiatives. Do interest groups deserve being called the "bad guys"? Are interest groups detrimental to the democratic process? Was James Madison on target when he lamented in *Federalist #10*, "that the public good is disregarded in the conflicts of rival parties [factions, or interest groups], and that measures are too often decided, not according to the rules of justice and the rights of the minor party, but by the superior force of an interested and overbearing majority?"[4] Or do interest groups play a vital role in strengthening the democratic process? Did not the sole voice of the American Association of Retired Persons (AARP) representing millions of the nation's seniors had a positive impact on the development of Obama's health-care plan? Has not the lone voice of Communities Organized for Public Service (COPS) brought to the residents of San Antonio's southwest side the sidewalks, drainage, and new roads that the area needed for decades? Why do people desire to affiliate themselves with interest groups? What benefits do they seek from them? What makes one interest group more powerful than another?

Who Controls the Public Policy Process in America?

The fundamental question particularly in a representative democracy is what outside force exerts its influence on and plays a dominate role in the public policy process. There are basically two schools of thought—elitism and pluralism. As in the case of elitism, the decision making process is dominated by a small group of powerful players. On the other hand, pluralist theories are based on the involvement of numerous groups usually referred to as pressure or interest groups.

Elitism is "the view that political power and the ability to influence the most important policy decisions are held by a few individuals who derive power from their leadership positions in large institutions."[5] Elitism is not a new theory of governance. In the *Republic*, Plato believed that society should be divided into three distinct classes: rulers, fighters, and producers. "A numerically small aristocracy of rulers, in command of a well-trained body of soldiers and administrators, governs the third class, or producers [farmers, artisans, etc.], which constitutes four fifths or more of the total population."[6] The chosen few of the aristocracy were the recipients of the education and training required of future rulers. Italian political theorist Gaetano Mosca wrote:

In all society—from societies that are very meagerly developed and have barely attained the dawnings of civilization, down to the most advanced and powerful societies—two classes of people appear—a class that rules and a class that is ruled. The first class, always the less numerous, performs all the political functions, monopolizes power, and enjoys the advantages that power brings, whereas the second, the more numerous class, is directed and controlled by the first, in a manner that is now more or less legal, now more or less arbitrary and violent.[7]

The concept of a landed and entitled aristocracy dominated throughout the emerging empires and eventually nation states. The composition of the elite changed as the economic mainstay of the nation state shifted from an agricultural to an industrial one. The traditional landed nobility that dominated the chambers of upper legislative houses and throne rooms was gradually replaced by the moneyed entrepreneurs. The rise of democracy or popular rule challenged elitism. Fearful of turning governing authority over to the masses, even the Framers of the United States Constitution wanted some guarantees that the elite would still have the upper hand. An advocate of elitism, Alexander Hamilton once wrote:

All communities divide themselves into the few and the many. The first are the rich and the wellborn, the other the mass of the people. . . . The people are turbulent and changing they seldom judge or determine right. Give therefore to the first class a distinct, permanent share in the government. They will check the unsteadiness of the second, and as they cannot receive any advantage by a change, they therefore will ever maintain good government.[8]

What has emerged in the United States, is a political elite defined by Harold Lasswell as "the power holders of a body politic. The power holders include the leadership and the social formations from which leaders typically come, and to which accountability is maintained, during a given generation. In other words, the political elite is the top power class."[9] Furthermore, sociologist C. Wright Mills contended in his publication *The Power Elite*, that the United States was indeed controlled by a political, business, and military elite that despite democracy, actually controlled the decision making process. The elites basically share the same political, social and economic perspectives. Texas experienced elitism with the plantation class that first settled lower portions of East Texas. The agricultural elite eventually gave way to the cattle baron, then the oil man and, finally, to the wealthy businessman. The elite group is usually composed of a homogeneous group drawn from the upper and upper-middle income Anglo classes. They tend to be well educated at prestigious colleges and universities and belong to the same civic and social organizations, in other words, the "country club set." Members of the elite are economically dependent upon each other through their participation in various business-oriented organizations such as the Chamber of Commerce and serve together on numerous boards of directors. An **interlocking directorate** occurs when two or more individuals representing different interests serve together either as board members or officers of key business and civic organizations. Interlocking directorates are mutually beneficial to all involved participants. For example, the board of regents for a local college decides to build a new classroom building. Benefiting from that decision is the board member who is president of a major bank who will provide the funding, the owner of a construction company who will probably build the building, a primary shareholder of a land development company who owns a convenient parcel of land, etc. In the political arena, the economic elites in Texas either run one of their own for office or actively recruit someone who will promote their interests. For example, between 1938 and 1957, Texas politics was heavily influenced by **The Establishment** "a loosely knit plutocracy comprised mostly of Anglo businessmen, oilmen, bankers and lawyers.[10] In the 1940s and 50s, Herman Brown, the founder of Brown and Root, would gather his multimillionaire friends into his suite at the Lamar Hotel in Houston. Known as the **8F Group** they would conduct interviews of political wannabes to ensure that any candidate they monetarily backed would, if elected, pursue their interests.

While one cannot deny that elites do exist in the United States, the prevailing dominance in political wheeling and dealing is centered on a multiplicity of actors or interest groups. **Pluralism** is "the view that competition and the subsequent negotiation and bargaining among multiple centers of power is the key to understanding how decisions are made. This framework starts from the assumption that a society is composed of many different groups and that the interactions of some of these groups in the political process shape actual decisions by state and local governments."[11] In *The Governmental Process*, political scientist David Truman emphasizes that **pluralist theory** "assumes that within the public arena there will be countervailing centers of power within governmental institutions and among outsiders. Competition is implicit in the notion that groups, as surrogates for individuals, will produce products

representing the diversity of opinions that might have been possible in the individual decision days of democratic Athens.[12] Whereas elitism assumes that one group will be the dominating force behind the choice of the issues addressed and the responses delivered, pluralism is more fluid as the levels of participation from various groups is determined by the issues at hand. In other words, the issue determines which groups will dominate the policy process, not the other way around. For example, those groups focusing on pro-choice and anti-abortion issues will not be involved in issues concerning gun ownership. The National Rifle Association will be a strong voice against gun control but will not usually play a role in industrial pollution issues. It is the issue that for that moment binds different groups together. During the 2011 Texas Legislative session groups of teachers, parents, members of professional education organizations, and, yes, even students staged rallies in Austin protesting the proposed budgetary cuts to education. Several years ago, diverse religious groups that usually find fault with each other's religious perspectives, joined forces with seniors loudly protesting on the steps of the state capitol demanding that the Texas Legislature defeat a measure imposing a state tax on bingo winnings.

It was political scientist Theodore Lowi who tied interest group activities with liberal political theory into a new ism—**interest group liberalism**. In *The End of Liberalism*, Lowi contends that the interplay among interest groups and governing institutions is liberalism "because it expects to use government in a positive and expansive role, it is motivated by the highest sentiments, and it possesses strong faith that what is good for government is good for the society."[13] He based his concept on the assumption that:

1. Organized interests are homogeneous and easy to define, sometimes monolithic. Any "duly elected" spokesperson for any interest is taken as speaking in close approximation for each and every member.
2. Organized interests pretty much fill up and adequately represent most of the sectors of our lives, so that one organized group can be found effectively answering and checking some other organized group as it seeks to prosecute its claims against society.
3. The role of government is one of ensuring access particularly to the most effectively organized, and of ratifying the agreements and adjustments worked out among the competing leaders and their claims.[14]

Unfortunately, the intensity of the conflict coupled with the inability to reach a compromise can result in hyperpluralism and legislative gridlock. **Hyperpluralism** is a governing situation wherein so many groups so successfully compete for political power that power becomes decentralized and nothing much can get done."[15] Conflicts among interest groups spills over into the conflicts within legislative houses and can lead to a long-term breach between the legislative and the executive branches of government. The term **gridlock** refers to "the freezing of action on an issue as a result of the sometimes overly effective operation of the separation of powers and the checks and balances system provided by the U.S. Constitution and the natural functioning of the two-party system."[16] For example, several interest groups have exerted their influence on numerous bills promoting a statewide water sharing plan to address chronic drought conditions. The intense fighting between these groups as to whose recommendation is the best option has resulted in the Texas Legislature becoming equally divided, meaning that Texas still does not have a statewide-mandated water sharing program.

Interest Group Dynamics

Called a faction by James Madison, an **interest group** is "an organized collection of individuals who are bound together in shared attitudes or concerns and who make demands on political institutions in order to realize goals which they are unable to achieve on their own."[17] Whether it be a homeowners association, the parent/teacher association at the elementary school or a hiking club, interest groups unite people under one small umbrella. Basically, Americans love the dynamics of group activity. In his *Democracy in America* published in 1835, Alexis de Tocqueville marveled over the propensity for Americans to organize into groups:

> In the United States, political associations are only one small part of the immense number of different types of associations. Americans of all ages, all stations in life, and all types of dispositions are forever forming associations. There are not only commercial and industrial associations in which all take part, but others of a thousand different types—religious, moral, serious, futile, very general and very limited, immensely large and very minute. Americans combine to give fetes, found seminaries, build churches, distribute books, and send missionaries to the antipodes. Hospitals, prisons, and schools take shape that way. Finally, if they want to proclaim a truth or propagate some feeling by the encouragement of a great example, they form an association.[18]

What was true in his 1830s observation still holds today. In the United States, interest groups do play an extremely important role in all aspects of the public policy process. The rise of interest groups has strengthened rather than weakened the democratic zeal for participatory politics. Beginning in the 1960s, the rise of liberal citizen groups was attributable to the anti-Vietnam pro-civil rights and women's rights movements. These organizations were "largely responsible for catalyzing an explosion in the growth of all interest groups. Efforts to limit the impact of liberal citizen groups failed, and the policy-making process became more open and more participatory."[19]

There are noticeable pros and cons to interest group involvement in the public policy arena:

> On the positive side, interest group politics creates a dynamism, often through conflict, that draws out diversity in policy proposals, a diversity producing innovation and social change. Interest groups also provide access for the public to affect government decision-making. Citizens align themselves with like minded people, and later develop coalitions with other groups that feel similarly on a particular issue. On the negative side, interest groups fighting for their special goals can fragment the policy process. This struggle reduces the leadership's capacity to direct citizen demands toward an effective solution, promoting instead a compromise that may partially satisfy each group but not resolve the initial issue.[20]

Regardless of the positive or negative impact of interest groups, lawmakers must accept the reality that interest groups will continue to grow in number and will remain ardent watchdogs over every single item of legislation that is introduced in the legislature. In a democratic system, the key to legislative successes is a healthy combination of compromise, accommodation, and negotiation. Basically, "democracy requires adequate representation of interests as well as institutions capable of addressing difficult policy problems. For policy makers who must balance the demand for representation with the need for results, the key is thinking creatively about how to build coalitions and structure negotiations between large groups of actors."[21] In a pluralist environment, every interest group, whether it be a local church group, sewing circle or the Chamber of Commerce, can conceivably earn the distinction of being a **pressure group**, that is, an organized group that seeks to influence the policies and practices of government.

Organizational Structure

Basically, interest groups fall into two structural patterns—nationally affiliated groups and grassroots organizations. A **nationally affiliated group** such as the League of Women Voters or the National Rifle Association is structured in a traditional pyramid fashion. The national organization serves as the catalyst for development of state and local affiliated chapters. The national organization provides the overall development of the group's philosophy, goals and objectives, bottom-line issue positions, rules of operation, etc. In turn, state organizations are to provide the appropriate framework, guidelines and oversight to ensure that their local chapters are in compliance with the policies and practices of the national organization. Periodically, the national organization will hold a national convention whereby the state and local affiliates will send voting delegates to approve a new slate of national officers and proposed changes to either the group's bottom-line issues or its overall operations. In turn, state organizations usually hold conventions for their local organizations.

While being affiliated with a national organization gives local organizations credibility and clout within their community surroundings, there are some significant negatives. First, local groups must pay both their state and national organizations for the right to exist within the protective embrace of its national organization. Individuals are more apt to join a local group that has the backing of a national organization. However, it comes at a price. For example, the local chapter of a nationally affiliated environmental group charges its members $75 in yearly dues. What many local members forget is this chapter must pay $35 per member to the national organization, and $25 to the state organization, leaving the local organization with only $15 per member per year to run the organization. Second, local concerns oftentimes do not fit into the overall philosophy or the bottom-line issue positions of the national organization. It leaves the local group with the choice of either not supporting their local community because to do so violates national directives or violating national policy in order to fulfill its obligation to its community-based membership.

On the other hand, **grassroots organizations** or **citizens' groups** develop at the community level first primarily to address unique locally-based issues that do not fit under a national umbrella. In San Antonio, Communities Organized for Public Service or COPS began in the west side of the city with the assistance of the local Catholic parishes. A predominately low- to lower-middle income Hispanic community, individual residents began to realize that their individual concerns over the lack of adequate drainage, sidewalks, and decent streets were collective concerns. By drawing themselves together, they decided the one collective loud voice carried more weight than the many individual soft voices at city hall. It was the tenacity and dedication of their leadership that turned the tide. As early as the 1960s, the leadership of COPS started their drive to bring an institute of higher learning to the south side of San Antonio. Finally, their collective voice was heard. In 1974, their president introduced a resolution at the group's first convention to open a community college either on the west side or southside of the city. In 1982, Texas Attorney General Mark White was running for governor. He pledged COPS that if the group endorsed him, he would, if elected, push the Texas Legislature to allocate the necessary funds to build this college. In March 1983, the Texas Legislature fulfilled newly elected Governor Mark White's request by officially chartering the construction of Palo Alto College. "Voters passed a bond the same year to build a $13 million campus with an initial capacity of 2,500 students."[22] The addition of Texas A & M at San Antonio, a four-year university campus with the hopes of offering masters and doctoral degrees located just across the expressway from Palo Alto College, has fulfilled COPs dream of bringing higher education opportunities to the southside of San Antonio! Today, no candidate running for any office in a district that includes a portion of the west side has a chance of winning that race without the endorsement of COPS. However, the longevity of grassroots organizations is dicey because they are basically acting alone. COPS has a successful track record because it continues to have consistent and committed strong internal leadership and maintains strong external support of its immediate community.

Types of Interest Groups

There are several broad categories of interest groups. For example, **advocacy groups** are "organizations created to seek benefits on behalf of groups of persons who are in some way incapacitated or otherwise unable to represent their own interests."[23] Advocacy groups are generally national-based organizations with state or local chapter affiliations. Depending upon their audience, advocacy groups fall into several broad-based categories such as single issue groups, citizen or public issue groups, economic or business organizations, religious and ideologically-based interest groups, workers organizations or unions, professional organizations, and government advocacy groups.

Single issue groups only advocate issues pertinent to their group's goals and objectives. Their overall aim is to protect their group from any unfavorable treatment, particularly legislative actions that would weaken the viability of their organization. Unfortunately, those that tend to be steadfast in their advocacy oftentimes are not prone to compromises. For example, the National Rifle Association (NRA) and all of its Texas-based local organizations had been actively involved in the 2011 Texas Legislative session by openly throwing their support behind Sen. Jeff Wentworth's bill allowing those with concealed handgun licenses to carry their weapons on public-supported college and university campuses. Founded in 1871 to promote marksmanship, the NRA is commonly known as the gun lobby. The organization has taken upon itself the task of preserving the Second Amendment to the United States Constitution and simply will not budge from this bottom-line issue. The same reluctance to compromise and make policy concessions can be said of the pro-life groups such as the National Right to Life Committee, which supports an amendment to the United States Constitution banning all abortions. Founded in 1973 after the United States Supreme Court ruling in *Roe v Wade*, this organization has launched an all-or-nothing campaign to overturn the Court's ruling.

One of the state's oldest single issue interest groups is dedicated to the preservation of the state's traditions, the contributions of its founding families, and, of course, significant historical sites and monuments including the Alamo. In 1891, while visiting her father's law library in Galveston, Texas, Betty Ballinger and her cousin Hally Bryan decided to launch an organization to preserve the "memory of the Texas pioneer families and soldiers of the Republic of Texas by forming an association of their descendants."[24] Subsequently garnering the support of fourteen other women, the Charter of the Daughters of the Republic of Texas (DRT) was officially filed on March 9, 1895. The objectives of the DRT are "(1) to perpetuate the memory and spirit of the men and women who achieved and maintained the independence of Texas; (2) to encourage historical research into the earliest records of Texas, . . . to foster the preservation of documents and relics; (3) to promote the celebration of Texas Honor Days."[25] A genealogical organization, the DRT is statewide with approximately 106 chapters spanning across ten districts. DRT organizations oversee historical sites across the state to include the French Legation Museum in Austin, the Ezekiel Cullen House and Museum in San Augustine, and the Gaines-Oliphint House in Milam.

On the other hand, **public interest groups** are "organized pressure groups seeking to develop positions and to support national causes relating to a broader definition of the public good."[26] With the awakening of the nation's conscious over civil rights and the turmoil of the Vietnam War, the late 1960s and 70s ushered a wide variety of numerous public interest groups seeking to influence the political process by awakening and mobilizing Americans who simply had not been overly involved in "politics." The **New Politics Movement** began in 1970 when former Secretary of Health, Education and Welfare under President Lyndon Johnson, John W. Gardner, and several other well-connected individuals founded **Common Cause**. Gardner believed that millions of Americans wanted to express their ire at their government but they lacked the guidance and leadership to channel their millions of single voices into one powerful politically-smart voice capable of moving lawmakers to their causes. Common Cause was the one organization that was able to shift the political tactics of the disgruntled from the very visible mass protests that caught the nightly headlines on the evening news to a more subdued but highly effective behind the doors approach to influencing the outcome of public policy—lobbying. During its hay day, Common Cause "claims credit for enactment of federal election reform, helping to wind down the Vietnam War, enactment of many 'good government' measures at the state level, reform of congressional procedures, blocking subsidies for a supersonic transport (SST), and cutbacks in the oil depletion allowance."[27] Common Cause served as the organizational model for the majority of the public interest groups that emerged from the New Politics Movement.

Public Interest Groups: Good Government

In the late 19th century, a loose group of reformers collectively joined forces to address the severity of the problems confronting the nation's newly arrived immigrant population groups, the urban poor, factory workers, etc., and to compel governing bodies to make the necessary legislative changes to improve the quality of life for all Americans. Emerging in the 1890s, members of the **Progressive Era** "tended to be white, educated, middle-class men and women who believed society needed to respond to the changes caused by industrialization, urbanization and immigration."[28] The politically corrupt antics in city governments throughout the nation caught the attention of newspaper columnists and reformers alike. Therefore, the Progressive Era launched a series of corrective actions to address the corruption of political bossism throughout major metropolitan cities such as New York, Chicago, Cleveland, Boston, etc. In 1900, the **National Civic League** was founded by businessmen advocating government regulation of business practices, improving working conditions for employees, and reforming city government. Other nationally-based organizations included the National Child Labor Committee, the National Housing Association, the Conference of City Managers, and the National Short Ballot Association. In particular, the National Municipal League, a Denver, Colorado based group founded in 1894, advocated municipal reform efforts. In 1981, the group changed its name to the National Civil League. In 1924, the American Municipal Association now known as the National League of Cities was organized to advocate reform of city governments. A nonpartisan community service agency, the National Urban League was founded in 1911 with the goals of bringing to light the economic and social concerns of African Americans and other minority and immigrant population groups. Today, the major nationally-based public interest groups are the Council of State Governments (CGS), National Governors Association (NGA), National Conference of State Legislatures (NCSL), National Association of Counties (NACo), the National League of Cities (NLC), United States Conference of Mayors (USCM), and the International City Management Association (ICMA). Holding yearly conferences, these associations enable such officeholders as governors, mayors and city managers to meet together to discuss and devise options to address their common concerns and public policy issues.

Public Interest Groups: Women

The Progressive movement was particularly attractive to the growing number of college educated middle- and upper-class women desiring to have a career and a presence outside of their traditional roles as wives and mothers. Across the nation, woman's organizations were focused more on raising money for charitable events, advancing the arts, and conserving historical landmarks. An accomplished pianist, Anna Hertzberg established the Tuesday Musical Club in 1901 in San Antonio. Her organization was well known for its "artist series concerts, young artist competitions, and its chorus, dance, piano and string ensemble programs."[29] Hertzberg is credited with founding the San Antonio Symphony. The Woman's Club of San Antonio was founded in 1898 by Eleanor Brackenridge, a wealthy socialite, and Marion B. Fenwick, a columnist for the *San Antonio Express* and the *San Antonio Evening News*. The group raised money to restore the city's historical buildings, promote the arts

and assist local agencies in meeting the needs of the city's poor.

One of the first community-based conservation groups in the United States, the San Antonio Conservation Society was founded in 1924 by Emily Edwards and Rena Maverick Green. Today, this organization is in the forefront of securing the renovation and preservation of historical buildings. "The group's biggest long-term crusade may have been to save and preserve San Antonio's Spanish colonial missions and historical mission irrigation canals and farmlands. That journey began in 1926, when the society acquired the last original doors of the Mission San Jose granary, followed by purchase of the granary and a 1930s restoration of the mission, with help from the Depression-era Civil Works Administration."[30] Today, the group's Historical Farm and Ranch Committee has identified significant historical farm and ranch homesteads and buildings dating back to the 1700s. This organization was the catalyst for founding of thirty-five conservation groups throughout Texas to include the Abilene Preservation League, the Dallas Heritage Village, the Hispanic Heritage Center of Texas, Historic Fort Worth, Preservation Austin, and Preservation Houston.

Although women did not have the right to vote until 1920, they soon changed the venue of their issue advocacy from their parlors to the halls of city council and state and national legislative houses. They realized that the key to addressing workers' abuses, lack of affordable housing, poorly funded schools, proper sanitation, drainage, etc., needed the muscle of governing bodies to enact the appropriate corrective legislation backed with stiff regulations and sanctions to successfully address their concerns.

Founded in 1920, the League of Women Voters is a non-partisan nationally-based organization dedicated to voter service. With fifty state organizations and hundreds of local leagues, this organization actively conducts voter registration drives, distributes voters guides to their local communities, and sponsors candidate debates and forums. Although the organization does not endorse candidates, it does actively solicit support from lawmakers concerning their program issues including quality education, economic development, affordable and available health care, housing, justice-related concerns, affordable quality child care, promotion of local libraries, protection and preservation of natural resources, and protection of voting rights. League members are strong supporters of government-reform efforts that lead to accountable, cost-effective and responsible public policies.

The preeminent non-partisan women's groups include the National Organization for Women (NOW) founded in 1966. According to its official Statement of Purpose:

The purpose of NOW is to take action to bring women into full participation in the mainstream of American society now, exercising all the privileges and responsibilities in thereof in truly equal partnership with men. . . NOW is dedicated to the proposition that women first and foremost are human beings who, like all other people in our society, must have the chance to develop their fullest human potential. We believe that women can achieve such equality only by accepting the full challenges and responsibilities they share with all other people in our society, as part of the decision-making mainstream of American political, economic and social life.[31]

The National Women's Political Caucus (NWPC) is a nationally-Washington based organization that actively recruits, supports, and endorses women for elective offices. In the 1990s, its national president, Harriett Woods, was instrumental particularly through the media, in convincing the United States Senate to take punitive action against Senator Robert Packwood, well known for his decades-old sexual harassment of women. At all levels of the organization, the goal of the organization is to ensure that women's issues are addressed by replacing men with women in elective offices. The abortion issue is paramount to women's organizations. In Texas, the Texas Abortion Rights Action League (TARAL) is up against the religious right and anti-abortion groups in its battle to uphold the Supreme Court's decision in *Roe v Wade*. A powerful voice at both the state and local level, Mothers Against Drunk Driving (MADD), promotes stiffer penalties for anyone driving under the influence of alcohol as well as those establishments serving and selling alcoholic beverages.

Public Interest Groups: Environmental

Particularly in the 1970s, the number of groups advocating environmental issues increased dramatically. In 1892, John Muir founded the Sierra Club, which has served as the model for subsequent environmental groups. Environmental interest groups span a broad spectrum from locally-based environmental preservation and protection organizations to Greenpeace, an international organization that lobbies governments across the world

to protect whales, dolphins, and seals from fishing fleets and hunters as well as other species of marine life that are in peril due to radical climate changes and even at-sea underground nuclear testing. Other groups include the National Audubon Society, Wilderness Society, and the Environmental Defense Fund.

Public Interest Groups: Civil Rights

The primary group advocating and defending the protections given to the American people through the United States Constitution's Bill of Rights is the **American Civil Liberties Union (ACLU),** headquartered in New York City. Closely associated with the goals of the ACLU, the Anti-Defamation League is a New York-based non-partisan organization that monitors and reports racism, bigotry, and anti-Semitism in America. Both of these organizations are watchdogs against discriminatory practices and acts of racism against all citizens and residents of the United States.

The largest and most preeminent civil rights organization is the National Association for the Advancement of Colored People (NAACP) founded in 1909 by W.E.B. Dubois, an educator and one of the founders of the Niagara Movement of 1905. The NAACP was formed as a result of the race riots that occurred in Springfield, Illinois, in 1908. An ardent socialist, William English Walling, wrote a magazine article calling for the unification of the African-American community to fight against racism and discrimination. Joined by fellow white social workers Mary White Ovington and Henry Moskowitz, Walling solicited the support of Oswald Garrison Villard, grandson of William Lloyd Garrison. Originally a primarily Anglo organization, the NAACP gained the support of both Dubois and Booker T. Washington. Dubois merged his Niagara Movement, an African-American protest group, with the emerging NAACP. Headquartered in Baltimore, Maryland, the NAACP has been the driving force behind key United States Supreme Court decisions such as *Guinn v United States* (invalidated the grandfather clause); *Moore v Dempsey* (exclusion of African Americans from juries was inconsistent with the Sixth Amendment to the Constitution); *Buchanan v Warley* (barred municipal ordinances segregating housing); *Shelly v Kraemer* (struck down restrictive covenants); *Sweatt v Painter* (ruled against segregated professional colleges and universities); and, of course, *Brown v Board of Education of Topeka Kansas* (ended separate but equal doctrine). Joining forces with Dr. Martin L. King, Jr., the NAACP was instrumental in securing the passage of the Civil Rights Act of 1964, the

Voting Right Act of 1965, and the Fair Housing Act of 1968. It is estimated that the current membership of the organization is over 500,000 with over 2,200 affiliated or chapter organizations across the nation.

On February 17, 1929, a small group of Hispanics in Corpus Christi, Texas, banded together and launched the League of United Latin American Citizens (LULAC). This organization holds "the record as the longest continually active civil rights organization for Mexican descent citizens in the United States."[32] LULAC successfully challenged the practice of excluding Hispanics from serving on juries, a direct violation of the Sixth Amendment to the United States Constitution guaranteeing one's right to be judged by an impartial jury. Chapters across the state actively protested against the white-only primary. Initially aimed to prevent African Americans from voting in Democrat primary elections, the white-only membership requirement also excluded many Hispanics. Traditionally, LULAC has based "its creed on a duality: Mexican consciousness in culture and social activity; but U.S., consciousness in philosophy and politics. While LULAC favored the learning of English, it called for the maintenance of Spanish. Its agenda also advocated social and racial equality, the development of political power, and economic advancement."[33] The Mexican American Legal Defense Fund (MALDF) legally challenges discriminatory practices and actions against the Hispanic community. Other notable groups include the American GI Forum, Mexican American Business and Professional Women's Association, Mexican-American Youth Organization (MAYO), and the Southwest Voter and Education Project.

Issue groups: Ideological

Ideological groups basically promote issue positions that are in keeping with their philosophical or ideologically based agenda. Religious organizations do play a pivotal role in national and state politics. Particularly in Texas, it has been oftentimes the coalition of the Baptists and Methodists who have pressured the Texas Legislature to support religious-based issues. In particular, it has been the Christian Coalition that has supported candidates from both political parties who support the reinstitution of school prayer into public classrooms and pro-life positions.

The American Conservative Union (ACU) founded in 1964 is a Washington-based organization dedicated to conservative causes. A secretive far right ultraconservative organization founded in 1954 by Robert H. Welch, the John Birch Society is dedicated to fighting communism and communist influences in American life. The organization was named after John Birch, a U.S. army

Mexican pecan shellers at work in a small non-union plant in San Antonio, Texas. March 1939.
Credit: Library of Congress.

captain killed by Chinese Communists in 1945, who is considered to be the first American casualty of the cold war. Initially advocating the impeachment of Earl Warren from the United States Supreme Court, the John Birch Society still wants the United States to withdraw from the United Nations, end its participation in NATO, and eliminate welfare. On the opposite end of the political spectrum, Americans for Democratic Action (ADA) is a liberal organization founded in 1947 to promote domestic social welfare policies.

Economic Interest Groups: Business

Across the nation, the largest category of interest groups lobbying in the nation's capitol and state legislative houses are business-oriented organizations. The preeminent advocate in Washington, D.C., for both large and small businesses is the U.S. Chamber of Commerce. The concept of the business community coming together to protect its collective interests actually began in the fourteenth century as northern German merchants joined into a hansa or a defensive alliance known as the Hanseatic League to protect international trade routes and promote free trade agreements among their membership. At its height, the Hanseatic League had over eighty-five local organizations with an overseeing national body headquartered in Lubeck. With the national economy shifting from an agricultural to an industrial base, many business owners in the United States duplicated the Hanseatic League model by forming chambers of commerce. The notion of a national organization overseeing state and local chapters took hold when President William H. Taft in a message delivered to Congress in 1911, mentioned the need for an unified body located in the nation's capitol that would represent the entire business community. Since opening its doors in 1925, the U.S. Chamber of Commerce has over 3 million members. The organization's bottom line issue is to promote free enterprise. Chambers are the advocates for less government regulation, low business taxes, and imposition of import taxes to promote domestic markets. The Chamber of Commerce is a prime example of a **peak association**, that is, an interest group that advocates for the entire broad spectrum of its constituency, i.e., the business community. Other business-oriented groups represent a segment of the business community such as the National Association of Manufacturers.

In Texas, several of the leading groups include the Texas Association of Business, Texas Association of Taxpayers, Texas Motor Transportation Association, Texas Automobile Dealers Association, Texas Independent Producers and Royalty Owners Association, Texas Chemical Council, Texas Restaurant Association, Association of Fire & Casualty Companies in Texas, Associated General Contractors of Texas, Texas Good Roads Association, and the Texas Bankers Association. These business-centered interest groups are crucial to the economic viability of this state. Since the discovery of Spindletop, the oil and gas business has pumped millions into the state's economy. When the price of crude is high, the state earns considerable revenue to fund everything from roads to schools. However, the price of oil and gas declined beginning in 2016 resulting in the loss of 35,800 jobs in the state's mining and logging industries.[34] Lobbyists hired by the oil and gas interest groups are actively pursing legislative actions to help the industry recover its economic dominance to include support for new pipe lines, expanded drilling rights in the Gulf of Mexico, and relief from environmental regulations that they see as standing in the way to opening up new drilling sites. Texas is also very dependent upon tourism. Interest groups associated with this industry working directly with transportation-related interest groups to promote faster and more efficient ways to travel to and from the state's major convention and tourist centers. "Construction was the only one of three goods-producing industries to have a net increase in employment in 2016, adding 8,800 jobs (1.3 percent) to reached 693,000 in August 2016."[35] Interest groups connected with the construction industry are closely watching Washington's on-going trade wars as the imposition of tariffs are resulting in price increases of construction materials. Regardless of their affiliations, it is essential that all business-related interest groups keep a watchful eye on their policymakers!

Economic Groups: Organized Labor

In 1907, Samuel Gompers, president and founder of the American Federation of Labor, defended both the trade union movement and his organization, which had grown to more than two million members:

> It must be borne in mind that the American Federation of Labor speaks for labor—that is, for the masses as a whole, whether organized or unorganized. The trade union is the only successful attempt to give voice to the "voiceless masses." In every trade, in every community where trade unions exist, they are recognized as the spokesmen of the workers and in fact of all except the employing and the idle rich classes. None conceded this more promptly than the unorganized themselves, who from ignorance or adverse environment may not yet be able to join the ranks of the organized workers, but they look to that protector of their rights as wage-workers and are glad to be represented by their more advanced fellow-workers.[36]

While the captains of industry were making their vast fortunes, the average American in the nation's factories was subjected to working exceptionally long hours with little pay under far too often horrific working conditions. The workforce was composed of mostly immigrants and unskilled workers who could not complain about their working conditions for fear of losing their jobs. The only avenue to gain better working conditions and wages for individual workers was come together as one strong voice under the umbrella of trade unions.

The nation's first attempt to organize workers was a secret society formed in 1869 as the Nobel and Holy Order of the Knights of Labor. Terence V. Powderly, an Irish American, was elected as its Grand Master Workman in 1879. Downplaying the need for worker strikes, Powderly believed that workers could negotiate with their employers for better working conditions, shorter working hours, and higher wages. Formed in 1881 under the guidance of Samuel Gompers, the American Federation of Trade and Labor Unions changed its name in 1886 to the American Federation of Labor (AFL). Gompers, however, took the approach that the only way workers could achieve their objectives was to press management for concessions, and, if all else failed, stage a worker's strike until management conceded. By the end of the 1890s, the AFL replaced the Knights as the nation's leading labor union.   In 1955, it merged with the Congress of Industrial Organizations

(CIO) into the AFL-CIO. For federal government employees, the American Federation of Government Employees (AFGE) was founded in 1932. Founded in 1936, the American Federation of State, County and Municipal Employees (AFSCME) is the largest union of state and local government employees.

The growth of organized labor groups was severely hampered when the United States Congress passed the **Taft-Hartley Act** in 1947. The aim of the legislation was to outlaw several labor union tactics viewed as threatening and, oftentimes, violent towards business owners. The law prohibited jurisdictional, wildcat and political worker strikes, mass picketing, closed shops and direct campaign donations by unions to political candidates. Section **14B** of Taft-Hartley permitted state legislative houses to legally outlaw closed-union shops. A closed-shop meant that employment opportunities would be available to all workers regardless if they were card carrying members of a trade union. Basically, union membership was an option, not a requirement. The Texas Legislature adopted Section 14B, severely limiting the power of organized labor within its state boundaries. "In 2018, union members accounted for 4.3 percent of wage and salary workers in Texas. . . Nationwide, union members accounted for 10.5 percent of employed wage and salary workers in 2018, down from 10.7 percent in 2017."[37]

However, this does not mean that organized labor no longer has the political clout to influence the public policy process. For example, the Firefighters Union in San Antonio has been at odds with the city council and the city manager over its labor contract for nearly ten years as periodic contract negotiations have fallen by the way side. The issue at hand centers on employee health insurance coverage and a long overdue pay increase. In 2018, frustrated union leadership decided to take their concerns to the public by advocating the adoption of three city charter amendments designed to reign in the power of city hall. Both city leadership and the firefighters launched expensive intense campaigns to persuade voters to their side of the issue. On election night, two of the three amendments passed. Now, the firefighters union has the "sole authority to declare an impasse in contract negotiations and submit the dispute to binding arbitration" and the city manager's term of office is limited to eight years with the proviso that he/she "cannot be paid more than 10 times what the city's lowest paid full-time employee earns."[38] Although Texas does not allow teachers' unions, other states do. For example, teachers in the Los Angeles, California school district successfully staged a strike for better pay, smaller classroom sizes, and paid mental-health counselors for each school in their district.

Economic Groups: Agricultural

Although Texas prides itself on its oil and gas businesses and high-tech firms, this state still reaps considerable benefits from its farming and ranching industries. Ranked as the third highest state in total cash receipts from agricultural crops and livestock, "farm and ranch cash receipts in 2015 totaled $23.49 billion, with estimates of $944.8 million for federal farm program, conservation, and indemnity payments. Realized gross farm income totaled $29.51 billion, with farm production expenses of $22.99 billion and net farm income of $6.51 billion."[39] Texas continues to be the nation's number one producer of cotton. Despite a historical record of periodic droughts, floods, wildfires and coastal hurricanes, livestock production and products associated with the cattle industry "accounted for 70.6 percent of the $23.49 billion cash receipts from farm marketings in 2015."[40] The cattle industry in Texas is indeed big business. "The state ranks first nationally in all cattle, beef cattle, cattle on feed, sheep and lambs, wool, goats and mohair. . . . The Jan. 1, 2017, inventory of all cattle and calves in Texas totaled 12.3 million head, valued at $12.67 billion, compared to 11.8 million head as of Jan. 1, 2016, valued at $16.52 million."[41]

Nationally, the first organization for Anglo farmers was the Order of the Patrons of Husbandry or the **Grange**, founded by Oliver Kelley in 1867. In February 1874, the organization issued its "Declaration of Purposes of the National Grange." Specifically the document detailed the group's numerous purposes along with its pledge to:

> Advocate for every state an increase in every practicable way of all facilities for transporting cheaply to the seaboard, or between home producers and consumers, all the productions of our country. We adopt it as our fixed purpose "to open out the channels in Nature's great arteries that the life-blood of commerce may flow freely." We are not enemies of railroads, navigable or irrigating canals, nor of any laboring classes. . . . We are not enemies to capital, but we oppose the tyranny of monopolies. We long to see antagonism between capital and labor removed by common consent, and by an enlightened statesmanship worthy of the nineteenth century.[42]

Today, the American Farm Bureau Federation (AFBF) represents the interests of large-acre farms and ranches while the National Grange, National Farmers Union, and National Farmers Organization advocate the unique concerns of the small acre-sized farmer and rancher. Preeminent agricultural-based groups include the Texas and Southwestern Cattle Raisers Association, Texas Nurseryman's Association, the Texas Corn Producers Board, and the Texas Farmers Union. Promoting the next generation of farmers and ranchers in Texas, it is the yearly stock shows and rodeos throughout the state that allow future farmers and ranchers to show their animals and perhaps win a blue ribbon or the grand prize. These awards bring not only a trophy for the family mantle but also very lucrative college scholarships.

The concerns over working conditions for migrant farm workers moved the late César Chávez to found the United Farm Workers Union. A nationally based organization, the United Farm Workers Union has been successful in securing higher and steadier wages for migrant farm workers. Beginning with a lettuce boycott in Texas, migrant workers under the guidance of Chávez staged a strike against the vineyards of California in 1965. Four years later, the striking workers called for a nationwide consumer boycott of all California wines. In their Boycott Day Proclamation the workers stressed:

> We have been farm workers for hundreds of years and boycotters for two. We did not choose the grape boycott, but we had chosen to leave our peonage, poverty and despair behind. Though our first bid for freedom, the strike, was weakened, we would not turn back. The boycott was the only way forward the growers left to us. We call upon our fellow men and were answered by consumers who said—as all men of conscience must—that they would no longer allow their tables to be subsidized by our sweat and our sorrow: They shunned the grapes, fruits of our affliction. . . . We marched alone at the beginning, but today we count men of all creeds, nationalities, and occupations in our number. . . . Grapes must remain an un-enjoyed luxury for all as long as the barest human needs and basic human rights are still luxuries for farm workers.[43]

Working conditions in vineyards and the agricultural fields across the county have changed resulting in better housing for migrant workers, improved sanitary conditions in the fields, protection for workers from hazardous chemicals and pesticides, and, in some areas, workers compensation and health-care coverage. Today, the primary issue confronting migrant farm workers is the anti-immigration sentiment sweeping across the nation.

Economic Groups: Professional Associations

Nationally-based professional organizations are charged with the task of ensuring that their members are given every opportunity to practice their "trade" in a fair and equitable fashion free of undo interference from government. Founded in 1878, the American Bar Association (ABA), headquartered in Chicago, Illinois, is the most high-profile professional association for lawyers. Its Committee on Federal Judiciary evaluates federal judicial nominees, rates their qualifications, and submits their recommendations to the United States Senate Judiciary Committee. The American Public Works Association (APWA), founded in 1894, is the Chicago-based professional organization for city engineers and others involved in the construction, management or maintenance of public works. In Texas, professional organizations include Lawyers Involved for Texas (LIFT), the Texas Trial Lawyers Association, the Texas Association of School Administrators, the Texas State Teachers Association, Texas Daily Newspaper Association, the Texas Association of Broadcasters, and the Texas Medical Association.

Benefits of Joining Interest Groups

Whether it be the local garden club, the American Civil Liberties Union or the Chamber of Commerce, people join groups for a variety of reasons. Far too often, an individual wants to contribute time, money, or tangible goods to help his/her community, but they simply do not know how to do it on their own initiative. They are seeking a private **purposive incentive**, that is, by joining a group, they will be able to gain the satisfaction of contributing to what they regard as a worthy goal or purpose.[44] For example, in San Antonio, The Elf Louise project started with one individual wanting to give new toys to children whose parents simply could not afford to give them Christmas gifts. Today, hundreds of volunteers begin gathering toys during the summer months and have them individually wrapped and delivered by Christmas morning to homes throughout the city. Many members of environmental groups did not join to fight anti-environmental forces in Washington, D.C. or Austin. These are the individuals who derive the personal satisfaction of saving a stranded dolphin or patiently cleaning crude oil from a bird's feathers. Meals on Wheels is a viable organization due to its volunteers who deliver meals to seniors and to the physically and mentally handicapped.

Many join groups simply because a membership entitles them to benefits. For example, many of the nation's seniors join the American Association of Retired Persons (AARP) because their modest yearly dues open the door to the association's travel club, low-cost life and health insurance programs, a credit card program, etc. Obviously, the costs of the benefits far exceed the individual cost of the yearly membership dues. Awards, perks, and benefits are collectively known as **selective benefits**. "Organizations in the best positions to offer such benefits are those initially formed for some nonpolitical purpose and that ordinarily provide material benefits to their clients."[45] Once the group crosses into a more politically active environment, the focus of membership benefits shifts with the organization using its funds to hire lobbyists and promote candidates for public office. In *The Logic of Collective Action*, Mancur Olson places selective benefits into three broad categories:

- **Material benefits**—tangible awards that have monetary value
- **Solidary benefits**—socially derived, intangible rewards of association, i.e., camaraderie, fun, status or prestige
- **Expressive or purposive benefits**—derived from advancing a particular cause or ideology.[46]

All interest groups are confronted with the **free rider**, "the individual who does not belong to an organized group, such as a union or a political party, but who nevertheless benefits from its activities."[47] Senior citizens do not have to belong to AARP in order to reap the benefits of the group's efforts to lobby for better health care for the elderly. The same holds true for veterans who do not pay any dues towards the Veterans of Foreign Wars chapters but benefit from the group's efforts. The League of Women Voters produces voters' guides for the community at-large. Without personally contributing any money towards the production costs, many individuals use these pamphlets to help them select their voting preferences. Many Americans hail themselves as loyal Democrats or Republicans, but they will not contribute any money to help their local parties man the office nor will they contribute their time to walk blocks to distribute election literature or take a person to the polls on election day. Basically, these perks are known as **collective benefits** whereby one enjoys the benefit derived from the group's initiatives but that individual contributed nothing to the group that brought him the benefits.

Another benefit to joining a particular group is **networking** whereby several groups with diverse memberships but similar goals and objectives meet periodically to exchange ideas and discuss common concerns. Chambers of Commerce have been in the forefront of promoting mixers. At these events, the host group provides the food and entertainment while the attendees mix with each other. It is of mutual benefit to the sponsoring interest groups since they have the opportunity to market their organizations and hopefully entice someone to join their groups. It can be beneficial to the attendees who can exchange their business cards with each other in hopes of making new friends or bringing in new business to their firms. For example, twice a year the major women's organizations in San Antonio come together for a program called "Can We Talk." Participating organizations are allowed to distribute membership information, a calendar of upcoming events, etc., to the attendees. It is a win-win situation.

Political Action Committees

To win an election, one must spend money, lots of money. Initially, only the wealthy ran for public office because they had the economic means available to them without undue solicitation from others. Although his opponent accused him of buying votes, "when George Washington ran for office in 1757, he followed a standard electoral practice of that time and used his own money to purchase liquor for potential voters."[48] Campaigning for both money and votes developed as those with political talent but without the personal wealth to finance their own campaigns decided to run for office. The creativity of soliciting campaign donations led to a series of federal and state laws placing restrictions on the amounts and sources of campaign dollars. One of the most criticized practices was **patronage** whereby an elected official would give lucrative government jobs to those who contributed the most to his/her campaign coffer. In response to the Tea Pot Dome scandal of 1824, Congress passed the **Corrupt Practices Act** that both limited and regulated the amounts and sources of both campaign contributions and expenditures, and barred contributions from labor organizations to any federal election campaign. After the assassination of President James Garfield, Congress enacted in 1883 the **Civil Service Reform Act** commonly known as the **Pendleton Act**, which established procedures for individuals seeking government employment to take competitive examinations. The **Political Activities Act** (1939), commonly known as the **Hatch Act** prohibited federal employees from participating in any political activities, forbade any political committee from spending more than $3 million in any campaign, and limited individual contributions to $5,000 per political committee. The **Tax Reform Act** (1986) prohibited the practice of using campaign donations as deductible expenses for income tax calculations.

In 1974, Congress enacted the **Federal Elections Campaign Act (FECA)** authorizing the creation of **Political Action Committees**, commonly known as **PACs**, and provided public financing for presidential general elections. Basically, PACs are "interest groups that collect money from their members and contribute these funds to candidates and parties."[49] The **Federal Elections Commission (FEC)** composed of six members appointed by the president with Senate confirmation was created to oversee the implementation and regulation of the act's provisions. Initially, the legislation called for:

- Limiting individual contributions to a maximum of $1,000 for a candidate in a national primary or general election with a $25,000 limit on any person's total contributions during an election year.
- Limiting special interest groups and PACs to no more than $5,000 per candidate in a national primary or general election.
- Repealing the portion of the Hatch Act prohibiting federal employees from participating in campaigns and elections. The new provision enabled them to engage in off-duty activities such as campaigning and fund raising.[50]

The FECA and subsequent legislation put limitations on direct or hard money contributions. The FEC yearly adjusts for inflation contribution levels. For the 2017-2018 election cycle, an individual could contribute up to $2,700 to each candidate or candidate committee per election, $33,900 to a national party committee per calendar year, $10,000 combined limit to state, district and local party committee per calendar year and $5,000 to any other political committee per calendar year.[51] According to federal law, foreign nationals are prohibited from making any contributions; however, "green card" holders are not considered foreign nationals and can make campaign contributions. While current state and federal laws limit hard money donations, the problem of unlimited amounts falling into the category of soft money remains an issue. Subsequent decisions by the United States Supreme Court have tied limits to campaign donations as a violation of the First Amendment's guarantee of free speech. For example, in *Federal Elections Commission v National Conservative Political Action Committee* (1985), the Court struck down a section of the Presidential Election Campaign Fund Act limiting spending by a political action committee to $1,000 for a presidential candidate as a violation of free speech.[52]

In 2010, the United States Supreme Court muddied campaign finance reform efforts in its controversial ruling in *Citizens United v FEC*. The background of the case involved a conservative lobbying group Citizens United seeking advertising time to air a film critical of Hillary Clinton, which was deemed as a violation of a provision of the 2002 **Bipartisan Campaign Reform Act** or **McCain-Feingold** banning the airing of any campaign commercial using a candidate's name within 60 days of a general election or 30 days before a primary election. It furthermore prohibited such expenditures from corporations or unions. The Supreme Court's decision ruled this provision as a violation of the 1st Amendment's protection of free speech. This ruling effectively "tossed out the corporate and union ban on making independent expenditures and financing electioneering communications. It gave corporations and unions the green light to spend unlimited sums on ads and other political tools, calling for the election or defeat of individual candidates."[53] The Court's ruling did not overturn federal campaign finance laws prohibiting direct campaign contributions from companies and labor unions that were originally banned with the passage of the **Taft-Hartley Act** in 1947. However, this ruling has created a new type of political action committees—**Super PACs**.

For candidates, accepting money from PACs can be problematic. On one hand, almost every candidate vows to their potential voting base that their loyalties rest with their supporters, not the corporate giants with their overflowing cash coffers. They oftentimes paint PACs as diabolical influence peddlers. Instead, the candidates pledge to only accept small monetary donations from individuals. On the other hand, it takes a significantly large number of small monetary donors to make up for that one check of $5,000 or $10,000 so desperately needed to fund a campaign. Despite a laundry list of regulatory policies, PACs contributed $444,000,000 to national, state and local candidates in just the 2015-2016 election cycle alone. Leading the donation pack was the usual suspects – corporations who collectively gave $182,000,000 through their employee PAC organizations.[54]

The general membership of any interest group may approve the formation of a PAC. However, the PAC must be officially registered with the FEC and comply with all required reports. If the PAC endorses or raises money for any candidates for a state office, the PAC must be registered in that state and comply with all of the rules and regulations including submitting all required reports within established timeframes. For example, an interest group decides to form a PAC. The general membership of the organization approves the selection of members to the PAC board. In turn, the PAC board is responsible for interviewing potential candidates for endorsement, verifying their credentials, and submitting their recommendations for approval to the organization's general membership. If an event is held to solicit donations for the PAC, money received at the event must be used for PAC-related activities. Usually smaller interest groups will not form their own PACs simply because of the complexity of the registration and reporting requirements.

Acceptable Interest Group Tactics

While the local garden club may be a very valuable social organization, rarely will its leadership have to enter the political arena. However, the survival of many of the more politically-oriented organizations is dependent on how they approach lawmakers and how they exert influence over the public policy process. The ultimate goal of any political interest group is to gain **access**, defined as "the ability to gain the attention and to influence the decisions of key political agents."[55] No matter how noble and justified the cause may be, an interest group without access to the key players in the legislature or the governor's office will not be able to effectively push their cause into the public policy arena. A single group acting alone is less successful than many groups coming together with a common cause. **Interest aggregation** is "the process of bringing together the concerns of diverse groups into a workable program."[56] To be successful, the process of bringing groups together must be a two prong approach. First, the various groups need to come together and actively and, perhaps, vocally articulate their concern. For example, Texans witnessed teachers, education administrators, parents and students rally periodically in Austin as the 2011 session of the Texas Legislature debated drastic cuts in public and higher education budgets. Many carried signs warning lawmakers to remember that protesters are voters who will not forget the draconian actions of their lawmakers the next time those same lawmakers need their votes to remain in office. The crowds were impressive and, for the moment, they collectively felt that they had persuaded lawmakers to rethink their budgetary strategy. It did not work. But these groups cannot afford to retreat! Consequently, the second step is the vital long-term strategy of keeping the coalition together by meeting periodically and devising a well-thought out plan to carry out their pledge to show-up at the polls on election-day. What is needed is an **issue network** composed of the various groups' leadership,

sympathetic lawmakers, and lobbyists who will continue to push the issue with both their fellow lawmakers and the general public. The issue must remain "alive."

Lobbying is "an effort designed to affect what government does."[57] The majority of the state's interest groups rely upon their general membership to articulate their issue. **Grassroots lobbying** or **indirect lobbying** is "influencing government decision makers through pressure usually in the form of letters, postcards, telegrams, and phone calls from a large number of constituents."[58] Nationally affiliated organizations instruct their state and local chapters on proper grassroots techniques. For example, form letters or canned statements are very ineffective since one letter is the same as all of the others. Lawmakers are more incline to read and actually respond to an originally written letter, post card or e-mail. The most effective is the personal phone call. Many organizations have several members who are in charge of alerting the membership of an upcoming legislative action and urging them to call their elected officials. Indirect lobbying also includes attending electoral activities, issuing public opinion statements, protesting and staging marches, and speaking at the "citizens to be heard" segment of a council meeting. Indirect lobbying is a very effective tool since it ties the organization to its surrounding community. A national organization's leadership is speaking to the nation as a whole. A locally-based organization draws its strength from the community. The more visible that organization is in that community, the more support it will draw from it. For example, individuals in Dallas, Fort Worth, Houston, Austin, and San Antonio know that there is a local office of the NAACP or LULAC because they see the leadership of these two organizations on the evening news being interviewed by a local reporter. They see the membership of these organizations actively participating in community-based activities. Rarely, will they see the national president of the NAACP or LULAC in their neighborhoods. Indirect lobbying gives an organization its visibility.

On the other hand, interest groups must also use **direct lobbying** activities such as assisting a legislator in drafting legislation, working directly with legislative supporters in planning a legislative strategy needed to take a bill and make it into a law, making personal visits to the capitol offices, and, if needed, testifying at hearings. The most influential interest groups in Austin are the ones that the lawmakers seek out for assistance in crafting, promoting, and implementing legislation. Just testifying at a legislative hearing by one of its members brings prestige to an organization. An interest group has "made it" in Austin when the lawmaker or a member of his/her staff asks for the organization's help to pass a bill or to provide needed research or testimony in support of a legislative item.

The most influential interest groups in the Texas Legislature are those who can hire a professional spokesperson or lobbyist to advocate for the group and articulate its issues directly before members of the legislature or the governor's staff. A **lobbyist** is "a person usually acting as an agent for a pressure group, who seeks to bring about the passage or defeat of legislative bills or to influence their contents."[59] Unfortunately, the media usually portrays the lobbyist as a vile individual who uses whatever means possible to achieve his/her employer's objectives. Far too often campaign ads usually run by opponents about incumbent candidates are about lobbyists handing over an envelope full of cash to a legislator right before a key vote. While a few may have participated in this activity, the majority do not. Another myth is that lobbyists are running amok, free of restrictions and oversight. The federal government requires that any person participating in a paid lobbying activity at the national level must comply with the **Regulation of Lobby Act** (Title III, Legislative Reorganization Act of 1946). The law specifies that:

a) persons or organizations receiving money to be use principally to either pass or defeat legislation before Congress must register.
b) persons or groups registering must, under oath, give their name, address, employer, salary, amount and purpose of expenses, and duration of employment.
c) each registered lobbyist must report quarterly giving full information on his or her activities.
d) failure to comply with any of these provisions will result in severe penalties ranging up to a $10,000 fine and a five-year prison term as well as a three-year ban against further lobbying activities.[60]

The **Open Government Act** passed by Congress in 2007 amended the Lobbying Disclosure Act of 1995 and clarified who must register as a lobbyist and what activities they can legally participate in.

Every state including Texas has implemented registration and reporting requirements for any lobbyist doing business in their state. The Texas Legislature has periodically enacted legislation placing restrictions on both interest groups and lobbyists particularly over their money raising and spending activities. In 1907, the Texas Legislature passed its first lobbyist registration law. The statute barred any extra-ordinary actions to unduly influence lawmakers. However, it was never enforced. A 1957 law was also unenforceable because it had just too many loopholes. In 1991, voters approved a constitutional amendment establishing the eight-member **Texas Ethics Commission (TEC)** to establish a code of conduct for members of the Texas Legislature. The measure was in response to a 1989 well-publicized incident involving Lonnie "Bo" Pilgrim of Pilgrim's Pride Chicken walking onto the floor of the Texas Senate in the middle of a special session, passing out $10,000 blank checks to nine state senators. Even though eight of the nine returned the money, the public was outraged that members of the Texas Legislature were so easily approachable to a bribe. There were, of course, the usual practices of legislators accepting trips, free meals, tickets to sporting events, European excursions, etc. As detailed in Article III, Section 24A of the amendment, the governor appoints the board's membership consisting of one Democrat and one Republican from lists submitted separately by members of the Texas House, Senate, the governor, and the lieutenant governor. The board's duties include proposing legislative salary increases, establishing the parameters for expense allowances, and keeping track of lobbyist registration forms, financial disclosure statements from legislators, and records of campaign contributions and expenditures as well as investigating formal ethics complaints filed against state-executive officials and legislators. The TEC oversees the registration of lobbyists and monitors the activities of both interest groups and lobbyists. According to the current laws:

a) A lobbyist must register with the TEC if he/she receives more than $1,000 in compensation in a calendar quarter for engaging in any communication with members of the Texas Legislature or the executive branch that are intended to influence the development, outcome, and implementation of laws or administrative rules.
b) A person must register if he or she spends more than $500 in a calendar quarter on any activity that might influence the development, outcome, and implementation of laws or administrative rules.
c) Any registered individual must provide detailed reports of their activities, money sources, and expenditures.
d) Registered lobbyists are prohibited from providing loans, transportation and lodging costs, and expenditures for entertainment, awards, and gifts that exceed $500 in a calendar quarter to any recipient of their lobbying activities.[61]

Furthermore, the law defines communications as a "broad array of activities, including the provision of food, beverages, entertainment expenses, gifts, awards and mementos, media advertising, and fund-raisers."[62]   If warranted, the Commission can level a maximum fine of $5,000. A person filing a frivolous or false complaint against a lawmaker faces a $10,000 fine. However, the effectiveness of the Commission is questionable. It takes a majority of six members to convict anyone of a violation. If a campaign-related complaint is filed, the Board cannot take any action until after the November general election. In 2010, the TEC fined Governor Perry $1,500 for failure to report rental property in College Station and for filing incomplete reports as to the value of the property. And, Bo Pilgrim was still involved in influence peddling. This time his target was the governor's office. Pilgrim gave $100,000 to the Republican Governors Association, a national interest group chaired by Perry. Six days later Perry's staff requested an ethanol waiver from the Environmental Protection Agency on the grounds that EPA restrictions would adversely impact the state's livestock industry.

Lobbyists have also been portrayed as individuals roaming state and national capitol buildings waiting to verbally attack any lawmaker in their wake. The scenario of the lobbyist pointing his finger into the face of the lawmaker as he threatens the future of the lawmaker's career if he does not bend to the lobbyist's wishes for the most part is a myth. The primary job responsibility of a lobbyist is to protect the interests of the group who hires him/her. When the legislative pre-filing period begins, it is the lobbyist who must scrutinize proposed legislative items that could positively or negatively impact their clients. The state's most successful lobbyists are themselves former legislators. They know "the ropes" and are very well versed in how the system works. Lobbyists are policy experts in their particular fields. Oftentimes, legislators will turn to lobbyists for information on pending legislation. Let's face it, few legislators are experts on every legislative item up for their consideration. Seeking expert advice enables the legislator to feel comfortable with his/her vote. Having a professional watchdog in Austin is a valuable tool for any interest group.

Another effective tool is the endorsement or non-endorsement of a candidate for public office. Several interest groups and organizations endorse candidates. For example, the Texas Women's Political Caucus endorses women candidates for statewide offices while local chapters endorse for offices within their territory. In every race with a woman candidate, a questionnaire is sent to all candidates running for that particular office. The questionnaire targets the specific bottom-line issues of the organization. If the candidate completes the questionnaire and the responses are receptive to the organization's endorsement committee, the candidate is scheduled for a personal interview. Based upon the committee's recommendation, the entire membership will then vote whether or not to endorse the candidate. The endorsement for the candidate is extremely important. First, the candidate is publically acknowledged as the organization's endorsed candidate. The voters may not know much about the candidate but, for example, if the local police officers association endorses a candidate, they are telling the public that this candidate supports initiatives favorable to law enforcement. Second, the organization is obligated to give their endorsed candidates their membership lists. While the organization cannot give the candidate a lot of money, members within the organization certainly can and will. Third, an endorsement means that members within that organization will work for the campaign. This gives the candidate a cadre of volunteers for block walking, phone banking, stuffing envelopes, and monitoring the polling sites on election-day. A non-endorsement also sends a powerful message that this candidate was not in tune with the bottom-line issues of the organization. In the 2010 governor's race, the powerful Texas Farm Bureau opted not to endorse any candidate in that race. Since its founding in 1988, the organization has always endorsed Republican candidates. The non-endorsement for Perry was troubling since he is a Republican, once served as the state's agricultural commissioner, and was raised on a Texas farm. The Perry snub was partially attributable to the governor's veto of a 2007 bill protecting private property rights, an issue near and dear to the Farm Bureau's membership. The organization has approximately 421,000 members with chapter organizations in at least 200 of the state's 254 counties.

Each election cycle involves candidates seeking endorsements from those organizations and interest groups that complement the candidate's political philosophy and issue positions. A conservative Republican and former spokesperson for the Republican Party's Tea Party faction, Senator Ted Cruz had a long list of conservative groups endorsing and at times funding his 2018 re-election bid. His stand for legal immigration policies and Trump's border wall drew the endorsement of the Americans for Legal Immigration and the National Border Patrol Council. A pro-life advocate, Cruz garnered the support of the Texas Alliance for Life and the Texas Right to Life Committee. His conservative political viewpoints drew the support of the John Birch Society, the Heritage Action for America, the American Conservative Union, Americans for Prosperity, the Eagle Forum, and so forth. His opponent Democrat Beto O'Rourke had a more liberal political perspective that earned him support from Equality Texas and the Human Rights Campaign. Governor Greg Abbott obtained endorsements from some of the same groups that backed Cruz plus nods of approval from Empower Texans for Fiscal Responsibility, the National Federation of Independent Business, the National Rifle Association, Texans for Lawsuit Reform, Texans for Toll-Free Highways, and the Texas State Rifle Association. His opponent Democrat Lupe Valdez received endorsements from the Feminist Majority Political Action Committee, the Human Rights Campaign, the Latino Victory Project, LPAC, Planned Parenthood of Texas, the Texas AFL-CIO, and the United Auto Workers.

Organized or unionized labor in the United States has been able to use collective bargaining as an effective tool to win concessions from employers. **Collective bargaining** is "bargaining on behalf of a group or employees, as opposed to individual bargaining, where each worker represents only himself or herself."[63]   In the private-sector, collective bargaining as been useful in obtaining better working conditions, shorter working hours, higher salaries, and better benefit packages for union members. When talks break down, the threat of a workers' strike has oftentimes brought management back to the table. Unionized government employees, however, have the right to collective bargaining but cannot go out on strike. States faced with looming long-term budget deficits are legislatively restricting the stretch of collective bargaining particularly for wages and benefits.

Groups such as the NAACP and the ACLU have been successful in litigating their concerns in the courtroom. The doctrine of separate but equal was ended when Thurgood Marshall, an attorney and head of the NAACP's Legal Defense and Education Fund, successfully pointed out to the Justices that although public schools were surely separated by race, they definitely were not equal in accessibility to a quality education and, thus, this constituted a violation of the Fourteenth Amendment's equal protection clause. The reputation of the ACLU as the defender of the Bill of Rights has been sealed with a series of victories before state and federal benches.

Unacceptable Tactics

Interest groups must be able to accomplish their agenda in ways that are generally acceptable to both their membership and the general public. Obviously violence is not an acceptable tactic. For example, immediately after the police arrested Timothy McVeigh for his role in the bombing of the federal building in Oklahoma City, law enforcement announced that he was a member of a militia group in Michigan. Within hours, the presiding officer of that militia organization took to the airwaves denouncing McVeigh's actions and empathically denied that McVeigh was a member of their group. Why? Although Americans understand that even those groups whose issues run against the values shared by most Americans have a constitutional right to express those viewpoints, violence is not the appropriate venue for expressing those views. Non-violence has always been a more acceptable tacit. When India was fighting for its independence from the British, it was Mahatma Gandhi who repeatedly drove home the point that the only way the international community was going to back independence for India was for the people of India to show to the world that they deserved it. Consequently, he opted for non-violent protests over violent massive mobs who threw rocks at each other, beat each other, and burned buildings and cars. Martin L. King, Jr., employed the same non-violent technique during the height of the Civil Rights Movement as well as Nelson Mandella in South Africa.

An equally unacceptable tactic, **bribery** is "the giving or offering of anything of value with intent to unlawfully influence an official in the discharge of his or her duties."[64] Bribery and corruption go hand and hand and has always been viewed with disdain by the American people. In a 1948 interview, President Harry Truman commented that:

> There would be no corruption if it were not for the corrupters. There are always weak people in every human setup. . . We must find a way to make the corrupter as guilty legally as the one who is corrupted. . . . I have always felt deeply about this subject of corruption. There is nothing I detest so much as a crooked politician or corrupt government official. But the type of businessman who is a fixer is even lower in my estimation. There are termites that undermine respect for government and confidence in government and cast doubt on the vast majority of honest and hardworking federal officials.[65]

Rarely used, offering any lawmaker a bribe is a dicey option. First, the bribe itself must be so attractive that the lawmaker simply cannot turn it down. Second, if the bribe is attached to a threat for non-compliance, then the person or group offering the bribe must carry out the threat. Third, state and federal laws punish both the parties involved with stiff penalties and, possibly, jail time. If a lawmaker were to accept a bribe and get caught, it is the end of his/her political career. Few lawmakers are willing to even consider taking the bait. As Thomas Jefferson wrote in 1782, "the time to guard against corruption and tyranny is before they shall have gotten hold of us. It is better to keep the wolf out of the fold than to trust to drawing his teeth and talons after he shall have entered."[66]

Does Pluralism Work?

In theory, pluralism implies that the issue at hand drives the key players in the public policy arena with each vested party playing a vital role in the drafting, approval, and implementation of public policy initiatives. Pluralism implies an even playing field whereby each vested interest equally competes with each other. Pluralism is democratic theory, based only on group interaction rather than or individual endeavors. Democratic theory tells us that decision making is rooted in open discussion, debate, consensus and, ultimately, reaching a compromise. In actuality, pluralism has its flaws simply because the playing field is not equal. Far too often a group with a valid noble cause looses simply because the opposing side has the competitive edge. For example, environmentalists used the BP oil spill as their pulpit to convince both President Obama and the American people that deep off-shore drilling was simply too hazardous to both fragile marine animal and plant life and humans. Report after report of the black goo heading for the pristine coastline of Texas, Louisiana and the southern Gulf coast states drove home the point of potentially irreversible damage. Initially, the president called for a moratorium on off-shore deep drilling activities in the Gulf of Mexico. However, big oil interests backed by rising costs at the pump changed public opinion and, subsequently, the White House eventually changed its mind. In the long run, big oil won. So, what makes one group more powerful than another?

Consistent and committed leadership is absolutely essential to the survival of any organization. It is the core leadership that speaks for the entire organization, upholds its guiding principles and mission, mobilizes its membership into action, and represents the organization before the media, elected officials, and the community it serves. It is the responsibility of the membership to elect the right people to represent their organization. Unfortunately, too many organizations suffer from inconsistent patterns of strong and weak leadership. A prolonged period of weak leadership can ultimately lead to the demise of the organization. The core leadership must also speak as one

voice. In-fighting among board members misdirects the organization from its primary goals and objectives and leaves the rank and file membership without consistent and cohesive guidance.

Interest groups simply cannot survive without money. The usual source of funding is the general membership through annual dues and, oftentimes, letters from the board asking for personal donations. Establishing the appropriate amount of annual dues is always problematic. As previously mentioned, once the local organization subtracts the amounts paid for state and national affiliations, there is very little left to pay rent, utilities, print the monthly newsletter, and, or course, hire a lobbyist. It is a given that individuals will join groups that offer them an array of benefits at the cheapest cost possible. Groups lose membership with each increase in its dues. The only option for many groups is to reach outside of the general membership through creative fund-raising activities. Roasting a popular elected official or honoring a well-known civic personality or advocacy for a popular cause such as the homeless is a viable option. However, the actual money an organization raises is determined only after the costs of hosting the event are deducted.

In the 1960s and 1970s, there were very few viable interest groups to choose from. NOW and the NWPC were the primary choices for feminists while the NAACP and its rainbow coalition brought millions into its fold. The Sierra Club boasted of its large membership particularly in the 1970s with the release of Rachel Carson's *Silent Spring* and the establishment of Earth Day. However, the New Politics Movement encouraged the development of splinter groups that departed from their founders. Today, women can choose from numerous interest groups advocating interests pertinent to them. The same holds true for the Sierra Club and the NAACP. In order for groups such as NOW and the NAACP to survive they must incorporate inclusiveness rather than exclusiveness into their purpose statements and bottom-line issues. For example, critics have charged, and rightfully so, that NOW is stuck in the 60s by continuing to drive home the point that American women want and need an equal rights amendment added to the United States Constitution. Passage of the ERA was their primary objective in the 1970s and 1980s, and it failed to win passage. The majority of today's women are interested in a broader spectrum of concerns such as health care, affordable child care, better child support programs, etc., not an equal rights amendment. The NAACP has had the same problem—stuck with the same agenda that drove individuals to join their rainbow coalition. The failure of the NAACP to attract new members into its organization led to a drastic change in their leadership. To be in the forefront of similar organized interests, interest groups must constantly review, update, and revise their bottom-line issues or they will exist no longer. Groups that embrace inclusiveness last while those who continue to narrow their agenda and "preach to their choir" become more exclusive and isolated from the mainstream of their service group.

Conclusions

James Madison was right when he remarked that interest groups divide people. But they divide people for the right reasons. As individuals, many of us are concerned about the direction our lawmakers are taking us. Many look around them and see the social, economic, and political problems confronting this state. But many are unwilling to personally speak to their lawmakers, write a letter to the editor, or publically speak out. Interest groups enable the many to act as one. Everyone who joins a group has something unique to offer. A group with strong leadership will be able to draw together singular unique talents to form a stronger more viable group. So by their very act of division, interest groups are unifiers.

The more political savvy interest groups in Texas are directly impacting the decision-making process in Austin by assuming some of the duties normally associated with political parties. These are the interest groups that actively recruit candidates for public office. They offer them training from how to write a speech to how to muddle through the campaign finance regulations and reporting requirements. It is the leadership of these groups that mobilize their members to work for their chosen candidates by walking blocks, manning phone banks, raising money, etc. It is the interest groups in this state that conduct voter registration drives, arrange for seniors and the physically challenged to obtain a mail-in ballot or get a ride to the polls. In short, Madison was wrong about the baneful effect of factions. When interest groups work within their legal boundaries, they are indeed an effective and necessary partner in the law making and public policy processes.

Chapter Notes

[1] V. O. Key, Jr., *Politics, Parties and Pressure Groups*, 4th ed., (New York, New York: Thomas Y. Crowell Company, 1958), 23.

[2] R. G. Ratcliffe and Joe Holey, "White, Democrats Target Perry Over Ethics," *San Antonio Express-News*, (Wednesday, July 7, 2010) 3B.

[3] Gilbert Garcia, "Texas Realtors Association Again Backs Perry," *San Antonio Express-News*, (August 21, 2010), 13A.

[4] James Madison, "No. 10: Violence or Parties Restrained by a Strong Federal Union," *The Enduring Federalist*, 2nd ed., Charles A. Beard, ed., (New York, New York: Frederick Ungar Publishing Co., 1964), 69.

[5] L. Tucker Gibson, Jr., and Clay Robison, *Government and Politics in the Lone Star State: Theory and Practice*, (Englewood Cliffs, New Jersey: Prentice Hall, Inc., 1993), 94.

[6] William Ebenstein, *Great Political Thinkers*, (New York, New York: Rinehart & Co., 1951), 6.

[7] Key, Jr., 7.

[8] Steffen W. Schmidt, Mack C. Shelley, II, Barbara A. Bardes, *American Government and Politics Today: 1995-1996 Edition*, 5th ed., (St. Paul, Minnesota: West Publishing Co., 1995), 14.

[9] Harold D. Lasswell, Daniel Lerner, C. Easton Rothwell, "The Elite Concept," *The American Political Arena: Selected Readings*, Joseph R. Fiszman, ed., 4th ed., (New York, New York: Little, Brown and Company, 1992), 89.

[10] Gibson, Jr., and Robison, 95.

[11] Steven A. Peterson and Thomas H. Rasmussen, *State and Local Politics*, (New York, New York: McGraw Hill, 1994), 187.

[12] Burdett A. Loomis and Allan J. Cigler, "Introduction: The Changing Nature of Interest Group Politics," *Interest Group Politics*, Allan J. Cigler and Burdett A. Loomis, eds., 7th ed., (Washington, D.C.: CQ Press, 2007), 5.

[13] Theodore J. Lowi, *The End of Liberalism*, (New York, New York: W. W. Norton and Company, 1969), 71.

[14] Ibid.

[15] *The HarperCollins Dictionary of American Government and Politics*, Jay M. Shafritz, ed., (New York, New York: HarperCollins Publishers, Inc., 1992), 432.

[16] Jack C. Plano and Milton Greenberg, *The American Political Dictionary*, 10th ed., (Orlando, Florida: Harcourt Brace & Co., 1997), 79.

[17] Gibson, Jr., and Robison, 90.

[18] Alexis De Tocqueville, *Democracy in America*, translated by George Lawrence, J.P. Mayer, ed., (Garden City, New York: Anchor Press, 1969), 513.

[19] Jeffrey M. Berry, "Citizen Groups and the Changing Nature of Interest Group Politics in America," *The Annals*, Vol. 528, July, 1993, The American Academy of Political and Social Science, (Newbury Park, California: Sage Publications), 31.

[20] Gerry Riposa and Nelson Dometrius, "Studying Public Policy," *Texas Public Policy*, Gerry Riposa, ed., (Dubuque, Iowa: Kendall/Hunt, 1987), 9.

[21] Berry, "Citizen Groups and the Changing Nature of Interest Group Politics in America," 41.

[22] ____, "S. Side Community Pressed for College," *San Antonio Express News*, (Friday, October 19, 2018), A8.

[23] Neal Tannahill, *Texas Government: Policy and Politics*, 4th ed., (New York, New York: HarperCollins College Publishers, 1993), 472.

[24] www.drtinfo.org/

[25] Ibid.

[26] *The HarperCollins Dictionary of American Government and Politics*, 475.

[27]Theodore J. Lowi and Benjamin Ginsburg, *American Government: Freedom and Power*, 3rd ed., (New York, New York: W.W. Norton & Company, 1994), 507.

[28]*Encyclopedia of Women and American Politics*, Lynn E. Ford., Ed., (New York, New York: Facts on File, Inc., 2008), 372.

[29]_____, "Classical Music Was Hertzberg's Legacy," *San Antonio Express News*, (Tuesday, October 23, 2018), A8.

[30]Scott Huddleston, "Many Battles for Conservation Group," *San Antonio Express News*, (Sunday, July 7, 2017), A18.

[31]"NOW's Statement of Purpose: 1966," *Major Problems in American Women's History*, Mary Beth Norton and Ruth M. Alexander, eds., 2nd ed., (Lexington, Massachusetts: D. C. Heath and Company, 1996), 445.

[32]*Las Tejanas: 300 Years of History*, Teresa Palamo Acosta and Ruthe Winegarten, (Austin, Texas: The University of Texas Press, 2003), 90.

[33]Daniel D. Arreola, *Tejano South Texas: A Mexican American Cultural Province*, (Austin, TX: The University of Texas Press, 2002), 191.

[34]*The Texas Almanac: 2018-2019*, (Denton, Texas: The Texas State Historical Association, 2018), 624.

[35]Ibid.

[36]*The Issues of the Populist and the Progressive Eras 1892-1912*, Richard M. Abrams, ed., (Columbia, South Carolina: The University of South Carolina Press, 1969), 152-153.

[37]*https://www.bls.gov/regions/southwest*

[38]Josh Baugh, "Amendments: Defeated Item Would Alter Budget Process," *San Antonio Express News*, (Wednesday, November 7, 2018), A1-A8.

[39]The Texas Almanac: 2018-2019, 694.

[40]Ibid.

[41]Ibid., 704.

[42]"Declaration of Purposes of the National Grange, February, 1874," *Documents of Texas History*, Ernest Wallace, David M. Vigness and George B. Ward, eds., 2nd ed., (Austin, Texas: State House Press, 1994), 222.

[43]"Grape Workers Issue the Boycott Day Proclamation, 1969," *Major Problems in Mexican American History*, Zaragosa Vargas, ed., (Boston, Massachusetts: Houghton Mifflin Company, 1999), 413.

[44]Thomas E. Patterson, *We The People: A Concise Introduction to American Politics*, 8th ed., (New York, New York: McGraw Hill Higher Education, 2009), 305.

[45]Loomis and Cigler, "Introduction: The Changing Nature of Interest Group Politics," 9.

[46]Ibid., 9-10.

[47]*The Harper Collins Dictionary of American Government and Politics*, 245.

[48]Mariana Currinder, Joanne Connor Green and M. Margaret Conway, "Interest Group Money in Elections," *Interest Group Politics*, Allan J. Cigler and Burdett A. Loomis, eds., 7th ed., (Washington, D.C.: CQ Press, 2007), 183.

[49]*The HarperCollins Dictionary of American Government and Politics*, 435.

[50]Plano and Greenberg, 123.

[51]*https://www.fec.gov/help-candidates-and-committees*

[52]Plano and Greenberg, 124.

[53]www.publicintegrity.org

[54]ProQuest LLC., *Proquest Statistical Abstract of the United States, 2019*, 7th ed., (Bethesda, Maryland, 2018), Table 461, 291.

[55]*The HarperCollins Dictionary of America Government and Politics*, 4.

[56]Tannahill, 479.

[57]Anthony Nownes, *Total Lobbying*, (New York, New York: Cambridge University Press, 2006), 6.

[58]*The HarperCollins Dictionary of American Government and Politics*, 264.

[59]Plano and Greenberg, 86.

[60]Ibid., 181.

[61]Paul Benson, David Clinkscale and Anthony Giardino, *Lone Star Politics*, (New York, New York: Pearson Education Inc., 2011), 137-138.

[62]Ibid., 137.

[63]*The HarperCollins Dictionary of American Government and Politics*, 121.

[64]Ibid., 72.

[65]*Treasury of Presidential Quotes*, Caroline Thomas Hansberger, ed., (Chicago, Illinois: Follett Publishing Co., 1964), 47.

[66]Ibid.

Chapter 3

Political Parties
of Texas

Official photograph of the National Democratic Convention,
Houston, Texas, 1928
Credit: Library of Congress

Party is a body of men united, for promoting by their joint endeavors the national interest, upon some particular principle in which they all agreed.[1] Edmund Burke

The value of political parties in the democratic process cannot be understated or underestimated. President Warren G. Harding summed it up in a speech he delivered in 1923:

> I believe in political parties. These were the essential agencies of the popular government which made us what we are. We were never perfect, but under our party system we wrought a development under representative democracy unmatched in all proclaimed liberty and attending human advancement. We achieved under the party system, where parties were committed to policies, and party loyalty was a mark of honor and an inspiration toward accomplishment.[2]

Both interest groups and political parties bring individuals of similar ideological persuasions and concerns under their protective umbrellas. What differentiates the two is the width of their umbrellas. Interest groups are narrower in their perspectives and issue concerns. Individuals join the Sierra Club because they know that this organization is devoted entirely to preserving the environment. Workers join labor unions because they know that organized labor advocates specific concerns to the nation's workforce, i.e., wage and benefit treatment, anti-discrimination at the work site, safety, etc. The survival of individual interest groups is totally dependent on how the group's leadership is capable of successfully advocating for their group's specific concerns and issues. On the other hand, political parties unite as many diverse groups as possible under their wide umbrellas. The Democrat Party draws its primary membership from the nation's workers, women, Hispanics, African Americans, the bulk of the nation's middle- and lower-income groups, and those who affiliate themselves with the liberal camp; whereas, the Republican Party's umbrella embraces the business community, upper-middle and upper-income groups, and those who uphold to conservative viewpoints. Once every four years, Americans align themselves into two major corners—Democrat and Republican, with those who simply do not want to totally affiliate themselves with either party—the independents.

The fabric that holds each umbrella together is its unique political philosophy. While most Americans have never read the platform of their political party, they recognize the Republican Party as the conservative group and the Democrats as the more liberal camp. This chapter examines the broad political philosophies that guide the issue positions of both political parties.

Whereas the majority of the world's democracies work within a multi-party system, the American two-party system simplifies the election process for the American voter. It is the political parties through the primaries that select the two candidates for each office for the general election. Therefore, it is a simplified process since the voter in November usually has only two choices—Democrat or Republican. Third party movements will arise from time to time, but their survival is very dicey and extremely short. Texas has had its share of third party movements. This chapter highlights their development, issue positions, and, unfortunately, their electoral demise. Historically, it is the nation's two major political parties that articulate the issues, register the voters, recruit candidates, assist in funding the campaigns, etc. However, there is a balancing act between political parties and state's interest groups. If a particular state has a strong two-party system, it usually has weak interest groups. In other words, the political parties take the lead in the election process with interest groups playing a vital but secondary role. On the other hand in states with weak political parties, it is interest groups that fulfill the functions traditionally associated with political parties. In Texas, political parties fall into the relatively weak role, leaving interest groups to pick up the slack. However, even in their weakened position to interest group activity, political parties in Texas do exert considerable influence in the election process and in the development of public policy initiatives that drive the governing structures in this state. This chapter examines the influence that the Republican and Democrat Parties as well as the state's numerous third party movements have had and will continue to have on the development not only of the state's political landscape but also on the state's ability to address pressing social and economic issues.

The Concept of a Political Party

A **political party** is "an organization whose members are sufficiently homogeneous to band together for the overt purpose of winning elections which entitles them to exercise governmental power, in order to enjoy the influence, prerequisites, and advantages of authority."[3] One of the basic factors that differentiates interest groups from political parties is interest groups really do not have a universal organizational structure. Any association of people with a shared purpose or goal can be called an interest group. On the other hand, "the political party is no mere bundle of activities, no ghostly presence or 'unseen hand' in the political process. It is a definable, observable social structure which, in order to organize political interests, must itself be organized."[4] Viable political parties "consist of three inter-related components: the **party in the electorate**, those who identify with the party; the **party in government**, those who are appointed or elected to office as members of a political party; and the formal **party organization**, the party 'professionals' who run the party at the national, state, and local levels."[5]

Political parties fulfill their role as the party of the electorate by:

- developing a concrete political philosophy that attracts individuals to affiliate themselves with the party,
- recruiting and supplying candidates for public office,
- overseeing the internal selection process usually through the intraparty primary selection process of candidates for the general elections,
- developing and articulating the issues,
- providing a venue for individuals to criticize government and its elected officials in a legal and hopefully, non-violent atmosphere,
- and, developing intraparty loyalty.

Once elected it is the responsibility of the public official to represent his/her political party in the development of public policy initiatives that embrace the underlying political perceptives of the party's entire party membership. This poses a significant conflict for many lawmakers who are elected from precisely defined constituencies whose issues may oftentimes conflict with the overall guiding principles of the party. Basically,

in the efforts to secure control of the machinery of government, American political parties have assumed the responsibility for organizing the governments, for recruiting leaders and staffing the bureaucracies, for getting out the voters, and for welding together alliances of disparate interests in support of party tickets and programs. Although these functions are not directly concerned with public policy, they do have a rather substantial impact on policy outcomes in the government. Through their officeholders the parties become major participants in conflict resolution, policy leadership, and policy adoption and administration. Though the control and discipline of their members of the legislatures is limited, the parties are a major influence on voting in these policy-making bodies. Thus party outputs in the areas of recruiting and staffing the policy-making machinery have significant bearing on policy outcomes.[6]

Party organization can only be achieved if a political party has a strong talented and committed staff of professionals at every level of the party's organizational structure. Regardless of whether it is a two-party or multi-party system, membership in a political party is strictly voluntary. Those who initially affiliated themselves with one party can surely switch to another when they feel that their original party choice is no longer fulfilling their individual political needs. Internal conflicts with these two major political parties are the norm, not the exception. The inner core of a party's organization is composed of representatives of the various factions within the party that come together:

for the purpose of fighting and government. It is not concerned with matters of fact, or doctrine, or even of principle, except as they bear upon the great cause for existence: success at the polls. Such organizations not only contain men of divergent views; they must also appeal to voters of differing opinions, prejudices, and loyalties. It is folly to talk of finding an actual basis [for political parties] in any set of principles relating to public welfare.[7]

The survival of any political party is tied directly to success at the polls. A political party may have solid political perspectives that garner wide-spread support among party diehards and potential party members. The party could well have a very functional organizational structure. It may very well field strong, capable and intelligent candidates for public office. Yet, these features matter very little if the party's candidates fail to win their elections. The key to a party's survival is to get people elected to those key public offices that directly craft, guide and influence the outcome of public policy initiatives.

The Historical Development of Political Parties

The exact date of the origin of the political party is sketchy. However, most historians see the evolution of the modern political party concept emerging in England during the mid-1600s and truly began to take shape during the Cromwellian revolution and the Restoration of the monarchy in 1660. Thomas Osborne, the Earl of Danby, was the founder of the Tory Party (the pro-king group) while Anthony Ashley-Cooper, the Earl of Shaftesbury, became the founder of the opposition party known as the Whig Party (the anti-king group). By 1675, the ideological lines were drawn with the Tories taking a conservative approach while the Whigs took the liberal side of the political spectrum. Under the banner of "no Popery!" the Whigs developed perhaps the first political party platform by taking strong stands on advocating Protestantism, religious toleration, personal liberties, promotion of commerce and business development, and the supremacy of Parliament over the monarchy. Basically the rise of political parties was directly tied to a changing regime from entrenched enfranchised aristocracies ruled under the absolutism of the divine right theory of kings to the rise of democratic governments that enabled the un-enfranchised common man to finally realize the same political rights and personal freedoms that for so long belonged only to the enfranchised aristocrats. The works of Jean Jacques Rousseau, Charles de Montesquieu, and John Locke were read and discussed by the economic and social elites of their time, the privileged few who had the benefit of a good education. It was the political party that enabled both the common man and the aristocrat to adjust to democratic principles and institutions.

> As democratic ideas corroded the old foundations of authority, members of the old governing elite reached out to legitimize their positions under the new notions by appealing for popular support. That appeal compelled deference to popular view but it also required the development of organization to communicate with and to manage the electorate. Thus members of a parliamentary body, who earlier occupied their seats as an incident to the ownership of property or as a perquisite of class position, had to defer to the people—or to those who had the suffrage—and to create electoral organizations to rally voters to their support.[8]

Although not a partnership "made in heaven," political parties permanently joined the political fortunes of the lawmaker to the empowered mass electorate. Where once gaining one's seat in the House of Commons was guaranteed, now the future of who held that seat belonged to the voters.

After achieving its independence from Great Britain, the United States merely duplicated the British two-party format. In 1790, Alexander Hamilton laid the foundation for the Federalist Party while by 1797 Thomas Jefferson had founded the Republican Party, also known as the Jeffersonian Republicans. These two early political parties did not have the same mass appeal as today's Democrat or Republican Parties. Both Hamilton and Jefferson were members of their respective elites. Hamilton represented the emerging industrial and commercial interests of the north while Jefferson was a member of the southern plantation aristocracy. Eventually, the Federalist Party would fall on hard times with the defeat of John Adams by Thomas Jefferson in 1800 and it ceased to exist by 1815. The Jefferson-Republican Party was indeed Jefferson's party. During the 1800 presidential campaign run, Jefferson "had already drawn up a set of party policies— frugal government, reduced national debt, smaller national defense, 'free commerce with all nations' but 'political connections with none,' freedom of religion, press and speech—and during the year his followers used these policies as a rough party platform in their own campaigns."[9] Jefferson took a grassroots approach to his campaign by taking his message to the people rather than waiting for the people to come to him, something the opposition failed to do. Himself a presidential candidate in the 1800 race, Aaron Burr concluded that the Federalists "erred in relying so much on the rectitude and utility of their measures as to have neglected the cultivation of popular favor by fair and justifiable expedients" and thus, lost the election.[10] Meanwhile by 1828, the Jeffersonian Republicans split into two separate political parties, namely the National Republicans and the Jacksonian Democrats. The National Republicans would be replaced by the Whigs in 1832 who by 1860, were replaced by the Republican Party. The Jefferson-Republicans and Jacksonian-Democrats are today's modern Democrat Party. Basically, today's Republican Party is the only third-party movement in the United States that evolved into a major political party.

Party Systems

The most predominate configuration of political parties is the **multiparty system** defined as "an electoral system, usually based on proportional representation, that often requires a coalition of several parties to form a majority to run the government."[11] In France, Germany, and Italy there are numerous political parties with no one party polling enough strength to dominate the electoral process. Consequently, the leadership of the various parties form coalitions with each other. Their combined electoral strength will put one of their coalition members into office. However, once in office the winning party leadership stays in power only as long as they are able to fulfill the promises made to the other parties in return for their support at the polls. The political dynamic in France, Germany, and Italy is a **conflictual party system** whereby "the legislature is dominated by parties that are far apart on issues or highly antagonistic toward each other and the political system."[12] Consequently, the longevity of the coalition is highly doubtful, leading to frequent elections and unstable governments. On the other hand, nations such as Norway and Sweden have a **consensual party system** whereby "the parties commanding most of the legislative seats are not too far apart on policies and have a reasonable amount of trust in each other and in the political system."[13]

The American political party system is basically a **two-party system** at the national level with one-party systems in several of the states. The two-party system fits nicely into the developing dichotomy of American-style politics. The debate over the ratification of the Constitution developed into two camps—the Federalists who favored it and the Anti-Federalists who opposed it. The nation's economic future was divided into two camps—the industrial north and the agricultural south. On the issue of slavery, one was either for its survival and extension or for its abolition. The dichotomy holds true today. Whatever position the Republican Party takes on the economy, the environment, social service issues, transportation, foreign policy, etc., the Democrat Party takes the opposition position. The party that wins the election in the halls of Congress or in either or both houses of the Texas Legislature is the majority party with the losing party becoming the minority party which bears the title of the **loyal opposition**, the party out of power. Of course, the two-party system does not mean that internally all members agree with all of the issue positions, but externally they try their best to portray themselves as unified bodies.

While the national two-party system thrives, many states have developed into a one party state, such as Texas. From its days as a Republic, Texans voted for Democrats with the exception of Reconstruction Texas when former Confederates were denied voting privileges. Once Republican E. J. Davis left Austin, Texans once again swayed towards the Democrat Party. The Democrat Party elite were members of the Texas **establishment**, the power brokers of Texas society. Basically, conservative in political persuasion, the establishment would occasionally allow the liberal wing of the party to elect one of its own such as U.S. Senator Ralph Yarborough (1957-1971) and, of course, Governor Ann Richards. In the 1940s, it was the threat of the Truman administration to declare the state's massive offshore oil deposits and its potential revenue for the federal treasury that moved solid Yellow Dog Democrats to vote for Republican Dwight Eisenhower for the presidency. It was not that painful since Eisenhower was born in Texas. The field of Democratic candidates became so congested that viable potential candidates and elected officials wanting higher office jumped ship to the Republican Party. John Connally, John Tower, and even Rick Perry were once Democrats that eventually became Republicans. The rise of the Republican Party was a gradual one with John Tower elected to the United States Senate in 1961; Kay Bailey Hutchison captured a United States Senate seat in 1992; George W. Bush took the governor's mansion in 1994; and in 1996, the Republican Party overtook the Democrats as the majority party in the Texas Senate. Today, the Republican Party holds all of the top state executive offices, the governorship, solid majorities in both the Texas House and Senate, and the majority of the Texas Supreme Court and Court of Criminal Appeals benches. The only bright spot for Democrats is the county-level and non-partisan local elections.

Factions with the Party Organization

Whether a party survives in the long term depends on how the core leadership deals with the factions within the party's wide umbrella. A **faction** is "a political group or clique that functions within a larger group, such as a government, party or organization."[14] Currently, the Tea Party Movement is basically a faction operating under the umbrella of the Republican Party. The task for the national leadership of the party is to determine how to keep individuals supportive of the underlying themes of the Tea Party that fit so nicely into the Republican political agenda from bolting from the mainstream of the party and forming their own third party movement. Factions lack longevity but they surely can wreck havoc with the base support of the two major political parties. Consequently, one needs to

consider the element of discontinuity in factionalism. Although conditions differ from state to state and from time to time, in many instances the battle for control of a state is fought between groups newly formed for the particular campaign. The groups lack continuity in name—as exists under a party system—and they also lack continuity in the make-up of their inner core of professional politicians or leaders. Naturally, they also lack continuity in voter support which, under two-party conditions, provides a relatively stable following of voters for each party's candidates whoever they may be. . . . loose factional organizations lack the collective spirit of party organization, which at its best imposes a sense of duty and imparts a spirit of responsibility to the inner core of leaders of the organization.[15]

Organizational Structure

On paper, the organizational structure of a political party resembles the modern corporate structure. At the top of the pyramid is the national party organization with its national chairperson and national committee overseeing the day-to-day operation of the national organization and establishing policy and practices for state and local party organizations. On the bottom rung of the pyramid are the local precincts or, as known in some states, the wards. The pyramid structure leads one to believe that the parties operate under a centralized structure whereby the national committee controls the activities of the party structure from top to bottom with the state and local levels having little or no authority. In practice, however, the pyramid is inverted, for the most important level in the party structure are the local precincts. American political parties are decentralized organizations. The primary objective of the national committee is to meet once every four years to select a presidential-vice presidential ticket for the general election. The national committees rarely get involved in United States congressional races and even less involved in gubernatorial contests.

Decentralization of power is by all odds the most important single characteristic of the American major party; more than anything else this trait distinguishes it from all others. Indeed, once this truth is understood, nearly everything else about American parties is greatly illuminated. . . . The American major party is, to repeat the definition, a loose confederation of state and local bosses for limited purposes.[16]

The lack of a cohesive relationship between the various levels of the nation's two major political parties can best be described as **stratarchy**, with each level acting independent of each other.[17] A closer look at the duties and responsibilities assigned to each level of the party pyramid gives an insight into the internal operations of a political party.

The National Party Organization

One of the most prestigious assignments any loyal party member can have is to hold a seat on the Democratic National Committee (DNC) or the Republican National Committee (RNC). Initially the membership of both committees was to consist of just the national chairperson and one man and one woman from each of the fifty states. Today, however, each committee has added members to the point that the RNC has over 150 members and the DNC over 300. The DNC continues to have two (one man and one woman) of each state's highest ranking party leaders as well as "two hundred additional members allocated to the states on the same basis as delegates are apportioned to the national convention; and a number of delegates representing such organizations as the Democratic Governors' Conference, the U.S. Congress, the National Finance Council, the Conference of Democratic Mayors, the National Federation of Democratic Women, the Democratic County Officials Conference, the State Legislative Leaders Caucus, and the Young Democrats of America."[18] Obviously, both political parties use an appointment to their national committees to recognize those who either work hard for the party or donate considerable amounts of money to the party. However, the effectiveness of such a large group is questionable. Meeting infrequently, the primary duties of both committees are confined to policy making, selecting the site of their national conventions and establishing the selection criteria for convention delegates. In *Political Parties*, Robert Michels observed that although both political parties have millions of members, in the end their organizational structure and the internal operations are run by a relatively few high ranking party insiders forming an oligarchy. Accordingly, the **Iron Law of Oligarchy** underscores that "in every organization, whether it be a political party, a professional union, or any other association of the kind, the aristocratic tendency manifests itself very clearly. The mechanism of the organization, while conferring a solidity of structure, induces serious changes in the organized mass, completely inverting the respective position of the leaders and the led. As a result of organization, every party or professional union becomes divided into a minority of directors and a majority of the directed."[19]

The real day-to-day operation of both parties rests with their respective national chairpersons. Although the national committee officially elects the chairperson, the selection is actually made by the president whose party controls the White House. For example, the 2012 Democratic National Convention was to a large extent controlled by President Obama's team, not the DNC. For the party out of power, the national committee would indeed select its national chairperson. The primary responsibility of the national chairperson is to raise and spend money on behalf of their party's candidates. The majority of the money, however, is spent on the presidential races, leaving state organizations to augment the coffers for its United States congressional and senatorial candidates, governors, etc. Additional duties include recruiting candidates, conducting campaign/strategy oriented training programs for candidates and campaign staff members, conducting issue and voter research, and assisting their party's presidential candidates in setting up field offices in the various states.

Obviously, the staff is focused on their party's **national convention** composed of delegates from all fifty states and United States territories meeting once every four years to officially nominate their slate of candidates for the presidential election as well as to draft and approve their national **party platform**. Perhaps one of the most important committees is the platform committee whose primary job is the craft a document that embraces the overall political philosophy of the party while at the same time, highlights issue positions and concerns of the various groups under their party's umbrella. A **platform** is "a statement of principles and objectives espoused by a party or a candidate that is used during a campaign to win support from voters."[20] A national party platform is more than just a document enumerating party political positions. As the official representative of their respective political party, every presidential candidate incorporates party platform issues into the campaign effort. Once elected, it is the responsibility of the president to ensure his/her policy choices and decisions mirror the positions articulated in his/her political party's platform. President Dwight Eisenhower emphasized that "there may be some cynics who think that a Platform is just a list of platitudes to lure the naïve voter—a sort of façade behind which candidates sneak into power and then do as they please. I am not one of those."[21] In keeping with the themes of the national platform, state and county or district conventions write their own platforms. Platforms issues will vary from state delegation to state delegation. As evidenced in both

the Texas Republican and Democratic platforms from their 2018 state conventions, state parties will blend their own issue concerns into the national party's overall philosophy. Resolutions made at the state conventions to amend the official party platform are entertained at the next national convention as that platform committee drafts the new document.

Although over the years nationally televised programming of the national conventions has been limited, all of the cameras focus on each party's presidential nominee's **keynote address**. This is perhaps the most highly anticipated and important speech a presidential candidate has to deliver. In the text of the speech, the nominee officially accepts his/her party's nomination and lays out his/her agenda for the upcoming general election. The speech is interrupted numerous times with clapping and cheering. At the end of the speech, the candidate, his/her family members, and key members of the party gather on the main platform to watch the balloons drop, the confetti fly, and the convention members cheer on the candidates. This is prime time television exposure for both the party and the candidate.

However, the real business of a convention and the internal wheeling and dealing between the national committee members and state party leaders usually escapes media attention. For example, the official seating of delegates falls upon the **credentials committee** who prior to the convention establish the process of certifying a state's official delegation. Each state's party organization will send their officially elected pledged and unpledged (independent delegates) as well as a cadre of alternate delegates. Credentialing a state's delegation can pose serious problems. During the 2008 presidential election cycle, the DNC was debating whether to credential delegates from several states whose state organizations decided not to respect the DNC's primary election schedule by moving their state primary elections from the Super Tuesday calendar. In the end, the questionable state delegations were credentialed and did cast their votes for the presidential/vice presidential candidate slate. Even the United States Supreme Court has played a role in settling credentialing issues. In 1891, the Court ruled in the *Democratic Party v LaFollette* that a state's party leadership could not force the DNC's credential's committee to accept a delegation that was selected in violation of DNC rules. In *Cousins v Wigoda* (1975), the Court ruled that only the credentials committee of a national political party has the authority to settle credential disputes between rival state delegations.

Both national party organizations have faced criticism that their traditional way of doing business was more exclusive than inclusive. In other words, the "good ole boy" wheeling and dealing between a few well-entrenched elites controlled the entire party from top to bottom, leaving the ordinary rank-and-file member to believe that his/her political party only needed them to vote on election-day for the party's anointed candidates. Particularly for the DNC, their 1968 national convention was an eye opener. At the height of the Vietnam War and civil rights protest movements, the DNC selected Chicago, Illinois, as their national convention site. All mayhem broke loose as Chicago's convention security force harassed, beat, and arrested scores of convention protestors outside of the facility while in the halls of the convention, charges were levied that backroom politics had predetermined the outcome of platform issues and selection of the candidates. Reform measures had to come or the party was doomed. In response to the criticism, DNC chairperson Fred Harris appointed then Senator George McGovern to head a special committee to investigate the operation of the party and make needed recommendations. Filed in 1971, the McGovern Commission advocated a more grass-roots approach by broadening the delegate pool to include more women and minorities. Also, the report recommended that state party officials could no longer demand that their delegates promote a "favorite son" candidate in lieu of their own personal candidate selections, and that at least 75 percent of a state's national convention delegation had to be chosen at their state conventions specifically from their congressional districts or smaller units. The RNC also formed its own committee to initiate possible reforms. Since then both the RNC and DNC have taken strides to make the delegation selection process more equitable including a broad representation of the entire party membership with particular emphasis on minorities and younger party supporters.

State Party Organizations

The United States Constitution does not even mention political parties nor does any amendment recognize their existence, overall responsibilities, or operational procedures. Every state legislative house, however, has set overall ground rules for establishment and operation of political parties as well as rules governing the election processes. The **Texas Election Code** enacted by the Texas Legislature is the primary source of the state's election laws. The Texas party system is composed of a permanent and temporary party organization format. The temporary party organization involves party members (loyal party-line voters) selecting their candidate preferences in the primary

elections, and, if need be, the primary run-off elections and, hopefully, attending their precinct conventions. The permanent organization is composed of all of the precinct chairs and the executive committee members of both the county/district and state organizations.

For both political parties, the state executive committee is composed of a chairperson, vice chairperson, and one man and one woman from each of the state's thirty-one state senatorial districts. All are selected at the state's biennial party convention with the chair and vice-chair selected at-large for two-year terms of office. Delegates from each state senatorial district meet to select their committee representatives. For the party in-power, the state chairperson position is basically ceremonial since the governor serves as head of his/her political party. The basic functions of the state organization include canvassing statewide election results, certifying a candidate's qualifications for office, receiving the filling forms, collecting the filling fees, and overseeing the site selection and coordination of the upcoming state convention. The state chairperson is the party's official "cheer leader" in that he/she promotes party unity, loyalty and strength at both the county and precinct levels, encourages precincts and county organizations in their grassroots efforts of registering and encouraging people to vote, raising money for statewide and local races, and working with the national party leadership.

In Texas, state conventions are held in June of even-numbered years. At the state convention, delegates certify the party's slate of candidates for the upcoming November general election, draft and approve the state's party platform, elect the party chair, vice-chair and state executive committee members to serve until the next convention convenes, adopt resolutions, and select their members to the national party executive committee. During presidential election cycles, delegates to the national party convention are selected as well as the party's slate of potential presidential electors at each party's respective state conventions.

Both parties select their delegates to the national convention differently. The Republican Party takes the simple route by basing the number of delegates for a particular candidate from the results of the presidential preference primary. The majority of the delegates are chosen on an at-large basis by the entire state convention delegates. These delegates are pledged for the candidate they are selected to represent. If a presidential candidate wins 50 percent or more of the popular vote in the primary in a particular United States congressional district or, as in some cases, statewide vote, the candidate is entitled to all of district or at-large delegates. A nominating committee selects the unpledged delegates. Texas Democrats, however, use a unique but confusing process known as **The Texas Two-Step**. The first step selects national convention delegates pledged to a candidate based on the vote tally of the primary election. The second step selects the reminder of the delegates at the precinct conventions. Under normal circumstances, most Democrats do not even participate in the two-step. They merely vote in the primary election and skip attending the precinct convention. The 2008 Democratic presidential primary was a different story. Both the Hillary Clinton and Barack Obama camps made sure Democrats loyal to their causes showed up at the precinct conventions. The Clinton camp was overjoyed because she won the popular vote in the primary election. One would think that she would now have more Texas delegates to the national convention than her opponent. However when the precinct conventions adjourned for that evening, Obama won the delegate tally with 99 to Clinton's 94. The Clinton camp protested the delegation selection process up until the week before the Texas Democratic State Convention. In 2012, Democrats gathered at their state convention held in Corpus Christi to discuss the future of the two-step. Despite a two-year battle from Clinton supporters, the two-step survived.

County/District Organizations

The county organization is governed by an executive committee composed of all the precinct chairs from that particular county. In larger counties such as Harris, Bexar, Dallas and Tarrant, the county is divided into districts. The county or district chairperson is popularly elected to a two-year term of office. The county/district organization is responsible for preparing the election ballot, receiving the filing forms, collecting the candidate filing fees, and determining the ballot order for the candidates. The practice in Texas is for each office to be listed in descending order of importance with the top position in a vertical ballot or the left-hand column on a horizontal ballot reserved for all candidates from the governor's political party. For the 2018 general election, all Republican candidates were in the first spot on the ballot for their specific offices since Governor Abbott is a Republican. The county/district organization is also responsible for canvassing the returns for the primary elections for local positions and arranging for the county/district conventions.

State election laws require that county/district conventions must take place eleven days after the primary election. At the county/district convention, delegates select their representatives to the state convention, adopt resolutions for consideration at the state convention, and for district conventions, select their district chairpersons and a recording secretary to take convention minutes. Each county/district convention selects one delegate to the state convention for every 300 votes cast in the county or district for the party's gubernatorial candidate in the last general election. The Republican Party requires that state delegates be elected directly from the county/district convention while the Democrats allow individual precinct delegations to select their own delegates. Regardless, if the county/district delegates do not select enough state convention delegates, the county/district nominations committee will fill the remaining slots.

The Precinct

The lowest level of the political party structure, the **election precinct** or **precinct** is chaired by a precinct chairperson officially selected on the primary election ballot or at the precinct convention held after the primary election polls have closed. Precinct chairpersons serve a two-year term of office. The precinct convention is open to all individuals who voted in their party's primary election. At the precinct convention, attendees select a pre-determined number of delegates to the county or district convention, as well as adopt resolutions for consideration at the county/district convention. For both the Democratic and Republican Parties, each precinct is authorized to send a delegate for every twenty-five votes cast in that precinct for their party's gubernatorial candidate in the last election. The primary duties of a precinct chair are to mobilize voter turnout, select poll watchers for the primary and general elections, arrange for the precinct convention, and serve on the county executive committee.

The precinct is the core of grassroots politics. It is the responsibility of the precinct chairperson to canvass the residents within his/her precinct to determine the party diehards from those vacillating between party loyalties and those who are not even registered to vote. It is the precinct chairperson who coordinates voter registration drives and assists voters who need mail-in ballots or special assistance in filling out the ballot. Precinct chairpersons oftentimes host coffees in their homes for those candidates running at the bottom of the ballot, i.e., judges, county commissioners, etc., so the candidate can establish a physical presence within the precinct and hopefully encourage attendees to fill the campaign jar. It is the precinct chairperson who assists in distributing campaign literature, posting signs, and offering voters a ride to the polls on election day.

Unfortunately, both political parties have far too many precincts operating without a chairperson. The party leadership is hard pressed to find those willing to fill these very important grassroots positions.

The Political Philosophical Spectrum

The **political spectrum** is merely a straight horizontal line on which political scientists place the political philosophical positions or the ideological perspectives of a given group. An **ideology** is "a comprehensive system of political beliefs about the nature of people and society."[22] The middle position on the political spectrum is always reserved for centrist positions. While any placement to the right of the middle indicates a conservative political ideology, left of the middle is reserved for more liberal perspectives. A brief overview of prevailing political philosophies reveals the underlying principles guiding the issue positions of those adhering to a particular political perspective.

Conservatism—The Right of the Spectrum

Holding the interior position on the right side of the political spectrum, **conservatism** is "the political outlook which springs from a desire to conserve existing things, held to be either good in themselves, are at least safe, familiar, and the objects of trust and affection."[23] A true conservative is the defender of the status quo against the onslaught of major changes not just in the political arena but also to economic and social institutions. The term **incrementalism** is "a doctrine holding that change in a political system occurs only by small steps, each of which should be carefully evaluated before proceeding to the next step."[24] There are six major elements to conservatism:

- First, conservatives generally have a religious bent. They believe a "divine intent rules society as well as conscience." Thus the existing order is somehow sanctioned by more than human forces.
- Second is an attachment to traditional life, in spite of its variety and apparent disorder.
- Third, conservatives believe "civilized society requires orders and classes." Thus society cannot be leveled. Though all people are equal morally, they must be unequal in social terms.
- Fourth is a close relationship between freedom and private property. The former is made possible only by the existence of the latter, and so conservatives support the existing distribution of property, even with its inequalities.

- Fifth is faith in **prescription** [the action of laying down authoritative rules or directions] and distrust of reason. Reason is not an adequate guide to human conduct.
- Finally, though conservatives are willing to countenance a measure of reform, they distrust more substantial change: "innovation is a devouring conflagration more often than it is a touch of progress."[25]

Consequently, a true conservative supports upholding and enhancing the existing social and political order. Although they acknowledge society's inherent inequalities of wealth, political power, economic upper mobility and social status, conservatives embrace a class system based on wealth and lineage. British political philosopher Edmund Burke is considered by many to be the father of conservative political thought. "His conservatism consists, in essence, of a few simple generalizations: that the present state of things is the sum total of all past developments; that it is too complex to understand; that meddling with it is therefore dangerous; and that arrangements that work well enough are best left alone."[26]

Adhering to the general principles of conservative thought, **cultural conservatism** is based on "support for traditional western Judeo-Christian values not just as a matter of comfort and faith, but out of a firm belief that the secular, the economic, and the political success of the western world is rooted in these value."[27] In Texas, cultural conservatism developed from the traditional political sub-cultural found in the southern plantation states particularly with its emphasis on elitism and entrenched social traditions. "This American cultural conservatism is directed towards conserving the fragments of old European culture, usually with an exile's consciousness of the difficulty of the task; but like the English version, it often striking claims for the rule of culture in determining the quality of life, not just of those who possess it, but also those who do not."[28] Further to the right, the **New Right** or the **religious right** focuses more on religious than cultural values. The agenda of the religious right sees an extremely limited role for government in all policy areas including the economy, welfare programs, the environment, etc. It takes a strong anti-communist and anti-socialist position. The religious right upholds traditional moral values including strong anti-abortion positions and advocacy for prayer in the public schools. An individual proclaiming him/herself as a true conservative would favor the free enterprise system, capitalism, a strong military, less government regulation, a less intrusive role for government, private property ownership and rights, cultural conservatism, and a strong-sense of moral and religious values.

Moderates—The Center of the Spectrum

The bulk of the American electorate is positioned in the middle of the political spectrum. A **centrist** is "an individual or political group advocating a moderate approach to political decision making and to the solution of social problems."[29] A moderate believes in:

- A desire for conciliation or compromise rather than confrontation. For example, the on-going budget battle in the Texas Legislature clearly shows the cleavage between Democrats and Republicans, leaving the moderate to view the body as polarized and unable to reach reasonable compromises.
- A preference for reform over revolution. Moderates prefer those policy options that correctly assess the problem and offer reasonable solutions to fix it.
- Political transformations gradually occurring without violence against the governing institutions.
- Tolerance towards views which do not match the consensus but are voiced in a non-violent manner.[30]

The majority of Texans share political views that place them in the middle. In many respects, the **mainstream** of the political spectrum is the most advantageous of political positions simply because it does not attract those whose political views are too far from the extremes of the traditional left (liberal) or right (conservative). To be in the mainstream means that one swims in the political center where most of the voters are to be found. Few are diehard conservatives or liberals.

Both the Texas Democratic and Republican Parties have their share of **ideologues**, that is, "those who believe intensely in a certain system of political beliefs; those who put faith in abstract principles without regard to the realities of a situation."[31] The term "**Dyed in the Wool**" labels the most partisan of the partisans. These are the ones who cannot be converted to other political perspectives and who go all out for his or her party. However, many Republican Texans proudly call themselves "**Bleeding Heart Conservatives**" because even though they follow the Republican Party's basic values, they also support efforts "to alleviate poverty and inadequate housing through conservative programs that empower people to help themselves as opposed to traditional government handouts."[32] And while many Texans are Democrats, they do not follow the traditional political positions of the "die hard liberal" ring of the Democratic Party.

Today, many voters simply do not want a party-label attached to them, preferring instead to declare themselves as **independents**. In other words, they are not true Republicans or Democrats in either ideological prospectives or candidate selections. These are the ones who will vote for some Democrat as well as Republican candidates. They cross party lines on the issues. For example, an individual may be against government regulation of personal freedoms but support strong regulation of the nation's financial industries. Some will embrace the Democrats on pro-choice but defend the Republican position on anti-abortion positions. Regardless of whether they call themselves independent, moderates, or mainstream voters, they have their own comfort zone whereby they can pick and choose between the two parties, issue positions, and the candidates that best fit their own individual political perspectives.

Liberalism—The Left of the Spectrum

While conservatives dread change, liberals embrace it. Originally, **liberalism** was "a political doctrine that espoused freedom of the individual from interference by the state, toleration by the state in matters of morality and religion, laissez-faire economic policies, and a belief in natural rights that exist independently of government."[33] Liberalism grew out of the Enlightenment with the writings of John Locke, Charles de Montesquieu, Jean Jacques Rousseau, Jeremy Bentham, John Stuart Mill, Immanuel Kant, and Baruch Spinoza. In the emerging United States, it was Thomas Jefferson and, in particular, James Madison who left lasting liberal imprints on both the United States Constitution and the Bill of Rights. In his *Spirit of the Laws*, Montesquieu defines **liberty** as "in a state, that is, in a society where there are laws, liberty can consist only in having the power to do what one should want to do and in no way being constrained to do what one should not want to do."[34] He differentiates between **positive liberty**, which is to force someone to be free versus **negative liberty** which to Montesquieu is "that tranquility of spirit which comes from the opinion each one has of his security, and in order for him to have this liberty the government must be such that one citizen cannot fear another citizen."[35] In other words, a government cannot force someone to vote (positive liberty), however, government must provide unrestrained accessibility to the voting process so someone can make a choice whether or not to vote (negative liberty).

Liberalism is based on the following concepts:

- The belief in the supreme value of the individual, his freedom and his rights. Therefore, liberalism embraces the concept of **individualism** defined as "the political, economic and social concept that places primary emphasis on the worth, freedom and well being of the individual rather than on the group, society or nation."[36]
- The belief that every individual has natural rights, i.e., life, liberty and property, which exists independently of government. It is government's responsibility to protect an individual's rights from interference from others (civil rights) and from the government (civil liberties). The Framers of the United States Constitution kept life and liberty as natural rights but changed property to the pursuit of happiness.
- The belief of the supreme value of freedom by limiting the power of governing institutions from inhibiting one from exercising that freedom. This belief underscores the basic representative democratic concepts of limited government, separation of powers, and checks and balances. John Locke wrote in his *Second Treatise of Government*, "the liberty of man in society is to be under no other legislative power but that established by consent in the commonwealth, nor under the dominion of any will, or restraint of any law, but what the legislative shall enact, according to the trust put in it."[37]
- Tacit consent and the social contract. According to John Locke, **tacit consent** means that an individual who enjoys some benefit from living in a particular country consents to obey the rules of that country, therefore, acknowledging its right to govern. "Locke emphasizes that possessing property in a country constitutes consent to its government. Because it is impossible to remove one's land from a country, accepting ownership of land requires membership in a society and so consent to obey its laws."[38] According to the **social contract**, people who are absolutely free as individuals come together as a community to form a governing body that will establish the rules for the exercise of basic fundamental rights. If the government fails to protect those rights, then the very people who established the government in the first place, have the absolute right to abolish it and create a new governing structure.[39]

The far left-side of the spectrum is reserved for those who adhere to a socialist agenda advocating public ownership of the means of production and a strong welfare state. The far left is impatient with those advocating gradual or incremental changes. They want rapid radical revolutionary economic, social, and political changes. Those under the radical umbrella include democratic socialists, Marxian socialists, communists, and anarchists. The United States experienced its own far-left movement commonly called the New Left during the 1960s. Launched across the nation on college campuses, students in particular staged protests challenging the established political, social and economic order of the nation. The New Left was fueled by the convergence of three major movements—anti-Vietnam war sentiments, the Civil Rights and the woman's liberation movements. Although there was no cohesive massive convergence of the three camps, what emerged was an agenda of common themes, i.e., anti-Vietnam War, hostility towards the traditional military-industrial complex, advocacy against racial discrimination, promotion of women's issues, and sincere empathy towards the nation's economic deprivation of the poor.

Major Parties: The Republican Party of Texas

Historical Overview

The southern states were first introduced to Republican presidential politics with the election of Abraham Lincoln in 1860. Severely divided over the future of slavery, the once solid Democratic base split with four candidates running for the presidency. There was no formal Republican Party in Texas. When the party called for its national convention, Texas had no Republicans delegates to send nor did they have a slate of Republican electors to cast their votes in the Electoral College. Faced with the inevitability that Lincoln would become the nation's next president, pro-union Texans to include Governor Sam Houston tried to rally Texans to support the idea that the election of Lincoln did not automatically mean succession from the union or even war. Of course, Texans like the majority of Southerners would not be confronted with the Republican Party again until after the South's defeat in the Civil War. As previously pointed out, the Radical Republicans in Washington, D.C., desired not only to punish the southern states for leaving the Union; they wanted to establish a very strong Republican Party presence in the south. Stripping former Confederate soldiers and those backing the southern cause of their voting rights during Reconstruction certainly helped the Republican Party to achieve its objectives. The state's first Republican state convention was held in Houston in 1867. Among the delegates to the 1868 state constitutional convention were nine African Americans whose support from the Republican Party earned them the honor of being the first African Americans elected to a public position. By giving former slaves citizenship and voting rights, the Republican Party not only in Texas but throughout the defeated South could count an overwhelming majority of the African-American vote into their column. Nationally, the elephant emerged as the party's official symbol. First appearing in a *Harper's Weekly* cartoon in 1874, creator caricaturist Thomas Nast used the elephant because he believed that the Republican Party was the best option for voters muddling through the "political jungle."[40]

Once former Confederates regained their voting rights, the Democrat Party dominated the state's political landscape for decades. Cracks in the Democrat Party's hold on Texas began with the presidential election of 1948 as traditional conservative Democrats saw the party leadership leaning too left for comfort towards the liberal perspective. "In 1948, President Harry Truman (D) infuriated much of the South by ordering an end to racial discrimination in federal hiring and an end to segregation in the armed services, and by calling for an anti-lynching law, elimination of the poll tax as a suffrage requirement, and the creation of a Fair Employment Practices Committee."[41] The anger with Truman's agenda hit an all time high when Truman eyed the rich offshore oil deposits commonly known as the Tidelands and its potential revenue generation for the federal coffer, not the state's treasury. Gradually more electable Democrats turned to the Republican Party as their chance to gain public office. Today, the Republican Party is in the driver's seat with the Democrats taking the back seat.

Political Ideology—The Party Platform

The first Republican to be elected to the governorship since Reconstruction, Bill Clements served two non-consecutive terms of office from 1979 to 1983 and 1987 to 1991. In his first inaugural speech delivered in 1979, Clements clearly laid out his own political philosophy embracing the Republican Party's viewpoint of the appropriate role for government in Texas:

> I want to conduct government in a **business-like manner**, with elected officials and government leaders responsible to the taxpayers just as a board

of directors and company officials are responsible to the stockholders. . . . I will persist because I believe you, the people, had made it clear your desire for better government and for **less government**. I will persist with my plans to return to you, the taxpayers one billion dollars of the state's surplus. I will persist with my plans to give your long-term, constitutional safeguards—including the right of initiative and referendum—to protect **against excessive taxation** and **wasteful government spending**. I will persist with my plans to **reduce the size of our state bureaucracy**.[42] (Emphasis added by author.)

In 2018, Republicans across the state gathered at their state party's convention to support their nominees for statewide races and a slate of candidates for both state legislative and national congressional seats as well as pen the platform that would guide their party and its candidates for the next two years. The political positions articulated by Governor Clements in 1979 are basically the same as those of the 2018 preamble to the party's platform with few exceptions:

Affirming the belief in God, we still hold these truths to be self-evident, that all men are created equal, that they are endowed by their Creator with certain unalienable Rights, that among these are Life, Liberty, and the Pursuit

Thomas Nast used the elephant in this cartoon relating the Republican defeat of Tammany Hall candidates in the 1875 elections. Credit: Library of Congress

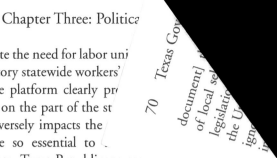

of Happiness. Throughout the world, people dare to dream of freedom given to us by God, implemented by our Founding Fathers and embodied in the Constitution. We recognize that the traditional family is the strength of our nation. It is our solemn duty to protect innocent life and develop responsible citizens. We understand that our economic success depends upon free market principles. If we fail to maintain our sovereignty, we risk losing the freedom to live these ideals.[43]

The party's platform listing of key principles underlines its traditional conservative political perspectives. We support:

- The strict adherence to the original language of the Declaration of Independence and the Constitutions of the United States and Texas.
- The sanctity of innocent human life, created in the image of God, which should be protected from fertilization to natural death.
- Preserving American and Texas sovereignty and freedom.
- Limiting government power to those enumerated in the United States and Texas constitutions.
- Personal accountability and responsibility.
- Self-sufficient families founded on the traditional marriage of a natural man and a natural woman.
- Having an educated population with parents having the freedom of choice for the education of their children.
- The inalienable right of all people to defend themselves and their property.
- A free enterprise society unencumbered by government interference or subsidies.
- Honoring all of those that serve and protect our freedom.[44]

Traditionally, Texas Republicans are strong supporters of legislation that protects business and industry from any form of government regulation and promotes free enterprise without any government interference whatsoever. They want to abolish federal regulations that impact intrastate commerce, that is, commerce within the state's boundaries. Furthermore, Texas Republicans have traditionally taken anti-worker and anti-union positions as a means of promoting business development. The platform calls for the state to eliminate all collective bargaining rights for public employees. They also oppose all state prevailing wage laws and continue to advocate for the abolition of the federal minimum wage law. Texas Republicans stress the need for a national right to work law that would essentially eliminate the need for labor uni[on] mandatory statewide workers'

The platform clearly pr[...] actions on the part of the st[...] that adversely impacts the [...] that are so essential to [...] Therefore, Texas Republicans are ag[ainst] the provisions covered in the Environmental [...] Act as well as opposed to all pro-environmental law[s] enacted by the Obama administration. For example, the platform states that the Party opposes any effort to declare carbon dioxide as a pollutant, supports the defeat of "cap-and-trade" legislation, seeks to abolish all barriers that would impede the production, reformation, refining and distribution of traditional energy sources such as oil and gas, the repeal of all legislation "mandating ethanol as a fuel additive and/or primary fuel.[45] Texas Republicans take a strong stance against any environmental laws that adversely impacts legitimate business interests and interferes with the absolute rights of private property ownership. They also advocate support of defunding any 'climate justice' initiatives, the abolition of the Environmental Protection Agency, and repeal of the Endangered Species Act. The platform emphasizes the Party's continuing efforts to protect the Tidelands and coastal areas from unwarranted federal regulation. In particular, Republicans "demand that the State of Texas and all coastal states enjoy and maintain jurisdiction and control of their offshore waters up to the international water boundaries as well as state inland waterways in regards to all natural resources therein" to include everything from minerals, game, fisheries, etc.[46]

However, the platform does address the adverse impact fracking production has had on county governments. This extraction process bought a "gold rush" of oil workers to counties in the southern sector of the state. These country and city governments saw their highways and roadways severely damaged by the continuous onslaught of oil tankers and heavy equipment trucks upon their thoroughfares. Acknowledging that county government simply lack funds to repair their roadways, the platform states that "counties with oil and gas production, and adjacent counties, should receive a portion of the production taxes that the state collects so that the road system can be maintained for the dual purpose of accommodating the needs of the industry and providing adequate public safety."[47]

Traditionally, Texas Republican Party platforms have emphasized the need to preserve both the sovereignty of the state's government and state's rights by restricting the power of the federal government over their state. "Pursuant to Article I, Section I of the Texas Constitution [the 1876 he federal government has impaired right f-government. Therefore, federally mandated n that infringes upon the 10th Amendment [of ited States Constitution] rights of Texas, should be red, opposed, and nullified. Regulation of Commerce Article I, Section 8 [of the United States Constitution] has exceeded the original intent. All attempts by the federal judiciary not expressly enumerated by the United States Constitution should likewise be nullified."[48] As stated in the 2014 platform, the Republican Party continues to support the repeal of the 17th Amendment to the United States Constitution. This amendment calls for the citizens of each state to directly elected their two United States senators. Instead, Texas Republicans want the Texas Legislature to nominate and appoint the state's senators to Washington, D.C. They also want the federal government to revoke all executive orders issued during the Obama administration that they feel violate the Party's platform positions. The platform also calls for term limits of twelve years for all federal and state elected officeholders.

The Texas Republican Party's platform continues to stress the party's strong support of the 2nd Amendment [right to bear arms] to the United States Constitution. The platform states that "we affirm that lawful gun ownership and carry by the people protects us from those who wish to do harm and guards against tyranny by our government."[49] They advocate constitutional laws at both the state and national level to uphold right-to-carry legislation while at the same time, abolishing gun-free zones to include public schools. Texas Republicans want the legal age to purchase a gun lowered from 21 to 18. They oppose any form of mandatory gun safety training as a requirement for gun ownership. Basically, the platform states "we call upon gun owners of Texas to regulate themselves through exercising safe handling procedures, voluntarily receiving training and helping others to train others, and safely carrying firearms as a deterrent to crime."[50] Gun right's advocates within the party stress through their platform that it is the responsibility of the gun owner and not the state or federal government to determine how a weapon is to be stored when not in use. Furthermore, they support "legislation and policies that reduce restrictions on legal gun owners to purchase, own, or carry any type of gun, ammunition, accessory, knife, or other weapons, and oppose all that hinder the same."[51]

The promotion and protection of traditional family values has always been a policy issue to Texas Republicans. The current platform reaffirms many of the Party's positions taken in previous platforms. Basically, Texas Republicans support the "affirmation of traditional Judeo-

Christian family values and oppose continued assaults on those values."[52] Republicans want the Texas Legislature to abolish no-fault divorce laws, reinstate covenant marriages, ban common-law marriages, and outlaw same-sex unions. The platform takes a strong parent's rights position by stating that "we support legislation ensuring that the parents' rights to raise and educate their children are protected in Texas law as a fundamental constitutional right and that there is a presumption that fit parents act in the best interest of their children. So long as the parent is fit, there will normally be no reason for the state to interject in the private realm of the family to question the ability of that parent to make the best decisions concerning the rearing of that child."[53] Furthermore, they advocate the abolishment of Child Protective Services (CPS). The platform also calls for the state to outlaw the teaching of sex education, sexual health, and sexual choice in the public schools, while at the same time, calling for the abolition of the federal government's Department of Education and oppose any effort towards a national core curriculum.

The Texas Republican Party continues its promotion of school choice and home-schooling. The 2018 state Republican Party platform reemphasizes the party's decades old pro-life and anti-gay positions. The Republican platform calls for the abolishment of all federal and state hate crimes laws. There is a position upholding the right of religious institutions to perform only those marriages that are consistent with their religious doctrines.

Border security particularly the shared border with Mexico, was a key campaign issue for Republican candidate Donald Trump. The Texas Republican Party has several platform positions addressing the need for more border security. They want every resident of Texas to provide proof of legal residency when they seek to obtain a driver's license or voter registration card. Furthermore, they want all employers to screen potential hires to ensure that they are indeed, legal citizens of the United States. The platform stresses the party's disdain for sanctuary cities and the granting of amnesty of anyone living in the nation illegally.

The platform also dabbles into foreign policy issues that of course, are not considerations for state governments to legislatively tackle. However, the Texas Republican Party wants the United States to withdraw from the International Monetary Fund (IMF), the World Trade Organization (WTO), the World Bank and any international trade agreements that conflict with the nation's economic viability. In particular, the United Nations (UN) has drawn the ire of state Republicans who demand in this platform that the United States withdraw its membership, not pay its dues, and move UN headquarters out of the United States.

A faction within the Republican Party, the **Tea Party Movement** aligns itself farther to the right of traditional conservative political ideology. The movement's bottom line issues include the elimination of the national debt through fiscally conservative policies enacted at all levels of government, elimination of deficit spending, protection of the free market system, strict adherence to the provisions detailed in the United States Constitution, promotion of civil responsibility, reduction of the overall size of government at all levels, and maintenance of local independence through the elimination of federal regulations covering everything from wages to the environment. Tea Party members adamantly support reducing the federal deficit by eliminating all federally and state funded social programs, the elimination of the income tax and the reduction and/or elimination of other tax generating programs, and the repeal of Obamacare. The movement has successfully recruited and elected several Texans to political office Under the protective umbrella of the Republican Party including Lt. Governor Dan Patrick, State Senator Donna Campbell, U.S. House Representative Will Hurd and U.S. Senator Ted Cruz. As the 2018 mid-term elections approached, leaders of the Tea Party decided to office realign themselves with the Republican Party rather than forming an independent third political party.

Major Parties:
The Democratic Party of Texas

After winning its independence from Mexico, the citizens of the newly formed Republic of Texas had to elect its governing officials. In 1836, there were no official political parties in the infant Republic. Subsequently, the elections focused more on the personal personalities and political positions of the candidates. Sam Houston, the newly crowned hero of the Texas Revolution, overwhelmingly won the presidency over Henry Smith, the governor of the provisional government of Texas, and Stephen F. Austin, soon to be named the Father of Texas. Texans were formally introduced to the Democratic Party when Texas was annexed into the United States in 1845. The Democratic Party with its pro-slavery positions attracted Texans to join its ranks resulting in a clean slate of Democratic victories from the White House to the governor's mansion up to 1860. Once former Confederates in the South regained their political freedoms taken from them by Reconstruction Radical Republicans, the supremacy of the Democratic Party

returned to the South and Texas. It was the Democrats that sent E. J. Davis packing and, unfortunately, penned the very restrictive Constitution of 1876.

Reconstruction had a significant impact on the future development of the Democratic Party. The abolition of slavery coupled with the granting of citizenship and the power of the vote to African Americans by the Republican-controlled federal government pushed the Democratic Party to take what they perceived to be prudent measures to protect the basically all Anglo Democratic Party base from the encroachment of the newly enfranchised African-American voters. It was the conservative wing of the Democratic Party that pushed for the enactment of the poll tax, a fee for voting. Setting it at $1.50 in 1901, the poll tax made it too expensive for many lower-income African Americans, Hispanics and Anglos to vote. It was the Democratic Party that established the white-only party primary election. This practice actually prohibited African Americans from having an impact in the general election since the Republican Party rarely ran candidates in opposition to the Democrats on the ballot. It took a series of United States Supreme Court rulings to finally drive home the point that the white-only primary was indeed unconstitutional. It was the Democratic Party that imposed the Grandfather Clause and the literacy test upon potential African-American voters. One test administered in a southern state required all potential African-American voters to name all of the presidents in order. Minor spelling errors on the registration card were grounds to declare the applicant as illiterate and, therefore, ineligible to vote. It was the Democratic Party in the South that fought against anti-lynching laws and staged an all out battle to defeat civil rights for African Americans. Throughout the South and, in particularly Texas, many were proud to be supporters of the **boll weevils**, "a long-used term for southern Democrats in the U.S. House of Representatives who supported conservative policies."[54]

Basically, the Democratic Party was anti-everything from taxes to civil rights to government regulation. It was the election of Woodrow Wilson (D) to the White House that changed the party's political perspective towards the federal government's responsibility to its citizens. Wilson believed that it was the government's responsibility under the Preamble to the Constitution that plainly charged the federal government with the tasks of "promoting the general welfare" of the American people and "providing for the common defense" of the nation. Consequently, the Democratic Party shifted from the party of the elite to the party of the people. It was Franklin Roosevelt (D) who used Wilson's philosophical shift to justify the creation of his New Deal programs. Where once the domination of the Democratic Party in Texas politics was unquestionable and seemed insurmountable. Today, Texas Democrats have seen their political clout diminished in this once one-party donkey state by an onslaught of Republican election victories. Lately in presidential general elections, Democrat contenders simply do not even consider Texas a toss-up state, firmly putting the state's electoral votes into the Republican column, and spending as little time as possible campaigning even in the major urban areas.

Political Ideology – The Party Platform

Ann Richards began her political career as a supportive mate for her husband's political ambitions. Realizing that she too could have a meaningful role in the political arena, Richards eventually was elected to two terms as state treasurer and soundly beat another Republican self-made millionaire oilman and rancher Clayton Williams for the governorship in 1991. In her inaugural address, Richards echoed the political rhetoric of a traditional Democrat:

> Today, we have a vision of a Texas where **opportunity knows no race or color or gender**—a glimpse of the possibilities that can be when the barriers fall and the doors of government swing open. . . . Today, we have a vision of a Texas with **clean air and land and water**, a Texas where a strong economy lives in harmony with a safe environment. . . . Today, we have a vision of a Texas where every child receives an education that allows them to claim the full promise of their lives. . . . Today, we have a vision of Texas where government treats every citizen with respect and dignity and honesty, where **consumers are protected**, where business is nurtured and valued, where good jobs are plentiful, and where those in need find compassion and help, where every decision is measured against a high standard of ethics and true commitment to the public trust.[55] (Emphasis added by author)

The preamble to the platform of the 2018 Texas Democratic Party begins with the statement that "Texas Democrats believe government exists to achieve together what we cannot achieve as individuals; and government must serve all people. A representative democracy is the only truly representative if every single citizen is guaranteed the inalienable right to vote in fair and open elections."[56] Furthermore, the preamble enumerates the basic principles of the Party:

- Equality and Freedom – Texas Democrats believe in equal opportunities and freedom for all human beings no matter a person's race, disability, religion, gender identity, sexual orientation, socioeconomic or immigration status.
- Smart Government – Texas Democrats believe in a fair criminal justice system serving all people; robust public and higher education opportunities are critical for our future; and our economy must benefit all Texans.
- A Healthy Texas – Texas Democrats believe healthcare is a right; women's rights are human rights; we owe future generations a clean and healthy planet; and a strong social safety net creates opportunity for all Americans.
- Principles of the Texas Democratic Party – Texas Democrats believe democratic government exists as a community, state, and nation what we cannot achieve as individuals; and that it must serve all citizens.
- We believe every Texan has inalienable rights that even a majority may not take away: the right to vote; the right to fair and open participation and representation in the democratic process; the right to health care; and the right to privacy.
- We believe in freedom: from government interference in our private lives and personal decisions; from discrimination based on race, ethnicity, national origin, disability, gender, sexual orientation, gender identity/expression or any other improper grounds; to exercise civil and human rights; and of religion and individual conscience.
- We believe in responsibility: that religion and individual conscience can never serve to excuse hatred and discrimination; that people are responsible for their actions; that we, who have benefited so greatly from our state and country, have a responsibility to support and give back to all our communities and public institutions; and that corporations are not people and should not be used to shield individuals from the responsibilities of their actions.
- We believe in equal rights: guaranteed in Section 3 of the Texas Bill of Rights; equality under the law guaranteed in Section 3a of the Texas Bill of Rights; and that no state may deny any person equal protection of the laws or due process under the law as guaranteed in the 14th Amendment to the U.S. Constitution.
- We believe in equal opportunity: to receive a quality public education from childhood through college; to find a good job with dignity; to buy or rent a good home in a safe community.

• We believe a growing economy should benefit all Texans: that the people who work in a business are as important as those who invest in it; that every worker would be paid a living wage of at least $15-an-hour; that good business offers a fair deal for customers; that regulation of unfair practices and rates is necessary; that the burden of taxes should be fairly distributed; that government policy should not favor corporations that seek offshore tax shelter, exploit workers, or pollute our environment; and all people, including those with disabilities.

• We believe that our lives, homes, communities and country are made secure: by appropriately staff, trained and equipped military, law enforcement and emergency services; by retirement and pension security; by responsible gun ownership; by encouraging job security where it is possible and providing appropriate assistance and re-training when it is not; by the preservation of our precious natural resources and quality of life; by ensuring that families have easy access to good food with clear understanding of the food quality and source, so they may make informed decisions on their family's health and well-being; by compassionate policy that offers a safety net for those most vulnerable and in need; and by family values that are promoted through policies that value all our families.[57]

Like their Republican counterparts, Texas Democrats propose various policy proposals to address their concerns. A topic already in the forefront for the 2019 legislative session, both Texas Democrats and Republicans want to enact needed reforms to the state's judicial system. Democrats are focusing their attention on bail reform. As detailed in the party's platform, they see the current bail system as "systematic racism and discrimination. Money, or the lack thereof, determines whether those pretrial detainees will be released or held in custody. . . . People who cannot afford to be released on money bail languish in deplorable conditions for months."[58] Consequently, Texas Democrats propose enacting legislation requiring pretrial release on personal recognizance and deferred adjudication, mandating immediate release of low-risk defendants, and requiring judges to make decisions to remand within forty-eight hours of the initial arrest. To alleviate both prison overcrowding and recidivism, Texas Democrats place their emphasis on rehabilitation programs to include education programs for inmates, increased accessibility to re-entry programs, substance abuse programs, repealing the state's "three strikes your out" and streamlining the state's parole

and probation systems. They also propose "treating dug use as a public health challenge rather than as a crime; and reducing possession of small amounts of controlled substances, per the prescribed schedules in the Controlled Substances Act, to a misdemeanor."[59]

In their platform, Texas Democrats believe that "law enforcement must engage the communities they serve and establish relationships with their citizens based on mutual respect and trust."[60] The platform stresses the need for statewide education and training programs with a special emphasis on "civil rights, racial sensitivity, implicit bias, and cultural diversity" for all peace officers.[61] Furthermore, they promote using community-based policing strategies and emphasizing the need to create more racially and culturally diverse law enforcement agencies. In addition, the platform clearly states the party's intentions to introduce legislation ending any form of racial profiling in searches and traffic stops, ensuring that any use of firearms and tasers by law enforcement is absolutely the only viable option to apprehending the accused, and "requiring independent or special prosecutors to investigate police officer involved actions that result in fatalities among citizens."[62]

Voting rights have come under attack with accusations of voter fraud. The Democratic Party has always been for the expansion and not the contraction of voting rights. Positions in the Texas Democrat platform call for the repeal of Texas photo voter identification laws that restrict the number of acceptable items such as a college student identification cards while at the same time, advocating for same day and online voter registration, and adherence to the federal Voting Rights Act and the Texas Voting Rights Act. The platform also calls for the abolition of the Electoral College, opting instead for the president to be chosen by a nationwide popular vote. Closely akin to voting rights is redistricting. The Texas Legislature has long been accused of gerrymandering through redistricting ploys to keep the dominate party whether it be Republicans or Democrats, in office for as long as possible. The Texas Democratic platform calls the creation of a nonpartisan redistricting commission. Campaign finance reform is a key issue for both parties. In the case of the Democrats, they want to overturn the United States Supreme Court ruling in Citizens United as well as introduce legislation requiring full disclosure of funding sources for any political activity from television ads to online campaign spots. They also want to see federal legislation reinstating the equal time rule that allows candidates to respond to statements made by their opponents.

While Texas Republicans uphold legislation favoring business development, Texas Democrats have always been on the opposite end due to their promotion of worker-friendly legislation. The 2018 platform emphasizes their efforts to pass legislation outlawing human trafficking, instituting a living wage, and if that fails, setting the minimum wage at $15 per hour and indexing it to inflation. In addition, they support organized labor unions, collective bargaining, the concept of equal pay for equal work, paid sick leave for all Texas workers, flextime, compensatory time, and paid family leave as well as workplace time for child nursing.

Both political parties want to tackle reforming the state's methods of funding public school systems and higher education institutions. Stressing the importance of a world class education, the Texas Democratic Party's platform calls for reducing the state's reliance on the "Robin Hood" plan and replacing it with a "100% equitable school finance system with sufficient state revenue to provide every child the opportunity to learn in an exemplary program."[63] An advocate of public education, Texas Democrats want mandatory full-day Pre-K for all children and additional state funds to support adult literacy programs. No fan of charter schools, Texas Democrats want a "moratorium on new charter schools and on the expansion of existing charter school networks and a thorough study of charter school impact on students and taxpayers" as well as "strengthen state oversight and academic and financial standard for charter schools."[64] Recognizing the high-turnover rate for teachers, the Texas Democratic Party platform calls for an increase in teacher pay as well as an increase in the state's contribution towards educational employees' health insurance and retirement programs. To entice more qualified people into the education field, Texas Democrats call for guaranteeing a teaching job to "students in the top 20% of their class who commit to a teaching career upon graduation."[65] In addition, they call for a college loan forgiveness program based on the number of years a person teaches in public schools. The Texas Democrat platform calls for abolishing high-stakes tests in the public schools, lowering class-size limits for all grades, and promoting dual credit and early college programs. The Texas Democratic Party platform also emphasizes measures to promote school safety and curtail bullying. They call for legislation promoting school-wide programs that promote positive behavior interventions while at the same time, prevent school violence, disruption of classes, bullying and harassment. They also stress that all public schools and institutions of higher learning must be drug- and weapon free.

Currently funding for the state's higher education institutions is based on enrollment. The Texas Democratic platform calls for the current formula to be adjusted to account for economic inflation, and of course, increased student enrollment. Their concerns about the rising cost of college tuition and the inability of students to repay their student loans is evident in their platform. Calling for increased funding of TEXAS grants, they also want to develop "alternative repayment plans for students struggling under monthly payments and/or refinancing existing loans to a lower rate tied to the current prime rate."[66] The governing bodies of the state's colleges and universities rarely have student representation on their boards of trustees. The Democratic platform calls for a voting student regent to serve on those governing bodies. Acknowledging the vital role community colleges play in the education of Texas residents, the Democratic platform calls for a tuition-free program for all high school graduates enrolling in a community college. It also calls for more state funding for new campuses and new or expanding programs. In particular, the Democrats place a strong emphasis on adult base programs such as ESOL (English as a Second Language) and GED (General Education Degree). The platform also calls for the Texas Legislature to enact the appropriate rules to "ensure full transferability of community college credit hours to four-year institutions."[67]

Both Texas Republicans and Democrats take strong positions on gun ownership, 2nd Amendment rights, and gun violence prevention. The Texas Democratic Party strongly believes that the answers to preventing gun violence rest with the imposition of strong legislation mandating background checks prior to the purchase of any firearm whether it be purchased at a gun shop, a gun show, or through a private party. They also want passage of laws requiring law enforcement to confiscate any firearms and ammunition in the household of any person arrested for any incidence of family violence, human trafficking, sexual assault, or stalking. Furthermore, any individual granted bail must surrender any weapons as a condition of being released until trial. Democrats call for laws forbidding the sale and distribution of extended ammunition magazines and all military-style assault weapons to civilians. In addition, they want legislation allowing "families to anonymously request pre-emptive judicial action restricting the possession or purchase of firearms for loved ones in crisis threatening harm to themselves or others."[68] Additionally, Texas Democrats advocate repealing the state's campus carry law currently enforced upon state-support colleges and universities.

Unfortunately, domestic violence and sexual assault continues to be a nationwide problem. As stated in their platform, "Texas Democrats believe violence and abuse affects Texans of all demographics and effective programs must be established at the individual, family, and community levels to combat this scourge on our society."[69] To accomplish this, the Democratic Party platform places an emphasis on strong enforcement of all Texas laws holding those accused of these criminal actions accountable, the creation of early prevention programs at all levels of government, and mandating school districts to promote "social emotional learning, safe and healthy relationships, and age appropriate sex education as part of their curriculum."[70] They also call for additional state funding for family violence shelters and the implementation of battering and prevention programs in all 254 counties. Democrats also want the Texas Legislature to sufficiently fund the state's Child Protective Services (CPS) in hopes of reducing the case load assigned to its social workers and end any efforts to privatize the agency.

Recognizing the need to support higher paying jobs, the Texas Democratic Party platform calls for raising the state's minimum wage to $15 an hour. Striking out against corporate giants, the state's Democratic Party leadership stresses that "no longer should corporate profits be subsidized by letting corporations pay poverty-level wages that leave the taxpayer footing the bill for public benefits" such as welfare and food stamps.[71] Democrats also decried the passage of the Trans-Pacific Trade Agreement negotiated by President Obama and all other free-trade agreements that Democrats feel hurt American workers, consumers, the environment, and so on. They emphasize that any international trade agreement must end child labor abuses and sweat-shops or if not, the United States should not be trading with these nations. At home, the Texas Democrat platform continues the party's historical track record of advocating for the 'appropriate' regulation of utilities companies, financial institutions and insurance companies.

Currently, Texas has the highest number of uninsured children in the nation. This is a reoccurring trend that Democrats believe must be corrected. They advocate the passage of the Healthy Texas Act of 2019 which provides a wide-range of universal health care coverage for medical, dental, hearing, and vision care, prescription drugs, surgical care, emergency room services, outpatient services, mental health and substance abuse counseling as well as home health and long-term care. This plan would allow patients to choose their own doctors. Basically, this proposed legislation would expand the advantages Democrats see in Obama's Affordable Care Act (ACA). Obviously, Texas Democrats oppose any actions to cut, cap or block existing Medicaid, Medicare, and CHIP services.

This platform reaffirms the same pro-choice position taken in every Texas Democratic platform since the 1960s.

Specially, this platform states that Democrats "trust Texans to make personal and responsible decisions about whether and when to bear children, in consultation with their families and physicians."[72] Additional platform positions stress the need to continue to reduce teen pregnancies, uphold the right to acquire all forms of contraception, and support for both family planning and affordable prenatal childcare programs.

Texas Democrats have always taken strong positions on the protection of the state's environment. This platform is no exception. It calls for the United States to rejoin the Paris Climate Accord and promotes programs for alternative energy sources to include solar, wind and geothermal, as well as efforts to encourage energy efficiency. It also mandates a moratorium on fracking to include shutting down existing wells and prohibiting the drilling of new ones. The problems caused by droughts and water shortages are also key issues for the state's Democrats. They advocate for a well-funded state water education campaign focusing on conservation. They also want the state to finally develop an effective state-wide drought relief program. In addition, they want more comprehensive state oversight to protect Texas bays, estuaries and wetlands. To address climate change, the Texas Democratic platform targets the coal mining industry. Democrats call for "retiring the oldest, heavy-polluting, coal burning Texas power plants that are so outdated that pollution controls are not an economically viable option" as well as outlawing strip mining.[73] Furthermore, they call upon the Texas Railroad Commission to "use their regulatory power as means of protecting the health, welfare, and property of Texans, rather than using it is a political tool."[74]

Texas Democrats take a strong position on immigration. Basically, they oppose President Trump's policies to include the administration's zero-tolerance policy, actions to separate children from their parents, and of course, a border wall. While they support the need for protecting and securing the border, they want all asylum seekers to be treated humanely. The platform calls for the closure of all family detention centers, the establishment of federally-backed faith-based refugee programs, support for the Deferred Action for Childhood Arrivals (DACA), the Deferred Action for Parents of Americans (DAPA), the Dream ACT, and upholding the 14th Amendment to the United States Constitution making all persons born in this country citizens. They also condemn any "xenophobic, racist, vigilante, and bigoted efforts which scapegoat immigrants."[75]

The Texas Democratic Party platform reemphasizes the party's support of women's rights as well as the protection of the rights of the LBGTQ community. They advocate for the inclusion of gender conformation surgery and inclusive transgender health care coverage in both Medicaid and Medicare and all employer-based insurance programs. They want a ban on "reparative" therapy. Texas Democrats also want legislation that promotes and guarantees additional measures to uphold the rights, privileges and necessary accommodations for the disabled community.

Third Party Movements in Texas

Periodically, Texas politics has been caught up in a national third party movement that usually runs an unsuccessful candidate for the presidency. By definition, a **third party** is "a temporary political party that often arises during a presidential election year to affect the fortunes of the two major parties."[76] Although it is extremely difficult for third party candidates running in state and local elections to even secure a place on the ballot, the political ideology of a third party or movement can have an impact on the overall issue positions taken by both the Democratic and Republican Parties. Usually third parties are formed around a specific individual who simply cannot secure a nomination to elective office from one or both of the major parties. For example, Theodore Roosevelt sought a second nomination for the presidency from his Republican Party. Failing to do so, Roosevelt's support base opted to run Roosevelt under a third party banner—the Bull Moose Party. Although he did not win the presidency, Roosevelt's strength in the ballot box split the Republican base in half, allowing Woodrow Wilson, the Democratic candidate to win the White House. In several recent presidential election cycles, both Ralph Nader and Ross Perot have run unsuccessful presidential bids as third party candidates. Occasionally, third parties such as the Tea Party or the Dixiecrats emerge as an organized protest effort against government policies or social issues such as in the case of the Dixiecrats, civil rights. They too are short-lived efforts since usually their political issues or concerns are eventually incorporated into the party platform of either the Democratic or Republican Parties. On the Texas scene, a few third party movements have placed candidates on a ballot with little or no success. But several third party movements have played a key role in redirecting the political agenda of the major political parties and resulted in the passage of meaningful legislation.

The two active third party movements in Texas are the Libertarians and the Green Party. The **Libertarian Party** was founded in 1971 by David F. Nolan of Colorado,

over concerns about the course of the Vietnam War, conscription or the draft, and the end of the gold standard for American currency. Promoting civil liberties, free market trade practices, and laissez-faire capitalism, the leadership of the party places their ideological positions as "more socially liberal than the Democrats but more fiscally conservative than the Republicans."[77] Although no Libertarian Party candidate has ever won an election in Texas, the Party faithful do hold periodic conventions and write a platform detailing their issue positions. In their 2014 platform, the preamble states that Libertarians:

> Seek a world of liberty; a world in which all individuals are sovereign over their lives and no individuals are forced to sacrifice their values for the benefit of others. We believe that respect for individual rights is the essential precondition for a free and prosperous world that force and fraud must be eliminated from human relations, and that only through freedom can peace and prosperity be realized. Consequently, we defend each person's right to engage in any activity that is peaceful and honest. . . . Our goal is a world set free in our lifetime, and it is to this end that we take these stands.[78]

As detailed in the Statement of Principles, Libertarians hold to their beliefs that:

- The Party exists to challenge the cult of the omnipotent state and to defend the rights of the individual.
- All individuals have the right to exercise sole dominion over their own lives, and have the right to live in whatever manner they choose, so long as they do not forcibly interfere with the equal right of others to live in whatever manner they choose.
- Government must not violate the rights of any individual: Namely (1) the right of life – accordingly we support the prohibition of the initiation of physical force against others;
(2) the right to liberty of speech and action – accordingly we oppose all attempts by government to abridge the freedom of speech and press, as well as government censorship in any form; and
(3) the right to property – accordingly we oppose all government interference with private property, such as confiscation, nationalization and eminent domain, and support the prohibition of robbery, trespass, fraud and misrepresentation.
- We oppose all interference by government in the areas of voluntary and contractual relations among

individuals. People should not be forced to sacrifice their lives and property for the benefit of others.

• "Libertarians reject the notion that groups have inherent rights. We support the rights of the smallest minority, the individual."[79]

Specifically, Libertarians support:

• Policies upholding the 4th Amendment to the United States Constitution, in particular protection against unreasonable search and seizure.
• Pro-choice positions because "government should be kept out of the matter, leaving the question to each person for their conscientious consideration."[80]
• Parental rights as long as the actions of the parents are free from abuse and neglect.
• Abolishment of all state and federal laws criminalizing gambling as well as any laws prohibiting the use of drugs for medicinal or recreational purposes.
• Abolishment of the death penalty.
• Policies promoting the free market system.
• Abolishment of any law restricting the use of private property.
• Policies holding government accountable for environmental damage.
• A federal balance budget amendment.
• The decriminalization of prostitution.
• Abolishing school boards and state/federal education agencies and "restoring authority to parents to determine the education of their children, without interference from government."[81]
• A free market health care system.
• A foreign policy freeing the United States from foreign entanglements.

The Libertarian Party ran a full slate of candidates for the 2018 Texas election cycle. Mark Tippets and Kerry McKennon were the Party's choices for governor and lieutenant governor. No statewide, congressional or state legislative Libertarian candidate won their election bids.

Founded in 1999, the Green Party of Texas has had a rough time making a lasting presence on the state's political scene. In 2000, the Secretary of State granted the party ballot access to run candidates for state and local elections. In the 2002 election cycle, Greens ran twenty-eight candidates for office. However, the election tallies resulted in the Greens receiving less than the mandated 5 percent mark to retain its ballot access. In Texas, political parties receiving less than 5 percent of the total votes cast in the governor's race must gather petition signatures from at least 1 percent of the vote cast in the governor's race from the last election. These signatures must be from potential voters who have not already declared their party affiliations nor have voted in a primary election of another party. The Texas Green Party simply could not produce the required number of petition signatures for the 2004, 2006 and 2008 elections. However, they did acquire the required number of signatures for the 2010 ballot. In the 2012, election the Texas Green Party regained ballot status and ran on the Texas ballot their national presidential candidate Jill Stein, David Collins for the Texas United States Senate seat as well as candidates for the Texas Supreme Court, Railroad Commission, congressional and state legislative seats, and local city and county races. Only two of their candidates won their races – Debbie Russell for a school board position in Austin, and LaShadion Shemwell for a city council seat in McKinney. In 2014, the Party ran a slate of fifty candidates for various offices. However, once again, the Party came up against the petition signature requirement. For each of the subsequent elections (2016 and 2018), the Texas Green Party failed to gain ballot access and did not run a slate of candidates. The Texas Green Party, however, does have a platform addressing approximately twenty-six main issues ranging from political reform to housing, gun safety, education, and, of course, environmental concerns focusing on water, transportation, sustainable agriculture, biotechnology, energy, waste management, land use, and so on.

The Know-Nothing Party

The formative years of the Know-Nothing Party began nationally in the late 1840s with the development of The Supreme Order of Star Spangled Banner, formed by secret far-right patriotic societies. The Order's political agenda focused on strong legislative efforts to restrict immigration, raising the residency requirement for citizenship to twenty-one years of age, and prohibiting both Catholics and the foreign-born from holding any elective office. Since it was a secret society, members were bound to reply "I know nothing" when asked about the organization's activities. In the early 1850s the party changed its name to the American Party and actually won some state elections in New England. In Texas, the Know-Nothing Party gained support particularly among those who disliked the increasing influence of both the Mexican and German communities in Texas politics. In 1855, the party nominated David C. Dickson to run as the lieutenant governor. While the party faithful lost that race, the Know-Nothings were capable of sending twenty of their members to the Texas House and an additional five to the state Senate.[82] The presidential election of

1856 was the demise of the Know-Nothing or American Party. The Republicans ran John C. Fremont, the Know-Nothing ran Millard Fillmore, and the Democrats ran James Buchanan. The Democrats soundly defeated both but dealt a fatal blow to Fillmore, basically ending the Know-Nothing movement. The anti-Catholic and anti-immigrant positions of the party were incorporated into the Republican Party platform.

The Grange or the Farmers Alliance

The initial group supporting agricultural interests of the small farmer and rancher was the **Grange**, founded in 1867 by Oliver H. Kelley. While they did not run candidates for public office, the movement did have a tremendous impact at the 1875 state constitutional convention, sending approximately forty delegates to hammer out the provisions of the state's current document that was ratified in 1876. In was the Grange that successfully pushed for strong regulatory measures against the railroads, banks, and insurance companies. The golden days of the Grange organizations across the country were the 1880s with the establishment of cooperative organizations including all-purpose retail shops commonly called Grange stores. The Grange movement declined in the 1890s as the newly formed **Farmers Alliance** incorporated the Grange agenda into their own organization. The Alliance promoted programs for the poor including increased efforts to regulate the railroads, improvements in public education, reforms in land-sale policies to favor the "little man" and prohibition of alcoholic beverages. The organization's party platform drafted in Cleburne in 1890 was eventually incorporated into the platform of the Democratic Party.

The Populist Movement and the Progressive Parties

A national movement, the Progressive Era brought third party politics to Texas. The political agenda of the **Greenbacks** focused on making more money or capital available for the growing middle class as well as the poor. They demanded that "the federal government issue more paper money, or greenbacks, on the theory that if more money were in circulation, more would naturally filter down to the farmers, who were hurting."[83] Their agenda included more funding for public education, a nationwide income tax, more state regulation of railroads, and less federal regulation. The Texas Greenback Party successfully elected George Washington Jones to the United States Congress from 1879 to 1887. They also made an unsuccessful attempt at the governor's office in 1882. Like most third party movements, the Greenbacks' longevity was short as their major agenda items were gradually incorporated into the Democratic Party.

Perhaps the most viable third-party movement in the United States, the **Populist Party** carried many of the same agenda items as the Farmers Alliance and the Greenbacks. The national organization of the Populist or the People's Party held its first convention in Cincinnati, Ohio, in May 1891. Their platform issues included using silver rather than paper money as the nation's currency, passing laws denying property ownership to aliens, confiscating excess state lands given to the railroads and other corporations, requiring both state and national governments to balance their budgets, creating free public education systems, reforming the prison system, passing legislation protecting workers, establishing an eight-hour work day, and abolishing the national Electoral College by mandating that the president and vice president of the United States be chosen by a direct vote of the people. The Populist Party was able to win both state and national offices, only to see their platform issues incorporated into the Democratic Party. In Texas, the leader of both the Progressive and Populist's movements was James S. Hogg. Elected as the state's attorney general in 1886, Hogg openly attacked the practices of the railroads and denounced discriminatory practices against farmers. He aggressively opposed the discriminatory business practices of insurance companies particularly leveled against rural communities and became the state's poster child for trust-busting. As governor of Texas, Hogg created the Texas Railroad Commission, a regulatory agency designed to halt the price fixing practices of the railroads as well as laws promoting prison reform, and revamping the state's education system. In the 1894 state elections, the Populists held 22 of 128 seats in the lower house of the state legislature and elected two state senators as well as a small host of county and precinct officers. The party's strength waned as the Democratic Party successfully incorporated key progressive and populist agenda positions into the Democratic Party platform.

La Raza Unida

The South Texas region commonly known as **the Valley**, is comprised of twenty-seven counties that directly share the international boundary with Mexico or are abutting border counties. All of these counties have been mired in poverty for decades with Starr County having the dubious distinction of being frequently one of the nation's poorest counties. The residents of the state's agricultural "Magic Valley" are predominately lower-income, undereducated Hispanics whose primary source of employment is either field work or service-sector low paying tourist-related jobs. While the American Civil Rights Movement focused primarily on the denial of equality to the nation's African Americans, the same discriminatory practices were used against the Hispanic community in Texas, especially in these twenty-seven counties. However, for a brief period the South Texas Hispanic community launched its own political party—**La Raza Unida**. The founding fathers of the party were Mario Compean and Jose Angel Gutierrez, who as college students in the 1960s realized that the potential electoral power of the Hispanic community lay dormant due to the lack of leadership. The African-American community had Dr. Martin Luther King, Jr., but the Hispanic community had no one of that stature to lead them. The 1970s was the hay-day for the La Raza movement. A grassroots movement, it began in 1969 in Crystal City, a predominately small Hispanic community in Zavala County. The desire to form a third party was in part due to the belief that the Democratic Party had abandoned the bottom-line issues of the Hispanic community. Gutierrez underscored the primary reason for La Raza:

> But, you see there is another, more important, reason, and that is that Mexicanos need to be in control of their destiny. We need to make the decisions that are going to affect our brothers and maybe our children. We have been complacent for too long. . . . This third party is a very viable kind of alternative. It's a solution. For once you can sit in your own courthouse and you don't have to talk about community control because you are the community.[84]

Several La Raza candidates were elected to the local school board as well as to city and county positions. Gutierrez and Compean promoted the development of La Raza organizations in Dimmit, LaSalle and Hidalgo counties. The party held its convention in 1972 and adopted a platform embracing the following positions:

- on labor: the right to strike for farmworkers' unions, parity in employment opportunities, end to exploitation of illegal aliens, guarantee of minimum annual income and benefits, and repeal all "right to work" laws.
- On education: bilingual, bicultural education throughout the education system, and increased opportunities for Chicanos in higher education.
- On justice: ability to run for judgeships and serve on juries and free legal aid to Chicanos.

The platform also underscored the needed for "Chicano self-determination" to exert themselves into the policy making roles in their communities to address economic, social, political and education concerns.[85]

In 1972, La Raza backed candidate Ramsey Muñiz ran for governor. The fear among conservative Democrats was that Muñiz would capture the majority of the Hispanic Valley vote for himself, thus depriving Democratic candidate Dolph Briscoe from beating the Republican gubernatorial candidate Henry Grover. Although Muñiz garnered a considerable number of votes, Briscoe still won the race. By 1978, La Raza's influence had diminished for several reasons including dissention within the party's leadership core, and legal and criminal issues faced by Muñiz, as well as seeing the bulk of the party's agenda incorporated into the Democratic Party.

The Fate of Political Parties in Texas

Although many question the long-term viability of both the Democratic and Republican Parties at both the national and state levels, political parties play a historically vital part in both the American political and electoral processes. The focus in American electoral politics has never been directed solely on party ideology. Few Americans who call themselves Republicans or Democrats attend their party caucuses, serve as delegates to party state and national conventions, volunteer to be precinct chairpersons, or have even read their respective party platforms. The small inner circle of hard-core party loyalists in both parties are the ones that draft the platform, set the credentialing rules, and plan the conventions. The important roles political parties play have been overshadowed by their nominees. The focus now is less on the internal operations of the party and more on the individual candidates. In other words, the emphasis has shifted from party-centered to candidate-centered elections. The American electorate listens and pays more attention to the candidates than they do to their respective party leadership. "Politics most of the time has been no center of ideological conflict but has been a center for office and perquisites in which segments of the public would join from time to time as they became involved. Aside from the materialistic objectives, most people could adopt an attitude of indulgent benevolence or of disinterest or of disdain toward the party battle and let the politicians fight out their troubles among themselves."[86]

Obviously, advances in communication have gradually rendered political parties almost invisible to the American electorate. National networks only cover a few hours each evening of the national conventions. Local news affiliates barely give five minutes of their broadcast time to state political conventions. However, it is the candidates themselves that garner the air time. Now candidates have their own websites that draw more "hits" than the official party websites. But one cannot blame the media alone for the almost non-existent presence of political parties. The decentralized organizational structure of the political party significantly detaches the national party leadership from state and, in particular, local organizations. With its narrow focus on presidential and, to a limited extent, congressional elections, the national leadership rarely puts a full campaign support effort into gubernatorial or even state legislative races. And, state organizations rarely get involved in county or precinct affairs unless they are called upon by county party officials. Political candidates need their respective parties to officially nominate them. Once the confetti has fallen on the convention floor, the candidate is basically on his/her own. They are the ones who have to run their own campaigns, and raise their own money. Decentralization has opened the door for interest groups to assume more of the roles traditionally assigned to political parties.

Regardless of their weakened status, political parties continue to play an extremely important role in maintaining the nation's two-party system. For example, the 2016 presidential election season began with eight to ten officially announced candidates running for the Republican nomination. Through a series of tough candidate forums and Republican primary elections, the field was narrowed to just one candidate. Imagine that without both the Republican and Democratic Parties conducting inner-party primary elections, the American voter would have ten or more choices for one office on a general election ballot. Since no candidate would receive a majority vote (50 percent plus one), the nation would be thrown into a series of runoff elections that would make the campaign season even longer than what it is now. These two political parties also provide a loud sounding board for various small splinter or interest groups that have valid issue positions but lack the tools to effectively impact the public policy process.

The Framers envisioned the system of checks and balances to keep the legislative and the executive branches of the government from overstepping their authority. However, the system of checks and balances is also applicable to the two-party system. Whether it be the United States Congress or the Texas Legislature, the Democrats are always keeping a watchful eye over the Republicans and vice versa. When one party oversteps its authority, the other is quick to respond, oftentimes

through the media. Politics without a party structure would be extremely difficult.

To say that the people can cast aside the domination of the national party regime is, however, to disregard the control of a powerful organization, a part of whose strength comes from the very multiplicity of local interests; to disregard the influence of prejudice and pride and party allegiance; to fail to reckon with the imagination to which national party leaders and party contests strongly appeal; and, above all, not to estimate correctly the force of inertia and the sheer difficulty of maintaining state or local organizations distinct from the national party system.[87]

A plausible solution to reversing the invisibility of the nation's two political parties is to move from a decentralized structure to a centralized one. A less detached presence of the national organization at the state and local level would reemphasize the value of one affiliating more with their party than their party's chosen candidates. In 1912, Republican Senator Robert LaFollette, Sr., pledged to his party that he would "do all in my power to restore it to the high place in the service and confidence and affection of the American people, which it held when it was the party of Abraham Lincoln."[88] Former Democratic national chairperson James Farley echoed similar sentiments: "As your national chairman, I have announced with all sincerity and without reservations that the national committee is behind every Democrat nominee. That has to be the guiding tenet of every honest Democrat if we are to continue in power in state and nation."[89] If the two-party system is to continue to be a force in national politics, it must reinvent itself into a body that can successfully recruit candidates, provide more than adequate campaign support including money, and work from top to bottom to bring strong committed leadership to every level of the party from the national committee to the precinct chairperson. Particularly in Texas, both the Democratic and Republican Party leadership simply cannot continue to relinquish their responsibilities to both the electorate and their candidates to politically-oriented interest groups.

Chapter Notes

[1]George Sabine, *A History of Political Theory*, 3rd ed., (New York, New York: Holt, Rinehart, Winston, Inc., 1961), 611.

[2]*A Treasury of Presidential Quotations*, Caroline Thomas Harnsberger, ed., (Chicago, Illinois: Follett Publishing Company, 1964), 238.

[3]William Goodman, *The Two-Party System in the United States*, 3rd ed., (Princeton, New Jersey: D. Van Nostrand Company, Inc., 1964), 6.

[4]Frank J. Sorauf, *Party Politics in America*, (Boston, Massachusetts: Little Brown and Company, 1968), 55.

[5]Susan Welch, John Gruhl, Michael Steinman, John Comer and Susan M. Rigdon, *American Government*, 5th ed., (Minneapolis/St. Paul, Wisconsin: West Publishing Company, 1994), 146.

[6]Thomas W. Madron and Carl P. Chelf, *Political Parties in the United States*, (Boston, Massachusetts: Holbrook Press, 1974), 302-303.

[7]V. O. Key, Jr., *Politics, Parties, and Pressure Groups*, 4th ed., (New York, New York: Thomas Y., Crowell Company, 1958), 232.

[8]Ibid., 220.

[9]James MacGregor Burns, *The Deadlock of Democracy: Four Party Politics in America*, 2nd ed., (Englewood Cloffs, New Jersey: Prentice-Hall, Inc., 1967), 32-33.

[10]Key, Jr., 222.

[11]Jack C. Plano and Milton Greenberg, *The American Political Dictionary*, 10th ed., (Orlando, Florida: Harcourt Brace and Company, 1997), 88.

[12]Gabriel A. Almond, G. Bingham Powell, Jr., Kaare Strom and Russell Dalton, *Comparative Politics Today: A World View*, 8th ed., (New York, New York: Pearson Longman, 2004), 90.

[13]Ibid.

[14]Plano and Greenberg, 77.

[15]Sorauf, 18-19.

[16]Ibid., 108.

[17]L. Sandy Maisel, *Parties and Elections in America: The Electoral Process*, 2nd ed., (New York, New York: McGraw-Hills, Inc., 1993), 54.

[18]William J. Keefe and Marc J. Hetherington, *Parties, Politics and Public Policy in America*, 9th ed., (Washington, D.C.: CQ Press, 2003), 16.

[19]*The HarperCollins Dictionary of American Government and Politics*, Jay M. Shafritz, ed., (New York, New York: HarperCollins Publishers, 1992), 305.

[20]Plano and Greenberg, 95.

[21]*Treasury of Presidential Quotations*, 244.

[22]*The HarperCollins Dictionary of American Government and Politics*, 286.

[23]Roger Scruton, *A Dictionary of Political Thought*, (New York, New York: Harper & Row Publishers, 1982), 90.

[24]Plano and Greenburg, 13.

[25]George Klosko, History of Political Theory: An Introduction, Vol. 2, Modern Political Theory, (Belmont, California: Wadsworth Group/Thompson Learning, Inc. 1995), 266-267.

[26]Ian Adams and R. W. Dyson, *Fifty Major Political Thinkers*, (New York, New York: Routledge, 2003), 90-91.

[27]*HarperCollins Dictionary of American Government and Politics*, 139.

[28]Scruton, 109.

[29]Plano and Greenberg, 5.

[30]Scruton, 302.

[31]*HarperCollins Dictionary of American Government and Politics*, 285.

[32]Ibid., 65.

[33]Ibid., 335.

[34]Klosko, 200.

[35]Ibid.

[36]Plano and Greenberg, 14.

[37]Adams and Dyson, 63.

[38]Klosko, 111.

[39]Scruton, 302.

[40]*The HarperCollins Dictionary of American Government and Politics*, 202.

[41]Randolph B. Campbell, *Gone to Texas: A History of the Lone Star State*, (New York, New York: Oxford University Press, 2003), 414.

[42]"A Republican and A Woman Inaugurated as Governors of Texas-January 19, 1979, and January 5, 1991," *Documents of Texas History*, Ernest Wallace, David Vigness and George B. Ward, eds., 2nd ed., (Austin, Texas: State House Press, 1993), 310-313.

[43]https://www.texasgop.org/platform

[44]Ibid.

[45]Ibid.

[46]Ibid.

[47]Ibid.

[48]Ibid.

[49]Ibid.

[50]Ibid.

[51]Ibid.

[52]Ibid.

[53]Ibid.

[54]HarperCollins Dictionary of American Government and Politics,

[55]"A Republican and A Woman Inaugurated as Governors of Texas-January 19, 1979, and January 5, 1991," *Documents of Texas History*, 313.

[56]*http://www.tx.democrats.org*

[57]Ibid.

[58]Ibid.

[59]Ibid.

[60]Ibid.

[61]Ibid.

[62]Ibid.

[63]Ibid.

[64]Ibid.

[65]Ibid.

[66]Ibid.

[67]Ibid.

[68]Ibid.

[69]Ibid.

[70]Ibid.

[71]Ibid.

[72]Ibid.

[73]Ibid.

[74]Ibid.

[75]Ibid.

[76]*The HarperCollins Dictionary of American Government and Politics*, 417.

[77]https://www.LibertarianParty.org

[78]https://www.lp.org/platform

[79]Ibid.

[80]Ibid.

[81]Ibid.

[82]Joe B. Frantz, *Texas: A History*, 2nd ed., (New York, New York: Norton, 1984), 136.

[83]"La Raza Unida Party: 1970," *Documents of Texas History*, Ernest Wallace, David M. Vigness and George B. Ward, eds., 2nd ed., (Austin, Texas: State House Press, 1994), 302-303.

[84]"La Raza Unida Convention Announces Its Priorities, 1972," *Major Problems in Mexican American History*, Zaragosa Vargas, ed., (Boston, Massachusetts: Houghton Mifflin Company, 1999), 417.

[85]Goodman, 636.

[86]Ibid., 650.

[87]Ibid., 638.

[88]Ibid., 639

[89]Ibid.

Chapter 4

Elections and Political Participation

It is essential to such a government that it be derived from the great body of the society, not from an inconsiderable proportion, or a favored class of it; otherwise a handful of tyrannical nobles, exercising their oppressions by a delegation of their powers, might aspire to the rank of republicans, and claim for their government the honorable title of republic. It is sufficient for such a government that the persons administering it be appointed, either directly or indirectly, by the people; and that they hold their appointments by either of the tenures just specified; otherwise every government in the United States, as well as every other popular government that has been or can be well organized or well executed, would be degraded from the republican character.[1]

James Madison, *Federalist #39*

Texas has had its share of "interesting" people and intriguing elections. Perhaps the most colorful to date has been W. Lee O'Daniel, who won as his first elective office the governorship in 1938. O'Daniel owned and operated Hillbilly Flour during the day and hosted a hillbilly radio show at night. While broadcasting his program one evening, he asked his listeners to send to him a one-penny post card if they believed that he should run for governor. His decision was sealed when he received nearly 50,000 post cards![2] With the campaign slogan of "Pass the Biscuits Pappy," O'Daniel toured Texas in a bus accompanied by his band the "Hillbilly Boys," formally known as "The Light Crust Doughboys." O'Daniel's election defies logic. Here was an individual who had no previous political experience, never voted, ran his campaign without a manager or any headquarters, and won the election. He could not even cast a vote for himself because he failed to pay his poll taxes. However once in office, his track record as governor was basically non-productive. After defeating Ma Ferguson for a second term, O'Daniel resigned from the governorship to run a successful campaign for the United States Senate.

Inadvertently, O'Daniel's retirement from the Senate in 1948 resulted in one of the closest and most controversial electoral contests Texans have ever witnessed. The Republicans did not run a candidate. Consequently, the winner of the Democratic primary election was a sure bet to win the general election. Both former governor Coke Stevenson and rising political star former United States Congressman Lyndon B. Johnson vied for the seat. Since voting machines were nonexistent, voters placed paper ballots into election boxes. The initial primary vote count gave the very tight race to Stevenson. A requested recount gave the edge to Johnson. Stevenson demanded a recount. The third recount did not happen because the ballot box in question, Box 13, disappeared or according to the more unbelievable tale, the box was destroyed by internal combustion. The box came from Jim Wells County, which was under the control of George Parr, an ardent supporter of Johnson. The difference in the victory

in the second recount was eighty-seven votes for Johnson. "Actually the figure was closer to 150, but the '87 vote landslide' became an identifying catchword whenever Senator Johnson was later introduced."[3] The election antics of Box 13 were typical of South Texas politics. It was a well established practice for politicians from both political parties to hire "political workers known as politiqueras to round up the votes, and complaints about hanky-panky with mail-in ballots surfaced with almost every election. . . . The politiqueras are very manipulative. Whatever it takes, they'll do it. And people are very easily intimidated, especially if they are old or handicapped."[4] Of course, no one was better at delivering the vote than George Parr, the Duke of Duval County. Until his suicide in 1975, Parr "operated it [Duval County] like a fiefdom and his followers believed and trusted him. . . George was a very able politician, but he was utterly ruthless and absolutely without principles."[5] In case of Box 13, it appeared that the opposition had enough evidence to overturn the Johnson victory at both the state and federal level. However, Supreme Court Justice Hugo Black finally declared the election for Johnson.

The antics of Pappy O'Daniel, the Duke of Duval, and perhaps Lyndon Johnson are legendary in Texas politics. Today's elections are rather lack luster. In the three gubernatorial general elections, Governor Rick Perry won impressive elections over his opponents. However, the Democratic Party's field facing Perry had been relatively weak candidates lacking statewide appeal. In 2002, the Democrats ran self-made millionaire Tony Sanchez, in 2006 it was Chris Bell, and in the 2010, it was Bill White, former mayor of Houston.

With Perry opting out of seeking a fourth term, the Democrats were hopeful that their candidate for the governorship would have a viable shot. For the Republicans, the likely candidates were State Attorney General Greg Abbott or perhaps David Dewhurst, Perry's long serving lieutenant governor. Boosted by her filibuster against the state's restrictive abortion bill, state Senator Wendy Davis survived the primary season and became the Democrats' general election candidate for governor. From the very beginning Davis had an uphill battle. She "started out nearly $21 million behind Abbott, never had his spending power despite raising tens of millions. She was hampered by an unpopular president, the Ebola crisis that drained attention from her race, identification with the abortion issue, a party infrastructure under construction and campaign misfires."[6] The hopes of the Democratic Party in Texas were dashed on Tuesday, November 4, 2014, as Abbott soundly beat Davis by a margin of 60 percent to 38 percent, and all of the state's top executive offices were carried by Republican candidates. In 2018, the Democrats ran for a statewide race a relatively unknown candidate Lupe Valdez against a well-known, well-financed, and seasoned politician incumbent Governor Greg d. It was not even a close race. For the Democrats, it was once again, back to the drawing board.

Particularly in the United States, running for public office has never been an easy process. During his first presidential bid, George Washington was even accused of trying to buy votes by offering individuals whiskey in return for their support. Today's elections are multi-million dollar media-driven campaigns that force candidates to become more focused on fund raising than on articulating their positions on the important issues. And yet despite all of the money raised, the constant barrage of television commercials, the endless candidate forums and campaign stops, the outcome of every election boils down to just one factor—voter turnout. If the voters who seemed to be enthusiastic about a candidate's message stay home on election day, the chances of scoring a political victory fade quickly. Unfortunately, many smart, articulate, and talented individuals who run for public office wind up on election night making concession speeches.

Voter apathy is a nationwide problem. A frustrated President Obama has even suggested that perhaps it is time to fine eligible voters for not voting as a means of improving voter participation. Already several European countries follow this practice with the end result of 90 percent or better voter participation. However, do individuals in these countries vote because they care about who runs their countries or do they vote just to avoid paying the fine? This chapter examines both the election process and the campaign strategy that might score an electoral victory.

Texas is not the only state confronted with voter apathy. When Barack Obama was running for his first term of office in the White House, his campaign staff launched voter registration drives on every major Texas college campus to turnout the vote. However in the 2008

John Locke, an English philosopher, greatly influenced the thinking of our Founders and provided the rationale for our break with England.

presidential election, only 46.5 percent of voting age Texans actually registered to vote, and only 59.5 percent of those individuals actually voted.[7] For the 2012 presidential election, "the total number of votes, 7,993,851, was 58.57 percent of the registered voters. The voting age population [in Texas] was estimated at 18,279,737."[8] Only 43.7 percent of the registered voting age population (VAP) voted in this race. The pattern held true in the 2016 race for the White House. The VAP for Texas in this race was 20,172,000. However, only 58.1 percent of these individuals registered to vote and only 47.7 percent of these individuals cast a ballot on election day.[9] In both elections, the majority of Texas voters continued the state's trend of voting for the Republican candidate. In 2012, 41.4 percent voted for Obama while 57.2 percent cast a ballot for Romney. In 2016, Clinton garnered 43.2 percent of the total vote while Trump carried the state's electoral votes with 52.2 percent of the total vote.[10] This was not an anomaly since for the past ten presidential elections less than 50 percent of the state's voting age population actually cast a ballot. Even fewer Texans vote in off-presidential election cycles when the state's entire slate of state executive officers is on the ballot. Despite the hoopla of the 2018 mid-term general election, Texas voter turnout statistics simply do not support the contention that Texas is turning from red to purple with an outpouring of newly registered and long-term registered but never-voted-before Texans marching to the polls. For this election, there were 19,900,980 voting age eligible Texans, but only 15,793,257 registered to vote. Of these individuals, only 8,371,655 representing 42.0 percent voted![11]

As evidenced in San Antonio's mayoral and city council elections, any voter turnout over 10 percent is hailed as a successful election effort. Every two years, the Texas Legislature puts forth before the state's electorate a list of constitutional amendments. Traditionally, voter turnout is at best, terrible. In November 2017, this trend held true as only 4.5 percent of the VAP voted in this election.[12] This chapter explores the political socialization process of Texans and examines the unfortunate trend towards voter apathy and low turnout at the polls.

The Mechanics of Elections

The Importance of Elections

The survival of a representative democracy rests on the premise that once elected, officials will be held accountable for their actions. In *The Social Contract*, John Locke places the credibility of government directly upon the citizens under that government. For Locke, the social contract is the people coming together to form a government that in turn will establish the appropriate rules while at the same time protect the citizens' rights to life, liberty, and property. If that government fails to govern effectively or does not protect the inalienable rights of its citizens, then those who created it can dissolve it and begin again. For Locke,

> the legislative has the ability to make laws, which makes it the supreme power *within* the political system, but the people retain an essential right to judge the legislative's performance. Thus the people are the supreme power, while the legislative is only appointed to perform certain tasks. If the people find that the legislative does not function properly, they can remove it, and place its power in other hands."[13]

The term **participatory democracy** is defined as the "maximum direct participation in political, economic, and social decision making by interested, active and knowledgeable local groups."[14] In other words, government and its governing officials are only accountable to the will of the people if the people hold them accountable. Popular periodic elections are the means people hold their governing authorities accountable. Therefore, an **election** is "a process of selecting one person or more for an office, public or private, from a wider field of candidates."[15]

Partisan versus Nonpartisan Elections

At both the national and state level, gaining an elective office is a two-step process. If a candidate is running in a **partisan election**, the individual must declare a party affiliation and gain an official nomination from the party's members. The first step in the process entails a **primary election** or an interparty election held to determine the party's representative for that elective office. The second step is the **general election** whereby voters regardless of party affiliation cast a vote to choose among the candidates nominated in the party's primary election to serve in an elective office. The president/vice presidential ticket, all members of the United States Congress, and in Texas, all members of the state legislative houses, executive officers (with the exception of the Secretary of State), county offices, and judges run in partisan elections. A **nonpartisan election** enables candidates to run without a party label. Usually, nonpartisan elections in Texas are conducted for municipal, or city, and school board elections. A nonpartisan election can be a two step process if the leading candidate does not win the election by a majority vote, that is, 50 percent plus one of the total votes in his/her favor. A runoff election will occur between the two top contenders for that particular office. The winner of the runoff is simply the one who has a **plurality** of the votes cast, that is, winning at least one more vote than their opponent received.

A strategy used quite often by both political parties is to discourage two candidates from seeking the same office, particularly for offices on the lower-end of the ballot. For example, there are seven district judge positions up for election. The respective party leadership would meet with the seven seeking to run for those benches. The goal is to have each one run for one bench, rather than having two run for the same bench. Running as an **uncontested candidate** without opposition on the primary ballot, enables the candidate to gain a position on the ballot with little or no effort. The candidate can save his/her campaign war chest for the general election where, in all likelihood, they will face an opponent.

Primary Elections

Although primary elections are technically interparty affairs, state legislative houses and to some extent the United States Supreme Court determine the format for the election process. In Texas, the process for conducting all elections is detailed in the **Texas Election Code**, a set of standards enacted by the Texas Legislature. The Code requires that all political parties whose candidate for governor in the last election received at least 20 percent of the total vote must hold a primary election. Third party candidates who received less than 20 percent in the last gubernatorial race or did not run any candidates for that position are required to use the convention system as well as file with the Texas Secretary of State a list of party members or supporters equal to one percent of the vote for the governor in the last election. Supporters must be registered voters who have not participated in the primary elections or conventions of either the Republican or Democratic Party. When Carole K. Strayhorn ran as an independent candidate in the 2006 general gubernatorial election, she had to gain a place on the ballot by collecting signatures on petitions. But the signees could not have voted in the primary elections held by the Democratic or the Republican Parties. Candidates from both parties accused her of diluting the vote for both parties by actively telling people that if they supported her, they could not vote in the primary elections. In order for a candidate from the Republican or Democratic Party to be listed on the primary ballot, the candidate must either pay a filing fee to offset the costs of the primary election or submit a petition of 5,000 registered voters for a statewide office. A petition listing totaling 2 percent of the total vote the party's gubernatorial candidate received in the last election for a maximum of 500 signatures for those running for district or lower offices is needed in lieu of a filing fee. For example, the filing fee for a United States senatorial candidate in Texas is $5,000. While the fee helps to cover the cost of the election, it also tests the seriousness of the candidate to run for that office since the fee is nonrefundable.

The major political parties in all fifty states periodically hold a **direct primary**, which is an "intraparty election in which the voters select the candidates who will run on a party's ticket in the subsequent general election."[16] The **Terrell Election Law** of 1905 mandates the use of the direct primary rather than the usual "behind the close door" selection of primary party candidates. The Republican Party held off enacting the direct primary until 1926. It was not until 1996 that all of the state's 254 counties used the direct primary format. The direct primary has proven to be a useful tool in "weeding out" or narrowing the field of prospective candidates. For example, seven individuals filed to run to be the Republican nominee for the governorship. Through the primary election and in the case of seven candidates, a runoff primary election, the party will have one candidate who will face the challenger from the other parties on the ballot. The United States Constitution does not specify how individual states and their respective political parties will select their candidates.

It is, therefore, up to the individual states and their political parties.

States usually adopt one of four primary formats. A few states use the **caucus** format whereby each political party holds public party membership meetings in cities and communities within their state with the candidates vying for elective offices. Each candidate is given the opportunity to articulate their issue positions. Once the candidates leave, the caucus membership votes as to which candidates they want to represent their party on the general election ballot. A **blanket primary** is "an open primary election that allows voters to participate in the nominations of candidates from multiple parties on the same day."[17] On primary election day, the voter would be given ballots from the Republican Party, the Democratic Party, and any other political party putting forth a slate of candidates in the primary election. An **open primary** is "a voting system also known as the **crossover primary** that permits voters to choose the party primary of their choice without disclosing party affiliation or allegiance, if any."[18] Consequently, a potential voter enters the polling place and is given a ballot for each political party participating in the primary election. The voter selects one ballot and discards the others. The voter presents his/her voter registration card. However, the card is not stamped to indicate a political party preference, enabling the voter to cast a vote in a runoff primary election for a candidate from a party different from the one they voted for in the primary election. The term **crossover** refers to the technique used by both major political parties to enhance the chances of a victory for their candidates. For example in the 2018 Texas governor's race, the Democratic Party leadership would look at the candidates on the Republican Party's ballot. Understanding that Greg Abbott is the strongest of the Republican gubernatorial candidates, they would want Democrats to crossover to the Republican side and vote for the weakest candidate on that ballot in hopes that the weakest candidate would win the Republican primary election. This situation would definitely help the Democratic candidate's chances to win the general election. The voter is not penalized for crossing over because in the open primary format, the voter can then cast a ballot in his/her original political party's runoff primary election.

However, Texas uses the **closed primary** whereby "the selection of a party's candidates in an election is limited to avowed party members."[19] In a Texas primary election, the voter goes specifically to a polling place of his/her political party or if the parties are sharing a polling place, to a specific table manned by election judges from their respective political parties. Prior to casting their vote, the voter must present a voter registration card, which is stamped to indicate the voter's political party membership. A registered Republican is now barred from voting in a Democratic Party primary runoff election. The crossover scenario can still occur but the Democrat who crosses over to the Republican Party's primary election will now have a voter registration card stamped indicating that the voter is now a member of the Republican Party! Under current law, the declaration of a party membership occurs on the day the voter casts a ballot for the primary election. Occasionally, Republican members of the Texas Legislature have introduced unsuccessful efforts to enact a **party purity law**, which would mandate that the voters declare their party affiliations three to six months prior to the primary election. With such a declaration, the ability for each party to participate in crossover tactics would be marginalized or possibly eliminated.

It is the responsibility of the county's executive committee to hold the primary election. However, the state does reimburse the county party organization for the cost of the election. It is up to the county party officials to determine whether to hold their own primaries, combine with the other parties in a joint primary, or pay the county to oversee the election. Regardless, it is each party's responsibility to have at least one election judge and alternate at each polling place. It is the responsibility of the election judge to open the polls during early and regular voting sites at 7:00 a.m., and on election night, close them when the last voter in line at 7:00 p.m., has cast his/her ballot. Once the polls have officially closed, it is the responsibility of the election judge at each precinct to bring the ballots or in the case of touch screen voting machines, the machines themselves to the designated counting center for validation.

As previously pointed out, the winner in the primary election must carry a **majority vote** margin of 50 percent plus one of the total votes. If not, then the two top contenders in the vote tally will face off in a runoff primary. The winner in runoff only needs to win more votes than his/her opponent. In the 2010 Republican primary election, Rick Perry avoided a runoff with U.S. Senator Kay Bailey Hutchison by carrying the election with 51 percent of the vote to her 30 percent.[20] In the 2014 Republican primary gubernatorial race, Greg Abbott won with 91.5 percent of the total vote over his opponents Lisa Fritsch, Mariam Martinez, and Larry Kilgore and on the Democratic side of the ballot, Wendy Davis carried 79 percent of the vote over her only opponent Ray Madrigal.[21] In both the 2010 and 2014 gubernatorial races, the leading candidate from both political parties successfully avoided a runoff election.

In the 2018 primary season, Greg Abbott avoided a run-off by receiving 90.4 percent of the total primary vote. However, the Democratic Party tally was a different story. Lupe Valdez got only 42.9 percent of the vote while one of her four opponents Andrew White got 27.4 percent. Valdez successfully defeated White in the run-off primary election.[22] To avoid costly primary and perhaps runoff elections, both political parties try to discourage other candidates from running against incumbents or those they feel already have an advantage over potential rivals. Running an unopposed primary election means that the candidate can spend only a marginal amount of campaign cash, if any at all, thus, saving the bulk of the money for usually a contested general election come November.

Every four years, Americans across the country cast their votes in the **presidential primaries**. Although the media focuses on the total vote each potential presidential contender receives, these primaries are **indirect election** interparty events that determine the number of delegates each contender will receive from their respective political parties in that state for the national convention nomination process. The majority of the Republican presidential primaries are **winner-take all**, meaning that whichever candidate gets the most votes, captures all of the national convention delegates from that state. On the other hand, the majority of the Democratic presidential primary elections are **proportional**, meaning that if a candidate wins 49 percent of the popular vote, he/she receives 49 percent of that state's delegates to the national convention. As previously pointed out in Chapter 3, the Texas Democratic Party uses the two-step system in determining the delegate distribution for its presidential contenders.

General Election

National law mandates that the elections for the presidency and members of Congress (all members of the House of Representatives and one-third of the United States Senate) be held on the first Tuesday after the first Monday in November in even numbered years. Of course, the president's term of office is four years. Texas voters go to the polls every two years to also elect the entire membership to the Texas House and one-half of the Texas Senate. Judicial seats and county seats are four-year staggered terms of office, with the exception of judges on the Texas Supreme Court and the Court of Criminal Appeals who serve six-year staggered terms. In Texas, elections for the governorship and all other state executive offices are held in non-presidential even-numbered years. One's declared party affiliation does not apply to general elections as the voter can cast a vote for candidates representing all parties on the ballot. General elections are plurality races whereby the person with the most votes wins.

Special Elections

A **special election** is "an election specifically scheduled to fill an office that has become vacant before the term of its expiration."[23] Special elections apply to vacated United States House and Senate seats, all state legislative seats, and home-rule city council positions. In Texas, the special election ballot is nonpartisan, meaning that candidates for all political parties or even an independent can run for the position. If the field is crowded and unless one candidate can capture 50 percent plus one vote, a runoff special election will occur. Only the two top vote getters in the special election would be eligible to face each other off in the runoff.

Tracking Elections

Political scientists study election results to determine whether a shift in public opinion or political preferences has a lasting impact on the course of future elections. Whereas their focus is primarily on presidential elections, any meaningful political shift in Washington, D.C., does have a domino effect on state election patterns. One election outcome in and of itself does not signal a long-term shift in one's party affiliation or political philosophical preferences. The political scientist looks at a series of consecutive elections to determine whether a particular election result can be labeled as critical, deviating, maintaining or converting. The ultimate aim is to pin-point if a long-term **realignment** within one political party can ultimately change the political philosophy or the political fortunes of the other parties.

> To recapitulate, then, eras of critical realignment are marked by short, sharp reorganizations of the mass coalitional bases of the major parties which occur at periodic intervals on the national level; are often preceded by major third-party revolts which reveal the incapacity of "politics as usual" to integrate, much less aggregate, emergent political demand; are closely associated with abnormal stress in the socioeconomic system; are marked by ideological polarizations and issue-distances between the major political parties which are exceptionally large by normal standards; and have durable consequences as constituent acts which determine

the outer boundaries of policy in general, though not necessarily of politics in detail.[24]

After analyzing the patterns attributable to these elections, political scientists have identified the presidential elections of 1800, 1828, 1860, 1896 and 1932 as critical elections. A **critical election** is "an election that heralds a new political alignment, that produces a new political majority, or that indicates a long-term shift in electoral behavior."[25] For example, the election of 1800 is directly attributable to the demise of the Federalist Party while the election of 1860 ushered in the dominance of the Republican Party until the election of 1912 when Democratic Woodrow Wilson won the White House. The election of 1932 is significant because of the shift in voting preferences and party loyalties. In particular, the African-American vote was solid Republican since Abraham Lincoln, a Republican president, ended slavery. Under Republican leadership former slaves were granted citizenship and voting rights. In 1932, Franklin Roosevelt, the Democratic nominee for the presidency, captured the majority of the African-American vote, which continues to vote over 95 percent or better for Democratic candidates.

Using the 1932 critical election as the benchmark, one can categorize subsequent elections. An election can be called a **maintaining election** because party loyalties that were present in the critical election remained stable with the majority party winning the election. The elections of 1936, 1940, and 1944 were essentially maintaining elections since Franklin Roosevelt easily won re-election and his party-base virtually remained the same. The election of 1948, however, is a **converting election** whereby the majority party wins, but there are some noticeable basic changes in the distribution of the party membership and philosophical preferences. Harry Truman's victory in 1948 was an extremely close election to the point that Gallup pollsters actually predicted Thomas Dewey, Truman's Republican opponent, would win the election. In the case of the elections of Republican Dwight Eisenhower and Democrat Jimmy Carter, one would possibly categorize these election results as a **deviating election** "in which a new party wins, not because there has been a realignment in political party preferences but because the winning party just happened to have an attractive candidate or some other factor in its favor (such as a scandal in the other party)."[26] In both of these elections, existing party loyalties were temporarily displaced by short-term forces. Eisenhower won his election in part because of the popularity gained by his impressive military record particularly during World War II. Jimmy Carter's path to the White House was definitely helped by the discontent the American people held for both Gerald Ford and the Republican Party for pardoning Richard Nixon for his actions in the Watergate Scandal.

Determining the outcome of any election falls upon the pollsters who measure the ebb and flow of public opinion on a weekly and, as the election day approaches, almost daily basis. A **poll** is "an attempt to determine public opinion concerning issues or to forecast an election."[27] Polls are only helpful to a campaign effort if the data obtained is reliable and verifiable. In looking at any poll, the key to reliability is the margin of error. If the poll has a + or – of less than 2 percent, then the results are far more accurate than a poll with a margin of + or – 10 percent. Both incumbent and challenging candidates use polling to determine what issues they should be emphasizing and how they should articulate them. For example, one of the "hot button" issues is immigration. All polls indicate that Texans are concerned about how to control the flow of illegal immigration coming across the Mexican border. Yet accurate polling will tell the candidate that potential voters in the southern sector of the state are less supportive of building a fence separating the United States from Mexico than potential voters in the Panhandle or the upper part of the East Texas region. The candidate does not have to compromise his/her philosophical position on immigration. However, reliable polling information will tell the candidate how to package his/her position to fit the particular political viewpoints of a designated area. Polling the entire area is difficult and time-consuming. Pollsters usually rely upon a **poll sample** defined as "a selected representative portion of a large population for the purpose of determining through extrapolation of the views, actions or intentions of that population."[28] The polling sample targets a certain segment of the population such as young college students and the instrument used will ask them questions pertinent to issues the pollster feels are important to them. Types of polls include face-to-face interviews, telephone surveys and mail-in instruments.

Predicting the outcome of elections used to be a relatively uncomplicated process. Traditionally voters would cast a **straight ticket** by merely turning the red lever on the voting machine that triggered a vote for all candidates from that particular political party. Nationally, there are more registered Democrats than Republicans. If the total vote turnout in a presidential election, for example, is over 51 percent, then Democrat candidates on the ballot fare better than Republicans. The reverse helps Republican candidates. Although less in numbers, Republicans tend to vote more frequently than their Democratic counterparts. However, today more voters are opting to vote **split ticket** by choosing candidates regardless of the candidate's declared party label, making far more difficult for pollsters to call elections based on just voter preference daily exit polls. However, one polling technique that seems to hold true is **bellwether polling**. On election night, commentators will declare the winner of the election oftentimes within ten minutes of the polls closing and before a substantial number of votes have been counted. They are basing their predictions upon their bellwether polling instrument. A bellwether is a poll sampling that is absolutely reflective of the entire potential voters in a designated region. The reliability of the polling is extremely dependent on the composition of the sample. For example, if the poll sample of less than 1 percent of an area composed of one million potential voters is a complete and accurate microcosm, the predicted election outcome will be correct.

The Ballot

The word ballot originated with the ancient Greeks. Throughout the Greek city-states, all males native-born to their city state were members of the government. They would cast their voting preferences by placing a white stone for yea and a black stone for nay in a container. Today, all elections in the United States use the **Australian ballot,** a secret ballot that is officially provided by a governing body, usually the county or city elections office, that is collected and tabulated by a government official, usually the election judges. In Texas, candidates run on a partisan or nonpartisan ballot. For both nonpartisan and partisan primary ballots, the candidates are listed in place on the ballot, that is, the candidates draw a number indicating what place they will have on the list of candidates for that particular office. Obviously, an alphabetical listing for a candidate whose last name begins with an "A" would have a more favorable ballot placement over the candidate whose last name begins with a "Z." For a general election partisan ballot, commonly known as the **party-column ballot**, candidates are listed by political parties. Traditionally, the candidates from the party of the incumbent governor are listed in order of importance on the left-hand side of the ballot. This is the preferred placement since voters tend to read from left to right. With the increased use of touch-screen computer voting devices, the trend has been to implement the **office-block ballot** whereby the elective office is listed across the top of the page and the candidates are listed in separate columns. Once again, candidates from the incumbent governor's political party are listed first on the ballot screen.

Texas prefers to use the **long ballot** also known as the bed sheet or jungle ballot since it lists all candidates running for office from, as in the case of a presidential election, president down to the lowest elective positions, usually justice of the peace or constables. At the end of the ballot there are also several binding and non-binding propositions requiring voter attention. The length of the ballot is problematic. Most voters will cast their votes for individuals listed at the top and middle part of the ballot. However, they do have a tendency to "run out of gas" as they near the bottom portion of the ballot. The touch-screen computers are not user friendly for the long ballot. Each page of the screen can only hold perhaps two to three offices at a time. Oftentimes, the long ballot means the voter must page through twenty-plus screens before pressing the red vote button, only to have to review those same twenty-plus pages to make sure their initial touch was the correct one.

Traditionally, voters used paper ballots that once marked by the voter were placed in boxes. After the polls closed, the sealed boxes were opened by election officials and hand counted. Texas has used a wide variety of balloting devices. The paper ballots were replaced by large voting machines. The ballots were pre-printed and scored to fit into the machines. By closing the curtain, the voter was insured privacy and would turn down the lever for each candidate for each office on the ballot. A voter could cast a straight ticket ballot by simply turning a red lever. These machines were very expensive to maintain and too bulky to store between elections. Consequently, several Texas counties opted to use punch card ballots whereby the voter would use a short-pointed tool to note their voting preferences. A clear punch is easy to tally. But election officials were oftentimes confronted with the same problems witnessed in Florida in the 2000 presidential race in determining whether the voter's true indication was a partial, hanging or pregnant chad. Gradually, Texas counties are opting for high-tech by using touch-screen computer generated voting devices. Although improvements have been made in the tabulation of votes, the major problem with the touch-screen system is the lack of a verifiable paper trail. Various organizations including the League of Women Voters have petitioned state officials to mandate that these computer generated voting systems provide both the voter and the election judge with a paper copy indicating the voter's preferences. The fear is that the computers can be compromised. For general elections, counties can choose to use traditional paper ballots, the manual operating voting machine, punch-card ballots, optical scanners or touch-screen devices.

Absentee and Early Voting

All states allow for **absentee voting** "that enable qualified voters to cast their ballots in an election without going to the polls on election day.[29] Prior to 1987, voters casting ballots for primary and general elections had to vote on election day. The only exceptions were those individuals brave enough to apply for an absentee ballot by swearing under oath to a county official that they were indeed not going to be in town on election day. Technically, lying under oath is a criminal offense. The Texas Legislature finally nullified the oath requirement and offered absentee balloting services at substations located in urban areas. Today, absentee voting has been extended for twenty-two days, ending six days before election day. Hours at the substations have been extended to twelve hours Monday through Friday with shorter hours for Saturdays and Sundays. Mail-in ballots are available to the elderly and handicapped. County voting officials will even make home visits to assist the physically handicapped and the visually-impaired in filling out their ballots.

In 1991, the Texas Legislature went a step further by instituting early voting periods for both primary and general elections. Registered voters do not have to vote in their precincts. Early voting for both primary and general elections is a 17-day period that ends four days before the election day. For a runoff primary election, the early vote period is for ten days ending four days before the election. Usually, early vote sites are open with extended hours on Monday through Fridays. State law mandates that polling sites be open on Saturdays and Sundays if fifteen registered voters in any given county request it.

Election Recounts

Once the results have been counted and certified, candidates can request a recount if they lose the election by less than 10 percent of the vote. The recount is for the entire representative district. If a candidate for State Attorney General requests a recount, all precincts in the state of Texas will be recounted. A recount in a district judge race would mean a recount of all precincts within that district. The Texas Election Code mandates a manual not an electronic recount. Initially the candidate requesting the recount must pay all of the costs of the procedure including hiring election officials to count those votes. If recount shifts in favor of the candidate, the money is reimbursed. For example, a losing candidate for a district judge position in Bexar County spent $42,000 just to find out that he still lost his election. The cost alone deters many losing candidates from requesting a recount.

Impact of Federal Legislation

Congressional legislation and United States Supreme Court rulings have changed how states traditionally conduct their elections. For example, the federal government addressed the needs of servicemen and their spouses who were stationed out of the country during presidential elections. Congress passed the **Federal Voting Assistance Act** in 1955 enabling all active duty members of any of the United States branches of the military, their spouses and qualified dependents, as well as other citizens temporarily residing outside the United States, to cast absentee ballots in presidential races. In 1975, The **Overseas Citizens Voting Rights Act** expanded voting privileges to those United States citizens residing outside of the country and its territories on other than a temporary basis. However, the law specifies that "these citizens must vote in the state in which they last resided immediately prior to departing the United States, even if many years have elapsed and the voter maintains no abode in the state and the intent to return to that state may not be certain."[30] As the events in the 2000 Florida presidential race unfolded, Al Gore's vice presidential candidate Joseph Libermann was anxiously awaiting the arrival and counting of the foreign ballots, particularly of Americans living is Israel who probably voted for the Gore/Libermann ticket. Today, the majority of the states including Texas only allow these individuals to cast votes for presidential candidates.

Unfortunately, state governments, particularly in the southern states, have not always upheld their responsibility to ensure that every eligible voter in their states actually has the opportunity to register and subsequently to cast a ballot. Voter irregularities were the norm rather than the exception. The leadership of the Civil Rights Movement was adamant that the voting process had to be more inclusive rather than exclusive. Dr. Martin L. King, Jr., and other civil rights leaders pushed both the United States Congress and the president to take a more active role in state elections. Both Presidents Kennedy and Johnson pushed for civil rights and voting rights legislation. Consequently, the most sweeping piece of federal legislation was the **Voting Rights Act** of 1965. The legislation mandated that states could not use any form of a literacy test to determine voter eligibility. Particularly in the South, the number of eligible voters far outweighed the number of actually registered voters. This legislation attempted to streamline and speed up the voter registration process. State leaders throughout the South were not pleased with the act's provision of authorizing federal registrars to assist in state-run voter registration efforts in those areas where less than 50 percent of those eligible were actually registered to vote. Renewed in 1970, the Voting Rights Act mandated that states lower the voting age from twenty-one to eighteen. It also prohibited states from disqualifying voters in presidential elections due to the potential voter's failure to meet state residency requirements beyond thirty days, and provided uniform national rules for absentee registration and voting in presidential elections. Gradually all states adopted the thirty day residency rule for all their state and local elections. The next renewal of the Voting Rights Act in 1975 included the requirement for bilingual ballots in those areas where English was not the primary language for 10 percent or more of the population. It also added voter and election protections for Spanish-Americans, Alaskan natives, American Indians, and Asian Americans. There have been numerous court challenges filed against the Voting Rights Act. In particular, the United States Supreme Court upheld the major provisions of the law in its 1966 ruling in *South Carolina v Katzenbach*. In 1980, the Court ruled in *City of Rome v Mitchell* that the provision of the law prohibiting any changes in voting practices that could have unintentional discriminatory impact were unconstitutional. Adopted in 1971, the **Twenty-sixth Amendment to the United States Constitution** lowered the voting age from twenty-one to eighteen. The constitutionality of the amendment was upheld by the Supreme Court in *Oregon v Mitchell* (1970).

The drama of the 2000 presidential election compelled the United States Congress to enact the **Help American Vote Act** commonly known as **HAVA** in 2002. A major problem with the Florida election count was the use of punch card ballots. The majority of the American electorate were totally unfamiliar with Florida's election laws and the problems determining what differentiated a pregnant from a hanging "chad." HAVA provided $325 million to help states who had not already phased out the old lever voting machines and the punch card balloting systems for updated voting mechanisms such as touch-screens. It also provided an additional pool of $325 million to help states improve the administration of their elections. It established an Election Assistance Commission composed of two Republicans and two Democrats charged with the tasks of certifying and testing alternative voting systems and studying election-related issues. HAVA specifically requires that states must:

- Provide voters with the opportunity to check for and correct ballot errors in a private and independent manner. This is called **second chance voting** for if a voter mistakenly over votes or forgets to cast a vote

in an election, the device will notify the voter that a change is necessary.
• Have a voting system with manual audit capability.
• Provide at least one voting device per precinct that is accessible to the disabled.
• Provide alternative or bilingual ballots.
• Have a voting system whose error rate does not exceed the existing rate established by the Federal Elections Office of Election Administration.
• Clearly define what constitutes a legal vote for each type of voting machine used in the state.
• Provide provisional ballots to ensure that no individual is turned away at the polls.
• Implement a single, uniform, official, centralized, interactive computerized statewide voter registration list that contains the name and registration information of every legally registered voter in the state.[31]

HAVA also requires the use of **provisional ballots** designed to allow a voter whose name does not appear on the official voter roster due to an administrative error, to vote. With the provisional ballot, the voter fills out an affidavit attesting that they did indeed fill out or received a voter registration card and then votes with a paper ballot. Kept separately from regular ballots, each provisional ballot is reviewed by the provisional voting ballot board. The ballot is counted in election results only if the voter is determined to be a registered voter in that precinct. Provisional voters will receive a notification in the mail by the tenth day after the local canvassing board has met advising the voter if the provisional ballot was counted and, if not, the reason why. Each state accepting HAVA funds must establish an Administrative Grievance Procedure for hearing complaints. Initially states are responsible for conducting hearings, and, if necessary, providing the appropriate remedy. The law gives the United States Department of Justice the authority to seek injunctive or declaratory relief for any violations of HAVA.[32] As detailed in Chapter 3, a recent United States Supreme Court decision has invalidated section 4 and indirectly section 5 of the Voting Rights Act.

Impact of State Legislation

In 2011, the Texas Legislature passed Senate Bill 14 mandating that all voters show a photo identification card when voting in person. Acceptable identification items are:

• Texas driver's license issued by the Texas Department of Public Safety (DPS)
• Texas Election Identification Certificate issued by DPS
• Texas personal identification card issued by DPS
• Texas concealed handgun license issued by DPS
• U.S. military identification card with the person's photograph
• U.S. citizenship certificate with the person's photograph
• U.S. passport

The law also mandates that with the exception of the U.S. citizenship certificate, all of the above identification items must be current or have expired no more than sixty days before being presented for voter qualification at the polling site. If the person's name does not exactly match the name on the identification card but is almost similar, the voter can cast a vote only if he/she signs an affidavit stating that he/she is the same person as listed on the roster of registered voters. If the voter does not have proper identification, he/she can use a provisional ballot with the understanding that if he/she does not present the required identification within six days, their vote will be invalidated. A permanent exemption may be granted to voters with a disability rating of at least 50 percent. Voters can cast provisional ballots with the same affidavit or appear six days later with an appropriate identification item if they declare a religious objection or have lost their identification cards due to natural disasters such as hurricanes, floods, etc. Voters are not required to show proof of identification if they use a mail in ballot.

Immediately, civil rights organizations and voter service groups filed federal lawsuits to halt implementation of the voter identification law. Initially, U.S. District Judge Nelva Gonzales Ramos of Corpus Christi struck down the law only to have the 5th U.S. District Court of Appeals stay the lower court's ruling while then Texas Attorney General Greg Abbott filed an appeal. Judge Ramos ordered the Texas Legislature to reevaluate their official list of valid voter identification items to address the lawsuit's charges of discriminatory practices aimed at minority voters. In 2017, the Texas Legislature passed Senate Bill 5 (SB5) as a remedy for the deficiencies noted in the original law (SB14). If a potential voter did not have the photo identification items listed in SB14, he/she could use their voter registration card, a utility bill or a bank statement. Judge Ramos was not impressed and blocked the implementation of SB 5. The judge simply repeated the same concerns he had with SB 14. He noted in his written opinion that "because those who lack SB 14 photo ID are subjected to separate voting obstacles and procedures, SB 5's methodology remains discriminatory because it imposes burdens disproportionately on Blacks and Latinos."[33] Finally, the Unite States Supreme Court ruled that the law was indeed constitutional. In writing the Court's dissent opinion, Justice Ginsburg believed that the Texas law "may prevent more than 600,000 (about 4.5 percent of all [Texas] registered voters from voting in person for lack of compliant identification. The greatest threat to public confidence in elections in this case is the prospect of enforcing a purposefully discriminatory law, one that likely imposes a poll tax and risks denying the right to vote to hundreds of thousands of voters."[34]

Voting advocates are heading back to court charging the state with voter discrimination once again. This time they are addressing the Texas Secretary of State's releasing of a list of approximately 95,000 individuals suspected of illegally registering to vote. The list includes approximately 58,000 who have been on the list since 1996. Taking the Republican Party's argument that voter fraud is prevalent throughout the nation, Texas Attorney General Ken Paxton stressed that "every single instance of illegal voting threatens democracy in our state and deprives individual Texans of their voice. Nothing is more vital to preserving our Constitution than the integrity of our voting process, and my office may do everything within its abilities to solidify trust in every election in the state of Texas."[35] Voting rights advocates question the validity of the study and the rationale behind it. They point out state databases are often riddled with errors, are not up-to-date and don't reflect the most recent information with regard to individuals. . . It will be very important for the state to provide more information about how they carried out their analysis, and we will have to test the veracity of their claims."[36] Several state legislative houses have passed their own legislation requiring voters to present a form of valid identification at polling sites.

The Candidate

Whether one is seeking to become president, governor or mayor, running for public office is an expensive time consuming effort with absolutely no guarantee that one will be celebrating an electoral victory in the wee hours after the polls close on election night. It is at best a two year process to become one's party nominee for the presidency. For governorships, United States congressional and state legislative house seats, the campaign with its primaries and general elections is a year and a half process from start to finish. Judicial races are just as expensive. Mayoral candidates are spending over a million dollars to run for a seat that in most cities across the nation, pays only a marginal yearly salary or at worst, a per diem for presiding over the council meetings. Those running for just a seat on the city council or the local school board must raise thousands of dollars.

Unfortunately, candidates running for public office must face the reality that it is an expensive process and one must be exceptionally good at fundraising. In his reelection bid, Governor Greg Abbott raised $75.6 million to battle in a race against his less-known Democrat challenger Lupe Valdez. Relatively new to "big time" politics, she was only able to raise $1.7 million.[37] Oftentimes, candidates must dip into their own piggybanks to fund their campaigns. In the case of Abbott, he used $1.1 million of his own money while Valdez chipped in approximately $38,000 to her campaign chest.[38]   Furthermore, the Federal Elections Commission campaign reports indicated that Republican candidate Kathleen Wall spent $6.2 million in her unsuccessful primary bid against incumbent Republican U.S. Rep. Dan Crenshaw and Gina Ortiz Jones, the Democrat candidate running against incumbent Republican U.S. Rep. Will Hurd spent $6 million. In turn, Hurd spent $5 million on his campaign. Democrat Lizzie Fletcher spent $6.1 million in her successful bid to unseat Republican U.S. Rep. John Culbertson from Houston.[39] In the hotly contested race for the U.S. Senate, incumbent Republican Ted Cruz spent $45.6 million on his successful run against Democrat Beto O'Rourke who spent $79 million on his campaign.[40]   The Ted Cruz campaign received $21.6 million from oil and gas interest groups, $15.2 million from Republican/conservative groups, $12. 2 million from air transport interests.[41] Meanwhile, O'Rourke raised $54 million from real estate affiliated interest groups, $46.5 million from health professional groups, and $11 million from non-profit organizations.[42] One could reasonably ask "where does the money go?" The expenses tied to a political campaign include salaries for the hired campaign strategists and campaign managers, rent for campaign headquarters and satellite offices, print advertising, commercial production costs, television air times, travel, campaign venues, and so on.

The success or failure of a candidate is directly tied to "the competitive effort of rival candidates for public office to win support of the voters in the period preceding an election." We commonly call this period the **campaign**.[43]

Prior to announcing one's candidacy, the candidate needs to at least hire a campaign manager and name a treasurer. The primary duties of the campaign treasurer is to coordinate the collection of campaign donations and file all of the required solicitation reports to ensure compliance with the appropriate state and federal campaign finance laws. Federal laws restricting campaign solicitations began in earnest with the passage of the **Hatch Act** (or the **Political Activities Act**) in 1939 prohibiting all political activities by federal employees as well as forbidding any political committee from spending more than $3 million in any campaign, and limiting individual contributions to $5,000.[44] Candidates for presidential and United States congressional elections must adhere to the rules established by Federal Election Campaign Acts of 1972 and 1974. Both were enacted to limit the amount of and the expenditure of campaign donations. The 1972 law:

- limited the amount a candidate could spend for political advertising to 10 cents for every eligible voter in a congressional district for House contests, statewide for Senate races and nationwide for presidential races with a limit of 60 percent of that sum usable for broadcast advertising and
- required complete disclosure of contributions in excess of $10 and expenditures in excess of $100.[45]

The 1974 revision of the **Federal Elections Campaign Act**:

- provided for public funding of presidential general elections.
- limited individual contributions to a maximum of $1,000 for a candidate in a national primary or general election with a $25,000 limit set on any person's total contributions during an election year.
- Mandated that special interests and political action committees could contribute no more than $5,000 to any candidate in a national program or general election.
- Created a six-member Federal Elections Commission appointed by the president with Senate approval.
- Repealed provisions of the Hatch Act by giving federal employees permission to engage in off-duty political activities.[46]

In addition, the federally enacted **Revenue Act** (1971) allowed for income tax fillers to check a box on their returns that would allocate three dollars to a federal fund available to presidential candidates vying for the White House in the general election. Candidates for all other positions must comply with the Texas Election Code and subsequent legislation regarding the collection, expense, and reporting

of campaign donations. To be in compliance, candidates must select their campaign treasurer prior to accepting any campaign contributions. Candidates and state-registered political action committees cannot accept cash donations over $100. All contributions and expenditures must be reported periodically with the Secretary of State's office. Judicial candidates in Texas have a different set of campaign finance guidelines from those seeking other elective offices. Regardless of the level of their bench, all judges in Texas are elected through partisan elections. They too need to raise money for their campaigns. In 1994, the Texas Legislature passed the Judicial Campaign Fairness Act. This legislation limits judicial campaign donations from individuals to $5,000 per candidate for a statewide office and between $1,000 to $5,000 for other judicial seats. Law firms can only contribute $50 per candidate.[47] Violators are subjected to both criminal and civil penalties.

State and federal laws place restrictions on the amount and use of direct contributions commonly known as **hard money contributions**. However, the laws are vague as to what differentiates a legal from illegal donation. Although the candidates may file the reports in a timely fashion, there are absolutely no requirements that the FEC reviews, investigates, and reports campaign solicitation irregularities in an expedient manner. For example, during his 2010 congressional race "the Federal Election Commission ordered Rep. Ciro Rodriguez to refund $89,000 in contributions from a 2004 Democratic primary."[48] The FEC also penalized Rep. Henry Cuellar "with a $28,500 fine after an audit showed he failed to disclose information on a $200,000 bank loan he received during the same controversial race [2004]."[49] It took five years for the FEC to complete these audits. The release of an FEC violation can have serious repercussions on the candidate's current campaign efforts. Within a matter of days after the FEC released its findings on the Rodriquez 2004 campaign, his opponent in the 2010 race was quick to accuse Rodriguez of knowingly accepting illegal campaign donations, leading voters to ponder whether the oversights on the part of the Rodriguez campaign staff were mere oversights or intentional actions.

Equally troubling are **soft money contributions**. These donations are indirectly given to a candidate to offset campaign expenses. For example, a candidate may want to host a fundraising effort. A donor could provide the rental for the facility, another provides the food, and someone else would cover the costs of the entertainment. Since these donations did not go directly to the candidate, they do not count towards the monetary limitations of hard money contributions. As a presidential candidate, Senator

This painting depicts delegates voting on the 1836 Constitution, on the evening of March 16, 1836, at Washington-on-the-Brazos, Texas, amidst the "Runaway Scrape." Credit: UTSA's Institute of Texan Cultures, #074-0445, Courtesy, artist Bruce Marshall.

John McCain made campaign finance reform one of his major campaign promises. In 2002, he and Senator Russell Feingold successfully sponsored the **Bipartisan Campaign Reform Act** attempting to limit soft money donations. The legislation banned soft money contributions to political parties, placed restrictions of end-of-campaign television commercials and advertisements, and allowed corporations, unions and interest groups to sponsor issue advertisements to run up to sixty days before a general election and thirty days before a primary election.

The United States Supreme Court has taken a dim view to campaign finance laws that they see as infringements upon the First Amendment's protection of free speech. In *Buckley v Valeo* (1976), the Court ruled that provisions of a 1974 campaign and finance bill limiting amount of money candidates could spend and limitations on how a candidate can spend his/her own money were an unconstitutional infringement upon constitutionally protected rights to free speech. The Court once again championed the cause of free speech by ruling in *Citizens United v Federal Elections Commission* (2010) that a provision in the Bipartisan Campaign Reform Act barring the airing of advertisements days before an election was unconstitutional.

Also, the timing of a campaign donation can come back to haunt a candidate. During the 2010 governor's race, Democratic candidate Bill White openly accused Republican Governor Rick Perry of illegal campaign solicitation and the granting of special concessions or kickbacks from the governor's office as a reward for a sizable donation to the campaign coffers. The allegation stemmed from nearly $500,000 in campaign donations over several years given to Perry by Peter Holt, chairman of a family-owned Caterpillar business and principal owner of the San Antonio Spurs. The supposed kickback "came in the form of a $8.5 million subsidy to Caterpillar Inc., from the Texas Enterprise Fund, created by the Texas Legislation at Perry's behest in 2003.[50] Accusing an incumbent of possibly accepting bribes or kickbacks is a favorite ploy used by challengers to convince voters that the incumbent is tainted and corrupt.

The message and the delivery of that message are keys to the success of any election campaign. Potential voters do not know everything about a candidate nor do the candidates expect them to research every single issue position and speech delivered by the candidate. What the candidate wants is a one or two words or an accomplishment as an incumbent that distinguishes them from his/her opponent.

When Rick Perry announced that he would not seek a fourth term, the governor's race became wide open, but both political parties did not have a favorite in mind. Serving as the state's attorney general for over eleven years, Greg Abbott was well known among his Republican cohorts. Pleased with his announcement to seek the governorship, Republicans saw Abbott as one who "possesses a conservative, principled, forward-looking vision that will improve the future of the Lone Star State, and build on the past successes under Perry."[51] A native Texan, Abbott earned his bachelor's degree from the University of Texas at Austin and his law degree from Vanderbilt University Law School. While in private practice, Abbott became a paraplegic in 1984 when an oak tree fell on him while he was running. Appointed by then Governor George W. Bush to the Texas Supreme Court, Abbott was successfully elected to two terms on the Court. In 2001, he resigned from the bench to run for lieutenant governor. However, John Cronyn serving as the state attorney general resigned his position to run for the United States Senate. Abbott then switched his race from lieutenant governor to state attorney general. As the state's attorney general, Abbott had already demonstrated his dislike for the perceived intrusiveness of the federal government. Under his watch, a wide variety of lawsuits were filed challenging numerous federal laws and federal mandates covering everything from Obamacare to environmental regulations. Abbott successfully convinced voters that his physical disability was not a deterrent to holding the state's highest office. To his credit, he demonstrated that his handicap made him a stronger and more determined person. During the campaign his staff issued a commercial of Abbott in his wheelchair traveling level by level down a parking garage. In contrast, Franklin Roosevelt ran for the presidency without a single photo or public appearance of him seated in his wheelchair. He perceived that the American public would see his disability as a weakness rather than as a strength. On election night, Abbott proudly proclaimed that he was "living proof that a young man can have his life broken in half and still rise up and be governor of this state."[52] His campaign focused on traditional conservative Republican Texas politics including a pro-life position, stronger border security, anti-environmental regulation, non-expansion of Medicaid, and, of course, overturning Obamacare.

The first woman to run in the general election for the governorship since Ann Richards, Wendy Davis's credentials to run for the state's highest office were not as impressive as her opponent's. She served on the Fort Worth City Council for nine years and successfully ran for the District 10 Texas Senate seat in 2008. Initially, she declared herself as a Republican but switched party allegiance to the Democrats in 2006. With only two years of state elective office experience, Davis simply could not compete against Abbott's impressive record. On the campaign trail, her speeches focused on her pro-education agenda of providing full-day pre-kindergarten to all eligible children, increase salaries for teachers, more financial aid for college students, in-state tuition for undocumented immigrants, and equitable funding for the state's public school system. She supported Obamacare and the expansion of Medicaid

benefits. However, her campaign took a wrong turn as the media focused more on her personal life than on her issue positions. Her book, *Forgetting to Be Afraid*, was about her personal life including a failed marriage, an abortion, and her struggles to get through law school as a single parent. She simply could not compete against a well-qualified candidate with a well-funded campaign war chest.

The 2018 governor's race was a relatively smooth ride for Abbott. There was really no major controversial issue that could have uprooted his campaign nor put him on the offensive. The Lupe Valdez campaign focused more on establishing her statewide identity than it did on attacking Abbott's administration and his political positions. There was only one statewide televised debate between Abbott and Valdez. With a limited war chest, the Valdez campaign simply lacked the resources to launch the type of intense campaign needed to unseat an incumbent candidate. The governor's race is a major political event that should have grabbed the bulk of the state's media outlets. Instead, the governor's race fell by the wayside as both the national and state media's attention was focused on the tight race between Ted Cruz and Beto O'Rourke for that Senate seat.

As true with a presidential election, a governor seeking re-election can either help or hinder the election possibilities for other candidates from his/her political party. The **coattail effect** is the tendency for a candidate heading a party ticket to attract votes for other candidates of his or her party on the same ballot.[53] High approval ratings for an incumbent governor means that his/her coattails are wide enough to carry other candidates with him or her to an electoral victory on election night. Consequently, the strategy is for candidates on the lower-end of the ballot to seek campaign support from the incumbent governor. Candidates want their party's incumbent governor to speak at their rallies, join them in photo-ops, and run commercials of the candidate supporting the governor's programs. However, a governor with low approval ratings has short coattails meaning that candidates from his or her party simply do not want to be seen with the governor. At best, candidates want to "divorce" themselves from an unpopular governor. In the 2010 race, Perry had exceptionally long coattails as all of the state's top executive offices, the majority of the United States congressional and state legislative seats and judgeships went the Republican way. The same pattern held in 2014 as all of the state's executive offices were won by Republican candidates and both houses of the Texas Legislature remained under Republican Party domination. Although several state legislative seats flipped from Republicans to Democrats, the 2018 election results reaffirmed the Republican Party's hold on this state. The Republican Party's candidates swept all of the state's top executive offices as well as maintained its majorities in both houses of the Texas Legislature.

The Franchise—Voters

Regardless of the amount of money spent, the hours on the road, the number of commercials hitting the airwaves, the outcome of any election falls upon the shoulders of the voter. However, gaining the franchise or the privilege to vote has not always been an easy task. Initially, voting privileges in the United States were tied to property ownership. The rationale was that property ownership meant that an individual had a vested interest in the political future of the nation and would cast a well-thought out vote come election time. Each state had a different definition of property ownership ranging from actually owning a certain number of acres to not having any outstanding tax obligations. The property requirement for voting ended with the election of Andrew Jackson to the White House. According to the Texas Constitution of 1836, "all persons (Africans, the descendants of Africans, and Indians excepted,) who were residing in Texas on the day of the declaration of independence, shall be considered citizens of the republic, and entitled to all the privileges of such."[54] Furthermore the Constitution of 1836 required that all free Anglos immigrating into the state in the future had to establish a six-month residency before being granted citizenship rights including voting privileges. The Texas Constitution of 1845 denied suffrage to free white males convicted of bribery, perjury, forgery and any other high crime. Throughout the development of Texas, African-American slaves and Native Americans were not considered to be citizens and therefore, were denied voting privileges.

With the end of the Civil War and the implementation of Reconstruction, southern whites saw the Radical Republicans in Washington, D.C., openly encouraging freed African Americans to take social, economic, and, in particular, political vengeance against Southerners. "You must see that the negroes [African Americans] will not be satisfied with a nominal, but deceptive equality, but are everywhere determined to become masters of those who late owned them as slaves. . . . So soon as they become invested with the right of suffrage, will [they] become masters of the situation, for they constitute a majority on every acre of good land from the Atlantic to the Mississippi, and from the Rio Grande to Memphis. By mere voting, and selecting none but negroes [African Americans] as county, state and federal officers, in the most favored regions where they constitute the majority, in two or three years

they might expel the whites from all the fertile sections of the South."[55] By February 1868, African-American Texans cast their first ballots in a special election to rewrite the state's constitution. Denied the political clout to oust the Radical Republicans, white Southerners resorted to their own tactics to preserve their superior status over African Americans. Texas followed other southern states by enacting a series of legislative acts known as **Black Codes** or **Jim Crow Laws**, denying freedoms and political rights to African Americans, while at the same time openly defying the national government. The implementation of Jim Crow began to adversely impact the ability of African Americans to access the ballot box and gain full political participation. The **grandfather clause** required passing a literacy test for those potential voters whose grandfathers could not vote before 1860. Of course, all former slaves were subject to take this test, which was so difficult that very few passed it. Despite these impediments, African Americans did win a handful of elective positions. With the exception of the 1877 Legislature, all Texas legislative sessions between 1868 and 1894 had African-American representation. In 1902, Texas joined other southern states by adopting a **poll tax** or voting fee ranging from $1.50 to $1.75 per year. In 1924, the Texas Legislature passed laws creating the **white-only primary**, limiting primary participation in the Democratic Party to Anglos only.

Using its power of judicial review, the United States Supreme Court began to chip away at discriminatory voting practices as early as 1915 when the court ruled in *Guinn v United States* (1915), that Oklahoma's grandfather clause was an unconstitutional direct violation of the Fifteenth Amendment. In *Nixon v Herndon* (1927), the Court invalidated the Texas White Primary Law of 1924 that stated: "In no event shall a negro [African American] be eligible to participate in a Democratic primary election in the State of Texas, and should a negro [African American] vote in a Democratic primary election, such ballot should be void and election officials shall not count the same."[56] The Court ruled that the Texas Legislature could not legislatively deny African Americans the right to vote in primary elections. The Texas Democratic Party continued the practice by circumventing the Court's ruling declaring itself a private club with the rights to establish its own membership criteria without government interference. However, the United States Supreme Court dealt a fatal blow to the white-only primary system by ruling in *Smith v Allwright* (1944) that the Texas Democratic Party was not a private club but an agent of the state of Texas and must adhere to both state and federally mandated rules and regulations for voting and elections with the understanding that no government agency can deny voting privileges to any qualified voter.

Enacted by the majority of the former Confederate States, the poll tax effectively prevented the poor and African Americans from voting. Despite the pleas of President Kennedy in 1962 for the states to voluntarily abolish the practice, five states including Texas held steadfastly to assessing the fee. The poll tax was outlawed with the passage of the **Twenty-fourth Amendment to the United States Constitution** in 1964. President Johnson openly supported the abolishment of the poll tax. He believed that eliminating it would "reaffirm the simple but unbreakable theme of this Republic. Nothing is so valuable as liberty, and nothing is so necessary to liberty as the freedom to vote without bans or barriers. A change in our Constitution is a serious event. There can now be no one too poor to vote."[57] Of course, several southern states interpreted the Twenty-fourth Amendment as only pertaining to federal elections. The United States Supreme Court ruled against them in 1966 in *Harper v Virginia State Board of Elections* by declaring that the use of a poll tax in any election was unconstitutional.

The literacy test was dismantled in a piecemeal fashion. The **Civil Rights Act of 1964** required states to accept a sixth grade education as meeting literacy and voter testing requirements. Minor errors on the test or a voter registration card could not be used to deny voting privileges. The **Voting Rights Act of 1965** suspended the use of discriminatory tests. A staunch supporter of the measure, President Johnson told the nation that:

> Our fathers believed that if this noble view of the rights of man was to flourish, it must be rooted in democracy. The most basic right of all was the right to choose your own leaders. . . . Every American citizen must have an equal right to vote. There is no reason which can excuse the denial of that right. There is no duty which weighs more heavily on us than the duty we have to ensure that right. Yet the harsh fact is that in many places of this country, men and women are kept from voting simply because they are Negroes [African Americans]. Every device which human ingenuity is capable has been used to deny this right. The Negro [African-American] citizen may go register only to be told that the day is wrong, or the hour is late, or the official in charge is absent. And if he persists and if he manages to present himself to the registrar, he may be disqualified because he did not spell out his middle name or because he abbreviated a word on the application. And if he manages to fill out an

application, he is given a test. The registrar is the sole judge of whether he passes this test. He may be asked to recite the entire Constitution, or explain the most complex provisions of State law. And even a college degree cannot be used to prove that he can read and write.[58]

The motivation behind the Voting Rights Act and corrective legislation and court decisions reversing Jim Crow tactics was to make both the registration process and voting more accessible and easier for qualified voters to participate in the election system. Today, in Texas potential voters must meet the following qualifications:

- Citizenship—a native-born or naturalized citizen of the United States
- Age—eighteen years of age on or before election day
- Residency—at least thirty days residency in the state and county immediately preceding election day; resident of area covered by the election on election day
- Registration to vote—at least thirty days immediately preceding election day
- Criminal status—not a convicted felon unless one's sentence, parole and/or probation period has been completed
- Mental status—not declared to be mentally incompetent by a court of law

If a person moves within his/her county, they may vote for candidates in county or statewide elections at their previous precinct if their voter registration card has not been cancelled or transferred to their new address. For municipal or city elections, the voter must cast their ballot on election day in their resident precinct. If a person moves from one county to another, they must re-register in the county of their new residence. Texas uses the permanent registration process whereby if a voter actually uses their card within a three-year period, they are not dropped from the voting roster. New voter registration cards are mailed automatically to every registered voter every two years, in January of even-numbered years. However, if the voter changed addresses and failed to notify the county elections office, they will need to re-register.

Political Participation

Despite improvements in both the registration and voting process, Texas is still grappling with low voter turnout.

There is a definitive tie between the level of competition in the election and voting participation levels. Political scientists know that levels of participation definitely increase during presidential elections but fall off in the mid-term election cycle. Also, a high profile competitive field of candidates will generate more intense interest on the part of the voters. However, the composition of the field of candidates and the election process itself is not the definitive answer as to why some people participate while others do not. Several political scientists focus on the cultural background of the individual as well as his/her political socialization process.

Culture and Politics

Why do people of German ancestry residing in the Hill Country tend to be politically and socially conservative and vote Republican while people of Spanish/Mexican descent living in South Texas rally around more liberal political issues and vote Democrat? Why do historical voting patterns reveal that individuals affiliated with the Baptist and Methodist religions vote against gambling legislation more frequently than any other religious group? Why is the political climate in East Texas totally different from South, West or North Texas?

Particularly in South Texas, the dramatic growth in the Hispanic population base should correlate to an equally dramatic increase in the number of Hispanics voting on election day and running for public office. However, the lingering question is why has this not happened? Throughout the development of Texas, Texans of Mexican descent have not enjoyed the same political, economic, and social advantages as those enjoyed by their Anglo counterparts. Although marginal improvements have been made, Texas has several of the poorest counties in the country predominately populated by Hispanics, located near the Mexican border. Year after year the Hispanic community continues to suffer from the adverse effects of poverty, high unemployment, low wages, illegal immigration, high public school dropout rates, limited education, and high illiteracy rates. In Texas, Jim Crow Laws also have adversely impacted the Hispanic community. Like their African-American counterparts, accessibility to the political process has been slow and sporadic. Traditionally, their political leanings have sided with the liberal wing of the Democratic Party. The power of the Hispanic voting bloc has occasionally been the primary reason why a candidate won or lost a race. For example, the Hispanic vote in South Texas was the key bloc that elected liberal Democrat Ann Richards to the governorship in a tight race against Republican candidate Clayton Williams. During her re-election bid against Republican George W. Bush, the South Texas Hispanic voting bloc that had once stood solidly behind Richards did not materialize for her in this race and she lost. In the 2000 race for the governorship, the Democratic Party hoped the candidacy of Tony Sanchez would draw a large voter turnout from the Hispanic community. Sanchez, however, did not attract a large Hispanic following and, subsequently, lost the race to incumbent Republican Governor Rick Perry.

The Hispanic community is the fastest growing minority population group in the nation. Hispanics became the majority population in San Antonio in the early 1990s. The potential power of the Hispanic voting bloc is very well known to politicians from both political parties. George W. Bush realized that his ticket to the governor's mansion depended to a large degree upon his ability to capture the Hispanic vote. He was unable to win favor with Hispanic voters, however, the low voter turnout among the traditionally Democratic Hispanic community in that election was enough for Bush to win the race. As a presidential candidate, Bush campaigned heavily in the Hispanic strongholds in California, New Mexico, Arizona, and Florida. Al Gore also competed for the same bloc. Thankfully for the Bush campaign, the Hispanic voting bloc did not flex enough muscle to harm Bush's bid for the White House.

Demographers note that "the Hispanic population of Texas grew by 41.9 percent between 2000 and 2010, while the non-Hispanic white population grew only by 4.2 percent."[59] By 2040, indications are that Hispanics will account for 78 percent of the state's population.[60] For the Texas Republican Party, the continuous growth in the Hispanic population and its political clout is problematic for a party whose platform issues include abolition of bilingual education programs, support of legislation banning noncitizen children from attending public schools, and, of course, the Republican-dominated State Board of Education's rewrite of the state's history curriculum that eliminated several notable Hispanics from the textbooks. Unless the Republican Party makes significant efforts to court the Hispanic vote, the potential outcome of elections may swing in the other direction. "Nobody knows when the magic time is, but if Democrats get 65 [percent] to 70 percent of the Mexican American vote, they are going to start winning all the elections."[61] So, why has the clout of the Hispanic vote base failed to deliver a resounding long lasting punch?

The pledge of allegiance is a typical scene in most schools across the nation. In this way children learn the political values of the country and develop pride in their heritage. Such values and commitment are a necessary ingredient to an orderly and just society.

The answers to these questions point toward cultural characteristics and patterns of behavior deeply rooted in each of us. What we believe in, how we express it, and how we react are the end results of our individual unique cultural heritage, historical background, family affiliations, religious preference, educational attainment, and socio-economic status. All of these factors stem from our diverse cultures. The broad scope of politics is in many respects a response based on the influence of culture and cultural differences. The remainder of this chapter focuses on the connection between one's political culture and the acquisition of political awareness through the political socialization process and the degree of participation one demonstrates in the political process itself. Political scientists study elections and voter patterns and preferences. Regardless of how talented and gifted a candidate may be, the outcome of every single election hinges on whether a person registers to vote, educates themselves about the candidates and the issues, trusts the integrity of the election system, and actively decides to cast his or her vote.

What Is Political Culture?

In *Comparative Politics: A Developmental Approach*, Gabriel Almond and G. Bingham Powell define **political culture** as "the pattern of individual attitudes and orientations towards politics among members of a political system."[62] Political culture plays a key role in the development and implementation of public policy. Political culture has "deep emotional dimensions involving the passions of loyalty and community identity, and the sentiments of human and geographical attachment. In relating emotions, rational considerations, and ethical values, political culture colors a person's expectations about their realities of politics and instills in them shared ideals as to what their public life might be."[63] For example, every legislative initiative is a reflection of a nation's political culture. Every piece of legislation is a compromise document combining various viewpoints and attitudes on a public policy issue. The implementation and subsequent success of a law is dependent upon receptive attitudes on the parts of both lawmakers and the citizens subjected to that law. One should consider that the need for United States Congress to enact corrective legislation to address civil rights abuses would have been more readily accepted and successful in a shorter period of time if public attitudes would have been more willing to the expansion of political rights to those traditionally prohibited from exercising those freedoms. Legislative houses can create laws but the laws themselves cannot change attitudes. Cultural differences can make or break a well-needed legislative action.

Almond and Powell contend that one's political culture is composed of three basic elements: "(a) **cognitive orientations**, knowledge, accurate or otherwise, of political objects and beliefs; (b) **affective orientations**, feelings of attachment, involvement, rejection and the like, about political objects; and (c) **evaluative orientations**, judgments and opinions about political objects and events which usually involve applying value standards to political objects and events."[64] For example, an individual has knowledge of a political issue such as public school funding, health-care reform, etc., (cognitive orientation). This issue will directly impact this person since his or her children attend Texas public schools or lack health care coverage (affective orientation). This individual has developed opinions about what should be done to ensure state funds are disbursed properly and equally among the school districts, or in the case of health care, whether affordable coverage can be guaranteed to those who do not have health insurance (evaluative orientation). One's political culture determines the course of action and level of participation that person will take in ensuring that these issues are appropriately addressed. Political culture also teaches an individual the patterns of acceptable political behavior. Texans, for example, are taught that the acceptable means of expressing an opinion range from discussions to public protests and demonstrations. However, violence is an unacceptable form of political expression. Political culture teaches the rules of citizenship and sets the criteria for separating the "good" citizen from those whose behaviors are unacceptable.

The acquisition of political culture is basically a generational process. "Each generation must receive its politics from the previous one, each must react against that process to find its own politics, and the total process must follow the laws that govern the development of the individual personality and the general culture of a society."[65] This tenet helps to explain why some people have a cultural-identity crisis; they feel compelled to conform to generational pressure while trying to incorporate their own individual feelings, which are oftentimes in conflict with the accepted norm. One's generational political culture can either be an asset or a liability in one's quest to form independent decisions about the political process.

The Political Socialization Process

Individuals acquire their political culture and their levels of participation in the political arena through the **political socialization process**. An informal training process, political socialization instills in us our sense of identity, belonging, and community. Nationalism and patriotism are essential to the viability of any nation state. Citizens must develop respect for their government or that government will never achieve internal sovereignty and legitimacy. Governments do not always please their citizens in their policy choices, but patriotism instills in those citizens a fighting spirit to defend their country at all costs. Texans pride themselves on their loyalty and staunch identification with the Texas image. We learn the significance of the symbols associated with our state such as the Lone Star flag and the state song—*Texas Our Texas*—through the political socialization process. Parades, memorials, and monuments constantly reinforce the guiding principles of our society and the sacrifices individuals have made to preserve those principles.

The process also teaches citizens the ideological framework guiding their political system. The cornerstone of the American governmental system is the firm belief in representative democracy, joined with the economic theories of capitalism and free enterprise. The political socialization process introduces individuals to the underlying concepts of democratic governments: protection of natural rights, the concept of limited government, popular sovereignty, free elections, majority rule/minority rights, and so on. The free enterprise system, with its emphasis on economic individualism, capitalism, anti-socialism, and the American dream is taught to us beginning at the elementary school level. The political socialization process also teaches citizenship duties and obligations. We learn how to be a "good" citizen and how to exhibit appropriate behavior. A good citizen may not always agree with the decisions government makes, but he/she will respect the laws levied by the government. The code of acceptable behavior does not advocate breaking laws or violent civil disobedience against governing institutions.

The end result of the political socialization process is the formulation of political opinions on which each of us base our political preferences on both issues and candidates. The success of the process is demonstrated by the level of **political efficacy** achieved by each individual. The term political efficacy is the belief that one's political participation has an effect on the course of political events. Individuals with high levels of political efficacy vote on a regular basis, actively participate in their political party, and often seek elected offices. Those with low political efficacy believe that their current political, social, or economic status will remain the same regardless of which political party or candidates win the election. These individuals rarely vote, if at all.

Agents of Political Socialization

We acquire our political culture through the **agents** of the political socialization process. The family, educational system, religious affiliation, peer groups both as adolescents and adults, the media, and important events, combined with an individual's historical and cultural background, are agents of the political socialization process. Each agent exerts its influence in the formation of issue positions and political preferences.

The most important agent is the influence of one's immediate family. Children emulate their parents; consequently, parents play a pivotal role in determining the degree of political involvement of their children. Children whose parents are more politically active will be more inclined toward an elevated level of political participation as adults than children from less politically involved parents. In some families, such as the Bushes, Kennedys, and Rockefellers, high levels of political participation are not an option but a family obligation. The discussion of political issues within the family environment encourages children to be more aware of events and issues. Although as adults they may express different viewpoints, most young adults share their parents' party loyalties. The term "**yellow-dog Democrat**" referred to the generational obligation to vote straight party Democrat, even if a yellow dog was on the ballot. The parents' ethnic background, social class, religion, educational attainment level, occupation, and income affect their child's political culture. Political scientists agree that the most predictable factor as to whether a person will vote is his/her socio-economic level or class. Those whose incomes are in the middle to upper levels tend to vote more often on a regular basis than those whose incomes are in the lower levels. Minorities tend to vote less often than their Anglo counterparts. These trends are in part linked to the influence of the family union.

The public or private school system gives children their first experience with a power structure other than their parents. A school is a self-contained political system with peers, levels of authority, and rules with rewards and punishments. Children develop long-lasting impressions about rules and authority figures from their early experiences with their parents and their schools. A teacher's influence is also seen through the choice of instructional materials, the interpretation of political, historical, and economic developments, and the treatment of political issues. Today in Texas the selection of textbooks in the public school system is a highly politicized issue with liberals, conservatives, and the radical right arguing over the materials, subject matter and philosophical concepts covered in public school textbooks. The textbook not only teaches but also indoctrinates children at a very young age about our government institutions, economic system, social structure, and societal behavior patterns.

Religion plays a key role in the political socialization process. Catholics, Protestants, and the Jewish faith hold different views on issues such as abortion, capital punishment, school prayer, gambling, and alcoholic beverages. The traditional Southern Baptist/Methodist Bible Belt is strongly opposed to gambling and alcohol consumption. It was the Bible Belt that successfully lobbied the Texas Legislature to pass a series of Sunday closings laws, known collectively as the **Blue Laws**. The first round of Blue Laws was a city ordinance passed in Houston in 1839 banning the sale of malt liquor on Sundays. The

more exclusive list of banned items was enacted by the Texas Legislature in 1961. Basically, consumers could not purchase air conditions, bed coverings, china, any item of clothing, footwear, hardware, headwear, home appliances, furniture, jewelry, kitchen utensils, lawn mowers, motor vehicles, musical instruments, television sets, and toys on Sundays. In 1985, the Texas Legislature finally repealed the Blue Laws by opting to allow all retail outlets and grocery stores with the exception of liquor stores to open at noon on Sundays with no prohibition on what items could be purchased.

For centuries, the traditional Catholic Church doctrine has stressed a pro-life position. In the United States, the Catholic Church was one of the founders of the anti-abortion movement. In 1973 under the leadership of Jesuit priest Edmundo Rodriguez, the Catholic Church joined forces with the Mexican-American community living on the Westside to create Communities Organized for Public Service or COPS. In 1979, Virginia Baptist minister Jerry Falwell created the Moral Majority. Desiring a return to traditional family values, this organization favors the reinstitution of prayer in the public schools and opposes abortion and sexual permissiveness. The Moral Majority entered the political arena by financing political candidates for elected offices ranging from local school boards to the presidency. Regardless of one's religious affiliation, politics and political issue positions are to some degree a part of the weekly sermon, to the point that some believe that the doctrine of separation of church and state has ceased to exist.

Studies indicate that peer pressure has played an important role in shaping one's political culture. For adolescents, peer pressure emphasizes conformity to a group's ideals or behavior patterns. The overwhelming desire to belong to a group or organization compels individuals to change their traditional habits for those of the group or organization they wish to join. In many respects, peer conformity uniquely defines a generation: the hippies of the 60s, bobby-soxers, and so on. As adults we are confronted with a new set of peer pressures as we settle into our chosen occupations. Sometimes individuals may totally switch their political party affiliations as peer pressure requires conformity to a party affiliation more acceptable to that peer group.

The media, particularly with the invention of the television, have become a major force in the shaping of one's political viewpoints. Nearly two-thirds of the adult population in the United States rely upon television news programming as their sole source of information. The credibility of a political party, candidate, or issue is directly tied to the degree of positive or negative televised coverage the item or issue receives. The early stages of the civil rights movement received more negative than positive coverage as the networks aired more violently specific pieces. Daily televised programming of the Vietnam War drove home vivid details of the horrors and reality of war and contributed to the development of the anti-war protest movement. Over-reliance on television does have its drawbacks. Communication outlets, whether newspapers, magazines, radio, the internet or television stations, are operated as profit-making businesses. The market of public opinion does dictate programming decisions. Television news is condensed and does not present in-depth analysis of political events and issues. Television on the whole does a poor job of explaining political issues, often presenting superficial facts and highlighting controversy to entice viewers and higher ratings.

Events and personal experiences can alter or reinforce one's political viewpoints and level of participation. The Great Depression of the 1930s changed the country's perspective on the role of the national government in quality-of-life issues. Before the Depression, public opinion held that economic deprivation was basically self-inflicted and recovery was the individual's responsibility. The Depression put millions out of work who had worked hard all of their lives. Obviously, they were not to blame for their plight. Public opinion blamed the national government and turned to it to solve the problems and to alleviate the suffering. The Great Depression ushered in the modern welfare state.

All of these agents help to develop and mold our political perspectives and determine our levels of participation in the political system. It cannot be definitively proven that one agent at any given time is the sole influence to changing one's political perspectives. These agents act in conjunction with each other.

General Political Trends in Texas

The impact of diverse political cultures has produced several political trends in Texas that often prevent this state from having a progressive-oriented and efficient governmental system. Texans have a love/hate relationship for government as a whole. They are well known to be very suspicious of government at any level, leery of politics, and distrustful of politicians. Political races often focus more on the candidate's character, personal life, and prior mistakes than on pressing public policy issues. Many hold that government is operated by elected officials with ulterior motives for personal gain. In addition, legislation should be passed only when deemed absolutely necessary

to meet an identified demand or pressing problem. Laws should serve people, not place unrealistic barriers and restrictions to one's personal good will. "Texans love for government to build highways, military installations and dams. They hate it when government collects taxes and requires them to operate a safe workplace or to provide equal opportunity to everyone regardless of race, color, or sex."[66] To put it simply, Texans do not like to be told what to do! Texans prefer a weak state government over a stronger system; the national government is treated with even more disdain and suspicion.

Texans have a natural distrust of President Obama's favorite 2008 campaign word—change. In the 1970s, for example, the state legislature appointed a special committee to re-evaluate and rewrite the current state constitution. This much amended document was, and still is, in need of complete revision. The committee's revised document was well written, eliminating many of the out-of-date provisions that no longer applied to state government, but despite a hard-sell effort on the part of the state legislators, voters turned down the revised document by a margin of three to one. The general sentiment was if the current constitution has been in use for over one hundred years, why change it? This reluctance to change hampers the development of much-needed innovative public policy alternatives.

Mention tax increases to the average Texan and he/she will "go ballistic." Pari-mutual betting and the lottery passed with flying colors when voters were threatened with the alternative—a state income tax. Texans are no different from other American citizens who seem to want more services from the government while paying less to the government that provides those services. This aversion to taxes has a negative impact on the public policy process; improperly funded programs are only marginally successful and usually fail to deliver adequate services. Every two years the state legislature is faced with the task of funding existing and new programs without initiating additional tax programs to raise revenue. Also, Texans prefer regressive general sales and excise taxes to progressive tax programs.

Social legislation, particularly programs for low-income groups, is not enthusiastically supported by the majority of Texans. "Sympathy for the down-trodden isn't a part of our history; within Texas, people have had to fend for themselves under harsh circumstances, and there has not been much dissatisfaction with the results."[67] Although the Texas Legislature boasts about the percentage of the state budget they allocate for social programs, Texas ranks in the lowest percentile among her sister states in the amount of money actually spent. There are many low-income people in Texas who need financial assistance but never see any benefits from the state's social service programs. The cries of the poor sometimes fall onto deaf ears.

Texas has low voter turnout in every election, particularly constitutional amendment referendum elections. The highest levels of low voter turnout are found among minority populations and low-income groups. Despite mass voter registration drives, the actual voter turnout on election day is somewhat higher in presidential and gubernatorial races but dismal in referendum, city and county elections. Low voter turnout feeds into the hands of those who want to uphold the status quo. Discouraging a mass voter turnout defeats change every time.

Conclusions

Texas is not the only state faced with low voter turnout. In the 2008 presidential election, nationally there were 225,499,000 individuals of voting age but only 64.9 percent of them registered to vote and only 58.2 percent of those registered voters actually voted. The numbers for Texas were lower than national figures with 58.5 percent of eligible voters registering to vote but only 48.8 actually casting a ballot.[68] In the 2012 presidential election, 16,062,000 Texans were eligible to vote but only 10,749,000 or 57.7 percent actually registered to vote. On election day, only 8,643,000 registered Texans actually voted. Basically, 46.4 percent of registered voters made the all-important decisions of who was going to represent Texas at both the state and national level for the 53.6 percent of Texans who were eligible to vote but opted not to participate.[69] The VAP for the 2016 presidential election was 245,502,000; but only 64.2 percent of these individuals registered to vote and only 56.0 percent of those registered actually voted.[70] Only the presidential elections held in 1952 (Eisenhower), 1956 (Eisenhower), 1960 (Kennedy), 1964 (Johnson) and 1968 (Nixon) had nationwide voter turnout above 60 percent of the voting age population. Since 1932, all of the other presidential races had voter turnout below 60 percent.[71]

Studies point to several factors behind low voter turnout in all levels of election activity. First, the election process in the United States is a long drawn out process. It takes over two years for a presidential candidate to plow through and actually survive all of the presidential primaries, win the official nomination at a national convention, and then hit the road running in August for the general election in November. United States congresspersons are constantly running for re-election. As soon are they are officially sworn-in to office for the current congressional session they must begin to focus their energies on actually legislating while at the same time campaigning for their next term of office. Critics claim that the United States exhausts both its candidates and its voters. In Britain, the campaign period lasts only a few weeks, not years. Perhaps the critics have a point. If the election cycle in the United States was compressed into just six months, would not the attention span of the voter be more in tune throughout the entire campaign effort up to election day?

Second, the negativity of the campaign actually turns voters away from the polls. Elections have always had the usual underhanded accusations levied by one candidate against his/her opponent. Today's voters on the whole are more intelligent and focused more on issues than personal barbs and insults hurled by one camp against the other. Perhaps voter turnout would have been higher if candidates actually discussed the state's problems and what their plans of action were to address those issues. The congressional races were laden with negative television commercials that focused more on the personal life of their opponents than, once again, on the issues. Poll after poll indicates that the American voter is fed up with the negativity. Negativity on the television set translates to voters staying home on election day.

Perhaps the most glaring observation is the timing of the election. Before early voting, the majority of the voters had to cast their ballots on a Tuesday, a work day. Many workers across the nation simply do not vote because their precinct is at least an hour's drive from their work site. Although federal law protects workers from being fired or disciplined for taking longer than their usual thirty minute or one hour lunch period to vote on election day, many are fearful that they will lose their job if they attempt to vote. Waiting until after work to vote is problematic since the polls close at seven. In the majority of other nations, elections are held on weekends with extended voting hours to accommodate workers.

Obviously, low voter turnout erodes the very principles of participatory democracy. This nation was founded on the ideals of majority rule/minority rights, not the other way around. The election process is a viable one. Candidates run for public office. They articulate their issues and demonstrate why they are the better candidate for public office over their opponents. In return, voters go to the polls and render their decisions. In democratic governments, elections are the ultimate tool of accountability. If a candidate is doing their job, then the voters should allow them to continue to govern. If not, voters should legally and peacefully remove them from office. The blame for low voter turnout in Texas and across the nation is shared between the political parties, the candidates, the media sources, and, of course, the voter.

Chapter Notes

[1]Charles A. Beard, *The Enduring Federalist*, 2nd ed., (New York, New York: Frederick Ungar Publishing Co., 1964), 163.

[2]Dede W. Casad, *My Fellow Texans: Governors of Texas in the 20th Century*, (Austin, Texas: Eakin Press, 1995), 48.

[3]Joe B. Frantz, *Texas: A History*, 2nd ed., (New York, New York: Norton, 1984), 187.

[4]John McCormick, "A South Texas Tradition," *San Antonio Express-News*, (Sunday, April 4, 2004), 16A.

[5]Ibid.

[6]Peggy Fikac, "Abbott Held All the Cards in Gov Race," *San Antonio Express-News*, (Wednesday, November 5, 2014), A1 and A14.

[7]*Texas Almanac: 2010-2011*, (Denton, Texas: Texas State Historical Association, 2010), 429.

[8]Texas Almanac: 2014-2015, (Denton, Texas: Texas State Historical Association, 2014), 416.

[9]ProQuest LLC, ProQuest Statistical Abstract of the United States: 2019, 7th ed., (Bethesda, Maryland, 2018), Table 439, 275.

[10]Texas Almanac: 2018-2019, (Denton, Texas: Texas State Historical Association, 2018), 501.

[11]Whitley, David, "Turnout and Voter Registration Figures (1970-Current), www.sos.state.tx.us/elections/historical

[12]Ibid.

[13]George Klosko, *History of Political Theory: An Introduction*, Vol. 2: Modern Political Theory, (New York, New York: Thomson, 1995), 108.

[14]Jack C. Plano and Milton Greenberg, *The American Political Dictionary*, 10th ed., (Orlando, Florida: Harcourt, Brace College Publishers, 1997), 93.

[15]*The HarperCollins Dictionary of American Government and Politics*, Jay M. Shafritz, ed., (New York, New York: HarperCollins Publishers, 1992), 198.

[16]Ibid., 72.

[17]Ibid., 464.

[18]Plano and Greenberg, 93.

[19]Ibid., 65.

[20]R. G. Ratcliff, "It's Down to Perry, White," *San Antonio Express-News*, (March 3, 2010), 1A.

[21]http://www.texastribune.org

22. https://apps.texastrubine/org/elections/2018/primary

[23]*The HarperCollins Dictionary of American Government and Politics*, 200.

[24]Walter Dean Burnham, *Critical Elections and the Mainsprings of American Politics*, (New York, New York: W. W. Norton and Company, Inc., 1970), 10.

[25]*The HarperCollins Dictionary of American Government and Politics*, 198.

[26]Ibid., 198.

[27]Plano and Greenberg, 100.

[28]Ibid., 101.

[29]Ibid., 59.

[30]*The HarperCollins Dictionary of American Government and Politics*, 50.

[31]www.ncls.org/helpamericavoteact, 1-3.

[32]Ibid.

33. http://www.huffingtonpost.com/entry/texas-voter-id-law-struck-down

[34]Guillermo Contreras, "Voter ID Law Stays in Place," *San Antonio Express-News*, (Sunday, October 26, 2014) A1 and A6)

[35]Liam Stack, "Texas Secretary of State Questions Citizenship of 95,000 Registered Voters", https://www.msn.com

[36]Ibid.

[37]https://votesmart.org/candidate/campaign-finance

[38]Ibid.

[39]https://www.fed.gov

[40]https://www.votesmart.org/candidate/campaign-finance

[41]https://www.opensecrets.org

[42]Ibid.

[43]Plano and Greenberg, 71.

[44]Ibid., 69.

[45]Ibid., 122.

[46]Ibid., 123.

[47]Texas Almanac: 2018-2019, 501.

[48]Gary Martin, "FEC Orders Rodriguez to Refund $89,000," *San Antonio Express-News*, (Friday, May 15, 2009), 7B.

[49]Ibid.

[50]Joe Holley, "White Asks If Grant Was Really A Kickback," *San Antonio Express-News*, (Friday, May 21, 2010), 5B.

[51]Plano and Greenberg, 66.

[52]Mike Ward, "He Is Fiercely Independent," *San Antonio Express-News*, (Sunday, October 26, 2014), A1 and A 20.

[53]Fikac, "Abbott Held All The Cards In Gov Race", 1A.

[54]"The Constitution of the Republic of Texas: March 17, 1836," *Documents of Texas History*, Ernest Wallace, David M. Vigness and George B. Ward, eds., 2nd ed., (Austin, Texas: State House Press, 1994), 104.

[55]"George Fitzhugh Reveals Southern White Fears of the Negro [African-American] Vote, 1867," *Major Problems in the History of the American South*, Vol. 1, The Old South, Paul D. Escott, David R. Goldfield, Sally G. McMillen and Elizabeth Hayes Turner, 2nd ed., (New York, New York: Houghton Mifflin, 1999), 404-405.

[56]Henry J. Abraham and Barbara A. Perry, *Freedom and the Court: Civil Rights and Liberties in the United States*, 8th ed., (Lawrence, Kansas: University of Kansas Press, 2003), 420.

[57]Billy Hobby, "High Time to Eliminate the Poll Tax," *San Antonio Express-News*, (Sunday, June 3, 2007), 5H.

[58]Bruce J. Schulman, *Lyndon B. Johnson and American Liberalism: A Brief Biography with Documents*, 2nd ed., (Boston, Massachusetts: Bedford/St Martins, 2007), 216-217.

[59]Texas Almanac: 2018-2019,427.

[60]Gary Scharrer, "Population Shift Could Alter Politics in Texas," *San Antonio Express-News*, (Sunday, May 16, 2010), 15A.

[61]Ibid.

[62]Gabriel A. Almond and G. Bingham Powell, Jr., *Comparative Politics: A Developmental Approach*, 1st ed., (Boston, Massachusetts: Little, Brown, 1966), 50.

[63]Ibid., 9.

[64]Ibid., 50.

[65]Lucian Pye, "Introduction: Political Culture and Political Development," *Political Culture and Political Development*, Lucian Pye and Sidney Verba, eds., (New Jersey: Princeton University Press, 1965), 7.

[66]Randall W. Bland, Alfred B. Sullivan, Robert E. Biles, Charles P. Elliott, Jr., and Beryle E. Pettus, *Texas Government Today*, 5th ed., (California: Brooks/Cole, 1992), 18.

[67]Nicholas Lemann, "Power and Wealth," *Texas Myths*, Robert O'Connor, ed., (College Station, Texas: Texas A & M University Press, 1986), 163.

[68]*U.S. Census Bureau, Statistical Abstract of the United States: 2010*, 129th ed., (Washington, D.C.: 2009), Table 407, 255.

[69]http://www.census.gov

[70]ProQuest Statistical Abstract of the United States: 2019, Table 439, 275.

[71]Ibid., Table 408, 255.

PART II

THE FOUNDATIONS OF GOVERNMENT

Chapter 5

Intergovernmental
Relationships

Capitol of Austin, Texas c. 1909

I proceed to inquire whether the federal government or the State governments will have the advantage with regard to the predilection and support of the people. Notwithstanding the different modes in which they are appointed, we must consider both of them as substantially dependent on the great body of the citizens of the United States. . . . The federal and State governments are in fact but different agents and trustees of the people, constituted with different powers, and designed for different purposes.[1] James Madison

On paper, the concept of federalism places the national government in the superior role over the state governments and, of course, the people. Article VI of the United States Constitution, commonly known as the **Supremacy Clause,** "makes very clear the subordinate relationship of the states to the national government: 'This constitution, and the laws of the United States which shall be made in pursuance thereof; . . . shall be the supreme law of the land; and the judges in every state shall be bound thereby . . ."[2] In practice, however, the relationship between the various states and the national government has never been a solid one. From day one, the relationship has been at best, very fragile with periods of close cooperation followed by episodes of clashes pitting one against the other in a struggle for control and power. In the middle of the controversy are the American people who as a whole, fearing the intrusion of the "big brother" muscle of the national government while at the same time, demanding federal assistance when a national crisis occurs or when they feel that their individual state governments are incapable of meeting their needs. In the aftermath of the terrorist attacks on the World Trade Center on September 11, 2001, Americans turned to their national government and not to their individual state governments for guidance and protection from future attacks. When Hurricanes Katrina and Rita ganged up and destroyed the Gulf Coast and New Orleans in 2005, coastal residents relied on the belief that when all else failed, the federal government would step in and provide the relief and assistance their local and state governments simply were unable to provide.

Immediately after President Obama delivered his first State of the Union address in 2009, the Republican Party's response to the speech was delivered by Louisiana's Governor Bobby Jindal. He berated President Obama's stimulus package of federal funds for state and local communities as a means of addressing the slumping economy by using federal dollars to put the unemployed back to work. Jindal saw it as just another ploy of the federal government to exercise its big muscle over the American people. He told the American audience that evening that "there has never been a challenge that the American people, with as little interference as possible by the federal government, cannot handle."[3] As a presidential candidate, then Governor George W. Bush expressed the same concerns about the intrusiveness of the federal government into state matters as did Presidents Ronald Reagan, Jimmy Carter and Bill Clinton, all former governors.

What a difference a few months make! In April, 2010, an off-shore oil rig owned by British Petroleum (BP) exploded and the deep-water well broke, releasing billions of barrels of crude oil into the Gulf of Mexico off the coast of Louisiana. How quickly Governor Jindal was to blame the federal government for what he called a slow response. Before a barrage of flashing cameras, "Jindal said the administration [Obama] has not provided enough equipment—including booms, skimmers, vacuums and barges—and that it stood in the way of his proposal to erect artificial barrier islands."[4] And, of course, it was a somber President Bush who apologized to the people of New Orleans and the Gulf Coast region for the federal government's inept response to the devastation caused by Katrina. Even before the winds and rain bands of both Rita and Katrina broke apart, it was both Governors Blanco of Louisiana and Perry of Texas who rushed to have the federal government declare areas of their states as disaster zones so federal monies would be available for disaster relief. Should the federal government have the power to force state governments to follow its dictates? Is this the relationship the Framers envisioned for the national and state governments in their collective quest to promote the general welfare of the American people? Just who is in charge, the states or the federal government? Should the federal government stand by allowing the states to provide the first response to an internal crisis and serve only as a backup plan?

The above situations are prime examples of a very fragile relationship between the states and the national government, a relationship we commonly refer to as **federalism**. The relationship has never been clearly defined. Not even the collective wisdom of the Framers could clearly delineate under all conceivable circumstances what belonged to the national government or to the states.

In *Federalist Paper, No. 45*, James Madison attempts to clarify the confusion by stating that "the powers delegated by the proposed Constitution to the federal government are few and defined. Those which are to remain in the State governments are numerous and indefinite. The former will be exercised principally on external objects, as war, peace, negotiation, and foreign commerce; with which last the power of taxation will, for the most part, be connected. The powers reserved to the several States will extend to all objects which, in the ordinary course of affairs; concern the lives, liberties, and properties of the people, and the internal order, improvement and prosperity of the State."[5] Basically, Madison envisioned a national government focused more on external affairs while state governments would manage the regional or internal needs of the nation. However, his clearly drawn lines of responsibility have become extremely intertwined and almost impossible to separate. This chapter explores and analyzes the concept of federalism and its impact upon the state of Texas. For over two hundred years, lawmakers at all levels of government have vacillated over whether the federal government should have an active role in the internal affairs of this nation.

The topic of intergovernmental relationships extends beyond a mere theoretical discourse. Beginning with the New Deal legislation of Franklin Roosevelt's administration, the national government has given billions of dollars to the states to fund everything from welfare to highways. To correct a slumping economy, President Obama allocated billions of federal dollars to state and local governments to "stimulate" the economy into high gear. Whether it be Roosevelt's New Deal or Obama's stimulus package, states have become very dependent upon receiving federal money.

Types of Intergovernmental Relationships

The interrelationship between national governments and their states or sub-governmental units usually conforms to either a unitary or confederation relationship. In both systems, one level of government has complete authority over the other. In the unitary system, the national government holds complete governing authority and power over the sub-governmental units. The **unitary system** is "one in which principal power within the political system lies at the level of a national or central government rather than at the level of some smaller unit, such as a state or province."[6] Created exclusively by the national government, the states and other sub-governmental units are severely weak in authority, serving as administrative agents to the national government. Sub-governmental units can be changed or eliminated by the national government. Power and governing authority flows from top to bottom. More than 90 percent of all modern nation-states use the unitary arrangement. In Texas, the relationship between state and county governments follows the unitary format. The Texas Constitution of 1876 specifically denies counties the right to pass ordinances. Subsequent attempts to pass legislation giving counties ordinance making authority have failed. Consequently, county governments remain basically powerless because, with few exceptions, they cannot act independently of the state legislature. The advantages of the unitary system are uniformity of public policy enforcement and centralized governing power. The primary disadvantage to this system is that sub-governmental units are so weak they cannot adequately address or respond to immediate emergencies and regional demands.

Power flows from bottom to top under a confederation system of government. A **confederation** is "a loose collection of states in which principal power lies at the level of the individual states rather than at the level of the central or national government."[7] Created by its sub-governmental units, the national government has only those governing powers given to it by the individual units. The national government has very narrowly defined governing authority and functions, and must act indirectly through the states to reach the citizens. The individual sub-governmental units decide whether a national law can be enforced upon citizens living in their states. The national government usually does not have the power to tax and may only request funding from the individual states. The national government usually has the power to declare war but does not have control over a national army or navy. Once again, the individual states have the option whether to commit their military in support of the national government. The relationship is so loose and delicate that a state or sub-governmental unit may at any time sever its association with the confederacy. And, the national government lacks the authority and the military power to force that state to remain a member of the confederacy. The United Nations (UN) follows a confederative format. As evidenced by several international crises, political directives issued by the UN are weakened by the inability of a central authority to compel compliance, cooperation, and obedience from member nations. The newly formed Soviet Republics are loosely joined in a confederative system. The president of Russia serves as both president of the individual state of Russia and the entire Confederation of Soviet Republics.

The federal system takes the best of the unitary and confederative forms by creating a hybrid system whereby governing authority and power flows up and down at the same time. **Federalism** is "a form of governmental structure in which power is divided between a central government and lower-level governments."[8] It is a system of shared governance. All sub-governmental units have the authority to pass legislative acts and enforce them upon the citizenry. The primary features of the federal system are:

(1) the central government is stronger than its member states in regard to the size of its budget and the scope of its jurisdiction; (2) national law is supreme; (3) the central government acts directly upon individuals in such matters as taxation and raising an army . . . and (4) states may not withdraw from the union.[9]

The United States uses the federal system. The main advantage to federalism is every level of government, whether it be a school district, water district or state government, has the legitimate authority to actually govern the people within their individual jurisdictions. The Framers opted for this form of government since "a federal system offered unity without uniformity. By reserving to the states considerable power, it lessened the likelihood of centralized tyranny."[10] Having lived under the thumb of the British government, the Framers definitely did not want to create a national government that could possibly become more authoritarian than the one they revolted against. However, a major weakness of this system is the failure to clearly delineate the powers and authority assigned to each governing unit. As evidence in the United States, "the distribution of power between the national and state governments has never been fixed. There has been a continual reshuffling of power, followed by a considerable resistance when one level is forced by legislative or judicial action to give up power."[11]

Why A Federal System?

After winning their independence from Britain, the former colonies opted for a confederation form of government as detailed in the **Articles of Confederation**. The newly formed states wanted to keep their individual autonomy by creating a very weak national government. The National Congress was comprised of representatives from each state. Collectively, each state had one vote in the Congress regardless of the number of delegates from each state. Once an act passed the National Congress, nine of the thirteen state legislative bodies had to approve it before it could be implemented in any state. The National Congress was empowered to declare war, conduct foreign policy and make treaties, but could not levy and collect taxes or regulate trade and commerce. The ineffectiveness of the confederation system became evident through the counter-productive actions of the individual states, and the inability of the national government to provide effective leadership. The states argued among themselves over everything from boundary lines to tariffs. Some states negotiated separate treaties with foreign governments to the detriment of their sister states. Several states issued their own currency and toll fees. The confederation system divided rather than united the American people. In *Federalist Paper, No. 5*, John Jay wrote:

Instead of their being "joined in affection" and free from all apprehension of different "interests," envy and jealously would soon extinguish confidence and affection, and the partial interests of each confederacy [state], instead of the general interests of all Americans, would be the only objects of their policy and pursuits. Hence, like most other bordering nations, they would always be either involved in disputes and war, or live in constant apprehension of them. . . .They who well consider the history of similar divisions and confederacies will find abundant reason to apprehend that those in contemplation would in no sense be neighbors than as they would be borderers; that they would neither love nor trust one another; but on the contrary would be a prey to discord, jealousy, and mutual injuries; in short, that they would place us exactly in the situations in which some nations doubtless wish to see us, viz., *formidable only to each other.*[12]

The economic viability and security of the nation was highly questionable as the leaders of this nation feared internal chaos and potential invasions from foreign powers, particularly Great Britain.

In *Federalist Paper, No. 41*, James Madison expressed the need for a stronger national government that would provide:

1. Security against foreign danger; 2. Regulation of the intercourse with foreign nations; 3. Maintenance among the States; 4. Certain miscellaneous objects of general utility; 5. Restraint of the States from certain injurious acts; 6. Provisions for giving due efficacy to all these powers.[13]

The Framers joined Madison's quest to create a stronger national government that would unite rather than divide; that would lead rather than be led; and that would be a formidable opponent for any potential invader. They believed that "this country and this people seem to have been made for each other, and it appears as if it was the design of Providence, that an inheritance so proper and convenient for a band of brethren, united to each other by the strongest times, should never split into a number of unsocial, jealous, and alien sovereignties. . . . To all general purposes we have uniformly been one people; each individual citizen everywhere enjoying the same national rights, privileges, and protection. As a nation we have vanquished our common enemies; as a nation we have formed alliances, and made treaties, and entered into various compacts and conventions with foreign states."[14] The problem confronting them was a form of government that was eroding the unity created by the American Revolution. The solution was to change that government from a confederation system that divided people, to a federal system that would hopefully, reunite people.

Constitutionally Mandated Intergovernmental Relationships

Through the Constitution, the Framers dismantled a confederation government and replaced it with a federal system. Adopted in 1789, the Constitution "created a national government with sovereign powers of its own—powers that once belonged exclusively to state governments. The proud sovereignty of the states was radically undermined; the "state's rights" which remained, although robust in the Founding Period, bore scant resemblance to the autonomy enjoyed by the states under the Articles."[15] The Framers created a government based on separation of powers, checks and balances, and a delicate intergovernmental relationship between the national government and the states.

> The constitutional place of the states in the federal system is determined by four elements: the provisions in the federal and state constitutions that either limit or guarantee the powers of the states vis-à-vis the federal government; the provisions in the federal constitution that give the states a role in the composition of the national government; the subsequent interpretations of both sets of provisions by the courts (particularly the United States Supreme Court); and the unwritten constitutional traditions that evolved informally and only later become formally recognized through the first three, directly or indirectly.[16]

The Framers actually created two distinct levels of federalism. The relationship and lines of authority between the national government and the various state governments were cemented by vertical federalism. Horizontal federalism eased the tensions between the various states by constitutionally mandating a mutually beneficial harmonious relationship.

Vertical federalism is the distribution of power flowing from the national government to the states and from the states to the national government. Vertical intergovernmental relations "take place when the national government interacts with the states or localities or when the states interact with localities."[17] Vertical federalism ushered in the concept of shared governance whereby all levels of government have some governing authority. "In the American federal system, sharing of functions by all planes of government is and always has been the norm."[18] The concept of vertical federalism is detailed in the Constitution through enumerated, implied, concurrent and reserved power distributions between the national government and the states.

Enumerated powers are those delegations of authority that are *expressly* written and granted to the national government. The Framers took from the states those specific powers that they felt were detrimental to the political and economic stability of the nation and reallocated them to the national government. In **Article I**, the United States Congress was granted the exclusive power to levy and collect taxes for the national government, borrow money, regulate interstate commerce, coin money, raise an army, establish post offices, establish naturalization laws, issue patents and copyrights, and declare war. These enumerated powers enable the national government to exercise considerable control over all levels of government. For example, the enumerated power to regulate interstate commerce has been used quite frequently to force the states, businesses, and citizens to obey congressional enactments. The United States Supreme Court, beginning with its ruling in **Gibbons v Ogden** (1824), has liberally interpreted the jurisdiction of the national government's control over interstate commerce as anything that has crossed or will eventually cross a state boundary line. Both the United States Supreme Court and Congress have used their control over interstate commerce to force state compliance of congressional acts involving everything from civil rights, desegregation, the environment, welfare, work safety regulations, fair wage treatment, to highway speed limits, and so on.

The Framers realized that they could not enumerate all the powers the national government would need to adjust to changing circumstances. Consequently, they brilliantly added to **Article I Section 8** to the United States Constitution stating that Congress can "make all Laws which shall be necessary and proper for carrying into execution the foregoing powers vested by this Constitution in the government of the United States, or in any department or officer thereof." This is the **implied powers** doctrine, commonly referred to as the **necessary and proper clause** or the **elastic clause**. The implied powers doctrine has given considerable leverage for the national government to pass legislative acts addressing concerns that should be the privy of state governments. Once again, the United States Supreme Court has historically strengthened the national government's use of implied powers. The implied powers doctrine provides the national government with the muscle to be a major player in the development of all public policy initiated at any level of government, whether it be at the state or local level.

Those opposed to the ratification of the Constitution, the **Anti-Federalists**, were particularly skeptical of the Framers' motives behind the necessary and proper clause. They feared this clause in combination with the Supremacy Clause (Article VI) gave too much power to the national government:

> How far the clause in the 8th section of the 1st article may operate to do away all idea of confederated states, and to effect an entire consolidation of the whole into one general government, it is impossible to say . . . But what is meant is, that the legislature of the United States are vested with the great and uncontroulable [uncontrollable] powers, of laying and collecting taxes, duties, imposts, and excises; of regulating trade, raising and supporting armies, organizing, arming, and disciplining the militia, instituting courts, and other general powers. And are by this clause invested with the power of making all laws *proper and necessary*, for carrying all these into execution; and they may so exercise this power as entirely to annihilate all state governments, and reduce this country to one single government. And if they may do it, it is pretty certain they will; for it will be found that the power retained by the individual states, small as it is, will be a clog upon the wheels of government of the United States; the latter therefore will be naturally inclined to remove it out of the way. Besides, it is a truth confirmed by the unerring experience of ages, that every man, every body of men, invested with power, are ever disposed to increase it, and to acquire a superiority

over every thing that stands in their way. This disposition, which is implanted in human nature, will operate in the federal legislature to lessen and ultimately to subvert the state authority, and having such advantages, will most certainly succeed, if the federal government succeeds at all. It must be very evident then, that what this constitution wants of being a completed consolidation of the several parts of the union into one complete government, possessed of perfect legislative, judicial, and executive powers, to all intents and purposes, it will necessarily acquire in its exercise and operation.[19]

Their fears were unjustified. The national government has never used its power to expel a state from the union!

Several of the enumerated powers are held **concurrently** by both national and all levels of government below it. For example, the power to levy and collect taxes is extended to all governing authorities. However, each level of government taxes a different commodity and/or taxes only a specified portion of the taxed item such as state and federal income taxes. Traditionally, the national government taxes individual and corporate incomes, while the Texas Legislature relies heavily upon sales and energy taxes, and regressive tax programs. Counties are funded through property taxes, while urban centers concurrently tax property and charge an added percentage to the state sales tax rate. Without the concurrent power to tax, sub-governmental units would not have enough revenue to provide services to its citizens; governments, regardless of the level, cannot operate without money. The national and state governments concurrently have the powers to establish judicial courts, make and enforce laws, exercise eminent domain, and with the exception of a few states, borrow money. (The Texas Constitution does prohibit the state government from borrowing money.)

Section 9, of **Article I** of the United States Constitution places restrictions on both state and national governments. The **Writ of Habeas Corpus** cannot be suspended except in cases of rebellion and insurrection. Bills of attainder, ex post facto laws, titles of nobility, and taxes on exports are prohibited. **Section 10** of **Article I** places restrictions on state governments: states are prohibited from entering into treaties, granting Letters of Marque, coining money, levying taxes on imports without congressional approval, maintaining an army or navy, forming interstate compacts without congressional approval, and declaring war.

The constitutional grant of power to the states is embodied in the **Tenth Amendment**: "the powers delegated to the United States by the Constitution, nor prohibited by it to the States, are reserved to the States, respectively, or to the People." Often called the reserved powers clause, the Tenth Amendment does not clearly define which powers are reserved to the states. However, state powers traditionally fall into four board general areas: **policing authority** including safety, health and morals; **taxing authority** to raise needed revenues; **propriety powers** over public lands used for public conveniences such as parks and airports; and eminent domain, a power shared by all levels of government to take private lands for a justifiable price for public use.

Article VI of the United States Constitution is an absolutely essential to the concept of vertical federalism. It clearly states that "this Constitution and the laws of the United States which shall be made in Pursuance thereof; and all Treaties made, or shall be made, under the Authority of the land; and the Judges in every State shall be bound thereby, any Thing in the Constitution or Law of any States to the Contrary not withstanding." Commonly known as the **Supremacy Clause**, Article VI makes vertical federalism work by declaring the Constitution as the supreme law of the land. This one article cements the relationship between the states and the national government, and mandates that all levels of government comply with the spirit and meaning of the Constitution.

Horizontal federalism or interstate relations are "those that occur between equals—that is, when states deal with other states or cities deal with other cities."[20] The Framers were concerned about the inability of the states to cooperate with each other. The Articles of Confederation had encouraged rivalry rather than cooperation. To ensure that the states would work with each other, the Framers inserted **Article IV** or the **Full Faith and Credit Clause** into the Constitution. Section 1 of Article IV states "full faith and credit shall be given in each State to the public Acts, Records and Judicial Proceedings of every other state." All legal documents including property deeds, marriage licenses, divorce records, and birth and death certificates, are legal in all of the states regardless of the state originating the documents. Article IV also requires states to cooperate with each other in returning fugitives from justice. According to Section 2, "the Citizen of each State shall be entitled to all the Privileges and Immunities of Citizens of the Several States." This provision clearly places the individual as a citizen of his/her country above residency in a state. The citizen is guaranteed freedom of movement and residency in any state under the jurisdiction of the United States government. Individual rights and privileges were strengthened with the addition

of the **Fourteenth Amendment**'s guarantees of equal protection and due process. The states do have limited authority to treat newcomers differently. States are not required to honor professional and occupational licenses issued by other states. For example, a licensed attorney in New York could not practice law in Texas until he/she had successfully passed the Texas Bar Exam. The same standards apply to teachers, hairdressers, plumbers, and so on. Public colleges and universities can charge a higher out-of-state tuition fee to those students who do not meet state residency requirements. Most states use a 30-day residency requirement for voting privileges.

The Framers were also appalled by the states arguing with each other over state boundary lines and ownership of lands located in the Northwest Territories. **Article III** of the United States Constitution gives original jurisdiction to the federal courts in all cases involving "controversies between two or more States; between a State and Citizens of another State; between Citizens of different States; between Citizens of the same State claiming lands under Grants of different States . . ." Obviously, the Framers had little faith that the individual states could successfully settle disputes between each other!

Federalism and the United States Supreme Court

The **Judiciary Act** of 1789 specifically grants the right of judicial review to the federal court system. Section 25 empowers the United States Supreme Court to render:

a final judgment or decree in any suit, in the highest court of law or equity of a state in which a decision in the suit could be had, where is drawn in question the validity of a treaty or statute of, or an authority exercised under, the United States, and the decision is against their validity; or where is drawn in question the validity of a statute of, or an authority exercised under, any State, on the ground of their being repugnant to the constitution, treaties, or laws of the United States, and the decision is in favour of such their validity, or where is drawn in question the construction of any clause of the constitution, or of a treaty, or statute of, or commission held under, the United States, and the decision is against the title, right privilege, or exemption, specially set up or claimed by either party, under such clause of said Constitution, treaty, statute, or commission, may be re-examined, and **reversed** or **affirmed** in the Supreme Court of the United States, in the same manner and under the same regulations, and the writ shall have the same effect as if the judgment or decree complained of had been rendered or passed in a circuit court, and the proceedings upon the reversal shall also be the same, except the Supreme Court, instead of remanding the cause for a final decision as before provided, may, at their discretion, if the cause shall have been once remanded before, proceed to a final decision of the same, and award execution. **But no other error shall be assigned or regarded as a ground of reversal in any such as aforesaid**, than such as appears on the face of the record, and immediately respects the before-mentioned questions of validity or construction of said constitution, treaties, statutes, commissions, or authorities in dispute . . . [21] (Emphasis added by author.)

All levels of government can pass laws; however, those legislative acts that do not conform with the spirit and meaning of the United States Constitution can be judged as unconstitutional acts by the federal courts with the Supreme Court serving as the **court of last resort**. In exercising this authority, the United States Supreme Court plays a crucial role in defining the relationships between the national and state governments under federalism.

In decisions immediately following the adoption of the Constitution, the United States Supreme Court advocated a strong national government or **nation-centered federalism**. In *McCullough v Maryland* (1819), the questions before the Court involved whether the national government could use its power of eminent domain over the state of Maryland to construct a branch of the National Bank as prescribed in the implementation of a national banking law; and whether the state of Maryland could levy a property tax on federal property. This case openly challenged Article I, Section 8, the necessary and proper clause. Chief Justice John Marshall's court strengthened the national government's power over the states through the implied powers doctrine by ruling that "after the most deliberate consideration, it is the unanimous and decided opinion of this court, that the act to incorporate the Bank of the United States is a law made in pursuance of the Constitution and is part of the supreme law of the land."[22] Furthermore, Marshall stressed the power of the national government over the states by noting that the Court's decision was based on the "conviction that the states have no power, by taxation or otherwise, to retard, impede, burden, or in any manner control, the operations of the constitutional laws enacted by Congress to carry into execution the powers vested in the general government. This is, we think, the unavoidable consequence of that supremacy which the Constitution has declared."[23]

In *Cohen v Virginia* (1821), Chief Justice John Marshall and the members of the United States Supreme Court artfully defended their right to review judicial decisions issued by state courts. The *Cohen* case involved the arrest and subsequent conviction of Cohen for illegally selling Washington, D.C., issued lottery tickets in Virginia. The Virginia state legislature had passed a law prohibiting the sale of lottery tickets within its state boundaries. Initially, the state court ruled against Cohen. Although the Supreme Court upheld the state's ruling, the *Cohen* decision opened the door for the Supreme Court to exercise authority to review the judgments issued by state courts. Marshall wrote:

> The American States, as well as the American people, have believed a close and firm Union to be essential to their liberty and to their happiness. They have been taught by experience, that this Union cannot exist without a government for the whole; and they have been taught by the same experience that this government would be a mere shadow, that must disappoint all their hopes, unless invested with large portions of that sovereignty, which belongs to independent States. Under the influence of this opinion, and thus instructed by experience, the American people, in the conventions of their respective States adopted the present Constitution. If it could be doubted, whether from its nature, it were not supreme in all cases where it is empowered to act, that doubt would be removed by the declaration, that "this constitution, and the laws of the United States, . . . shall be the supreme law of the land, and the judges in every State shall be bound thereby; anything in the constitution or laws of any State to the contract notwithstanding." This is the authoritative language of the American people; and . . . of the American States. It marks, with lines too strong to be mistaken, the characteristic distinction between the government of the Union, and those of the States. The general government, through limited as to its objects, is supreme with respect to those objects. This principle is part of the Constitution; and if there be any who deny its necessity, none can deny its authority.[24]

The questions of whether the states or the national government had the authority to control shipping on the Hudson River was addressed by the United States

Supreme Court in *Gibbons v Ogden* (1824). Once again, the Supreme Court dealt a blow to the states by favoring the national government. The Marshall Court ruled that "this power [regulation of commerce], like all others bested in Congress, is complete in itself, may be exercised to its upmost extent, and acknowledges no limitations other than are prescribed in the Constitution."[25] Chief Justice Marshall went to considerable lengths in defining actually how the Court was interpreting the term "interstate" commerce:

> The words are "congress shall have the power to regulate commerce with foreign nations, and among the several states, and with the Indian tribes." The subject to be regulated is commerce; and our constitution . . . one of enumeration, and not of definition, to ascertain the extent of the power, it becomes necessary to settle the meaning of the word . . . Commerce, undoubtedly, is traffic, but it [is] something more—it is intercourse. It describes the commercial intercourse between nations, and parts of nations, in all its branches, and is regulated by prescribing rules for carrying on that intercourse. . . . The power over commerce including navigation, was one of the primary objects for which the people of America adopted their government, and must have been contemplated in forming it. . . . The word used in the constitution, then, comprehends, and has been always understood to comprehend, navigation within its meaning; and a power to regulate navigation, is as expressly granted, as if that term had been added to the word "commerce." To what commerce does this power extend? The constitution informs us, to commerce "with foreign nations, and among the several states and with the Indian tribes." It has, we believe, been universally admitted, that these words comprehend every species of commercial intercourse between the United States and foreign nations . . . The subject to which the power is next applied, is to commerce "among the several states." The word "among" means intermingled with. . . Commerce among the states cannot stop the external boundary line of each state. . . . The grant of this power carries with it the whole subject, leaving nothing for the state to act upon.[26]

Basically, the Court's ruling granted the national government the authority to oversee all commercial activity that crosses any state boundary line, leaving the states with just the authority to control commerce within their individual boundary lines, commonly known as **intrastate commerce**.

Since 1789, the Supreme Court has vacillated over whether the national government should exert a strong and, oftentimes, intrusive role in state affairs. Initially taking a strong national government position, the Court shifted to a pro-state position in the early Nineteenth Century. However, the necessity of the federal government interceding into state affairs during the Great Depression compelled the Court to reverse its position once again by becoming a strong advocate of the national government from the 1930s to mid 1990s. "The expansion of the federal role has been greatest, for example, in matters involving individual rights, civil rights, voting rights, and legislative apportionment. It has not been as extensive in programmatic areas that affect state and local finances more directly, such as welfare and education."[27] In **Garcia v San Antonio Metropolitan Transit Authority** (1985) the Court ruled that the National Fair Labor Standards Act applied to all employees of state and local governments. In **South Carolina v Baker** (1988), the Court declared that Congress could tax the interest earned from an individual's savings accounts as well as state and local bonds.

An advocate of returning more power to the states, President Ronald Reagan ensured that his appointees to the Court supported his position. Consequently, "not since before the New Deal-era constitutional revolution in 1937 has the states received such protection in the U.S. Supreme Court from allegedly burdensome federal statutes."[28] A pro-state decision was rendered in **United States v Lopez** (1995) when the Court declared a state law banning the possession of guns near public schools unconstitutional. The Court backed the states in **Plintz v United States** (1997) by declaring the provision of the Brady Bill, requiring local law enforcement to conduct background checks before issuing handguns, as both an unfunded mandate and an unconstitutional intrusion upon the states. However, the Court did not eliminate the federal government's right to place limits on the states or to force laws upon the states and local governing bodies.

States Rights vs. National Power

In 1860 the battle lines were drawn between North and South over the national government's attempt to control the South's economic future by abolishing slavery. In the 1960s, Governor Ross Barnett of Mississippi defiantly faced his own state's national guard, which had been ordered by President Kennedy to protect James Meredith as he became the first African American admitted to the

University of Mississippi. In 1994, an angry group of Texas ranchers openly challenged the Environmental Protection Agency's (EPA) desire to protect the breeding grounds of the tiny Golden Warbler. In 2010, Governor Rick Perry openly criticized and sued the EPA over the implementation of new clean air standards that if enforced, would definitely put the majority of the state's cities into noncompliance, subjecting them to fines and placing higher and more expensive fuel admission standards onto all Texas's motorists and transportation-dependent businesses. Another lawsuit challenged several provisions of the Clear Air Act stating that "air quality is the primary responsibility of the states and local governments," while another section says each state "shall have the primary responsibility for assuring air quality within the entire geographic area comprising the state."[29] States along the shared border of Mexico have filed court challenges to President Trump's implementation of a national emergency as his means to evoke the federal government's powers of eminent domain to seize state-owned and private-held property to build a wall separating the United States from Mexico. Whether the argument centers on slavery, desegregation, a bird, or air pollution standards, the root of the argument is states' rights. It is a part of traditional Texan and southern cultures to view any intrusion by the federal government into the internal operations of their states as an obvious breech of states' rights. Just how far the federal government can exercise control over the states has been an ongoing debate since the adoption of the United States Constitution. Those who favor states' rights over national rights include Thomas Jefferson, John C. Calhoun, the United States Supreme Court from 1920-1937, Ronald Reagan, and Greg Abbott.

John C. Calhoun was the foremost advocate of states' rights. Former vice president and distinguished senator from South Carolina, Calhoun believed in the **compact theory** of government. In his *Discourse of the American Constitution*, Calhoun observed that the American government was "federal and not national because it is a government of a community of States, and not the government of a single State or nation."[30] Consequently, the Constitution was an intergovernmental treaty among sovereign states. "The sovereignty of the States, in the fullest sense of the term, is declared to be the essential principle of *the* Union; and it is not only asserted as an incontestable right, but also claimed as an absolute political necessity in order to protect the minority against the majority."[31] In turn, these sovereign states created a limited national government. States' rights advocates view the national government as an agent of the states, not the other way around. Powers not specifically given to the national government by the Constitution are exclusively reserved to the states.

States' rights advocates firmly believe that the national government should not use any of its enumerated and implied powers to interfere in state governance. Calhoun developed three actions that both the states and the American people could take to halt intrusions by the national government into state affairs. Calhoun positioned the states as middlemen or buffer zones between the national government and the people. The United States Congress could pass any law it wanted, including the abolition of slavery; however, each state's legislature had to approve any national congressional act before it could be enacted within their states. This concept of **interposition** places each state as the protector of its people by preventing the enforcement of unwanted or unnecessary national laws upon them. Calhoun believed that "the states have the right 'to interpose' when the Federal government is guilty of a usurpation, because, as there is no common judge over them, they, as the parties to the compact, have to determine for themselves whether it has been violated."[32] The concepts of **concurrent majority** and **nullification** went a step further. Calhoun advocated that national laws were binding only if a majority of the nation's citizens concurred with these enactments. Calhoun wrote that "the government of the concurrent majority . . . excludes the possibility of oppression by giving to each interest or portion, or order—where there are established classes— the means of protecting itself by its negative against the measures calculated to advance the peculiar interest of others at its expense."[33] For example, if the United States Congress wanted to abolish slavery, it could do so only with the approval of the majority of the American people. To protect those citizens living in frontier areas not under the protection of statehood, Calhoun believed that "each sectional majority or large interest that was not territorially based has the constitutional power to an absolute veto over any action of the federal government that, while representing the national majority, threatened the welfare of the minority."[34] Calhoun's argument will prove to be one of the justifications the southern states used to secede from the union in 1860. If the national government could not stop its intrusions into the affairs of the states, the states were left with little choice but to sever or nullify their contractual affiliation with the national government and form their own governing structure.

The question of whether a state could secede from the union was settled by the United States Supreme Court in its ruling in *Texas v White* (1869). The justices reinforced the philosophy of the Framers that a united strong central government was paramount over regional differences. The majority opinion of the Court echoes the sentiments of Alexander Hamilton, George Washington and James Madison:

> The Union of the States never was a purely artificial and arbitrary relation. It began among the Colonies and grew out of common origin, mutual sympathies, kindred principles, similar interests, and geographical relations. It was confirmed and strengthened by the necessities of war, and received definite form, character, and sanction, from the Articles of Confederation. By these the Union was solemnly declared to "be perpetual." And, when these Articles were found to be inadequate to the exigencies of the country, the Constitution was ordained "to form a more perfect union." But the perpetuity and indissolubility of the Union by no means implies the loss of distinct and individual existence, or of the right of self-government by the States. On the contrary, it may be not unreasonably said, that the preservation of the States, and the maintenance of their governments, are as much within the design and care of the Constitution, as the preservation of the Union and the maintenance of the National government. *The Constitution, in all of its provisions, looks to an indestructible Union, composed of indestructible States*.[35] (Emphasis added by author.)

States' rights arguments are essential to understanding intergovernmental relationships between Texas and Washington, D.C. Throughout the South, southern conservative Democrats and Republicans preach the same tune—a fear of national government intrusion into state affairs. National laws are historically viewed with suspicion, skepticism, and as just one more odious encroachment upon the states' ability to govern themselves.

The Changing Faces of Federalism

Whether state interests overshadow national interests or vice versa, the direction of federalism changes periodically. It does not, however, change in precise cycles where every fifty years, for example, the states are in the driver's seat only to see the national government turn the cycle to its side for fifty years, and so forth. "In conservative periods the roles of state governments have been enhanced, whereas in liberal or pro-government periods, the role of the national government has grown."[36] Perhaps the answer rests less with politics and changing cycles and more on the inaction of the states among themselves and with the national government. Far too often the might of the national government will supersede the right of the states to manage their own affairs when the states demonstrate their inability to handle their own problems or they simply ask for federal assistance. The United States Constitution gives the national government the task of promoting the general welfare of the country and its citizens. The national government is motivated to take the upper hand over the states, not in response to periodic cycles, but in response to particular problems and crises threatening the general welfare.

From 1787 to 1932, intergovernmental relationships were viewed as **dual federalism** "when autonomous national, subnational, and local governments all pursued their own interests independently.[37] Dual federalism is often called the **layered cake** approach to intergovernmental relationships. Each level of government represents a layer of a cake, with the national government as the top layer and subsequent layers belonging to sub-governmental units, ranging from the states to the lowest possible governing unit. The layers of the cake are separated and protected from interference from each other by thick layers of icing. The United States Supreme Court on rare occasions extended the role of the national government over the states but for only specific situations where the states could not address the issues on their own. For example, the need for a national banking system was evidenced by the individual states' inability to control the evolving banking industry within their states. Banks were operating without charters, charging inconsistent interest rates, and operating under unfair practices detrimental to the growth of business and industry. In *McCullough v Maryland* (1819), the Supreme Court upheld the national government's right to provide a national banking program. With few exceptions, the prevailing belief was that the national government would not intercede into the traditional role of the states. For example, an advocate of federally-sponsored social reforms, President Woodrow Wilson could not convince Washington or state governments to support his initiatives. Consequently, it was the states that were "left to take action regarding such problems as care of dependent children. Federal domestic programs in the late 1920s were so limited that state spending was double federal spending. States also were dominant over cities as policy makers, spending about three times as much money as local governments."[38]

The collapse of the Stock Market in 1929 and the subsequent Great Depression of the 1930s changed intergovernmental relationships from dual to cooperative federalism. The states were totally unprepared to handle Depression-era problems of unemployment, hunger, and homelessness faced by millions of Americans. **Cooperative federalism** is based on the sharing of responsibilities and joint financing of programs to address citizen needs. The New Deal programs of the Roosevelt administration openly cooperated with state and local governments to provide jobs, food, and economic development, in hopes of preventing another economic downturn of the magnitude of the Great Depression. Cooperative federalism is often called **marble cake federalism** since there is no clear-cut delineation of program development, financing, responsibilities, and accountability between national and state governments. Cooperative federalism resulted in billions of federal dollars allocated to state and local governments for infrastructure improvements, economic development, job creation, and social service programs. The era of cooperative federalism ended in 1964.

The cornerstone of Lyndon Johnson's presidency was the Great Society programs, designed to improve the quality of life for all through a series of federal programs. The Johnson era ushered in a new breed of federalism known as **creative federalism**. Particularly for social programs, creative federalism emphasized "relationships between Washington and many other independent centers of decision in state and local governments, in new public bodies, in universities, in professional organizations and in business. Creative federalism includes a deliberate policy of encouraging the growth of institutions that will be independent of and, in part, antagonistic to the federal government power. Almost every party of every new program transfers federal funds to some outside agency."[39] Johnson truly believed that it would take a multi-leveled highly talented think tank to address the nation's chronic social ills. While the social agenda called for cooperation, the 1960s also ushered in a series of legislative acts dealing with civil rights, voting rights, affirmative action, desegregation, open housing, equal employment and so on. The enforcement and implementation phases were legislatively given to the individual states.

Initially state governments, particularly in the South, were unwilling to actively enforce federal laws. Creative federalism offered the federal government the leverage and the incentives for states to implement these laws by cementing the flow of ample grant money to federal mandates including civil rights. To continue to receive money for low income housing, highways, education, and

so on, states had to enforce federal laws. Non-compliance would place their federal grant money into jeopardy. Creative federalism dealt another severe blow to the states. Under the program, any agency, city, or county government could apply and receive a federal grant without prior approval from the governor's office, and if awarded, the money went directly to the grant recipient, bypassing the governor's desk. "As a result, by 1980 about 30 percent of all federal aid bypassed state governments, compared to 8 percent in 1960."[40] Consequently state governments lost some of their control over their own sub-governmental units.

Former governor Ronald Reagan entered the White House with a firm resolve to reverse the direction of intergovernmental relationships. Reagan was particularly critical of the numerous federal mandates or requirements placed upon grant recipients, viewing them as intrusions upon state and local governments, and as a blatant violation of the Tenth Amendment to the United States Constitution. Reagan's fears were the same sentiments expressed by John C. Calhoun over a hundred years before. In a nationwide address, Reagan told his audience that "it is my intention to curb the size and influence of the Federal establishment and to demand recognition of the distinction between the powers granted to the Federal Government and those reserved to the states or to the people. All of us need to be reminded that the Federal Government did not create the states; the states created the Federal Government."[41] The goals of Reagan's **New Federalism** were "to make states' rights the effective policy of the land by reducing the role of the national government in state and local affairs, by slowing the flow of federal dollars to states and municipalities as part of a national strategy to discourage their dependency on the federal government, and by returning to state and local officers more control over how money should be spent."[42] Reagan told the governors that they would have more freedom in allocating federal funding. However, Reagan also saw New Federalism as a national debt reduction plan whereby the financial burden for needed service programs would be shifted from the federal purse to state pocketbooks.

The concept of New Federalism was actually launched during the Nixon administration. In a radio message delivered on Labor Day in 1972, President Nixon warned workers that "when Government tampers too much with the lives of individuals, when it unnecessarily butts into the free collective bargaining process, it cripples the private enterprise system on which the welfare of the worker depends."[43] Nixon consolidated numerous federal agencies charged with coordinating grant programs with state and local governments into ten regional councils. Federal regulations were simplified and streamlined to allow state and local governments more autonomy in the decision-making process. The Reagan administration went a step further by cutting federal funding to state and local governments. Reagan redirected federalism by securing permission from Congress to consolidate fifty-seven categorical grant programs into nine broad block grants. Another sixty categorical grants were eliminated in 1981.

The Reagan administration had a plan to force state governments to assume full financial and administrative responsibility for the two costliest federal programs—food stamps and Aid to Families with Dependent Children—and forty-one smaller programs. In return the federal government would assume control over the Medicaid program, the health-care provision for the poor. This creative swapping was stalled in Congress when the state governors complained about their lack of financial resources to fund these programs. Congressional actions fueled by the discontent of Democrats and minority groups led Reagan to abandon New Federalism by the start of his second term. Reagan did ease federal intrusion into state and local governments by issuing **Executive Order 12612,** which eliminated and/or relaxed several federal regulations dealing with service programs. Under Reagan, New Federalism was only marginally successful. Federal funds for state and local government programs were decreased considerably; however, the major federal budget reductions envisioned by Reagan did not materialize. The national debt grew in part to Reagan's increased spending on defense initiatives. Cuts in spending did not eliminate the need for the services. However, Reagan merely shifted the financial and administrative burden onto state governments. While Reagan boosted about how he was reducing the national deficit, "thirty-eight states increased taxes in 1983. Overall, the tax revenues of state governments rose by 14.8 percent from 1983 to 1984."[44] The promised reduction of federal mandates was short-lived as Congress passed legislation placing more regulations upon state and local governments.

The direction of federalism changed once again with the election of Bill Clinton to the White House. Serving as a governor during the Reagan presidency, Clinton knew the frustration of trying to solve poverty, crime, and unemployment without ample financial assistance from the federal government. The individual states simply did not have the resources to address these issues. He also realized that the federal government could not afford just to give states and local governing authorities a blank check. Consequently, his concept of **Constrained Empathetic Federalism** rested upon the creation of **empowerment zones** whereby non-federal resources are combined with modest federal-cash outlays to achieve a zone's targeted objectives. Clinton requested that Congress fund six urban and three rural zones. Initially, the federal government would fund the majority of the projects with the understanding that once a zone achieved increased economic development, the financial burden would shift to the empowerment zone, alleviating the federal government's commitment.

The pendulum changed once again when George W. Bush entered the White House with his intention of reintroducing Reagan's New Federalism. During the beginning of his presidency, Bush introduced the concept of **Pragmatic Federalism** by forming a special committee to evaluate which federal programs would fare better under state and local control. However, it is questionable whether pragmatic federalism ever made it out of the starting gate. Bush's "No Child Left Behind" program gave the federal government a primary role into public education policies and practices that have been traditionally reserved to the state and local communities. In response to the attacks on the World Trade Center, the Bush administration expanded the federal government's role in intelligence matters through the creation of a cabinet-level position called the **Department of Homeland Security**. The **Patriot Act** empowers federal authorities to conduct criminal investigations traditionally falling under the authority of state and local law enforcement agencies. The Obama administration did not coin a new term for his administration's approach to federalism. He did emphasize the need for the federal government to come to the assistance of the states when the nation's economy took a turn for the worse. His response to the economic crisis patterned the actions taken by the Roosevelt administration during the Great Depression. Obama used federal dollars to stimulate the nation's economy in hopes of jump starting economic recovery in state and local communities. Another package resembled Roosevelt's Works Progress Administration whereby federal dollars were allocated to state and city governments to address infrastructure needs while at the same time, putting the unemployed back to work.

Federal Grant Programs

Federal grant programs were designed to give federal money to state and local governments to fund programs and services for the general welfare of the American people. The grant concept ushered in a **Robin Hood approach** to distributing federal tax dollars collected from those citizens in upper income brackets and redistributing them to those in lower-income groups. This is the old Robin Hood principle of taking from the rich and giving to the poor.

The use of federal money was intended to encourage state and local governments to provide better services and to experiment with new approaches to solve old urban problems ranging from lack of affordable housing to replacement of out-dated sewer lines. The ample flow of federal dollars to resource-starved and hungry sub-governmental units allowed the federal government to force grant recipients to implement federal nondiscriminatory laws and regulations particularly related to the workforce. Grants were supposed to reinforce the partnership between the states and the national government: the federal government would provide the funding, overall regulations, program goals and objectives through congressional legislation; the states, cities, counties, and, in some cases, educational institutions and private agencies would administer the programs, deliver the services, and implement federal mandates.

However, federal grant programs have major drawbacks. Federal mandates and compliance requirements place a strain upon the limited resources of grant recipients. A National Governor's Conference held in the 1970s echoed the same complaints heard today:

- Lack of coordination among federal departments or agencies limits the effectiveness of programs in addressing problems they were designed to solve and increases the administrative burden on the states.
- The federal executive branch has exceeded its proper authority in some areas, encroaching on matters which are in the proper jurisdiction of the states.
- Federal regulations are prescriptive in methodology rather than oriented toward end results.
- Excess reporting and paperwork requirements must be met by states participating in federal programs.
- Funding and program implementation held up by lengthy approval processes, absence of program guidelines, and other administrative practices cause serious dislocation and inequities at the state level.
- Lack of federal coordination and consistency in implementing indirect cost determination procedures creates continuing administrative confusion for the states.[45]

Unfortunately, states and local communities are caught in the middle. Sub-governmental units cannot shrink from their responsibilities to their citizens. They simply cannot delegate the burden to other entities. However, they are dependent upon some form of federal funding since very few states and local governments even before the 2009 economic downturn, can afford to support and deliver the services demanded from their citizens. Emergency situations such as a hurricane in the Gulf Coast, wildfires in California, and an oil spill heading for Louisiana must be addressed. A territorial possession of the United States, the people of Puerto Rico are still trying to recover and rebuild after Maria, a category 5 hurricane, hit their island on October 4, 2017. What federal assistance they have received has been slow in coming and simply not enough to help their cash-strapped economy to recoup the island's losses. Once again, the states simply do not have the funds or the resources to handle these situations by themselves.

The redistribution of federal dollars to assist state and local governments began with the **Northwest Ordinance** of 1785, providing federal lands for public education in the Western territories. Federal cash outlays helped to build roads, railroads, and canals. The increased use of federal grants began in the 1950s. **Grants-in-aid** are "federal payments to states and federal and/or state payments to local governments for specified purposes and usually subject to supervision and review by the granting government or agency in accordance with prescribed standards and requirements."[46] There are several types of grant programs including categorical, project, formula and block.

A **categorical grant** was a federal payment to a state or local government for a specific purpose. Categorical grants were awarded for social service programs, education, highways, airports, and so on. Interested parties applied and competed for grant money. The potential recipient provided a detailed proposal with planning documents indicating how the grant money would be used. Usually categorical grants contained a matching requirement whereby the recipient was required to contribute some of its own funds toward the project. Matching agreements ranged from 10 to 50 percent of the costs, insuring that the recipient would be anxious to complete the project since its own money was committed to it. The two basic types of categorical grants were project and formula. **Project grants** in the 1960s were used to build federally funded housing projects across the nation. The money would be allocated to state and local governments on an as need basis, as demonstrated through the application process. Under a **formula grant program**, federal money was allocated by Congress based on a predetermined formula used to determine the amount each state would receive. Constituting 80 percent of all federal grants, categorical grants were preferred by Congress since they had an influential role in determining how federal dollars would be spent. The federal government reserved the right to periodic on-site inspections and audits to guarantee compliance. Perhaps the one major weakness in the program was the confusion and duplication of grant projects. Virtually all federal agencies offered categorical grants creating an uncoordinated and confusing plan to address the nation's infrastructure problems. Whereas categorical grants were designed for specific projects, **block grants** are given for prescribed but broad activities ranging from health care to public education. These grants have fewer federal guidelines and regulations attached to them giving the recipient more discretion and flexibility in using the money. Presidents George Bush and George W. Bush and most state governors preferred block grant programs.

The cornerstone of the Robin Hood approach was the **General Revenue Fund** created in 1972 by President Nixon. This **revenue sharing** program provided federal money without strings and mandates to state and local governments. Funding allocations were based on a formula that took into account the area's population size, income level, tax effort, etc. The largest sums were awarded to urban communities with a high percentage of below poverty-level residents who were making efforts to raise revenues on their own through higher taxes. Revenue sharing was gradually phased out beginning in 1980 when President Carter eliminated state governments from the program. In 1986, President Reagan terminated the entire program since he felt that "legislators and bureaucrats should not collect taxpayers' money from each state only to turn around and send that same money back to the states."[47]

The primary compliant about all federal grant programs is the ability of the national government to force recipients to comply with federal laws and regulations by attaching strings or **mandates** to the grants. Noncompliance can spell disaster since the recipient may see the existing grant cancelled or even be denied future opportunities to apply for another grant. There are four major categories of mandates. First, a is a congressional law or regulation that must be enforced or state and local officials may be held accountable by civil or criminal penalties. For example, all federal grant recipients must comply with the provisions of the Equal Employment Opportunity Act, Occupational Safety and Health Act, Americans with Disabilities Act, Title VII of the Civil Rights Act, all of the civil rights acts, Fair Labor Standards Act and Environmental Protection

Act. Failure to comply carries a very stiff price. Second, **crosscutting regulations** apply to every category of grants such as environmental impact statements. Many grants contain **crossover sanctions** whereby states and local governments will lose federal funding for noncompliance. Finally, a **partial and outright pre-emption mandate** is applied when a state or local government fails to establish its own requirements thereby the federal agency overseeing that functional area can assume partial or, if all else fails, outright jurisdiction over the project. President Reagan in particular, saw the increase in federal mandates as an intrusion into the operations of state and local governments. However, Congress saw it differently and continued the practice of using federal grant programs as a means of forcing state and local governments to follow its dictates or lose billions of dollars in federal funding.

Both federal and state legislative houses were guilty of applying unfunded mandates to their sub-governmental units. An **unfunded mandate** is "one level of government requiring another to offer—and pay for—a program as a matter of law or as a prerequisite to partial or full funding for either the program in question or other programs."[48] For example, the core curriculum was amended to require four years of both science and mathematics in the high schools. If schools do not comply, the Texas Legislature has threatened to reduce and/or deny state funding to that school district. However, in both instances, the Texas Legislature did not provide additional funds to hire more teachers or to build additional classrooms. In 1994, the Republican Party issued its "Contract with America" that included a push for Congress to eliminate all federal unfunded mandates. A compromise was reached. Signed into law by Bill Clinton in 1995, the bill requires the Congressional Budget Office to provide at least the cost of the proposed legislative mandate prior to a bill's approval.

Texas and Federal Money

Although Texans may complain about the regulations and the strings attached to federal funding, the state does receive an ample amount of federal dollars ranging from government defense contracts to grants and cash outlays for roads, bridges, housing, and income support programs. The state also receives direct federal payments for Social Security, Medicare, federal retirements, veterans' benefits, food stamps, and other programs. The *2018 Annual Cash Report* issued by the Texas Comptroller of Public Accounts indicates

Table 5.1 – Federal Revenue by Agency Excluding Trust Funds – Year Ended August 31, 2018

State Agency	2017	2018
Health and Human Services Commission	$24,418,809,828	$25,483,441,961
Texas Education Agency	5,074,619,538	5,168,826,769
Texas Department of Transportation	4,250,529,667	3,875,223,749
Texas Workforce Commission	1,235,162,617	1,296,873,870
Department of Public Safety	250,967,871	957,173,605
Department of Agriculture	580,582,299	611,332,945
Department of Family and Protective Services	447,521,097	446,330,039
Department of State Health Services	865,847,278	402,924,419
General Land Office	287,929,230	340,981,572
All Other Agencies	953,660,607	1,035,459,381
Total All Agencies	$38,365,630,033	$39,618,568,311

Source: *State of Texas Annual Cash Report: Revenues and Expenditures of State Funds for the Year Ended August 31, 2018*, Austin, Texas: Texas Comptroller of Public Accounts, 2018, Table 6, page 15.

Texas' federal funding increased by 3.3 percent in fiscal 2018, totaling $39.6 billion. Federal funds accounted for 33.0 percent of total net revenue, making then the second largest revenue source in fiscal 2018. . . . Health and human service programs received more federal money than any other governmental function in fiscal 2018, at $27.6 billion. The federal money was used for medical aid and public assistance programs, with some being distributed to other agencies that administer the programs. Education and highways construction programs also benefit from large amounts of federal funding. In fiscal 2018, the Texas education system received $5.2 billion in federal funds, which was unmatched revenue. The Texas Department of Transportation (TxDOT) received $3.9 billion of federal money, all of which must be matched.[49]

Table 5.1 indicates the amount of federal funds received by all state agencies for years 2017 and 2018. The allocations include both matched and unmatched money. Under federal guidelines, recipients of federal matching funds must first spend its appropriated amounts before receiving the allocated federal funds.

The allocation of federal funds is, in part, based on a state's demographics including poverty rates, income levels, employment trends, educational attainment, and health care statistics. Unfortunately, Texas still has high poverty rates and low income levels offset with high secondary public school dropout rates. Regardless of the outcome of Obamacare, state leaders cannot dodge the fact that Texas has for many years led the nation in the number of uninsured children. The stark truth is that Texas continues to receive a lion's share of the federal funding allocated annually to every state in the union. Unfortunately, Texans need to remember that the state's treasury would be hard pressed to fund many of its budgetary items if the federal government severely decreased or totally eliminated its funding allocations. Although the proud individualist Texan hates to admit it, this state needs the billions it receives from the federal government.

In turn, the Texas Legislature reallocates some of its federal funding to city and county governments, junior college districts, public school districts, judicial districts and other political subdivisions. Table 5.2 illustrates the redistribution of federal funds for fiscal year 2018. In addition, these sub-governmental units can submit their own applications for federal grant monies. Of course, one cannot overlook that individual Texans also receive federal funds in the form of direct payments for retirement and disability insurance benefits, Medicaid services, income maintenance programs, unemployment benefits, veterans' benefits, and federal education and job training assistance.

Rising Interstate Conflicts

The Framers understood that the states would have conflicts with each other. They envisioned that the **interstate compact,** an agreement between two or more states requiring congressional approval, would reconcile these differences. Interstate compacts have been used to

Table 5.2 – Flow of Funds to Local Governments Year Ended August 2018
(Allocations from the State and Federal Sources)

	Cities	Counties	Community Colleges	Public School Districts	Other*
State and Federal Grants					
Highways/Transportation	$ 68,892,209	$ 37,648,232	$ 256,937		$ 90,910,793
Public Safety/Corrections	185,851,327	417,293,996			305,501,897
Education	4,141,192	29,652,553	984,662,000	26,785,253,378	182,395,682
General Government	166,795,564	333,238,107	2,522,390	5,620,549	225,632,311
Health and Human Services	102,767,039	105,251,543	48,221,997	14,584,484	116,253,908
Natural Resources /Recreational Services	125,460,935	68,304,652		9,202,312	72,446,144
Total State & Federal Grants	**$653,908,267**	**$991,389,084**	**$1,035,663,324**	**$26,814,660,723**	**$993,140,734**
Shared Revenue					
Mixed Beverage Taxes	104,006,051	113,046,296			
Bingo Prize Fees	14,469	20,395			
Hotel Occupancy Tax	7,087,960				
Total Shared Revenue	**111,108,480**	**113,066,692**			
Taxes Collected in Trust					
City Sales Taxes	5,803,790,706				
County Sales Taxes		547,998,227			
MTA Sales Tax					1,944,514,706
Special District Sales Taxes Allocations					619,304,465
Other Special Events /Venues Tax Allocations					57,592,943
Total Taxes Collected in Trust	**5,803,790,706**	**547,998,227**			**2,621,410,114**
Total Funds to Local Governments	**$6,568,807,453**	**$1,652,454,002**	**$1,035,663,324**	**$26,814,660,723**	**$3,614,552,848**

*Other includes funds to judicial districts and additional political subdivisions.

Source: *State of Texas Annual Cash Report: Revenues and Expenditures of State Funds for the Year Ended August 31, 2018, Austin, Texas: Texas Comptroller of Public Accounts, 2018, Table 9, page 20.*

settle transportation disputes, river boundary changes, commerce issues and extradition of criminals. However, the Framers never envisioned the commercial and business rivalries of today. States openly compete with each other over everything from major plant relocations and national political conventions to expansion sports franchises.

States market themselves by emphasizing their positives and downplaying their negatives. The best known sectional conflicts are East-West, and "sunbelt" versus "frostbelt" or "rustbelt" states. The rivalries are intense for several reasons. First, beginning with the 1980 census, there have been significant migration shifts in population across the country. The traditional industrial states have and are continuing to lose population, while western and southern states have seen offsetting increases. A significant loss in population equates to loss of business and economic development, decreases in tax revenues and federal funding, and loss of political clout in the United States House of Representatives. For every loss of a United States congressional seat in the north, a southern or western state gains a seat. People are leaving the rustbelt for the sunbelt. The northern states must market themselves to regain these population losses.

Second, the economic downslides of the 1980s and the mid-2000s have placed several states on the brink of bankruptcy. State governors and legislative houses can no longer be complacent about business development, economic diversity, and success in education. The industrialized and highly unionized states in the north have seen their traditional economic mainstays close their plants and relocate to the south. The south can offer a pleasant climate, lower wages, and, better yet, a non-union working environment. The tense marketing efforts for economic development and plant relocations have created bitter contests between the states.

Third, environmental concerns and responsibilities have created problems for all of the states. A state may be fined for environmental damage it did not create. For example, should Kentucky and Tennessee be held financially responsible for the cleanup of a river that was environmentally destroyed by a factory located in Ohio, which was guilty of dumping waste into that river? In the case of the federal government, how much monetary responsibility should it bear for the adverse damage caused by an international oil company's deepwater oil well rupture? The issues of accountability, responsibility, and cost liability are difficult to reconcile.

The Future of Federalism

Vertical and horizontal federalism are based on shared governance. The Framers desired a balanced government with all levels of government actively participating in promoting and providing for the general welfare of the nation's citizens. Basically,

> Federalism has been praised because (1) it permits a flexible policy that can be adopted to individual circumstances, and, therefore, reduces conflict between levels of government; (2) it disperses power widely and thus, in its pluralism it minimizes the risk

of tyranny; (3) it encourages public participation in governance, and hence, makes office holders more accountable and more responsive to the needs of the people; (4) likewise, a more decentralized system tends to be a more equitable distribution of benefits and burdens; (5) it improves efficiency (by reducing the delays and red tape usually associated with a central bureaucracy), and encourages experimentation and innovation at subnational levels of government. On the other hand, federalism has been criticized because (1) it protects the interests of a local majority, often at the expense of racial and other minorities; (2) it permits states to thwart the efforts of the national government to achieve uniform standards, and equal treatment, across all the states, and this leads to inequalities; and (3) in asking states and localities to rely more on themselves it gives advantages to rich states and disadvantages to poor states.[50]

Unfortunately, no model of government has or ever will be perfect. Despite its inherent flaws, federalism has proven to be the best plan including *all* levels of government into the decision making and public policy processes. Americans must also realize that we cannot have it both ways. Texans enjoy the tangible benefits that federal dollars bring to this state, but grossly frown upon federal rules, regulations, and guidelines. Like her other forty-nine sister states, Texas is not in the financial position to fund all of its service and infrastructure needs without outside assistance. Until Texans can provide for themselves the services, highways, bridges and schools that $39,618,568,311 in yearly federal funds provides, they will have to bite the bullet and accept those federal rules, regulations and guidelines.

Chapter Notes

[1]James Madison, "No. 46: Relative Strength of the Federal and State Governments," *The Enduring Federalist*, Charles Beard, ed., 2nd ed., (New York, New York: Frederick Ungar Publishing Co., 1964), 203.

[2]David C. Saffell and Harry Basehart, *State and Local Government: Politics and Public Policies*, 8th ed., (New York, New York: McGraw Hill, 2005), 40.

[3]Leonard Pitts, "Big, Bad Government? Sure, Until They Need It," *San Antonio Express-News*, (Saturday, May 29, 2010), 9B.

[4]Karan Tumulty and Steven Mufson, "Officials Feuding Over Oil Cleanup," *San Antonio Express-News*, (Tuesday, May 25, 2010), 1A.

[5]James Madison, "No. 45: Federal Powers Not Dangerous to the States," *The Enduring Federalist*, Charles Beard, ed., 2nd Ed., (New York, New York: Frederick Ungar Publishing Co., 1964), 202.

[6]D. Grier Stephenson, Jr., Robert J. Bresler, Robert J. Frederich, and Karlesky, *American Government*, 2nd ed., (New York, New York: HarperCollins, 1992), 59.

[7]Ibid., 58.

[8]Steven A. Peterson and Thomas H. Rasmussen, *State and Local Politics*, (New York, New York: McGraw-Hill, 1994), 21.

[9]Saffell and Basehart, 39.

[10]Ibid.

[11]Ibid., 33.

[12]John Jay, "No. 5: Perils of American Discord," *The Enduring Federalist*, Charles Beard, ed., 2nd ed., (New York, New York: Frederick Ungar Publishing Co., 1964), 50-51.

[13]Peterson and Rasmussen, 24.

[14]John Jay, "No. 2: The True Basic of a Federal Union," *The Enduring Federalist*, Charles Beard, ed., 2nd ed., (New York, New York: Frederick Ungar Publishing Co., 1964), 39.

[15]Russell L. Hanson, "Intergovernmental Relations," *Politics in American States: A Comparative Analysis*, Virginia Gray, Herbert Jacob, and Robert A. Albritton, eds., 5th ed., (Illinois: Scott, Foresman/Little Brown, 1990), 41.

[16]Danial J. Elazar, *American Federalism: A View from the States*, 3rd ed., (New York, N. Y.: Harper and Row Publishers, 1984), 41-42.

[17]Richard Bingham and David Hedge, *State and Local Government in a Changing Society*, 2nd ed., (New York, New York: McGraw-Hill, 1991), 42.

[18]Elazar, 31.

[19]Michael Kammen, *The Origins of the American Constitution: A Documentary History*, (New York, New York: Viking Penguin, Inc., 1986), 306-308.

[20]Bingham and Hedge, 42.

[21]Kammen, 382-383.

[22]Ralph A. Rossum and G. Alan Tarr, *American Constitutional Law: Cases and Interpretation*, (New York, New York: St. Martin's Press, Inc., 1983), 120.

[23]Ibid., 122.

[24]Ibid., 215.

[25]Saffell and Basehart, 42.

[26]Rossum and Tarr, 261 and 264.

[27]Richard P. Nathan, "The Role of the States in American Federalism," *The State of the States*, Carl E. Van Horn, ed., (Washington, D.C., Congressional Quarterly, 1989), 23.

[28]Steven G. Calabresi, "Federalism and the Rehnquist Court: A Normative Defense," *The Annals of the American Academy of Political and Social Science*, Vol. 574, March, 2001, 25.

[29]Peggy Fikac, "Pollution Fight Going to Court," *San Antonio Express-News*, (Tuesday, June 15, 2010), 1A.

[30]*John C. Calhoun: A Disquisition on Government and Selections from the Discourses*, C. Gordon Post, ed., (New York, New York: Bobbs-Merrill, 1953), 86.

[31]Hermann E. von Holst, *John C. Calhoun: American Statesman Series*, Arthur M. Schlesinger, Jr., ed., (New York, New York: Chelsea House, 1980), 78-79.

[32]Ibid. 79.

[33]*John C. Calhoun: A Disquisition on Government and Selections from the Discourses*, 30.

[34]Peterson and Rasmussen, 28.

[35]"*Texas v White*: The Constitutionality of Reconstruction—1869), *Documents of Texas History*, 2nd ed., Ernest Wallace, David M. Vigness and George B. Ward, eds., (Austin, Texas: State House Press, 1994), 208-209.

[36]Nathan, 17.

[37]Malcolm L. Goggin, "Federal-State Relations: New Federalism in Theory and Practice," *Perspectives on American and Texas Politics: A Collection of Essays*, Donald S. Lutz and Kent L. Tedin, eds., (Dubuque, Iowa: Kendall/Hunt, 1989), 187.

[38]Saffell and Basehart, 43.

[39]David B. Robertson and Dennis R. Judd, *The Development of American Public Policy: The Structure of Policy Restraint*, Glenview, Illinois: Scott, Foresman and Company, 1989), 145.

[40]Saffell and Basehart, 45.

[41]Goggin, 194.

[42]Ibid, 183-184.

[43]"Richard Nixon: Labor Day Radio Address-1972," *The Rise of Conservative America, 1945-2000: A Brief History with Documents*, Ronald Story and Bruce Laurie, eds., (Boston, Massachusetts: Bedford/St. Martins, 2008), 91.

[44]Nathan, 27.

[45]Bingham and Hedge, 45.

[46]*The HarperCollins Dictionary of American Government and Politics*, Jay M. Shafritz, ed., (New York, New York: HarperCollins Publishers, Inc., 1992), 262.

[47]Peterson and Rasmussen, 39.

[48]*The HarperCollins Dictionary of American Government and Politics*, 352.

[49]*State of Texas Annual Cash Report: Revenue and Expenditures of State Funds for the Year Ended August 31, 2018*, (Austin, Texas: Comptroller of Public Accounts, 2018), 14-15.

[50]Goggin, 186.

The Texas Constitution

Congress Avenue, Austin, Texas, with the State Capitol
in the background, c1901

"Our Constitution is like our island, which uses and restrains its subject sea; in vain the waves roar. In that Constitution, I know, and exultingly I feel, both that I am free; and that I am not free dangerously to myself or to others. I know that no power on earth, acting as I ought to do, can touch my life, my liberty or my property. I have that inward and dignified consciousness of my own security and independence which constitutes, and is the only thing which does constitute, the proud and comfortable sentiment of freedom in the human beast." Edmund Burke, 1784, *Speech on the Representation of the Commons in Parliament.*[1]

Displeased with the current state constitution, voters went to the polls in 1875 and approved a constitutional convention to completely revamp the document. Just like the Framers who met in Philadelphia, the convention delegates diligently evaluated the document and, unfortunately, completely rewrote it. The final product incorporated the popular themes of the time—low salaries for governing officials, biennial short legislative sessions, a mandate for balanced state budgets, popular election of particularly every government official including judges, and a systematic approach to weaken the governor's powers. Approved in a low voter turnout election, the 1876 Texas Constitution is the document today that guides the governing institutions of this state. Whenever the Texas Legislature or the governor's office fails to react in a favorable manner, critics point to the failure of the state's constitution to appropriately empower governing institutions to meet the state's pressing problems. Should this document remain as the "organic law" of the state or should another state constitutional convention be convened to reevaluate, update and, perhaps, completely write a new state constitution? This chapter explores this possibility.

Whether they be national or state, all constitutions give one an unique insight into the politics, social structure, business climate, key events and cultural perspectives that underscores their creation. Understanding the motives of those men at the tables who penned these documents allows one to transverse into their lives at that particular moment. For example, the current Texas Constitution placed severe restrictions on the railroad industry, banking institutions and insurance companies. Why? Because at that table in 1875 were members of the Grange, the farmers and ranchers in Texas who were extremely upset over the railroads' price fixing schemes, the interest rates and lending practices of the banks, and the inability of the insurance companies to honor claims relating to crop failures and adverse weather conditions. As we shall see, the document of 1876 definitely addressed their concerns. While following the governing structures and primary principles laid out in the United States Constitution, each state document is unique in that it covers the regional issues of the people residing in that state. Whenever a state convenes a constitutional convention, interest groups and political parties alike play a vital role in the drafting, ratification, and implementation of the document. Usually constitutional revision is driven by a particular group or groups that view the current document as detrimental to their goals and, in some instances, survival. They pit themselves against those who feel that the current document does not require change since it protects their interests. A constitutional convention is held in anything but a congenial setting. Deep-seated conflicts pit one against the other. The end result is democracy at its best—a compromised document. This chapter delves into the uniqueness of the state's several constitutions and the oftentimes contentious manner in which they are created. As the "organic law" of a nation state or a state government, it is the intent of all constitutions to guide the governing institutions it creates. The document itself is the key to understanding how efficient and effectively a government actually governs. The maxim is the document controls the role of the government; the government does not control the document. This chapter develops this concept.

Constitutionalism and Theories of Government

In 1215, a group of disgruntled noblemen insisted that their king meet them in a field called Runnymeade to address the arbitrariness of their monarch over them. Citing that they had fundamental rights that no government or king could take from them, they left King John with two options. Either he signed the **Magna Carta** agreeing to protect those rights, or he would lose their support and his throne. By signing this agreement, King John gave up his absolute authority and affixed his seal to a constitution. Although they did not realize it at the time, these barons ushered in a new "ism" to political science. **Constitutionalism** is "the political principle of limited government under a written contract."[2] Therefore, the **constitution** is "a fundamental or 'organic' law that establishes the framework of government of a state, assigns the powers and duties of governmental agencies, and establishes the relationship between the people and their government."[3] All constitutions whether at the nation-state or state level are the organic laws over their established jurisdictions.

Initially, ancient and medieval political philosophers beginning with Plato and Aristotle pondered whether government was necessary in the first place. They collectively concluded that once men left their nomadic individualist lifestyle behind and collectively formed societies in an urban or city environment, government with its rules and regulations was indeed necessary for the survival of the community. Basically, **government** is "the formal institutional structure and processes of a society by which policies are developed and implemented in the form of law binding on all.[4] It is the constitution that gives legitimacy to governing institutions and the officials deemed to execute the actions of the government. For centuries, political writers have argued over the purpose of forming a government in the first place. Most dismiss that it was just a mechanism of controlling people from harming each other or impeding upon another's right to survival. Jean Jacques Rousseau rationalized that "the great question of the best possible government seemed to me to reduce itself to this: 'What is the nature of the government best fitted to create the most virtuous, the most enlightened, the wisest, and in, fact, the best people, taking the word 'best' in its highest sense?'"[5]

The Enlightenment philosophers Jean Jacques Rousseau, Charles de Montesquieu and John Locke went a step further. They concluded that it was the people of any given territory that had the absolute right to life, liberty, and property. Collectively members of a society agreed to give up their absolute natural rights to form a governing body that would protect those rights for the benefit of the entire society. In other words, government was created by a **social contract**, commonly known as a constitution. In his *Reflections on the Revolution in France*, Edmund Burke wrote:

> Society is indeed a contract. Subordinate contracts for objects of mere occasional interest may be dissolved at pleasure—but the state ought not to be considered as nothing better than a partnership agreement in a trade of pepper and coffee, calico, or tobacco, or some other such low concern, to be taken up for a temporary interest, and to be dissolved by the fancy of the parties. It is to be looked on

> with other reverence, because it is not a partnership in things subservient only to the gross animal existence of a temporary and perishable nature. It is a partnership in all science; a partnership in all art; a partnership in every virtue and in all perfection. As the ends of such a partnership cannot be obtained in many generations, it becomes a partnership not only between those who are living, between those who are dead, and those who are to be born. Each contract of each particular state is but a clause in the great primeval contract of eternal society, linking the power with the higher natures, connecting the visible and invisible world, according to a fixed compact sanctioned by the inviolable oath which holds all physical and all moral natures, each in their appointed place."[6]

In *The Rights of Man* written in 1792, Thomas Paine connected a nation state's constitution and its governing institutions to the concept of the social contract by emphasizing that "a constitution is a thing antecedent to a government, and a government is only the creature of a constitution. The constitution of a country [or state] is not the act of its government, but of the people constituting a government."[7] Yet, what is the ultimate purpose of forming a government?

Whether at the national or state level, all constitutions detail a) the ideological approach to government, b) the structure of the governing body, and c) the responsibilities placed upon both the governing and the governed. An **ideology** is "the 'way of life' of a people, reflected in their collectively held ideas and beliefs concerning the nature of the ideal political system, economic order, social goals, and moral values."[8] After securing their independence from the British, there was little debate that the appropriate political future of the United States would be framed in a democratic driven ideology that vested ultimate political authority with the people. **Democratic ideology** is based on:

- Individualism, which holds that the primary task of government is to enable each individual to achieve the highest potential of development;
- Liberty, which allows each individual the greatest amount of freedom consistent with order;
- Equality, which maintains that all persons are created equal and have equal rights and opportunities; and
- Fraternity, which postulates that individuals will not misuse their freedom but will cooperate in creating a wholesome society.[9]

What would become the model for all state constitutions to come, the United States Constitution embodies the concept of **representative democracy** whereby "the people elect representatives to act as their agents in making and enforcing laws and decisions."[10]

However, in order for a representative democracy to work, the burden of governing falls upon the shoulders of both the governors and the governed. The governed must hold their governors accountable for their actions by awarding them for their efforts by re-electing them or punishing them for their inabilities to govern by removing them from office either through the ballot box or the impeachment process. James Madison in *Federalist #51* entitled "The Structure of the Government Must Furnish the Proper Checks and Balances Between the Different Departments" correctly assessed the need for government through a constitution to keep the governors honest and on track:

> The interest of the man must be connected with the constitutional rights of the place. It may be a reflection on human nature, that such devices should be necessary to control the abuses of government. But what is government itself, but the greatest of all reflections on human nature? If men were angels, no government would be necessary. If angels were to govern men, neither external nor internal controls on government would be necessary. In framing a government which is to be administered by men over men, the great difficulty lies in this: you must first enable the government to control the governed; and in the next place oblige it to control itself.[11]

In keeping with Madison's observations, the Framers underscored the need for the government to both protect the governors from overstepping their authority and to ensure that the governors did not trounced upon the inalienable rights of those they governed. Consequently, governing authority is divided among the three branches of government—executive, legislative and judicial. The notion that unchecked power in the hands of the governing would eventually lead to abuse of power fueled the concept of equally distributing governing responsibilities to each branch of government. In his *Spirit of the Laws*, Charles Montesquieu believed that "all would be lost if the same man or the same body of principal men, either of nobles or of the people, exercised these three powers: that of making the laws, that of executing public resolutions, and that of judging the crimes or the disputes of individuals."[12] The Framers heeded Montesquieu's warning by deliberately dividing any government function between at least the executive and legislative branches. Basically, the legislative branch is charged with creating and making laws while the executive branch serves as the implementing body of legislative acts. In foreign affairs, the executive branch can nominate ambassadors, but only an official confirmation from the Senate gives that appointee the position. While a president may commit troops to a combat situation, only Congress can officially declare war. In *Federalist No. 47—Separation of Powers within the Federal Government*, James Madison justified the actions of his fellow Framers: "The accumulation of all powers, legislative, executive, and judiciary, in the same hands, whether of one, a few, or many, and whether hereditary, self-appointed, or elective, may justly be pronounced the very definition of tyranny. . . ."[13] As a further guard against abuse of power, the Framers introduced the "notion that constitutional devices can prevent any power within a nation from becoming absolute by being balanced against, or checked by another source of power within that same nation."[14] **Checks and balances** on governing authority forces each branch of the government to keep the others within their constitutional boundaries. Every state constitution since the adoption of the United States Constitution includes the concepts of separation of powers and checks and balances. Above all, the Framers desired a democratic government that was accountable to the people who created it.

Development of State Constitutions

Initially, it was the constitutions of the original thirteen colonies that guided the Framers in crafting the national document. Once adopted, the national constitution became the blueprint for subsequent state documents. Consequently, all state documents have the following:

- A **preamble** or introductory paragraph detailing the ideological and political framework of the government
- Three branches of government—legislative, executive, and judicial
- With the exception of Nebraska, bicameral legislative houses
- Separation of powers between the three branches of government with a series of checks and balances
- Enumerated powers, and in several state documents, implied powers through a necessary and proper clause
- Qualifications for governing officials, i.e., citizenship, residency and age, and as in the case of judges, certain professional qualifications

- Terms of office and election procedures for elected officials and impeachment processes
- Process of appointing key governing positions including members of boards and commissions
- Power of **eminent domain**, that is, a government's right to take private property for the public's use
- Power of taxation and revenue generation
- **Police powers** to enact laws for public health, safety and morals
- Amendment processes
- A bill of rights listing protected freedoms and civil liberties, oftentimes more embracing of the freedoms detailed in the United States Constitution's Bill of Rights.

The relationship between the federal or national government and state governments is detailed in Chapter 5 entitled "Intergovernmental Relationships."

Texas Constitutions

As previously stated, every state constitution is a reflection of its time. Each document addresses the pressing political, social, and economic issues that compelled a group of individuals to seriously discard their existing constitution and replace it with one that they determined would best address their concerns. Unlike several of her sister states, Texans have been governed under seven different constitutions. And although the current document has major flaws, it is doubtful that Texans will be convinced to write an eighth constitution.

Mexican Federation Constitution of 1824

After an eleven year struggle, Mexico won its independence from Spain in 1821. Initially, the government consisted of an executive composed of a five-man regency and a legislative body known as the Congress. The intent was for the regency to dissolve once an emperor was designated. The leader of the independence movement, Agustín de Iturbide, was given the lofty title of Generalisimo de Tierra y Mar. By May 18, 1821, Iturbide became the emperor of Mexico. The Emperor's rule was a short one because by 1823, his government collapsed only to be replaced by a three-man junta. One of the junta's first actions was to select delegates for a constitutional convention. Officially titled the Acta Constituiva de Federacion de 1824, this document initially established a provisional government that became a permanent government by October 1824 for all of Mexican territory including Texas.

Underscoring the principals of Charles Montesquieu, the document called for a strict separation of powers among the executive, legislative and judicial branches or departments of government. Designed along the lines of a federal system, Mexico was divided into nineteen states and four territories. At the federal level, the government consisted of a bicameral legislature. The upper house named the Senate was composed of two senators from every state and territory. The lower house called the Chamber of Deputies was composed of one deputy for every 80,000 inhabitants. The president and his vice president were elected by the legislature for four-year terms.

Constitution of the State of Coahuila and Texas—1827

According to the 1824 Mexican Constitution, the Province of Texas was united with the Coahuila as one state of the newly created Mexican Republic. A constitutional convention was convened on August 15, 1824 at Saltillo to draft the document, which was finally approved in 1827. A lengthy document consisting of approximately 225 articles, Texas's first official state constitution outlined the governing structure for Texas until its own successful revolution from Mexican rule. The document echoes the Mexican government's establishment of the Catholicism as the state's official religion. The document provided a unique approach to the protection of civil rights and liberties:

> Art. 11: Every man who inhabits the territory of the State, although he may be but a traveler, enjoys the imprescriptible [sic] rights of *Liberty, Security, Property* and *Equality*, and it is the duty of the said State, to preserve and protect by wise and equitable laws, these universal rights of men.
> Art. 12: The State is obliged to protect all its inhabitants, in the exercise of that right which they have, of writing, printing and publishing freely their political ideas and opinions, without the necessity of any examination, revision or censure, anterior to the publication, under the restrictions and responsibility [sic] established, or which may hereafter be established by the general laws on that subject."[15]

However, the document includes an interesting article that if enforced, could suspend an individual citizen of his/her protected rights for "not having any employment, office, or known means of living; [and] for not knowing how to read or write."[16]

The constitution called for an executive branch consisting of a governor, vice governor and an Executive Council "composed of three voters proper, and two substitutes, of all whom only one can be an ecclesiastic. These councilors, along with the governor and the vice governor, were to be elected on the day after the election of deputies to the Congress of the State of Coahuila and Texas."[17] This executive council functioned along the lines of the United States president's cabinet to both provide advice and consultation with the governor and oversee the administrative functions of the executive branch.

Legislative powers were vested in a Congress consisting of twelve land holders and six suppletories called Deputies. Qualifications for office included eight years of residency in the state, possession of real property of least $8,000, or employment that generates $1,000 per year.[18] Meeting in annual sessions beginning in January of each year, the legislature was charged "to promote and advance, by laws, literature, public education and the progress of the sciences, arts and useful establishments; removing the obstacles which tend to paralyse such commendable objects."[19]

The final approval of any legislative action rested with the governor who could either sign a bill into law or exercise a form of veto authority known as **promulgation** whereby "if he [the governor] should not agree, he was to make observation upon the laws and decrees of Congress . . . suspending their publication until said Congress resolves thereon."[20] Additional duties given to the governor included appointment authority over all non-elective positions, overseeing the judicial branch, calling Congress into special sessions, and the right to discipline government employees. Basically, "the chief executive could suspend from office (up to three months) and deprive of one-half salary 'all officers of the executive department, and of his appointment or approval, on violating his orders or decrees, transmitting the data on the subject to the respective tribunal, should he think there is proper ground for action.'"[21] Although granting the governor extensive powers, this constitution also enabled Congress to check gubernatorial authority. For example, the governor could not take command of the state militia without prior permission from Congress nor could the governor exert his influence over the conduction and outcome of any criminal trial. The governor could not deprive a person of their protected civil rights and liberties. The governor was prohibited from leaving the capital for more than a month without the prior approval of Congress.

The downside to this document was the power of the Congress to issue and the governor to execute decrees. A **decree** is an administrative order having the force of law.

Texans viewed decrees with suspicion, fearing that the Mexican government was taking punitive action against them. It seemed that whenever a "dangerous" situation or emergency arose, the governor was apt to rule by decree. "Used on 325 occasions before Texas rebelled, the decree power covered such emergencies as those of 1826 and 1829, when the governor was authorized to arrest and confine without legal procedure any person whom he suspected as a disturber of the peace, and of 1834, when he was authorized to organize troops to defend federal institutions and take, on his own authority, any measures that might be necessary for securing public tranquility in the state."[22] The Texas Declaration of Independence lists the overuse of decrees as one of its grievances against the Mexican government.

Constitution of the Republic of Texas—1836

On March 2, 1836, the provisional government of Texas issued a Declaration of Independence from Mexico and convened a committee to write a constitution for the Republic of Texas. Meeting in the small community of Washington-on-the-Brazos, the fifty-nine delegates had two primary objectives, namely, "the preservation of their fledgling nation and the preservation of their own lives."[23] By the time they finished the document, the Alamo had fallen, a second large force of Mexican troops crossed the Rio Grande, and the future of liberated Texas looked dismal. Approved on March 17, 1836, this document would become the organic law of the newly created Republic of Texas, which was guaranteed by the defeat of Santa Anna by Sam Houston at San Jacinto on April 21, 1836. Although the verbiage of the document is similar to both the United States Constitution and several constitutions from other states, the Texas committee opted to design a government following the unitary format rather than the customary federal system. The document did encompass the concepts of separation of powers and checks and balances between the three branches of government—legislative, executive and judiciary.

The executive branch is laid out in Articles III and IV. Basically, the President of the Republic would be elected initially for two years, which was later changed to a three-year term of office with the proviso that he could not succeed himself. This addressed the Texans' concerns about the 1827 Constitution, which enabled the president to run for unlimited terms of office, eventually becoming a semi-monarch. Qualifications for the office included that candidates had to be at least thirty-five years of age, a citizen of the Republic, and an established resident in the

Republic for at least three years prior to election. Similar to Article II of the United States Constitution, the duties of the President of the Republic included the appointment of a Cabinet and other governing positions, power to remit fines and forfeitures, receive and reject ambassadors from foreign countries, fill vacancies, recommend legislation to the Congress, and negotiate treaties. The committee reversed another practice of the Mexican government by ensuring that the President of the Republic could not lead the army in the field without the prior consent of Congress. The Constitution mandated that the president just like his counterpoint in Washington, D.C., be charged with ensuring that "laws are faithfully executed."

The legislative body was a bicameral Congress consisting of a House of Representatives, the lower house, and a Senate, the upper house. Members of the House had to be at least twenty-five years of age, a citizen of the Republic, and established at least a six month residency in the Republic prior to election. According to the Constitution, the membership of the House "shall not consist of less than twenty-four, nor more than forty members, until the population shall amount to one hundred thousand souls, after which the whole number of representatives shall not be less than forty, nor more than one hundred: *Provided*, however, that each county shall be entitled to at least one representative."[24] To seek a seat in the Senate, the candidate had to be at least thirty years of age, a citizen of the Republic and reside in the country for at least one year prior to election. Another reversal of the Mexican-dominated Constitution of 1827, Article V, Section 1 states that "ministers of the gospel being, by their profession, dedicated to God and the care of souls, ought not to be diverted from the great duties of their functions: therefore, no minister of the gospel, or priest of any denomination, whatever, shall be eligible to the office of the executive of the republic, nor to a seat in either branch of the congress of the same."[25] Terms of office were one year for Representatives and three years for Senators. Both were chosen from representational districts based on population.

Articles I and II detail the duties and responsibilities of the legislative branch. Along the lines of the United States Constitution's Article I, the Republic's Congress was empowered to pass legislation into law with the approval of both houses, levy and collect taxes and imposts, borrow money, provide for the common defense and general welfare of the Republic, regulate commerce, coin and regulate the value of money, establish post offices and post roads, grant charters of incorporation, as well as patents and copy rights, declare war, provide and maintain the armed

forces and the navy, and call out the militia. Article II, Section 7 contains the same necessary and proper clause as the United States Constitution's Article I, Section 8.

The judicial branch of the Republic's government is outlined in Article IV. It calls for one Supreme Court and inferior courts, the number of which would be determined by Congress. Judges at all levels were to be elected for four-year terms with no limit on the number of terms. The document clearly sets the levels for both original jurisdiction at the district court level and appellate cases to be heard only by the Supreme Court as the "court of last resort." The Supreme Court would consist of a chief justice and associate judges hearing cases in annual sessions.

This document set the stage for the development of county governments by mandating that "the Republic shall be divided into convenient counties, but no new county shall be established, unless it be done on the petition of one hundred free male inhabitants" residing in an area no less than nine hundred square miles.[26] The Constitution mandated that all county governments be staffed with an appropriate number of justices of the peace, one sheriff, a coroner, and constables elected by the residents of the county for two-year terms of office. Justices of the peace and constables would be appointed by the executive branch of the Republic.

The document contains a Declaration of Rights similar to the United States Constitution's Bill of Rights. Of course, property rights are sacred to Texans. This document upheld the head right system established under both the Spanish and Mexican governments whereby the head of the family would be guaranteed one league and labor of land. It also mandated that if the property holder died without a will, the estate would be awarded to his children or heirs. The issue of slavery is also addressed in this Constitution in Section 9 of General Provisions:

All persons of color who were slaves for life previous to their emigration to Texas, and who are now held in bondage, shall remain in the like state of servitude: *provided*, the said slave shall be the bona fide property of the person so holding said slave as aforesaid. Congress shall pass no laws to prohibit emigrants from bringing their slaves into the republic with them, and holding them by the same tenure by which such slaves were held in the United States; nor shall congress have power to emancipate slaves; nor shall any slave holder be allowed to emancipate his or her slave or slaves without the consent of congress, unless he or she shall send his or her slave or slaves without the limits of the republic.

No free person of African descent, either in whole or part, shall be permitted to reside permanently in the republic, without the consent of congress; and the importation or admission of Africans or negroes [African Americans] into this republic, excepting from the United States of America, is forever prohibited, and declared to be privacy.[27]

Basically, the document preserved the institution of slavery by prohibiting the emancipation of slaves either by the government or the slave owner. Furthermore, freed slaves had to have the permission of the government to remain in Texas. The only prohibition on the slavery in Texas was the foreign importation of slaves from any area other than the United States.

This constitution was written during and before Texas won its independence from Mexico. Like all revolutions, there are those who support the incumbent government, in this case, Mexico and do not want to overthrow the government; those who favor overthrowing the incumbent government; and those who simply do not want to side with either group. This constitution specifically states that "all persons who shall leave the country [the country of Texas] for the purpose of evading a participation in the present struggle, or shall refuse to participate in it, or shall give aid or assistance to the present enemy, shall forfeit all rights of citizenship, and such lands as they may hold in the republic."[28]

Texas Constitution of 1845

As previously mentioned, by 1845 the political climate in the United States had changed, enabling the United States Congress to officially annex Texas into the Union. From the very beginning of the Texas Revolution, the goal was once independence from Mexico was won, Texans wanted to be a part of the United States. Consequently, the Annexation Agreement passed both houses of Congress as a joint resolution on March 1, 1845. The agreement stipulates that the Republic of Texas will now be called the state of Texas "with a republican form of government adopted by the people of said Republic, by deputies in convention assembled, with the consent of the existing Government in order that the same may be admitted as one of the States of this Union."[29] According to the document, Texas could divide into as many as five states; it was responsible for paying off its foreign debts; the Texas flag could fly at the same height as the U.S. flag; and Texas would retain title to its public lands.[30] As an independent country, the Republic of Texas had the absolute international right to maintain

a defensive force to block any invasions from a foreign country. As a state in the union of the United States, Texas now would be defended by the mighty might of the United States government. Therefore, the annexation agreement mandated that Texas would only be admitted to the union "after ceding to the United States all public edifices, fortifications, barracks, ports, and harbors, navy and navy yards, docks, magazines and armaments, and all other means pertaining to the public defense, belonging to the said Republic of Texas."[31] Opting to remain as one big state, Texans once again were called into a convention to write the constitution that would bind them at least for the short-term to the United States of America. Once all the agreements were signed and the state constitution was officially approved by the United States Congress, the official Joint Resolution for the Admission of the State of Texas into the Union was signed on December 29, 1845. Hailed as the state's best effort, "this constitution worked well and was considered a model for its time. Many provisions from the 1845 Constitution were incorporated into subsequent state constitutions, including the present state constitution."[32] This document introduced the **homestead provision** protecting personal properties of less than 200 acres from foreclosure. Ahead of its time, this constitution guaranteed a married woman's right to own separate property. It also established a permanent state-sponsored fund for the establishment of public school systems. It outlined a constitutional amendment process.

The document's Bill of Rights is detailed in the twenty-one sections of Article I. It guarantees freedoms of religion, speech, and association. All Texans are protected from unreasonable seizures, as well as guaranteed a speedy trial, fair and impartial juries, protection from double jeopardy, unreasonable bail, and protection from cruel and unusual punishment. All citizens of Texas are guaranteed the right to bear and to keep arms. The *writ of habeas corpus* could only be suspended in cases of rebellion or invasion. The document grants more rights and freedoms than the United States Constitution. For example, Section 16: "no citizen of this state shall be deprived of life, liberty, property or privileges, outlawed, exiled, or in any manner disfranchised [lost of voting privileges] except by due course of the law of the land."[33]

Once again, stressing the principles of separation of powers and checks and balances, Article III details the duties and responsibilities of the legislative branch. A bicameral branch composed of a House of Representatives and a Senate, the legislature met in biennial sessions, the length of each session to be prescribed by law. Serving two-year terms of office with no limit on the number of terms, members of the House had to be United States citizens, at least twenty-one years of age, and reside in the state for two years with one year in his representational district prior to election. For the State Senate, a member had to be at least thirty years of age, a United States citizen, and reside in the state for three years with at least one year of residency in his district. State senators served a four-year term with no limit on the number of terms. The document details the election of a Speaker of the House while the lieutenant governor served as the president of the Senate. Similar to the United States Constitution all bills originated in the legislature with the House initiating all revenue raising legislation. In order to become law, a bill had to pass both houses and then be signed into law by the governor. Both houses participated in the impeachment process with the House drawing up the articles or charges of impeachment and the Senate acting as the jury to determine whether a government official, such as the governor, was guilty of the charges.

Elected for two-year terms of office, the governorship was a term-limited position in that the governor could not hold office for more than four years in any term of six years. In order to run for the governorship, a candidate had to be at least thirty years of age, a United States citizen, and reside in the state for three years immediately preceding his election. Constitutionally, the governor was empowered to "take care that the laws be faithfully executed." The governor could grant reprieves and pardons, remit fines and forfeitures, and nominate candidates for key government positions to the Texas Senate for confirmation. A 1850 constitutional amendment mandated the popular election of key state officials. The governor was constitutionally bound to give a state-of-the-state message, similar to a president's State of the Union address. The governor also possessed veto authority over legislative acts. If the governor vetoed a bill, he had to send the legislation back to the house of its origin with his written objections to the bill. The legislature had a right to override the veto with a 2/3's vote in both houses. In addition, a governor did not have to sign a bill in order for it to become law. Within a five day period, the governor could either sign it into law, veto it, or after the five-day period, opt not to return the bill to the house it originated in, and thus it would become law automatically.

What is interesting about this document are some of the provisions listed under Article VII—General Provisions. Individuals convicted of bribery, perjury, forgery, or other high crimes were deprived of their voting privileges. Dueling was outlawed. All civil officers had to reside within the state while all district and county officials had to live within their districts or counties. The document outlawed lotteries and the right of the state to grant divorces. The legislature could exempt from taxation up to $250 in personal belongings such as household furniture. Overall the document was anti-business by requiring a 2/3's vote of approval from both houses to create any kind of a private corporation. It also forbade the incorporation of any bank. However, the document further upheld the homestead exemption by increasing the exempted level to $2,000 in value for a parcel of land less than 200 acres. Article VIII, addressed the issue of slavery. Section 1 states that "the legislature shall have no power to pass laws for the emancipation of slaves without the consent of their owners, nor without paying their owners previous to such emancipation, a full equivalent in money for the slaves so emancipated."[34] However, the Constitution did give slaves the right to a jury trial for crimes higher than petty larceny and "any person who shall maliciously dismember, or deprive a slave of life, shall suffer such punishment as would be inflicted in the case the like offence had been committed upon a free white person, and on the like proof, except in the case of insurrection of such slave."[35]

No constitutional convention has survived without its heated debates, introduction of controversial provisions, shouting matches from the disgruntled, and, in the end, negotiations sprinkled with compromises. One of the most heated debates at this convention centered on the voting franchise. One of the delegates proposed limiting voting rights to only white (Anglo-American) males, thus eliminating Mexicans and Tejanos from voting. Delegate Frances Moore from Houston warned of the potential harm of allowing non-Anglos to vote. He pointed out that "hordes of Mexican Indians may come here from the West and may be more formidable than the enemy you have vanquished. Silently they will come moving in; they may come back in thousands to Bexar, in thousands to Goliad, and perhaps Nacogdoches and what will be the consequences? Ten, twenty, thirty, forty, fifty thousand may come in here and vanquish you at the ballot box, though you are invincible at arms. This is no ideal dream: no bugbear, it is the truth."[36] His proposal met with resounding defeat as Bexar delegate Jose Antonio Navarro addressed the convention. Navarro was one of the three Tejanos that signed the Declaration of Independence from Mexico. He played a key role in the Texas Revolution fighting along the side of Sam Houston, survived as a prisoner of war in the ill-fated venture into Santa Fe, and was currently serving in the Republic's Congress. He stressed the sacrifices Mexicans and Tejanos made in the battle to free Texas from Mexico's domination.

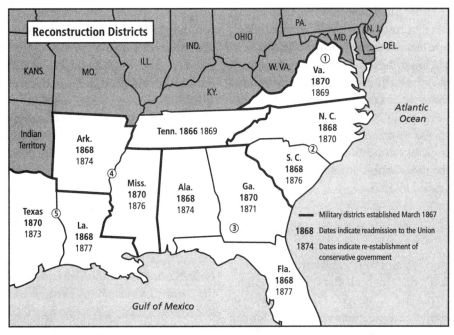

Reconstruction Districts

Military districts established March 1867
1868 Dates indicate readmission to the Union
1874 Dates indicate re-establishment of conservative government

Constitution—1861

In December 1860, the state's political leaders asked voters to send two delegates from each representative district to a state convention held January 1861. "By a vote of 152 to 6, this convention passed a resolution, later ratified, calling for secession from the Union."[37] Of course, the state constitution had to be rewritten to reflect that Texas was no longer a state of the United States but a state under the Confederate States of America. The only substantial change to the 1845 document was the requirement that public officials had to declare their loyalty to the Confederacy and protect the institution of slavery.

Constitution of Presidential Reconstruction (1866)

As previously pointed out, it was Lincoln's intention to bring the now former confederate states back into the union as soon as possible under the less punitive means possible. Lincoln proposed his **Ten-Percent Plan** whereby "if 10 percent of the people who had voted in the 1860 presidential election would swear their allegiance to the United States, then that state could elect their own state government."[38] An additional requirement was for each southern state to recognize the end of slavery and the need to grant citizenship rights to former slaves. Following Lincoln's death, President Andrew Johnson attempted to implement Lincoln's reconstruction plan. In Texas, he appointed A. J. Hamilton as provisional governor and tasked him to guide the legislature to convene a constitutional convention to write a new document that met the national government's requirements of abolishing slavery, repudiating the ordinance of session and the state's war debt, and clearly defining social, economic and political rights, short of granting the right to vote, for newly freed slaves. The constitutional convention delegates agreed to abolish slavery but refused to recognize the Thirteenth Amendment to the United States Constitution that officially ended slavery, refused to give blacks equality before the law in defiance to the Fourteenth Amendment granting former slaves citizenship, and refused to abide by the Fifteenth Amendment granting former slaves, now citizens, the right to vote and prohibited freed slaves to hold any public office.

To offset the possibility of a Radical Republican or a carpetbagger from becoming governor, the delegates strengthen the requirements for seeking the governorship. "The length of state residence was doubled, and candidates were required to have resided in Texas for six years preceding election."[39] And just in case the state capitol was overtaken by federal officials, the document gave the governor the right to convene a state legislative session in another location. Although the document basically reflected the 1845 state constitution, the 1866 document was the first to grant the governor a line-item veto authority over appropriations bills as detailed in Section 17:

The governor may approve any appropriation, and disapprove any appropriation in the same bill. In such case, he shall in signing the bill designate the appropriation disapproved, and shall return a copy of such appropriations, with his objections, to the House in which the bill shall have originated; and the same proceedings shall then be had as in the case of other bills disapproved by the Governor; but if the Legislature has adjourned before the bill is returned to the House, he shall return the same to the Secretary of State with his objections, and also to the next session of the Legislature."[40]

The document was approved by the voters in June 1866. With its official ratification, on August 1866, Johnson declared the insurrection in Texas over, and Texas was readmitted as a state in 1870.

Constitution of Congressional Reconstruction—1869

However, the 1866 Constitution was short lived since by November 1866, the Radical Republicans gained control of the United States Congress. They insisted on more punitive measures and sanctions against the former confederate states including denying political, social and economic rights to anyone who participated in or was sympathetic to the southern cause. Between March and April 1867, Congress passed laws dividing the South into five military districts with a military leader assigned to oversee the government in each district. In order to vote or to hold any elective office, Southerners had to take a loyalty oath pledging their allegiance to the United States government. Of course, every former confederate state had to rewrite their state constitutions. The Texas military governor Philip Sheridan appointed E. M. Pease as the provisional governor who quickly called for a constitutional convention. Convened on April 1, 1868, ninety delegates sat at the table and wrote the most punitive state constitution ever seen in Texas that effectively elevated the governorship to nearly a dictatorship. Noted Texas historical Walter Prescott Webb observed that this constitution was "the longest and most unsatisfactory of Texas Constitutions, but the greatest dissatisfaction of the people living under it came from abuses by state officials elected under it rather than from constitutional defects."[41] This is the document that motivated the constitutional delegates in 1875 to reverse almost every provision in this constitution, making a power laden executive and legislature into a weak executive branch and an equally vise gripped legislature.

The executive branch consisted of eight elected four-year term positions: governor, lieutenant governor, treasurer, comptroller of public accounts, commissioner of the General Land Office, and the superintendent of public instruction. Only the attorney general and secretary of state were appointive offices. The governor was empowered to appoint scores of government positions including judges and even mayors. Constitutionally, the governor controlled access to public information and controlled the press with the provision in the document that the governor could designate a newspaper in each judicial district as the official publication with the understanding that no advertisements or articles could be printed in it without official clearance. The document gave the governor the authority to establish voter qualifications and registration procedures. It created an election process that was basically a fixed one: "voters could cast their ballots only in their county seats in an election that would last from 8:00 a.m. to 4:00 p.m. for four consecutive days. . . . the returns could be 'adjusted' at the end of each day to favor the candidates acceptable to the reconstructionists."[42] Lawlessness was the norm, rather than exception in Reconstitution Texas. Naively, the convention delegates added a provision in the constitution enabling the governor to establish a state police force. The governor was also named commander in chief of the state militia with the legal authority to use it to respond to an invasion or insurrection, but most importantly, to effectively execute the laws of the state.

Mandated to meet in annual sessions, the House of Representatives was composed of ninety members elected to two-year terms with no term limits. The Senate was composed of thirty members serving six-year terms of office. Basically, they had the same duties and responsibilities as detailed in the 1845 state constitution.

"The convention assumed considerable responsibility beyond the writing of a constitution and spent much time chartering railroads, gathering evidence of the lawlessness in East Texas, debating proposals for the sale of a portion of the state to the United States, and dealing with the inappropriate conduct of its own members."[43] One item on the table for discussion was the possibility of dividing the state into three separate states. Radical Republicans had political motives in mind. "Radicals in East Texas and West Texas hoped to separate their sections from Central Texas, the region that had dominated the state politically and economically before the war. Politically the radicals hoped that they could maintain Republican control in the strongly Unionist West Texas and perhaps East Texas with its large African-American population."[44] Moderate voices squashed that proposal.

However, not everything was wrong with the document. The Constitution of 1869 called for a free public school system funded by the sale and lease of state lands. The state's school-age children were required to attend at least four months of school each year. The document also canceled all of the state's debts incurred by its participation in the Civil War. The state also increased its population through the creation of the Bureau of Immigration designed to entice settlers to Texas. The delegates upheld a married woman's right to separately own her own real and personal property. The Constitution even gave legal recognition to common law marriages. Once the Constitution was approved by the voters, President Grant signed by March 1870, an act of Congress ending military rule and Reconstruction in Texas.

The Constitution of 1869 left the door wide open for Radical Republican E. J. Davis to turn the governorship into a dictatorship within a matter of months. Although he served only one four-year term of office, Governor Davis definitely left a long lasting impression on the future political development of this state. In 1870, Davis convinced the Texas Legislature to enact a series of laws collectively known as the **Obnoxious Acts**. The first two measures gave him extra ordinary police powers. Concerned about lawlessness, Davis was able to place both the state militia and his newly created state police under his personal control. "Some of the worst desperados in the state took service in the [state] police, and under the shield of authority committed the most highhanded outrages: barefaced robbery, arbitrary assessments upon helpless communities, unauthorized arrests, and even the foulest murders were proven against them."[45] The third Obnoxious Act authorized Davis to fill all vacancies at city, county, district and state levels, successfully putting

Richard Coke, Texas Governor,
Photo taken between 1870-1880.
Photo credit: Library of Congress

approximately 8,500 of his loyal supporters in charge at every level of the government. To marginalize the efforts of the reinsurgent Democratic Party, Davis carefully monitored all elections and manipulated them towards continued Republican domination. On paper, the Constitution of 1869 followed a federal governing format, under Davis it was changed to a unitary one with the governor at the top of the pyramid controlling his puppets. Fearing that the Democrats would chip into his Radical Republican majorities in the Texas House and Senate, Davis postponed the legislative elections of 1870 to 1872. His Office of the State Printer successfully controlled the dissemination of all official matters. Although the state treasury was struggling to make ends meet, Davis was notorious in giving state officials high salaries.

Davis allocated large chunks of tax money to public education while at the same time gave away state lands as incentives for the railroads to come to Texas. During the 1870-72 biennium session, "the worst measure of the session, and perhaps the worst ever passed, was one granting to two parallel railroads, the Southern Pacific and the Memphis, El Paso, and Pacific, $6,000,000 of thirty-year 8 percent state bonds, under the sole condition that the roads unite at a point halfway across the state. It was provided that these bonds might later be exchanged for public land at the rate of twenty-four sections of every mile. Since the roads were already claiming sixteen sections under an old act, they ran a good chance of getting a total of over 22 million acres."[46] Basically "the governor so shaped the laws and the administration that his power over the people of Texas was as truly totalitarian as that which had been wielded by the military commanders. In actual fact the liberty and life of every citizen lay in the governor's hands."[47]

By 1871, former Confederates in Texas were gaining back their voting rights and political clout. In 1871, a special election resulted in four Democrats being elected to the United States Congress. In the 1872 presidential election, Republican Ulysses S. Grant failed to carry Texas. By 1872, Texans voted in more Democrats than Republicans to the state legislature, giving Democrats their first majority in the Texas Legislature since the end of the Civil War. Consequently, they were able to repeal many of Davis' punitive laws including the Obnoxious Acts. In 1873, Davis was driven out of the capitol with the election of Democrat Richard Coke to the governorship.

The Current Document—The Constitution of 1876

With the Democrats in the majority and the Republicans in a political retreat, the cry was to call for a constitutional convention to write a new state constitution. Convened in September 1875, the constitutional convention consisted of ninety delegates of whom "seventy-six were Democrats and fourteen were Republicans. The average age of the delegates was forty-five, and seventy-two of the men were immigrants from other Southern states; nineteen were from Tennessee. About fifty of the delegates had come to Texas between 1840 and 1870, and had first-hand experience of Reconstruction."[48] One-third to one-half of the delegates were members of the Patron of Husbandry or the Grange. Composed primarily of farmers and small-spread ranchers, the Grange's motto of "**Retrenchment and Reform**" underscored the group's commitment to anti-monopolistic business practices particularly of railroads, banks and insurance companies, legislative action favoring the farming and ranching industries, bringing big government down to size by decreasing the salaries of elected officials, setting and limiting terms of elective offices, and, in the case of Texas, reforming the appointment powers of the governor. Among the notable delegates were John H. Reagan, former Postmaster General of the Confederacy, later member of U.S. House, Senate, and Chairman of the Texas Railroad Commission; John "Rip" Ford, the Texas Ranger captain who forced Davis to leave the capitol; Thomas Nugent, later Populist Party candidate for governor in 1892 and 1894; and Lawrence "Sul" Ross, Indian fighter and later governor and president of Texas A & M University. Collectively, the delegates desired to:

- Restrict the power of state government, particularly curbing the abusive practices of the Davis administration
- Protect the interests of the agricultural and ranching communities
- Ensure the appropriate policies were in place to respond to the economic Panic of 1873 and the ensuring economic depression.

Adopted on February 15, 1876, the state's current constitution is definitely reflective of the Framers intentions "to insure that no one as powerful as Governor Davis could ever again hold office. The constitution signaled the return of Democratic control of the government and, along with that control, a weak governor and a decentralized state government. The constitution was a creature of a rural state dominated by populist white farmers who believed that if government was weak, if taxes were low, and if they were left alone from government's intrusiveness, they and the state would prosper. The philosophy is still the governing principle of the Texas Constitution, although it is debatable whether such a principle is appropriate in the diverse, urban state that Texas has become."[49] Unfortunately, this document punishes the governing institutions more so than its intended target, E. J. Davis. "Scholars believe that constitutions should be flexible, concise, and dedicated to the fundamental principles of government. The Texas Constitution fails all three tests."[50]

The 1876 Constitution clearly reigns in powers of both the executive and legislative branches. In contrast to the centralization of power and authority in the Davis administration, this constitution creates a plural executive that is extremely decentralized and lacking in accountability. The document calls for the election of all executive officers at the state level with the exception of the Secretary of State. Unlike the President of the United States, the Texas governor cannot appoint his/her executive team nor can he/she terminate them for poor performance. The governor of this state is dependent upon the voters to select individuals who are from the governor's same political party and/or his/her same political perspectives. Far too often, we have seen a governor elected from one party with a lieutenant governor from the opposition and a mixture of Democrats and Republicans filling top executive positions. Constitutionally, the executive "team" is not required to meet as one group nor are they constitutionally mandated to even work together.

The federal bureaucracy is an organized pyramid with each governing function tied to a cabinet officer. In Texas, state agencies are actually run by boards and commissions who simply are not required to report directly to the governor. Once the governor appoints members to these commissions and boards with the approval of the Senate, these groups operate basically independently of the governor's oversight. One of the major complaints about the Davis administration was the governor's ability to appoint every governing position from state to local levels. This constitution addresses this by calling for the popular election of all governing officials including judges, mayors, city council members, etc.

The document specifies that the governor's term of office is two years (later changed to four years) with no limits on the number of terms. The tradition of governors only serving two terms of office was broken by Governor Perry when he was elected to a third term of office in 2010. Powers given to the governor include a limited line-item veto for only appropriations and the traditional veto authority with a legislatively mandated 2/3's override provision. The most powerful authority the governor has over the legislature is to call the legislature into special session with the governor dictating its agenda. In comparison to other state governors, the powers granted to the governor by the Texas Constitution renders the person residing in the governor's mansion one of the weakest state executives in the nation.

The delegates also aimed their collective wrath at the legislative branch. Article 3 details the organizational structure, qualifications for and terms of office, as well as the duties and responsibilities of the Texas House and Senate. Of particular note, the document prevents both Houses from expanding its membership. Initially mandated to consist of only ninety-three members, the document specifies that "the number of Representatives [of the Texas House] shall never exceed one hundred and fifty."[51] Likewise the Senate is constitutionally confined to thirty-one members. As one of the fastest growing states in the nation, Texans are confronted with the reality that with every census-driven redistricting plan, their representatives in Austin are acting on the behalf of more residents within their districts. One of the benefits of the 1869 Constitution was annual legislative sessions. The 1876 Constitution changed that to biennial regular sessions of only 140 days with the provision that the governor could call a 30-day special session with him/her setting the agenda for the session. The shortness of the legislative session has proven to be problematic since this body is constitutionally mandated to produce a two-year balanced budget as well as to pass all of the needed legislation for a two-year period. The 1876 Constitution even mandates the flow of the legislative process. According to Section 5 of Article 3:

> When convened in regular Session, the **first thirty days** thereof shall be devoted to the introduction of bills and resolutions, acting upon emergency appropriations, passing upon the confirmation of the recess appointees of the Governor and such emergency matters as may be submitted by the Governor . . . provided that during **the succeeding thirty days** of the regular session of the Legislature the various committees of each House shall hold hearings to consider all bills and resolutions . . . provided further that during the **following sixty days** the Legislature shall act upon such bills and resolutions as may be then pending. . . ."[52] (Emphasis added by author.)

One of the most contentious complaints about the Davis administration was the high salaries paid to the governor, state executive officers and legislators. Initially,

it was proposed to give the governor only $5,000 per year. While some believed that the stature of the office commanded higher compensation, the other side argued that "the office should never be sought as a remunerative one and the salary of $333 a month plus house was fairly reasonable and ought to be sufficient."[53] The group compromised on an annual salary of $4,000 per year, which remained in effect until 1936. Members of the state legislature fared worse as their compensation was lowered to a mere $600 per month. Since the regular session lasted only five months in a two-year cycle, a legislator could receive only $3,000 during their term of office. Subsequent legislation has changed the governor's salary to well over $100,000 per year while members of the legislature still receive their $600 per month but it is paid on a twelve-month schedule, amounting to $7,200 per year. While in keeping with the belief that government service should be viewed as voluntary servitude to one's community, the compensation plan outlined in the 1876 document drew mixed reviews. While the convention was still in session, an article in the *Houston Telegraph* pointed out that:

> Texas has been advertised as an El Dorado with inexhaustible resources, a sort of paradise. But now we have proposed to engraft her organic law a feature which indicates a narrow, contract, parsimonious policy, and proclaims to the world that her public servants must be salaried as if they were paupers . . . The few thousand dollars which, by the cutting down of salaries, is hoped to be save to the state, will be a most costly economy to Texas . . .[54]

Under the Davis administration, the governor had the power to appoint all of the judges. The state Supreme Court was viewed by many as a powerful body bent on exercising its own brand of punitive and discriminatory justice upon Texans. After all, if the governor appointed one to a judicial bench, that judge knew that in order to keep his position, his mandate was to follow the governor's game plan. The 1876 Constitution addressed those concerns by mandating the popular election of all judges for specified terms of office with age as the only limit on the number of terms one could serve. Article 5, Section 1a states that "the office of every such Justice and Judge shall become vacant when the incumbent reaches the age of seventy-five (75) years or such earlier age, not less than seventy (70) years."[55] This provision has been overturned by a constitutional amendment eliminating the age limitation. To avoid a single state Supreme Court from exercising unlimited authority, the 1876 Constitution created a two-headed or bifurcated court composed of the State Court of Criminal Appeals and the State Supreme Court. Furthermore, the majority of the rules governing the process and decision making authority of the courts comes from the Texas Legislature. Far too often judges in the Texas court system decry the ability of the legislature to enact criminal and civil statutes that vise grip the ability of the judges and their juries to render their own judgments and levels of penalties.

On a good note, the Grangers were able to ensure the protection of a person's personal property from forced sale (Article 16, Section 49) and the forced sale of one's homestead (Article 16, Section 50). The document also provided for homestead grants of 160 acres to the head of families and 80 acres to single men over 18. To address the abuses of the railroads, the convention delegates mandated the establishment of an elected three-member Railroad Commission (Article 16, Section 30) to oversee their operations. As detailed in Article 16, Section 16 "no foreign corporation, other than the national banks of the United States domiciled in this state, shall be permitted to exercise banking or discounting privileges in this State."[56] In other words, no bank or insurance company not headquartered in Texas could do business in Texas. This restriction remained in effect until President Carter signed into law in 1980, the Bank Deregulation Act, allowing out-of-state banks to operate within other states. The document also reversed the governor's control over public education by calling for local control of public schools and ending compulsory education.

Constitutional Reform Effort

Obviously, the 1876 Constitution successfully addressed the issues with the Davis administration. However, it is the architect of a governing structure that oftentimes simply does not work effectively and efficiently in meeting the state's needs. A decentralized governing structure has created a headless system with no one actually in charge. The legislative duties are divided between the governor, the lieutenant governor, and the speaker of the Texas House. The governor has no real control over the state's bureaucracy since every executive officer with the exception of the Secretary of State is elected. Bureaucratic operations and policy development are controlled by separately elected or appointed members to numerous boards and commissions who meet periodically throughout the year, leaving the day to day operations to state employees. At the local level, the 1876 Constitution places very rigid restrictions on both county and city governments. The state legislature establishes the tax rates for both city and county governments. Counties in Texas are constitutionally denied ordinance making capability, making them wards of the state legislature.

Governor Perry even joined the ranks of those pushing for another constitutional convention to completely rewrite the state constitution. Perry even advocated constitutional revisions to include the governor appointing all state executive officers, creating a cabinet organization similar to the president's cabinet that would distribute bureaucratic functions to various cabinet members thus eliminating the multiplicity of boards and commissions, and granting the governor the power to appoint members of both the Texas Supreme Court and Court of Criminal Appeals. While these changes seem reasonable to the establishment of a more efficient government, others see this as a ploy for Perry to return state government back to the Davis days.

A major flaw of the document is the lack of a "necessary and proper clause." In the United States Constitution, the necessary and proper clause as detailed in Article I, Section 8, enables the Congress to enact laws that are necessary to run the government but do not violate the provisions of the Constitution itself. In other words, Congress can make laws to cover items not specifically noted in the Constitution without adding amendments to the document. For Texas, the absence of the necessary and proper clause means that far too often the only way the Texas Legislature can implement provisions of its own Constitution is through the amendment process. Currently, the Texas Constitution has over 650 amendments. With each legislative cycle, the number of voter approved amendments only adds to the length of and the confusing organizational structure of the state's constitution. Revision is not a welcomed option. Truthfully, mention the words change and state constitution in the same sentence, and the suspicions of Texans are aroused.

From 1876 to 1973, "there has been little talk from the public about constitutional revision. Other than the League of Women Voters, which has consistently shown an interest, no other group has come forth to push for revision. Most members of the general public must be pleased with the current state constitution, satisfied with the piecemeal revisions that have been occurring for the past 120 years, or they don't care."[57] Attempts have been made to create a new constitution. For example, in 1973, the Texas Legislature created a 37-member Constitutional Revision Commission to make recommendations for changes by 1974. The key groups in supporting revisions to the current document were the academic community, all of the state's major newspapers, the Texas Municipal League, the Texas State Bar, the AFL-CIO, the National Farmers Union, Common Cause, the League of Women Voters, the Texas Association of College Teachers, the American Association of University Women, and the American Association of Retired Persons or AARP. In particular, the League of Women Voters in Texas has continuously advocated to state lawmakers, the governor and any other interested party that the 1876 Constitution is out dated and totally unworkable. As soon as the convention was approved, special interest groups protected in the 1876 document raised their concerns. Would the current constitution that does not require candidates for justice of the peace be licensed attorneys be changed to require them to be lawyers? If so, would the state be constitutionally bound to pay a higher salary for these justices? Would the Permanent University Fund that constitutionally only provides funding for the University of Texas and Texas A & M systems be expanded including all state supported colleges and universities? Would the dedicated Highway Trust Fund that provides money for all state road projects be dismantled? Would a constitutional rewrite change Texas from a right-to-work state to a unionized one?

The committee met and opted to revise the 1876 document. The Texas Legislature approved the revisions and a special statewide election was called to adopt the newly written state constitution. Fearful of the distrust factor, the committee in conjunction with the legislature prepared booklets detailing current wording, proposed changes to the wording, and the rationale for the changes. Unfortunately, the revised document was overwhelmingly defeated at the polls! The League of Women Voters of Texas tried once again to push for constitutional reform in early 2000. They invited Bill Hobby, former lieutenant governor, former speakers of the House, and former legislators to join them in a televised forum. The League pressed them on the weaknesses of the document hoping the panelists would join their revision chorus. While agreeing the document has its noticeable flaws, the panelists were adamantly against revising the constitution.

Basically, the state's constitution has been revised through the amendment process. Over the years, voters have approved or disapproved numerous amendments proposed by each legislative session. Since the legislative session of 1879, the Texas Legislature has put before the voters 672 constitutional amendments. On the November 7, 2017 ballot, the legislature put forth for approval seven more constitutional amendments:

SJR 1 – The constitutional amendment authorizing the legislature to approve for an exemption from ad valorem taxation of all or part of the market value of the residence homestead of the surviving spouse of a first responder who is killed or fatally injured in the line of duty.

SJR 6 – The constitutional amendment authorizing the legislature to require a court to provide notice to the attorney general of a challenge to the constitutionality of a state statute and authorizing the legislature to prescribe a waiting period before the court may enter a judgment holding the statute unconstitutional.

HJR 21 – The constitutional amendment authorizing the legislature to provide for an exemption from ad valorem taxation of part of the market value of a residence homestead of a partially disabled veteran or the surviving spouse of a partially disabled veteran if the residence homestead was donated to the disabled veteran by a charitable organization.

SJR 34 – The constitutional amendment limiting the service of certain officeholders appointed by the government and confirmed by the senate after the expiration of the person's term of office.

HJR 37 – The constitutional amendment relating to legislative authority to permit credit unions and other financial institutions to promote savings plans for lotto winners.

SJR 60 - The constitutional amendment to establish a lower amount for expenses that can be charged to a borrower and removing certain financial expense limitations for a home equity loan, establishing certain authorized lenders to make a home equity loan, changing certain options for the refinancing of home equity loans, changing the threshold for an advance of a home equity line of credit, and allowing home equity loans on agricultural homesteads.

HJR 100 – The constitutional amendment on professional sports team charitable foundations conducting charitable raffles.58

All seven amendments were approved! Unfortunately, few if any of the now 672 constitutional amendments failed to win voter approval. And unfortunately, few if any of them attempt to address and correct the weaknesses of the current state constitution.

The practicality of constitutional amendment elections is questionable since these elections constantly draw low voter turnout. The Texas Legislature does a poor job in providing information that adequately explains the provisions of the amendments. For example, the Texas Legislature approved a constitutional amendment to allow homeowners to obtain a reverse mortgage on their homes. The measure passed, but few Texans actually knew what a reverse mortgage was in the first place. While not the best path to follow, it appears that Texans will continue to change their state constitution in piecemeal fashion, one amendment at a time.

Conclusions

In subsequent chapters, we will be examining the office of the governor, the legislature, the state bureaucracy, and the court system. While we detail the duties and responsibilities of each functional area, we must understand that the framework for their existence is tied directly to the state's current constitution. Governing bodies can only govern effectively when their constitution allows them to do so. In the case of the Texas Constitution, its restrictiveness does not adequately provide the flexibility government needs to govern. Far too often Texans criticize their governor and the legislature for not taking action on a particular issue. But perhaps their inaction is because the state constitution does not allow them the mechanism to address the issue. Few Texans have read the state constitution. If they did, they would have an understanding as to why governing institutions in this state cannot do what Texans want them to do. In other words, the document has tied the hands of the governor, state executive officers, and 181 members of the Texas Legislature. While admitting that the state's constitution is a very flawed document, few lawmakers have the desire to advocate writing a new one!

Chapter Notes

[1]George Klosko, *History of Political Theory: An Introduction*, Vol. 2: Modern Political Theory, (New York, New York: Thomson/Wadsworth, 1995), 274.

[2]*The American Political Dictionary*, Jack C. Plano and Milton Greenberg, eds., 10th ed., (Orlando, Florida: Harcourt Brace & Company, 1997), 7.

[3]Ibid., 34.

[4]Ibid., 12.

[5]Klosko, 230.

[6]Ibid., 296.

[7]*The Harper Collins Dictionary of American Government and Politics*, Jay M. Shafritz, ed., (New York, New York: HarperCollins Publishers, Inc., 1992), 141.

[8]*The American Political Dictionary*, 13.

[9]Ibid.

[10]Ibid., 24.

[11]James Madison, "No. 51—Internal Checks on the New Constitution," *The Enduring Federalist*, Charles A. Beard, ed., 2nd ed., (New York, New York: Frederick Ungar Publishing Company, 1964), 225.

[12]Klosko, 202.

[13]James Madison, "No. 47—Separation of Powers within the Federal Government," *The Enduring Federalist*, 221.

[14]*The Harper Collins Dictionary of American Government and Politics*, 103.

[15]"The Constitution of the State of Coahuila and Texas: March 11, 1827," *Documents of Texas History*, Ernest Wallace, David M. Vigness and George B. Ward, eds., 2nd ed., (Austin, Texas: State House Press, 1994), 61.

[16]Ibid.

[17]Fred Gantt, Jr., *The Chief Executive in Texas: A Study in Gubernatorial Leadership*, (Austin, Texas: The University of Texas Press, 1964), 20.

[18]"The Constitution of the State of Coahuila and Texas: March 11, 1827," *Documents of Texas History*, 61.

[19]Ibid.

[20]Gantt, Jr., 21.

[21]Ibid., 22.

[22]Ibid.

[23]L. Tucker Gibson, Jr., and Clay Robinson, *Government and Politics in the Lone Star State: Theory and Practice*, (Englewood Cliffs, New Jersey: Prentice Hall, 1993), 37.

[24]"The Constitution of the Republic of Texas: March 17, 1836," *Documents of Texas History*, Ernest Wallace, David M. Vigness, and George B. Ward, eds., 2nd ed., (Austin, Texas: State House Press, 1994), 100.

[25]Ibid., 102.

[26]Ibid.

[27]Ibid., 104.

[28]"The Constitution of the Republic of Texas: March, 17, 1836," *Documents of Texas History*, 103-104.

[29]*Texas Almanac: 2018-2019*, (Denton, Texas: Texas State Historical Association, 2018), 482.

[30]Lawrence W. Miller, "The Texas Constitution," *Texas Politics: A Reader*, Anthony Champagne and Edward J. Harpham, eds., (New York, New York: W. W. Norton and Co., 1997), 21.

[31]*Texas Almanac: 2018-2019*, 482.

[32]Miller, "The Texas Constitution," *Texas Politics: A Reader*, 22.

[33]"The Texas Constitution of 1845," *Documents of Texas History*, Ernest Wallace, David M. Vigness and George B. Ward, eds., 2nd ed.,

(Austin, Texas: State House Press, 1994), 150.

34Ibid., 156.

35Ibid., 157.

36John MacCormack, "Tejanos' Fortunes Fell in the 19th Century," *San Antonio Express News* (Friday, November 17, 2017), A12.

37Miller, "The Texas Constitution," *Texas Politics: A Reader*, 22.

38Ibid., 22.

39Gantt, Jr., 28.

40Ibid.

41Ibid., 31.

42Ibid., 30.

43Miller, "The Texas Constitution," *Texas Politics: A Reader*, 23.

44Rupert Richardson, Adrian Anderson, Cary D. Wintz, and Ernest Wallace, *Texas: The Lone Star State*, 9th ed., (Upper Saddle River, New Jersey: Pearson/Prentice Hall, 2005), 226.

45Wilbourn E. Benton, *Texas Politics: Constraints and Opportunities*, 5th ed., (Chicago, Illinois: Nelson-Hall Publishers, 1984), 47.

46Ibid., 47-48.

47Gantt, Jr., 31.

48Miller, "The Texas Constitution," *Texas Politics: A Reader*, 25.

49Ibid., 16.

50Ibid., 17.

511876 Texas Constitution, Article 3 – The Legislative Department, Section 2.

52Ibid., Article – The Legislative Department, Section 5.

53Gantt, Jr., 34.

54Ibid., 36.

551876 Texas Constitution, Article 5 – The Judicial Department, Section 1-a.

56Ibid., Article 16 – General Provisions, Section 30.

57Miller, "The Texas Constitution," *Texas Politics: A Reader*, 30.

58Texas Almanac: 2018-2019, 482.

The Texas Legislature

George Bush
for Congress

ON NOVEMBER 7,
VOTE FOR WEST TEXAS.
VOTE FOR
George Bush for Congress

Dear Voters,
  Laura and I would like to take this opportunity to thank you for the many kindnesses you've shown us during my campaign for the Congress.
  You've listened to me, and you've told me what you think. And hundreds of you have actively worked in my campaign.
  I am very grateful to all of you.
  During the past twelve months I have told you how much I want to represent you in the Congress. I mean that. I know I can do a good job.
  Again, our thanks.

George W. Bush

*Parliament is not a **congress** of ambassadors from different and hostile interests, which interests each must maintain, as an agent and advocate, against other agents and advocates; but Parliament is a **deliberative** assembly of **one** nation, with **one** interest, that of the whole—where not local purposes, not local prejudices, ought to guide, but the general good, resulting from the general reason of the whole. You choose a member, indeed; but when you have chosen him, he is not a member of Bristol, but he is a member of Parliament.[1]*

Edmund Burke, ***Letter to the Sheriffs of Bristol***[1]

The above quote from noted political philosopher Edmund Burke was taken from a speech he delivered in the British Parliament after his election to a seat in the House of Commons representing the people of Bristol, England. He lamented upon the complexity of the decision every lawmaker has to make whenever a bill is before his/her consideration. Do I vote based upon the will or wishes of the people who elected me to represent their particular interests and concerns or do I consider my voting options on what is best for the entire nation or in this case, state? Once every two years the 181 members of the Texas Legislature head for Austin for its biennial session. Once the gavel bangs the body to order, each legislative house is faced with the task of creating and passing all of the laws they deem necessary to run this state for the next two years while at the same time, crafting a balanced biennial budget. When times are good and the money is rolling in, the Texas Legislature has an easy task. Everyone has ideas on how their legislative district can benefit from a budget surplus. But when times are hard, the Texas Legislature like her sister legislative chambers across the nation, has to make some extremely difficult decisions. The 85th Texas Legislature began on a very gloomy note—the state was facing a financial crisis. When it ended both its regular and special session, those same 181 members that came to Austin finally left with the realization that yes they did indeed balance the budget by slashing appropriations left and right, and, yes they did not raise taxes nor did they touch the state's rainy day fund. But, they also should have left their respective legislative chambers with the realization that their actions may have helped the state to regain its economic foothold but did their votes hurt those they were sent to represent? After the votes were counted in November 2018, the Texas Republican Party won all of the state executive offices and maintained majorities in both houses of the Texas Legislature. The majority of these Republican candidates ran campaign promises dear to the state's conservative base: "lower taxes, trim bureaucracy, improve schools, secure the border, improve roads and eliminate in-state tuition for undocumented immigrants."[2] In his inaugural speech, newly sworn in Lieutenant Governor Dan Patrick stressed that he was going to once again introduce legislation to reduce property taxes. While people gathered in Austin to hear this speech clapped and cheered in support of his pledge, once lawmakers gathered in Austin in January 2019, the reality of their election promises hit home. The state of Texas is not funded by property tax revenue, but city, county, community college districts and school districts consider property tax revenue as one of their major sources of revenue. Cutting this revenue stream from them would mean serious budgetary setbacks. Others are complaining that if taxes are reduced and revenue streams are adversely impacted, many state programs will be severely underfunded or not funded at all! This poses a political problem for state Republican elected officials. Tax cuts on one hand and increased requests to fund state needs on the other. Does a lawmaker keep his/her election campaign promise to slash budgets and taxes or does he/she vote to approve these budgetary requests for more money and, perhaps, raise taxes?

With the horrific killings at the church in Sutherland Springs coupled with the Santa Fe High School shooting resulting in the deaths of 10 students and teachers, lawmakers were quickly prefiling bills dealing with gun safety issues. Before them are at least 19 different pieces of proposed legislation demanding a long laundry list of items to include closing the gun-show loophole on background checks, allowing constitutional carry of firearms and a red flag law removing guns from these deemed too dangerous to carry a weapon. Also on their plate is legislation reforming the public school finance system that includes a long-awaited pay increase for the state's public school teachers. There are numerous proposed measures dealing with everything from environmental regulations, higher education costs, infrastructure transportation needs, water conservation plans to address droughts, to once again, sanctuary cities, annexation guidelines, and property tax reform.

Every candidate who runs for a legislative seat pledges he/she will listen to constituent concerns, articulate them before the body, and strive to successfully pass the needed legislation. No wonder constituents are often left thinking that their legislator has abandoned them. This chapter examines the awkwardness Burke and every legislator before and after him who had and will have to ponder this fundamental question—what is more important, the needs of the few or the needs of the many?

By their very nature, legislative houses are knee-deep in traditions and parliamentary processes. It is not an easy task to turn a proposed idea into a bill that a governor will possibly sign into law. In each legislative session, thousands of bills are introduced, but only 10 percent successfully make it through the process of becoming a law. Every newly elected legislator must go through a "'legislative boot camp" where they learn the ins and outs of the legislature. It is also important for the average citizen to have a general knowledge of the operations of a legislative body and its relationship to both the executive and judicial branches of the governing structure. Author of *The Leviathan*, Thomas Hobbes likened his theory of matter in motion to government:

> For everything is best understood by its constitutive causes. For as in a watch, or some small engine, the matter, figure and motion of the wheels cannot well be known, except to be take insunder and viewed in parts; so to make a more curious search into the rights of states and the duties of subjects, it is necessary, I say, not to take them insunder, but yet that they do be so considered as if they were dissolved; that is, that we rightly understand what the quality of human nature is, in what matters it is, in what not, fit to make up a civil government, and how men must be agreed amongst themselves that intend to grow up into a well-grounded state.[3]

Therefore to understand how a legislature works, we need to take it apart and examine its integral parts.

The Mechanics of the Texas Legislature

Unicameral Versus Bicameral

It was the intention of the Framers to guarantee that all government policy initiatives would originate in an elected assembly, regardless of the level of government. However, the Framers were also concerned that without a system of checks and balances and separation of powers that are usually guaranteed with a bicameral legislative body, a unicameral or one house legislature would have the potentiality for seizing power and ultimately using its authority to control the entire governing process. At the Constitutional Convention, "concern over a unicameral legislature [was] reflected in John Adams's warning that 'a single assembly is liable to all the vices, follies, and frailties of an individual;

subject to fits of passion, flights of enthusiasms, partialities or prejudices, consequently productive of hasty results and absurd judgments."[4] Both national and state leaders heeded Adams's concerns by creating with the exception of Nebraska, two-house legislatures. Guided by the wisdom of constitutionally mandated checks and balances and the concept of separation of powers, the bicameral format ensures that one legislative house cannot act on its own nor can it exert power and authority over the other chamber. It is a partnership. Of course, partnerships are not perfect. The contests between the two houses of the Texas Legislature oftentimes resemble the "fits of passion, flights of enthusiasms, [and] partialities or prejudices" Adams warned of over two hundred years ago.

Legislative Sessions

The state's constitution mandates that the legislature meet once every two years for 140 calendar days beginning on the second Tuesday in January of odd-numbered years. Additional or **special sessions** of 30 days can be called only by the governor who also sets the agenda. The only constitutionally mandated **joint session** whereby both houses meet as one group is the delivery of the governor's the state of state message. Biennial **regular sessions** of only 140 days have proven to be problematic for several reasons. First, the development of effective legislation is a deliberative process. Committees must be given the opportunity to put each item presented before them "under the microscope." In other words, like the analogy of the watch, all of the component parts of a proposed legislative act must be carefully scrutinized, analyzed, and researched to ensure that the legislation does indeed address its intended purpose. Unfortunately the shortness of the session does not allow this to happen. The end result is far too many poorly written laws that simply fail to successfully address the policy concerns of this state. Second, a part-time legislature empowers a full time governor to assume extra ordinary authority that would be checked by a full time legislature. The United States Congress meets in annual sessions with few breaks during the year. Their day to day presence upholds the system of checks and balances in that they constantly watch the actions of the presidency and can at any given moment remind the president of his constitutional limitations. Over the years there have been several Texas constitutional amendments changing the session from part to full time, however, voters have overwhelmingly defeated every one of them.

The Membership of the Legislature

The Texas House is composed of 150 members and the Senate composed of 31. To be eligible as a candidate for the Texas House, one must be at least twenty-one years of age, a United States citizen, and live in the state for two years in which one year must be in the legislative district prior to the election. A Senate candidate must be at least twenty-six years of age, a United States citizen, and live in the state for five years in which one year must be in the legislative district prior to the election. Legislators are constitutionally mandated to live in the district they represent throughout their elective term of office. The term of office for House members is two years while Senators serve four-year terms. Constitutionally, the election cycle mandates that the entire membership of the House and one-half of the Senate is up for election every two years. Texas does not have term limits.

The compensation package is one of the lowest in the nation. The base pay for legislators and even the lieutenant governor is $7,200 per year, as specified by the Texas Constitution. Embarrassingly, the 2016 poverty level for a single person is $12,228, $5,028 above the base pay for the state's lawmakers. Several years ago the Texas Legislature approved a constitutional amendment for voter approval that would have raised their base pay to approximately $23,358 per year. The amendment, however, was soundly defeated. Legislators must maintain at least one office in their legislative district and employ someone to manage it. In addition, lawmakers need support staff to assist them with the preparation of their own legislation, research on pending items, addressing the needs of constituents, etc. Legislators are also reimbursed for necessary office expenses and do receive a per diem for every day the legislature is in session. At the start of the 84th legislative session, the Texas Ethics Commission garnered the support of both the lieutenant governor and the Speaker of the Texas House to raise the per diem "from $150 to $190, which amounts to a $5,600 raise for lawmakers over the course of a 140-day session. It would also slap about $1 million in overall new expenses onto the tab for the upcoming session."[5] By combing the base pay with the per diem, a state lawmaker earns about $33,800 a year for the regular 140-day session for a total pay for a two-year term of $41,000. State campaign finance laws do allow elected officials to use their campaign war chests to cover additional living expenses during a legislative session. However, many legislators must use their own funds to augment staff salaries and the cost of living in Austin. On a positive note, legislators do qualify for retirement benefits when they reach the age of sixty if they have served eight years. The range of compensation packages offered to various state legislators range from a high of $107,241 for members of the California state legislature to a low of $6,000 per session for South Dakota's state lawmakers. Nevada, New Mexico, North Dakota, Utah, Washington, and Wyoming do not offer a base pay to their state lawmakers opting instead for per diems and payment of usual expenses. But Texas at $7,200 is the second lowest among those states that do offer a base pay rate to their lawmakers.[6]

Low compensation discourages long-term tenure in the Texas Legislature as many lawmakers are merely using a state legislative seat as a stepping stone to higher elective or to an appointed government office with a more lucrative salary. It is estimated that the turnover rate in both houses is between 20 to 25 percent every session. Seasoned lawmakers are an asset to any governing body because they continue to bring valued expertise to the lawmaking process. They are the mentors and role models for the newly elected members. Both houses of the United States Congress have members who have served thirty or forty years in their respective houses. When Joe Biden was chosen to be Obama's running mate, he had served over forty years as the Democrat Senator from Delaware. The expertise he brought to the White House particularly in foreign policy proved to be invaluable to President Obama. Unfortunately, the Texas Legislature rarely awards one of its own with a twenty-year service pin! Rick Perry served longer in the governor's mansion than the majority of the state's lawmakers have held their respective seats. Constant turnover means that every legislative session is bogged down with repetitive legislative initiatives. Reinventing the wheel does not lead to innovative lawmaking. Lack of seasoned expertise is definitely a very noticeable weakness of the Texas Legislature.

Ideally, there is the belief that for a representative body to be truly representative of its membership must be reflective of the population it is elected to represent. In reality, legislative houses at both the state and national level do not mirror the population at large. In Texas, the majority of the state's legislators are older Anglo males that are established professional businessmen and lawyers. More women and minorities are being elected to legislative seats, but they are still in the minority in both houses. Obviously, the costs of running an election offset by the meager compensation offered to legislators prevents many individuals especially women and minorities from running for office.

Key Legislative Officers

The legislative process itself involves political wheeling and dealing along with compromises initiated through committee actions, floor debates, and bargaining for political concessions and trade-offs. The state legislature is "an institution in which procedures reflect, and in turn, perpetuate the messiness, openness, pragmatism, compromise, and deliberateness so characteristic of much American policymaking."[7] Consequently, the leadership of each chamber plays an essential role in the development of public policies. An effective leadership guides the entire process from start to finish. Whether it is the Speaker of the House or the lieutenant governor, the leadership group of a legislative body acts as:

1. *Gatekeepers* in the lawmaking process who can use their power to delay or block the adoption of a proposed law.
2. *Coalition builders* and *negotiators* who can put together majority support for a proposal that will determine whether it is enacted in the form it was introduced or becomes a "watered-down" version.
3. *Communicators* who explain legislative intent to the public. By communicating their own interpretations of the how and why of new laws they can aid public understanding and acceptance.[8]

There is a direct relationship between quality leadership and effective policy development. Strong leadership unites various factions into one voice capable of developing sound reasonable policy directives. Conversely, weak leadership only perpetuates factional differences that are incapable of producing effective legislative initiatives.

In both chambers of the Texas Legislature, both the Speaker of the House and the lieutenant governor in the Senate wield significant power. Each appoints members of their respective legislative houses to committee positions, appoints both the chair and vice-chair to all committees, assigns bills to the various committees for consideration, controls parliamentary procedure on the floor including the right to or not to grant a member permission to speak, establishes points of order, interprets the rules governing the flow of business in his/her respective chamber, and acts as a mediator when conflicts arise. In addition, both individuals serve as the joint chairpersons of the important Legislative Council and **Legislative Budget Board (LBB)**. Meeting as an interim body, the LBB studies the revenue streams as well as state expenditures and prepares the budget and appropriations bills for the beginning of the next legislative session. Between legislative sessions, the

LBB also has the authority to cut appropriated agency spending and transfer money between agencies. The Speaker and the lieutenant governor also appoint all of the members to the Legislative Audit Committee and the Sunset Advisory Commission. An interim committee, the **Legislative Council** plans the upcoming legislative agenda by exploring and studying state problems and tentatively planning legislative proposals to address these concerns.

Whereas the members of national and state constitutional conventions knew exactly what their chief executive officer should be doing, they have always been at a lost as to the responsibilities of the second man—the vice president or, in the case of state governments, the lieutenant governor. Both simply cannot be elected to doing nothing except to be on stand-by waiting for either the governor or the president to suddenly leave office. In the case of the vice president of the United States, his/her day job is to preside over the Senate. However, the vice president is not really the true presiding officer since his/her only official duty is to cast a vote to break a tie vote on the Senate floor. In Texas, however, the most politically powerful position is the lieutenant governor. Elected separately from the governor, the lieutenant governor is both a legislative and executive officer of the state of Texas. Since they are not running as a team, both the governor and the lieutenant governor can conceivably be from different political parties or of the same party but with different political perspectives. The role of the lieutenant governor as an executive officer will be discussed in Chapter 8. The state's current lieutenant governor is Republican Dan Patrick. Other notables include Bob Bullock (D) and Bill Hobby (D). To date, no woman or minority has held the office.

Whereas the lieutenant governor is selected in a statewide race, the Speaker of the House is initially elected as a state representative from his/her respective district. The membership of the House determines who will be its presiding officer. To date, no woman or minority has been elected Speaker by the House membership. Traditionally, the Speaker served only one term of office, which was gradually changed to two. However, the mold was broken with Bill Clayton serving four terms from 1975 to 1983, and both Gib Lewis and Pete Laney served five terms. Usually, the Speaker for the next session is temporarily approved at the close of the last session. Once the next session is convened, a cursory vote is taken.

Lately, however, the selection of a Speaker has proven to be anything but cursory. The 2007 legislative session ended on a sour note. While bills were lined up awaiting crucial floor action, Republican Speaker Tom Craddick's attention was focused more on keeping his job since he now had to openly fend off challenges from members of his own party,

Table 7.1   **Texas House and Senate Committees—86th Session**
(Unless specified, the committee is substantive and either standing or permanent.)

Joint legislative Committee – Joint Committee on Oversight of HHS Eligibility System

House of Representatives
(36 Standing Committees)
Agriculture & Livestock
Appropriations
  Sub Com. On Article II (Texas Constitution)
  Sub Com. On Article III (Texas Constitution)
  Sub Com. On Articles I, IV, V (Texas Constitution)
  Sub Com. On Articles VI, VII, VIII (Texas Constitution)
Border and Intergovernmental Affairs
Business & Industry
Calendars
Corrections
County Affairs
Criminal Jurisprudence
Culture, Recreation & Tourism
Defense & Veterans' Affairs
Economic & Small Business Development
Elections
Energy Resources
Environmental Regulation
General Investigation and Ethics
Government Efficiency and Public Safety
Higher Education
Homeland Security & Public Safety
House Administration
Human Services
Insurance
Judiciary & Civil Jurisprudence
Land & Resource Management
Licensing & Administrative Procedures
Local & Consent Calendars
Natural Resources
Pensions, Investments and Financial Services
Public Education
Public Health
Redistricting
Rules and Resolutions
State Affairs
Technology
Transportation
Urban Affairs
Ways & Means

Senate
(18 Standing Committees)
Administration
Agriculture & Rural Affairs
Business & Commerce
Criminal Justice
Economic Development
Education
Finance
     Sub Com.—Articles VI & VII (Texas Constitution)
Government Organizations
Health & Human Services
Higher Education
Intergovernmental Relations
Internadtional Relations and Trade
Jurisprudence
Natural Resources
Nominations
State Affairs
Transportation and Homeland Security
Veteran Affairs & Military Installations

than on acting on pending legislation. Essential pieces of legislation were put on the back burner in favor of the very open display of internal party backbiting and bickering. Usually, the opposing party gives the Speaker grief. This time it was members from Craddick's own political party that found fault with his vindictive and overbearing leadership style. Using legal but rarely used parliamentary tactics, Craddick was technically "re-elected" for the next session, pending his re-election bid to his legislative seat.

However, when the 2009 session began, the gavel belonged to the new Speaker, Joe Straus, Jr., a Republican from San Antonio. During the 2009 session, colleagues from both sides of the aisle appreciated Straus's ability to draw members from both parties together. He even appointed some Democrats to key committee positions. As tradition holds, Strauss was unofficially re-elected to the Speaker's position. Yet as the opening of the 2011 session approached, conservative members of Straus's own party called for a change in leadership. The 2010 mid-term elections resulted in approximately twenty more Republicans gaining seats usually held by Democrats. These newly elected House members added more conservative Republicans to the ranks seeking to oust Straus. Wanting a more conservative member to serve as their Speaker, this group of Republicans openly attacked Straus's leadership style and even his religion. This small group of Christian conservative Republicans felt that Straus's Jewish faith was standing in the way of the Speaker from taking a more conservative position on their bottom-line issues. Despite the attacks on his religious beliefs, Straus was able to pull together enough Republican and Democrat support to retain his position for another term; and at the end of the 2011 term, he was once again, tentatively re-elected as Speaker for both the 2013 and 2015 sessions. However, the beginning of the 2015 session witnessed a contested election for the Speaker's position. Challenging Straus was Scot Turner, a first-term African-American state representative from Frisco whose claim to fame is nine years in the National Football League (NFL) as a cornerback. Although the final vote was overwhelmingly for Straus, the Tea Party wing of the Republican Party continued to try to oust him at the end of the session simply because "toppling a speaker that some have deemed as too moderate [is] much more about something else: drawing some of the clearest battle lines to date within the Texas GOP. 'This is meant to intimidate those who support Speaker Straus and provide tangible evidence as to who we supported and provide ammunition in any contested primary race that might occur.'"[9]

After serving five terms as Speaker, Joe Strauss announced as early as October 2017 that he would not seek re-election. On January 8, 2019, State Representative Dennis Bonnen, a Republican from Angleton, was officially sworn in as Speaker. First elected to the Legislature in 1996, Bonnen was unanimously elected to guide the state's lower house. In private life, he is the chief executive officer of the Heritage Bank in Pearland. He actively campaigned for the position after Strauss announced he would be giving up his seat in the legislature. Bonnen pledged to the House membership that he would "keep the Texas Legislature from getting 'caught up in the things that don't lead to real results.' He named public school funding as his top priority, in addition to school safety, combating human trafficking and reforming property tax collection."[10]

While both houses of the United States Congress use the majority/minority leadership format, the Texas Legislature has eliminated this layer of leadership opting to place more responsibilities on the shoulders of the committee chairpersons. To rally the troops, both the Democrats and Republicans meet separately in their own party caucuses. A **caucus** is "a meeting of party members in one of the houses of a legislative body for the purpose of making decisions on selections of party leaders and on legislative business."[11] Both the Speaker and the lieutenant governor have the option to appoint a **pro tempore** or **pro tem** member of their respective houses to act in their place whenever they are unavailable to attend a daily session.

All members of the Texas Legislature are granted **legislative immunities** as detailed in the Texas Constitution. No member can be sued for slander or held accountable for any statements or comments made during any official legislative activity, i.e., debate in a committee or on the floor of their respective houses. Also, members cannot be arrested while in attendance in a legislative session or while traveling to and from a legislative session unless they have been charged with a felony, breach of the peace, or treason. However, the governor does have the right to call for the arrest of legislators who fail to attend the legislative session. This occurred in 2003 when the Senate Democrats fled to New Mexico and the House Democrats to Oklahoma over the legislature's redistricting plan.

The Committee System

While the media focuses its attention on floor activities, it is actually the committees that perform the bulk of the legislative work. The presiding officers in both houses determine committee membership. The chairperson and vice chairperson positions are usually held by members of the majority party. Since the Texas Senate has only thirty-one members, several committee chair- and vice-chair positions are held by members of both political parties regardless of which party holds the majority of the seats. Legislators serve on at least one committee with several serving on two or more. Committees fall into several broad categories. **Standing committees** are regular or permanent bodies that consider legislation within their particular subject areas. Standing committees are further subdivided in the substantive and procedural bodies. **Substantive standing committees** focus on the crafting of legislative actions whereas **procedural standing committees** handle the internal process or the flow of proposed legislation through the various steps leading up to the final vote. In the Texas House, the key procedural committees are Calendars, Local and Consent Calendars, Rules and Resolutions, General Investigating and Ethics, House Administration, and Redistricting. In particular, the **House Rules and Resolutions Committee** plays a very vital role in the legislative process since this is the body that provides the rules under which all bills are debated, amended, and given final consideration on the floor. Several standing committees have specialized **subcommittees**. Created by the leadership of each legislative house, **ad hoc** or **select committees** are short-term committees assigned to investigate a particular issue or policy concern. Once the committee has submitted its findings, the committee is disbanded. These bodies can be composed of members from one house or both houses of the legislature. When the legislature is not in session, the majority of the standing and select committees convert to **interim** committees that meet on a regular basis. Table 7.1 lists the committees in both houses of the 86th Texas legislative session.

Each legislative house can act as a **Committee of the Whole**, a procedure used by a legislative body to expedite business by resolving the official entire body of a house of the legislature into a committee for the consideration of bills and other matters. Oftentimes, both houses of the legislature are addressing the same issue or conducting similar legislative investigations. To expedite the process, their separate committees will form a **joint committee** composed of members from both houses. Joint committees are created by a special proclamation issued by the presiding officers of both houses to study particular issues or concerns. They meet when the legislature is not in session since both House and Senate rules do not allow for any bills or resolutions to be referred to a joint committee while the legislature is in session. If both houses of the legislature pass a similar bill but with different provisions, an ad hoc committee formally called a **conference committee** composed of

five members selected by the presiding officers from each house, is convened to reconcile differences in the legislation in hopes of crafting a single legislative item that will pass both houses.

Assigning members to the various committees has always been a politically dicey situation. Traditionally, both houses followed the national congressional practice of the **seniority system** whereby the individual of the majority party that has served on that committee the longest is appointed as its chairperson with the individual of the majority party serving the second longest becoming the vice-chairperson. Whenever there is a change in the majority party, the chair- and vice-chair positions merely shift along the same seniority pattern. A major drawback to the seniority system is that the presiding officers have no authority to appoint their own people to key committee positions. Both the Speaker and the lieutenant governor needed the ability to appoint those who shared their political philosophy and work ethic. In order to be successful, the presiding officers had to have the capability to put together their own team. To appease the old guard who held steadfastly to the seniority system, a 1973 Texas House reform measure created a modified seniority system. Under this compromise, any House member could request a committee assignment based on his/her seniority ranking, that is, the total number of years they have served in the House. Committees assignments would be based 50 percent on seniority. If the committee had less than 50 percent seniority appointments, then the request would be granted. The Speaker retained the power to appoint the chair and vice chair and the remaining 50 percent of the committee membership. Due to its size, Texas House members usually serve on two committees. One of the charges levied against Speaker Craddick was his propensity to appoint to committee leadership positions only those who were loyal to him. With Speaker Straus the complaint had been from his own party rank and file that he was just too moderate of a Republican and his leadership style was one of non-partisanship, meaning that he appointed both Republicans and according to his critics, too many Democrats to key committee positions.

The Texas Senate opted for a more complicated method based on the total membership of the committee. For a committee with a total membership (excluding the chair and vice chair) of ten or less, three seats are reserved to those who are have served on that committee during the last session while committees with more than ten members, four seats are similarly reserved. Furthermore, no Senator can be a chairperson of more than one committee. Senators usually serve on three committees. With only

31 members, both Democrats and Republicans oftentimes chair committees regardless of the party in power.

Primary Responsibilities of the Texas Legislature

Architects of Public Policy—Law Making

The primary task of any legislative house is to *initiate* public policy. "Any self-respecting legislature should not be content merely to deal with the governor's legislative program or routinely approve members' bills. It has a responsibility to initiate action and to deliberate on a wide variety of proposals dealing with the most important and controversial problems of the day, such as abortion, crime, gun control, welfare, and education, to name a few."[12] All official responses submitted for legislative consideration are called bills. A **bill** is merely a proposed law that either changes an existing one or creates a new one. A bill becomes a law once it has passed both houses of the Texas Legislature, signed by the governor within a specified period of time, or if vetoed by the governor, the veto is successfully overridden by both houses of the legislature by a two-thirds vote. There are several types of proposed legislation:

• **Statutes** or **acts** are laws enacted by a state legislature. Originally, they are introduced as bills and are coded according to their house of origination. For example, a bill introduced in the Texas Senate is noted by a S. A bill introduced in the Texas House is noted by an H, i.e., SB 1 or HB 1. Bills fall into two general subcategories—public and private. A **public bill** or a **general bill** applies to all affected parties. For example, a bill is passed increasing the tuition for all state supported colleges and universities. On the other hand, a **private bill** or **special bill** provides "an exception to a law for an individual rather than trying to change the entire bill."[13] For example, although approving the tuition hike bill, a legislator introduces a bill that would exempt returning soldiers from paying the increased tuition as a way of honoring them for their service to their country. Lawmakers may also consider **local bills** whose scopes are limited to a specified geographical area of the state or a unit of local government such as a city, county, school district, precinct, etc. Using the tuition bill as an example, a local bill would grant an exemption to a small community hard hit by one of the state's raging wildfires that severely damaged their only college. The state would be giving tuition relief to enable that college to repair its damage while at the same time remain open to students.

Of particular note, special legislation is oftentimes needed to implement a new federal law. In order to accomplish this, two separate pieces of legislation are required. First, an **authorization bill** "creates a program, specifies its general aims and how they are to be achieved, and unless open-ended, puts a ceiling on monies that can be used to finance it."[14] Second, an **appropriations bill** approving the money to fund the program must be passed.

• **Resolutions** are formal expressions of opinion or decisions that are offered by a member of either the Texas House or Senate for approval by one or both houses of the legislature. A **simple resolution** is "a measure adopted by one chamber of a legislative body. It does not require approval either by the other house or by the governor."[15] Usually simple resolutions take the form of a commendation of a fellow member of the chamber, a memorial to recognize the accomplishments of a deceased individual, a statement of congratulations acknowledging a particular accomplishment or a statement of legislative sentiment. These legislative items are coded as SR for Senate resolution or HR for House resolution.

• **Joint resolutions** must be approved by both houses of the Texas Legislature but do not require the approval of the governor. Joint resolutions are used primarily to proposed constitutional amendments, to ratify amendments to the United States Constitution or to request convening a state convention to consider amendments to the United States Constitution. Before becoming effective, all amendments to the state constitution must be approved by the voters. Joint resolutions are coded as SJR to indicate a Senate joint resolution and HJR for a House joint resolution.

• **Concurrent resolutions** must be approved by both houses of the Texas Legislature and the governor. The majority of concurrent resolutions express the same sentiments as simple resolutions but from both houses. Concurrent resolutions that deal with administration matters between both chambers, such as setting the time of adjournment for a joint session, do not require the governor's approval. These items are coded as SCR for Senate concurrent resolutions and HCR for House concurrent resolutions.

The process of transforming a bill into a law is an arduous one as just one negative vote along this complicated path kills the measure. Of the thousands of bills introduced during the session, only 10 percent or less actually become law. One of the contributing factors is the shortness of the session. With precious little time, far too many bills fail to make it to the governor's desk. Let us begin our journey onto the legislative pathway with a bill introduced initially in the Texas House of Representatives:

Step 1—The bill is introduced with the first of three readings; numbered, and assigned to a committee by the Speaker of the Texas House. Beginning in November of even-numbered years, members can **pre-file** a bill by submitting it to the clerks of their respective houses. Once the session begins, all of the pre-filed bills are the first ones to receive a number and begin the process. A bill must be officially introduced by a state representative. Bills relating to any subject can be introduced within the first sixty days of the session. After the 60-day deadline, any bill other than a local bill deemed by the governor to be an emergency can be introduced only upon the approval of at least four-fifths of the members on the floor present and voting. Of the approximately 8,000 bills filed during the 84th Texas legislative session, 928 bills were filed on the last day of the filing period bringing the total number of bills "to 4,114 House bills, 1993 Senate bills, and 1,771 resolutions."[16]

Step 2—The committee or, if need be, a sub-committee examines the legislation. If the committee believes the bill is too flawed for further consideration, they can vote to **pigeonhole** it, effectively killing it. It is the committee or the sub-committee that conducts public hearings, reviews the legislation, and, if necessary, adds amendments to the original bill and submits a committee report. The "notice of the hearing" must be posted at least five calendar days before the scheduled hearing in a regular session or at least twenty-four hours before the scheduled hearing in a special session. Both sides must have enough time to rally their troops for their testimony. The committee report includes a record of the committee's activities and recommendations, including placement on the appropriate calendar, the text of the bill, any proposed amendments, a detailed bill analysis, any recommendations for funding, and any other attachments to the legislation. A favorable report moves the bill forward while a negative report kills the measure. A bill receiving an unfavorable report can be revived by a minority report or a motion adopted by a majority vote from the Texas House membership. The motion is commonly known as a **discharge petition**, a legislative procedure that forces a bill out of committee. In our scenario, the bill receives a favorable nod. In the Texas House, all committee reports are submitted to the committee coordinator who, in turn, forwards them to the printer.

Step 3—The bill is printed and distributed to the entire Texas House membership.

Step 4—The bill is forwarded to the Calendars Committee for assignment to one of six different calendars:

• **Consent Calendar**—all bills not expected to draw serious opposition from passing

• **Emergency Calendar**—all bills demanding immediate attention including those submitted by the governor as emergency items; all revenue, tax and appropriations bills

• **Major State Calendar**—all legislative items effecting the entire state that are not emergency items

• **General State and Area Calendar**—all bills having less than a statewide effect or apply to more than one county

• **Local Calendar**—all legislative items pertaining to one county, locality, or group

• **Constitutional Amendment Calendar**—all proposed amendments to either the state constitution or the United States Constitution

The Rules and Resolutions Committee also establishes the time limits for debate of items for consideration on the Texas House floor.

Step 5—On the House floor, the bill is given its second reading. Debate follows with any amendments to the original legislation requiring a majority vote for approval.

Step 6—On the House floor, the bill is given its third reading. Debate follows. Any proposed amendments at this point must be approved by a 2/3's vote. The bill passes the House.

Step 7—Approved amendments are added to the bill. The bill is now forwarded to the Senate for its consideration.

The same steps are followed in the Texas Senate with the exception of Step 4, since the Senate does not have a Calendars Committee. Also, the Senate has open ended debate with the infrequently used option to filibuster the legislation. A **filibuster** is an attempt to grab control of the Senate floor and literally talk the bill to death. Usually a filibuster is conducted by senators who simply do not have the support of their fellow lawmakers. The hope is by tying up all of the other pending business of the Senate, they will effectively convince the membership to set this bill aside for another day, thus freeing up all of the back logged bills for floor consideration. Perhaps the only way to spoil a filibuster attempt is to evoke **cloture,** a parliamentary technique used by a legislative body to end debate and bring the matter under consideration to a vote.[17] Perhaps she did not realize it at the time but Texas Democrat State Senator Wendy Davis became a national household name overnight and launched her bid for the governorship on Tuesday, June 25, 2013, when she staged an 11-hour filibuster that successfully stalled for the short-term a bill practically closing all abortion clinics in the state of Texas. Her filibuster was unique in that the Republicans in the Texas Senate passed procedural rules mandating that she had to speak about the subject matter of the bill, nothing less than that, or the filibuster would end. She could not like United States Senator Ted Cruz read from Dr. Seuss' *Green Eggs and Ham* while he was filibustering against a federal bill. Also, Davis was restricted from any conveniences including bathroom breaks, a chair to sit in, food or water breaks, etc. In the end, both houses of the Texas Legislature passed the bill, and Governor Perry signed it into law.

If the bill passes the Senate and no amendments are added to it, then the bill is forwarded to the governor for his/her consideration. However, if the bill passed in the Senate has been significantly changed from the House version, or if new amendments have been added to the House version, or if bills introduced in each chamber are identical in subject matter and intent but differ in other ways, a **conference committee** is required to hammer out the differences in hopes of combining both bills into one piece of legislation that will pass in both houses. The presiding officers from both houses appoint five members to serve on the committee. Senate rules require that at least two of the Senate conferees be members of the Senate committee that originally handled the legislation. A conference committee's charge is limited to just reconciling only the identified differences in the existing legislation. The committee cannot alter, amend, or omit text unless specifically directed to do so. The committee's final report has to be approved by at least three committee members from their respective houses. An inability to reconcile differences in the conference committee basically kills the chances of the bill from passing in either chamber of the legislature. If the committee's actions are successful and the bill passes both houses, it is then forward to the governor's office.

There are several voting options used in legislative houses. Votes can be recorded with each legislator either verbally saying yea or nay or he/she can simply indicate his/her preference by pushing a bottom on their desk with their response recorded on a electronic scoreboard. Parliamentary procedures allow for voice votes, a show of raised hands, or members standing indicating their preferences when called upon. A teller counts either the number of raised hands or the standing members. The voice vote is perhaps the most flawed voting method because it is up to the presiding officer to determine the difference in the volume between the yeas and the nays. The method of casting and tallying votes has plagued all legislative houses. Traditionally, how your legislator voted on a particular bill was difficult to determine particularly in the Texas House. Votes were noted on a large electronic board whereby a representative simply pushed a button to approve, disapprove, or to abstain. The board would light up in the appropriate category by each

representative's name. In the Senate, it was just a roll call vote. Particularly in the House, there were allegations of "**ghost voting,**" whereby someone other than the lawmaker assigned to that desk pushed the button. There was even the situation where a lawmaker died in the middle of the session, but mysteriously the board continued to show him voting throughout the rest of the session. Finally in 2007, voters approved a constitutional amendment requiring that all final votes be recorded. The rationale behind the amendment was the concern from voters that they simply had no way of knowing how their representatives voted. A recorded vote puts the pressure on the legislator to defend his/her choices to their constituents. In the heat of the campaign, recorded votes keep the lawmaker honest in articulating his/her issue positions and gives the opponent no room to the say that his/her incumbent opponent cast a vote different from the one officially recorded.

The governor has three options: sign the bill into law; refuse to sign it and it automatically becomes law; or veto it. If the bill is vetoed, the governor must send the bill back to the house of origin along with his/her written objections. If there is time remaining in the legislative session, both houses can override the veto with a 2/3's majority in both chambers. If not, the legislation can only be revived at the beginning of the next legislative session. The implementation time period of laws passed by the Texas Legislature is established in Section 39, Article III, of the Texas Constitution: "no law passed by the Legislature, except the general appropriation act [the budget bill], shall take effect or go into force until ninety days after the adjournment of the session at which it was enacted, unless the Legislature shall, by a vote of two-thirds of all the members elected to each house, otherwise direct."

While the legislature may pass them and the governor may sign them into law, many state laws have been overturned by both state and federal courts as unconstitutional acts. Lawmakers cannot overlook that the judiciary does make public policy whenever it rules on the constitutionality of a law. State appellate courts and the Texas Supreme Court hear cases challenging the merits of whether any state law, local statute, or city ordinance is an unconstitutional breach of the Texas Constitution. Historically, the state court system has played a key role in a full range of policy issues from public education funding to water conservation plans. Of course, the potential impact of the United States Supreme Court cannot be overlooked. **Article VI** of the United States Constitution, called the **Supremacy Clause,** made this document the supreme law of the land, meaning that any law passed at any level of government can be invalidated by the United States Supreme Court if that law conflicts with the spirit and meaning of the United States Constitution. The power of judicial review was granted to the federal courts including the United States Supreme Court through the passage of the **Judiciary Act of 1789**.

Budgeting

Discussed in more detail in Chapter 10, one of the primary duties of the Texas Legislature is to pass a biennial balanced budget for the interval between legislative sessions.

Representing the Constituents

How a lawmaker casts his/her vote is reflective of how they individually view their relationship with their constituents. Their style of representation, in part, hinges on how long the each lawmaker has served in the legislature. Newly elected lawmakers tend to follow the **instructed-delegate** view of representation whereby a legislator is duty bound to vote according to the dictates of his/her constituents. Consequently, it is the responsibility of the lawmaker to constantly seek the opinion of his/her constituents before casting a vote on any item before the legislature. Lawmakers are not to vote along party lines or according to their own consciousness. Rather it is the opinions and issue positions of the constituents that guide the lawmaker's decisions. On the other hand, those who have served their legislative districts for several years usually opt for the **trustee** view of representation. According to Edmund Burke, "your representative owes you, not his industry only, but his judgment and he betrays, but instead of serving you, if he sacrifices it to your opinion."[18] In other words, lawmakers are empowered to vote according to what they consider to be in the best interests of the people they were sent to represent. Voters must trust their lawmakers to make the right decisions even though those decisions at the time they are made contradict the sentiments of the constituents. For example, few will support their lawmakers approving a new tax simply because no one likes to pay taxes. But, in the future if those new tax revenues mean new schools, better roads, and more convenient services to the lawmaker's district, then the lawmaker who casts his/her vote to approve those taxes made the right decision. The hybrid option is the **politico** view of representation, combining the trustee and delegate models. Consequently, lawmakers can opt to use their own discretion as to whether to consult or not to consult with their constituents prior to casting his/her vote on the floor of their respective legislative houses. Of the three models, the politico is the most practical option.

In the view of his/her constituents, the lawmaker that is always seeking concurrence before casting a vote is seen as weak and indecisive. On the other hand, a lawmaker that consistently votes on legislative matters without input from his/her constituents can be viewed as out of touch and detached from the very people he/she courted for their support at the polls.

Basically what the average constituent wants is a lawmaker that can make the tough decisions while at the same time bring advantages back to his/her district. **Pork barrel legislation** is "appropriations made by a legislative body providing for expenditures of sums of public money on local projects not critically needed."[19] In the United States Congress all broad-based sweeping pieces of legislation granting billions of dollars in new projects such as interstate highway expansion plans divide the potential funding into at least fifty or more parcels. Now each member of the Senate and the House of Representatives has a vested interest in voting for that bill. The same tactics are employed in state legislative houses. For example, a bill before the Texas House of Representatives is a multi-billion dollar highway construction package that will bring better roads and more jobs to the state's major metropolitan areas. Would you continue to support your lawmaker who decided to vote against the measure because it went against the philosophical approach of his/her political party leadership who sees it as a frivolous expenditure, or would you support the lawmaker that not only voted for the measure but made sure that your district received a large chuck of the money for highway and road projects in your city?

Impeachment and Censure Processes

All state legislative houses have the power of impeachment over the governor, judges, and state executive officials. **Impeachment** "a formal accusation, rendered by the lower house of a legislative body that commits an accused civil official for trial in the upper house."[20] Patterned after the United States Congress, the Texas House of Representatives could form a committee to investigate any illegal activities, breach of constitutional duties, or, as in the case of a judge, judicial misconduct. The committee would report its findings to the membership of the House. In turn, they may find no substance to the allegations, or they could vote to officially charge the individual with an impeachable offense. Once the charges are made, then the impeachment process begins. The Senate as a whole acts as the jury, while the Chief Justice of the Texas Supreme Court serves as the presiding judge. To date, the Texas Legislature has only impeached one governor—Jim Ferguson in 1917. Internally, all legislative houses have provisions to officially discipline or **censure** a member for inappropriate behavior, dereliction of official duties, or malfeasance. Article III section 11 of the Texas Constitution states that "each House may determine the rules of its own proceedings, punish members for disorderly conduct, and with the consent of two-thirds, expel a member, but not a second time for the same offense." Few legislative houses have expelled any of its members, opting instead to selectively and rarely use censure. Escaping the punishment of the Texas Legislature does not exempt the individual from possible criminal charges if their actions violated state or federal laws. For example, between legislative sessions, Representative Tara Rios Ybarra (D) representing the South Padre Island district was arrested and charged by federal agents for Medicaid fraud. If convicted she was facing at least five years in prison and a hefty fine. The adverse publicity caused her to lose her primary race in 2011. In March 2013, a federal judge dismissed all of the charges for oral surgery fraud against her and three other dentists.

Approving U.S. and Proposing Texas Constitutional Amendments

The United States Constitution mandates that any amendment to the document must be approved by three-fourths of the states by either a vote of the state legislatures or a state convention. In Texas, national constitutional amendments are ratified by a majority vote in both houses of the legislature. During the 2017 legislative session, the Texas Senate passed several measures to convene a national constitutional convention to amend the United States Constitution with the aim of reducing federal control over state governments. Introduced by Texas Senator Brian Birdwell, a conservative Republican from Granbury, the measures called for "imposing fiscal restraints on the federal government, including a balanced budget amendment; limit federal jurisdiction in favor of increased states' rights; limit terms of office for federal officials and members of Congress; and allow the states the right to ratify decisions by the U.S. Supreme Court that overturned law."[21] His proposals ran against a brick wall since the Texas House did not approve them and even if they did pass both houses of the Texas Legislature, it still takes the action of twenty-four other state legislative houses to call for a national constitutional convention.

For the Texas Constitution, amendments are proposed by a two-thirds vote in each chamber with final approval left up to the voters. Since its adoption in 1876, the current Texas Constitution has over 650 amendments, making it one of the longest and most amendment documents among the fifty states.

Confirming Appointments

As a check on a governor's authority, all legislative houses are constitutionally required to approve all appointments made by the governor to non-elective government positions within his constitutional authority. According to Article IV, Section 2 and 3, "all vacancies in the State or district offices, except members of the Legislature, shall be filled unless otherwise provided by law by appointment of the Governor. An appointment of the Governor made during a session of the Senate shall be with the advice and consent of two-thirds of the Senate present." Advice and consent enables the Senate to conduct investigations and, if necessary, hearings regarding the qualifications of the nominee. Of course, the governor should exercise **senatorial courtesy** by conferring with nominee's state senator before submitting the name to the full Senate. Whatever a governor can do before hand helps his/her nominee clear the hurdles. **Confirmation** is "the power of a legislative body to approve nominations made to fill executive and judicial positions."[22] If the legislature is not in session, the governor can opt to use a **recess appointment** whereby the individual will assume the duties of the position pending official confirmation when the legislature convenes its next session. In the case of an elective office vacancy, the governor would appoint a temporary replacement until a special election can be called. Basically, the bulk of the governor's appointees fill positions on state boards and commissions.

Administrative Oversight

The separation of powers doctrine divides the operation of government between the legislative branch that creates the laws and the executive branch charged with the implementation and execution of the laws. Legislative houses create the budget and allocate the funding to the various state agencies charged with implementing state laws. It is the responsibility of the legislature to ensure that the taxpayers' money is spent wisely and appropriately. In Texas, state agencies are required to submit regular reports to the legislature detailing their operations and budgetary expenditures. The **Legislative Audit Committee (LAC)** requires that the state auditor conduct random periodic inspections of both the books and the operations of each state agency. A six-member commission, the membership includes the Speaker of the Texas House, the chairpersons of the House Appropriations Committee and the Senate Finance Committee, the lieutenant governor, and a senator appointed by the lieutenant governor. In 1997, the Texas Legislature went a step further in its oversight function with the passage of the **Sunset Act,** establishing the **Sunset Advisory Commission**. This body is composed of ten legislators (five from each house) and two chosen from the public at-large. The task of the commission is to at least once every twelve years review each state administrative agency and recommend whether it should continue as is, be combined with another agency, or abolished. In 1981, the commission was given the authority to review the rules and regulations of administrative agencies. On paper, it appears that the commission is well armed to play a heavy hand in the day to day operations of state agencies. However, the effectiveness of the commission is questionable in that it rarely chastises an agency for lax rules and regulations and is even more reluctant to actually abolish an agency. Unlike Texas, some states have enacted strong sunset laws mandating an automatic expiration date for many of its non-essential state agencies.

Casework

An informal function of a legislative house, **casework** is collectively "the services performed by legislators and their staffs at the request of and on behalf of constituents.[23] Oftentimes legislators and their staff members are the troubleshooters and problem solvers for their constituents. It can be as simple as referring the caller to the appropriate state agency to investigating a claim of fraud or illegal business practices. Unfortunately the decentralized structure of the state's bureaucracy does not encourage cooperation of or the sharing of basic information between the numerous state agencies. Ignoring a constituent's concerns can hurt the re-election chances of an incumbent candidate more so than a negative campaign ad aired from the opponent's camp. When a constituent visits the capitol, he/she has the expectation that when they knock on their representative's office door, someone will be there to open it and provide them with a greeting, a handshake and, perhaps, a quick tour. When a concerned citizen calls to express an opinion or to report a concern, the caller expects someone to answer the phone and listen to them. Constituents like to feel that they are important to their elected representatives.

Legislative Redistricting

Redistricting has been and always will be the most contentious task assigned to any state legislative body. **Apportionment** is "the allocation of legislative seats."[24] 4The process of apportionment is known as **redistricting**, defined as the action of a state legislature or other body in redrawing legislative electoral district lines following a new population census.[25] Simplistic terminology for such a complicated process! Legislative and congressional districts are apportioned by a ratio. The number of seats of both houses of the Texas Legislature was fixed by the 1876 Texas Constitution. The easy method is to simply divide the total population of the state into 150 House districts and 31 Senate districts. The same method would apply to United States Congressional districts. However, *where* those boundary lines are drawn can determine the political fate of any single state lawmaker and United States congressperson as well as their respective political parties. What lawmakers want to avoid is the taint that their efforts have resulted in **gerrymandering**, "the drawing of legislative district boundary lines to obtain partisan or factional advantage."[26] The United States Constitution does not demand the redrawing of legislative and congressional districts but merely requests a review of district apportionment at least once every ten years after an officially federally conducted census to ensure equal representation among the representational districts. Across the state, the charge of gerrymandering was initially levied by urban population groups who saw their legislative houses ignoring the growing lopsided increase in urban population coupled with a declining rural population. The Texas Legislature followed several of her sister legislative houses by opting not to redistrict, thus keeping the existing boundary lines census after census. Rural interests were overrepresented while urban areas were underrepresented. The districts were indeed gerrymandered to favor rural interests. In 1948, voters approved a constitutional amendment to the Texas Constitution that stipulates in Article III, Section 28 that "the Legislature shall, at its first regular session after the publication of each United States decennial census, apportion the state into senatorial and representative districts. . . . In the event the Legislature shall at any such first regular session following the publication of a United States decennial census, fail to make such apportionment, same shall be done by the Legislative Redistricting Board of Texas." The **Legislative Redistricting Board (LRB)** is composed of the Speaker, lieutenant governor, comptroller, land commissioner and the state attorney general. Constitutionally, the Board, when called upon, is required to assemble in Austin within ninety days after the adjournment of the regular legislative session and has sixty days to develop a redistricting plan. An acceptable plan must bear the signatures of three LRB members and once filed with the Secretary of the State, it becomes effective with the next general election. If the Board fails to develop a plan, the Texas Supreme Court has the jurisdiction to compel the commission to perform its duties until a plan emerges.

Despite the creation of the LRB, the charges of gerrymandering against urban districts continued into the

1950s and 60s. The **Baker v Carr** case of 1962 clearly indicated that the United States Supreme Court was deeply concerned over the infrequency of and the methods employed in redistricting plans. The case involved the validity of a 1901 Tennessee law requiring its legislature to base any redistricting plan on the number of "qualified" voters in the state. The Court not only ruled that mal-apportioned and, in several states, non-apportioned legislative districts were unconstitutional but that the federal courts did have jurisdiction over apportionment issues. In 1964, the Court stepped further into the fray with its ruling in **Reynolds v Sims** questioning the lack of legislative redistricting by Alabama's state legislature. Stating "legislators represent people, not trees or acres," the Court mandate that all seats in a bicameral legislature must be appropriated on an equal population basis.[27] The **Reynolds** case along with its 1963-64 decisions in **Gary v Sanders** (each person's vote must be counted equally in statewide primary elections) and **Wesberry 'v Sanders** (congressional districts must be as close as possible equal in population) introduced a new concept to redistricting— "**one man, one vote.**" In other words, the Court basically ruled against multimember legislative districts and under/overrepresented legislative and congressional districts. The 1965 **Voting Rights Act** requires that all redistricting plans receive a pre-clearance from the United States Justice Department prior to implementation. The map would have to be redrawn if the review showed that the districts were gerrymandered. In 1982, a provision was added to the Voting Rights Act requiring the Justice Department to reject any redistricting plan that denied representation to minorities. In 1986, the United States Supreme Court ruled in **Thornburg v Gingles** that redistricting plans had to maximize minority representation in both national and state legislative redistricting efforts. A 2001 Court decision in **Hunt v Cromartie** limited the practice of racial gerrymandering by ruling that race could not be the primary factor in determining legislative district boundary lines. However, the Court did uphold partisan considerations as a primary factor.

Texas redistricting plans became the focus of the Court's ruling in **Kilgarlin v Martin** in 1965 mandating that Texas adhere to the "one man, one vote" principle. The Texas Senate had always been configured into single member districts. However, seats in the Texas House were multimember districts whereby voters in a county would cast separate votes for two or more legislative seats. Clearly a violation of "one man, one vote," by 1975, these districts were all redrawn into single member districts. The 1990 census proved to be a problem for Texas redistricting plans as the legislature worked with census data that was flawed.

Since the Census Bureau falls under the direction of the United States Department of Commerce then Secretary of Commerce Robert Mosbacher, a Texan, informed the Texas Legislature that approximately 560,000 Texans had not been counted in the census tallies. However, the legislature proceeded to redistrict, prompting Governor Ann Richards to opt not to signed the redistricting bill and allowing it to become law while Attorney General Dan Morales was trying to get the Census Bureau to adjust the tallies. Mosbacher did not adjust the totals.

The biggest issue in redistricting in Texas is the twin problems of **minority vote packing** and **minority vote dilution**. For example, the census indicates that Harris County has increased its population enough to mandate four rather than three United States congressional seats. To minimize the opportunity of the African-American community to elect two or more African-American congresspersons, the district boundary lines are drawn packing as many African-Americans into one district as possible, enabling them to elect only one African-American candidate. In a minority vote dilution plan, the lines are drawn to disperse the African-American community throughout the four districts in order to severely weaken their voting power in hopes that no African Americans are sent to Congress from these four districts. Minority population groups are the watchdogs over redistricting plans, poised at any moment to file a legal challenge.

However, the scope of redistricting changed dramatically with the 2003 Texas redistricting efforts. In 2001, the Texas Legislature and the LRB failed to create an acceptable redistricting map for its United States congressional seats. The task now fell to a panel of federal judges who redrew the congressional districts to favor incumbent Democrats. The Republicans were not pleased at all. Despite a heavy Republican voter turnout, the 2002 congressional elections saw more Democrats headed for Washington than Republicans. Republican candidates fared much better in the Texas Legislature since they were in the driver's seat in redrawing the Texas House and Senate district boundary lines. Since there is no provision in the Texas Constitution limiting redistricting to just once every ten years, Republicans in both legislative houses decided to redo the districting map. The majority leader of the United States House of Representatives, Tom DeLay, and to some extent Karl Rove jumped into the fray by taking a very active role in the Texas redistricting scheme in hopes of strengthening Republican domination of the Texas Legislature for decades to come. Of course, Democrats were beside themselves. The 2003 legislative regular session began with redistricting on the horizon. However, Lieutenant Governor David Dewhurst (R) and his fellow senators were not enthusiastically supporting another redo. Another roadblock was the Senate's requirement that a two-thirds vote of the members is required for any bill to come before the Senate floor. Although the Democrats held only one-third of the seats, they had enough muster to defeat the redistricting bill from gaining floor consideration. Lacking a majority in the House, Democrats decided they would prevent redistricting from surfacing on their floor by all fifty-five jumping ship and going to Oklahoma. They remained there throughout the rest of the legislative session, leaving the House without a quorum to pass any legislation. Governor Perry decided to call a special session with redistricting being the only agenda item. Again, Senate Democrats used the two-thirds rule to successfully block redistricting from gaining floor action. Dewhurst hinted that if a second special session was needed that he would entertain a motion to suspend the two-thirds rule in the Senate in order to pass the redistricting plan. The House Democrats returned as Perry contemplated calling the second special session. As the Senate Democrats pondered as to whether it was their turn to leave the state, Governor Perry tried to surprise them by ending the first special session a day early and immediately called the second, thus trapping the Democrat senators in Austin. The Democrats, however, spoiled that plan by quickly fleeing this time to Albuquerque, New Mexico. The governor then called a third special session. Unfortunately for the Democrats, Houston Senator John Witimire returned to Austin. Witimire feared that the governor would continue to call special sessions until redistricting was a done deal. The boycott ended, and the Republican plan won approval, ultimately giving the Republicans large gains in congressional seats in the 2004 general election. The Justice Department upheld the redistricting plan. The Democrats joined forces with minority groups in challenging the plan.

In 2006, the United States Supreme Court ruled in **League of United Latin American Citizens v Perry** that the United States Constitution only requires at least one revisit of district boundary lines after a census, meaning that states can redistrict as many times as they wish within that ten-year period. The only ruling favoring the Democrats was that the Court did conclude that two congressional districts located in west Texas were indeed gerrymandered against Hispanics. The Court mandated the redrawing of the 23rd Congressional District that stretched from the northwestern part of San Antonio to El Paso. The boundary lines were basically shifted back to the original plan. The judge called for a special election slated for November 7, 2006. The fate of Congressman Ciro Rodriguez was definitely impacted by these shifting

redistricting plans. The 23rd was his congressional district. Under the 2003 Republican plan, Rodriguez's district so changed that it resulted in Rodriguez running against another incumbent Democrat Congressman Henry Cuellar. Cuellar bet Rodriguez in the primary election. The 2003 redraw was a Republican attempt to help incumbent Republican Congressman Henry Bonilla successfully replaced Rodriguez in the 28th congressional district. In the 2004 election, Bonilla won in the 23rd district with Rodriguez winning his seat in the 28th district. In the 2006 races, Henry Cuellar successfully challenged Rodriguez in the 28th district race. As a result of the 2006 Supreme Court decision, the shifting boundary lines for the 2006 special congressional elections put Rodriguez back into the 23rd district where he soundly beat Bonilla.

Redistricting was once again a hotly debated issue in the 2011 legislative session. The preliminary census tallies showed that the rapid growth in the state's population would mean that the state's congressional delegation would change from 32 to 36. The four new seats would mean one more additional seat in Bexar and Harris counties, one in the Fort-Worth Metroplex and another one in the Rio Grande Valley. With a super-majority in the Texas House and a strong majority in the Senate, the Republican plan passed with partisan flying colors. If the plan held, the Republicans would likely take 26 of the 36 seats with all Republicans in "safe seats." However, Democrats filed lawsuits challenging the redistricting plans. A lower federal court ruled against the Republican plan and drew maps of their own favoring Democrats and minority population groups. "In trying to fix this imbalance, the district court's plan created three new districts in which minority voters would be the majority, with the Democrats possibly gaining four seats."[28] The new plan still had to undergo pre-clearance by the Justice Department as mandated by the Voting Rights Act of 1965. Meanwhile, Republicans sued on the grounds that legislative houses and not judges are charged with redistricting responsibilities. On January 20, 2012, the United States Supreme Court told the three-judge federal district court in San Antonio to put aside redistricting plans it created and design new maps based on those made by the Texas Legislature. "The Court's unanimous decision said that redistricting is primarily a job for elected state officials and that the lower court had not paid enough deference to maps drawn by the State Legislature."[29]

On June 25, 2013, the United States Supreme Court ruled in **Shelby County v Holder** that Section 4 of the Voting Rights Act of 1964 is unconstitutional. Section 4 sets the guidelines for whether a state's redistricting plans are subject to preclearance. Section 5 details the procedures for preclearance. According to the Court, the problem with Section 4 is that the criteria for preclearance is forty years old and has never been updated. In its 5-4 decision, the Justices did not strike down the Voting Rights Act but clearly emphasized that "Congress could have updated the coverage formula at that time, but did not do so. Its failure to act leaves us today with no choice but to declare [Section 4] unconstitutional. The formula in that section can no longer be used as a basis for subjecting jurisdictions to preclearance."[30]   Basically, if the formula to determine what constitutes a preclearance is unconstitutional then Section 5 is ineffective since the Justice Department cannot conduct any preclearance analysis. As expected, voting rights activists and civil rights leaders were outraged. Jon Greenbaum, chief counsel for the Lawyers' Committee for Civil Rights Under Law, stated "the Supreme Court has effectively gutted one of the nation's most important and effective civil rights law. Minority voters in places with a record of discrimination are now at greater risk of being disenfranchised than they have been in decades. Today's decision is a blow to democracy. Jurisdictions will be able to enact policies that prevent minorities from voting, and the only recourse these citizens will have will be expensive and time-consuming litigation."[31]

After the Court's decision, the Texas Legislature opted to use the court's redrawn maps with only minor changes for the upcoming 2014 election cycle. Back in court again, both sides were arguing over the legality of the 2013 district maps. In 2017, a three-judge federal court issued its ruling that "the 2011 maps were drawn by Republicans to intentionally discriminate against minority voters, who tend to favor Democrats" and "determined intentional discrimination remained a problem in the 2013 maps because the 11 problem districts were almost entirely unchanged from the 2011 maps."[32]   To remedy this problem the justices "ordered two congressional districts and nine Texas House districts to be redrawn to correct improper racial gerrymandering or efforts to reduce minority voting strength."[33]   Obviously, the LRB did not like the Court's ruling. Still holding to the legality of the 2013 district lines, the LRB stood firm as the legal team representing various minority rights groups pressed onward to the United States Supreme Court. The Supreme Court ruled in 2018 that the 2013 districting maps were legal and did not violate the Constitution or the Voting Rights Act. "The court said it found no evidence that Republican lawmakers drew the districts in 2013 with the intent to discriminate, in part because they had adopted court-drawn districts."[34]   The upcoming 2020 census tally will indicate a shift in population from rural to urban areas as well as population growth in the state's major cities. The LRB will meet again to redraw those state and congressional legislative districts. And once again, whatever configuration

they come up with will be challenged before the federal courts once again for the same issues that have plagued redistricting plans for reapportioning the state's representational districts for decades.

Conclusions

The Texas Legislature has strengths and weaknesses. On the whole, the limitation of the biennial session coupled with the shortness of the session to only 140 days does compromise the effectiveness of the body. There simply is not enough time to carefully examine, investigate, and analyze every piece of legislation. Despite the hard work of committee members, there are always problems with the final product. Far too often the legislation suffers from substantive (textual) and procedural (implementation and enforcement) problems that ultimately makes the law unenforceable. The high turnover of lawmakers in both houses is alarming. The solution to both of these problems would be annual sessions and higher pay that would entice a legislator to continue to want to serve his/her state government. However, both cost money. If the taxpayers rejected a measure to increase legislative salaries from $7,200 to $23,358, they certainly are not going to want to pay the tab for annual sessions, salary increases for legislators and their staff members, and the costs of day to day legislative expenses. From 1949 to 1975, Texas voters soundly rejected five state constitutional amendments changing the legislative session from biennial to annual.

The Texas Constitution basically stripped the governor of real governing power. However, the practices of the Texas Legislature have given the governor more authority than he/she should have. The shortness of the legislative session backlogs bills. The rush is on in the final weeks to pass as many bills as possible and pile them on the governor's desk hours before adjournment. Yet, this leaves the door wide open for the governor to selectively choose which bills to enact and which to veto. The governor knows that once the legislature has adjourned and the lights are turned off, there is no one home in those chambers to override the veto. Senator Jeff Wentworth did introduce a proposed constitutional amendment allowing the legislature to call itself into special session if it wanted to override the governor's veto. However, the proposal went nowhere. The shortness of the session enables the governor to wait until the legislature has adjourned to make a recess appointment of an individual knowing that the individual could not pass the muster with the current Senate in hopes that in next session, the Senate would see what a wonderful job this person has done and deem him/her worthy of the permanent position.

Whether it is the United States Congress or the Texas Legislature, democratic bodies must be able to debate in a friendly professional manner and ultimately reach a compromise. "All government, indeed every human benefit and enjoyment, every virtue and every prudent act, is founded on compromise and barter. We balance inconveniences; we give and take; we remit some rights that we may enjoy others; and we choose rather to be happy citizens than subtle disputants."[35]

With the close of the 2017 legislative session, the word compromise cannot be used in the same sentence with the Texas Legislature. Nor does gridlock apply when both houses of the legislature are controlled by Republican majorities.   Particularly in this legislative session, the spirit of bipartisanship was absent even before the session began. In particular the 2017 session witnessed heightened "noisy gallery protests to rules fights, filibusters, walkouts, hideouts, and speaker insurrections. . . the 85th session was marked by an unusually harsh tone, deep divisions, and a lack of civility."[36] In the regular session, state Senator Donna Campbell, Republican representing New Braunfels, introduced a bill curbing a city's right to annex unincorporated subdivisions into its city limits without prior approval of subdivision residents. After very heated debate, "that bill, SB 715, nearly made it to Abbott's desk but was killed in the waning hours of the session, after a filibuster by state Senator Jose Menendez, D-San Antonio."[37] Placed on the agenda for the special session, once again heated debate blocked its passage. Another item before this legislative session was a bill outlawing sanctuary cities. If passed, this law would ban cities, counties and even colleges and universities from prohibiting law enforcement from asking individuals about their immigration status. It would have allowed the state to file criminal charges against law enforcement officers who did not ask the question and provided for the removal of any state elected official who blocked the ban. This bill alone created a hostile environment in both chambers. "On the [regular] session's final day, a scuffle occurred on the House floor after hundreds of protestors chanted opposition to SB4 in the Capitol rotunda. A member of the Texas Freedom Caucus in the House said he called U.S Immigration and Customs Enforcement (ICE) to report the protestors were illegal immigrants, enraging some Hispanic legislators and leading to a tussle with each side accusing the other of threats and violence."[38] The lack of cooperation between the Democrats and Republicans is legendary. Unfortunately, the same pattern appears to be developing in the 2019 legislative session with one exception. The great divide seems to be mirroring the dynamics of the Republican Party at the national level where moderate Republicans and conservative-backed Tea Party members are more at odds with each other than they are collectively battling their Democrat counterparts.

Chapter Notes

[1]George Klosko, *History of Political Theory: An Introduction*, Vol. 2: Modern Political Theory, (New York, New York: Thomson/Wadsworth, 1995), 279.

[2]Mike Ward and Peggy Fikac, "Eyes on Capitol For New Session," *San Antonio Express News* (Monday, January 12, 2015), A5.

[3]Klosko, 40-41.

[4]David C. Saffell and Harry Basehart, *State and Local Government: Politics and Public Policies*, 8th ed., (New York, New York: McGraw Hill, 2005), 155.

[5]David Saleh Rauf, "Lawmakers Poised for Pay Bump," *San Antonio Express-News,* (Wednesday, December 3, 2014), A3.

[6]*2018 Legislator Compensation Information,* National Conference of State Legislatures.

[7]Walter J. Olezek, *Congressional Procedures and Policy Process*, 3rd ed., (Washington, D.C.: The Congressional Quarterly, Inc., 1989), 25-26.

[8]Saffell and Basehart, 167.

[9]David Saleh Rauf and Patrick Svitek, "Straus Challenged for Speaker Post," *San Antonio Express-News*, (Tuesday, January 13, 2015), A3.

[10]Cassandra Pollock, Edgar Walters, Alex Samuels and Emma Platoff, "Texas House Names Dennis Bonnen New Speaker on Celebratory Opening Day, " *Texas Tribune*, January 8, 2019, (*https://www.texastribune.org*)

[11]Jack C. Plano and Milton Greenberg, *The American Political Dictionary*, 10th ed., (Orlando, Florida: Harcourt Brace and Company, 1997), 134.

[12]Saffell and Basehart, 263.

[13]*The HarperCollins Dictionary of American Government and Politics*, Jay M. Shafritz, ed., (New York, New York: HarperCollins Publishers, Inc., 1992), 62.

[14]Ibid., 59.

[15]Plano and Greenberg, 169.

[16]Madlin Mekelburg, "Last Day of Filing Brings in 928 Bills," *San Antonio Express-News*, (Saturday, March 4, 2015), A3.

[17]Plano and Greenburg, 135.

[18]Klosko, 279.

[19]Plano and Greenberg, 158.

[20]Ibid., 150-151.

[21]Mike Ward, "Senate Votes to Try to Change Law of U.S., *San Antonio Express News*, (Wednesday, March 1, 2017), A3 and A10.

[22]Ibid., 138.

[23]*The HarperCollins Dictionary of American Government and Politics*, 96.

[24]Ibid., 128.

[25]Plano and Greenberg, 162.

[26]Ibid., 148.

[27]Ralph A. Rossum and G. Alan Tarr, *American Constitutional Law: Cases and Interpretation*, (New York, New York: St. Martins Press: 1983), 683.

[28]http://www.nytimes.com/2012/01/21/opinion/redistricting-in-texas

[29]http://www/nytimes/com/2012/02/21/us/supreme-court-rejects-judge-drawn-maps-in-texas-redistricting

[30]http://www.huffingtonpost.com.2013/06/25/voting-rights-act-supreme-court

[31]Ibid.

[32]Chuck Lindell, "Feds Flip, Back Texas in Redistricting Fight," *San Antonio Express News*, (Friday, Feb. 1, 2019), A4.

[33]Ibid.

[34]Ibid.

[35]Klosko, 286.

[36]Texas Almanac: 2018-2019, (Denton, Texas: Texas State Historical Association, 2018), 479.

[37]Vivanna Davila, "Senate Oks Curb on Annexation," *San Antonio Express News*, (Thursday, July 27,2017), A3.

[38]*Texas Almanac: 2018-2919*, 479.

The Executive Branch

President and Mrs. Kennedy and Texas Governor John Connally and his wife.
Motorcade in Dallas, Texas, November 22, 1963.

The governorship is "to the people, it is a symbol of the unity of society within the state; to the governor, his[/her] staff, and his[/her] many advisors, it is an image to be carefully constructed and them disseminated through the mass media of communication until it influences every politically conscious person in the state. The governorship is many things, as is the Presidency, and the governor must play many social roles and must learn to help the public to keep them individually identifiable. The governor is chief of state, the voice of the people, chief executive, commander-in-chief of the state's armed forces, chief legislator, and chief of his party."[1]

Far too often, Americans see their governor as a co-equal to the President of the United States in power and prestige. Particularly in the twenty-first century, Texans "look to the governor more than to the legislature and the judiciary; they expect the governor to be able to carry the legislature with him[/her] on important policies, and hold him[/her] responsible if he[/she] fails. On the other hand, if he[/she] succeeds, they honor and exalt him[/her]. He[/she] becomes a national figure."[2] Unfortunately, the Texas Constitution does not give its governor the same sweeping authority granted by the United States Constitution to its chief executive officer—the president. The success or failure of the state's governor is tied more directly to the political and "people" skills of the individual elected to occupy the governor's chair. Like any other state, Texas has had a few governors that Texans can be proud of intermingled with those who had lackluster and even embarrassing tenures as the state's chief executive officer.

Even the hero of the Battle of San Jacinto found that his own strong political skills oftentimes failed him. The early years of Texas's struggles were definitely bound to the fortunes of Sam Houston. On the positive side, Houston devoted the majority of his life in Texas to public service. He was commander of the Texas forces in the fight for independence, served twice as the president of the Republic, served as governor of the State of Texas, and served for fourteen years as the United States Senator from Texas. An adamant supporter of the federal union, Houston resigned his senate seat to run for the governorship of Texas in an attempt to prevent secession from the union. Although he was elected once again as the state's chief executive officer, he resigned after the people of Texas voted to join the Confederacy. He was a man of virtue, honor, truth, and loyalty, yet his personal life did not reflect these traits. One either loved him or hated him. The man who was once courted for the White House was so unpopular when he died that at his funeral on July 27, 1863, only thirteen people attended to pay their respects. Like so many before and after him, Houston was the victim of the fickleness of politics and public opinion. If things go well, you are a hero. If things go wrong, you are vilified.

This chapter examines the transformation of the governor's office from a very strong one created by the 1869 Texas Constitution into a relatively weak one under the 1876 Texas Constitution. In a matter of eight years the office changed from a strong single executive into a weak plural executive. Did the gentlemen who wrote the 1876 document make "a conscious attempt at decentralization and disorganization designed to prevent concentrated authority at any point in state government?"[3] If so, has this structure prevented the state's governors from fulfilling their obligations as the "chief of state, the voice of the people, chief executive, commander-in-chief of the state's armed forces, chief legislator, and chief of his party?"[4] Should Texans continue to strip their governors of meaningful governing authority and mandate that whoever is elected to this position use merely their personal political skills to run the state's government? What changes and recommendations have been made or proposed to convert the office back from one of constitutionally mandated weakness to strength?

The governor's office fulfills the traditional constitutional responsibility of implementing the laws passed by the state's legislative houses. This chapter examines the role state agencies and their boards and commissions play in the enforcement of the state's laws and policies. At both the national and state level, the "bureaucrats" with their rules and regulations are themselves victims of widespread criticism for their lack of efficiency, effectiveness, and their intrusive natures. President Herbert Hoover once lamented that "bureaucracy is ever desirous of spreading its influence and its power. You cannot extend the mastery of the government over the daily working life of a people without at the same time making it the master of the people's souls and thoughts."[5] However, state agencies provide government-sponsored services that average citizens simply cannot provide for themselves. This chapter analyzes the mechanics of the state bureaucratic agencies and addresses many of the criticisms leveled at them.

The Governor

On the presidential campaign trail, George W. Bush was constantly questioned about his qualifications for the presidency. Rightly or wrongly, Bush addressed the criticism by pointing out that he was the powerful governor of the second largest state in the nation. Few actually know that many comparative studies of state executive officers rank the constitutional power and authority of the Texas governor as one of the weakest in the nation. The Council of State Governments' annual survey indicates that in only ten states including Texas do governors share rather than have complete authority over the development of their state's budget. While the Texas governor has line-item veto authority, its use applies only to appropriations. It is further limited since the governor can only line it out, that is, eliminated it from the budget. The governor cannot simply replace one amount with another since that task belongs to the Texas Legislature. Following a presidential-executive model, thirty-two states constitutionally mandate that their governors form a cabinet of key executive officers that meet either on a constitutionally required schedule or at the governor's discretion. Selection of cabinet officers is primarily achieved through gubernatorial appointments or a combination of election and appointment. However, the Texas Constitution opts for a plural executive composed of key executive officers that are popularly elected to their positions with no provision for the governor to remove them from their office. The plural executive further weakens the authority of the Texas governor.

In "The Governors" published in *Politics in the American States: A Comparative Analysis*, Thad Beyle ranks the effectiveness of state governors on both their constitutional duties and the personal attributes they use to execute their gubernatorial duties. The personal rating is based on whether the governor's margin of victory constituted an electoral mandate; the governor's personal ambitions, i.e.; whether this is the highest office he/she is seeking or do they have presidential aspirations; does the governor intend to seek another term of office; and their overall performance ratings. Using a scale of one to five, Beyle gave the Texas governor a 4.5. The second part of the survey looks at the institutional powers granted to governors. The variables include whether the state executive branch follows a single or plural executive format; the length of and limits on the term of office; the governor's control over the state budgetary process; the extent of the governor's veto authority; the governor's ability to work with his/her legislature and their own political party; and the depth of a governor's appointment powers. Unfortunately, the final results place the Texas governorship at 3.1 on a one to five scale. The lowest ranking state governorship belongs to Alabama with a 2.7 rating.[6] A closer examination of the constitutional powers granted to the governor leads one to believe that, indeed, Texas has a weak governor. However, this perception is misleading. In evaluating the performance of any Texas governor, one must realize that "particular powers may be inadequate for this or that purpose, but put together the various powers, the prestige of the governorship, the leadership that is expected from the incumbent, and a shrewd, genial, and dynamic man [or woman] in the office, and the combination becomes an engine of public power that can accomplish great things."[7]

Qualifications for Office, Tenure and Succession

As specified in Article IV, Section 4 of the Texas Constitution, candidates for the governorship must be at least thirty years of age, a citizen of the United States, and must have resided in the state at least five years immediately preceding his/her election. Although not constitutionally mandated, Texans prefer to elect gubernatorial candidates that have either a track record of elective experience or a well-establish successful business background. Very few have been elected without any public office experience. For example, Jim Ferguson proudly ran under the banner of "Farmer Jim" and boasted that his lack of experience in government was actually what the voters wanted in a candidate for the governorship. Pappy O'Daniel also successfully ran his gubernatorial campaign on a similar vein by pointing out that he had never voted in an election or served in any public office. Although never holding an elective office, Dolph Briscoe's resume included positions on civic organizations as well as heading such organizations as the Cattleman's Association, Sheep and Goat Raiser, and the South Texas Chamber of Commerce. He made his fortune in the cattle industry. However, the majority of the state's candidates have held at least one or two elective positions prior to running for governor. Joseph Sayers (1899-1903) served in the state legislature and was elected as both lieutenant governor and United States congressman prior to his election to the governorship. Coke R. Stevenson (1941-1947) was a state representative, and served two terms both as speaker of the Texas House of Representatives and lieutenant governor. Price Daniel (1957-1963) served three terms in the Texas House with one term as speaker, three terms as state attorney general and one term in the United States Senate. Preston Smith (1969-1973) had an attractive elective office track record including three terms in the Texas House, two terms in the

Texas Senate and three terms as lieutenant governor. Rick Perry served initially in the Texas House of Representatives and was subsequently elected as the state's Commissioner of Agriculture and lieutenant governor under Governor George W. Bush. Ann Richards served as the state's Comptroller of Public Accounts prior to her election to the governorship. Greg Abbott was appointed then elected to the Texas Supreme Court and served as the state's attorney general for eleven years. Although they lacked elective office experience, William Clements and George W. Bush impressed voters with their successful oil business ventures that made both of them multi-millionaires. Basically, the unwritten qualifications for the governorship for most voters is whether the candidate has "(1) brilliance of mind, (2) legal knowledge, (3) political experience, (4) administrative skill, (5) sound knowledge of business and industry, and (6) a nationwide acquaintance."[8]

With the exception of Miriam Ferguson and Ann Richards, all of the state's governors have been males. No minority has ever been elected to the governorship. Politically, all of the state's governors with the exception of Ann Richards and, perhaps, James Hogg have been moderate Democrats or conservative Republicans. As discussed in Chapter 4, Texans are very leery of any candidate from the liberal side of the political spectrum.

Passed in 1975, a constitutional amendment changed the term of office from two- to four-years with no limitations on the number of terms a governor can serve. Usually governors served two terms of office. Preston Smith actually ran for a third term but was soundly defeated due to his involvement in the Sharpstown Bank scandal. John Connally is the only Texas governor elected to three consecutive two-year terms of office while Rick Perry is the only Texas governor to be elected to three consecutive four-year terms of office. While the salaries of the members of the Texas Legislature are constitutionally mandated at $7,200, the governor's salary is not mandated and has been increasing steadily. Today, Governor Abbott earns $150,000 per year, making him one of the highest paid governors in the nation. Of course, the governor resides in the state mansion. All of the governor's official expenses including offices at the Capitol and staff salaries are paid out of the state budget. Table 8.1 lists the individuals who have served as either a president of the Republic of Texas or as governor of Texas, with the exception of Sam Houston who was elected as both president and governor of Texas.

Constitutionally, the line of succession to the governorship falls initially upon the lieutenant governor. When Bush was elected to the presidency, Lieutenant Governor Rick Perry automatically became governor. The Texas Senate then elects one of their own to serve as a temporary lieutenant governor while still holding his/her Senate seat until the next general election. If both offices of the governor and lieutenant governor are vacated, the Texas Constitution elevates to the governorship the next in line, the president pro-tempore of the Texas Senate. From there the line of succession is the Speaker of the House, state attorney general, and the chief justices of the fourteen courts of appeals in ascending numerical order, beginning with chief justice of the First Court of Appeals. The state constitution does provide for the lieutenant governor to assume the governor's chair if the governor is temporarily unable to serve due to illness or being temporarily disqualified for the office, or impeached from office. The lieutenant governor automatically serves as governor when the governor is out of the state. Likewise, if both the governor and the lieutenant governor are out of the state, the president pro-tempore of the Texas Senate serves as the acting governor.

Duties of the Texas Governor

Legislative Responsibilities

Initially, governors were supposed to assume the traditional role as the primary implementers of legislative acts. Both presidents and governors, however, have assumed more leadership duties including exerting their influence into the policy arena. It is the single voice of the governor and not the numerous voices of the legislators that the citizens of Texas turn to for leadership and guidance in both good and bad times. A former governor, President Theodore Roosevelt once commented about the evolving role of governors in the legislative process:

> In theory the Executive [governor] has nothing to do with legislation. In practice, as things are now, the Executive [governor] is or ought to be peculiarly representative of the people as a whole. As often as not the action of the Executive [governor] offers the only means by which the people can get the legislation they demand and ought to have. . . . More than half of my work as Governor was in the direction of getting needed and important legislation.[9]

Table 8.1 –Presidents of the Republic and the Governors of Texas

Presidents of the Republic of Texas

David G. Burnet	Mar. 16, 1836-Oct. 22, 1836
Sam Houston	Oct. 22, 1836-Dec. 10, 1838
Mirabeau B. Lamar	Dec. 10, 1838-Dec. 13, 1841
Sam Houston	Dec. 13, 1841-Dec. 9, 1844
Anson Jones	Dec. 9, 1844-Feb. 19, 1846

Governors of Texas

J. Pickney Henderson (1846-1847)[1]	Thomas M. Campbell (1907-1911)
George T. Wood (1847-1849)	Oscar Branch Colquitt (1911-1915)
Peter Hansbrough Bell (1849-1853)	James E. Ferguson (1915-1917)[5]
J. W. Henderson (1853-1853)	William Pettus Hobby (1917-1921)
Elisha M. Pease (1853-1857)	Pat Morris Neff (1921-1925)
Hardin R. Runnels (1857-1859)	Miriam A. Ferguson (1925-1927)
Sam Houston (1859-1861)[2]	Dan Moody (1927-1931)
Edward Clark (1861-1861)	Ross S. Sterling (1931-1933)
Francis R. Lubbock (1861-1863)	Miriam A. Ferguson (1933-1935)
Pendleton Murrah (1863-1865)	James V. Allred (1935-1939)
Fletcher S. Stockdale (1865)	W. Lee O'Daniel (1939-1941)[6]
Andrew J. Hamilton (1865-1866)	Coke R. Stevenson (1941-1947)
James W. Trockmorton (1866-1867)	Beauford H. Jester (1947-1949)
Elisha M. Pease (1867-1869)	Allen Shivers (1949-1957)[7]
Edmund H. Davis (1870-1874)[3]	Price Daniel (1957-1963)
Richard Coke (1874-1876)[4]	John Connally (1963-1969)
Richard Hubbard (1876-1879)	Preston Smith (1969-1973)
Oran M. Roberts (1879-1883)	Dolph Briscoe (197301979)[8]
John Ireland (1883-1887)	William P. Clements (1979-1983)[9]
Lawrence Sullivan Ross (1887-1891)	Mark White (1983-1987)
James Stephen Hogg (1891-1895)	William P. Clements (1987-1991)
Charles A. Culberson (1895-1899)	Ann W. Richards (1991-1995)
Joseph D. Sayers (1899-1903)	George W. Bush (1995-2000)
S. W. T. Lanham (1903-1907)	Rick Perry (2000-2014)[10]
	Greg Abbott (2015 to present)

[1]Albert C. Horton actually served as the governor while Henderson was fighting in the Mexican War.
[2]Houston submitted his resignation when Texas voted to join the confederacy.
[3]After initially winning the election, Davis was appointed as the provisional governor of Texas.
[4]Coke resigned his governor's seat to become a United States Senator.
[5]Ferguson was impeached in 1917.
[6]O'Daniel resigned his governor's seat after he appointed himself to the United States Senate.
[7]Lieutenant Governor Shivers became governor when Jester died in office in 1949.
[8]A 1975 constitutional amendment changed the governor's term of office from two to four years.
[9]Clements was the first Republican elected as governor since Reconstruction.
[10]Lieutenant Governor Perry became governor when George W. Bush was elected president; only governor to be elected to three terms of office.

The relationship a governor has with his/her legislature is oftentimes the only factor a voter has in determining the reelection of an incumbent governor. Particularly during a legislative session, the news media focuses on the wheeling and dealing between the governor's staff, key legislative members, and the leadership of his/her political party. A governor with a good working relationship with the legislature will see the bulk of his/her legislative priorities successfully passed. While on the other hand, a governor seen as unwilling to compromise usually is confronted with a hostile legislature equally unwilling to work with the governor. Even though Greg Abbott has Republican majorities in both houses of the Texas Legislature, there are divisions within the party that can lead to friction and legislative impasses. To the voter, the quality of the working relationship a governor has with his/her legislative houses demonstrates whether this governor has the appropriate leadership skills needed to guide the state for another term of office.

Governors use both informal and formal means of informing the legislature of the direction it should take in addressing public policy concerns. At their inauguration, all in-coming governors clearly indicate their legislative preferences in their inaugural addresses heard by both members of the legislature and, more importantly, the public. The Texas Constitution mandates that the governor deliver a "**state-of-the-state**" message at the beginning of each legislative session. Traditionally, these messages were suppose to update the legislature about the condition of the state's economic picture. However, governors have become accustomed to seizing this opportunity to tell the legislators about their own policy priorities while, at the same time, strongly reminding legislators of what actions the governor's office will take if the legislature does not bow to his/her wishes. Delivered on February 5, 2019 before a joint session of the Texas Legislature, Governor Abbott recognized the state's growing population primarily fueled by those migrating from other states. He pointed out that:

On this very day, about 1,000 new residents will call Texas home. That happens almost every day. Whether you like that or not, we can never lose sight of the reasons so many people make life altering decisions to uproot their families and businesses and chart new paths –paths that guided them to Texas. They were fed up with big government policies increasingly running their lives and imposing burdensome regulations. They were taxed out of their states that some of their families had lived in for generations. The cost of doing business imposed by heavy-handed special interest groups simply became too oppressive. They needed an escape. They longed for freedom. They wanted hope. They found it in Texas. We may not be perfect, but to all the newcomers I talk to, they think Texas is a governmental Holy Grail."[10]

He challenged the 2019 legislature to "tackle some challenges that have plague Texas for more than a generation."[11] His legislative wish list included "emergency legislation" for the creation of an incentive package to retain qualified and talented public school teachers to the tune of a "six-figure salary" and reforming the state's current public school finance system away from the Robin Hood plan to a more equitable financing system benefiting all of the state's public schools.[12] Other items included school safety, providing mental health professionals for both public schools and state-funded colleges and universities, fulfilling the traditional pledge of property tax reform, funding to help those adversely impacted by Hurricane Harvey, additional funding for Texas Anti-Gang Centers, legislation addressing human trafficking and the protection its victims, and charging the legislature with providing the funding the Texas Veterans Commission needs to help veterans receive appropriate heath care benefits. Throughout the legislative session, governors use informal means of communicating policy changes and new initiatives by working directly with their own party's leadership in each house or through members of the governor's staff. "Anyone familiar with the realities of political life is aware that the 'great game of politics' entails at one time or another varying degrees of cajolery, conniving, capitulation, cunning and compromise. Nowhere is the give-and-take nature of politics more demonstrable than in the lawmaking process, and probably no better example of practical politics in operation can be cited than the techniques utilized by the chief executive [governor] in his[/her] dealings with the lawmakers.[13] Make no mistake about it, governors do pay close attention to the daily activities of each legislative house.

Governors have an arsenal of constitutionally mandated authority over the public policy process. Potentially, it is the governor and not the legislature than can exert more direct influence on the development of policy initiatives. Essentially, "the governor wields more influence because of his [/her] more prominent position, which is due to:

1) his [/her] uniqueness as the head of the executive branch, which makes him [/her] a prime source of

news; 2) his [/her] power of veto; 3) his [/her] power to send messages to the legislature and to secure wide publicity for his [/her] recommendations; 4) his [/her] exclusive power to convene special sessions (which should never have been permitted to slip out of legislative hands) and even to determine the agenda for such sessions (a) lamentable violation of separation of powers as well as a denial of wholesome legislative independence); 5) his [/her] power of appointment to executive posts, which may be used to influence legislative action or inaction; and 6) his [/her] power to initiate the budget estimates (which few legislatures are equipped to examine with care and discrimination) . . ."[14]

The governor also has the authority to prod the Texas Legislature into action on items he/she deems to be of extreme importance. For example, at the beginning of the 82nd Texas Legislative session, Governor Perry declared as "emergency" on high priority legislative items including bills requiring a sonogram for any woman seeking an abortion, requiring voters to show photo identification at the polls, and outlawing sanctuary cities.

The **veto** or the threat of a veto is a formidable power given to governors. Particularly in Texas, the shortness of the legislative session can help a governor achieve his/her legislative agenda. Since the Texas Legislature usually waits until the last few weeks of the legislative session to pass the majority of its bills, a governor can successfully work behind the scenes to massage legislation to his/her favor knowing very well that the legislature simply cannot afford for the governor to veto essential legislation. The constitutional guidelines favor the governor since he/she has ten days when the legislature is in session and twenty days when it is not in session to consider whether bills should become laws. If the session ends before the ten days have expired, the governor can veto it and send it along with his/her objections to the Secretary of State. No legislative action can be taken on the measure until the legislature convenes two years from the close of the session.

It seems to be the general opinion of experienced legislators that instances are rare indeed in which vetoed bills are reintroduced and passed without first having undergone sufficient amendment to meet, or at least compromise, the objections to the veto. The single factor which might serve to make such later passage of a vetoed bill possible, namely, a change in administration, serves but to illustrate the political and legislative nature of the present power of veto.[15]

Even if the item is vetoed while the legislature is in session, few vetoes are ever overridden by both houses of the Texas Legislature. A **post-adjournment veto** is the governor's action of vetoing a bill after the legislature has officially adjourned. Post-adjournment vetoes are absolute since they cannot be overridden by the legislature. Bill Clements vetoed 51 bills in just his first two years as governor. Governor Perry used it frequently. By the end of the 2001 legislative session, Perry's vetoing rage became known as the **Father's Day Massacre,** as he vetoed 82 of 1,600 bills passed by the legislature.[16] Several of the items were measures that he assured his own party leadership that he would sign into law. He even vetoed a bill that overwhelming passed both houses of the Texas Legislature. Perry was governor during seven sessions of the Texas Legislature beginning with the 77th and ending with the 83rd. In total, Perry used his regular and line-item veto authority 301 times.[17]

Although limited in scope, the **line item veto** enables the governor to veto appropriations items without vetoing the entire bill. Usually passed at the end of the session, appropriations bills normally arrive on the governor's desk after the legislature has adjourned. Now his/her line item veto is a post-adjournment one, meaning that it is absolute with no chance of being overridden. Technically the line item veto zeroes out the appropriated amount for that particular budget item. The governor simply cannot substitute one figure for another since only the Texas Legislature is empowered to originate appropriations bills. Consequently, it is incumbent for the legislature to work arduously with the governor's office to win tentative approval of the appropriations before the bill makes it to the governor's desk. What the Texas Constitution does not give to the governor is a **reduction veto,** "which would allow him[/her] to reduce an appropriations item without eliminating it."[18] With the reduction veto, it is the legislature's responsibility to either override it and replace it with another amount or reinstate the original appropriation. Yet a prudent use of the line-item veto can show Texans that their governor is indeed watching the financial bottom-line by keeping the legislature from overspending or spending money on frivolous unnecessary projects and programs. For example, Governor Bill Clements bragged that his gubernatorial pen eliminated $252 million from the $20.7 billion from the 1980-81 biennial budget.[19]

The mere threat of a veto can send legislators scrambling to address the governor's discontent with the legislation. "The real power of the governor's veto lies not in his[/her] use if it, but his[/her] threat of it. Members of the legislature will often consult the governor before introducing doubtful legislation, and if the governor warns them that he will veto the measure, they will usually withdraw the offending bills."[20] Obviously, it is incumbent upon the bill's sponsor and his/her party leadership in the legislature to work closely with the governor's staff to iron out the differences to ensure both the passage of the measure and the governor's signature making it law.

The governor's veto options also include the proviso to not take action and allow the bill to automatically become law. This option can be a smart political ploy for a governor caught between a rock and a hard place. Governor Mark White was faced with a political hot potato over the pari-mutuel betting bill. If he signed it into law, he feared a political backlash from conservative Baptist-Methodists who openly condemn gambling. It he vetoed it, he feared repercussions from the business community who believed that without pari-mutuel betting the only viable option for raising additional revenue would be to increase business taxes and, perhaps, implement a statewide income tax. So, White decided to take no action and simply allow the bill to become law without his official signature. Ann Richards did the same with the 1991 legislative redistricting plan crafted and passed by the Texas Legislature. Those same minority groups that helped her to win the governorship felt that the new plan was discriminatory to minorities. She simply could not offend the very group that was instrumental in putting her in the governor's mansion. However, vetoing the bill would have put extreme pressure on the legislature to draft another plan within a relatively short period of time. She faced no political liability by allowing the bill to become law without her official approval.

As previously pointed out in Chapter 7, the Texas Constitution empowers only the governor to call a special session of the legislature. While it may appear to be a trivial action, the meaningful power is the governor's absolute authority to set the agenda for the special session. No item outside of the official agenda can be discussed on the floor of either house of the legislature. Governor Bill Clements called the legislature into three special sessions with only one agenda item—public school financing. The federal courts had given the Texas Legislature a deadline to address funding inequities or the public schools would not open for the upcoming school year. Clements vowed that he would keep them in session forever until they came up with an acceptable plan that he would sign into law. From 2002-2006, Governor Perry called seven special sessions primarily to address redistricting issues (three in 2003) and four others to iron out, once again, state funding of public

schools. At the end of the 82nd Texas Legislative session, he called another special session to address windstorm insurance coverage issues, among other items. He also called a special session at the end of the 83rd legislative session to secure approval of the abortion bill that Wendy Davis successfully filibustered.

Governor Abbott called for a special session at the close of the 2017 regular legislative session. His agenda covered a wide variety of items that the legislature simply either failed to address or to pass for his signature. Specially the agenda called for:

- Abortion – prohibit local governments from funding abortion providers to include Planned Parenthood; restricting health care plans from providing any abortion coverage; stronger abortion reporting requirements

- Development – prevent cities from regulating tree-cutting activities on private property; preventing local governments from changing the rules of a development project during the construction phase; speeding up local constitution permitting processes; mandating that residents in unincorporated areas have a vote to approve proposed annexation plans

- Education – giving teachers a $1,000 pay increase; creating a more flexible teacher performance review process for rewarding salary and benefits increases; establishing a commission to study state school financing; allow school vouchers for students with special needs

- Financial – passing a property tax reform bill; placing caps on state and local spending; and prohibiting union dues from being collected from government paychecks

- Medical – review of sunset legislation for five medical regulatory agencies; strengthening patient protections for do-not-resuscitate orders; extending the maternal mortality task force

- Privacy- pass legislation for the use of multi-occupancy showers, locker rooms, restrooms, and changing facilities for transgender people

- Voting – legislation protecting against mail-in ballot fraud[21]

Even before the special session was called, legislators were busy lining up proposed bills for the session to include "proposals to give winners of the Purple Heart Medal a tax break, prohibit property owners associations from nixing Christmas displays, mandate that school districts reimburse teachers for supplies they buy with their own money or allow schools to use toll roads for free."[22] Despite their legislative creativity, those items only would be considered in a special session if they fit into the governor's specified agenda.

Abbott used the special session to solicit campaign donations for his upcoming 2018 reelection campaign. It is against state law for a sitting state legislator to call for campaign donations during regular legislative sessions. The law does not apply to special sessions. Abbott's campaign staff issued an e-mail pointing out that "during the next 30 days, lawmakers are going to tackle important issues to Texans from out-of-control local regulations to skyrocketing property taxes to runaway state and local spending. Contribute right away if you support Governor Abbott's special session agenda."[23] The governor was not the only one as many members of the Texas Legislature were holding campaign fundraisers and e-mail solicitations during the special session. Only about half of the governor's special session agenda passed the legislature. Abbott got approval of legislation banning state funding of abortion coverage on primary health care plans, a measure cracking down on mail-in ballot fraud, limits on city tree ordinances, and the creation of a special task force to study public school finance reform. But the governor lost on his proposals for property tax reform and the controversial bathroom bill.

Appointment Powers

The Texas Constitution empowers the governor to appoint approximately 2,000 positions to approximately 300 various boards, commissions, committees and councils as well as filling vacancies for elected executive officers, members of the State Railroad Commission, State Board of Education and judicial positions with the exception of municipal, county and justice of the peace benches until the next general election. The only state executive officer appointed by the governor is the secretary of state. The governor appoints a successor to a vacated United States Senate seat until a special election can be held to fill the position. In this case, the governor can, as Pappy O'Daniel did, appoint him/herself to the position. If a vacancy occurs in either house of the Texas Legislature or in the Texas delegation in the United States House of Representatives the governor cannot name a successor but must instead call for a special election. In a special election, all candidates filing for the office run at one time with a runoff election option if the leading candidate does not win with a majority vote.

The ability to appoint members to serve on the states' various boards and commissions enables a governor to reward those who work on or donated substantial funds to the governor's campaign efforts. However, governors must avoid the perception that an appointment can be purchased for the right price. For example, more than half of Perry's appointees to state boards and commissions including the boards of regents at state-supported colleges and universities donated substantial funds to his campaigns. Reportedly, "Perry has collected nearly $90 million in donations over the past decade. At least $10 million has come from appointees to boards and commissions, and more than half that money has come from regents."[24] All appointments must be approved by the Texas Senate.

Since becoming governor in 2015, "Abbott has appointed 889 people to boards or elevated them to chairmanships. Two hundred fifty-nine of those picks-and their spouse in some cases – have donated a combined $14.2 million to Abbott's campaigns since June, 2001."[25] In the 2017 legislative session, Lyle Larson, Republican from San Antonio, won House approval of a bill that "would have barred the appointment of gubernatorial campaign donors if they had given more than $2,500 in the previous year. It would have prohibited appointees from giving more than $2,500 annually while serving."[26] The bill did not pass in the Senate. Of course, the practice of **senatorial courtesy** holds whereby the governor should gain approval of the appointee's state senator prior to announcing the nomination. An appointment to a state board or commission is usually a safe one in that these are non-salaried positions. Secondly, boards and commissions meet infrequently only to establish broad-based policies over the agencies assigned to them. The only drawback is the majority of these appointees serve for six-year terms. A first term incoming governor would have to live with those appointees made by the previous governor simply because their terms of office have not yet expired.

A gubernatorial appointment can open the doors particularly for women and minorities. Governor Clements appointed the first two women to the Texas Supreme Court and the first African American to the Texas Court of Criminal Appeals. Throughout his first term in the governorship the majority (71.8%) of Abbott's appointees were Anglo.[27] In comparison, "the late Democratic former Gov. Ann Richards appointed a larger percentage of women, African-Americans and Hispanics than the Republicans that followed her."[28] A presidential or gubernatorial appointment to fill the unexpired term of an elective office enables the appointee to not only demonstrate his/her ability to do the job but establishes vital name recognition with the potential electorate. Those who initially received their position through an appointment are more than likely to run for that position. Come election time, they will have the advantage over their challengers.

However, an appointment can be an embarrassing incident for both the governor and the appointee. For example, Ann Richards was faced with the rare opportunity of filling a vacancy on the Texas Railroad Commission. Numerous individuals submitted their applications to Richards' staff. One, in particular, caught the governor's eye. Lena Guerrero's resume was impressive including a degree from the University of Texas. Guerrero's appointment would give Richards the opportunity to place a minority woman on a traditionally dominated all white male commission. The nomination sailed through the Texas Senate. Guerrero's job performance was exceptional, leading her to run for her position in the next general election. However, her opponent uncovered what Guerrero knew and the Richards' staff did not. Despite her campaign commercials that she remembered her graduation day from UT she did not complete her academic program, nor did she graduate or receive a diploma. Consequently, she had to resign her position on the Railroad Commission and withdraw from the race. Both Governor Richards and her staff were embarrassed because they should have verified the information on Guerrero's resume prior to submitting her name to the Texas Senate. And, of course, Guerrero should have been truthful on her resume.

Infrequently, the Texas Senate will reject a governor's nominee. The governor, however, has the option to use a **recess appointment**, whereby he/she can wait until the legislature adjourns, and appoint that person to fill that position until the legislature reconvenes. Since the legislature meets biennially, that gives the appointee at least two years or more in the position. Once the legislature convenes, the governor is required to resubmit the nominee for official Senate confirmation. Governor Perry used the recess appointment on three different occasions to fill the position of chairperson of the State Board of Education. His first two picks, Gail Lowe and Don McLeroy, did not pass Senate scrutiny because of their ultra-conservative positions on education. For the third pick, Perry nominated Barbara Cargill, another social conservative. By using his recess appointment after the

legislative session ended in 2013, Cargill served as the chair of the State Board of Education for almost two years before the start of the 83rd legislative session. Of course, the Texas Senate unanimously confirmed her appointment once the new session began.

Initially, Governor Abbott appointed Carlos Cascos as his secretary of state. Casocs subsequently resigned, leaving Abbott to make an interim appoint of David Whitley to the position. With the start of the 2019 legislative session, Abbott officially placed Whitley's appointment before the Senate Nominations Committee. Usually a non-controversial confirmation process, Whitley's nomination has been held up by the committee for Whitley's release of the contentious list of approximately 100,000 plus supposedly of individuals who were unqualified to even register to vote. The reliability of Whitley's list is questionable and is being challenged in several lawsuits filed by voting rights, civil rights and minority group organizations. Whitley has tried to mend fences by meeting with key members of the Texas Senate and "even issued something of an apology for the way his agency bundled its rollout of the controversial citizenship review, which was based on deeply flawed data and seemingly pulled in tens of thousands of registered voters for review because they were naturalized citizens."[29]

Administrative Powers

As the state's chief administrative officer, the governor is directly accountable for all of the various state agencies charged with the running this state. Whenever a law is passed by the legislature, governors do have some flexibility concerning the implementation process and the ultimate marching orders to state agencies. An **executive order** is "any rule or regulation issued by a chief administrative authority that, because of precedent and existing legislative authorization, has the effect of law."[30] Both presidents of the United States and the nation's governors have the authority to use executive orders to reorganize the executive department and create or abolish task forces, boards or commissions. These actions do not require prior approval from legislative houses. For example, President Harry S. Truman used an executive order to desegregate the nation's officer corps to enable minorities to be admitted into officer training programs. President Eisenhower used an executive order to completely reorganize the nation's executive branch of government. Governors will also use the executive order mandating that an agency under his/her direction implement a certain procedure or policy. For example, Governor Perry used an executive order to mandate that all of the state's public schools set aside a fixed percentage of their revenue for certain classroom instruction activities. All executive orders issued by the governor bear the governor's initials and are officially chronologically numbered. For example, an executive order with the code GA36 stands for Greg Abbott executive order number 36. Usually of a ceremonial nature, governors can issue **proclamations** as official public announcements honoring a notable individual or recognizing an important event in Texas history. More importantly, proclamations are used to declare a particular region or community as a disaster area, which qualifies affected parties for special disaster relief and, perhaps, federal assistance.

Removal Powers

Whereas the Texas Constitution grants the governor extensive appointment powers, the document does not give him/her independent authority to remove from office the majority of those he/she appointed. The governor can only independently remove members of his/her personal staff, the executive director of the Department of Housing and Community Affairs, and the commissioners of Health and Human Services, and Insurance. With few exceptions, the governor cannot remove any appointee initiated by his/her predecessor. Of course, the governor cannot fire any member of the state executive team. A 1980 constitutional amendment does allow the governor to remove his/her appointees with prior consent of the Texas Senate. Obviously, the most effective way of removing an appointee is for the governor or his/her staff to talk the individual into resigning their position or accepting another position within the executive branch. This practice saves both the governor and the appointee from public scrutiny and embarrassment. If an appointee refuses to resign, the options available for removal are a) a formal impeachment process similar to removing a governor; b) an **address** whereby the legislature by a 2/3's vote in both houses requests to remove a judge from office; or c) **quo warranto proceedings**, a process whereby the courts would remove the appointee from office.

Budgetary Powers

According to the Texas Constitution, budgetary responsibilities are shared between the Texas Legislature and the governor. Like the president of the United States, the governor would prepare his/her own budget plan for submittal to the Texas Legislature for consideration and reconciliation with the budget document drafted by the pertinent legislative budget committees. By law, the governor is required to submit a budget within five days after the legislative session begins. The state even provides an executive office to assist the governor, namely, the Budget, Planning and Policy Division. This can be a useful tool for the governor since the document indicates his/her budget priorities and his/her public policy initiatives for the upcoming legislative session. The governor's budget document should also indicate which items he/she would be likely to veto. Governors submitting their version of the budget can also help to forestall lengthy budget battles between the legislature and the governor, as well as to prevent an overuse of the governor's line item veto authority after the budget has been developed and passed by the legislature.

Military Powers

Constitutionally, the governor is commander-in-chief of the state's military forces, i.e., the Texas National Guard. Article IV, Section 7 of the Texas Constitution states that the governor "shall have power to call forth the militia to execute the laws of the State, to suppress insurrections, repel invasions, and protect the frontier from hostile incursions by Indians or other predatory bands." The governor has the authority to appoint the Guard's adjutant general who serves as the governor's military aide and advisor. Usually, the governor calls the Guard into action whenever the state is threatened by a natural disaster such as a hurricane or, as seen throughout the summer of 2011, wildfires. The Guard assists in disaster relief, rescues, and protection against looting and destruction of property.

In extreme situations, the governor can declare **martial law** whereby the Guard rules temporarily as the state's military force due to civil disorders deemed unmanageable by local authorities. Governor Jim Ferguson (1915-1917) placed the city of Houston under martial law due to a racial confrontation between Anglos and the African-American community over the building of Camp Logan for the U.S. army during World War I. Governor William Hobby (1917-1921) declared martial law in Galveston in 1920 due to a violent longshoremen's strike. "Between 1917 and 1931, therefore, martial law was used more frequently than during any other period in Texas history. Of the eight times it was invoked, three instances involved race trouble, two were brought about by labor troubles, two quieted periods of lawlessness, and one coped with a storm disaster. The duration of martial law ran from three days to four months."[31] During the wildcat oil days in the East Texas oil fields, Governor Ross Sterling (1931-1933) declared martial law in Rusk, Gregg, Smith and Upshur counties.

Chinese American boys from the Chinese Optimist Club with Texas Governor Allan Shivers, Austin, Texas. c. 1949-1957. Photo credit: UTSA Institute of Texan Cultures

Judicial Powers

According to Article XV, Section 8 of the Texas Constitution, the governor is empowered to remove the judges of the Supreme Court, Court of Appeals, and District Courts "on the address of two-thirds of each House of the Legislature, for willful neglect of duty, incompetency, habitual drunkenness, oppression in office, or other reasonable cause which shall not be sufficient groups for impeachment. . ." To date very few judges have been removed from office on the governor's recommendation. The governor's judicial powers have been effectively used to appoint judges to benches that have been vacated either by the death, resignation, or removal of a sitting judge.

As oftentimes seen on television, a condemned convict is escorted into the death chamber and just as the lethal drugs are nearly injected into the prisoner, the phone rings. The call is from the governor either granting a stay of execution or executive clemency. This is for the most part pure fiction. In Texas, the governor is restricted to granting only one thirty-day reprieve for a death row inmate. In 1936, the Board Pardon Advisors was renamed as the Texas Board of Pardons and Parole. The change was necessitated by the accusation that Governor Miriam Ferguson's husband Jim, the former and impeached governor, was selling pardons and paroles to convicted felons. Not only was the name of the agency changed,

but the Texas Legislature severely limited the governor's authority to grant concessions to those convicted of criminal activity. Appointed by the governor, the eighteen-member board recommends the action the governor should take including parole, executive clemency, a full or conditional pardon, a reprieve of a death sentence, a commutation, or remittance of fines and forfeitures. A **parole** is "the freedom granted to a convicted offender after he or she has served a period of confinement and so long as certain conditions of behavior are met."[32] **Executive clemency** actually sets aside or reduces a convict's sentence. A **pardon** is "an executive's granting of a release from the legal consequences of a criminal act."[33] A **commutation** is merely the reduction of a sentence. The governor still has the authority to override the board's recommendations.

Informal Powers

Traditionally, the governor's role as the state's chief of state was basically ceremonial. The governor would officially represent the state whenever the president of the United States or a foreign dignitary visited the state. The role, however, is changing as governors across the nation are meeting more frequently in Washington, D.C., to discuss common problems, issues, and possible solutions. Oftentimes, a governor is called upon by the president to act as his/her representative on foreign soils or to assist in the

Mrs. James E. (Miriam) Ferguson
Photo credit: Library of Congress

implementation of international agreements. For example, Governor Ann Richards was called upon by President George H. W. Bush to assist in the implementation of the North American Free Trade Agreement with Mexico.

The governor serves as the state's Chamber of Commerce by officially advocating for business development and economic growth. Governor Allen Shivers (1949-1957) secured billions of dollars for the state's public and higher education funds by battling President Harry Truman over the state's offshore oil deposits, commonly known as the Tidelands. John Connally promoted tourism across the state and was the catalyst behind the 1968 Hemisfair, a world's fair held in San Antonio. The Toyota plant in San Antonio probably would have never happened if it had not been for Governor Perry working with local, state and federal officials to meet Toyota's conditions to include a private spur railroad line built at the plant to enable the shipment of parts in and finished trucks out of the facility.

Also, the governor serves as his/her political party's leader. At the party's national convention, it is the governor that leads his/her party's delegation and usually casts the delegate votes for the presidential nomination. The governor also plays an integral role in drafting the state's party platform as well as appointing individuals to key executive party leadership positions.

Impeaching the Governor

The Case of Jim Ferguson

Although many legislators over the years have pondered impeaching the governor, only one has ever been officially charged by the Texas House of Representatives, tried and convicted by the Texas Senate, actually removed from office, and prohibited from running for a state office. The dubious distinction belongs to James Edward Ferguson. In 1914, Texans elected a newcomer to the governor's mansion—James Ferguson. Running for office as "Farmer Jim," Ferguson worked as a migrant farm laborer in the fields of California, Nevada, Colorado, and Texas. With only a few months of formal education, Ferguson passed the Texas State Bar Exam and began practicing law. He was successful enough to acquire several businesses, including Temple State Bank. As governor, Ferguson passed several reform packages including measures to assist tenant farmers, establish rural schools, and reform the state court system. In 1916 he ran for reelection on the platform of promoting public and higher education, and regulating the emerging state highway system.

However, his second term of office began on a sour note as campaign opponent wealthy banker Charles H. Morris leveled charges that Ferguson was using state funds for his own personal gain. A Travis County grand jury launched an investigation leading to an indictment against Ferguson for illegal use of public funds. The charges included using his own bank as the state's primary depository, consequently using state money to make his bank and himself more profitable. Ferguson was forced to call a special session, which began impeachment proceedings on twenty-one different charges of misappropriation and fraud. Ferguson was eventually convicted on ten counts. The now former governor of Texas, Ferguson decided that if he could not be a candidate, his wife could. **Miriam Ferguson** (oftentimes called Ma) ran successfully for two terms as governor. Of course, it was well known that "Ma" was acting only on the directions of her husband, "Pa." Every official photograph of Governor Miriam Ferguson shows her sitting in the governor's chair, but Jim Ferguson was always standing either by her side or behind her chair. Mrs. Ferguson's administration was often unpleasant, as her "enemies subjected her to continual derision and abuse, undoubtedly out of hate for Farmer Jim, presumably the puppeteer pulling her strings, and from leftover antifeminist sentiment."[34]

Almost an Impeachment—Preston Smith

In 1971, Governor Preston Smith artfully avoided impeachment over his role in the Sharpstown Bank Scandal. By the time the taint of the scandal had ended in 1978, Sharpstown had successfully destroyed "the political careers of a former governor [Preston Smith], a former lieutenant governor [Ben Barnes], a former Texas speaker [Gus Mutscher] who was married to a former Miss America, two former attorney generals [Waggoner Carr, for one] a former state insurance board chairman [John Osorio], a former state Democratic chairman [Elmer Baum] and several lesser figures [Rep. Tommy Shannon, for one]"[35]

The initiator of the scandal, Frank W. Sharp, was a multimillionaire Houston land developer, owner of the Sharpstown Bank and the National Bankers Life Insurance, and majority stockholder in other key businesses. With advanced warning that the Federal Deposit Insurance Corporation (FDIC) was looking into potential irregularities at his bank, Sharp was the primary advocate and lobbyist behind a bill introduced in the 1969 Texas legislative session exempting state banks from FDIC audits. Mutscher guided the bill through both the regular and special sessions as Sharp attempted to secure favorable legislative votes by offering very lucrative stock deals from his insurance company and unsecured loans from his bank. Several, including Smith, bought stock and subsequently "sold their stock to a Jesuit organization, which listened to Sharp's advice and paid over the market price for the shares. Smith and Dr. Elmer Baum, chairman of the state Democratic Executive Committee, netted about $125,000 from the transaction."[36] Subsequently, the bill sailed through both houses and only needed Smith's signature to become law. Smith, however, vetoed the bill. On the day that Smith was inaugurated for his second term as governor, the Federal Securities and Exchange Commission filed official claims of stock manipulation and bribery against Sharp. "The SEC alleged Sharp had bribed Gov. Preston Smith, House Speaker Gus Mutscher, Jr., and other state officials by providing them more than $600,000 in loans from Sharpstown State Bank."[37] In the end, Mutscher, his aide Rush McGinty, and Shannon were convicted of conspiracy to accept bribes on March 14, 1972, and each was sentenced to five years probation. Frank Sharp, however, was granted immunity from further prosecution since he agreed to testify against all involved parties in exchange for pleading guilty to two minor banking violations, paying a $5,000 fine, and serving a sentence of three years of probation. The entire scandal involved over seventy-five individuals. Perhaps the smartest person of those involved was Smith. If he had signed that bill into law, he would have been officially charged with impeachable offenses by the Texas House and subjected to the embarrassment of an impeachment process.

An Indicted Governor

On April 12, 2013, Travis County District Attorney Rosemary Lehmberg was arrested on a DWI (Driving While Intoxicated) charge. She was charged and booked into the Travis County jail. "According to the arrest affidavit, Lehmberg's attitude was cooperative and polite but also insulting and cocky. Her speech was slurred and mumbled. The deputy started to perform a field sobriety test but Lehmberg would not stand still or listen to instructions."[38] After her release, she issued a letter of apology and "stated that she wishes to enter the guilty plea without request for delay, without legal argument by counsel, without any plea bargain, and without any request for leniency or consideration of any type."[39] Charged with a Class A Misdemeanor, a judged sentenced her to 45 days in jail, a $4,000 fine, and suspended her driver's license for 180 days.[40] She complied with the judge's ruling. In addition to her duties as district attorney, Lehmberg also is the director of the Public Integrity Unit, a state-funded program. One of the Unit's assignments was an investigation of contracts issued by the Texas Department of Public Safety to implement the state's border security program. One of the contracts was issued as a "no-bid" thus avoiding the competitive contracting process established for all levels of government. Among those calling for her resignation was Governor Rick Perry. Her repeated refusals to resign led Governor Perry to threaten to veto funding for the Public Integrity Unit. However, Lehmberg absolutely refused to resign, and Perry followed through with his threat and vetoed the funding amounting to approximately $7.5 million.[41]

The group Texans for Public Justice pushed for a full scale investigation charging that Governor Perry abused his constitutional authority. A grand jury subsequently handed down an official indictment in August 2014, charging Perry with two criminal counts "of abuse of official capacity and coercion of a public servant."[42] If convicted, a first-degree felony charge of abuse of power carries a punishment ranging from five to ninety-nine years in prison and the second charge, a third-degree felony is punishable by two to ten years in prison. Becoming the first governor indicted since Jim Ferguson in 1917, Perry was officially charged, booked, fingerprinted, and had his mug shot taken. A defiant Perry claimed "the veto in question was made in accordance with the veto authority afforded to every governor under the Texas Constitution."[43]   The other side contended that the governor of Texas has every right to use his/her veto authority as detailed in the state's constitution. However, in this case, it is the threat used against an official elected by the people of Travis County that is illegal and thus, an abuse of the governor's constitutional powers. The timing of Perry's veto was questionable. His argument was that he had lost confidence in Lehmberg's ability to do her job. Others believe that his veto was revenge due to the Public Integrity Unit's investigation of the no-bid contracting practices used by the Perry administration. For months, the Perry legal team had unsuccessfully used numerous arguments before the courts to have the charges dropped. Before officially leaving office, Perry "used state taxpayer money to defend himself in the case, racking up at least $80,000 in legal expenses for one lawyer."[44] The matter was settled on February 24, 2016, when the Texas Court of Criminal Appeals dismissed the charges against Perry.

Success of the Office

With few exceptions, the governors of Texas have been able to exert their influence to bring positive changes to the state's political, social, and economic landscapes. Joseph Sayers (1899-1903) was the first Texas governor to request federal assistance for a natural disaster. Samuel Lanham (1903-1907) was instrumental in the passage of the Terrell Elections Law, which helped to eliminate election fraud and provided uniformity in the party nomination process. Thomas Campbell (1907-1911) helped to secure passage of the state's first pure food law as well as promoted strengthening the state's anti-trust laws, instituted much needed prison reform measures, and established the Texas State Library. Nicknamed Little Oscar or the Napoleon of Texas politics, Oscar Colquitt (1911-1915) advocated against statewide prohibition. He also promoted prison reform including outlawing prisoner abuse, leasing of prisoners to farmers, and wearing striped prison uniforms. Daniel Moody (1927-1931) wanted to reorganize the executive branch by converting the plural executive into a model more aligned with the president of the United States whereby key state executive officers would be appointed by the governor rather than elected to their positions in popular elections. James Allred (1935-1939) proposed the Public Utility Commission to regulate in particular rural electrical cooperatives, pushed for regulation of lobbyists, and instituted the Texas Retirement Program for all state

workers. Coke Stevenson (1941-1947) was the catalyst behind the creation of the Texas Good Roads Association and actively lobbied for the passage of a measure giving Mexican legal and illegal immigrants the same rights and privileges as legal residents of Texas. William Hobby (1917-1921) signed into law a 1918 bill giving women the right to vote in primary elections, a year ahead of the passage of the Nineteenth Amendment to the United States Constitution. Public education was reformed with the passage of the Gilmer-Aiken Bill under the guidance of Beauford Jester (1947-1949). The major accomplishment of Mark White's governorship (1983-1987) was education reform including raising teacher's salaries, establishing a state-support research fund for higher education institutions, and limiting class sizes in the public schools.

State Executive Officers

The Plural Executive

One of the major complaints about the Davis administration was the sweeping appointment powers given to the governor by the Texas Constitution of 1869, enabling him to appoint all state executive officers, every state judge from the Texas Supreme Court to a justice of the peace, and even local officials such as mayors and city council members. Their ire was clearly evident when they wrote Article IV, Section 2 that "all the above officers of the Executive Department [lieutenant governor, comptroller of public accounts, commissioner of the general land office and attorney general] (except Secretary of State) shall be elected by the qualified voters of the State at the time and places of election for members of the Legislature." Basically,

> the delegates were determined to curb the powers of the governor to avert renewal of despotic control over state and local administration. Consequently, they adhered to the principle of decentralization of authority and provided for popular election of all officials in the executive branch, with the exception of the secretary of state, in effect making the department heads independent of gubernatorial control and responsible only to the electorate.[45]

Today, all of the state's top executive officers with the exception of the Secretary of State are popularly elected to four-year terms of office with no limits on the number of terms. This list includes the lieutenant governor, state attorney general, commissioner of the general land

Table 8.2

State Executive Officers

Office	Office Holder	Term Expiration	Party	Elected or Appointed
Governor	Greg Abbott	2020	Republican	Elected
Lieutenant Governor	Dan Patrick	2020	Republican	Elected
Secretary of State	Not Confirmed			Appointed
Attorney General	Ken Paxton	2020	Republican	Elected
Comptroller of Public Accts.	Glenn Hegar	2020	Republican	Elected
Land Commissioner	George P. Bush	2020	Republican	Elected
Agriculture Commissioner	Sid Miller	2020	Republican	Elected
Railroad Commissioner	Christi Craddick	2020	Republican	Elected
Railroad Commissioner	Wayne Christian	2020	Republican	Elected
Railroad Commissioner	Ryan Sitton	2020	Republican	Elected

office, comptroller of public accounts, commissioner of agriculture, and all members of the Texas Railroad Commission and the State Board of Education. While the concept of elected state executive officers supports the premise of participatory democracy, in practice, the plural executive weakens the effectiveness of both the executive branch and the governor. Governors are victims of the voters' preferences. In other words, the voters can give the governor a cadre of well qualified talented individuals or individuals who are not very knowledgeable about the ins and outs of state government or are just unqualified for their positions. Just because someone has enough money or political smarts to win an election does not mean that they are qualified for the position they are seeking. Governors can only work with what the voters hand them. Also, those who are popularly elected cannot be removed by the governor. They are elected officials who can only be removed by the electorate in the next election cycle.

Furthermore, the plural executive format places these officials on the same level of the organization chart with the governor. There is no constitutional requirement that the governor consider state executive officers in the same light as the president must his/her cabinet. They do not meet on a regular basis with the governor. Even with the lieutenant governor, the second in line for the governorship, the Texas Constitution does not require that the governor share information and coordinate political directives with him/her or any other state executive officer. Consequently, the state's executive branch is decentralized and fragmented. Whereas you can hold a president accountable for the mistakes of his/her cabinet members, one cannot hold the state's governor to the same scrutiny. Fragmentation and decentralization at the top means that all state agencies within the executive branch are also organized along the same structure. Regardless of

the structure, each state executive officer is charged with specific duties and responsibilities that are essential to the overall operation of state government. Unfortunately, in Texas each executes their duties independently of each other. Table 8.2 lists the key members of the state's executive offices.

Lieutenant Governor

As previously discussed in Chapter 7, the state's lieutenant governor is constitutionally and, perhaps, politically the most powerful elective position in the state. The lieutenant governor is both an elected member of the executive branch and by constitutional authority the presiding officer of the Texas Senate. In other words, he/she is both an executive and legislative officer of the state of Texas. If the governor has a good working relationship with his/her lieutenant governor, the path for a smooth relationship with the Texas Legislature is sealed. However, since both the governor and lieutenant governor run as separate candidates, not as a "ticket," oftentimes, the two are from different political parties and, unfortunately, have different political philosophies. In 1998, Rick Perry was elected as the state's only Republican lieutenant governor since Reconstruction. The trend of Republican lieutenant governors has continued with David Dewhurst elected to the position in 2002 and Dan Patrick in 2014 and 2018.

Many have used the position as lieutenant governor as a stepping stone to higher office, such as Perry. Yet, a few have had very distinguished careers equal to Bob Bullock (1991-1999). As lieutenant governor, Bullock created the Texas Performance Review as a tool to assist the state's comptroller to work with state agencies to implement cost-saving measures. He was instrumental in securing passage of both education and welfare reform packages.

Bill Hobby held the position from 1973-1991, making him the longest serving lieutenant governor.

Attorney General

The state attorney general is the state's legal representative in any litigation involving the state of Texas. However, the attorney general is party to civil litigation only. Criminal cases are handled at the county level through the district attorneys. Several years ago former Attorney General Jim Mattox decided to run for governor. In his campaign, Mattox wanted voters to see him as a person "tough on crime." So, his ads pictured him in a vacant prison, slamming cell doors as he stated that as the state's attorney general he personally filled those cells with hardened criminals. Yet, Mattox could take no credit for filling any of the state's prison cells.

The state's attorney general heads the Office of the Attorney General (OAG) that employs approximately 4,000 individuals including four hundred plus attorneys. The OAG has thirty-four divisions and approximately seventy regional offices strategically located throughout the state. In particular, the Consumer Protection Division acts on complaints filed against companies for unfair business practices. The state's "lemon" law, for example, mandates that anyone who purchased an automobile has the right to demand a new vehicle if the original vehicle has been in repair three times for the same mechanical problem within one year of purchase. While the Comptroller's Office collects tax dollars, it is the OAG's Collections Division that assists in recovering delinquent taxes. The most visible and oftentimes criticized agency is the Child Support Enforcement Division that not only oversees the collection of child support payments but handles issues of paternity identification and location of absent parents.

Both houses of the Texas Legislature rely upon the OAG to issue legal opinions concerning pending legislation. Obviously, no legislative house should pass legislation that they know will not pass the litmus test of their own state constitution or the United States Constitution. It is incumbent that the state attorney general inform them of such a probability and indicate the action the legislature should take to rectify the potential constitutional problem. Once legislation is passed, it is the OAG that assists state agencies in drafting implementation procedures to ensure, once again, that their actions are constitutional.

Serving from 1991-1999, Dan Morales (D) was a rising star in the Democratic Party. He initiated a lawsuit joined by several other state attorney generals against the major tobacco companies. The major issue centered on the

James S. Hogg, Governor of Texas, 1891-1895.
Photo credit: UTSA's Institute of Texan Cultures

illnesses attributable to tobacco products and the medical costs states were incurring to address tobacco-related ailments. Morales hired several high ranking attorneys to battle the case, which they won, resulting in a $17.3 billion judgement. After he left office, his successor now United States Senator John Cronyn questioned the cost of approximately $3.3 billion incurred in battling this case. The ensuring investigation led to Morales being convicted and "sentenced to four years in prison in 2003 for crimes related to his attempt to funnel part of the legal fees to a friend."[46]

Comptroller of Public Accounts

Initially, the Texas Constitution divided the state's financial responsibilities between a state treasurer who paid the bills and the comptroller of public accounts (CPA) who collected tax revenues due to the state. In 1994, Martha Whitehead (D) ran for the treasurer's position on the platform that once elected, she would push to abolish her own office. In 1995, voters approved a constitutional amendment consolidating the functions of the treasurer into the comptroller's hands thus effecting abolishing the state treasurer's office.

Table 8.3   **Selective List of State Agencies**

Commission on Jail Standards	Texas Commission on the Arts
Commission on State Emergency Communications	Texas Dept. of Banking
Credit Union Department	Texas Dept. of Criminal Justice
Department of Agriculture	Texas Dept. of Insurance
Department of Family & Protective Services	Texas Dept. of Motor Vehicles
Department of State Health Services	Texas Dept. of Parks & Wildlife
Department of Information Resources	Texas Dept. of Public Safety
Employees Retirement System	Texas Education Agency
Health & Human Services Commission	Texas Facilities Commission
Office of Consumer Credit Commissioner	Texas Historical Commission
Public Utility Commission of Texas	Texas Juvenile Justice Dept.
Texas Higher Education Coordinating Board	Texas Lottery Commission
Texas Racing Commission	Texas Medical Board
State Bar of Texas	Texas Military Department
State Office of Administrative Hearings	Texas School for the Blind and
State Office of Risk Management	Visually Impaired
Sunset Advisory Commission	Texas School for the Deaf
Texas Animal Health Commission	Texas State Library and Archives
Texas Commission on Environmental Quality	Commission
Texas Commission on Law Enforcement	Texas Veterans Commission
Texas Dept. of Transportation	Texas Water Development Board

The most controversial CPA has been Carole Keeton Strayhorn who won the position in a close race in 1998. One of the major functions of the CPA is to certify that the proposed upcoming biennial budget passed by the Texas Legislature and officially signed into law by the governor is indeed a balanced budget whereby anticipated revenues equal anticipated expenditures. At the close of the 2003 regular session and a special legislative session, Strayhorn very publically took on both Governor Perry and Lieutenant Governor David Dewhurst when she refused to certify the budget claiming that it was not balanced. Due to a clerical error, the bottom line of debits and credits were indeed unbalanced. Instead of informing them privately about the error, she went public by declaring herself as the only truly responsible fiscal caregiver in the state, embarrassing both Perry and Dewhurst. Seen as a retaliatory move on the part of Dewhurst and Perry, the Texas Legislature while in another special session reassigned Strayhorn's performance review program (PRP) to the Legislative Budget Board. Originally designed by Comptrollers Bob Bullock and John Sharp, the PRP enabled the comptroller's office to audit and recommend budgetary efficiencies initially to public school districts. Strayhorn expanded its scope by offering assistance to all state agencies and took the credit

for saving the State of Texas billions of dollars by stopping frivolous spending. In what many saw as a retaliatory move on her part, Strayhorn decided to challenge Perry in the 2006 Republican primary election and ran once again unsuccessfully as an independent candidate in the 2010 general election.

Commissioner of Agriculture

Created in 1907, the state's commissioner of agriculture manages the Texas Department of Agriculture (TDA), acting as the state's official spokesperson and ambassador of the state's farming and ranching industries. In addition, the TDA in conjunction with the federal Department of Agriculture oversees the use of agricultural pesticides including providing training for the use of and the granting of licenses to users. The TDA actively supports local livestock shows and rodeos by working closely with Future Farmers of America (FFA) organizations and public schools in assisting students in raising and showing livestock and agricultural products. For many rural teenagers across the state, winning the blue ribbon at the state fair or the competition for the grand champion steer means very lucrative college scholarships and recognition for the family's farm and ranch. Interestingly, the Texas Constitution mandates that any candidate seeking the agricultural commissioner's job must be a practicing farmer or rancher. Traditionally a male-dominated office, Susan Combs won election to the office in both 1998 and 2002, becoming the state's first woman to hold the office.

Commissioner of the General Land Office

Overseeing the leasing and sale of the state's publically-owned land, the office of commissioner of the General Land Office (GLO) was initially created by the 1836 Texas Constitution. Originally, state lands were leased for mineral rights and grazing for cattle to repay state debts or, as in the case of the Davis Administration, given as gifts to railroad companies seeking to build railroad lines in the state. Today, the income generated through the lease and sale of state's approximately 20.3 million acres of public land funds the Permanent School Fund (PSF). The GLO also manages the state's Veterans Program created in 1946 by the Texas Legislature to provide loans for the purchase of farmlands and homesteads or the remodeling of an existing home. The money is provided through the sale of bonds with revenue recaptured by the repayment of the loans. The GLO also oversees all of the state's beaches since the Texas Constitution does not allow for private ownership of coastline properties. Former Commissioner Garry Mauro established the "adopt the beach" program whereby private citizens and various groups can officially adopt a portion of the Texas coastline. The adoption agreement requires that participants periodically sponsor or personally collect trash and clean up their area. In particular, the Archives and Records division of the GLO is the state's official holder of land titles dating back to the Spanish land grant programs.

Grandson of President Hubert Walker Bush, George P. Bush was elected as land commissioner initially in 2014 and easily won reelection in 2018. One of his "pet" projects is enhancing the prestige of the Alamo in San Antonio. He successfully removed the Daughters of the Republic of Texas from management of the mission by placing it under his office's supervision. Several plans have been presented to include a see-through wall encasing the Alamo and the surrounding area, restoring several historical buildings, and establishing a museum across the street from Alamo Plaza. The plans for the see-through wall have been shelved as a series of other plans have been introduced but not acted upon.

Secretary of State

The only appointed state executive office, the Secretary of State is the state's chief elections officer. Those duties entail working with county election officials to ensure that all federal and state election laws and processes are followed, and officially certifying the tabulation of all election returns for state and district offices. In addition, the Secretary of State's office issues all charters of operation for Texas-based corporations and permits to those out-of-state businesses conducting business in Texas. In accordance to Article IV of the United States Constitution, all states must assist other states in extraditing accused and convicted criminals back to the state of the origin of the criminal act for trial and punishment. The extradition agreements are issued and processed by the Secretary of State's office.

Texas Railroad Commission

One of the state's oldest regulatory commissions, the Texas Railroad Commission, was the dream of Governor James S. Hogg (1891-1895). Upon his election as the attorney general, Hogg, backed strongly by the Farmer's Alliance, desired to create a state agency that would end the price fixing practices and abusive wheeling and dealing of the railroads that were adversely harming the productivity and profitability of the state's farming and ranching industries. In his 1891 "Message to the Legislature," Hogg challenged the legislature to finally take action:

> For fourteen years the State constitution has provided that "the legislature shall pass laws to correct abuses to prevent unjust discrimination and extortion in the rates of freight and passenger fares on the different railroads in this State, and shall from time to time pass laws establishing reasonable maximum rates of charges for the transportation of passengers and freight on said railroads, and enforce all such laws by adequate penalties." At no time has this mandate been obeyed, though at each recurring session of the Legislature since its promulgation futile efforts have been made to do so.[47]

The bill passed and was signed into law by Hogg by the end of the legislative session. Hogg selected State Senator John H. Reagan, the leading advocate for railroad regulation, to head the newly created three-member Texas Railroad Commission.

By 1917, the Railroad Commission was given the authority to regulate oil and gas production in Texas. A 1919 oil and gas conservation law empowered the

Commission to set anti-waste production guidelines for the extraction of oil and gas. In the early 1930s, the Commission was given the task of regulating production as a means of stabilizing prices. By 1933, the Railroad Commission was given the responsibility to set maximum production limits for all wells operating in Texas. Currently, the Commission regulates oil, gas, and mining operations.

The Texas Bureaucracy

A **bureaucracy** is "the totality of government offices or bureaus that constitutes the permanent government of a state; that is, those people and functions that continue irrespective of changes in political leadership."[48] The primary responsibility of any bureaucratic organization is to implement the laws passed by their respective legislative houses. Regardless of the governing structure, bureaucratic agencies usually fall under the executive branch of the government. Consequently, the executive, whether it be the president of the United States or the governor of Texas, is fully accountable for the actions of the bureaucratic agencies under their charge. At the national level, all bureaucratic agencies are supervised by a member of the president's cabinet or as in the case of the military, the Joint Chiefs of Staff. In Texas, however, the state bureaucratic agencies do not take their marching orders from the governor or, in most instances, from state executive officers. Instead, agencies are normally run by an appointed board or commission whose membership meets either once or twice a year. The primary function of a board or commission is to establish the policy needed to implement a directive primarily issued by the Texas Legislature. In turn, the agencies themselves establish the procedures required to implement the policy directives issued by both their board or commission and the Texas Legislature. Whereas the federal bureaucracy is a centralized structure under the presidency, the Texas bureaucracy is the embodiment of fragmentation and decentralization from top to bottom with little or no coordination between the different agencies. Table 8.3 is a selective list of state agencies.

Boards and Commissions

There are over 250 boards and commissions overseeing some function of the state bureaucracy. All of the members of these bodies are with few exceptions gubernatorial appointments subject to Senate confirmation. Although the state lacks a comprehensive state water plan, there are over twenty-three state boards and commissions setting policies for selective bodies of water ranging from the board of directors of the Upper Colorado River Authority, the Canadian River Municipal Water Authority to the Edwards Aquifer Authority. Each acts independently of each other with little or no coordination among them. Under the heading of criminal justice, there is the Council on Sex Offender Treatment, Crime Stoppers Advisory Council, the Crime Victims' Institute Advisory Council, Juvenile Justice Advisory Board, Texas Judicial Council, Texas Juvenile Probation Commission, Texas Board of Pardons and Parole, Texas Youth Commission, to name a few. Every occupation in Texas requiring a license has its own examining or licensing board ranging from polygraph examiners, dietitians, plumbers, nurses to acupuncture technicians.

Role in Policy Development and Implementation

Traditionally, bureaucracies were viewed as mere implementers of public policy with little impact on the actual development of the directives. This perspective has changed dramatically. "It is axiomatic that politics and administration are blended, and that administrative agencies are often significantly involved in the development of public policy."[49] Bureaucracies do shape public policy. State bureaucratic agencies begin their influence at the initial stages of policy development. Lawmakers are not experts on every issue. They rely upon state agencies to provide research and testimony before committee hearings. As each piece of proposed legislation edges itself closer to a final floor vote, state bureaucrats will show their support or disfavor of the proposal by actively soliciting the backing of influential interest groups, lobbyists, and even members of the legislative houses. Bureaucracies can also make or break policy initiatives simply by the way in which an agency implements a new policy directive. The manner in which a legislature writes laws plays right into the hands of state agencies. For example, a legislature passes a law mandating that all public sidewalks must be handicap accessible. It is now the state agency charged with implementing this directive that will determine how to accomplish this task as well as how to fine those parties that decide not to obey this law. In order to implement state laws, agencies are oftentimes granted extraordinary authority. Basically, all state regulatory agencies must have the **quasi-legislative** authority of rule-making that enables them to determine how a law is to be implemented as well as **quasi-judicial**

powers to perform many functions ordinarily performed by the courts including investigative authority, and power to adjudicate and to judge those guilty of a policy infraction. Their judicial authority also empowers them to determine the punishment of the guilty party.

The Nature of State Agencies

Unfortunately, bureaucratic organizations in the United States are sorely underestimated for the important and vital role they play in the day-to-day operations of government. Few citizens would be capable of fulfilling the tasks they call upon both federal and state agencies to perform. The perception is that state agencies are riddled with inefficiencies, chronically operating in the red by spending their money on frivolous non-essential items, mired in duplication of functions, riddled with red tape, and out-of-touch with the true needs of the American people. One of the definitive experts on bureaucracies was German socialist Max Weber (1884-1920) who analyzed the ins and outs of bureaucratic agencies. A closer look at Weber's observations mirrors the perception and complaints many have of state agencies.

According to Weber, bureaucratic agencies are organized in a tight **hierarchical structure** resembling a pyramid. Those at the top of the pyramid are upper management while those at the bottom are the lowest ranking employees. The ideal communication model is one whereby information from management flows from the top to the bottom through each layer as information from the lowest level flows at the same pace to the top. However, in the real world, the major problem with bureaucratic organizations is the lack of communication. Far too often important and necessary information never makes it up and down the organizational structure.

The structure is linked by an entrenched **chain-of-command** whereby employees are encouraged to receive orders from and communicate with their immediate supervisor. Violating chain-of-command carries serious repercussions, which might include denial of a promotion, a substandard job performance evaluation, or termination. Legislative houses have implemented measures to encourage state employees to report incidents of waste, inefficiency, and mismanagement to upper management. However, an employee accusing their supervisor of wrongdoing is often the victim of punitive action rather than a candidate for employee of the month. Both the federal and several state legislative houses have enacted **whistleblower protection laws** to protect those employees who violated the chain of command by reporting misdeeds to upper management.

The rule of thumb is that "promotions go to those who don't 'make waves' which threaten the established procedures that survive when old goals are forgotten, or new adaptations or directions tempered by all the comfortable berths."[50]

The pyramid resembles the layer cake approach to federalism in that each layer is isolated from the other. Every functional task at each level is detailed in the job description. If an employee aspires to rise to the next level, the job description for that position lists the pre-requisite skills that an employee must possess to even be considered for a promotion in that area. Bureaucracies are also tied securely to the concept of division of labor. Imagine the assembly line of a major manufacturer whereby the unassembled product is gradually assembled at each juncture of the line. Bureaucracies work in the same repetitive style, encouraging area specialists while discouraging opportunities for promotion and job enrichment. Employees are oftentimes horizontally and vertically stuck in their job. One can become vertically stuck because in order to reach the next level within his/her department, the employee needs those pre-requisite skills or is faced with the reality that the incumbent in the next highest level is not going to be leaving their assignment anytime soon. The employee now has to face the reality that unless he/she goes back to school or enters an agency-sponsored management training program or has the patience to wait for his/her immediate supervisor to either get promoted or leave the agency, he/she has no alternative but to continue to work at the same job for years to come. Of course, a lateral or horizontal transfer to another functional area is also nearly impossible, once again, because the employee lacks the pre-requisite skills to work in another functional area. Immobility can ruin an employee's enthusiasm for his/her job. For those lucky enough to get a promotion, bureaucrats are often the victims of *The Peter Principle*, "under which each staff member is eventually promoted until he reaches his own particular level of mediocrity. There he stays, naturally resistant to any change, keeping his eye largely upon the length of the coffee break, the lunch hour, his annual and sick leave—and most of all upon the length of time which must elapse before he can retire with his maximum pension."[51]

On the whole bureaucrats are reluctant to accept any change that could adversely impact their entrenched routines. The election cycle can bring a new person to the governor's mansion or change the party leadership in the Texas Legislature. But the election cycle does not change the employment status of the civil servant. He/she is employed for the long-term, not the short-term. A newly elected governor, for example, may want to make sweeping changes. As pointed out before, the governor can appoint members to agency boards and commissions. However, the term of office for a board or commission member is usually six years. Unless a governor is elected to two consecutive terms, he/she cannot readily change the entire membership of any board or commission. Bureaucrats oftentimes use the ploy of "we're taking it under consideration" whenever an unwanted policy change hits their desks. Waiting it out until the next election cycle virtually guarantees that the requested change will never take place.

The most noticeable flaw of bureaucratic agencies is their strict adherence to rules and regulations. Far too often individuals seek assistance from state agencies only to be confronted with agency rules that are so inflexible and un-user friendly that people simply would rather do without the service. For an individual with limited education and poor English-language skills, a government issued form is intimidating. For an individual suspicious of government in the first place, providing income information, a social security number, or any personal information is intimidating. What these individuals need is for someone to assist and guide them through the paperwork. Perhaps with a little assistance, they would be more comfortable in filling out the requested forms that could eventually provide them with the assistance they need.

Budgeting and Staffing Issues

The effectiveness of any state agency is tied directly to its ability to deliver services to its clientele whether it is a business concern or, as in the case of the Texas Workforce Commission, unemployed workers. Since the election of Rick Perry to the governorship, budget cuts in an atmosphere of no new taxes has meant budgetary and staff reductions across the board for the Texas state agencies. In other words, state employees are working more for less. The usual suspects for budget cuts are programs for the state's poor. Under the banner of Health and Human Services Commission, for example, are the departments of Assistive and Rehabilitation Services, Aging and Disability, Family and Protective Services, and the State Health Services. In particular, Family and Protective Services have been severely criticized for their inability to remove children from abusive family environments in a timely manner. Too many children have just fallen through the cracks with disastrous and oftentimes fatal results due to numerous problems such as the lack of coordination between local police, district judges, and Child Protective Service Agencies. Working under the banner of "work

more with less," social workers, in particular, are taking on more cases and logging in more hours beyond the traditional forty-hour week. A high employee turnover rate is the norm rather than the exception across state agencies. It is extremely difficult to build cadre of long-term dedicated public-sector employees when one realizes that they could be making more money working less hours in the private-business sector. High turnover coupled with consistent draconian budget cuts are severely hampering the effectiveness of all of the state's bureaucratic agencies.

Clientele Agencies and Iron Triangles

Regulatory bureaucratic agencies are established to regulate a segment of the economy, not the other way around. A **clientele agency** is "a loose term for any government organization whose prime mission is to promote, serve, or represent the interest of a particular group."[52] All state agencies both oversee the operation of and the interests of their groups. The Texas Department of Agriculture is designed to promote the interests of the state's farming and ranching industries. The state's Credit Union Department not only enforces state laws pertinent to the viability of credit unions, but it also looks out for the interests of the industry by ensuring that no laws are passed that would adversely impact credit union operations. The problem with clientele agencies arises with the real or perceived perception that the regulated clients of the agency are pulling the strings of the agency to their favor. As a gubernatorial candidate, Ann Richards was very critical of the board overseeing the Texas Department of Insurance. She alleged that every year the insurance companies would seek and win approval of considerable increases in premium rates. Once she became governor, she moved quickly to replace as many members of the insurance board as she possibly could because the incumbent gubernatorial appointees to that board were indeed executives of insurance companies. Why would the owner of the company who happens to sit on the very board that regulates his/her company vote down a premium increase that would make his/her own business more profitable? Yes, clientele agencies need to promote the interests of their clients but it should be handled in a fair handed manner. Richards' solution was to appoint a mixture of industry or business-related specialists tied to the regulated agency along with individuals outside of that industry.

The bureaucratic relationship with their clientele agencies can lead to the formation of an **iron triangle** defined as "a pattern of stable relationships between an agency in the executive branch, a congressional [or in this case, a state legislative] committee or subcommittee, and one or more organized groups or clients."[53] This tight relationship is mutually beneficial to all involved parties. For example, the Texas Department of Transportation [agency of the executive branch] has been working closely with the transportation committees of both houses of the Texas Legislature to secure funding for a light rail system on a prototype designed by a highway construction firm specializing in both surface roadways and mass transportation designs [the clientele agency]. In the end, the Texas Legislature wins since both houses can jointly announce that they have approved sweeping legislation designed to alleviate traffic snarls on expressways and save motorists wear and tear on their vehicles while also easing their pocketbooks over the high price of gasoline. The Texas Department of Transportation wins because the agency will be the project manager over the light rail project. The highway contractor who submitted the prototype wins the bid to build the project. Iron triangles are detrimental to the democratic process because "they tend to dominate policymaking in their areas of concern. The triangles are considered to be as strong as iron, because the supportive relations are so strong that others elected or appointed to control administrative policy are representatives of the public's interests are effectively prohibited from interfering on behalf of the public."[54]

A major compliant against both iron triangles and clientele agencies is the propensity of businesses associated with these arrangements to be the recipients of lucrative government contracts. Governments and private businesses should operate under a competitive bidding process whereby bids from interested parties are submitted, studied, and awarded in a fair and equitable manner. However, far too often the cries of favoritism have merit as a government agency or a private business will by-pass the process and issue a no-bid contract to a business with close ties to those who make the final decisions.

Conclusions

Whether a governor is successful in overseeing the state's executive branch is tied more directly to the individual political skills and governing talent the individual brings to the office. The current Texas Constitution gives little real governing authority to the state's chief executive officer. The writers of the 1876 Texas Constitution completely dismantled the executive branch created under the 1869 Texas Constitution as a means of taking punitive action against the incumbent governor—E. J. Davis. What they did was to punish the office, not the man. In reality they

took no power from Davis for he had already left office. Their actions insured that every governor following Davis would govern from a constitutional position of weakness, not strength. If Texans are to hold their governors accountable for the actions of the state executive branch, then they need to give him/her the authority to do so. Governor Dan Moody (1927-1931) advocated the same changes for the executive branch that Perry (2000 to 2014) proposed during his second term of office. Both wanted to strengthen the governor's hand by allowing the governor to establish a presidential model whereby all state executive officers are appointed by the governor with Senate confirmation. In turn, these officers would be aligned similar to the president's cabinet with state agencies assigned to each. The state could surely save money by eliminating all of the boards and commissions with the exception of professional licensing boards. State agencies need constant oversight and direction, not marching orders from a commission that meets once or twice a year. By giving the governor more authority to run his/her own branch of government, Texans could truly hold him/her accountable for their actions.

Currently, the state's bureaucracy is so decentralized and fragmented that its weakened state renders it incapable of truly servicing the needs of Texans. Realignment under a state executive officer would, to some extent, address these deficiencies. Regardless of how they are aligned, state agencies must be given the proper tools to work with. Texans can rightfully level criticism and disdain when a properly funded and staffed state agency fails to fulfill its duties and responsibilities. No one wants to support a failing operation. However, Texans cannot justifiably criticize an agency for its failures when its budget continues to be severely cut, employee turnover is dismal, and the workload increases on the backs of the reduced staff. The bulk of the state's employees are doing a fine job with the tools that they are given by the state legislature. The problem is with the quality and quantity of the tools.

Chapter Notes

[1]Fred Gantt, Jr., *The Chief Executive in Texas: A Study in Gubernatorial Leadership*, (Austin, Texas: The University of Texas Press, 1964), 73.

[2]Ibid., 6.

[3]Ibid., 7.

[4]Ibid., 73.

[5]*Treasury of Presidential Quotations*, Caroline Thomas Harnsberger, ed., (Chicago, Illinois: Follett Publishing Company, 1964), 23.

[6]Thad Beryle, "The Governors," *Politics in the American States: A Comparative Analysis*, Virginia Gray and Russell Hanson, eds., 8th ed., (Washington, D.C.: CQ Press, 2004), 205-212.

[7]Gantt, Jr., 13.

[8]Ibid., 13.

[9]Gantt, Jr., 170.

[10]*https://gov.texas.gov*

[11]Ibid.

[12]Ibid.

[13]Gantt, Jr., 235.

[14]Ibid., 172-173.

[15]Ibid., 179.

[16]Paul Benson, David Clinkscale and Anthony Giardino, *Lone Star Politics*, 4th ed., (Mason, Ohio: Thomson, 2006), 179.

[17]http://www.lrl.state.tx.us

[18]Benson, 180.

[19]Clay Robison and Joe Holley, "Ex-Governor Dies at 94," *San Antonio Express-News*, (Monday, May 30, 2011), 6A.

[20]Gantt, Jr., 186.

[21]Mike Ward, "Governor Sets Special Session Agenda," *San Antonio Express News*, (Tuesday, July, 11, 2017), A2.

[22]Ibid.

[23]James Drew, "Campaign Giving OI Right Now," *San Antonio Express News*, (Sunday, July 23, 2017), A3.

[24]Matt Stiles and Brian Thevenot, "Perry's Picks for Regents Donate Millions to Him," *San Antonio Express-News*, (Tuesday, August 24, 2010), 1A.

[25]Peggy Fikac and Annie Millerbernd, "Donors Still Get State Appointments," *San Antonio Express News*, (Sunday, January 7, 2018), A1-A22.

[26]Ibid.

[27]Ibid.

[28]Ibid.

[29]Alexa Ura and Emma Platoff, "Opposition to Texas Secretary of State David Whitley's Nomination Mounts, Imperiling His Future in the Job," *Texas Tribune, https://www.texastribune.org*

[30]*The HarperCollins Dictionary of American Government and Politics*, Jay M. Shafritz, ed., (New York, New York: HarperCollins Publishers, 1992), 215.

[31]Gantt, Jr., 159.

[32]*The HarperCollins Dictionary of American Government and Politics*, 416.

[33]Ibid., 413.

[34]Joe B. Frantz, *Texas: A History*, 2nd ed., (New York, New York: Norton, 1984), 174.

[35]"The Sharpstown Scandal: 1971," *Documents of Texas History*, Ernest Wallace, David M. Vigness and George B. Ward, eds., 2nd ed., (Austin, Texas: State House Press, 1994), 305.

[36]Robert A. Calvert and Arnoldo De Leon, *The History of Texas*, (Arlington Heights, Illinois: Harlan Davidson, Inc., 1990), 306.

[37]Joe Holley, "Sharpstown Scandal Put Briscoe in Governor's Seat," *San Antonio Express-News*, (Sunday, July 4, 2010), 3B.

[38]http://www.myfoxaustin.com

[39]Ibid.

[40]http://www.statesman.com

[41]Brian M. Rosenthal and Mike Ward, "Perry' Veto Killed a Probe of No-Bid Pacts," *San Antonio Express-News*, (Saturday, January 17, 20150), 1A.

[42]Brian M. Rosenthal, "Watchdog Known for Bringing Down Pols," *San Antonio Express-News*, (Sunday, August 24, 2014), A6.

[43]Peggy Fikac and David Saleh Rauf, "Perry Indicted," *San Antonio Express-News*, (Saturday, August 16, 2014), 1A.

[44]David Saleh Rauf and Patrick Svitek, "Gov Spends $1 Million in Battling Indictment," *San Antonio Express-News*, (Friday, January 16, 2015), A1 and A9.

[45]Gantt, Jr., 33.

[46]http://www.laits.utexas.edu

[47]"Governor James Hogg on Railroad Regulation: January 21, 1891," *Documents of Texas History*, Ernest Wallace, David M. Vigness and George B. Ward, eds., 2nd ed., (Austin, Texas: State House Press, 1994), 244.

[48]*The HarperCollins Dictionary of American Government and Politics*, 80.

[49]James E. Anderson, *Public Policymaking*, 5th ed., (New York, New York: Houghton Mifflin Co., 2003), 53.

[50]Ernest S. Griffith, *The American Presidency: The Dilemmas of Shared Power and Divided Government*, (New York, New York: New York University Press, 1976), 84.

[51]Ibid., 83-84.

[52]*The HarperCollins Dictionary of American Government and Politics*, 117.

[53]Theodore Lowi and Benjamin Ginsberg, *American Government: Freedom and Power*, 4th ed., (New York, New York: W. W. Norton, 1996), 274.

[54]*The HarperCollins Dictionary of American Government and Politics*, 157.

Chapter 9

The Judicial Branch of Texas Government

"Lightnin" Washington, an African-American prisoner, singing with his group of immates in the woodyard at
Darrington State Farm, Texas
April 1934, Credit: Library of Congress

. . . . it is in the courts and not in the legislature that our citizens primarily feel the keen, cutting edge of the law. If they have respect for the work of the courts, their respect for law will survive the shortcomings of every other branch of government; but if they lose their respect for the work of the courts, their respect for law and order will vanish with it to the great detriment of society.[1]

Justice Arthur Vanderbilt

Today, approximately 252,000 Texas's residents are currently behind bars, with 163,000 housed in state prisons for capital, first, second, and third-degree long convictions, 55,000 in state jails convicted of state jail felony offenses, and another 27,000 are housed in federal prisons. The state's juvenile facilities house 4,300 youths. An additional 368,000 are currently on probation and 107,000 are on parole.[2] At the end of fiscal year 2018, the state of Texas spent $362,454,252 on staffing costs related to the State's two supreme courts and fourteen state Courts of Appeals, the Office of the State's Prosecuting Attorney, and so forth, accounting for an increase of 4.8 percent over 2017 expenditures. An additional $4,374,600,361 was expended for public safety and correctional facilities, accounting for a 9.1 percent increase over 2017 expenditures.[3] These figures do not include the millions spent by county governments to pay their judges, sheriffs and deputies, and to maintain their jails nor the millions also spent by municipal governments to pay and equip their police forces, maintain their city jails and city courts. In total, the judicial system in Texas is expensive. If the ultimate goal of maintaining a strong judicial and law enforcement function is to deter crime, then law enforcement and the judicial system across this nation has failed. Currently, Texas has more jail cells, executed more criminals, and has more inmates on death row than any other state. Candidates for judicial benches, sheriff, state legislative and congressional positions always pledged to the voters that if they elect them, they will reduce crime and make our streets safer. Is that possible?

The American judicial system is composed of three primary entities. It is the police departments across the state that arrest accused violators of criminal laws. It is the courts that render whether the accused is guilty of a criminal act, and, if so, what penalty will be accessed for that violation. It is the correctional facilities that ensure that the guilty party is appropriately serving his/her sentence. At both the federal and state levels, the three component parts of the judicial system seem to be independent of each other as well as fragmented and decentralized. Yet, the phenomenon is that in order for the judicial system to actually address crime, all three component parts are actually dependent upon each other. For example, a county

district attorney must rely upon the local police force to conduct the proper investigation and gather the evidence needed to bring a case to trial. The judge is dependent upon both to ensure that the defendant's constitutional rights have been properly protected from arrest to trial. The district attorney and the police officers are dependent upon the judge to conduct a constitutionally legal trial, to properly instruct the jury, to ensure that the appropriate evidence is introduced, and to assess the appropriate penalty if the accused is found guilty of the alleged offense. This chapter explores this unique partnership.

An indirect partner in the judicial process is the Texas Legislature. These are the "tough on crime" lawmakers that the voters send to Austin to enact legislation addressing criminal actions. The legislature directly impacts the operations of state and local police forces, the courts, and correctional facilities. On the state level, it is the legislature that determines how much money will be spent and where it will be spent on the state's judicial system. Of course, overriding all federal and state judicial systems is the United States Supreme Court whose decisions have impacted the way the judicial system at both the federal and state levels operates. This chapter examines their role in the judicial process.

There are basically two schools of thought on the direction states should take on their approach to crime. The first school is based on the "**just deserts**" concept, that is, the penalty or the sentence fits the severity of the criminal act. Advocates believe that once a person is sentenced, they should serve the entire sentence and not receive time off for good behavior, time served pending trial, or an early release. They believe that serving a full sentence is indeed a deterrent to crime. To fulfill their objectives, states need to put their budgetary dollars into building more prisons, hiring more correctional staff, and, of course, expanding local police forces and adding more courts. The other side of the argument believes that **rehabilitation** is the correct course to deter future criminal acts. **Recidivism** is "a relapse into criminal behavior."[4] Statistics support their contention that once a person is released from prison or the county jail, they are more apt to commit another crime within a relatively short period of time. To prevent this, they advocate intense in-prison job skills training, GED or college-level educational opportunities, and psychological evaluations and treatments. Once released, the prisoner should spend his/her probationary period in a series of graduated half-way houses that will give former inmates the chance to successfully leave their world of crime behind and never see the inside of a prison again. With the lack of budgetary funds, state governments cannot have it both ways. Lawmakers must select the option that will suit the attitudes of their constituents, meet their budgetary constraints, and actually reduce crime. This chapter explores those options as they apply to the Texas justice system.

The Law

Law is "the rules of conduct that pertain to a given political order of society, rules that are backed by the organized force of the community."[5] While the concept of law is universally accepted, the embodiment of laws varies from nation to nation for law is a cumulative reflection of a nation's culture, history, social structures, political development, governing structures, and, in some instances, its religious institutions. Noted Roman statesman and political theorist, Cicero (106-43 BC) emphasized the necessity and importance of formulating a body of laws:

Law is the highest reason, implanted in Nature, which commands what ought to be done and forbids the opposite. . . . the origin of justice is to be found in law, for law is its natural force; it is the mind and reason of the intelligent man, the standards by which justice and injustice are measured.[6]

"Law comprises three basic elements—force, official authority, and regularity—the combination of which differentiates law from mere custom or morals in society."[7] The legitimacy of a government is its ability to make laws along with its right to enforce them. A nation's people respect the right of their government to make laws if that government, in turn, makes reasonable laws and enforces them in an equitable, fair, just, and consistent manner. The United States Supreme Court deals with these issues every session particularly in matters relating to the application of the law. The statue in front of the United States Supreme Court is of Lady Justice with a blindfold over her eyes. She symbolizes the fairness and equal application of law for in her eyes, law is binding regardless of who you are and what position you hold in the society.

Common and Equity Law

The necessity of law became evident in the ancient world with the formation of villages, towns, and cities. Once man ceased to live by himself and sought a communal lifestyle, rules were needed to ensure that while all had the right to the tools of survival (food, shelter and clothing), there were definitive guidelines in place that established the means for all members of that social structure to acquire those tools without undo harm to others. Although the Sumerians developed rudimentary codes of law, it was the Babylonian King Hammurabi that collected from the various villages and towns nearly 300 separate laws and codified them into one body of law. Of course, his code is well known for its emphasis of "an eye for an eye" as the perfect retribution and punishment. The code also formed the basis for the modern judicial system of physical punishments and monetary fines. For example, if a free man took the eye of an aristocrat, he forfeited his own eye as a punishment. But, if that same man took the eye of a commoner, then he paid him one mina of silver.[8] However, the American judicial system is based on common law defined as "judge-made law that originated in England from decisions shaped according to prevailing customs."[9] In 1066, William the Conqueror of Normandy successfully invaded the British Isles and immediately began to bring continuity, order, and stability to the region's government and laws. Kings Henry I and Henry II continued the codification process. "The term **'common'** law was used for the law developed in the King's Courts and was generally employed in order to distinguish between it and that of the ecclesiastical courts" commonly known as **canon law**.[10] The longevity of common law is the use of **precedents** whereby a judge bases his decision upon a previously heard case similar to the one currently under consideration. The King's judges were required to put in writing not only the particulars of the case and their decisions but also the rationale behind their decisions so that judges hearing a similar case in the future could use these original decisions as a guide for rendering their own rulings. This practice gave legitimacy to the body of the law and ensured that the laws were equal, fair, and consistently applied. Precedents are based on the Latin term *stare decisis*, meaning to let the previous decision stand. The use of precedents is the cornerstone of the American judicial system. The practice enables a judge to feel confident that the decisions rendered in his or her court are validated by previous court rulings. Judges are less likely to stray from *stare decisis* since an errant ruling that violates the protected constitutional rights of the accused can be appealed to a higher state or federal court for review with the possibility of the judge's ruling being overturned. The importance of common law to the legitimacy of any judicial system simply cannot be underestimated. Associate Justice of the United States Supreme Court from 1902 to 1932, Oliver Wendell Holmes, wrote in his *The Common Law* in 1881:

> The life of the law has not been logic; it has been experience. The felt necessities of the time, the prevalent moral and political theories, institutions of public policy, avowed or unconscious, even the prejudices which judges share with their fellow-men, have had a good deal more to do than syllogism in determining the rules by which men should be governed. The law embodies the story of a nation's development through many centuries, and it cannot be dealt with as if it contained only the axioms and corollaries of a book of mathematics. In order to know what it is, we must know what it has been, and what it tends to become . . . the very considerations which judges most rarely mention, and always with an apology, are the secret root from which the law draws all the juices of life. I mean, of course, considerations of what is expedient for the community concerned.[11]

Closely related to common law, **equity law** begins where the law ends. Basically, "equity leaves the judge reasonably free to order *preventive* measures—and under some circumstances even *remedial* ones—usually in the form of a writ, such as an *injunction*, or restraining order, designed to afford a remedy not otherwise obtainable, and traditionally given upon a showing of peril."[12] Courts can order children removed from a home pending the conclusion of a divorce and custody hearing. Judges issue protective orders to prevent alleged spousal abusers from having contact with the abused party. However questions regarding the permanency and enforceability of protective orders have moved women's organizations to push for stronger sanctions against violators. A judge can also issue an **injunction** defined as "a court order that requires a person to take an action or to refrain from taking an action."[13] Injunctions are used primarily to stop the enforcement of a law or the construction of a project while the court reviews the legal questions posed by a pending suit. For example, a lower court federal judge issued an injunction to halt the implementation of Obama's executive order outlining his immigration reform measures until the United States Supreme Court determined the constitutionality of Obama's actions. Another federal judge used an injunction to prevent the implementation of the controversial Arizona immigration bill while the judges studied the fine print of this legislation to ensure that it did not promote racial profiling in the apprehension of individuals living illegally in the United States.

Civil and Criminal Law

The body of cases before a court usually falls into two broad categories of law—criminal and civil. **Civil law** "deals with disagreements between individuals—for example, a dispute over ownership of private property."[14] In Texas, civil law is codified in *Vernon's Annotated Civil Statutes*. The two parties in a civil suit are the **plaintiff**, who initiates the suit, and the **defendant**, the person accused of causing harm to the plaintiff. Civil litigation also involves disputes over contracts, domestic and business relations, destruction of property, jury claims from vehicle accidents, and medical malpractice. Under the American judicial system, a civil law conviction is based upon the **preponderance of the evidence**. The plaintiff is seeking a **remedy**, which is usually a monetary settlement to the injured party, a fine paid to the courts, or a prison term and a fine. One of the lingering campaign issues particularly with Republican candidates is the issue of **tort reform**. Tort law is "the law of civil wrongs. It concerns conduct that causes injury and fails to measure up to some standard set by society."[15] A civil suit is focused on determining the negligence of the defendant against the plaintiff. **Negligence** is "carelessness or the failure to use ordinary care, under the particular circumstances revealed by the evidence in the lawsuit."[16] Once negligence has been established, the question arises as to the monetary value of the remedy. There are two steps to the reward. For example, a worker falls from a building, suffering serious injuries. If his employer is found to be negligent, then the obvious remedy is to reimburse the employee for the costs currently incurred by his injury. What is more difficult to determine is future monetary loses. If the injuries were so severe the employee is now permanently disabled, what reasonable remedy can be offered to offset his future lost of earnings and the potential financial lost and hardships placed upon the victim's family members. Insurance companies support tort reform that places limitations on monetary awards in civil cases. Those opposed to tort reform believe that it is the unique circumstances that led to the negligence in the first place that drives the value of the remedy.

The cost of civil litigation with attorney's fees and court costs can be beyond the reach of an individual who has a valid claim of wrongdoing against another.

Beginning with William the Conqueror, the British implemented the **people's courts**, we now commonly call **small claims courts**. In this scenario, both the plaintiff and the defendant appear before a Justice of the Peace without attorneys present. Each side presents their argument backed by either physical evidence or witnesses. The judge, in turn, will listen to both sides, review the evidence, render a verdict, and if the defendant is indeed guilty, set the amount of the monetary award.

Criminal law applies to "offenses against the state itself—actions that may be directed against a person but that are deemed to be offensive to society as a whole."[17] In Texas, criminal law is defined and codified in both the *Texas Penal Code* and *Texas Criminal Code*. A conviction on criminal charges is based on guilt established **beyond a reasonable doubt**. In other words, if a member of a jury or a judge believes that there is even a glimmer of doubt as to whether the defendant committed the crime, then the ruling must be not guilty. If the individual is indeed convicted of the charges, then the defendant will face a jail or prison term, a monetary fine, or both.

Other Bodies of Law

The laws passed by both the United States Congress and state legislative houses are commonly known as **statutory laws** whereas home rule cities in Texas issue their own legally binding directives commonly known as **ordinances**. All ordinances and statutory laws must be in line with the spirit and meaning of the provisions of both the Texas Constitution and the supreme law of the land, the United States Constitution. **Constitutional law** is more than just the wording in a single document, in this case, the United States Constitution. It is also the "compilation of all court rulings on the meaning of the various words, phrases, and clauses in the United States Constitution."[18] The United States Supreme Court by constitutional empowerment is the **court of last resort**. This body has the final say on constitutional issues. The right of the federal appellate courts and the Supreme Court to review federal, state and local laws for their constitutionality against the United States Constitution was granted by the **Judiciary Act** of 1789. State appellate and supreme courts have judicial review over statutory laws and ordinances that could be in conflict with their own state constitutions.

Administrative law is "that branch of law that creates administrative agencies, establishes their methods of procedure, and determines the scope of judicial review of agency practices and actions."[19] Statutory laws grant bureaucratic agencies both quasi-legislative and quasi-judicial powers that are required for the implementation of regulatory legislation. Without them, bureaucratic agencies would not have the muscle to force compliance. Since the legislation creating the agencies is, at best, lacking in direction, it is the responsibility of the agencies to develop their own rules and regulations associated with the implementation and enforcement of the legislative directions assigned to them.

The Role of the Supreme Court in State Judicial Matters

The United States Supreme Court is the watchdog over both the federal and state court systems to ensure that the constitutional rights guaranteed to all citizens are equally and fairly applied, even to those accused of a criminal act. The American judicial system was founded on the **adversary system**, meaning that an individual accused of a crime is innocent until proven guilty. It is the burden of the accuser, not the accused, to prove beyond a reasonable doubt that the accused committed a criminal act. The accused has the same rights as any other citizen. Certain rights are forfeited only after the person has been convicted. "The Constitution strongly emphasizes the protection of rights of defendants in the criminal process. The original document contains no fewer than seven provisions specifically addressed to this matter—these are in keeping with the Founders' [Framers'] concern to protect minorities (in this case, unpopular defendants) from tyrannical excesses of an aggrieved or outraged majority . . . The Bill of Rights places an even greater stress on criminal procedure. Of the twenty-three separate rights enumerated in the first eight amendments, thirteen relate to the treatment of criminal defendants."[20] Initially, the first ten amendments known as the Bill of Rights were only applicable to the national government. Gradually, the United States Supreme Court through its rulings has selectively incorporated or tied several of the provisions of the Bill of Rights to the states.

The initial landmark case tying the states to the rights of the accused as detailed in the United States Constitution was *Palko v Connecticut* (1937). Initially, Frank Palko was tried and convicted in a state court on a second-degree murder charge. He was given a life sentence without the possibility of parole. The state prosecutors believing that the jury should have convicted him on a first-degree murder charge and given him the death penalty appealed the lower court's decision to the Connecticut Supreme Court of Errors. This Court overturned the initial conviction and mandated a new trial. The judgment of the jury at the retrial resulted in a first degree conviction and a death sentence. Palko's attorneys appealed this decision to the United States Supreme Court as a violation of their client's protection under the Fifth Amendment's guarantee against double jeopardy and the Fourteenth Amendment's guarantee of due process. The Court ruled against Palko. This decision is important because Justice Benjamin Cardozo's "carefully crafted opinion has long been regarded as the catalyst in the nationalization of the rights of the accused, as it established categorically that the states were obligated to the fundamental imperatives of the Bill of Rights through the Fourteenth Amendment. Cardozo distinguished rights that are fundamental—the very essence of a scheme of ordered liberty—from rights that are not quite so fundamental. Fundamental rights may always be applied to the states, whereas, others may be applied to the states only when state action violates the due process clause of the Fourteenth Amendment."[21]

Also every level of law enforcement and judicial proceeding must adhere to the Bill of Rights' guarantee of the writ of **Habeas Corpus**. Persons accused of committing a crime have the absolute fundamental right to know within a reasonable period of time of what they are accused of illegally doing. The arresting officer must justify his/her actions before a magistrate. If the officer's actions are justifiable, the accused will be charged and either held pending trial or released on bail. If the officer's actions are not justifiable, the magistrate will release the accused.

In 1966, the United States Supreme Court addressed the question of whether a person accused of a crime can voluntarily waive his protected constitutional rights against self-incrimination. The case concerned Ernesto Miranda who was arrested and interrogated for the kidnapping and rape of an eighteen-year old girl in Arizona. During questioning, Miranda signed a confession, acknowledging his guilt and waiving his protected constitutional right against self-incrimination. Miranda, of course, was convicted. His attorneys appealed the case to the Supreme Court on the grounds that Miranda did not understand what his protected rights were in the first place, nor had he ever read the Constitution or the Bill of Rights. Miranda did not speak English fluently. The Court ruled that Miranda's rights had been violated. Chief Justice Earl Warren "made it clear that the prosecution may not use a statement against the accused elicited during custodial interrogation unless it demonstrates the use of effective safeguards to secure, his or her constitutional rights, and they must be made known to the accused. Interrogation could proceed if the accused 'voluntarily, knowingly, and intelligently' makes a waiver of the rights to which he or she is entitled."[22]   Initially, the Court mandated that all arresting and interrogating officers verbally read from a 3 X 5 card the protected rights guaranteed to the accused party prior to making an arrest or initiating accusatory questioning. The decision established these ground rules:

1. He [the arrested suspect] must be told he has the right to stay silent.
2. He [the arrested suspect] must be told that anything he says may be used against him in court.
3. He [the arrested suspect] must be told he has the right to have an attorney with him before any questioning begins.
4. He [the arrested suspect] must be told that, if he wants an attorney but cannot afford one, an attorney will be provided for him for free.
5. If after being told this, an arrested suspect says he does not want a lawyer and is willing to be questioned, he may be, provided that he reached his decision "knowingly and intelligently."
6. If after being told all his rights, a suspect agrees to be questioned, he can shut off the questions at any time after they have started, whether or not he has an attorney with him.[23]

In addition, arresting and interrogating officers cannot assume that the accused understands English. If English is not the primary language of the accused, then the interrogation must cease until the appropriate interpreter is present. Although law enforcement is no longer required to read one's rights from a card, they still must apprise arrested individuals of these constitutional protections. These fundamental rights must be *voluntarily* and not *involuntarily* waived.

The federal courts have reviewed numerous challenges to **Miranda**. If the accused was not appropriately advised of his/her constitutional rights, appellate courts at both the state and federal level have more often than not granted the accused a new trial. The validity of *Miranda* was revisited by the United States Supreme Court in a case involving the constitutionality of a federal anti-crime law that allowed the use of voluntary confessions obtained without first Mirandizing the defendant to be introduced as evidence at trial. In a 7-2 decision, the Court reaffirmed its commitment to *Miranda*. Chief Justice William Rehnquist wrote that "*Miranda* announced a constitutional rule that Congress may not supersede legislatively. We decline to overrule *Miranda* ourselves. *Miranda* has become embedded in routine police practice to the point where the warnings have become part of our national culture."[24]   However, the Court has given law enforcement some leeway. In 2001, the Court ruled in **Texas v Cobb** that a defendant's murder confession is admissible even though his attorney, who was at the time of the interrogation was physically involved in another trial, was not present during the questioning. While the failure to Mirandize a defendant is usually grounds for a new trial, defendants do not have the right to sue the arresting officer for any monetary damages associated with civil litigation. The Court also ruled in **Chavez v Martinez** (2003) that a police officer's failure to issue Miranda Rights could not be used against him in a civil suit involving police brutality.

Citizens are protected against unreasonable searches and seizures by the Fourth Amendment to the United States Constitution. The United States Supreme Court has applied the reasonable restrictions rationale to determine what constitutes a legal from an illegal search. "As far back as 1886, in **Boyd v United States**, the Court in effect, tied the Fourth Amendment to the Fifth Amendment's self incrimination provision, indicating that the two 'run almost into each other.' An unreasonable [illegal] search and seizure, the Court felt, is in reality a 'compulsory extortion' of evidence that could result in compulsory self-incrimination."[25] Under normal circumstances, officers should obtain a search warrant prior to conducting a search.

The **Sixth Amendment** to the United States Constitution guarantees the right to legal representation or counsel. The question of affordability of legal representation was address by the United States Supreme Court in **Powell v Alabama** (1932). In this case, Powell and six other African-American youths were convicted and given death sentences for the rape of two Anglo women. Their one-day trials occurred six days after their arrests. The legal representation afforded to the six defendants consisted of court-appointed attorneys who saw their clients moments before the start of the trials. The Court ruled that all six had been denied their protected rights of due process and equal protection of the law because "(1) they [the defendants] were not given a fair, impartial and deliberate trial; (2) they were denied the right to counsel with the accustomed incidents of consultation and opportunity of preparation of trial; and (3) they were tried before juries from which qualified members of their own race were systematically excluded."[26] Speaking on behalf of the Court, Justice Sutherland stated that "in light of the facts—the ignorance and illiteracy of the defendants, their youth, the circumstances of public hostility, the imprisonment and close surveillance of the defendants by the military forces, the fact that their friends and families

were all in other states and communication with them necessarily difficult, and above all that they stood in deadly peril of their lives—we think the failure of the trial court to give them reasonable time and opportunity to secure counsel was a clear denial of due process."[27]

In addition, the Court has steadfastly upheld the right of legal counsel for indigents. In the 1930s, the Court ruled that attorneys must be appointed to any indigent accused of committing a federal crime. The right to court appointed legal counsel to indigent defendants in state courts was mandated in the United States Supreme Court's 1963 landmark decision in **Gideon v Wainwright**. Like so many defendants, Clarence Gideon could not afford to hire an attorney. Exercising the only option available to him, Gideon tried unsuccessfully to act as his own counsel. However, the justices of the Supreme Court saw this as a grave injustice and emphasized "that the government hires lawyers to prosecute and defendants who have the money hire lawyers to defend are the strongest indications of the widespread belief that lawyers in criminal courts are necessities, not luxuries. The right of one charged with a crime to counsel may not be deemed fundamental and essential for fair trials in some countries, but it is in ours."[28] Basically, the *Gideon* decision "nationalized the right to counsel in *all*—save certain misdemeanor—criminal cases, *be they capital or noncapital*" charges.[29] The Court reaffirmed the importance of court-appointed counsel in **Alabama v Shelton** in 2002 by ruling that a defendant charged with even a minor offense must have legal representation.

Traditionally the appointment of legal counsel for indigent defendants was a function of the county courts. County judges assign indigent cases to those attorneys frequently trying cases in their courts. Court-appointed attorneys receive a set fee paid by the county to cover legal services. Of course, the fee is much less than what the attorney would normally charge a client. The state, therefore, believed it was fulfilling its constitutionally mandated responsibility by providing attorneys for indigents. With the passage of the **Texas Fair Defense Act,** the Texas Legislature reemphasized its commitment to provide legal counsel to indigent defendants by offering state funding to those counties unable to appropriate money for court-appointed attorneys. Funding alone, however, does not guarantee that the indigent defendant receives the same quality of legal defense as one who can afford to privately hire an attorney. In 2003, the United States Supreme Court ruled in **Wiggins v Smith** that "the failure of an inexperienced defense attorney to conduct a reasonable investigation of the defendant's troubled personal background constituted ineffective assistance of counsel."[30]

The death penalty is still debated as a possible violation of the **Eighth Amendment**'s protection against cruel and unusual punishment. It has become an international issue as individuals accused of committing crimes in the United States flee to those countries that decry the death penalty. These nations will not extradite an accused person if a conviction in an American court results in a death sentence. Opponents question the effectiveness of the death penalty as a deterrent to crime. In 1972, the United States Supreme Court ruled in three separate cases collectively heard as *Furman v Georgia* that the death penalty, as applied in this case, was indeed an abuse of the Eighth Amendment. "Although the Court never decided that execution was necessarily cruel and unusual punishment, the justices outlawed mandatory death sentences and approved a two stage process for capital cases, with guilt determined first and punishment fixed by predetermined standards."[31] The *Furman* case did address the cruelty of the death penalty. In determining the intent of the Eighth Amendment, Justice Brennan wrote:

First the clause prohibits the infliction of uncivilized and inhumane punishments. Second, the clause demands that, in the name of human dignity, the state refrain from inflicting punishment arbitrarily or unevenly; namely, imposing the death penalty on some but not on others who are guilty of the same crime. Third, the clause requires that a punishment must not be "unacceptable to contemporary society." The fourth and final principle inherent in the cruel and unusual clause is that a punishment must not be excessive. A punishment is excessive if it is an "unnecessary" or "pointless inflection of suffering." If there is a less severe form of punishment that will adequately accomplish society's penal goals, then the present form of punishment is probably excessive.[32]

In 2002, the federal courts made three key rulings limiting the use of the death penalty. By declaring the federal 1994 Death Penalty Act unconstitutional, U.S. District Judge Jed Rakoff halted the use of the death penalty in all federal cases. He based his decision on the fact that "the best available evidence indicates that on one hand, innocent people are sentenced to death with materially greater frequency than was previously supposed and that, on the other hand, convincing proof of their innocence often does not emerge until long after the convictions."[33] In *Williams v Taylor* (2000), the Court ruled 6-3 that the execution of the mentally handicapped was an unconstitutional breach of the Eighth Amendment's prohibition against cruel and unusual punishment. Subsequently, any defendant with an IQ of 70 or less could not be given the death penalty. The Court's decision overturned laws in approximately twenty states, including Texas, that executed the mentally impaired. In *Ring v Arizona* (2002), the Court ruled that juries, not judges, must decide whether a convicted murderer should receive the death penalty. In support of its 7-2 decision, Justice Ruth Bader Ginsburg noted that "the Constitution guarantees a trial by a jury, and that right extends to weighing whether a particular killing merits death or life in prison."[34]

In February 2003, the United States Supreme Court granted a Texas inmate the right to present his case before a federal appellate court. Miller-El was tried, convicted, and given the death sentence for murdering a Dallas Holiday Inn employee during a 1985 robbery. Miller-El's attorneys sought to appeal the conviction on several constitutional issues including the deliberate exclusion of African Americans from the jury. The United States Supreme Court had already ruled that preemptory challenges made by attorneys in an effort to deliberately exclude potential jurors because of their race was unconstitutional. Initially, Miller-El's appeals to both the Texas Court of Criminal Appeals and the federal courts were denied. "Texas officials maintained that prosecutors had legitimate reasons for striking the excluded blacks [African Americans] from the jury pool, such as their view on capital punishment. State trial and appeals courts agreed, and federal courts said Miller-El had not made a persuasive enough case for them to step in."[35] Miller-El's attorney presented to the Court a historical tract record of the Dallas County courts' deliberate efforts to encourage the exclusion of minorities from trial juries. Placed in evidence was a "1963 circular by the district attorney's office instructing that prosecutors 'not take Jews, Negroes [African Americans], Dagos [Italians], Mexicans or a member of any minority race on a jury, no matter how rich or how well-educated."[36] Court records during the Miller-El original trial indicated "prosecutors asked a different set of questions to minority potential jurors than those asked of Anglos and successfully excluded 91 percent of the eligible black [African-American] jurors with preemptory strikes but used preemptory strikes against only 13 percent of eligible non-black jurors."[37] Verbally admonishing the lower federal courts for both ignoring the weight of the evidence and not granting the appeal, the Supreme Court ruled 8-1 in Miller-El's favor.

Table 9.1 is a selective list of Supreme Court rulings that have directly impacted how law enforcement, the courts, and correctional facilities operate in the United States. In the majority of the Supreme Court rulings discussed earlier and those listed in Table 9.1, the United States Supreme Court had questions arising about procedural and substantive issues with either the body of the law in question or the process used by the judicial system. As will be covered in further detail in Chapter 11, substantive issues focus on how a law, statute, or ordinance was written. If the law lacks clarity as to its meaning, then both the general public and law enforcement officials do not have a clear understanding as to what constitutes a violation of the law. Procedural concerns arise as to how the law is applied. Holding one person accountable to violating a law and then exempting another violator from punishment of the same law is unconstitutional.

Initially, law enforcement did not openly embrace the Court's ruling in *Miranda v Arizona*, seeing the reading of constitutional rights as an unnecessary step in the apprehension and interrogation of suspects. Today, however, *Miranda* has saved many well investigated and tried cases from having their verdicts appealed and successfully overturned because the convicted felon claimed

Table 9.1 Selective United States Supreme Court Cases

Case	Year	Decision
Alabama v Shelton	2002	Court-appointed counsel must be granted to a defendant facing a suspended jail term for a minor offense.
Argersinger v Hamlin	1972	Non-felony defendants have the right to court-appointed counsel.
Arizona v Fulminate	1991	A coerced confession does not automatically turn over a conviction.
Ashcraft v Tennessee	1944	A confession obtained through psychological coercion is not voluntary and therefore not admissible in court.
Atkins v Virginia	2002	The death penalty cannot be used for defendants with an IQ under 70.
Baldwin v New York	1970	Individuals accused of petty offenses do not have the right to a jury trial.
Ballew v Georgia	1978	Six is the minimum number for a jury panel.
Baze v Rees	2008	Kentucky's use of lethal injections does not violate the 8th Amendment to the U.S. Constitution.
Beck v Alabama	1980	A jury must be allowed to consider a lesser included offense, not just a capital offense or acquittal as verdict options.
Berger v U.S.	1935	The primary task of a prosecutor's job is the pursuit of justice, not just winning cases.
Betts v Brady	1942	Indigent defendants accused of a noncapital crime are not guaranteed court-appointed counsel (overturned in 1963 *Gideon v Wainwright* decision).
Bond v U.S.	2000	Passengers on a bus or train have an expectation of privacy when they place their luggage in an overhead storage rack.
Booth v Maryland	1987	Victim impact statements are unconstitutional in capital cases because the statements can result in an arbitrary and capricious application of the death penalty.
Boykin v Alabama	1969	Whenever a defendant enters a plea of guilty it is up to the judge to determine if the plea was knowingly entered and absolutely voluntary.
Brady v Maryland	1963	Due process is violated with prosecutors withhold evidence from the defense that might be favorable to the defendant.

Branzburg v Hayes	1972	Journalists cannot release confidentiality of sources when they are subpoenaed before grand juries and are compelled to give testimony.
Brigham City v Stuart	2006	Police can enter a home without a warrant when they have a reasonable assumption that an occupant is seriously injured.
Brown v Mississippi	1936	A confession obtain by physical coercion is an unconstitutional violation of the due process clause of the 14th Amendment to U.S. Constitution.
Buckley v Fitzsimmons	1993	Prosecutors have qualified immunity from civil law-suits for their actions during criminal investigations, news/press-related statements they may make.
Burns v Reed	1991	Prosecutors have qualified immunity from lawsuits concerning advice to the police.
Chavez v Martinez	2003	Failure of a police officer to apprise the suspect of Miranda cannot be used against the officer in a civil suit.
Chinnel v California	1969	During a search, police can only search the person and the area within the immediate vicinity.
Coleman v Alabama	1970	Counsel is required during the critical stages of defendant's initial appearance, bail and preliminary hearings.
Coker v Georgia	1977	Rape is not a capital death penalty offense.
County of Riverside v McLaughlin	1991	A judicial determination of probable cause with 48-hours of the arrest complies with the "promptness requirement."
Deck v Missouri	2005	The U.S. Constitution prohibits the use of visible shackles during a trial's penalty phase as well as during the guilt phase unless that use is justified as an essential interest specific to the defendant.
Dickerson v U.S.	2000	Upheld *Miranda v Arizona*.
Douglas v California	1963	Indigents have right to court-appointed counsel for their first appeal.
Duncan v Louisiana	1968	The due process clause of the 14th Amendment binds the 6th Amendment right to a jury trial to the states.
Enmund v Florida	1982	Death penalty cannot be imposed for an individual who played a minor role in a felony, and does not kill, attempt to kill, or intend to kill.
Faretta v California	1975	Defendants have the constitutional right to self-defense.
Florida v J.L.	2000	Police cannot stop a motorist and conduct a search based solely on an anonymous tip.
Ford v Wainwright	1986	Execution of the insane violates the 8th Amendment to the U.S. Constitution.
Francis v Resweber	1947	Re-execution after a failed execution violates the 8th Amendment to the U.S. Constitution.
Furman v Georgia	1972	Invalidated all existing death penalty laws.
Georgia v McCollum	1992	The defense cannot exclude jurors based on their race.
Georgia v Randolph	2006	If the police do not have a search warrant, they cannot search a home if one of the occupants objects, even if another grants police permission.

Gerstein v Pugh	1975	An arrested individual is entitled to a prompt hearing; a wait of thirty days is unconstitutional.
Glass v Louisiana	1985	Electrocution does not violate the 8th Amendment to the U.S. Constitution.
Glossip v Gross	2015	States may use a drug linked to botched executions to carry out death sentences.
Godfrey v Georgia	1980	The death penalty is not a possible sentence for ordinary murder.
Gregg v Georgia	1976	Death penalty laws do not necessarily constitute "cruel and unusual punishment."
Hall v Florida	2014	The IQ test cannot be the sole instrument for determining intellectual disabilities.
Hamilton v Alabama	1961	Counsel is required during arraignment.
Harris v New York	1971	Voluntary statements made prior to a defendant being apprised of constitutional rights can be used at trial to impeach the defendant's credibility.
Hill v McDonough	2006	Prisoners can invoke a provision of the Civil Rights Act of 1871 to challenge a state's choice of drugs used to administer a lethal injection.
Holt v Hobbs	2015	Arkansas correction officers violated the religious liberty of Muslim inmates when they forbade them from growing beards over security concerns.
Hudson v Michigan	2006	Even if the police fail to knock and announce themselves prior to entering a residence, any evidence obtained as a result of the search may be admitted at trial.
Hurtado v California	1884	States are not required to use the grand jury system for felony charges.
Illinois v Perkins	1990	A law enforcement officer can pose as an inmate to obtain a confession without apprising inmate of Miranda rights.
Illinois v Rodriguez	1990	Good faith exception search is constitutional even though the victim allowed entry into an apartment she no longer resided in with the accused.
Illinois v Wardlow	2000	A suspect running from the police can be subjected to a stop-and frisk search.
Imbler v Pachtman	1976	Prosecutors have absolute immunity from civil liability during a criminal prosecution.
In re Gault	1967	Juveniles have right to counsel under the 6th Amendment to the U.S. Constitution.
Jencks v U.S.	1957	Prior inconsistent statements made by a witness must be made available to the defense.
Johnson v Zerbst	1938	Indigent defendants in federal court are guaranteed court-appointed counsel.
Kalina v Fletcher	1997	Prosecutors can be sued for making false statements of fact in affidavits.
Kastigar v U.S.	1972	Use immunity is not a violation of the 5th Amendment's guarantee of protection from self-incrimination.
Knowles v Iowa	1998	Just issuing a speeding ticket does not give police the right to search the vehicle.
Lanzetta v New Jersey	1938	A law is unconstitutional if the meaning of the law is so vague that "men of common intelligence must necessarily guess as to its meaning."

Mapp v Ohio	1961	The exclusionary rule applies to both federal and state law enforcement agencies.
Martinez v Court of Appeals of California	2000	Defendants cannot self-represent on appeal cases.
Missick v Mississippi	1990	Once the defendant has asked for legal representation, interrogation cannot resume until the attorney is present.
Miranda v Arizona	1966	Counsel must be guaranteed when requested by the accused during interrogation; defendant must be apprised of constitutional rights before waving those rights.
Morgan v Illinois	1992	Defendants may challenge for cause a prospective juror who would automatically vote to impose the death penalty in a capital case.
Morrison v Olson	1988	Use of independent counsels is constitutional.
Muchler v Mena	2005	In this case, the use of handcuffs to detain a defendant during the execution of a search warrant was reasonable and did not violate the 4th Amendment to the U.S. Constitution.
New York v Quarles	1984	Issues of public safety can justify an officer's failure to provide Miranda Warnings before questioning about the location of a weapon.
Payne v Tennessee	1991	The introduction of victim's impact statements during sentencing is not a violation of the 8th Amendment's protection against cruel & unusual punishment.
Payton v New York	1980	An arrest warrant is necessary to enter a suspect's private resident with the exception of the suspect's consent or an emergency situation.
Pennsylvania v Muniz	1990	Police officers can ask routine questions and video tape the responses of those suspected of DWI violation.
Powell v Alabama	1932	Court-appointed counsel is guaranteed to indigent defendants accused of a capital case.
Press Enterprises v Superior Court	1986	All preliminary hearings must be open to the public.
Republican Party v White	2002	Judicial candidates to include incumbent judges can discuss issues during their campaigns.
Riley v California	2014	Police need a warrant to search the cellphones of people they arrest.
Ring v Arizona	2002	Only juries can decided the critical sentencing issues in death penalty cases.
Roe v Flores-Ortega	2000	A lawyer's failure to file an appeal does not constitute ineffective counsel.
Roper v Simmons	2005	The death penalty for a defendant under 17 years of age is unconstitutional.
Ruiz v Estelle	1980	U.S. District Court declared prison overcrowding in the Texas prison system unconstitutional.
Samson v California	2006	The 4th Amendment does not prohibit a police officer from conducting a non-suspicious search of a parolee.
Scott v Harris	2007	A police officer's attempt to stop a dangerous high-speed chase that threatens innocent parties does not violate the 4th Amendment to the U.S. Constitution.

Sheppard v Maxwell	1966	Defendant denied fair trial due to prejudicial pretrial publicity.
Simon & Schuster v New York Crime Victims Board	1991	Ruled unconstitutional the state's "Son of Sam" law making illegal for criminals to profit from their offenses.
South Carolina v Gathers	1989	Introducing characteristics of the victim during a death penalty deliberation is irrelevant.
Spaziano v Florida	1984	Judges can override a jury's recommendation of a life sentence and impose the death penalty. (Overturns *Ring v Arizona*)
Strickland v Washington	1984	One's defense attorney can be judged as ineffective only if the court proceedings were unfair and the judgment would have been different.
Taylor v Louisiana	1972	Women cannot be excluded from jury duty.
Thompson v Oklahoma	1988	The death penalty cannot be given to defendants under the age of fifteen.
U.S. v Leon	1984	Upheld a limited use of the good faith exception to search warrants.
U.S. v Lopez	1995	Congress cannot use its authority under the commerce clause to prohibit guns in schools.
U.S. v Scheffer	1998	Polygraphs cannot be used in court as evidence.
Wiggins v Smith	2003	A lawyer's inability to conduct a complete investigation into the client's background does not constitute ineffective defense.
Williams v Florida	1970	State court juries can have less than twelve members.
Witherspoon v Illinois	1968	Prospective jurors cannot be eliminated due to their views on the death penalty, for their actions during criminal investigations, and for news/press-related statements they may make.

that his or her constitutional rights were not explained to them prior to signing that confession or admitting to incriminating activities that enhanced that guilty verdict.

Although the United States Supreme Court has vacillated in its own rulings on the subject, decisions relating to the claimed that his or her constitutional rights were not explained to them prior to signing that confession or admitting to incriminating activities that enhanced that guilty verdict. The Court's decision in **Boykin v Alabama** (1969) led to law enforcement officials to require that the defendant sign a statement that he/she understood the repercussions of their confession and voluntarily admitted to their criminal activity.

Although the United States Supreme Court has vacillated in its own rulings on the subject, decisions relating to the death penalty have led many state governors and legislators to question the validity of their state's use of it. Over the years, the Texas Legislature has expanded the range of crimes subject to the death penalty. As a presidential candidate, then Governor George W. Bush defended the state's supposed eagerness to execute death row inmates. In an interview, Bush commented that "I'm confident that every person that has been put to death in Texas under my watch has been guilty of the crime charged, and has had full access to the courts."[38] However, data disputes Bush's claim. "Seven death row inmates were exonerated in Texas from 1993 to 1997 after evidence of witnesses who had lied [on the stand] mistaken witnesses, and prosecutorial misconduct."[39] Governor Rick Perry took a more cautious approach to the death penalty. He even entertained an execution moratorium similar to the one issued in Illinois. Perry held that only those who are guilty beyond a reasonable doubt of a heinous crime should suffer the ultimate penalty. But, Perry also vetoed legislation that would have provided state funding for those death row indigent inmates whose cases were judged before DNA became a definitive test of innocence or guilt.

Texas Judicial System: Law Enforcement

The state's law enforcement community consisted of 41,912 full-time sworn officers as of October 31, 2017. The average number of officers for every 1,000 inhabitants of Texas was 1.5. The ratio of law enforcement officers to inhabitants decreased 19.2% from 2016.[40] In addition, there were 26,039 "civilian" (not in uniform) support staff employed with state and local law enforcement agencies. Civilian employment has decreased 22.6% since 2016. Civilian employment accounts for 38.3% of the Texas law enforcement workforce.[41] The 2017 report indicates that during 2017 alone:

- In 2017, there were 46,414 juvenile and 759,550 adult arrests.
- There were a reported total of 842,055 index offenses in Texas in addition to 3,294 cases of arson and 345 human trafficking offenses.
- The 2017 state crime rate was 2,975 crimes per 100,000 persons, a decrease of 6.6% from 2016.
- A reported 123,211 violent crimes occurred during 2017, a 2.1% increase from 2016.
- There were 718,844 property crimes, a 6.1% decrease from 2016. Burglary accounted for 18.5% of all property offenses.
- A reported 14,332 rapes occurred in 2017, an increase of 7.6% over 2016 figures.
- 67,285 motor vehicle thefts were reported in 2017, a decrease of 1.8% over 2016 reported cases.
- In 2017, the total value of reported stolen property was $1,980,079,125 with law enforcement recovering $518,811,568 value of stolen property.
- There were 190 hate crime incidents reported in 2017, an increase of 6.7% over 2016 reported incidents.
- In 2017, there were 195,315 family violence incidents involving 212,207 victims and 207,213 offenders, a decrease of 0.6% compared to 2016.
- In 2017, there were 18,122 sexual assault incidents involving 18,750 victims and 18,774 offenders, a decrease of 1.3% over 2016 reported incidents.[42]

Sadly in 2017, seven law enforcement officers were killed feloniously in the line of duty and an additional seven were killed in duty-related accidents. There were 4,553 officers assaulted during 2017.[43]

The majority of the crimes committed in Texas are handled through the local police chief and his/her officers and the county sheriff and his/her deputies. At the state level, the Department of Public Safety (DPS) Highway Patrol's primary task is to police the state's highways. The elite Texas Rangers primarily investigate major crimes and allegations of police brutality and misconduct. Unfortunately, the crime lab investigation television series leads viewers to believe that all local police departments have the same type of sophisticated laboratories and forensics experts as seen on these programs. Particularly in smaller communities and bedroom cities, the police force's primary duty is traffic control and the issuance of moving violations. If a murder occurs in their jurisdiction, more than likely they will need to call upon the Texas Rangers for expert assistance.

In the old West, it was the person who could draw and shoot the fastest that usually wore the sheriff's badge. Today in Texas, the county sheriff is elected to a four-year term of office. Usually the candidates are former police officers or county deputies. The local police chief is usually appointed to his/her position by the city council. Every candidate for a police officer's position must complete basic training courses as mandated by the Texas Commission on Law Enforcement. Whereas once a high school diploma was sufficient, the majority of the state's police departments are requiring some college-level work or a bachelor's degree. Upon graduating from their local police academy, officers are required to attend regular in-service training programs to keep them up-to-date on current criminal activities such as identify theft, family violence, and drug trafficking, as well as breakthroughs in new forensic and investigative equipment and software, and anti-racial profiling and sensitivity courses. With budget shortfalls, city governments are hard pressed to maintain the appropriate number of officers and provide them with the sophisticated equipment they need to effectively police the streets and keep innocent people safe from harm. Salary and benefit issues are always a concern. Just how much is enough to pay a person to put their life on the line on a daily basis?

The most vital component part of the judicial process is the actions of the local police officers for they investigate the crime scene, gather the evidence, apprehend and interrogate the suspect, and build the case against the accused. By the time the case goes to trial, the county could have the best prosecuting team in the state, but if the evidence gathered by the local police is flawed or compromised, then the prosecution will lose the case. The majority of the United States Supreme Court decisions have dealt with the investigative and pre-trial actions of law enforcement from illegal search warrants or, as in this case, the lack of one, in *Mapp v Ohio*.

Figure 9.1   The Texas Judicial System
States Highest Appellate Courts

Supreme Court	Court of Criminal Appeals
One Court with Nine Justices	One Court with Nine Justices
Jurisdiction—Final appellate court in civil and juvenile cases	Jurisdiction—Final appellate court in criminal cases

Courts of Appeals
(State Intermediate Appellate Courts)
14 Courts – 80 Justices
Regional Jurisdiction—
Intermediate appeals from trial courts
in the respective courts of appeals districts

District Courts
(State Trial Courts of General and Special Jurisdiction)
447 Courts—437 Judges
Jurisdiction
Original jurisdiction in civil actions over $500, divorce,
titles to land, and contested elections
Original jurisdiction in felony criminal matters
Juvenile matters
13 district courts are designed criminal district courts;
Others are directed to give preference to certain specialized areas

Death Penalty
Appeals

County Level Courts
(County Trial Courts of Limited Jurisdiction)
494 Courts—494 Judges

Constitutional County Courts (254 courts—one court in each county)	County Courts at Law (222 courts in 84 counties)	Statutory Probate Courts (18 courts in 10 counties)
Jurisdiction: Original jurisdiction—civil actions between $200 and $10,000 Probate (contested matters may be transferred to District Court) Exclusive original jurisdiction over misdemeanors with fines greater than $500 or jail sentence Juvenile matters Appeals de novo from lower courts or on the record from municipal courts of record	Jurisdiction: All civil, criminal, original and appellate actions prescribed by law for constitutional county courts. Jurisdiction over civil matters up to $100,000 (some courts may have higher maximum jurisdiction amount).	Jurisdiction: Limited primarily to probate matters

Local Trial Courts of Limited Jurisdiction

Justice Courts (821 Courts—821 Judges) (Established in precincts within each county)	Municipal Courts (917 Cities—1,414 Judges)
Jurisdiction: Civil actions of not more than $10,000 Small Claims Criminal misdemeanors punishable by fine only (no confinement) Magistrate functions	Jurisdiction: Criminal misdemeanors punishable by fine only (no confinement) Limited civil jurisdiction in cases involving dangerous dogs Magistrate functions

The legalities of the **search warrant** and the interrogation process can be problematic for law enforcement. A search warrant is "a written document, signed a by judge or magistrate, authorizing a law enforcement officer to conduct a search."[44] Under normal circumstances, a search must be in compliance with the Fourth Amendment to the United States Constitution, which clearly states that there must be probable cause that a crime has taken place and that the evidence sought is directly tied to that criminal action. If evidence is improperly seized, a judge may evoke the **exclusionary rule**, meaning "that evidence which is otherwise admissible may not be used in a criminal trial if it is a product of illegal police conduct."[45] A search warrant includes the officer's sworn affidavit indicating the reason for the search, a list of the items subject to the search, and the location of the search. Once signed by a magistrate, the officer can now use the warrant to conduct the search. But what if the officer believes that by the time he/she gets the warrant, the evidence being sought might disappear or be destroyed? The officer can conduct a **warrantless search** under certain circumstances. If the owner of the house consents to a search, the search can take place without a warrant. With or without a warrant, evidence seized during a search is legal if it is in **plain view** of the officer. For example, the officer is looking for a stolen flat-screen television as indicated in the warrant. In the process of the search, the officer finds the television but besides it in plain sight is an illegal firearm. The officer can seize the weapon and charge the defendant with an additional violation since the object in question was indeed in plain sight of the officer. However if in the course of the search, the officer finds that same illegal weapon hidden in the back of the closet, then it is questionable whether the weapons violation will be upheld in court. Also, there are situations that occur frequently while in the midst of a search, an officer will want to seize items directly linked to the crime, but not originally listed in the warrant, constituting a **good faith exception**. In this situation, the seized illegal weapon has been identified by witnesses as being used by the accused during the robbery of that flat-screen television. In *Illinois v Krull* (1967), the United States Supreme Court ruled that the good faith exception did apply to warrantless searches. However, any defense attorney will definitely question the admissibility of the evidence obtained by a warrantless search during pre-trial motions, and the judge can invoke the exclusionary rule and render the evidence inadmissible.

Another area of concern is the interrogation of the suspect. **Investigative** questioning can continue without an attorney present. However, when the investigative questioning shifts to accusatory questioning and the accused evokes the right to legal counsel, the questioning must cease until the attorney is present, as re-enforced by the United States Supreme Court's ruling in *Minnick v Mississippi* (1990). Confessions obtained through physical or psychological coercion are inadmissible in court. Oftentimes, the accused will agree to confess to the crime as part of a plea bargain deal. **Plea bargaining** is "the process through which a defendant pleads guilty to a criminal charge with the expectation of receiving some consideration from the state."[46] While critics frown on plea bargaining as just a way for the accused to escape trial and possibly jail time, police departments as well as lawyers and judges like these agreements for several reasons. First, the police have obtained actually what they wanted in the first place—a confession. Second, it saves the state the time and money of a trial. Third, more importantly, it can lead law enforcement to apprehend an individual accused of a more serious crime. For example, a drug dealer signs a plea deal for a reduced sentence or even probation in exchange for information leading to the arrest of his/her supplier.

The United States Constitution mandates that anyone accused of a crime must be apprised of the charges against him or her within a reasonable time by the arresting officer in front of a magistrate. This constitutes the **initial appearance** of the accused that occurs within a few hours or days of the arrest. For misdemeanor offenses, the accused merely enters a plea, and the magistrate disposes of the case. For felony charges, a plea at this stage is not allowed. Once the **charging document** detailing the particulars of the charge is present, the accused is now officially referred to as the defendant. The magistrate will determine the disposition of the defendant by either setting **bail** (a cash payment for release), releasing the defendant on **recognizance** based on the defendant's prior criminal record, employment, ties to the community, not deemed to be a flight risk, etc., or **remanded** in jail until after the preliminary hearing whereby the judge hearing the case will determine whether to grant bail or continue to remand the defendant. With the exception of serving as witnesses during the trial, the role of local law enforcement has ended.

If the police handle the process appropriately from start to finish, then the next level of the decision rests with the county/district attorney. Elected to a four-year term of office, candidates for district attorney must be licensed practicing attorneys. The district attorney's office is composed of a cadre of well qualified defense attorneys whose primary job is to get a conviction. However, it is up to the district attorney's office to prosecute the case. The political future of the district attorney could hang in the balance particularly with high-profile cases. For example, the Casey Anthony trial in Florida attracted millions of viewers to turn in to the evening news or to watch the proceedings over the internet. The district attorney's office made headlines of its own by promising that the evidence presented to them by the local police department conclusively demonstrated that Anthony did indeed murder her daughter. However as the trial progressed, the experts outside of the courtroom predicted a not guilty verdict simply because the so-called conclusive evidence was flawed and inclusive. To avoid the situation in Florida, it is incumbent that the district attorney's office has a solid professional working relationship with their local police departments.

The Texas Court System

Legal Jurisdiction

Jurisdiction is the "authority vested in a court to hear and decide a case."[47] All courts have a prescribed level of **original jurisdiction** "defined as the authority of a court to hear a case in the first instance."[48] As indicated in Figure 9.1, justice of the peace courts and municipal courts have original jurisdiction for criminal misdemeanors punishable by fines only. These judges do not have the authority to order jail time for a minor traffic violation. Constitutional county courts, however, do have original jurisdiction over misdemeanor offenses with fines over $500 or a jail sentence. Only the district courts have original jurisdiction to hear felony cases. Courts can also have **appellate jurisdiction** defined as the "authority of a court to review decisions of an inferior court."[49] In Texas, misdemeanor convictions are not appealed in the usual format but are presented in the county level courts as *de novo* (Latin for a new trial) or **on the record** from the municipal courts of record. The Court of Appeals has exclusive jurisdiction to hear just appellate cases judged in the district courts. Texas has a dual Supreme Court or a bifurcated system composed of the **Supreme Court,** which is the final appellate or **court of last resort** for civil and juvenile cases and the **Court of Criminal Appeals** that serves as the court of last resort for all felony criminal cases. Appellate courts oftentimes use the **Writ of Certiorari,** "an order issued by a higher court to a lower court to send up the record of a case for review."[50] The Texas Supreme Court also can hear cases on the constitutionality of a state law. Like the United States Supreme Court, the body can render a decision or declare

that the issue is a **political question** whereby the desired remedy can only be rendered by the legislative branch of government.

All criminal charges fall into two broad categories. A **felony** is "a serious crime punishable by death or by imprisonment in a penitentiary for a year or more."[51] The **Texas Penal Code** lists felony charges by the degree of the offense. The lowest level of a felony conviction carries a maximum fine of $10,000 plus a prison sentence in the state prison system ranging from 180 days to two years for the crime of using an unauthorized vehicle and vehicle theft. A **third degree felony** conviction carries a prison term ranging from two to ten years and a fine up to $10,000. Crimes in this category include kidnapping, escape from a jail or prison, aggravate assault, and deadly conduct. Those convicted of sexual assault, intoxication manslaughter, home burglary, or robbery have committed a **second degree felony** that carries a sentence ranging from two to twenty years and a fine up to $10,000. A **first degree felony** entails the crimes of murder, indecency with a child, attempted capital murder, and aggravated assault. A conviction for a first degree felony carries a sentence ranging from five to ninety-nine years and a maximum fine of $10,000. A **capital offense** is levied for those who murder a peace officer, firefighter, or employee of a penal institution who is acting in his/her official capacity; murders a person while the defendant is in the process of committing or attempting to commit kidnapping, burglary, robbery, aggravated sexual assault or arson; commits a serial or mass murder; commits a murder for hire, murders a child under the age of six; murders a person while escaping or attempting escape from a penal institution; murders a judge for retaliation; and commits repeated sex crimes against children. The sentence ranges from life in prison without parole or the death penalty. With the exception of murder, all offenses fall under the **statute of limitations,** that is, "a state or federal legislative act that establishes a time limit within which lawsuits may be brought, judgments enforced, or crimes prosecuted."[52]

A **misdemeanor** is "a minor criminal offense."[53] The Texas Penal Code divides those offenses by classes. The lowest level is **Class C** for offenses associated with traffic and city ordinance violations, public intoxication, disorderly conduct, simple assault, and theft valued at under $50. A conviction carries a maximum $500 fine with no time served in the county jail. A **Class B** misdemeanor offense is levied against those charged with a first offense of driving while intoxicated (DWI), prostitution, possession of less than two ounces of marijuana, and harassment. These offenses carry a fine of $2,000 and a maximum jail sentence of 180 days. The highest misdemeanor category is a **Class A** offense for those charged with assault causing injury, resisting arrest, and a weapons violation. A guilty verdict results in a maximum fine of $4,000 and one year confinement in the county jail.

Qualifications and Selection of Judges

The qualifications for a judgeship depend upon the level of court the candidate seeks. For a seat of the Texas Supreme Court or the Texas Court of Criminal Appeals, candidates must be at least thirty-five years of age, a citizen of the United States, and a resident of Texas. In addition, candidates must be licensed to practice law in Texas and have at least ten years experience as a practicing attorney, a sitting judge on a court of record or a combination thereof. Elected for four-year terms of office, candidates for district judge must be licensed to practice law in Texas for at least four years, be residents of the judicial district in which they serve for at least two years, and be citizens of the United States. For County Courts at Law and statutory Probate Courts qualifications for office vary according to the specific Texas legislative statute that created the court. Overall candidates for these benches must be licensed to practice law in Texas and must be a resident of the county their court serves. Judges of the County Courts at Law must be at least twenty-five years of age. Judicial candidates for Constitutional County Court seats must only be well informed in the law of the state since the majority of the 254 counties do not require that their judges be licensed attorneys. Judges of Municipal Courts of record must be attorneys. However, all other judges for municipal courts and justice of the peace courts do not have to be licensed attorneys. Justice of the peace judges are required by law to complete a forty-hour course covering the proper execution of that office's duties the first time they serve. After that, they are required to complete twenty hours of course work per year. All county, municipal and justice of the peace judges serve four-year terms of office.

In Texas, all judicial benches are filled through the partisan election process. The written and, perhaps more important, unwritten code of judicial conduct can make it difficult for an incumbent judge to seek reelection. Whereas an incumbent legislator can brag about his or her accomplishments, a judge simply cannot discuss the particulars of cases heard before his/her court. The usual questions incumbent judges feel comfortable in addressing are those focusing on their ability to move cases quickly through the trial process as expediently as possible. Decisions made by judges have to be legally correct although they may not be politically correct. The average voter focuses on the political correctness of the judge's decisions. Few voters are well versed in the law! However, few Texans would support the idea of the governor's appointment powers extending to judges. In some states, the middle road has been the implementation of the **Missouri Plan** whereby judges are initially appointed to their benches by the governor with senatorial approval for a set probationary period. At the conclusion of probationary period, each judge's performance is reviewed by a panel of judicial experts. If the judge passes their evaluation, the judge can then run for the bench in a popular election.

The Trial Phase

For felony charges, the official trial process begins with the **preliminary hearing**. The prosecution presents to the presiding judge the charges against the defendant in the form of an **indictment**, defined as "the formal accusation drawn up by the prosecutor and brought by a grand jury, charging a person with the commission of a crime.[54] In turn, it is the judge's decision as to whether there is probable cause to proceed with a trial. If a trial is to take place, the judge will determine the further disposition of the defendant and place the trial on his/her calendar or **docket**. At this time, the judge will appoint an attorney if the defendant not cannot afford to hire one. Texas does have a **Speedy Trial Law** that requires that the prosecution must be ready to try a case in a specified time period. However, in most cases, the defense has not had adequate time to prepare.

Like most states, Texas uses a two jury system—the grand jury and the petit or trial jury. The primary role of the **grand jury** is to review the evidence gathered by the prosecution to determine whether the present body of evidence is sufficient to proceed to trial. A jury commission of three to five members appointed by a district judge draws up a list of potential jurors. In turn, the district judge selects twelve members to serve a three-month term as members of the grand jury. Only the prosecution participates in a grand jury hearing. Based upon the evidence, the jury will either **true bill** the case, which leads to the issuance of a formal indictment against the defendant, or **no bill**, meaning that the evidence is insufficient to take it to trial. The grand jury system is valuable to the entire judicial process. For the prosecution, the jury's no bill decision gives them the opportunity to "go back to the drawing board" and gather more compelling evidence that will ultimately pass the panel's scrutiny. It saves the courts time and money for if a grand jury finds fault with the evidence, both the judge and trial jury surely will. Oftentimes no matter how heinous the criminal act maybe, the evidence simply will not move a jury to a conviction. Obviously, the charge of murder has a better chance of standing if indeed the prosecution can produce **direct evidence**, i.e., the body of the deceased. A case built entirely on **circumstantial evidence** is difficult to successfully prosecute.

When most individuals receive their jury summons in the mail, they do their utmost best to find a reasonable excuse to avoid it. However, it is a constitutional guarantee that those accused of a crime must be judged by a panel of his/her peers. A **jury** is "an impartial body that sits in judgment on charges brought in either criminal or civil cases."[55] In Texas, felony trial juries must consist of twelve members, and their decision must be unanimous. The jury selection process is a "weeding out" of those jurors deemed by both the prosecution and defense as detrimental to the defendant's chances of being judged without prejudice. The defense, of course, wants to see a jury panel that will give his/her client the best opportunity to be judged fairly. For example, the chances of a defendant charged with rape receiving a fair trial is in peril if the jury is composed of twelve women. Likewise, a woman charged with murdering her husband would not receive a fair trial if the jury she is facing is composed of twelve men. A jury panel must be reflective of the community. As evidence in Los Angeles, California, the jury that ruled in favor of the police officers accused of brutally beating African-American Rodney King was an all Anglo jury with the exception of one Hispanic. Once the verdict was delivered and the jury dismissed, the media interviewed the Hispanic jury member who claimed that he was threatened by the others to vote their way. If a fair and impartial jury is not possible, the judge may order a **change of venue**, moving the trial to an area unfamiliar with the case in hopes of securing a proper jury panel.

The jury selection process is basically a two-step process. Initially, there are **statutory exemptions** excluding government officials, medical personnel, ministers, educators, and lawyers. Also, the judge may automatically dismiss a potential juror due to undue hardship. The final step is the **voir dire**, a French word meaning to speak the truth, whereby the prosecution and defense teams ask qualifying questions of potential jurors. If the juror indicates that he/she simply cannot render a fair judgment in this case, the juror will be challenged for cause by either the defense or prosecution and depending upon the judge's decision, can be removed from the panel. Both sides have a certain number of **preemptory challenges** to exclude those they feel would not be supportive of their side in the case. Usually, these challenges are not questioned. However, the United States Supreme Court did rule in **Baston v Kentucky** (1986), that prosecutors cannot use a preemptory challenge to remove in this case African Americans from the jury solely based on their race or can the defense as ruled in **Georgia v McCollum** (1992). Once selected, the judge will swear the jurors in and inform the jury of their official charge. Jurors are required not to discuss the particulars of the case with each other nor with anyone outside of the court room. In high profile cases, the judge may order that the jury be sequestered for the duration of the trial.

Once the evidence has been presented and both sides have stated their closing arguments, the judge will then instruct the jury beginning "with discussions of general legal principles (innocent until proven guilty, guilty beyond a reasonable doubt, and so forth). This follows with specific instructions on the elements of the crime in the case and what specific actions the government must prove before there can be a conviction."[56] The judge's instructions are paramount to the trial simply because incorrect or misguided instructions can lead a jury to make the wrong decision. When filing an appeal, defense attorneys have often used errors in the judge's instructions to the jury as justifiable reasons for an appeal.

In the Texas court system, the first phase of the punishment stage is to determine the guilt or innocence of the defendant. If the jury returns a **not guilty verdict**, the defendant is clear of all of the charges related to that trial. The Fifth Amendment's protection against double jeopardy automatically applies. The defendant could well exit the court house and admit to committing the crime without the fear of being tried for that offense again. If the jury cannot reach a decision, then it is a **hung jury**. This ruling does not exempt the defendant from another trial. It is up to the prosecution to determine whether to retry the case. A **guilty verdict** automatically triggers the second phase commonly referred to as the **sentencing phase**. Held several days after the original verdict, the sentencing phase entails the introduction of the now convicted defendant's previous criminal record and activities, testimonials from friends in support of the defendant, and statements from the victim or the victim's family members. The jury will reconvene and recommend a sentence to the judge.

Correctional Facilities

In Texas, those convicted of a felony offense will serve their sentences in a state prison overseen by the **Texas**

Department of Criminal Justice. While the unincarcerated believe that inmates have it easy, in reality the Texas prison system has never been known for its generous treatment of its inmates. Prison reform efforts have been sporadic. A handful of governors have addressed the issue by outlawing black and white striped prison uniforms, ending chain gangs, and prohibiting the "farming out" of prisoners to pick crops and work on private road construction projects.

Reform was just rhetoric until the United States Supreme Court tackled with the state's prison system in ***Ruiz v Estelle*** in 1980. David Ruiz was an inmate serving a twenty-five year sentence for armed robbery. In 1972, he and several inmates filed a class action lawsuit claiming the Texas prison system was in violation of their protected rights against cruel and unusual punishment. One of the allegations was that the prison staff was triple bunking prisoners due to overcrowded facilities. In 1978 in a lengthy trial, witness after witness revealed that Ruiz's claims were valid. The prison system on the whole was not providing for the prisoner's personal security and safety, denied them appropriate medical care, and forced them to work in unsafe environments. The federal district ordered the United States Justice Department to join forces with state officials to investigate the conditions in the state prison system. In 1980, the federal district court declared the Texas prison system practices were unconstitutional violations of the Eighth Amendment to the United States Constitution. Furthermore the Court cited the Texas prison system for:

- Overcrowded prison cells and dormitories with prisoners left unguarded to commit vicious acts of rape and assault upon each to other,
- Not providing for the safety and security of the prisoners,
- Not providing acceptable medical and psychiatric care,
- Not addressing the needs of special-needs inmates, i.e., physical and mental disabilities,
- Not holding discipline hearings for prison personnel who committed acts of cruelty against the prisoners,
- Overuse of solitary confinement,
- Lack of accountability on the part of prison administration, and,
- Impeding an inmate's accessibility to the court system by denying consultation with attorneys.

Since there is no state or national accreditation agency for prisons, the state of Texas issued their own reports hailing the Texas prison system for its efficiency and humane treatment of its inmates. Once this report was released, the state of Texas was placed in a very embarrassing position. With Ruiz, the federal government declared that all correctional facilities had to guarantee a pre-determined square footage allocation for each prisoner's protected right to privacy, or face a hefty daily fine for each prisoner that exceeded the capacity of the prison facility. The state was left with only three options: violate the federal court's ruling, reduce its prison population through early release, or build more prisons. The Texas Legislature opted to build more prisons.

In 2017, a federal judge issued a 100-page report demanding that the state "provide air-conditioned living quarters for elderly, disabled and other heat-sensitive inmates" at a prison unit hear Houston.[57] Specifically, the judge gave state prison officials only fifteen days to draft a plan guaranteeing the facilities "475 vulnerable inmates have living units cooled to no more than 88 degrees and that 1,000 have easy access to indoor respite areas. The prison must develop a heat-wave policy to prevent injuries and install insect-proof window screens."[58] The judge's ruling could prove to be an expensive one since the majority of the state's prison facilities do not have air conditioning.

Of course, inmates are not just sitting in their cells counting off the days until they are released. The primary function of any prison or jail is to hopefully turn the convicted into law abiding citizens that once they are released from prison will never commit another crime again. Upon arrival, convicts are assessed by prison psychologists and a plan for psychiatric and/or counseling sessions leading towards rehabilitation is established for the inmates. Medical and dental treatment is available as well as religious counseling. Since the majority of the state's inmates are not high school graduates, academic education programs from elementary to senior high school are available, as well as junior college-level courses and job training programs. If parole is granted, an inmate is generally assigned to a half-way house to prepare them for life after their release. While the Texas Legislature brags about the length of a prisoner's sentence, in reality a convict not given the death penalty or a sentence of life in prison without parole is eligible for parole after serving one-fourth of their sentence or fifteen years, whichever comes first. A convict can earn extra time off his/her sentence by making positive steps toward rehabilitation, demonstrating good behavior, and providing service to the prison such as working in the prison cafeteria, laundry room, etc. Whether the prisoner is granted parole is in the hands of the Board of Pardons and Paroles.

Juvenile offenders convicted of serious criminal acts are placed with the **Texas Department of Criminal Justice (DCJ)**. The agency replaced both the Texas Youth Commission and the Texas Juvenile Probation Commission. The Texas Youth Commission was investigated for a wide range of violations and criminal acts including assaults and rape committed by the guards and staff hired to protect the children in their custody. The legislature has shifted the emphasize for juvenile offenders from incarceration in a "boot camp" environment to one that encourages community and family-oriented rehabilitation programs. The primary tasks of this commission is to "support development of county-based programs and services for youth and families that reduce the need for out-of-home placement; seek alternatives to placing youthful offenders in secure state facilities, while also addressing treatment of youth and protecting the public; enhance the continuity of care throughout the juvenile justice system; and use secure facilities of a size that supports effective youth rehabilitation and public safety."[59]

Once released from prison, the former inmate is placed on probation and assigned a county probation officer to oversee his/her rehabilitation. In the ideal world of rehabilitation, the parole officer actually visits the residence of the parolee to assure that they have adequate shelter. The parole officer helps the parolee to enroll in school or get a job. The parole officer makes frequent visits at the parolee's place of employment to ensure that the parolee is indeed successful on the job. Supervision and guidance outside of the prison walls is essential in rehabilitation. The parole officer is supposed to be the former inmate's mentor, the one person he/she can turn to for advice and guidance. In the real world, however, county budgets have been slashed for so long that counties simply cannot afford to hire enough parole officers to provide the needed hands-on supervision. Instead, the parolees report to the parole officer who asks a few questions, fills out a form, and collects a monthly fee from the parolee. This is not appropriate rehabilitation. One should not wonder why Texas has a high rate of recidivism. For many former inmates, life on the streets is more hazardous to them then life in a prison cell.

Department of Family and Protective Services

A state agency that works closely with both local law enforcement agencies and the state courts, the divisions of the **Texas Department of Family and Protective Services (DPS)** have far too often garnered the disdain of the media

whenever an elderly person or a child is severely injured or tragically killed due to family and institutional violence. According to its mission statement, DPS is charged with protecting "children and adults who are elderly or have disabilities and regulates childcare."[60] The agency's several divisions investigate claims of abuse, neglect and exploitation of both the elderly and children, regulate all of the state's daycare, foster care, adoption agencies, before- and after-school programs and maternity homes as well as oversee community-based programs designed to prevent child and elderly abuse and juvenile delinquency.

Sadly, reported child abuse cases are and will continue to be a tragic problem for the state of Texas. In 2018 alone DPS served 82,888 children and 30,378 families with 52,546 children entering the agency's services.[61] DPS and its Child Protective Services Division (CPS) has been under fire for the DPS's inability to remove children fast enough to save their lives. Any reported incidence of abuse must be investigated by case workers of the Adult Protective Services (APS) and CPS. If the allegations of abuse are upheld then it is the responsibility of both agencies to report the incidence of violence to local law enforcement agencies. They, in turn, investigate, apprehend, and compile evidence for a potential arrest, indictment, and trial. Both APS and CPS have the authority to remove the abused party from their caregivers whether it be their parents in the case of children or a private residence or an elderly care facility for victims of elder abuse. Once removed, children are usually placed into the state's foster care system. Once the case is before a judge, the recommendations from CPS can range from permanently removing the child from the abusive environment by placing the child with other relatives or in foster care with possible adoption or requiring the abusive parent(s) to attend training programs designed to correct their behavior with the hopes that CPS will recommend that the children be returned to them.

Particularly with CPS, the agency has been fraught with problems ranging from consistent budget cuts across all of its programs from the Texas Legislature leading to staff reductions. The turnover rate for case workers is alarming. In 2016, Henry Whitman, commission of Family and Protective Services called upon both the Texas Legislature and the governor's office to provide an estimated $53.3 million to hire "550 front-line investigators, special investigators, and case workers. The agency will hire an additional 279 workers to provide supervision, support, hiring and training."[62] Whitman was facing a turnover rate ranging from "57 percent in Dallas to 31 percent in San Antonio."[63] The high turnover rate should be no surprise that for a base salary of $32,000, social workers were taking on a high volume of cases, putting in more than forty-hours per week and were confronted with a litany of issues from "dropped or delayed investigations into abuse and neglect, scores of children sleeping in offices because of a shortage of placement sites" and so on.[64] Although he did not receive the additional funding, Whitman did initiate measures to alleviate the strained workload. As a result, CPS turnover "fell from 25.4 percent in FY [fiscal year] 2016 to 18.4 percent by August 2017. . . . CPS investigation caseloads declined 32.5 percent, conservatorship caseloads by 12.1 percent, and family-based safety services caseloads by 29.6 percent."[65] The persistent charges that CPS simply moves too slowly to help abused and neglected children is, in part, still directly tied to the case worker's case load. Unfortunately while CPS and APS are confronted with constant budget cuts and high turnover rates, far too many children and senior citizens are being abused. No child or senior citizen should be a victim of abuse and, of course, no child or senior citizen should die because "the system" failed them.

Conclusions

If the purpose of the Texas judicial system is to arrest, convict, and incarcerate more criminals, then the Texas judicial system merits praise. The number of people serving time in the state's maximum and minimum security facilities is increasing daily. However, if the purpose of the judicial system is to not only punish those for criminal acts but to rehabilitate them and provide them a path to deter them from committing crimes in the future, the entire system is a failure. As previously stated, judicial systems have only two diametrically different paths to take—incarnation or rehabilitation. What the state of Texas has attempted to do for decades is to go in both directions at the same time with dismal results. Unfortunately, it will be the budget and not the collective wisdom of legal experts that will determine the future course of the state's judicial system. Recently, the Federal District Courts opened the Pandora's box of *Ruiz v Estelle* by ruling that the California state prisons are grossly overcrowded, and committing daily acts of cruel and unusual punishment. The remedy is for this nearly bankrupt state to begin to early release nearly 100,000 prisoners currently housed in Californian jail cells. Can you image state officials seating at a table trying to determine how far up the felony chain they can reasonably to go in order to bring down their prison population to the acceptable level that will prevent the state from paying the hefty daily penalties levied by the federal government. California's problem is also Texas's

problem for surely the federal government will begin to investigate other state prison systems for overcrowded and inhumane conditions. A prudent person would wonder why the state has so many people either behind bars, sitting on death row, or under some form of state supervision. What can be done to address this problem?

A large percentage of the blame can be placed at the footsteps of the Texas Legislature and the governor's office. Oftentimes the ticket to winning a seat in the Texas House, the Texas Senate and the governor's mansion is to take a strong stance on crime. Session after session, laws are passed that either lengthen the sentence for existing crimes or add new criminal acts to the growing list of offenses. For example, it goes over well with the public for a candidate to vow that if elected, he or she will make sure that the current Class A misdemeanor charge for resisting arrest will be reclassified to a third degree felony that will send the offender to prison. Or better yet, juries once had only two sentencing alternatives for a capital offense—the death penalty or life in prison with the realization that the defendant only had to serve one-third of the sentence in order to be eligible for parole. Juries usually opted for the death penalty. The legislature changed that by adding another option—life in prison without parole. What few think about is the cost behind this decision. Judges are also leery of the Texas Legislature's meddling into areas that should be reserved to the discretion of the judge and to the jury. Far too often crime-related legislation dictates the prison term without providing any leeway for a judge or jury to offer a more lenient or harsh sentence. Judges are elected to interpret the law and to merit levels of punishment on a case by case basis. Instead, the Texas Legislature is opting for the one-size-fits-all approach by mandating an established prison term.

The justice system is supposed to be based on fairness, in other words, everyone accused of a crime will be given the proper tools to defend themselves against the charges levied against them. After the not guilty plea was rendered, O. J. Simpson was asked if he received a fair trial. His response resonates today. He pointed out that he had the money to hire the best attorneys in the nation. Sadly, he felt that if he had been a poor African American, he would have probably been found guilty. This is the problem with the American justice system. Far too often it is the thickness of a person's wallet that determines the quality of defense he/she will receive during trial. States governments can surely address this by providing a meaningful public defender program. Texas does not have one.

The need to reform the state's judicial system is definitely on the minds of citizens and lawmakers alike.

"They want people accused of nonviolent crimes to be with their families and to stay employed. They want jail populations to be reduced, and defendants' risk to the public to be properly assessed. They want minor amounts of marijuana possession to be treated as a minor offense, on par with a traffic ticket. Not a black mark on someone's record."[66] Legislation calling for the decriminalization of small amounts of marijuana have already been placed before both houses of the legislature. Changing the state's cash bail system to a more equitable system has also been on the legislature's radar. Study after study emphasizes that the nation's current cash bail system forces a dis-apportioned number of the poor and racial minorities to remain behind bars pending trial simply because they cannot afford to pay 10 percent of their bail amount. Individuals accused of minor crimes are sitting in jail cells waiting weeks, months and even years for their cases to go the trial. The nation's county jails remind one of the dreaded English debtors' prisons whereby a person could be arrested for a minor debt, denied right to post bail, denied an attorney, denied a trial, and remain incarcerated until someone paid his/her outstanding debt. In 2007, the Texas Legislature did pass a cite-and-release bill allowing local law enforcement authorities to voluntarily decide to merely issue a citation for minor offenses such as "driving with an invalid license, graffiti, low-level theft and possession of small amounts of marijuana."[67] Many local law enforcement agencies opted not to grant cite-and-release. In August 2018, the California state legislature passed SB10, essentially abolishing the cash bail system throughout the state. The bail bonds businesses retaliated by securing enough petition signatures to call for a statewide referendum on the issue slated for November 2020.

Meanwhile, Governor Abbott has called for his own package of judicial reform measures. "Abbott said bond amounts would be set to better match the threat of accused criminals."[68] He recommended "having judges and magistrates who set bail be informed of the defendant's full criminal history and take that into account when setting bond amounts, adding the safety of law enforcement to the list of threats judges must consider when setting bail, and implementing a statewide case management system, so judges and magistrates would have all the relevant information at bail settings."[69] The emphasis on bail has shifted from setting a cash bail for every conceivable non-violent criminal offense to only those deemed as violent. Abbott pointed out that "our goal for people who are not dangerous to the community is to not house non-dangerous criminals behind bars, but put them on a pathway toward productivity and contributing back to society. Our goal at the same time is to make sure that if there are criminals who are dangerous who pose a threat to a law enforcement officer or the community, we're going to get them off the street and keep them off the street."[70]

On a final note, the citizens of Texas are fortunate that they have elected a cadre of smart talented legal-minded judges who are indeed committed to parceling out justice in a fair and equitable manner. Cities and counties are hiring more police officers and providing them with both the equipment and technology to apprehend criminals including the sensitivity training needed to understand the rationale behind why a person would commit a crime. More cities are moving towards bicycle patrols and foot-patrols to drive home the point that the police are here to **prevent** crime from happening in the first place. Minority officers are being assigned to patrol minority neighborhoods. Far too often the sight of the police car with its siren blaring and the lights flashing is intimidating especially among those who are fearful and distrusting of law officers in the first place. What is needed, however, is major positive reform to the state's prison system. Without meaningful rehabilitation efforts, the state's prison system will continue to be just a revolving door.

Chapter Notes

[1]Henry J. Abraham, *The Judicial Process*, 2nd. ed., (London, England: The Oxford Press, 1968), 3.

[2]*https://www.prisonpolicy.org*

[3]*State of Texas Annual Cash Report 2018: Revenues and Expenditures of State Funds for the Year Ended August 31, 2018*, (Austin, Texas: Comptroller of Public Accounts, 2018), 54 and 56.

[4]Jack C. Plano and Milton Greenberg, *The American Political Dictionary*, 10th ed., (Orlando, Florida: Harcourt, Brace College Publishers, 1997), 276.

[5]Henry J. Abraham, *The Judicial Process*, 2nd ed., (London, England: The Oxford Press, 1968), 9.

[6]Ibid., 7.

[7]Robert A. Carp, Ronald Stidham, and Kenneth L. Manning, *Judicial Process in America*, 6th ed., (Washington, D.C.: CQ Press, 2004), 3.

[8]William J. Duiker and Jackson J. Spielvogel, *World History: A Comprehensive Volume*, 3rd ed., (Belmont, California: Wadsworth Thomson Learning, 2001), 11.

[9]Plano and Greenberg, 254.

[10]Abraham, *The Judicial Process*, 10.

[11]Ibid., 15.

[12]Ibid., 17.

[13]David W. Neubauer, *America's Courts and the Criminal Justice System*, 8th ed., (Belmont, California: Wadsworth Thomson Learning, 2005), 37.

[14]Carp, Stidham and Manning, 7.

[15]Ibid., 258.

[16]Ibid.

[17]Ibid., 7.

[18]Ibid., 9.

[19]Plano and Greenberg, 248.

[20]Ralph A. Rossum and G. Alan Tarr, *American Constitutional Law: Cases and Interpretations*, (New York, New York: St. Martin's Press, 1983), 469.

[21]John C. Domino, *Civil Rights and Liberties: Toward the 21st Century*, (New York, New York: HarperCollins, 1994), 138.

[22]Lucius J. Barker and Twiley W. Barker, Jr., *Civil Liberties and the Constitution*, 6th ed., (Englewood Cliffs, New Jersey: Prentice-Hall, 1990), 263.

[23]Henry J. Abraham and Barbara A. Perry, *Freedom and the Court: Civil Rights and Liberties in the United States*, 8th ed., (Lawrence, Kansas: University of Kansas, 2003), 142.

[24]Mark Helm, "Miranda Warning: Court Upholds 'the Right to Remain Silent,'" *San Antonio Express-News*, (Tuesday, June 27, 2000), 1A.

[25]Barker and Barker, Jr., 249.

[26]Rossum and Tarr, 521.

[27]Ibid., 522.

[28]Neubauer, 150.

[29]Abraham and Perry, 74.

[30]Neubauer, 151.

[31]Domino, 98.

[32]Ibid., 174-175.

[33]Delvin Barrett, "Federal Death Penalty Halted," *San Antonio Express-News*, (Tuesday, July 2, 2002), 3A.

[34]Anne Gearan, "Justices Give Jury Last Say in Executions," *San Antonio Express-News*, (Tuesday, June 25, 2002), 6A.

[35]Jan Crawford Greenburg, "Supreme Court Sides with Texas Death Row Resident," *San Antonio Express-News*, (Wednesday, February 26, 2003), 15A.

[36]Ibid.

[37]Ibid.

[38]Sara Rimer and Raymond Bonner, "Texas Officials Weigh Fairness of the Death Penalty," *San Antonio Express-News*, (Monday, May 15, 2000), 9A.

[39]Ibid.

[40]The Texas Crime Report for 2017, (Austin, Texas: Texas Department of Public Safety,2017), 49.

[41]Ibid.

[42]Ibid., 1.

[43]Ibid., 2.

[44]Neubauer, 270.

[45]Domino, 140.

[46]Neubauer, 285.

[47]Plano and Greenberg, 267.

[48]Ibid., 272.

[49]Ibid., 250.

[50]Ibid., 251.

[51]Ibid., 263.

[52]Ibid., 278.

[53]Ibid., 271.

[54]Ibid., 265.

[55]Ibid., 268.

[56]Neubauer, 323.

[57]Gabrielle Banks, "Judge Orders Relief for Some Prisoners," *San Antonio Express New*s, (Thursday, July, 20, 2017), A3.

[58]Ibid.

[59]*Texas Almanac: 2018-2019*, (Denton, Texas: Texas State Historical Association, 2018), 511.

[60]http://www.dfps.state.tx.us

[61]*Texas Department of Family and Protective Services 2017 Annual Report, https://www.dfps.state.tx*

[62]Mike Ward, "Children's Agency Seeks 800 More Staff," *San Antonio Express News*, (Saturday, October 22, 016), A1-A10.

[63]Ibid.

[64]Ibid.

[65]*Texas Department of Family and Protective Services 2017 Annual Report, https://www.dfps.state.tx*

[66]Express Editorial Board, "Texans Want Bail Reform," *San Antonio Express News*, (Sunday, January 13, 2019), F1-F6.

[67]Ibid.

[68]Jolie McCullough, "Texas Gov. Greg Abbott Proposes Bail Reform After Death of DPS Trooper," *Texas Tribune*, (August 7,2018), *https://www.texastribune.org*

[69]Ibid.

[70]Ibid.

PART III

THE PUBLIC POLICY
PROCESS AND THE ISSUES

Chapter
10

The Public Policy Process

HOUSTON, TEXAS

Public policies in a modern, complex society are indeed ubiquitous. They confer advantages and disadvantages, cause pleasure, irritation, and pain, and collectively have important consequences for our well-being and happiness. They constitute a significant portion of our environment. This being so, we should know something about public policies, including how they are formed, budgeted, implemented, and evaluated.[1]

Good karma seems to follow Governor Greg Abbott. After handily defeating his opponent in the 2018 governor's race and taking the oath of office for his second term, Abbott's Comptroller Glenn Hegar predicted a rosy economic upswing for the state's coffers. "Hegar is projecting that the Legislature will have over $119 billion to spend in the state's next two-year budget-roughly $9 billion more than thecurrent plan."[2] According to Hegar, "state sales tax collections are driving much of the growth and are expected to make up more than half of the revenue."[3] In his State of State message delivered before a joint session of the Texas Legislature, Governor Abbott proudly proclaimed the greatness of the state, particularly its thriving economy. He pointed out that "Texas leads the nation in new job creation. And we have the fastest growing economy in America. A by-product of this success is a prosperity that touches all corners of our state. Texas recorded its lowest unemployment ever. And wages are rising. Digging deeper, you'll see that we lead the nation in jobs created by African-American business owners and Hispanic women business owners. And get this—Texas is now number one for women entrepreneurs."[4] Hegar backs up Abbott's comments. In the state's *Annual Cash Report: 2018*, Hegar reported that "from August 2017 to August 2018 the Texas economy added 394,500 nonfarm jobs, an increase of 3.2 percent. . . . Texas added more new jobs than any other state during this period. Private-sector employment rose by 3.8 percent while government employment (federal, state and local) grew by 0.2 percent. The state's rate of job growth was the highest among the 10 most populous states and the fourth highest among all states."[5]

Yet even while the governor was delivering his speech, the reality of the state's economic picture was not as rosy as Hegar and Abbott proclaimed. A portion of the $9 billion in new revenue has already been tagged to address budgetary shortfalls in the 2018-2019 state budget. "There's an expected shortfall in health and human services, along with costs associated with rebuilding after Hurricane Harvey, which wrecked havoc along the Texas coast."[6] The state's budgetary responsibilities have always been tied to generous infusions of cash from the federal government. President Trump's declared national

emergency to build "the wall" will eventually mean that money already allocated to the state from everything from roads and highways to income support programs for the state's poor could well be reduced or eliminated as the Trump administration strips funding from these budget items to address border security priorities. With the start of the 86th Legislative Session, the body's leadership is eager to implement their own campaign promises of "property tax reform, increasing teacher's pay and school finance reform . . . and to fund critical needs of our state such as infrastructure and health care."[7]

Regardless of the state's financial situation, lawmakers cannot ignore the depth of the social and economic problems confronting this state. An article published by the *Houston Chronicle* in 1997, pointed out that "in such areas as per-capita state spending on public health, education, welfare, and parks and recreation, Texas ranks behind most other states, and that basic pattern will remain unchanged. . . . Texas, meanwhile, is a leader in the percentage of residences who live in poverty or in prison, distinctions that some critics largely blame on things such as insufficient education, public health and drug treatment budgets."[8] Little has changed in eighteen years! Despite the countless number of bills designed to prevent crime, Texas usually leads her sister states in the both in the number of executions and death row inmates awaiting their lethal injections. Billions of dollars have been poured into public and higher education. Yet, the state is confronted with a historical track record of poor-performing schools, high dropout rates offset with low graduation rates from both high schools and colleges and universities, and an ever increasing pool of undereducated and ill-prepared workers for the state's emerging high-tech industries. In addition, state leaders are confronted with the startling reality that among her sister states, Texas ranks 26th in median household income and 15.6 percent of Texans live below the poverty level.[9] The economic status and poverty of the border region is akin to third and fourth world poverty. To add to the list of problems, lawmakers must also come to grips with the state's environmental damage that will take billions and billions of dollars to cleanup. Chronic periodic droughts offset by heavy rains and floods wreck havoc with the state's vital farming and ranching industries. To date, the Texas Legislature and all of the state's previous governors have failed to adequately address water conservation issues. With all of the tools and resources available to government, why is government at any level not adequately addressing the needs of those they were elected to govern? What went wrong?

In would be unfair to place blame solely upon the state legislature or the governor. Although public policy is created in a highly political environment, the blame also cannot be totally attributed to "just politics as usual." The primary cause of policy failures is poorly written and ineffectively implemented policy directives. Policy disasters are directly linked to lawmakers' inabilities to follow the process of creating policy from start to finish. A poorly crafted policy will with few exceptions ultimately fail to achieve its goals and objectives.

This chapter explores the public policy process from the inception of the idea to its final evaluation of the policy response. The "process" is a series of steps that must be weighed equally in importance. Overlooking just one step can condemn the policy response to failure before it is even written. What lawmakers fail too often to recognize is that the actual creation of the policy response is more important than the policy itself. The success or failure of any law, ordinance, or statute hinges more on how it was researched, debated, crafted, budgeted, implemented, and finally evaluated than on the problem or issue it was designed to address. Public policy is also more than just a legislative act, a response, or course of action. It is a reflection on the prevailing political, economic, social, cultural, and, sometimes, religious perspectives shared by those who write the policy responses. These influences impact the entire "process." Another crucial step is budgeting. What budgetary items should be increased or decreased is politics at its best and, often, worst. Every new tax law or increase in existing taxes will have a direct impact on the citizen's pocketbook. Conversely, every dollar cut from a social service program can have a devastating effect on our state's poorest citizens. The budget is more than just dollars and cents and a list of debits and credits. This chapter also delves into the state's budgetary process.

Planning and Budgeting

What is Public Policy?

In the private sector, **policy** is defined as a "purposive course of action followed by an actor or set of actors in dealing with a problem or matter of concern."[10] Policy

is, therefore, more than just a corporate response to an issue or concern. It is a deliberative action designed to achieve a defined purpose, goal, or objective. There is a noticeable difference between public and private policy directives. Created by governing bodies, "**public policy** can be defined simply as an officially expressed intention backed by a sanction, which can be a reward or a punishment."[11] Governing institutions at all levels make public policy. However, it is not crafted in a vacuum by lawmakers in isolated chambers; policy initiatives are government responses to the demands of its citizens for authoritarian action to address a public concern or need. Therefore, all public policies must have "an authoritative, potentially legally coercive quality that the policies of private organizations do not have. Indeed, a major characteristic distinguishing government from private organizations is its monopoly over the legitimate use of coercion. Governments can legally incarcerate people; private organizations cannot."[12] If citizens obey and follow the intentions of government, they are rewarded for their obedience. Conversely, the citizen who disobeys the law will be punished by a sanction, fine, imprisonment, or a combination thereof.

The development of public policy at any level of government is based on five fundamental principles. First, public policy initiatives created in a democratic government are based on conflict and accommodation. "There is opposition to virtually every policy proposal, and agreement is reached only after bargains have been struck and compromises have been agreed on."[13] Political bickering is a given in the creation of public policy. It is a high-stakes game with every interested and affected party desiring to be a winner, not a loser.

Second, public policy initiatives can be either positive or negative responses. "Some form of overt governmental action may deal with a problem on which action is demanded (positive) or governmental officials may decide to do nothing on some matter on which government involvement was sought (negative)."[14] Government cannot and should not respond to every citizen's demand. After careful deliberation and an assessment of available resources, government may find that simply doing nothing and allowing the concern to address itself is the appropriate response.

Third, the end results of a policy initiative are a series of outputs and outcomes. **Policy output** is "the action actually taken in pursuance of policy decisions and statements."[15] These are the measurable results of a policy, both positive and negative. For example, the end result of welfare reform can be measured statistically by evaluating a series of variables including job growth, unemployment figures, number of applications submitted for income support services, poverty studies, dollars spent, and so on. **Policy outcomes**, however, are oftentimes the unmeasureable consequences. For example, the rhetoric of welfare reform has changed the attitudes that some Americans traditionally hold towards the level of responsibility that government should bear in meeting the needs of the destitute. The outcome of a policy can have a far more lasting impact than the actual policy output.

Fourth, there is a difference between policy making and decision-making. **Policymaking** is "a flow and pattern of action that extends over time and includes many decisions, some routine and some not so routine"; whereas, **decision-making** "involves a discrete choice from among two or more alternatives."[16] Decisions are made on a daily basis, often without the benefit of a thoughtful planning process. Policymaking, however, can have a long-lasting impact upon the governing process. Therefore, it should never be allowed to become the victim of quick non-deliberative thinking. To be successful, policymaking must be treated as a deliberate product of an intense and often lengthy process.

Fifth, the taxpayer demands that lawmakers create policies that are both cost-effective and successful. Subsequently, "the need is to design realistic goals that embrace a balance between efficiency and effectiveness."[17] The taxpayer's expectations are lofty desires that cannot be totally fulfilled by Texas lawmakers. Effective and efficient public policy is difficult to create, particularly when the Texas Legislature meets only once every two years for only 140 days. The shortness of the legislative session does not allow state legislators the luxury of ensuring that every legislative act passed during that session will be effective in addressing its goals and objectives, fiscally responsible, and administratively efficient. Both lawmakers and citizens alike must realize that the quality and quantity of any government service can be severely compromised when the budget alone guides the policymaking process.

What is the Purpose of Public Policy?

Governments enact public policy in response to the public's demand to address an identified concern or issue. Usually, the initial approach taken by government failed to adequately address the issue at hand; consequently, corrective public policy presents a new alternative or change from the traditional approach. Government at any level must have the ability to enforce this change in direction through a sanction, fine, or imprisonment for noncompliance. "Consequently, it must be clearly understood that all public policies are coercive, even when they are motivated by the best and most beneficent of intentions. . . . For us, the coercive element in public policy should instill not absolute opposition but a healthy respect for the risks as well as the good that may be inherent in any public policy."[18] In other words, public policy through its enforcement mechanisms modifies our behavior and, in some cases, changes our perspectives. For example, few like to drive the posted speed limit. But we definitely modify our driving habits to the mandated speed limit when we see the police car in front of us because we all want to avoid a costly ticket.

The primary purpose of law enforcement is to serve as a visible deterrent to crime. Criminal statutes, civil fines, and penalties are attached to each criminal activity to warn an individual of the consequences of violating the law. The problem confronting law enforcement is ensuring that the penalties for noncompliance are severe enough to drive home the point of the consequences one faces for violating the law. The use of the death penalty in Texas continues to be a hotly debated issue. Opponents argue that the execution of convicted murderers has not been an effective deterrent to violent crime. Supporters believe that the death penalty is the only severe punitive sanction available to eventually curb violent crime. They are supportive of legislation limiting the number of appeals from death row inmates in hopes that executions carried out in a more expedient manner will eventually achieve the goal of preventing criminal activity.

Governments use a variety of tools beside laws to force behavior modifications. The direct approach is through contracting and licensing. **Government contracts** contain mandates that the recipient must enact or face losing the contract. A state highway contract specifies the type of paving materials to be used in constructing the road, the applied thickness of the asphalt and base materials, the distance between each highway stripe, and so on. To enforce these requirements, each segment of the construction project must be inspected by the appropriate state agency before the next phase of construction begins. Noncompliance means loss of existing and, perhaps, future contracts. Contract mandates ensure that taxpayer money will produce a high quality highway system at the best price possible. Contracting requirements also include mandated compliance with federal laws including the Equal Employment Opportunity Act, Occupational Safety and Health Act (OSHA), Environmental Protection Act, Endangered Species Act, Title VII of the Civil Rights Act, Americans with Disabilities Act, and all wage and labor laws.

A **license** is "a privilege granted by government to do something that it otherwise considers to be illegal."[19] A license compels behavior modification by forcing the recipient to comply with industry or professional standards. Noncompliance can mean revoking the license and denying the recipient the right to practice his/her profession. The threat of removing the license should ensure proper professional conduct. Teachers, doctors, lawyers, and even plumbers and hairdressers must be licensed to practice their trades in Texas.

Governments can also modify and limit our use of certain public services by charging us fees. **User fees** or charges are "specific sums that consumers of a government service pay to receive that service."[20] City governments provide parking services to their residents and visitors through city-sponsored parking lots, garages, or designated curb-side parking. Motorists, however, must pay a fee for this service. The state of Texas imposes a fee for the use of its state parks and recreational sites. The imposition of user fees allows government to control the accessibility and use of the service while, at the same time, providing additional revenue for the maintenance and preservation of parks, zoos, museums, and historical and recreational sites.

Indirectly, a citizen's spending habits are governmentally controlled through taxing, banking, and pricing policies. For example, raising the price of gasoline forces some drivers to use their vehicles less frequently than when gasoline prices are lower. The Comptroller's office decided to encourage retail sales when it enacted a "sales tax free" weekend before the start of the public school year. As a result, shoppers boost sagging retail sales simply to save a few dollars in sales taxes. An increase in mortgage and consumer loan rates will force people to think twice before purchasing a new home or automobile. Conversely, government encourages increased consumer buying and business investments by lowering taxes and interest rates and/or providing additional deduction allowances come income tax time.

The Public Policy Process

The development of public policy is "analogous to biological natural selection. In what we have called the policy primeval soup, many ideas float around, encountering new ideas, and forming combinations and recombinations . . . Through the imposition of criteria by which some ideas are selected out for survival while others are discarded, order is developed from chaos, pattern from randomness. These criteria include technical feasibility, congruence with values of community members, and the anticipation of cultural constraints, including a budget constraint, public acceptability, and politician's receptivity."[21] The **process** of developing the policy involves eight crucial steps. Each step is instrumental to the success of the policy initiative and must be afforded equal attention. If one step is marginally treated or actually overlooked, the policy initiative, no matter how necessary, will fail. Bad, ineffective public policy is the end result of poor planning. "Lawmakers can go a long way toward assuring effective policy implementation if they see that a statute incorporates a sound technical theory, provides precise and clearly ranking objectives, and structures the implementation process in a wide number of ways so as to maximize the probability of target group compliance. In addition, they can take positive steps to appoint skillful and supportive implementing officials, to provide adequate appropriations and to monitor carefully the behavior of implementing agencies throughout the long implementing process, and to be aware of the effects of changing socio-economic conditions and of new legislation (even supposedly unrelated areas) on the original statute."[22] The process begins with identifying the problem and ends with an evaluation of the resulting policy initiative.

Problem Identification

The first step confronting lawmakers is to properly identify the problem. A **problem** is defined as "a condition or situation that produces needs or dissatisfaction among people and for which relief or redress by governmental action is sought."[23] Too often legislation treats the consequences of or the adverse impact of the problem without actually solving the problem. "The effort to define a problem by identifying the causes of bad conditions rests on a certain conception of cause. In this conception, any problem has deep or primary causes that can be found if one only looks hard enough and does careful research . . . Once 'the' cause is identified, policy should seek to eliminate it, modify it, reduce it, suppress it, or neutralize it, thereby eliminating or reducing the problem."[24] The contributing factors or casual factors should be the targets of legislative actions if lawmakers truly want to solve the problem.

For example, the bubonic plague or Black Death killed thousands of people throughout major urban areas in continental Europe and England during the fourteenth and again in the seventeenth centuries. Lawmakers were soundly convinced that the disease was being spread by rats. Their decision was to simply kill the rats and destroy the homes and personal belongings of the dead. Although thousands of rats were killed, the plague continued. What went wrong? Basically, policymakers overlooked the real causes of the disease. True, it was the rats and their fleas that were spreading the disease from household to household. But the major contributing factor was the living habits of the residents. It was common practice throughout Europe to simply throw one's household and personal waste out onto the streets and into open sewers. The rats and their menacing fleas were thriving off the garbage. The solution to eventually ending the plague was the implementation of proper sanitation procedures, converting open above ground sewers into enclosed underground systems, and the development of indoor plumbing. Through corrective legislation backed by stiff sanctions, the rats, their fleas, piles of rotting garbage, and, of course, the plague disappeared considerably as personal and public sanitation habits improved. Thousands of lives might have been saved if lawmakers had properly identified the causes of the problem sooner.

The solution to crime is not just arresting more people and building more jails. Crime is the end result or the "disease" stemming from a multiplicity of complex casual factors. The solution to crime rests, in part, with adequately identifying the casual factors that motivated that person to indeed commit a crime. As evidenced by Katrina, hurricanes bring lots of heavy winds and rain that can produce short-term flooding. However, the lingering flooding of the city of New Orleans was caused by a multiplicity of factors including an out-date levee system, inadequate drainage systems, and local building codes that allowed a heavy concentration of residential and commercial construction to occur too close to the levees and in historically flood-prone areas.

Also policymakers must determine whether the identifiable problem requires a substantive or procedural policy response. "**Substantive policies** involve what government is going to do, such as constructing highways, paying welfare benefits, acquiring bombers, or prohibiting the retail sale of liquor. Substantive policies directly allocate advantages or disadvantages, benefits and costs to the people. **Procedural policies**, in contrast, pertain to how something is going to be done or who is going to take action. So defined, procedural policies include laws providing for the creation of administrative agencies, determining the matters over which they have jurisdiction, specifying the process and techniques that they can use in carrying out their programs, and providing for presidential, judicial and other controls over their operations."[25] For example, the federal government's response to environmental damage actually began with the passage of the Environmental Protection Act in the 1970s. Each subsequent legislative

act clearly states the government's intention to try to reverse environmental damage while, at the same time, to prevent it from happening by imposing stiff sanctions on those who violate the laws. The problem with environmental legislation has been with the procedural policies such as enforcement and the application of punitive sanctions.

There is a distinct difference between a crisis situation and a problem. The policy responses are significantly different in both situations. With both hurricanes Katrina and Rita, heavy flooding along the Texas and Gulf Coast areas drove people out of their homes, ruined agricultural crops, destroyed livestock, and caused extensive property damage and, unfortunately, resulted in the loss of human life. As the events unfolded, the crisis response was supposed to address the immediate needs of those adversely impacted by the storms. All of the people within the paths of the storms' wrath needed to be safely evacuated to shelters, provided with adequate food, clothing, and, if needed, medical assistance. Heavy equipment was required to clear roadways and restore public utilities. Emergency teams were supposed to be on-standby ready to bring much needed supplies to affected areas, especially an ample supply of clean drinking water. Unfortunately as evidenced with Katrina, government at all levels failed to provide the appropriate crisis response. In other words, communities must be prepared to handle a crisis situation that mandates advanced planning and preparation capable of delivering a quick and effective response. After the flood waters receded, the problems confronting decision makers in Louisiana focused on what caused the flooding in the first place and a plan to enable individuals to rebuild their destroyed properties. This is a deliberative long-term well developed plan of action. Whenever lawmakers treat long-term problems with short-term responses, the problems are never adequately addressed.

Lawmakers must also avoid the practice of allowing public opinion to turn a concern into a crisis. Public outcry is not necessarily a crisis situation. For example, in 1985 San Antonio experienced its first substantial snowfall in decades, thirteen inches of snow, very unusual. Mayor Henry Cisneros closed all of the expressways, essentially shutting down the city for the day. Several outraged individuals wanted the mayor to prevent a future snow-related crisis by buying a fleet of snow plows. But commonsense moved the City Council to consider this snow crisis as just a freak act of Mother Nature. Obviously, giving-in to a sporadic short-lived public outcry would have resulted in an expensive long-term expenditure that the city simply did not need over the longhaul.

Agenda Building

Once the casual factors have been identified, an agenda or plan of action must be developed. The agenda is the embodiment of the philosophical and technical approaches to an identified policy issue. An effective agenda should attack all of the identified casual factors at the same time. Doctors have realized that bombarding one side of a cancerous tumor with heavy doses of radiation and chemotherapy will halt the growth of the tumor on just the treated side, while the untreated side continues to grow. The same holds true for public policy. By treating and/or curing just one symptom, policy makers allow the other symptoms to grow stronger. For example, the drug policies passed during the Reagan administration sought to end the importation of drugs into the United States. Instead of focusing on *all* international drug sources, the agenda concentrated primarily on Columbia. Consequently, drug trafficking from Columbia was indeed substantially slowed, but the flow of drugs continued as other international drug cartels assumed the Columbian share of the market. Unfortunately, putting one's eggs into one basket happens far too often:

> In the issue of death and injuries resulting from drunk driving, both our laws and our cultural beliefs place responsibility with the drunk driver. There are certainly alternative ways to view the problem: we could blame vehicle design (for materials and structure more likely to injure or kill in a crash); highway design (for curves likely to cause accidents); lack of fast ambulance service or nearly hospitals; law enforcement of drunk driving penalties by police; or even easy availability of alcoholic beverages. . . . Even when there is a strong statistical and logical link between substance and a problem—such as between alcohol and car accidents, handguns and homicides, tobacco and cancer deaths, or illicit drugs and overdose deaths—there is still a range of places to locate control and impose sanctions. . . . In the case of alcohol, we have traditionally seen drinkers as the cause and limited sanctions to them, although sellers have more recently been made to bear the costs. In lung cancer deaths, we have blamed the smoker primarily, but to the extent that people have sought to place the blame elsewhere, they have gone after cigarette manufacturers, not sellers or tobacco growers. With handgun homicides, we have limited blame to the user of the guns, rather than imposing sanctions on either the seller or manufacturers.[26]

An essential component of any action plan is the development of well defined goals and objectives. These provide a clear understanding as to the intent of the policy directive. A **goal** is the targeted end result of an action or activity. For example, the ultimate goal of a water conservation plan is to ensure that there is enough water to cover everyone's needs during a drought. **Objectives**, on the other hand, are the strategies used to obtain the desired goals. The objectives to a water conservation plan could include limited periods for lawn watering, imposing higher costs for water, and so on. The objectives for a policy maker are just as important as a blueprint is to a homebuilder. "Statutory objectives that are precise and clearly ranked in importance serve as an indispensable aid in program evaluation, as unambiguous directives to implementing officials, and as a resource available to supporters of those objectives both inside and outside the implementing agencies."[27]

Action plans must include *measurable* and *attainable* goals and objectives. Far too often lawmakers attempt to sell their ideas as wondrous miracle cures. How many times have voters heard elected officials pledge that their program is the definitive answer to a problem, only to see it fail? Lyndon Johnson hailed his War on Poverty Program as the answer to eliminate poverty, a lofty, unreasonable, and, of course, unattainable goal. President George W. Bush vowed to the American people that his domestic and foreign policy directives following the attack on the World Trade Center would end international terrorism across the globe. Despite his good intentions, Bush's plan failed to achieve its anticipated goal. There are just too many variables at play that are beyond the reach of American policy makers. Lawmakers should be honest and realistic with their constituents. An anti-crime package designed to achieve a 5 percent reduction in crime each year over a five-year period has a far better chance of seeing its goal achieved or even exceeded than a policy with the lofty goal of completely eliminating all crime within a five-year period. Lawmakers are usually willing to continue financing a project with a proven track record of achieving its modest goals and objectives over proposals that fail to make their targeted overly ambitious goals.

Formulating Policy

The actual development of the policy response entails more than just designing the strategies and programs needed to address anticipated goals and objectives. First, lawmakers must determine their preferred policy approach and policy option as well as whether the ultimate implementation of the policy should be assigned to the public or the private sector.

Lawmakers usually opt for one of four policy approaches: preventive, alleviative, punitive, and, the rarely used, curative. The actual selection of the policy approach is dependent upon several factors including public opinion and support, the prevailing political philosophy embraced by policymakers, the seriousness of the problem, and the current status of the state's economic condition. Both the preventive and alleviative options are short-term options. The **alleviative approach** is designed to address the current suffering caused by the policy problem or issue without actually attempting to solve the problem or issue itself. With the collapse of the Stock Market and the nation's financial institutions in 1929, millions of Americans were immediately adversely impacted through the loss of their financial holdings, their jobs and, in some instances, the roofs over their heads. Consequently, the driving force behind President Roosevelt's New Deal programs was to provide temporary alleviative programs to address the current suffering caused by the collapse of the nation's economy. Initially created in 1939, the Food Stamp program was reintroduced in 1964 with the passage of the Food Stamp Act. It was designed to alleviate the pains of existing hunger by providing the poor with the means needed to obtain food. As the Katrina driven flood waters receded in Louisiana and the Gulf Coast areas, the focus of the national government's response was to address the immediate needs of the displaced by providing food, shelter, clothing, and medical assistance. On the other hand, the **preventive approach** recognizes the potential for future suffering by providing a safety net for those who could be adversely impacted by the problem or issue. The majority of the nation's social service programs contain an alleviative and a preventive provision. For example, the alleviative portion of the Food Stamp program is a pre-determined calculation of the income needed to provide a family with food. Consequently, 100 percent of those currently at or below that income level are eligible for the program. The preventive portion recognizes potential suffering by placing the income eligibility level at 125 or 150 percent. The preventive factor recognizes that many wage earners are on the edge of slipping into poverty and attempts to stop that from happening.

Both of these approaches, however, are designed to address the consequences caused by the problem without actually solving the problem. For example, several cities have implemented project warm and project cool programs, which provide heaters and air conditions to the poor to alleviate the current suffering of adverse weather conditions and to prevent illnesses and fatalities caused by weather extremes. Some programs even provide financial assistance for those who cannot afford to pay their utility bills. However, these programs do not address why these individuals cannot afford to purchase their own heaters or window units or to even pay their monthly utility bills. They simply address current and future suffering. The same observation can be made for the majority of the programs created by national and state legislative houses. Simply building more prison cells only alleviates the suffering the criminal element inflicts upon law-abiding citizens. Providing hot meals and a warm bed at night to the homeless temporarily alleviates and prevents the pain of homelessness. Merely recognizing and easing the pain does not remove the cause of that pain. Both the alleviative and preventive strategies should never be substituted for or mistaken for a cure for any policy problem or issue.

The **punitive approach** seeks to punish those deemed responsible for creation of the problem in the first place as well as those adversely impacted by it. For example, many Americans believe that poverty is a self-inflicted situation caused by an individual's own failure to achieve economic viability. Guided by a firm belief in the free market economy and the concepts of Social Darwinism, some believe that poverty is "the product of moral or character deficiencies in the individual. If people were poor it was their own fault" and ultimately their responsibility to rise above their economic reversals without assistance.[28] The majority of the state's social service programs are laden with punitive measures. First, state laws draw a distinction between deserving and undeserving poor. A series of means-tested requirements ensures that they are indeed truly deserving of financial assistance. The national government has given states the leeway to place additional punitive restrictions including work requirements, time limits on benefits, and strict eligibility requirements. Second, state lawmakers have used the punitive approach as a means of preventing abuse. Oftentimes, the mere threat of denying benefits to a recipient will deter abuse. For example, individuals receiving unemployment compensation are required to search for work and must accept any job offer. Benefits recipients are told in advance that benefits will be revoked if they do not seek work, refuse a job offer, or falsify reporting documents. State and federal environmental laws use a wide variety of punitive sanctions including costly fines and criminal charges. These laws were designed to identify and punish violators as well as to send a clear message to potential polluters to prevent future violations. Rarely does government at any level award businesses, industries, and individuals for not polluting. The ultimate objective of the punitive approach is punishing the violators rather than actually solving problems.

Finally, the most difficult policy option is the **curative approach**. This option actually attempts to eliminate or cure the problem. Although one can imagine that one day the world will be rid of crime, pollution, or even poverty, it is extremely difficult to accomplish these feats for several reasons. First, the curative approach's success depends upon an honest deliberative assessment that correctly identifies the factors that created the problem in the first place. Oftentimes, society as a whole, does not want to recognize that it was their collective actions and thoughts that helped to create the problem. For example, the root cause of racism is the social and cultural approaches taken by people of all ethnic backgrounds and races in their relationships with each other. Second, the complexity of the policy program mandates a long-term bipartisan support from all sectors of the political spectrum. The state's poverty-related problems simply cannot be solved in a five-, ten-, or even twenty-year period. A long-term policy commitment is exceptionally difficult to achieve in a democratic government based on periodic elections that oftentimes unseat incumbents and changes the party balance in Austin or Washington, D.C. Third, the curative approach is doomed to failure when it is tied to unattainable goals and false hopes. For example, "a central premise of President Johnson's War on Poverty was that investments in education and training, civil rights protections, and community organizations representing the have nots could dramatically lift this generation's poor out of deprivation and insure their children a decent life."[29] The programs simply could not meet the expectations. The majority of the public policy initiatives include a combination of at least three of these four approaches. For example, state environmental laws are designed to alleviate the suffering caused by previous incidences of pollution while using punitive sanctions against violators and preventive measures to avoid future damage. The curative approach is rarely used as a viable political option.

Policymakers must also determine the type of policy needed to both implement and ultimately achieve the anticipated goals and objectives of a policy initiative. These choices include distributive, redistributive and regulatory policy options. **Distributive policies** are "governmental actions that convey tangible benefits to individuals, groups or corporations."[30] For example as part of his plan to jump start the economy, President Obama created "cash for clunkers," which provided federal money to those who had an outdated car and wanted to trade it for a newer one but did not have the money or the available credit to make the

deal. The benefit helped both: the consumer brought a car and the car manufacturer and dealer sold a car. The most commonly used distributive policy, **subsidies** are "simply government grants of cash and other commodities."[31] Subsidies, however, are successful only when the recipient becomes totally dependent upon receiving the cash or the commodity. Initially, the gift is given with few strings or conditions attached. Once dependency is established, the government can begin to attach more and more demanding conditions with the threat that noncompliance means the loss of the benefit. The heightened dependency factor usually results in compliance.

Redistributive policies, on the other hand, are "conscious attempts by the government to manipulate the allocation of wealth, property, rights, or some other value among broad classes or groups in society."[32] Often known as Robin Hood programs, these policies are designed to reallocate wealth from the more affluent to the economically disadvantaged. Federal grant programs were initially designed to reallocate federal tax dollars to economically strapped state and local governments under the assumption that the wealthier states had more than enough to fund their own infrastructure projects such as roadways, airports, and housing.

Finally, lawmakers use regulatory options to address policy concerns. **Regulatory policies** are "governmental actions that extend government control over particular behavior of private individuals or businesses."[33] The federal government initiated the move towards regulation with the passage of the Interstate Commerce Act in 1887. Regulatory laws are laden with punishing civil, criminal, and monetary sanctions aimed to ensure compliance. Particularly with environmental laws, businesses, corporations, farmers, ranchers, and property owners openly resent the federal and state mandates attached to regulatory legislation. Lawmakers must realize that regulatory actions laced with costly mandates and punitive sanctions are not openly embraced by the regulated parties. However, sanctions and mandates may be the only means to ensure compliance.

The formulation process also includes determining which sector of the economy, namely public or private, will be responsible for implementing the policy response. Traditionally, all government services have been provided by the public sector. Each legislative act either creates a new agency or assigns additional duties to existing agencies. The public outcry to cut the state budget and reduce the size of government, led lawmakers to consider contracting to the private sector for the provision of a public service. **Privatization** is "a general effort to relieve the disincentives toward efficiency in public organizations by subjecting them to the incentives of the private market."[34] Privatization has been embraced as the primary means for government to save money in both personnel and equipment costs, while at the same time releasing government from the burden of providing a service. Enthusiastic supporters would like "to privatize the full gamut of public assets and services, including many forms of public provisions such as public schools, national parks, public transportation infrastructure, and prisons, whose origins and rationale fall within the gambit of the classical liberal state. In privatization they believe they have found a sovereign remedy against all ailments to the body politic, good for stimulating economic growth, improving the efficiency of services, slimming down the state, and expanding individual freedom, including the opportunities to disadvantaged minorities, too."[35] On the other side of the coin, "opponents contend that when the costs of monitoring contracts are considered, service delivery may be more expensive under privatization. . . Contracting, they argue encourages 'low balling,' where private firms bid low and then raise their charges to cover the real costs of the service. When costs are lower, opponents believe it often is because providers cut corners in their services and pay workers lower salaries."[36]

Shifting public responsibilities to the private sector should be used with extreme discretion for several reasons. First, contracting to the private sector relinquishes direct government control over that functional area or service. For example, the state legislature opted to use private companies to operate several of its prison facilities. Whenever a prisoner escapes or an inmate levels brutality charges against the guards, it is the state of Texas that bears the wrath of public opinion and the liability even though the state did not play a direct hand in the operation of that prison. The federal government has had its own public relations nightmares with incompetent private contractors. For example, the Department of Homeland Security's agency Immigration and Customs Enforcement (ICE) contracted to the private sector housing facilities for detained immigrants. Several of these facilities were closed by ICE after reports of neglect, abuse, sexual assault, poor housing conditions, medial mistreatment, were made public. It was ICE that had to face the uproar over the operation of these facilities—not the contractors! Second, the sensitivity of the program or function may preclude privatization. City officials, for example, could run into numerous constitutional challenges if it contracted to private security firms all of its law enforcement functions including the arrest and interrogation of suspects. Third, the quality of

customer service can be seriously compromised. The Texas Legislature received an earful of complaints about the lack of efficient, expedient, and courteous customer service about the provider of CHIP, a charge leveled far too often against private government service contractors. During a budget crunch, the Texas Legislature opted to contract with the Texas Access Alliance operating as Accenture, a company based in Bermuda to "oversee call center operations, process applications, and determine CHIP eligibility, maintain the benefits computer system and provide enrollment services."[37] The agency did fulfill its contractual obligation to save the state money by awarding CHIP benefits to only those who they determined met all of the eligibility requirements. However, the process of cutting the estimated $899 million costs down to $543 million within a two-year period resulted in an avalanche of complaints from denied applicants, plan participants, and healthcare providers to the point that one lawmaker declared that "Rick Perry and the Republican leadership owe the taxpayers and the children of Texas an apology for the millions wasted on Accenture."[38] Consequently, the contract was cancelled and the responsibility for CHIP was given back to the state's Health and Human Resources Commission.

Budgeting

A **budget** is "an estimate of the receipts and expenditures needed by government to carry out its program in some future period, usually a fiscal year."[39] A budget is more than just two columns listing debits and credits. A carefully crafted budget "contains words and figures that propose expenditures for certain objects and purposes. The words describe types of expenditures (salaries, equipment, travel) or purposes (preventing war, improving mental health, providing low-income housing), and the figures are attached to each item. Presumably those who make a budget intend there to be a direct connection between what is written in it and future events. . . . In the most general definition, budgeting is concerned with translating financial resources into human purposes. A budget, therefore, may also be characterized as a series of goals with price tags attached. Because funds are limited and have to be divided in one way or another, the budget becomes a mechanism for making choices among alternative expenditures."[40] No matter how worthy the policy initiative may be, it simply cannot survive without funding. Therefore, budgeting is not something that is considered in isolation of the policy process. It oftentimes drives the process and can determine the success or failure of a policy directive. Agenda items must reflect budgetary reality. "If a state is facing a serious financial shortfall, putting new items on the agenda may be an option foreclosed from the start. It makes little sense to debate whether something should be done about the homeless when the state's treasury is bare and revenues are inadequate for normal business."[41]

However, an improperly budgeted program can occur for several reasons. First, lawmakers may grossly underestimate the cost of the initiative. Usually this happens on long-term projects. The cost projections for each year should be increased to adjust for increases in salaries, equipment, maintenance, and customary expenses. It is exceptionally difficult to request a legislature to provide additional revenues for cost overruns. Second, lawmakers are extremely skeptical of appropriating large sums of money for an unproven project. The program must look good enough on paper and promise long lasting results to garner full budgetary treatment. Third, voters can influence the budgeting process. For example, an increase in the state's sale tax rate would have to be approved by the voters in a general referendum election. Consequently, lawmakers have opted to increase the items subject to the tax rather than put the future of the state's budget into the hands of the voters who consistently want tax rate decreases, not increases. Local governments and school boards have learned painful lessons of preparing prudent bond packages to build new parks, roads, and schools only to have the voters soundly reject them. Unfortunately, governments are faced with the unpopular position of raising revenues just to meet current service levels. Adding new service programs is a luxury few state and local government officials can afford.

Budgeting also involves finding funding sources. Cash-strapped state governments can no longer look towards Washington for money to offset declines in state revenues. Creative funding ranges from lotteries and casino gambling to horse racing and state income taxes. State governments are also turning to the private sector to share in funding socially sensitive policy issues. However, for many of the nation's governors and mayors, seeking additional funding sources is extremely difficult. Increasing sales tax rates will bring additional revenue only if people buy more taxable goods and services. Property tax revenues are extremely dependent upon the value of the taxable properties. Decreased property values mean less money in the coffer.

Political Implications

Regardless of the policy issue, all lawmakers must consider the potential political implications of their actions. Each

legislative action will provide benefits to one group and hardships to another. Legislative voting records are generally public documents. Any incumbent seeing re-election expects that his/her opponent will use that voting record as political ammunition. Interest groups also monitor these voting records to ensure that both their endorsed candidates and individuals seeking future endorsements have been supportive of the bottom line issues of their group. The key is to hurt those who cannot politically hurt you.

One cannot overlook the fact that "political culture helps shape political behavior; it 'is related to the frequency and probability of various kinds of behavior and not their rigid determination.' Common values, beliefs, and attitudes inform, guide, and constrain the actions of both decision-makers and citizens."[42] Unfortunately, the Texas Legislature is well known for its lack of innovative policy options. Often the traditional Texas approach to addressing its problems comes into direct conflict with the dreaded word—*change*. As a whole, Texans are anti-government, clinging to the frontier belief in the rugged individual. "The individualist thread in our culture considers the individual responsible for his or her own success or failure. Social forces, like poverty or racial discrimination, are used by individuals to excuse their own failures, but are not deterrents to those with true ability."[43] Obviously, a liberal Democrat advocating increased state expenditures for the needy would face sharp opposition and suffer political liabilities among mainstream Texas voters. The political implications would be too detrimental to support this policy alternative. "The Texan's distrust of government leads him to support it little, under the apparent belief that the less resources government has the less evil it can do."[44] There are far fewer negative political implications in advocating status quo public policies than there are in promoting sweeping innovative methods that "rock the boat."

Adoption/Selling

A policy must be sellable to both the recipient and, if required, the group targeted to fund the program. Politicians must package their programs by emphasizing the benefits and downplaying any negatives. Poor salesmanship can destroy a perfectly well-designed initiative. Effective public policy must have the support of public opinion behind it; if not, it falls short of its anticipated goals and objectives.

Long-term projects far too often become the victims of the short-sightedness of public opinion. The American public wants quick and effective responses to their needs, and they are not receptive when politicians call for patience with the announcement that it could take ten years or better to see anticipated results. "The rather episodic issues-attention span of the general public and the mass media tends to undermine and diffuse political support for any particular program among both the public and legislators."[45] For example, the Bush administration garnered widespread public support for its initial military actions against Iraq. Public opinion polls showed America's concern over Iraq's support of international terrorist organizations and the fear that the Iraqi government would use its arsenal of weapons of mass destruction against Americans. However, the American people soon learned that there was no direct tie between the Iraqi government and major international terrorists groups nor did Iraq have the reported large stockpiles of so-called weapons of mass destruction. Public support dramatically eroded as the Bush administration continued to try to convince both the public and Congress that a military and political victory was still a real possibility. In this case, lawmakers seeking a successful re-election bid had to turn into political candidates who must listen to the voices of their constituents. Policy makers can ill-afford to overlook the fickleness of the public's support. "There is a general tendency for organized constituency support for a wide variety of programs—including environmental and consumer protection, as well as efforts to aid the poor—to decline over time, while opposition from target groups to the costs imposed on them remains constant or actually increases. This shift in the balance of consistency for such programs gradually becomes reflected in a shift of support among members of the legislature as a whole and the committees in the relevant subsystem(s)."[46] A positive long-term selling process with periodic updates of successes and progress could offset this problem.

Implementation

Successful program implementation is dependent upon several factors. First, the policy creating the program must clearly delineate levels of responsibility and, more importantly, provide measurements of accountability. Far too often, legislatively created programs have failed because the agency targeted with implementing the program did not fulfill its responsibilities. Bureaucrats can determine the fate of any well-crafted legislative action simply by the manner in which they implement it. "Any new program requires implementing officials who are not merely neutral but also sufficiently committed and persistent to develop new regulations and standard operating procedures and

to enforce them in a face of resistance from target groups and from public officials reluctant to make mandated changes."[47] A successfully implemented policy directive is possible under the guidance of an agency staff committed to executing all of the required elements within the established time frame by appropriately using all of the essential tools including budgeted amounts, personnel, and equipment. Bureaucratic agencies are rarely held fully accountable for their failures. It is easier to condemn the program than to fault the responsible agency. Second, laws should be clearly written to the point that they provide clear-cut guidelines for the agency charged with implementing the program. Most legislation creates a policy concept but leaves the details to the implementing agency. Vaguely written policy initiatives leave the door wide open to poor implementation, policy failures, and, of course, legal challenges. Third, successful programs correctly anticipate the demand for the service and adequately allocate resources to meet the demand—personnel, equipment, site location, and revenue. For example, opening a new facility to handle food distribution to low-income families with one clerk in a building located in a higher-income neighborhood is missing the targeted service group. This is poor allocation of resources. Fourth, long-term policy initiatives are multiple year, phased-in projects. Each phase must be implemented to produce anticipated goals and objectives. Unfortunately, "an over-emphasis on pragmatism can produce a focus on immediate results rather than long-term or enduring programs."[48] Consequently, the tendency is to implement one or two phases and use a half-implemented program as the measurement of success or failure for the entire initiative. Also, a change in administrations and party leadership could conceivably prevent a program from achieving full implementation. It is just political reality that a Republican governor will not want to continue to carry out the policies initiated by a Democrat governor and vice versa.

Evaluation

The final stage of the policy process is a complete and honest evaluation of the policy itself. "At a minimum, policy evaluation requires that we know what we want to accomplish with a given policy (policy objectives), how we are trying to do it (programs), and what, if anything, we have accomplished toward attainment of the objectives (impacts or outcomes, and the relation of the policy thereto). And in measuring accomplishments, we need to determine not only that some change in real-life conditions has occurred, such as the reduction in the unemployment rate, but also that it was due to policy actions and not to other factors, such as private economic decisions."[49] Every policy has its problems; the evaluation process earmarks those areas of concern and recommends corrective actions. It is more cost-effective to fix minor program flaws than to start over again.

It's the Process

The public policy process is a series of eight steps, beginning with problem identification and ending with an in-depth evaluation effort. As we have seen, each step is equally vital to the development of what policymakers want— cost effective, administratively viable, and goal achievable public policy initiatives. It takes a carefully thought-out action plan to create good public policy.

The State Budgetary Process

Despite the best efforts of governors, legislators, mayors and city councils, the reality is that:

states and localities make taxing and spending decisions in economic, political and demographic contexts over which they have little control. National economic trends, for example, affect taxing and spending decisions. Federal government policies also affect state and local taxing and spending decisions. The federal government mandates that states and localities make public facilities accessible to handicapped persons, devise plans to reduce air pollution, and provide health care for the medically indigent. Politicians in Washington may change the level of funding available to carry out these mandates. The politician's dilemma is that voters and interest groups favor most government spending programs but dislike paying taxes to support them. . . Since most state constitutions prohibit state and local governments from running deficits, governors and legislators must put together balanced budgets of taxing and spending that will be tolerable to the electorate.[50]

The financial status of state and local governments has always been tied to the ups and downs of the nation's economy. If the national economy is booming, state and local governments reap the benefits from tax dollars generated by thriving businesses, near to full employment, and increased consumer spending. If the national economy is in a downward spiral, state and local revenues decline due to a lack of consumer spending, high unemployment, depressed business development, and business closures and liquidations. What happens in Washington, D.C., does have an impact on state and local budgets. For example, President Ronald Reagan began in earnest the effort to slash billions from federal aid packages to state and local communities as part of his plan to reduce national budget deficits. Since Franklin Roosevelt's New Deal programs, state and local budget planners had become dependent upon the generosity of the federal government, opting not to allocate their own money for social services, transportation, and, in some instance, public and higher education programs. Those presidents wanting to reduce the flow of federal dollars to state and local coffers used the rhetoric of returning more governing control and, of course, financial responsibilities back to the states. President Clinton's budgeting skills resulted in a national budgetary surplus boosted by a very healthy economy. The dawning of a new century, however, brought economic woes to the nation's economy. Even before the collapse of the World Trade Center on September 11, 2001, the economic picture was beginning to sour as stock trading declined; major corporations began to lay off thousands of workers; and consumer buying came to a near standstill. During the waning days of the Bush administration, the costs of funding two wars coupled with the collapse of the housing industry, the potential demise of several major financial institutions, financial scandals, rise of homeowner foreclosures, etc., took its toll on an already fragile economy. Both Bush and Obama were faced with the possibility of a economic collapse akin to the Great Depression unless the federal government stepped in to artificially jump start the private economic sector. Both opted for bailouts for the financial institutions and federally funded stimulus packages. Action or in some cases, inaction from lawmakers in Washington can have positive and negative impacts on state finances. After Congress opted not to fund President Trump's border wall, the president fought back by refusing to sign a congressional funding bill. His actions initiated a 35-day partial federal government shutdown. Federal employees in the affected agencies did not receive at least one maybe two paychecks. While the federal government did not lose money, state and local governments definitely did. Cash strapped unpaid federal workers cut back on their spending. Even though they did receive their backpay, federal workers are on edge that another shutdown may happen are holding back on their spending. Texas is a state heavily dependent upon sales tax revenues to fund the majority of the state's budget. Any decline in consumer spending means that the state of

Texas and its cities lost revenue during this 35-day federal shutdown.

At the state and local level, governors, mayors and county commissioners are scrambling to balance their own budgets. With rising deficits coupled with shrinking revenue streams, the options are limited to across-the-board cuts to existing programs, cutting salary and benefits for government employees, privatizing traditionally run government services, tapping into rainy-day funds, layoffs, expanding lotteries and gaming operations, assessing higher fees for state-funded colleges and universities, charging more for using public transportation, and, yes, even raising taxes. Against this backdrop, the art of budgeting has become extremely difficult, particularly in states mandating a balanced budget. The process of doling out billions of dollars is politics at its best and worst. Every state agency and interest group across the nation keenly watches the wheeling and dealing over budgetary decisions.

The Terminology of Budgeting

Fiscal policy is "public policy that concerns taxes, government spending, public debt, and management of government money."[51] The budget serves as the centerpiece of any fiscal policy endeavor. The Texas Constitution mandates a **balanced budget** whereby on paper, revenues equal expenses. The State Comptroller is constitutionally bound to guarantee a balanced budget, thus in theory, avoiding a deficit situation. A **deficit** occurs when a state spends more than it earns within a designated budgetary period. The current state constitution prohibits the legislature from borrowing money to offset budget shortfalls except in cases of invasion or insurrection.

The Texas budget is a **biennial** document prepared for a two-year budget cycle. The fiscal year begins on September 1 and ends on August 31. A biennial budget cycle has two major drawbacks. First, "budgeting for two years, rather than for one year, as most governments do, means that Texas budget makers must cope with more than the usual uncertainties about future needs, emergencies, and productivity of the state's major revenue sources."[52] Forecasting revenues and expenses for one year is difficult enough with the ups and downs of national and international economic conditions. Second, revenue sources can be dedicated and earmarked to fund certain items. **Earmarking** is the budgetary practice of allocating a specific tax revenue stream for a specific purpose such as the Texas Legislature specifying that a certain percentage of the revenue generated from the hotel occupancy tax be given to promote tourism throughout the state. In Texas, budget dollars are legislatively dedicated to fund the state highway program. **Dedicated funding** ensures that the money will be used for its intended purpose. However, once the revenue is dedicated it cannot be transferred to another budget item or used to offset an unexpected state crisis or natural disaster.

A sometimes ominous term far too often used by challengers to incumbent legislative candidates is "pork." **Pork barrel politics** is "the use of political influence by members of Congress [or in this case, state legislators] to secure government funds and projects for their constituents."[53] A legislator's job includes fighting for state funds for projects and needs within his/her legislative district. In Texas, the 150 members of the House and the 31 members of the Senate promote their district needs, often selfishly overlooking the needs of the whole state. State agencies also participate in pork barreling by consistently inflating their budget requests. "Typically, administrators ask for more money than they actually need, believing that those appropriating money will automatically cut budgetary requests. Also, they tend to spend all funds that are allocated for a specific time, such as a fiscal year, because to return funds can lead to a reduction of funds during the next budgetary period."[54]

The governor's office has an impact on the budget. Governors can veto the entire budget or use their **line-item veto** authority, which allows them to veto or zero out specific budgetary items without vetoing the entire budget. Another tool is **impoundment**, defined as "the withholding by the executive branch of funds authorized and appropriated by law" through the legislative branch.[55] Authority to use impoundments has been the exclusive right of the presidency dating from George Washington's administration. State legislative houses have gradually granted their governors impoundment authority. In 1987, the Texas Legislature passed a measure giving limited budget impoundment powers to the governor. Basically, "under this statute, the governor may prevent an agency from spending part of its appropriation, may transfer money from one agency to another, and may suggest the timing for particular expenditures."[56]

Budget Strategies

There are several budgetary strategies available to budget makers. Texas traditionally used the **incremental budgetary process,** a virtually automatic process whereby state agencies receive marginal budgetary increases or decreases with each new budget cycle. State agencies merely submit their budget requests with a built-in adjustment.

Without much review, budget makers normally accept the budget requests and increased or decreased the line-item allocation accordingly.   There are several severe drawbacks to using the incremental system since "there is little attempt to evaluate program results or compare across different program areas in a given fiscal year. Such systematic evaluation would require a number of actors not readily available to most state agencies: clear agreement or programmatic objectives, reliable methods of measuring progress towards those objectives, [and], personnel skilled in methods of policy analysis."[57]

Subsequently, Texas seems to be moving more towards a modified **planning program budgeting (PPB) concept** with a cost-benefit analysis feature. The focus is on programs, not line-item allocations. The budget process "initially sets out goals (the planning phase), develops and approves programs for reaching these objectives (the programming phase), and prices and allocates inputs required for reaching these objectives (the budgetary phase).[58] The cost benefit is a built-in feature since agencies must demonstrate the need for the money.

Once popular in the 1970s and 80s, **zero-based budgeting (ZBB)** is based on the concept that the allocation of funds for any expenditures begins anew with each budgetary cycle. "The past, as reflected in the budgetary base, is explicitly rejected: There is no yesterday; nothing will be taken for granted; everything at every period is subject to searching scrutiny."[59] In other words, the future of every state agency and program is on the table. "This approach encourages greater policy orientation, because out-of-date programs are dropped instead of being continued as existing budget items that are not questioned once they become part of a department's established budget. In some cases, departments rank their programs in order of priority and set performance levels for all programs."[60] Oftentimes, the ZBB strategy can be used to shift budgetary responsibilities from one level of government to another. Governor Rick Perry used this strategy in his version of the 2003-2005 state budget. By submitting a zero budget, he basically shifted the responsibility and the accountability from the governor's office to the state legislature. This signaled that Texas is moving in the direction of her sister states. "Today nearly all states require some kind of performance budgeting in which governments first decide what they want to accomplish and then develop their budgets. Programs then are evaluated on the basis of work performance—are objectives being accomplished?—and on how effectively services are being provided on a per-unit cost basis. This means the focus is on outcomes or results of programs."[61]

This budgetary strategy plays into the hands of skeptical taxpayers weary of funding programs that simply do not work.

The State Budgetary Cycle

The Texas budgetary cycle is a complicated process beginning months before the legislative session begins. The short legislative session of only 140 days once every two years mandates that key budget oriented committees convene as interim committees to draft the document. The process is further complicated by the **dual budgeting concept,** whereby two budgets may be submitted to the Texas Legislature, one from legislative budget committees and another from the governor's office. Of course, both budgets will be totally different.

The process begins with the **Legislative Budget Board (LBB)**. Created in 1949, the dominating actor in drafting the budget is composed of ten legislators including the lieutenant governor, Speaker of the Texas House, chair of the House Appropriations Committee, chair of the House Ways and Means Committee, chair of the Senate Finance Committee, chair of the Senate State Affairs Committee, two appointees by the speaker and two appointees by the lieutenant governor. The lieutenant governor is the chairperson with the Speaker serving as the vice chairperson. Meeting as an interim committee in-between legislative sessions, the LBB sends budget instructions for monetary requests to all state agencies and departments. Budget requests usually require a "five-year time frame, which includes actual expenditures for the last year of the previous biennium, estimated and budgeted expenditures for the current biennium, and a projection of needs for the next biennium."[62] The LBB meets with each agency and department to discuss budgetary requests. The final budget is submitted by the LBB in the form of an appropriations bill to the Senate Finance Committee and the House Appropriations Committee within five days after the legislative session begins.

Although the Texas Constitution mandates that all appropriations or spending bills originate in the Texas House, the **appropriations committees** in both houses are extremely influential in the state budgeting process and are plum committee assignments. "In all, not more than 15 of the 181 legislators in the House and the Senate participate meaningfully in the crucial decisions made in the preparation, formulation, and adoption of the Texas budget."[63] Both appropriations committees will parcel out segments of the budget to the proper committees for their consideration. Funding for education, social services, highways, and so on, needs to be reviewed by those committees with expertise in these areas. The time frame is extremely short since the final budget must be on the floor of each house within ninety days of the legislative session. Consequently the appropriations committees are responsible for the bulk of the budgetary duties.

Of course, the Senate and the House will pass separate budget bills that are totally different. A conference committee is formed from members of both houses to reconcile budget differences in order to produce one budget that will pass both houses. This is nail-biting time as the hours of the legislative session tick by without a budget. Normally, a final product will emerge almost on the last day of the session, hastily passed, and sent to the governor's office before the final gavel falls. If a rare budget impasse occurs and the Texas Legislature adjourns without a budget, it is the governor's responsibility to call a thirty-day special session devoted to the state budget.

The **Comptroller of Public Accounts** works closely with the LBB and the Texas Legislature to produce a balanced budget. The Comptroller is constitutionally required to issue a sworn statement guaranteeing that the state's cash-on-hand and projected revenues will cover anticipated budget expenses for the next biennium. All budget appropriations are cleared through the Comptroller's office before the final budget emerges. The Comptroller does have the authority to adjust allocated amounts, after all, the state should only spend what it can earn. The Texas Legislature, however, can override the Comptroller's recommendations and increase any amounts for budgeted items with a four-fifths vote of approval from both houses.

When the budget reaches the governor's desk, he/she has three viable options. First, the governor can sign the final appropriations bill, approving the entire budget. Second, the governor can approve the final budget after line-item vetoing those appropriates he/she does not want to support. The line-item veto cancels the entire budget for that item. For example, the governor feels that the allocation for public education is not enough so he line-item vetos this appropriation. Governors cannot simply pencil-in a new amount but must recommend an acceptable amount to the Texas Legislature. In turn, the Texas Legislature renegotiates in this case the entire budget for public education until an agreement is reached with the governor. Even the threat of using a line-item veto has proven to be a very effective tool for a governor to convince the Texas Legislature to conform to his/her wishes. Third, the governor can veto the entire budget and call for a special session to develop a new one!

Revenue Sources

With the discovery of Spindletop in 1901, the Texas Legislature found the pot of gold at the end of the rainbow. As long as the oil flowed, the Texas coffers were brimming over with budget surpluses. The Texas Legislature taxed every facet of oil from removing it from the earth to pumping it into a vehicle's gas tank. However, the Texas Legislature has finally learned a painful lesson about placing the state's future upon one natural resource. First, oil and gas are nonreplenishable natural resources; sooner or later oil and gas will be very scarce resources. Second, the production and pricing of oil and gas in Texas is totally dependent upon an unstable international marketplace guided by the **Organization of Petroleum Exporting Countries (OPEC)**.

The 1980s, for example, saw the price of oil plunge. Each decrease in the price of crude oil meant major decreases in state revenues. Consequently, the Texas Legislature has had to develop alternative sources of revenue. Because Texas is one of the few states without a state income tax, the Texas Legislature relies on a wide variety of regressive tax programs. Texas also collects revenue from the sale and lease of grazing and mineral rights from a twenty million-acre-plus tract of state-owned land. Beginning in the 1980s, the Texas Legislature approved pari-mutuel betting on horse and dog races, a lottery, and a tax on bingo game winnings. The revenue-seeking creativity of the Texas Legislature is severely hampered by the anti-tax sentiments of most Texans. Culturally and historically, Texans are extremely hostile to new or increased taxes. A serious attempt by the Texas Legislature to introduce a state income tax did make Texans overlook the adverse impact of gambling as they rushed to the polls to approve pari-mutuel betting. Before we delve into the various tax programs, a discussion of tax terminology is warranted.

The Terminology of Taxes

A **tax** is "a compulsory contribution for a public purpose rather than for the personal benefit of an individual."[64] Taxes have been the traditional source of revenue for governments. The money collected is eventually returned to the citizens in the form of public services ranging from sanitation to medical care. Generally, Americans are weary of paying taxes and do not support politicians and lawmakers advocating tax increases. However, citizens constantly demand more government-sponsored services. In developing a tax program lawmakers must select a plan that will provide a reliable ample source of revenue with a minimal impact on taxpayers' pocketbooks. There are several key factors that lawmakers must consider in selecting a tax option.

Elasticity is "an economic criterion applied to a tax that refers to the tax's ability to generate increased revenue as economic growth or inflation increases."[63] A highly elastic tax will expand and/or contract proportionally with economic growth or stagnation. **Elastic taxes** are the most reliable and predictable sources of revenue. The income tax is the best example of an elastic tax because as a person's income increases, his/her tax burden increases. A tax is tagged as **inelastic** when it does not generate increase revenues in proportion to economic growth. Sales taxes are inelastic taxes since the rate is fixed. It does not matter what the individual's income level is, the amount of the tax is fixed on the item. An individual whose income is $100,000 will pay the same amount in tax on an item of clothing as the individual earning $10,000.

Lawmakers must take into account the potential reliability of the tax as a dependable source of revenue. A tax that meets its anticipated level of revenue is a far better program than a tax that is highly unpredictable in revenue returns. "Sales, property and income taxes are reliable because experts can predict with only a small margin of error future economic growth and activity upon which taxes are based. Severance taxes on energy production can be unreliable because the income they generate is affected by rapidly changing and unpredictable international political forces."[66] **Tax accuracy** and reliability go hand in hand. Governments must have adequate sources to predict accurately the reliability of revenue sources to produce needed income. Revenue may be lost if the measurement tool to assess tax values is inadequate or antiquated. For example, most local and county governments in Texas have an adequate means of accurately assessing the taxable value of personal residential properties. However, governments do a poor job in assessing business properties since they oftentimes rely upon the business owner to honestly appraise their own property. The net result is an irretrievable substantial loss of revenue. The **tax effort** is "a measure of whether, given a state's economic situation, it is taxing above or below its capacity to raise revenue."[67] In other words, states with strong track records of economic growth have the potential to raise ample revenues at average tax rates, if willing to do so. Texas, considered to be a economically stable state with a high potential for revenue generation, is a low-tax effort revenue-generating state due to a historical dependency upon regressive tax programs.

How much money a tax will ultimately produce is called the **yield,** which is the difference between the money generated by the tax or income produced by the program and the administrative costs incurred in collecting the revenue. The easiest and cheapest taxes to administer and collect are income and sales taxes. These taxes produce a higher yield than property taxes, which are costly to administer because property must be assessed for its tax value on a regular basis. Initially hailed as a lucrative income generator, the Texas lottery has not lived up to its potential.

The **visibility** of a tax is an important political consideration for lawmakers. Although they are very reliable revenue sources, income and property taxes are highly visible since the taxpayer receives a property tax bill in the mail and is constantly reminded that April 15 is the filing date for income taxes. To add salt to the wound, taxpayers are constantly reminded to pay those taxes on time or face costly late charges, fines, and even imprisonment and/or loss of their property. On the other hand, sales taxes are low visibility taxes since the majority of the consumers do not keep records of sale tax expenditures. Politicians particularly in Texas prefer the safest course possible with the taxpayer by preferring to support low visibility tax options. **Tax equity** or the fairness of the tax is another major consideration for lawmakers. As long as the taxpayer believes that the tax is needed and fairly applied, he/she will pay the tax. However, this country separated itself from England in part over unequal taxes imposed on the colonists. The principle of fairness in taxation cannot be overlooked by lawmakers seeking reelection.

The application or allocation of the revenue generated by the tax program is another major consideration for budget makers. **Operating expenses** are yearly costs needed to run government such as salaries, benefits, equipment, rent, utilities, and supplies. **Capital expenses** are multi-year or amortized costs. A new mainframe computer system or a new building are expenses allocated over five-, ten- or thirty-year periods. Reliable sources should be found to cover operating costs, whereas unreliable funds should be reserved for capital expenses.

Lawmakers can determine who bears the burden of a tax simply by their choice of a tax program. There are four types of taxes a government may levy on its citizens. Income, property, and corporate taxes are progressive tax programs. A **progressive tax** is "any tax in which the tax rates increase as the tax base (that is, the amount subject to be taxed) increases."[68] For example, the rate of the tax would increase in increments for those with higher incomes paying more in taxes. In contrast, a **regressive tax** is "any tax in which the burden falls relatively more heavily upon low-income groups than upon wealthy taxpayers."[69] Sales, excise and energy taxes are regressive taxes since

Table 10.1 – Percentage of Net Revenues by Source – Year Ended August 31, 2018
(All Funds Excluding Trust)
Amounts in Billions

Category	Amount	Percentage of Net Revenue
Federal Income	$39.6	33.0%
Total Tax Collections	55.6	46.3%
Licenses, Fees, Fines and Penalties	6.5	5.4%
State Health Service Fees & Rebates	7.6	6.3%
Net Lottery Proceeds	2.2	1.9%
Land Income	2.1	1.7%
Interest and Investment Income	1.8	1.5%
Settlements of Claims	.5	.5%
Escheated Estates	.6	.5%
Sales of Goods and Services	.3	.2%
Other	3.3	2.7%

Total Revenue - $120.2 Billion

Source: *State of Texas Cash Report: Revenues and Expenditures of State Funds for the Fiscal Year Ended August 31,2018*, Austin, Texas: Texas Comptroller of Public Accounts, 2018, Chart 2, page 12.

they adversely impact incomes of middle- and lower-class individuals. The state coffers are very dependent upon revenue from sales taxes while the primary source of tax revenue for city, county, and special district governments such as school districts, is property taxes.

Advocated by former President Ronald Reagan, **proportional taxes** impose equal tax burdens regardless of one's income level. Reagan envisioned a flat tax with no deductions for federal income taxes. Subsequently, a 5 percent tax rate would produce the same tax burden regardless if one's yearly income was $10,000 or $100,000. A tax system could follow a **benefit principle system**. In this scenario, those who use the service more often than others would be assessed a higher user fee or tax burden; whereas, nonusers would be relieved of the tax or fee obligation. If people do not need to use the service, why should they pay for it?

Tax revenues can be adversely impacted by tax deductions and tax abatements. **Deductions** allow individuals to decrease their tax obligation by providing an allowance or tax break for certain investments and expenditures. Critics of the federal income tax believe that the more than ample number of deductions has made the income tax more regressive than progressive. **Tax abatements** are temporary tax relief programs granted by government as an incentive for future economic development and job creation. For example, a major Fortune 500 company wants to move to Texas. An attractive incentive would be to permit the company to delay its property tax obligations for five years, which would allow the company to get a solid foothold within the state. Although this company will not pay property taxes for the first five years, it will pay these deferred taxes in subsequent years.

The Revenue Side of the Budget

By the end of the 2018 fiscal year, the state of Texas collected a total of $120.2 billion excluding trust funds to pay for state expenditures. Table 10.1 illustrates the amount of revenue obtained from numerous revenue streams. The primary sources of revenue for the state are tax collections that accounted for 46.3 percent of total revenue with federal funds allocated directly to the state, accounted for 33.0 percent of the state's total revenue. Collectively, revenue generated from the issuance of licenses and permits, collected from fines, the sale of lottery tickets, and the sale and rental of state-held land accounted for only 20.7 percent of total state revenues for fiscal year 2018. Currently, the state has "more than 230 different types of licenses and fees, including health-related fees, higher education tuition, motor vehicle registration fees, professional fees and various inspection fees."[70] Table 10.2 provides a detailed analysis of the sources of state revenue for fiscal years 2017 and 2018. The greatest decline in revenue in 2018 was from taxes levied on the

Table 10.2 Net Revenue by Source – All Funds Excluding Trust – Years Ended August 31
(Amounts in Billions)*

Tax Collection by Major Tax	Total 2017	Percent of Change 2016-2017	Total 2018	Percent of Change 2017-2018
Sales Tax	$28.9	2.3 %	$31.9	10.5%
Motor Vehicle Sales/Rental Taxes	4.5	(1.8)**	5.0	9.7
Motor Fuel Taxes	3.6	2.0	3.7	2.5
Franchise Tax	3.2	(16.5)	3.7	13.7
Oil Production Tax	2.1	23.6	3.4	60.9
Insurance Taxes	2.4	6.7	2.5	5.6
Cigarette and Tobacco Taxes	1.5	9.7	1.3	(13.3)
Natural Gas Production Tax	10.0	69.8	1.4	45.6
Alcoholic Beverages Taxes	1.2	3.0	1.3	6.1
Hotel Occupancy Tax	.5	1.8	.6	13.3
Utility Taxes	.4	.9	.4	3.0
Other Taxes	.2	14.2	.3	51.5
Total Tax Collections	**$50.0**	**2.4%**	**$55.6**	**12.0**
Revenue by Source				
Total Tax Collections	$49.6	2.4%	$55.6	12.0%
Federal Income	38.3	(2.8)	39.6	3.3
Licenses, Fees, Fines and Penalties	6.2	2.1	6.5	3.5
State Health Services Fees and Rebates	6.7	201.9	7.6	13.4
Net Lottery Proceeds	2.0	80.2	2.2	8.5
Land Income	1.7	48.7	2.1	21.6
Interest and Investment Income	1.7	24.1	1.9	9.3
Settlements of Claims	.5	(19.1)	.5	3.2
Escheated Estates	1.0	78.5	.6	(35.0)
Sales of Goods and Services	.3	5.2	.3	(7.5)
Other Revenue	3.0	1.9	3.3	10.4
Total Net Revenue	**$111.0**	**(0.1)%**	**120.0**	**8.1%**

*Totals may vary due to rounding.
**() Indicates a negative percentage.

Source: *State of Texas Annual Cash Report: Revenue and Expenditures of State Funds for Year Ended August 31,2018*, Austin, Texas: Comptroller of Public Accounts, 2018, Table 3, page 13.

sale of cigarette and tobacco products. In 2011, the Texas Legislature increased the tax rates on these products as a means of encouraging individuals to quit smoking. The amount of tax revenue for these items has been declining steadily, resulting in a 13.3 percent decrease in revenue just between 2017 and 2018. Whether or not the state's lottery is a viable income generator has been questionable since its inception. For fiscal year 2018, "net lottery proceeds totaled $2.2 billion, 8.5 percent more than fiscal 2017. The proceeds figure represents retailer lottery sales, net of commissions and prize payment."[71] According to Table 10.3, per capita sales tax collections rose from a deficit in fiscal year 2016 to an increase of 10.4 percent in 2018 over revenues collected in 2017. Overall, at the end of fiscal year 2018, the state had an ending cash balance of $31,779,565,258.[72]

Sales Taxes

According to the Comptroller's report, "Texas's sales taxes are the state's largest single source of tax revenue, bringing in $31.9 billion in fiscal 2018, 10.5 percent more than fiscal 2017. Sales tax collections account for 57.5 percent of tax collections and 26.6 percent of net revenue for all funds, excluding trust."[73] The state sales tax rate has gradually increased from its inception in 1961 of 2 percent to its present level of 6.25 percent. Cities have the option of "piggy-backing" the state base rate by adding 0.5 to 1.0 percent. Sales tax revenues can be increased by upping the tax rate, the tax base, or both. Increasing the **tax rate** is a highly visible risk for state legislators. Even a marginal increase will be met with sharp opposition from voters. Usually, the Texas Legislature opts for the less visible

Table 10.3 – Texas Per Capita State Tax Collections – Years Ended August 31

Fiscal Year	State Tax Collections	State Population	Per Capita State Tax Collections	Percent of Change	Taxes as a Percent Personal Income
2014	$50,992,561,539	26,896,600	$ 1,896	4.9%	0.0%
2015	51,683,059,891	27,389,200	1,887	(0.5)*	4.0
2016	48,476,226,223	27,845,500	1,741	(7.7)	3.8
2017	49,643,421,639	28,255,300	1,757	0.9	3.8
2018	55,584,775,261	28,668,600	1,939	10.4	4.0

**() indicates a negative percentage change.

Source: *State of Texas Cash Report: Revenues and Expenditures of State Funds for the Fiscal Year Ended August 31, 2018*, Austin, Texas: Texas Comptroller of Public Accounts, 2018, Table 4, page 13.

approach by increasing the **base rate**, the items subjected to the tax. Currently unprepared food items, some articles of clothing, housing, medical care, some services such as car washes, and agricultural supplies are exempt.

The state sales tax is a regressive tax program. Lower- and middle-income Texans pay a larger percentage of their disposable income into sales taxes than those individuals in the upper-income brackets. Sales taxes are tied directly to the state's economy and the fickle buying habits of the consumer. If the economy slows, unemployment increases and job security declines, the consumer's spending habits become more cautious and conservative. Also, sales taxes are inelastic revenue sources. The sales tax rate is applied to items, not incomes. On the positive side, sales taxes are paid by non-Texans. Cities known for tourism are able to capture additional revenue with the piggy-back option. These taxes are high-yield revenue sources that are collected by local businesses and forwarded to the state, relieving the state of high administration and assessment costs.

While it is extremely difficult to separate out the amount of sales taxes generated by visitors and convention attendees to the state's major cities, one can point to the growth in the leisure and hospitality employment sector as a sign of the state's dependence upon tourism, conventions and special sporting events. "Employment in the leisure and hospitality industry increased by 49,000 (3.7 percent) over the [2018] fiscal year. The majority of the industry's job gains occurred in the food services and drinking places sector, which added 33,000 jobs (3.1 percent). The largest percentage increase was in the amusement, gambling and recreation industries sector, which grew by 4.2 percent (4,700). Total leisure and hospitality employment in August 2018 was 1,372,100, representing 11 percent of total Texas employment."[74]

Motor Fuels Tax

A regressive consumer-driven tax program, the motor fuels tax is levied on gasoline, diesel, and liquid petroleum gas. The current rate is 20 cents per gallon for gasoline or diesel fuels. The proceeds of this tax are totally dedicated, with three-fourths pegged for roads and highways, and one-fourth for the Available School Fund, the primary state funding source for the state's public school system.

Severance Taxes

Texas is a natural resource rich state. If it were an independent nation, Texas would be tied with Iran as the world's fifth-largest oil producer. Texas also has an abundant supply of natural gas, sulfur, and uranium; it seems only natural that the state would want to tax these resources. A **severance tax** is levied for the extraction of any natural resource from the earth including off-shore oil drilling operations. The state taxes crude oil, natural gas, sulfur, stone, sand, cement, salt, lime, clays, and gypsum. The oil production tax rate is 4.6 percent of the market value of oil produced in the state. The tax on natural gas production is 7.5 percent of the market value of gas produced. The severance tax on oil and gas is actually paid by the consumer, "passed off" either at the pump or on one's utility bill.

Other Tax Programs

Similar to the sales tax, excise taxes are applied separately to certain commodities. The state taxes all utilities and telephone services. An unique excise tax, **sin taxes** are charged on all alcoholic beverages whether they are purchased from a retail store, over the counter at a

Table 10.4   Tax Rates and Taxable Bases for Major Texas State Taxes

Fiscal Year 2018

Tax	Rate and Base
Sales Taxes	**Limited Sales and Use**: 6.25 percent of the retail sale of tangible personal property and selected servics; 1.5 percent Texas Emissions Reduction Plan Surcharge on the sale, lease or rental of off-road, heavy-duty diesel equipment (other than some agricultural equipment). **Boat and Boat Motor**: 6.25 percent of the total consideration paid for a boat or boat motor; $15 tax for each boat or boat motor brought in the State by a new resident.
Natural Gas Taxes	7.5 percent of the market value of natural gas produced in the state. 4.6 percent of the market value of condensate produced in the state.
Oil Production	**Production**: 4.6 percent of the market value of oil produced in the state.
Motor Fuels Taxes	**Motor Fuel**: 20 cents per gallon of gasoline or diesel fuel (eligible transit companies qualify for a refund of 1 cent per gallon on gasoline and ½ cent per gallon on diesel fuel). **Compressed Natural Gas and Liquefied Natural Gas**: 15 cents per gallon.
Motor Vehicle Sales and Use/ Rental, and Manufactured Housing Sales Tax	**Sales and Use**: 6.25 percent of vehicle sales price, less any trade-in; $90 tax for each motor vehicle brought into the State by a new resident; $10 tax paid by donee for each gift of a motor vehicle; $5 tax paid by each party in an even exchange of two motor vehicles; 1.0 percent or 2.5 percent Texas Emissions Reduction Plan surcharge on certain diesel truck purchases. **Rental**: 10 percent of gross receipts on rentals of 30 days or less; 6.25 percent on rentals of 31 to 180 days. **Manufactured Housing Sales**: 5 percent of 65 percent of the sales price on the initial sale or use of a new manufactured home.
Cigarette and Cigar/Tobacco Products Taxes	**Cigarette**: (1) $70.50 per 1,000 weighing 3 pounds or less ($1.41 per pack of 20) and (2) $72.60 per 1,000 weighting more than 3 pounds per 1000 ($1.452 per pack of 20). **Cigars and Tobacco Products**: (1) Cigar rates vary with weight per 1,000, constituents, and price: From 1 cent per 10 cigars weighing over 3 pounds or less per 1,000 to $15 per 1,000 cigars weighing over 3 pounds per 1,000. **Snuff, chewing tobacco, and roll-your-own-tobacco**: 0.75 percent of taxable margin or 0.375 percent of taxable margin for taxable entities primarily engaged in wholesale or retail trade. Taxpayers with total revenue of $20 million or less may elect to pay tax on revenue apportioned to Teas at a rate of 0.331 percent, $1.22 per ounce based on the manufacturer's list weight.
Alcoholic Beverage Taxes	**Beer**: $6.00 per 31 gallon barrel. **Liquor**: $2.40 per gallon. **Wine**: Alcohol volume not over 14 percent – 20.4 cents per gallon. More than 14 percent – 40.8 cents per gallon. Sparkling wine – 51.6 centers per gallon. **Malt Liquor** (Ale): 19.8 cents for gallon. **Mixed Beverage**: 6.7 percent of the permittees gross receipts and a retail sales tax of 8.25 percent
Insurance Premium Taxes	**Life Insurance and Health Maintenance Organizations**: 0.875 percent of the first $450,000 in taxable gross life premiums or HMO taxable gross receipts, and 1.75 percent of taxable gross life premiums or HMO taxable gross receipts in excess of $450,000. **Property and Casualty Insurance**: 1.6 percent **Accident and Health Insurance**: 1.75 percent **Unauthorized, Independently Procured, and Surplus Lines Insurance**: 4.85 percent of gross premiums written for the insured whose home state is Texas. **Title Insurance**: 1.35 percent of gross premiums written in Texas.
Utility Taxes	**Public Utility Gross Receipts**: one sixth of 1.0 percent of gross receipts **Gas, Electric and Water Utilities** – (1) Cities 1,000 to 2,499 population – 0.581 percent of gross receipts; (2) Cities 2,500 to 9,999 population – 1.070 percent of gross receipts; (3) Cities 10,000 population or more – 1.997 percent of gross receipts. **Gas Utility Pipeline**: 0.5 percent of gross utility receipts less the cost of natural gas sold.
Hotel Occupancy Tax	6 percent of consideration paid by occupant.

Source: *State of Texas Annual Cash Report: Revenues and Expenditures of State Funds for the Year Ended 2018*, Austin, Texas: Texas Comptroller of Public Accounts, 2018, pages 117-118.

Table 10.5—Percentage of Net Expenditures by Function—Year Ended August 31, 2018
(All Funds Excluding Trust)
Amounts in Billions

Category	Amount	Percentage of Net Expenditures
Education	$ 36.8	31.6%
Health and Human Services	50.4	43.3
Transportation	10.0	8.5
Public Safety and Corrections	5.4	4.6
Employee Benefits	4.8	4.1
General Government	3.4	2.9
National Resources/Recreational Services	2.7	2.4
Debt Service – Interest	1.6	1.4
Other	1.5	1.3

Total Expenditures = $116.6 Billion
(Total may not add due to rounding)

Source: *State of Texas Annual Cash Report: Revenue and Expenditures of State Funds for the Year Ended August 31, 2018*, Austin, Texas: Texas Comptroller of Public Accounts, 2018, Chart 3, page 16.

restaurant, or on an airline or train. The state's primary tax on businesses, the **franchise tax**, is levied on both domestic and foreign businesses operating in Texas. The state also charges a **motor vehicle sales tax** at 6.25 percent of the sale price, less any trade-in. Table 10.4 lists the various tax programs and their rates.

Federal Government

Although tax collections account for 46.3 percent of the state's revenue in 2018, 33.0 percent of all state revenue comes from the federal government. Through various grant programs, federal contracts and entitlement programs, "Texas' federal funding increased by 3.3 percent in fiscal 2018, totaling $39.6 billion."[75] During fiscal year 2018, the federal government gave the state of Texas $27.6 billion to cover costs for Medicaid, Medicare, the Children's Health Insurance Program (CHIP) and other public assistance programs.[76] In addition, the "Texas education system received $5.2 billion in federal funds. . . The Texas Department of Transportation (TxDOT) received $3.9 billion in federal money."[77] The federal funds are needed definitely to augment many of the state's financial responsibilities. Yet, the federal government's generosity is oftentimes fickle as lawmakers in Washington, DC have selectively scaled back on federal funding to the states. "In fiscal 2018, the Department of State Health Services, TxDot, and the Department of Family and Protective Services saw the only dollar decreases in federal

funds a, reduction of $462.0 million, $375.5 million and $1.2 million from fiscal 2017, respectively."[78] The costs associated with these functional areas have not decreased just because the federal government has decided to give less. The burden now merely has shifted upon state lawmakers and ultimately, the tax payers to offset any decreases in anticipated federal funds.

The Expense Side of the Budget

An overview of state expenditures is detailed in Tables 10.5 and 10.6. In 2018, $36.8 billion representing 31.6 percent of state expenditures in 2018 was spent on both public and higher education programs while $50.4 billion representing 43.3 percent of total state expenditures was spent on health and human services. Collectively only 25.2 percent of state expenditures covered other expense items such as transportation, public safety, corrections [the state prison system] and employee benefits.

These figures are misleading since both the state and the public school districts share funding responsibilities for elementary and secondary education. Both the state and individual community college districts share funding responsibilities for two-year college programs. In addition to state funding, state-supported four-year colleges and universities as well as community colleges are funded through student tuition, federal grants, and endowments and financial contributions from alums and the private sector. In other words, the state of Texas is not and has not

Table 10.6 Net Expenditures by Function – All Funds Excluding Trust – Years Ended August 31
(Totals May Not Add Due to Rounding)

Expenditure Item	Total 2017	Total 2018	Percent of Change 2017-2018
General Government			
Executive Branch	$2,783,421,232	$ 2,882,725,331	3.6%
Legislative Branch	150,078,904	139,159,263	(7.3)*
Judicial Branch	345,837,980	362,454,252	4.8
Education	35,504,880,963	36,783,411,379	3.6
Employee Benefits	4,775,179,125	4,760,439,498	0.1
Health and Human Services	49,075,263,713	50,421,211,916	2.7
Public Safety and Corrections	4,927,729,972	5,374,569,067	9.1
Transportation	10,260,658,371	9,951,962,725	(3.0)
Natural Resources/			
Recreational Services	2,045,995,022	2,746,428,813	34.2
Regulatory Services	349,818,908	312,409,589	(10.7)
Lottery Winnings**	557,026,044	627,932,600	12.7
Debt Service – Interest	1,255,690,046	1,592,837,164	26.8
Capital Outlay	613,540,131	598,534,083	(2.4)
Total Net Expenditures	$112,625,120,411	$116,554,075,690	3.5%

*() indicates a negative percentage.
**Does not include payments made by retailers.

Source: *State of Texas Cash Report: Revenues and Expenditures of State Funds for the Fiscal Year Ended August 31, 2018¸ Austin,Texas: Texas Comptroller of Public Accounts, 2018, Table 7, pages 16-17.*

totally funded the state's education systems. Also, the state is not bearing the total costs for programs lumped under the heading of 'Health and Human Services'.

Conclusions

The economic indicators point to a heathy growing Texas economic picture. In 2018, "employment in the service-providing industries grew by 2.7percent. Employment increased in all three of the goods-producing industries (mining and logging, manufacturing, and construction."[79] The oil and gas industry is recovering from the dismal drop in oil and natural gas prices so prevalent during 2014 through 2016. All the economic indicators point to a prolong period of prosperity for the state of Texas. A growing job market coupled with an increase of people migrating into Texas means additional revenues for the state. However, a state budget so dependent upon sales tax revenues is extremely dependent upon a healthy job market, low unemployment and consumer spending. Unfortunately, every state's budget is tied directly to the ups and downs of the nation's economy and the everchanging political climate in Washington and Austin. The rosy

economic picture painted by Governor Abbott is so dependent upon so many variables that he and the Texas Legislature have very little or no control over! There could be cloudy skies lurking over Abbott's rosy economic picture. "Oil markets and outlooks made a sharp turn in 2018, quickly shifting from predictions of global shortages and $100-a-barrel crude to concerns about increasing supplies, weakening demand and another oil glut."[80] This is not good news for a state economy so dependent upon the oil and gas business. In Texas, "we live and die by the price of oil" and any substantial decline in the oil and natural gas industry does create a domino effect in all other sectors of the state's economy.[81]

Chapter Notes
  [1]James E. Anderson, *Public Policymaking*, 5th ed., (New York, New York: Houghton Mifflin Company, 2003), 1.
  [2]Allie Morris, "$9 Billion More Expected for Texas' Budget," *San Antonio Express News* (Tuesday, January 8, 2019), A1 and A9.
  [3]Ibid.
  [4]*https://gov.tex.gov*
  [5]*State of Texas Annual Cash Report: Revenues and Expenditures of State Funds for the Fiscal Year Ended August 21, 2018,* (Austin, Texas: Comptroller of Public Accounts, 2018), 3.

[6]Morris, "$9 Billion More Expected for Texas' Budget," A1 and A9.

[7]Ibid.

[8]Clay Robison, "Tax Cut Will Cost Texans, Critics Charge," *Houston Chronicle*, (Sunday, July 27, 1997), 24A.

[9]*ProQuest, ProQuest Statistical Abstract of the United States: 2019*, 7th ed., (Bethesda, Maryland: 2018), Tables 709 and 735, 463 and 479.

[10]Anderson, 2.

[11]Theodore J. Lowi and Benjamin Ginsburg, *American Government: Freedom and Power*, 3rd ed., (New York, New York: Norton, 1994), 619.

[12]Anderson, 5.

[13]David C. Saffell, *State and Local Government: Politics and Public Policies*, 4th ed., (New York, New York: McGraw-Hill, 1990), 239.

[14]Anderson, 5.

[15]Ibid., 4.

[16]Ibid., 14.

[17]Gerry Riposa and Nelson Dometrius, "Studying Public Policy," *Texas Public Policy*, Gerry Riposa, ed., (Dubuque, Iowa: Kendall/Hunt, 1987), 11.

[18]Lowi and Ginsburg, 620.

[19]Ibid., 623.

[20]*The HarperCollins Dictionary of American Government and Politics*, Jay M. Shafritz, ed., (New York, New York: HarperCollins Publishers, Inc., 1992), 590.

[21]Steven A. Peterson and Thomas H. Rasmussen, *State and Local Politics*, (New York, New York: McGraw-Hill, 1994), 190-191.

[22]Paul Sabtier and Daniel Mazmanian, "The Conditions of Effective Implementation: A Guide to Accomplishing Policy Objectives," *Public Administration: Concepts and Cases*, Richard Stillman, ed., 4th ed., (Princeton, New Jersey: Houghton Mifflin Company: 1988), 387.

[23]Anderson, 81.

[24]Deborah Stone, *Policy Paradox: The Art of Political Decision Making*, (New York, New York: WW. Norton & Company: 2002), 188-189.

[25]Anderson, 6.

[26]Stone, 206.

[27]Sabtier and Mazmanian, "The Conditions of Effective Implementation: A guide to Accomplishing Policy Objectives," 380.

[28]Randall W. Bland, Alfred B. Sullivan, Robert E. Biles, Charles P. Elliott, Jr., and Beryle E. Pettus, *Texas Government Today*, 5th ed., (Pacific Grove, California: Brooks/Cole, 1992), 432.

[29]Sar Levitan, "How the Welfare System Promotes Economic Security," *Political Science Quarterly*, The Academy of Political Science, Vol. 100, No. 3, Fall, 1985, 453.

[30]Randall B. Ripley and Grace A. Franklin, *Congress, the Bureaucracy and Public Policy*, (Homewood, Illinois: The Dorsey Press, 1976), 16.

[31]Lowi and Ginsburg, 610.

[32]Ripley and Franklin, 18.

[33]Ibid., 18.

[34]Robert W. Bailey, "Uses and Misuses of Privatization," *Prospects for Privatization*, Steve H. Hanke, ed., The Academy of Political Science, 1987, Proceedings, Vol. 36, No. 3, 138.

[35]Paul Starr, "The Limits of Privatization," *Prospects for Privatization*, Steve H. Hanke, ed., The Academy of Political Science, 1987, Proceedings, Vol. 36, No. 3, 124.

[36]David C. Saffell and Harry Basehart, *State and Local Government: Politics and Public Policies*, 8th ed., (New York, New York: McGraw Hill, 2005), 205.

[37]Peggy Fikac and Gary Scharrer, "State's Contract with Accenture Ending," *San Antonio Express-News*, (Wednesday, March 14, 2007), 8A.

[38]Ibid.

[39]Jack C. Plano and Milton Greenberg, *The American Political Dictionary*, 10th ed., (New York, New York: Harcourt Brace College Publishers, 1997), 390.

[40]Aaron Wildavsky and Naomi Caiden, *The New Politics of the Budgetary Process*, (New York, New York: Pearson Education Inc., 2004), 2.

[41]Peterson and Rasmussen, 184.

[42]Anderson, 42.

[43]Nelson Dometrius, "The Texas Policy Environment," *Texas Public Policy*, Gerry Riposa, ed., (Dubuque, Iowa: Kendall/Hunt, 1987), 18.

[44]Ibid.

[45]Sabtier and Mazmanian, "The Conditions of Effective Implementation: A guide to Accomplishing Policy Objectives," 346.

[46]Ibid., 384.

[47]Ibid., 381.

[48]Dometruis, "The Texas Policy Environment," 18.

[49]Anderson, 135.

[50]Peterson and Rasmussen, 200.

[51]Bland, et al., 332.

[52]Ibid., 331.

[53]Grier D. Stephenson, Jr., Robert J. Bresler, Robert J. Freidrich, and Joseph J. Karlesky, *American Government*, 2nd ed., (New York, New York: HarperCollins, 1992), 15.

[54]Leon Blevins, *Texas Government in National Perspective*, (Englewood Cliffs, New Jersey: Prentice-Hall, Inc., 1987), 317.

[55]*The HarperCollins Dictionary of American Government and Politics*, 290.

[56]Eugene Jones, Joe E. Ericson, Lyle C. Brown and Robert S. Trotter, Jr., *Practicing Texas Politics*, 8th ed., (Boston, Massachusetts: Houghton Mifflin Company, 1992), 428.

[57]Susan B. Hanson, "The Politics of State Taxing and Spending," *Politics in American States: A Comparative Analysis*, 5th ed., Virginia Gray, Herbert Jacob and Robert Albritton, eds., (Illinois: Scott/Forseman/Little Brown, 1990), 362.

[58]Wildavsky and Caiden, 228.

[59]Ibid., 190.

[60]Saffell and Basehart, 201-202.

[61]Ibid., 202.

[62]Bland, et al., 333.

[63]Ibid., 336.

[64]Jones, et al., 433.

[65]Nelson C. Dometrius, "Government Revenues and Expenditure Policy," *Texas Public Policy*, Gerry Riposa, ed., (Dubuque, Iowa: Kendall/Hunt, 1987), 33.

[66]Ibid., 34.

[67]Hanson, "The Politics of State Taxing and Spending," 348.

[68]Plano and Greenberg, 411.

[69]Ibid., 415.

[70]*State of Texas Annual Cash Report: Revenues and Expenditures of State Funds for the Fiscal Year Ended August 21, 2018*, 11.

[71]Ibid.

[72]Ibid.

[73]Ibid., 11.

[74]Ibid.

[75]Ibid., 14.

[76]Ibid., 15.

[77]Ibid.

[78]Ibid.

[79]Ibid., 3.

[80]Sergio Chapa, "2018 Comes to a Close with Declines in Stocks, Oil," *San Antonio Express News* (Tuesday, January 1, 2019), B4.

[81]Rye Druzin, "With Oil Down, Texas' Manufacturing Dips," *San Antonio Express News*, (Tuesday, January 1, 2019), B4.

Chapter 11

Texas Civil Liberties & Civil Rights

Signing of Civil Rights Act of 1964.
July 2, 1964
by Cecil Stoughton.
Photo credit: LBJ Library Photo

This was the first nation in the history of the world to be founded with a purpose. The great phrases of that purpose still sound in every American heart, North and South: "All men are created equal"—"government by consent of the governed"—"give me liberty or give me death." Well those are not just clever words, or those are not just empty theories. Those words are a promise to every citizen that he shall share in the dignity of man. This dignity cannot be found in a man's possessions; it cannot be found in his power, or in his position. It really rests on his right to be treated as a man equal in opportunity to all others. It says that he shall share in freedom, he shall choose his leaders, educate his children, and provide for his family according to his ability and his merits as a human being. To apply any other test—to deny a man his hopes because of his color or race, his religion or the place of his birth—is not only to do injustice, it is to deny America and to dishonor the dead who gave their lives for American freedom.[1]

President Lyndon B. Johnson, Joint Session of the United States Congress, 1965

In June 2003, national media attention was drawn to the predominately African-American small town of Tulia, nestled between Amarillo and Lubbock. In compliance with Governor Rick Perry's order, twelve African-American men were released from prison by a district judge pending a review of the charges and sentences levied against them in 1999 for drug possession, leaving only four of the original thirty-eight behind bars. Their saga begins with Thomas Roland Coleman, a member of the Panhandle Regional Narcotics Trafficking Taskforce, assigned undercover to apprehend drug dealers and users in the area surrounding Tulia. One by one he gathered enough "evidence" to eventually bring to trial and subsequently convict thirty-eight men including thirty-five African Americans. The majority of the defendants plea-bargained for lesser sentences, while others received 90-year prison terms. At first, few questioned Coleman's tactics or the validity of his testimony at each trial. After all, Coleman was the only witness for the prosecution. In 2000, Coleman was the recipient of the state's narcotics officer of the year award. Gradually, the credibility of Coleman's evidence and testimonies became highly suspect. Defense attorneys charged that Coleman either planted or just made up evidence against the accused. While on the witness stand, Coleman also lied about his own problems with the law. By his own admission, Coleman is a racist and had been overheard making racial statements. Coleman was not the only guilty party in Tulia during those trials. Each trial was heard by a jury of twelve men and women, presided over by a judge. Were these individuals completely overwhelmed by Coleman's expert testimony or were they themselves guided by their own preconceived prejudices against Tulia's African-American community?

Shortly after leaving a family gathering in the early morning of June 2, 1998, James Byrd, Jr., an African-American resident of Jasper, Texas, accepted a ride home from three Anglo men. Byrd never made it home. The following morning, law enforcement officials found "the badly mutilated remains of the 49 year-old black [African American] and a trail of blood. Deputies followed the dark red stains for a mile and found Byrd's head. Then his right arm. Another mile they found tennis shoes, a wallet, even his dentures. And then the trail ended, at the churned-up patch of grass strewn with empty beer bottles, a lighter bearing white supremacist symbols and a wrench set inscribed with the name 'Berry.'"[2] The official autopsy report revealed that "much of Byrd's skin was stripped and shredded, and he had numerous broken bones and his elbows, kneecaps, lower back and both heels were ground to the bone. Court documents said Byrd's face had been spray-painted black."[3] Officials reacted quickly by arresting and charging three men with first degree murder. All three were subsequently convicted with two receiving the death penalty and one a life sentence. The state's first hate crimes bill finally secured the blessing of both the Texas Legislature and the governor. Effective September 1, 2001, the **James Byrd, Jr., Hate Crime Bill** calls for stiffer criminal penalties for crimes prompted by racial hatred or bias against race, religion, color, sex, disability, age, or national origin.

In 1993, national media focused their lenses upon the small predominately white East Texas community of Vidor, Texas. The racial relationship between the town's African-American and Anglo sections was more reminiscent of the Reconstruction era of the 1870s than the post civil rights period of the 1990s. Commentators were surprised to learn that African Americans had been historically bullied and threatened by white supremacists and Klan members from even thinking about moving into the city limits of Vidor. A constant reminder of "their place" was a sign reading "Nigger, Don't Let the Sun Set on You in Vidor."[4] For then Secretary of Housing and Urban Development

Henry Cisneros the problem was a federally funded low-income housing project built in the 1950s in the heart of Vidor's downtown whose residents were all Anglo. Since the majority of the African-American community had incomes qualifying them for the housing, Cisneros demanded immediate integration. He was, of course, met with defiance as federal agents had to recruit African Americans to move into the project.

At a 1988 surprise birthday party for their fellow officer, a cadre of state troopers from the Texas Department of Public Safety (DPS) decided to pull what they considered to be a harmless funny prank on the birthday boy. Eight Anglo officers dressed in traditional KKK attire including white robes, pointed hats and KKK emblems, danced around the honoree, State Trooper Darron Keith Anderson, an African American. "A rookie and the only black [African-American] officer in the Livingston office at the time, he suffered a nervous breakdown as a result of the birthday party and other acts of discrimination by co-workers, which he said included a racial slur."[5] The eight officers received suspensions.

In 1916, an all-Anglo jury in Waco, Texas, convicted 17-year-old African-American Jesse Washington of murdering Lucy Frayer, a 53-year old Anglo woman. The townspeople could not wait for the justice system to deliver Washington's punishment. "A mob seized Washington and dragged him to the town square. In front of more than 10,000 onlookers, Washington's attackers tore off his clothes, beat him, sliced off body parts with knives, hung him from a tree with a chain, and burned him to death. The body was then dragged through town until the head came off. Young boys extracted the teeth and sold them as souvenirs."[6]

Sadly, these incidents indicate a pattern of sustained racism that has and continues to divide our state and our nation. To the African-American and Hispanic communities, both the federal government and the state of Texas have failed to adequately address their needs. The frustration of a government moving too slowly to protect their guaranteed constitutional and statutory rights can be seen on their faces. The lofty words of the Declaration of Independence declaring that all men are created equal are meaningless when minorities are confronted with racial hatred, poverty, poor education, and the realization that one's plight will not be miraculously changed by simply casting a vote in an election. Our nation's first African-American president knows very well that once the euphoria of electoral victory faded, the focus and the burden was shifted to him to improve social, economic, and political conditions for the nation's minority populations.

Conversely, some Americans believe that an overzealous national government has become too powerful and arbitrary in granting civil rights to minorities, to the detriment of Anglo Americans. Socially conservative groups view the United States Supreme Court's ruling against mandatory school prayer and the federal laws prohibiting assault weapons as just two more examples of government narrowing the parameters of civil liberties. Although the majority of Anglo Americans support the concept of civil rights and liberties for all people and are themselves law-abiding citizens, a small group of white supremacists and militants have become extremely vocal and, in some instances, violent in venting their anger against government. The fear that government is systematically stripping away from them their "guaranteed" constitutional rights while granting preferential treatment and government protection to minorities, women, and immigrants has materialized into white backlash attacks against Affirmative Action, immigration, and social service programs. On April 19, 1995, a nine-story federal government building in Oklahoma City was blown apart, tragically killing 168 men, women and children. Timothy McVeigh, affiliated with predominately white-male state militia groups angry over the intrusion of government into their private lives and its perceived denial of their constitutionally granted civil liberties and rights, was convicted and executed for the Oklahoma City bombing,

The challenge before government at all levels is to protect the rights and privileges of all of its citizens. This would appear to be a simple charge for a country founded on the democratic principles of equality and freedom. However, racial tolerance, political equality, and social acceptability have eluded the American people for over 200 years. Men and women of diverse races, nationalities, and beliefs have endured and continue to battle racial discrimination, physical and verbal abuse, and threats, just to gain the rights to own property, receive an equitable education, hold a job at a decent wage, and vote. Although the United States Constitution's Bill of Rights guarantees freedom of speech, religion, and assembly, men and women have been branded as social outcasts, jailed, and even killed because their beliefs were unacceptable to others.

Equality is perhaps the most difficult policy issue confronting lawmakers today. The continual inability to achieve racial and gender equality is deeply embedded in the social, political, cultural and historical development of both the nation and this state. Particularly in the area of civil rights, government can pass laws mandating equality and provide sanctions against noncompliance. However, government cannot legislate attitude changes. Tragically, Texas has a dismal record in extending civil rights to *all* of its citizens. Although dramatic improvements have been made, Texas still must deal with racial and gender discrimination claims, ranging from employment and political abuses to police brutality.

The purpose of this chapter is to examine the scope of civil liberties and civil rights in Texas. Any discussion of rights cannot exclude the impact of the United States Constitution, the national government, and the United States Supreme Court in establishing the parameters for state actions. The Texas Legislature cannot enact any law that conflicts with the spirit and meaning of the United States Constitution. The quest for civil rights is a study of people. This chapter examines the cultural, social, political, and historical barriers that have traditionally denied equal treatment for the state's women and minority population groups. The struggle of these groups to achieve an equal place at the table indicates their determination to achieve social and political equality and economic viability. This chapter also examines the avenues lawmakers have taken to address these issues.

Civil Liberties

"Americans are much given to saying with pride—with more pride, perhaps than understanding—that they live under a government of laws and not a government of men. . . . What we really mean is that the men who wield power in the name of the public do so not arbitrarily or capriciously but in conformity with certain settled rules and certain fundamental standards of fairness. And we mean also that those who wield power are always subject to check and correction by other elements in the government."[7] Consequently, the Framers created a national government based on the principles of a democracy, guaranteeing fundamental rights to each citizen that could not be taken away by the arbitrary actions of government. **Civil liberties** encompass those inalienable rights "that belong to individuals by the nature of humanity and which cannot be taken away without violating that humanity."[8] In his *Second Treatise on Government*, John Locke declared that pursuits of life, liberty and property were inalienable rights. In the Constitution, the Framers changed Locke's selections to life, liberty and the pursuit of happiness. The first ten amendments, collectively known as the **Bill of Rights**, detail civil liberties guaranteed to each citizen. The Framers understood that protection of these rights was absolutely necessary to creating a democratic form of government. Furthermore, they ensured the permanency of these rights with the adoption of **Article VI**, commonly known as the **Supremacy Clause**, making the Constitution the supreme law of the land. Consequently, any national and state law or local ordinance that conflicts with the spirit and meaning of the Constitution is an illegal and unconstitutional act.

However, the Framers never intended for these civil liberties to be absolute rights. **Individual liberty**, defined as "the condition of being free from restrictions or constraints," does conflict with the collective spirit of the community.[9] Fearful of the problems that would arise from the unrestrained pursuit of democracy, the Framers opted to curtail an individual's absolute civil liberties in hopes of creating a harmonious unified community. Consequently, they rationalized that "if we were to live in a truly 'civil' society we must agree to respect the rights of others and subject our activities to reasonable restrictions enacted for the good of society."[10] Basically, **reasonable restrictions** are the logical and rational curtailments enacted by government upon the absolute unrestrained pursuit of inalienable rights in order to guarantee the protection of those rights to all members of a civil society. Religious freedom is not an absolute right to do anything one wants to do in pursuit of this freedom. The belief, however, is a protected right. One cannot be arrested because his/her religious beliefs are socially unacceptable. Yet, one can be arrested when his/her pursuit of those religious beliefs breaks a law or causes harm to other individuals or to their property. Freedom of speech ceases to be an absolute right when one's words become "fighting words" leading to a "clear and present danger" to others. These are logical, reasonable restrictions on civil liberties.

In most instances, the determination of what constitutes reasonable restrictions is not absolutely clear cut. For example, the Second Amendment guarantees the right to bear arms. Yet, this amendment does not define what an acceptable weapon is, nor does it specify under what conditions it can be legally used. What is reasonable bail? What constitutes a fair trial? Under what conditions can a witness declare protection from prosecution under the Fifth Amendment? What is cruel and unusual punishment?

The interpretation of the intent of the Framers in crafting the Bill of Rights has been a topic of discussion for legal experts, judges and lawmakers ever since these ten amendments were added to the Constitution. Basically, the Framers never provided either in the document itself or through individual writings, clear-cut definitions and guidelines for legislating and subsequently enforcing reasonable restrictions on civil liberties. If we see this omission as an oversight on their part then we cannot overlook that "the Constitution of the United States itself, the supreme law of the land, was framed by mortal men. Ordinary mortals legislate in Congress, administer the laws in the executive branch of the government, and interpret the laws in the judicial branch. These laws were not delivered to us on tablets from Mount Sinai; they are not self-executing; and they are inevitable conflicts about the application and construction of them."[11]   Perhaps their omission was purposeful, leaving the establishment of the parameters to future generations of lawmakers and jurists seeking to meet the changing needs of the American people:

[S]hould we not pay the authors [the Framers] the compliment of believing that they meant no more than they said? What they left unsaid, they left open for us to decide. What then are the judges looking for, if it is not the intent of those who made the Constitution? . . . The Constitution has become something in its own right. It is an integral part of what men do with it. It has long ceased to be more than what other men hoped they would do or intended them to do. The Constitution, together with the Court's work, is not so much pushed by the plans of the past as pulled by the hopes of the future. It is not stuffed, but pregnant with meaning. The intent of the Framers when it is not expressed is only that we, the Congress, the President, and the Court, should be allowed to make good on their best hopes and cash in on their boldest bets. What our forefathers said, they said. What they didn't say, they meant to leave to us, and what they said ambiguously, indefinitely, equivocally, or indistinctly, is in so far not said.[12]

Beginning with the **Judiciary Act of 1789**, the interpretation of the intent of these amendments and the establishment of reasonable restrictions has been left to the federal court system, through the use of judicial review. The power of **judicial review** "authorizes the United States Supreme Court to hold unconstitutional, and hence unenforceable, any law or official action based upon a law, and any other action by a public official that is deems— upon careful reflection and in line with the inherent tradition of the law and judicial restraint—to be in conflict with the Constitution."[13]   However, the problem confronting state lawmakers is that each new panel of jurists has its own interpretations as to the meaning and application of those civil liberties and rights granted by the Bill of Rights. The death penalty, for example, was ruled unconstitutional in 1972 by the United States Supreme Court as a violation of the Eighth Amendment's protection

against cruel and unusual punishment. Each state had to comply by changing the sentences of death row inmates to life in prison. In 1976, the Court reversed its decision, and the death penalty was reinstated. Although judicial review was designed to protect the erosion of civil liberties by government, the lack of consistency in United States Supreme Court rulings often baffles and confuses state lawmakers.

The initial question confronting the United States Supreme Court was whether the provisions of the Bill of Rights was enforceable only upon the national government or all levels of government. In **Barron v Baltimore** (1833), Chief Justice John Marshall ruled that the first ten amendments were indeed enforceable only on the national government by pointing out that "the Constitution was ordained and established by the people of the United States for themselves, for their own government, and not for the government of the individual states. . . . The powers they conferred on this government were to be exercised by itself; and the limitations on power, if expressed in general terms are . . . necessarily applicable to the government created by the instrument. They are limitations of power granted in the instrument itself; not of distinct governments framed by different persons and for different reasons."[14] Besides, all of the original states had adopted their own state constitutions embodying their own civil liberties and civil rights prior to the adoption of the United States Constitution, which in some instances, granted more rights to their citizens than the national government.

The passage of the Fourteenth Amendment with its provisions of equal protection and due process paved the way for the United States Supreme Court to reverse Marshall's decision. In **Gitlow v New York** (1935), Gitlow challenged the ruling of the New York State Supreme Court to declare his use of the *Communist Manifesto* in his class lectures as subversive and unconstitutionally protected speech. Not only did the Supreme Court uphold his conviction as a case of "clear and present danger," it clearly stated that "for present purposes we may and do assume that freedom of speech and of the press which are protected by the First Amendment from abridgment by Congress are among the fundamental personal rights and liberties protected by the due process clause of the Fourteenth Amendment from impairment by the States.[15]   Currently, the United States Supreme Court has not tied all of the ten amendments of the Bill of Rights to all levels of government. Instead, they have opted to use a piece-meal practice known as **selective incorporation**.   Basically, the justices have selectively applied the Fourteenth Amendment's due process clause to bind the states to the Bill of Rights whenever the constitutional issue before them suits their interests.

The Bill of Rights is portrayed as a document granting sweeping civil liberties to all Americans. Initially, these rights and privileges were granted to a small segment of the population. The freedom of expression through the ballot box was initially extended to only Anglo male property owners until the election of Andrew Jackson to the White House. Native Americans were declared citizens of foreign nations and not subject to the protections of the Bill of Rights until they were finally granted citizenship and voting privileges in 1924. Until the passage of the Thirteenth Amendment, slaves and indentured servants were not considered to be citizens. They too were excluded from the protective embrace of the Bill of Rights. In most instances, women were prohibited from owning property and denied voting privileges until the passage of the Nineteenth Amendment to the United States Constitution and a cadre of legislative acts at both the state and federal levels reversing these inequities. It has taken years of corrective legislation to provide inclusive rather than exclusive protection of civil liberties.

The Importance of the First Amendment

The **First Amendment** to the United States Constitution is the embodiment of the principles guiding the Framers in creating a democratic government for this country. The amendment states that "Congress shall make no law respecting an establishment of religion, or prohibiting the free exercise thereof; or abridging the freedom of speech, or of the press; or the right of the people peaceable to assemble, and to petition the government for a redress of grievances." This amendment addresses the fundamental civil liberties granted to the American people.

Freedom of Religion

The phrase "Congress shall make no laws respecting the establishment of religion" is called the **establishment clause**. The Framers did not want government to be in a position to sponsor one religious belief over others or to advocate one religious practice over other practices. The Framers justified their actions by emphasizing the problems the English government historically had when it sponsored one state religion over other beliefs, and the horrible loss of life and property resulting from religious conflicts. "The bitter memories of religious intolerance suffered by American colonists before coming to America can be seen in a 1774 statement issued by the First Continental Congress, declaring that the Church of England was ". . . a religion that has deluged [England] in blood, and dispersed

bigotry, persecution, murder, and rebellion through every part of the world."[16] The tendency for one religious group to believe that their teachings and practices should take preeminence over other beliefs and practices has led to religious conflicts and a breakdown of religious tolerance. The Framers separated church or religious issues from government thus creating the **separation of church and state doctrine**. United States Supreme Justice Hugo Black once wrote that the First Amendment's Establishment Clause meant that:

Neither a state nor the Federal Government can set up a church. Neither can pass laws which aid one religion, aid all religions, or prefer one religion over another. Neither can force nor influence a person to go to or to remain away from church against his will or force him to profess a belief or disbelief in any religion. No person can be punished for entertaining or professing religious beliefs or disbeliefs, for church attendance or nonattendance. No tax in any amount, large or small, can be levied to support any religious activities or institutions, whatever they may be called, or whatever form they may adopt to teach or practice religion. Neither a state or the Federal Government can, openly or secretly, participate in the affairs of any religious organization or groups and vice versa. In the words of Jefferson, the clause was intended to erect a wall of separation between Church and State.[17]

The choice of one's religious beliefs and practices rests with the individual, not the government.

The United States Supreme Court has become the champion for ensuring that the fragile wall separating church from state is still intact as well as preserving an individual's right to hold diverse religious beliefs and practices without recrimination. The guidelines for subsequent religious-based questions were established in the Court's ruling in **Lemon v Kurtzman** (1971). The *Lemon* case involved two issues of state funding for private schools. The Pennsylvanian case involved the allocation of state funds to private schools for textbooks, instructional materials, and teachers' salaries for nonreligious-based classes such as history, English, and math. The Rhode Island case questioned the legality of the state legislature giving a 15 percent pay increase to private school teachers in nonreligious-based subject fields. The Court ruled both of these programs unconstitutional violations of the exercise clause. Coined the **Lemon Test**, "a statute is constitutional under the establishment clause if (1) it has a secular legislative purpose, (2) its principal or primary effect neither advances nor inhibits religion, and (3) it does not foster excessive governmental entanglement with religion."[18]

The United States Supreme Court has addressed the issue of whether federal funds used to promote education in both public and private schools is a violation of the doctrine of separation of church and state. In ***Everson v Board of Education of the Township of Ewing*** (1947), the issue involved a New Jersey state law that provided public funding to children in low-income families to offset the costs of using the public transportation system to and from both public and private schools. Everson challenged the constitutionality of the law under the grounds that giving federal funds to a private religious-based school violated the wall separating church from state. The Court ruled 5-4 in favor of the program by basing their decision on the **child benefit theory** whereby public funding could be provided to students who attend both public and private or parochial schools as long as the funding benefits the child, not the school. Justice Black stressed that the New Jersey law "does no more than provide a general program to help parents get their children, regardless of their religion, safely and expeditiously to and from accredited schools."[19] President Lyndon Johnson alluded to the child benefit theory when he signed into law the Elementary and Secondary Education Act of 1965, bringing the first major infusion of federal money into the nation's public and private schools. In ***Mitchell v Helms*** (2000), the Court once again applied the child benefit theory by upholding a Louisiana state law providing public funds to public and private or parochial schools for the purpose of instructional equipment including maps, books, computers, and learning-based software. In another ruling, the Court upheld at 1977 Arizona state law giving a tax credit of up to $500 to individuals making monetary donations to private and parochial tuition assistance and scholarship programs.

The Texas Legislature has joined the ranks of other state legislative houses in advocating school voucher programs allowing students to attend the private, public, or parochial schools of their choice. The vouchers are both private and government cash payments to the parents to cover the costs of tuition, transportation, textbooks, and, in some instances, school supplies and uniforms. With few exceptions, state courts ruled against government-funded vouchers particularly to private and parochial schools as a violation of the separation of church and state doctrine. The test case before the United States Supreme Court centered on a pilot voucher program used in Cleveland, Ohio. Ohio's state legislature enacted a law that "gave parents $2,250 per child in tuition vouchers to be used in about 50 schools."[20] A lower federal court had initially ruled that the Ohio voucher system was unconstitutional since it "has the effect of advancing religion through government-sponsored religious indoctrination."[21] The United States Supreme Court reversed the lower federal court's ruling by declaring that the "Ohio program is entirely neutral with respect to religion."[22] Supporting the majority, Justice Sandra Day O'Connor stated she was "persuaded that the Cleveland voucher program affords parents of eligible children genuine non-religious options consistent with separation of church and state protections."[23] In other words, the Court applied the child benefit theory in rendering their decision.

Perhaps the most controversial religious issue addressed by the United States Supreme Court is school prayer. In 1962 and 1963, the Court heard two cases challenging government-sponsored religious activities in the public schools. School districts are considered special governing units since they enact policy, set tax rates, collect taxes, and are administered by elected boards. In ***Engle v Vital*** (1962), Steven Engle challenged a 1951 decision of the New York Board of Regents to approve a brief prayer for recital in the public school system. In 1958, the New Hyde Park School District adopted the prayer, requiring students to recite it each day in every class. Engle objected to having his two children recite the prayer on the grounds that it violated their freedom of religion, and compromised the doctrine of separation of church and state. The United States Supreme Court ruled eight to one in Engle's favor. Justice Black wrote "that by using its public school system to encourage recitation of the Regent's prayer, the State of New York has adopted a practice wholly inconsistent with the Establishment Clause. There can, of course, be no doubt that the New York's program of daily classroom invocation of God's blessing as prescribed in the Regents' prayer is a religious activity. It is a solemn avowal of divine faith and supplication for the blessing of the Almighty . . . [The] Constitution's prohibition against laws respecting an establishment of religion must at least mean that in this country it is no part of the business of government to compose official prayers for any group of the American people to recite as part of a religious program carried on by government."[24] The companion case was the ***Abington School District v Schempp*** (1963). In this case, a Pennsylvania law required the verbal reading of ten verses from the Bible at the beginning of each school day in all public schools. Children could be excused with parental consent. The Schempp family objected to the readings because their Unitarian faith does not interpret the meaning of the Bible in the same manner as other religions. They also felt that their children were the subject of ridicule by their fellow classmates because they were sent out into the hallway during the readings. Ruling 8 to 1 in favor of Schempp, the Court felt the biblical readings constituted a religious ceremony, an unconstitutional act in the public schools. In both cases, the Court never ruled that voluntary prayer was unconstitutional in the public schools. However, requiring involuntary compliance of advocacy of one's religious belief over other religious beliefs (Schempp) and the promotion of one's religious practice over other practices (Engle) by a governing body were unconstitutional actions violating the separation between church and state.

Since ruling in the *Engle* and *Schempp* cases, the Court continues to hear cases involving prayer in the public school systems. In **Wallace v Jaffree** (1985), the primary issue was an 1981 Alabama state law mandating that "at the commencement of the first class of each day in all grades in all public schools the teacher in charge of the room in which each class is held, may announce that a period of silence not to exceed one minute in duration shall be observed for meditation or voluntary prayer, and during such period no other activities shall be engaged in."[25] The constitutionality of the law was challenged by a parent on behalf of his children. A federal district judge ruled that the activity was constitutional. However, the federal appellate court overturned this ruling, opting instead to rule the state law unconstitutional. The United States Supreme Court affirmed the appellate court's decision. Justice Paul Stevens wrote that the legislation was "enacted for the sole purpose of expressing the State's endorsement of prayer activities for one minute at the beginning of each school day. The addition of 'or voluntary prayer' indicates that the State intended to characterize prayer as a favored practice. Such an endorsement is not consistent with the establishment principle that the government must pursue a course of complete neutrality toward religion."[26]

The constitutionality of student-led prayer at high school graduation ceremonies was addressed by the Court in 1992. In **Lee v Weisman**, the Court ruled that this practice was constitutional only "if school officials instructed students to keep them [the prayers] non-sectarian and non-proselytizing."[27] Texas high school football is teeming with decades-old traditions of cheerleaders, bands, the playing of the national anthem, and, of course, the pre-game prayer. The Court tackled the constitutionally of student-led pre-game prayers in a case involving the Santa Fe School District. In a 6-3 decision, the Court dealt a fatal blow to the traditional pre-game prayer. Once again, their decision hinged on the involuntariness of the pre-game prayer since members of the audience, regardless of their religious beliefs or practices, were asked to stand during the prayer. Traditionally, the United States Supreme Court has held steadfast in its belief that voluntary prayer is legal but involuntary prayer is not. In 2001, the Court upheld a lower court's ruling that Virginia's moment of silence law was constitutional. The justices believed that the Virginia law met the Court's criteria since it is "a moment of silence law that is clearly drafted and implemented so as to permit prayer, mediation, and reflection within the prescribed period, without endorsing one alternative over the others . . . . [because it does] not favor the child who chooses to pray over the child who chooses to meditate or reflect."[28]

Various forms of religious practices are constitutional as long as these activities are lawful and do not violate the personal rights or property of others. In **Church of Lukumi Babbalu Aye v Hialeah** (1993), the Court ruled that animal sacrifices in a religious ceremony are constitutional. However, not all religious practices garner the support of the Court. In 1862, the Court ruled in **Reynolds v United States** that the Mormon Church's practice of polygamy was not a protected constitution right. The polygamy issue resurfaced again in a case involving a Utah Mormon who had five wives and 28 children. He was convicted on all four counts of bigamy.

During the 2007 legislative session, the Texas Legislature passed two significant pieces of legislation that could possibly be challenged in the courts. The Religious Viewpoints Anti-Discrimination Act "requires public school districts to adopt policies specifically allowing spontaneous religious expression by students. A so-called model policy included in the law states that upperclassmen who are student leaders—such as council officers or the captain of the football team—should be designated as speakers. . . The new law creates a limited open forum that gives students the opportunity to speak about religious issues. If a student speaks at a sports event, a school assembly or graduation ceremony elects to express a religious viewpoint while addressing an otherwise permissible topic, school officials must treat the religious content the same as they would the secular content."[29] The law does not sanction prayer, only religious expression. However, the legislation does not cover whether students with opposing religious viewpoints would be given the opportunity to address the same audience. Another law directs the State Board of Education to include a Bible course as an elective in all state-supported public schools. The legislature felt that by offering the course as an elective, it would not be offensive to others since with parental consent, students would be able to take the course.

Pledges of Allegiance

The Texas Legislature passed in 2003 a law mandating that the Pledge of Allegiance to both the United States and Texas flags be recited by every student in the state's public school system at the start of each class day, and a 2007 law amending the Texas Pledge of Allegiance to include the words "under God." The Texas Legislature was reacting to a 2002 decision by the 9th Federal Circuit Court of Appeals that the use of the word "God" in the Pledge of Allegiance to the United States flag was an unconstitutional violation of the separation of church and state doctrine. Originally written in 1892 by Rev. Francis Bellamy, the pledge included the phrase "one nation indivisible with liberty and justice for all." The phrase "under God" was added in 1954 by an executive order issued by President Dwight Eisenhower during the height of the cold war. Voting against the wording of the present pledge, Federal Circuit Judge Alfred Goodwin stressed that "leading school children in a pledge that says the United States is 'one nation under God' is as objectionable as making them say 'we are a nation under Jesus,' a 'nation under Vishnu,' or 'a nation under no god,' because none of these professions can be neutral with respect to religion."[30] Public out-cry against the ruling prompted the federal court to put the decision on hold pending further review. On June 14, 2004, the United States Supreme Court reversed the ruling of the federal appellate court. However, "the majority of the justices declined to decide the issue of the pledge's constitutionality. Instead, the justices decided the case on a dubious technicality, ruling that the adult plaintiff in the case had no right or 'standing' to sue."[31] Actually, the pledge received a reprieve since the issue could come before the Court again if a plaintiff comes forward that does have the right to pursue it. Consequently, the United States Congress has continuously introduced without success a constitutional amendment guaranteeing the right to use the word "God" in the pledge.

Freedom of Speech

The right to express one's opinions is a sacred privilege to Americans. Although we may not like what some people say and do, we respect their rights to express their viewpoints. Any government action slightly resembling censorship is met with sharp criticism. However, we do not have the absolute right to say or do whatever we want to do. The United States Supreme Court has distinguished protected speech from unconstitutional utterances. **Pure speech** is "speech without any conduct."[32] A person's words are

constitutionally protected as long as those words do not pose harm to others. The Court distinguished acceptable from unacceptable speech by its ruling in **Schenck v United States** (1917). Schenck had been convicted in a lower court of violating the Espionage Act of 1917 by distributing Socialist-inspired leaflets encouraging men to resist the World War I draft. Ruling unanimously against him, the Court ruled that Schenck's actions created a **clear and present danger** to others. Justice Holmes wrote:

> We admit that in many places and in *ordinary times* the defendants in saying all that was said in the circular would have been within their constitutional rights. *But the character of every act depends upon the circumstances in which it is done . . .* The most stringent protection of free speech would not protect a man in *falsely* shouting "fire" in a theater and causing a panic. It does not even protect a man from an injunction against uttering words that have all the effects of force. . . . *The question in every case is whether the words used are in such circumstances and are of such a nature as to create a clear and present danger that they will bring about the substantive evils that Congress has a right to prevent.* When a nation is at war many things that might be said in time of peace are such a hindrance to its effort that their utterance will not be endured so long as men fight and that no Court could regard them as being protected by any constitutional right.[33]

Unconstitutionally protected, **fighting words** are words that by their very nature inflict injury upon those to whom they are addressed. For example, an individual speaking out against injustice is using his constitutional right to freedom of speech. However, if that same speaker calls a police officer a derogatory name and incites the crowd to attack the police officer, the speaker's words have ceased to be constitutional and become fighting words, thus creating a clear and present danger. The speaker can now be held accountable for the violent reactions of the audience.

Symbolic speech is "the use of symbols, rather than words, to convey ideas."[34] The majority of the symbolic speech cases emerged from protests in the 60s and 70s over the nation's involvement in Vietnam. In **Tinker v Des Moines School District** (1969), several high school students were suspended for wearing black arm bands as a symbolic silent protest against the war. The United States Supreme Court viewed the students' actions as protected constitutional speech that did not create a clear and present danger. In **Cohen v California** (1971), once again the Court ruled in favor of the protester. Cohen was cited for wearing a jacket bearing a four-letter word against the draft. However, the Court did take a dim view of burning government documents such as draft cards. In **United States v O'Brien** (1968), O'Brien's conviction of destroying his draft card as a protest against the Vietnam conflict was upheld.

The burning of the American flag was also used as a sign of protest in the 60s and 70s. The Court consistently ruled that these actions were indeed protected speech. In **Street v New York** (1969), the Court overturned a lower court's conviction of Street for destroying the American flag burned in protest over the 1960 ambush shooting of James Meredith, the first African-American student to enroll at the University of Mississippi. During the 1984 Republican National Convention held in Dallas, Gregory Johnson headed a political protest against President Reagan. Following a march, Johnson soaked an American flag in kerosene and set it on fire. None of the bystanders were physically injured. Johnson was arrested for the desecration of the flag, convicted of a Class A misdemeanor, sentenced to one year in prison, and fined $2,000. The Texas Court of Criminal Appeals overturned the conviction on the grounds that flag burning was protected by the First and Fourteenth Amendments to the United States Constitution. The state of Texas asked the United States Supreme Court to reverse this ruling, citing a threat of clear and present danger as well as upholding statutes against destroying a national symbol. In a 5-4 decision, the Supreme Court held that Johnson's actions were constitutionally protected. In addition, the presumption of clear and present danger was not sufficient grounds to arrest Johnson. Stressing that burning the American flag is not socially acceptable, Justice Brennan wrote:

> Our decision is a reaffirmation of the principles of freedom and inclusiveness that the flag but reflects, and of the conviction that our toleration of criticism such as Johnson's is a sign and source of our strength. We do not consecrate the flag by punishing its desecration, for in doing so we dilute the freedom that this cherished emblem represents."[35]

The exercise of freedom of speech is also unconstitutional when it is used to deliberately harm the character and reputation of another person. **Slander** is verbal malicious attacks against another person. **Libel**, however, is defamation in print or by other visual presentations. The reasonable restrictions involving slander and libel revolve around the intent of the initiating party. In 1964, the United States Supreme Court addressed the issue in **New York Times v Sullivan**. A police commissioner from Montgomery, Alabama, Sullivan was initially awarded $500,000 in damages by a lower court to settle his suit against the *New York Times* for printing an advertisement containing false statements charging his police force with brutality against African Americans. The United States Supreme Court reversed the lower court ruling on the grounds that (a) public officials are naturally expected targets of verbal and printed attacks; (b) erroneous statements are often unavoidable; and (c) "even false statements about official conduct, therefore, enjoy constitutional protection, unless they were made with 'actual malice,' that is, with the knowledge that they were false or with a reckless disregard of whether or not they were false."[36] Basically, the mere printing of false statements is not libel unless those statements were printed with a reckless disregard for the truth and for the purpose to maliciously harm the reputation of an individual.

With its free accessibility to and the amenity it affords, the internet and the cell phone have given individuals the perceived constitutionally protected right to say whatever they wish to say about anyone. Unfortunately, this has led to a new word in our vocabulary—cyberbullying. The intensity of the cruel, hostile and humiliating text messages and emails have caused the victims of these attacks to violently act out or more tragically commit suicide. It is a nationwide problem. Yes, the actions of the person(s) texting these horrible messages is wrong. Can the text message itself be considered slander and consequently, challenged in the courts as a civil damage lawsuit? Furthermore, if the target of the messages commits suicide, can the sender of the messages be held criminally liable for the person's death? Currently, there is no federal law addressing cyberbullying. Every state, however, has passed some type of law or policy regarding bullying. The bulk of these laws place the responsibility of monitoring bullying in public and private schools as well as colleges and universities at the feet of school/college administrators. During the 85th Legislative Session, the Texas Legislature passed and the governor signed into law Senate Bill 179. The law is named after David Molak, a 16-year old student from Alamo Heights High School in San Antonio, who was so subjected to intense cyberbullying from his classmates that he committed suicide. The law classifies any act of cyberbully as a misdemeanor offense. According to David's Law, school districts are now required to include an anti-cyberbullying statement in their student policies, notify parents if their child is a victim of cyberbullying, develop an anonymous reporting system, conduct the appropriate investigations, discipline or expel students participating in cyberbullying, and report the incident to law enforcement. The Texas law also places blame on those parents who knew their children were cyberbully but did nothing to stop it.

Obscenity

If art is in the eyes of the beholder, the same standard applies to what is or is not obscene. According to the United States Constitution, we have the freedom to express ourselves. Paintings, motion pictures, advertisements, dance, sculpture, literature, and so on, are modes of expression. Judging a work as art or obscenity should be a personal choice. However, far too often it is the courts that must, once again, determine reasonable restrictions. In *Roth v United States* (1957), Justice Brennan drew the line between constitutionally and unconstitutionally protected creative expression:

> The first Amendment was not intended to protect every utterance. . . . The protection given speech and press was fashioned to assure unfettered interchange of ideas for the bringing about of political and social changes desired by the people. All ideas having even the slightest redeeming social importance— unorthodox ideas, controversial ideas, even ideas hateful to the prevailing climate of opinion—have the full protection of the guaranties unless excludable because they encroach upon the limited area of more important interests. But implicit in the history of the First Amendment is the reject of obscenity as utterly without redeeming social importance. . . . We hold that obscenity is not within the area of constitutionally protected speech or press.[37]

In its decision in *Miller v California* (1973), the Court ruled that actions or items can be deemed obscene only if they meet all three of the following criteria:

1) Whether the average person, applying contemporary community standards, would find that the work, taken as a whole, appeals to prurient interest.
2) Whether the work depicts or describes, in a patently offensive way, sexual conduct specifically defined by the applicable state law.
3) Whether the work, taken as a whole, lacks serious literary, artistic, political or scientific value.[38]

Reasonable restrictions means that the personal possession of obscene materials by an adult of an adult is a protected right. However, the sale and distribution of sexually explicit materials to minors is a crime. Child pornography is a crime. Erotic dancing by an adult is a form of expression protected by the First Amendment. The distinction between legal and illegal actions in obscenity cases is usually determined by the age of the participant.

Freedom of the Press

A free press is essential to democratic governments. Citizens have the right to know what their government is doing. The United States Supreme Court has protected the sanctity of the Fourth Estate, the press. In 1931, the Court established the boundary of "**no prior restraint**" in its decision in *Near v Minnesota*. The only time government can legally "stop the presses" from publishing a story is when such actions would pose an imminent threat to national security. For example, it would have been a threat to national security for the press to publish the exact timing of the dropping of nuclear weapons upon Japan during World War II before the action occurred. It is not a breach of national security to publish this information after the fact.

The concept of no prior restraint was held to close scrutiny when the Court heard arguments in *New York Times v United States* (1971). The case revolved around the actions of Daniel Ellsberg, a temporary federal employee and anti-Vietnam war advocate who discovered a cache of secret government documents detailing the beginning of the United States' involvement in Vietnam. Collectively known as the Pentagon Papers, these documents revealed a conscious effort on the part of key national leaders to lie to the American public about the nation's initial involvement in Vietnam. Ellsberg voluntarily brought the documents to the *New York Times* and the *Washington Post*. Publishing the first excerpts from the documents, both papers were initially placed under a federal order not to continue. The federal government claimed that publishing these documents presented a present threat to national security, even though the United States was already heavily involved in Vietnam. The United States Supreme Court ruled against the federal government. Justice Black hailed the papers' actions for printing the documents by stating "in my view, far from deserving condemnation for their courageous reporting, the *New York Times*, the *Washington Post*, and other newspapers should be commended for serving the purposes that the Framers saw so clearly. In revealing the workings of government that led to the Vietnam War, the newspapers nobly did preciously that which the Framers hoped and trusted they would do."[39] The United States Supreme Court also ruled that the publication of an event that had already occurred was not a threat to national security. Ellsberg, however, was convicted of stealing government documents. Although we may not always like or agree with the articles published in our daily newspapers, censorship is a direct violation of freedom of the press.

Assembly and Association

In the aftermath of the tragedy of September 11, 2001, citizens and lawmakers alike were pushing the White House and Congress for legislation granting expanded authority for federal agencies to investigate, infiltrate, and identify members belonging to both international terrorist organizations and domestic-based interest groups hostile to the American government. With few exceptions, the international community was outraged and horrified as they watched the footage of three high-jacked planes plunging into the twin towers of the World Trade Center and the Pentagon. We, as a nation, have become more cautious of and alert to groups advocating anti-American sentiments. However, the Bill of Rights does give us the right to assemble in groups. And every American does have the right to associate with whomever he/she wants to as a protected right to freedom of speech and religion. Our history has been tainted by the actions of the Klan, the American Nazi Party, skinhead groups, and so on. However, the Framers never intended for government to legislate whether citizens can belong to certain groups. Sanctioning a person's membership in the PTA because their philosophy is socially and politically acceptable while arresting an individual for joining a white supremacist organization because their philosophy is socially and politically unacceptable, is unconstitutional. Also, the membership of a group cannot be arrested because the actions of a particular member created a threat to national security. For example, the anti-abortion movement is very vocal in condemning the actions of abortion providers. Subsequently, supporters of anti-abortion organizations have committed criminal acts against abortion clinics and their employees. However, it is the individuals directly involved and not the entire group membership of the organization that have been charged and convicted of criminal acts.

The Ku Klux Klan (KKK) has had its share of cases before both state and federal courts. For example, in 1969, Charles Brandenburg, a KKK leader, gave consent for a television station to film a Klan rally. The footage highlighted excerpts from Brandenburg's speech including

the statement that "if our President, our Congress, our Supreme Court, continues to suppress the white, Caucasian race, it's possible that there might have to be some revenge taken."[40] The state of Ohio convicted Brandenburg for violating the state's Criminal Syndicalism Act outlawing terrorism. In **Brandenburg v Ohio** (1969) the United States Supreme Court reversed Brandenburg's conviction based on the decision that they were "confronted with a statute [Ohio's Criminal Syndicalism Act] which, by its own words and as applied, purports to punish mere advocacy and to forbid, on pain of criminal punishment, assembly with others merely to advocate the described type of action. Such a statute falls within the condemnation of the First and Fourteenth Amendments."[41] In this case the mere advocacy of violence did not present a clear and present danger.

In 1978, the Supreme Court addressed the question of assembly in hearing the emotionally charged case **National Socialist Party v Village of Skokie**. Also known as the American Nazi Party, the National Socialist Party wanted to stage a public march through the predominately Jewish suburb of Skokie, Illinois. The majority of the townspeople were either survivors of or had lost relatives in the Nazi concentration camps during World War II. Residents were furious and petitioned their city council to deny the group a parade permit. A local judge and the Illinois state court upheld the city council's decision not to grant permission to the group on the grounds that this march would create a clear and present danger. The United States Supreme Court reversed the lower court ruling. Once again, a presumption of violence was not a valid reason to deny the march. The Court went a step further in this case by stating that the "use of the swastika is a symbolic form of free speech entitled to First Amendment protection. Its display on uniforms or banners by those engaged in peaceful demonstrations cannot be totally precluded solely because that display may provide a violent reaction by those who view it. Particularly is this true, where, as here, there has been advance notice by the demonstrators of their plans so that they have become, as complaint alleges, 'common knowledge' and those to whom be offended are forewarned and need not to view them."[42]

This decision was a reasonable restriction accommodating both parties. Although the Nazi Party opted to march in downtown Chicago rather than in Skokie, they retained their constitutional right to stage a public march. And, those who would have been offended by the march retrained their protected right not to watch! The Supreme Court has steadfastly stood behind its original ruling in the *Skokie* case. In a subsequent situation, a federal judge heard arguments concerning the right of the Aryan Nations to stage a march down the main street of Coeur d'Alene, Idaho. Fearful that the group's march would lead to violence, the city council decided to reroute the parade from the main street to back streets near a garbage dump. The Court ruled that the council's actions violated the Aryan Nation's rights to freedom of assembly under the First Amendment.

For decades, the statutes of Civil War Confederate generals and statesmen have been on public display in cities throughout the South. Many view these statues as reminders of the horrors of slavery. Public out cries have resulted in city councils, county officials, governors and university administrators to remove the statutes from public view. On August 12, 2017, a Unite the Right Rally was held in Charlottesville, Virginia in protest of city officials removing a statute of former confederate general Robert E. Lee. The protesting group was a montage of neo-confederates, neo-Nazis and Klan members. The rally turned violent with James Fields driving a car into the crowd killing Heather Heyer and injuring 19 other individuals. An additional 16 were injured by protesters on both sides of the protest, and two officers were killed in a helicopter crash. Those arrested were not arrested because of their views. They were arrested because their actions caused injury to others. Once again, words are constitutionally protected but violence motivated by those words is not.

Municipal governments across the state of Texas and the nation have attempted to curb juvenile gang activities by imposing curfew laws whereby unsupervised juveniles under a certain age are prohibited from being on city streets after a certain hour. Exceptions have been made for teens whose work hours or attendance at certain public events exceeds the legal time limit. Violators and/or their parents can be ticketed, fined, arrested, or even jailed. The United States Supreme Court gave sanction to curfew laws by ruling favorably in a case challenging a curfew ordinance enacted by the city council of Charlottesville, Virginia. However, the Court did not uphold the constitutionality of an anti-gang ordinance implemented in Chicago, Illinois. The ordinance mandated that the police breakup any gathering and possibly arrest individuals if "they stood or sat around in one place with no apparent purpose in the presence of a suspected gang member."[43] Justice Paul Stevens wrote that "the ordinance allowed the police to order people to move on without inquiring into their reasons for remaining in one place . . . It matters not whether the reason that a gang member and his father, for example, loiter near Wrigley Field is to rob an unsuspecting fan or just to get a glimpse of Sammy Sosa leaving the ballpark. Friends, relatives, teachers, counselors, or even total strangers might unwittingly engage in forbidden loitering if they happen to engage in idle conservation with a gang member."[44]

Often the potential fear of an organization's goals and objectives compels both the legislature and the courts to over react with repressive measures. The openness of the American lifestyle changed on September 11, 2001, as we watched the tragedy unfold at the World Trade Center. Americans were shocked and angered that their government did not do enough to prevent this terrorist attack. The collective "we" put pressure on both the president and Congress to apprehend and, subsequently, punish the responsible parties, identify and disband both domestic and foreign-based terrorist organizations, and protect this country from future attacks. The Bush administration responded with several key pieces of legislation leading to the creation of the Department of Homeland Security, a presidential cabinet-level position. However, questions persist and doubts are raised as to the impact these security measures have had and will continue to have on the meaning and exercise of civil liberties and personal rights protected by the United States Constitution.

The **Patriot Act** gives federal agents "more leeway to wiretap phones, lets investigators track e-mail and internet corrections, allows secret searches of terror suspects' property, enhances the ability of federal agencies to share data, includes legislation to fight international money laundering, and increases terror-related penalties."[45]

In time, however, the federal courts and, in particular, the United States Supreme Court may well dismantle the Patriot Act in the same manner as they did with the **Smith Act**. Passed in 1940, the Smith Act made it illegal to organize or knowingly become a member of any organization advocating by force or violence the overthrow of any United States government agency or branch. The primary targets of the legislation were the Communist Party and anyone sympathetic to socialist/communist ideology. The primary initiator of the "Red Scare," Senator Joseph McCarthy used the Smith Act to launch a "witch hunt" against anyone perceived to be unfaithful to the United States. Initially upholding key provisions of the act, the Supreme Court by 1957 began to gradually unravel it. Granting constitutional rights to others while denying those same rights to groups feared for their issues was, in itself, unconstitutional. Any attempt to narrow the meaning of constitutionally protected civil rights and liberties erodes the foundation of a democratic government. Gary Hart, a former U.S. senator and one-time presidential candidate, once commented that "I' don't think we will reach a perfect balance between security and liberty. We haven't done it in 225 years. That's why we have courts."[46]

The Second Amendment: The Right to Bear Arms

To survive the rigors and dangers of the American frontier, one had to be able to successfully defend oneself and protect one's property. The preferred weapons were the rifle and the handgun. Today, the majority of Texans own a weapon. Hunting is both a sport and a generational rite of passage. Joining the ranks of the National Rifle Association, many Texans hold the Second Amendment to the United States Constitution as their absolute protected right to own and use firearms. The amendment simply states that "a well-regulated militia being necessary to the security of a free State, the right of the people to keep and bear arms, shall not be infringed." The intent of this amendment has become one of the most contentious political and social issues dividing the American people. "Reflective liberals tend to want to ban all guns, and portray their owners as rednecks who don't seem to care that gangbangers and hate-mongers can get their hands on firepower. At the other extreme, entrenched gun lobbyists appear to believe that virtually any regulation is a threat to their constitutional rights."[47]

The strained tensions between the two camps came to a boiling point over the passage and subsequent implementation of the **Brady Bill**. Named for President Reagan's former press secretary, the Brady Bill requires a waiting period to enable law enforcement to conduct a background check on any individual seeking to purchase a handgun. The intent of lawmakers was to ensure that handguns were not sold to individuals with criminal records or documented mental deficiencies. The courts have never denied the right for law-abiding citizens to own weapons. However, the courts have backed federal legislation delineating the types of acceptable weaponry that can be purchased and used by private citizens. "No federal appellate court or the Supreme Court has ever ruled you can't put some limit on the Second Amendment."[48]

Horrific mass shootings in the nation's public schools, shopping centers and workplaces have compelled lawmakers across the country to revisit their state's gun possession laws. The Texas Legislature's response to the mass killings in the First Baptist Church in Sutherland Spring, and Santa Fe High School near Houston was to institute campus carry throughout the state's publicly funded colleges and universities. Only licensed handgun owners can carry a concealed weapon on these campuses. The logic is that the potential loss of life and injury to others can be minimized by a licensed gun owner taking defensive action.

Protection of Private Property

In *Democracy in America*, Alexis de Tocqueville observed that "in no other country in the world is the love of property keener or more alert than in the United States and nowhere else does the majority display less inclination toward doctrines which in any way threaten the way property is owned."[49] In Texas, property ownership is a sacred right dating to the Spanish land grant system. The United States Constitution addresses property rights in Article I, Section 10, known as the **contract clause**. This provision prohibits state government from passing laws that expand a debtor's right not to repay financial obligations and to back out of a contractual agreement. However, the contract clause does not give property owners the exclusive rights to do whatever they wish to do to their property. Once again, reasonable restrictions apply. In the 1880s, the United States Supreme Court ruled that contracts must contain reasonable police powers as a means of protecting the health, safety, welfare, and, in some instances, the morals of the general public. The Supreme Court upheld these property restrictions in *Home Building and Loan Association v Blaisdell* (1934). Therefore, it is reasonable for cities and counties to impose building codes and compliance inspections to protect the safety of both the homeowners and his/her neighbors. Ordinances can restrict the location of certain businesses such as sexually explicit establishments and liquor stores near public schools, and so on.

The United States Constitution through the Fourteenth Amendment gives all levels of government the power of **eminent domain** whereby private land can be confiscated by government for the promotion of the public good. However, the Constitution also recognizes that private property owners must be justly compensated for the loss of their property. All levels of government have used eminent domain as a means of building sports and convention arenas, highways and expressway systems, and urban development projects.

Civil Rights: Defined and Defended

"Although the Declaration of Independence had stipulated, as a self-evident truth, that 'all men are created equal,' it soon became obvious that in the words of George Orwell, "some men are created more equal than others."[50] Inequality and racial intolerance are not just American problems. The quest for **human rights**, that is, "the right of individuals and groups to be treated in humane ways and with respect for human dignity and personal well-being," is a centuries old dream that has yet to be fully realized.[51] The frustrating struggle of minorities and women finally to achieve an equal footing before their fellow mankind and the law continues to divide this country. The painful lesson of the turbulent and sometimes violent 1960s was the realization that laws alone will not make people of diverse cultures and races equal. Sadly, laws cannot change attitudes!

Collectively, **civil rights** are "the acts of government intended to protect disadvantage classes of persons or minority groups from arbitrary, unreasonable, or discriminatory treatment."[52] A series of civil rights laws passed by the United States Congress has identified protected classes: race, color, national origin, religion, sex, age, Vietnam veterans, and handicapped. A cornerstone of President Johnson's civil rights agenda was an attempt to reverse discriminatory practices through **affirmative action**, defined as the steps taken on the part of government to address previous incidences of discrimination particularly in the employment process. There are basically two major categories of discrimination. **De facto discrimination** is an undeliberate action that adversely impacts one group over another. For example, "white flight" in the 1960s and 1970s from downtown urban centers to the suburbs created racially segregated neighborhoods, primarily located in the central business districts of Texas's major cities. No laws or deliberate actions created this dramatic shift in migration patterns. However, **de jure discrimination** is a purposeful action to adversely impact one group over other groups. The question of whether the resulting discriminatory action was de jure or de facto usually arises over issues of legislative redistricting and reapportionment, single-member versus multi-member districts, school financing, housing, etc.

Either intended or unintended, discrimination does arise through the crafting and implementation of legislative acts. Both the Fifth and Fourteenth Amendments to the United States Constitution forbid both the national and state governments to deny to any person life, liberty, and property without due process of the law. "The concept of **due process** of the law and its application to our federal and state governments, is based on an extensive reservoir of constitutionally expressed and implied limitations upon governmental authority, ultimately determined by the judicial process, and upon those basic notions of fairness and decency which govern, or ought to govern, the relationships between rulers and ruled."[53] The courts usually determine a violation of due process as procedural and/or substantive breaches of equal treatment that created a discriminatory action. **Procedural due process** refers "to the manner in which a law, an ordinance, an adminristrative

practice or a judicial task is carried out"; and **substantive due process** refers to "the content or subject matter of a law or ordinance."[54] Laws must be equally enforced and violators must be held equally accountable. The body of cases dealing with civil rights violations is riddled with instances of unequal application of the law. Government at all levels is participating in discriminatory practices when in enforcing a law, they hold one individual more accountable than others. In matters arising over the context of a law, the primary issue is the vagueness of the meaning and interpretation and, ultimately, the application of that law. Unfortunately, some laws are so vague in context that people of common intelligence must guess as to their meaning and application. Basically, government cannot hold citizens accountable for obeying laws that are laden with vague operational definitions and provide inadequate guidelines for both those charged with obeying it and those charged with enforcing it. "In both the substantive and procedural due process concepts the judicial test of constitutionality or legality has become more or less the same: Is the governmental action 'arbitrary,' 'capricious,' 'unreasonable,' 'invidious,' 'irrelevant,' or 'irrational' either in context or procedure?"[55]

For example, in 1971, the United States Supreme Court heard arguments in *Coates v Cincinnati* that presented both procedural and substantive problems with a Cincinnati city ordinance. Dennis Coates was arrested with other protesters for violating this ordinance that made it illegal for three or more persons to assemble on any street corner, sidewalk or vacant lot and, thereby, conduct themselves in a manner annoying to persons passing by. The Court declared this ordinance unconstitutional for several reasons. First, the ordinance was procedurally unenforceable and too vague in substance. Without proper definition of what constituted "annoying behavior," both citizens and law enforcement officers were confused as to the differences between acceptable and unacceptable behavior. Individual interpretation leads to discrimination and unequal application of the law. Second, the ordinance was a direct violation of the right to assemble as guaranteed by the First Amendment to the United States Constitution. Once again, the power of judicial review rescued the citizen from unfair treatment.

State legislative houses also wrestle with providing the appropriate language and particularly the intent of a legislative item. During the 2019 Texas Legislative session, Democrat House member Joe Moody and Senate member Jose Rodriguez each pre-filed bills pertaining to a 'red flag' provision for gun ownership. On the surface, these two bills would address the possession of weapons by individuals who pose an obvious harm to the safety of others by "temporarily remove guns from people deemed dangerous by a judge."[56] A similar piece of legislature failed to win approval during the 2017 legislative session. The Rodriguez bill calls for a "red flag" for "evidence of substance abuse, the recent acquisition of firearms, ammunition or other deadly weapons, or making threats."[57] To cover a possible substantive due process problem, his bill would make "false reporting a criminal offense."[58] The bill still has a substantive due process problem because it does not clearly define what constitutes an abusive substance nor does it define what constitutes a threat or what identifies a person as dangerous. Also, the legislation does not address how long of a period of time can a judge legally ban someone from possessing a firearm. If one is deemed as dangerous, is it a lifetime ban or a ban effective until the person is judged to be no longer dangerous? And who determines whether or not a person is dangerous or subsequently, not dangerous to society? Without these precise definitions, the bill also has a procedural problem in that it would leave it up to the judge to determine whether or not the gun holder violated the law and therefore, must surrender his/her weapon and what timeframe would be appropriate to determine whether to return the weapon back to the gun owner.

The role of the United States Supreme Court particularly in the protection and promotion of civil rights is paramount to understanding the ground that has been made to eradicate racial prejudice and discrimination. "When the race controversy attained a degree of no longer ignorable public concern at the highest government level in the late 1940s, it was the judicial branch of the government, with the Supreme Court at its apex, which led the other branches in tackling the problem. While it probably did not lead eagerly or joyously, a people's rightful claims could no longer be ignored merely because the political, in particular the legislative branches, refused to become involved beyond the most cursory of levels, and in fact, consistently passed the problems on to the Court."[59] The 1960s civil rights movement actually began when the United States Supreme Court dismantled the concept of "separate but equal" in its ***Brown v Board of Education of Topeka, Kansas*** decision. The pattern seems to be that once the United States Supreme Court renders a landmark decision involving civil rights and liberties, it is the role of the legislative and executive branches to keep the momentum going by enacting the necessary corrective legislation.

The Roots of Prejudice

A learned behavior, **prejudice** is a "feeling or act of any individual or group in which a prejudgment about someone else or another group is made on the basis of emotion rather than reason."[60] Consequently, "prejudice is an unfavorable attitude towards people because they are members of a particular racial or ethnic group, and **discrimination** is an unfavorable action toward people because they are members of a particular racial or ethnic group."[61] Racism is the single most important problem confronting our nation today. This nation can hardly claim to be a melting pot when one group feels superior over others. This is not a unified country when minorities are targets of discriminatory racial slurs and stereotypical characterizations. This is not a cohesive society when women of all races are constantly reminded that they are less worthy than their male counterparts. For example, the cries for welfare and healthcare reform have been and probably will continue to be tainted with racial slurs and derogatory references against the nation's poverty-stricken minorities and, particularly, women. Despite the statistical evidence that the majority of the nation's poor are Anglos, welfare and health care are usually portrayed as "minority problems." The desire to shut down the shared borders between the United States and Mexico is oftentimes laden with racial comments and slurs against those illegal immigrants who are supposedly taking jobs away from native-born Americans. Of course, the majority of the jobs those legal and illegal immigrants are reportedly taking from Americans are the low-paying positions that most Americans would not want in the first place. Racism and prejudice have and will continue to divide rather than unite this nation.

The attitudes of racism and prejudice are deeply rooted in the history, culture, and traditions of all population groups. To some degree, racism has plagued every civilization on this planet. The most advanced civilizations including the Greeks and the Romans, used class distinctions, ethnic backgrounds, religious differences, and economic status to segregate one group from another. Although an advocate of democracy, even Aristotle "on the other hand was sure that all men possessed reason, but thought that the distinguishing mark of slaves was that they possessed only so much of the power of reason as to enable them to understand their masters, without being about to reason for themselves; and he concluded that manual workers ought not to participate in government on the grounds that their lives denied them the opportunity to cultivate the qualities essential to wisdom."[62] Unfortunately, Texas is well known for its own problems with racism and prejudice against African Americans, Hispanics, Native Americans, and women. As they crossed the United States border into Texas, Anglo American settlers brought with them their culture, farming and ranching skills, technology, and their long-held prejudices. Both T. R. Fehrenbach in his novel *Lone Star* and Arnoldo De Leon in *The Tejano Community 1836-1900* stress that the origin of the racism demonstrated by Anglo American settlers in Texas was a carryover from the sentiments passed to them through their ancestors who helped to create the original thirteen American colonies. According to De Leon:

> In actuality, such transgressions sprang from deeply rooted Anglo American attitudes. American responses to the native Tejanos were shaped by feelings against Catholics and Spaniards and antipathy to Indians and Negroes [African Americans]. Anti-Catholic sentiment and Hispanophobia had its origin in tracts in England in the mid-sixteenth century when propagandists, dissatisfied with the Roman Catholic Church, denounced the mass as blasphemous, the clergy for encouraging superstition, and the Pope for being anti-Christ. Since Spain was the most powerful of the Catholic nations and the self-proclaimed champion of Catholicism, Englishmen easily merged their Anti-Catholic and nascent Hispanic hatred. Political rivalry between England and Spain only exacerbated attitudes and soon the alleged atrocities inflicted by Spain against the New World natives begot a so-called Black Legend. Such prejudices arrived intact in North America where subsequent literary diatribes expanded upon them. Military conflict along the Georgia-Florida frontier and diplomatic animosity following the American Revolution abetted those feelings. Anglo-American immigrants to Texas carried those attitudes across the Sabine River. . . . The immigrants, then, did not arrive in Texas with open minds concerning the native Tejanos: their two-hundred-year experience with "different" peoples had so shaped their psyche that their immediate reaction was negative rather than positive. Most immigrants to Coahuila y Tejas, despite their honest, industrious habits, were racists. They had retained impressions acquired before their arrival in the state then reapplied and transposed those racial attitudes upon the native castas.[63]

These same beliefs were used against the Chinese who came to Texas to build the railroads, the Germans who were discriminated against during World Wars I and II because the United States was at war with their ancestral homeland (which few had never seen), and the Vietnamese who fled a war torn country to become successful fisherman on the Texas coast and also productive naturalized citizens. Texas laws and attitudes have not always been favorable to the changing role of women in American society. The gay and lesbian communities are confronted with discriminatory practices as state laws still place impediments to their chosen lifestyles. Basically, racism can be viewed from four concepts, namely, nativism, the superior/inferior explanation, the economic theory, and racial separation.

Nativism

The concept of **nativism** rests on the belief that only those born on the soil of their native country should be the ones to benefit from that birthright. For example, the first generation of English colonists to America believed that they were the "native" culture for this nation. These original immigrants began to serve as the **host culture** for subsequent immigrant groups. The United States Constitution recognizes the importance of nativism by mandating that any candidate for the presidency must be a "native born" citizen. The original English settlers developed their own class structure. On his travels across the country, Alexis de Tocqueville wrote: "the first that attracts attention, and the first in enlightenment, power, and happiness is the white [Anglo] man, the European, man 'par excellence,' below him comes the Negro [African American], and the Indian."[64] The host culture begins to exercise its perceived superior position by viewing other cultures as a threat to their economic viability and to the survival of the own culture and way of life.

The quest to preserve the "American way of life" began in the 1790s as Americans began to seek the means to secure and preserve their emerging traditions. Several state legislative houses entertained "English-only" laws and pressed the national government to initiate anti-immigration laws. "In the first flush of their new-found freedom, the Americans suspected that Catholics might be monarchist subversives and that immigrants from France might attempt to foment the kind of unrest that led to the French Revolution. These and other concerns about foreigners created a widespread xenophobia. The first federal laws concerning naturalization, passed in 1790, provided that 'any free white person' who had lived in the United States for 2 years could apply for citizenship. By implication, of course, Black slaves, Native Americans and indentured Whites were excluded as potential citizens. These laws also ruled out applicants who were not of 'good moral character.'"[65] It really did not matter what their country of origin was, every immigrant group that has crossed over a United States boundary line has suffered from some form of racial discrimination. In 1850, the Secret Order of the Star Spangled Banner was formed in New York. Under its new name, "The Order of United Americans," chapters were formed in every state, with 960 lodges in New York alone. The membership was limited to "only native-born male citizens of the Protestant faith, both of Protestant parents, reared under Protestant influence and not united in marriage with a Roman Catholic."[66] The height of the nativism movement was the formation of the Know-Nothing Party, a short-lived third party movement launched into the national scene in 1854. A grass-roots organization, the party began winning elections at the city, county, and state levels. In 1856, the party nominated Millard Fillmore in his first unsuccessful bid for the White House. When Sam Houston decided to resign his United States Senate seat in order to block Texas from joining the confederacy, he ran and won the governorship on the Know-Nothing Party label.

The same pattern occurred in early Texas as the Anglo-American settlers began to establish a dominating foothold onto the territory. As early as 1835 Stephen F. Austin vowed "that Texas should be effectually, and fully Americanized—that is—settled by a population that will harmonize with their neighbors in the *East*, in language, political principles, common origin, sympathy and even interest. . . . I wish a great immigration from Kentucky, Tennessee, *every where*, passports, or no passports, *any how*. For fourteen years I have had a hard time of it, but nothing shall daunt my courage or abate my exertions to complete the main object of my labors – to *Americanize Texas*."[67] Within a relatively short period of time, the Spanish/ Mexican traditions and culture that had served as the host culture for over three hundred years, had been simply superseded by a new host culture—Anglo American.

Superior/Inferior Explanations

Closely aligned with nativism, the **superior/inferior concept** of racism is the belief that one group or culture is intellectually, genetically, and culturally superior to any other group. In *Mein Kampf*, Adolph Hitler outlined his desires to create a superior Aryan nation composed of three groups: "the culture-creating Aryan race; the culture-bearing races which can borrow and adopt but cannot create; and the culture-destroying race, namely, the Jews."[68] In Hitler's world, the Aryan race had a moral obligation to remove that group that would eventually destroy their culture—the Jews. The superior/inferior

concept is the cornerstone of white supremacy groups who truly believe "the tall, blond, blue-eyed peoples of northern and western Europe were the modern remnants of a talented race called the Nordics (or Teutons) who were descended from the ancient Aryans of India. The Nordics were said to have a special talent for political organization that enabled their members to form representative governments and create just laws; hence, the Nordic portion of the White race was destined to rule over all races, including the shorter Alpine; and the darker-skinned 'Mediterranean' portions of the White race."[69] The enslavement of black Africans was justified under the concept of superior/inferior racism with a mixture of benevolence and the desire to save souls. In 1732, John Barbat, a slave trader and author of *A Description of the Coast of North and South Guinea*, wrote "that the slave's conditions in his own country were so appalling that it was kindness to ship him to the West Indies and more considerate masters, not to mention that 'inestimable advantage' they may reap of becoming Christians and saving their souls."[70] Never having stepped on African soil, well-respected political philosophers David Hume and George Hegel also condemned the African culture. In his *Essay and Treatises* published in 1768, Hume wrote: "I am apt to suspect the Negroes [Black Africans] to be naturally inferior to the white. There never was a civilized nation of any other complexion than white, nor even any individual eminent either in action or speculation. No ingenious manufacturers amongst them, no arts, no science."[71] In his *Philosophy of History,* Hegel condemned the entire continent of Africa by noting that their people are "capable of no development or culture, and as we have seen them at this day, such have they always been . . . At this point we leave Africa, not to mention it again. For it is no historical part of the world; it has no movement or development to exhibit."[72] The Spanish explorers, conquistadors and missionaries in Central and Latin America and to some extent in Texas, used the same rationale towards Native Americans. The Catholic Church, for example, "converted" Native Americans to Christianity because they firmly believed that the only true religion was indeed the Christian faith. Subsequently, the religious and social cultures of the Aztec and the Inca, among the most advanced civilizations in the ancient world, were viewed as barbarian, unsophisticated and pagan.

The basic philosophy of the KKK is based on the superior/inferior concept of racism. In 1868, the Klan required a potential member to take its solemn oath:

. . . I Swear to maintain and to defend the social and political superiority of the White race on this Continent; always and in all places to observe a marked distinction between the White and African races; to vote for none but White men for any office of honor, profit or trust; to devote my intelligence, energy and influence to instill these principles in the minds and hearts of others; and to protect and defend persons of the White race, in their lives, rights, and property, against the encroachments and aggressions of persons of an inferior race.[73]

Regardless of the rhetoric or the tactics, each act of cruelty levied by the superior over the perceived inferior is justified as the desire to save the inferiors from themselves!

Economic Theory of Racism

In his book *Jim Crow America*, Earl Conrad sees economics as the explanation for racism. The overwhelming desire for land, natural resources, and economic viability drove Anglo Americans to use whatever means possible to obtain these treasures. "Greed had come to America, along with democracy, and greed was built into the hearts and minds of many millions of white [Anglo Americans] who were the products of the past, not the creators."[74] Native Americans were the initial targets because of their vast landholdings. The greed factor reached a fever pitch when gold was discovered on Indian land. Greed drove Anglo-American settlers (with the blessing of the United States government) to do whatever it took, ranging from relocation to extermination of Indian tribes to obtain the land. The original Spanish-Mexican landowners in Texas saw their lands gradually forced from them through legal and, far too often, illegal means. African slaves were brought to Texas to enhance the economic viability of the southern plantation owner by toiling day after day planting and picking his crops. Once they were economically depressed, minorities were systematically denied access to the tools that could liberate them—education and voting. Minorities were constantly reminded of their inferior status by Jim Crow laws that created a wall of separation between Anglos and minorities. According to Conrad, racial explanations overshadowed the driving economic issue:

The issue comes down to pennies, then, and so it has been since the time when slave traders marched into Africa, handed out a few bottles of rum, and walked off with a hundred or so human commodities. The profit was enormous. . . . Twenty-five cents in the hands of two white [Anglo] men is twenty-five cents less in the hands of a black [African-American] laundress. Magnify that in terms of the economic process intensively at work in all Southern states, and almost as sharply operative in the North, and you can put an arrow through the heart of Jim Crow.[75]

The civil rights acts passed in the 1960s and 1970s gradually dismantled the legislated Jim Crow laws. However, the unlegislated vestiges remain today in parts of the deep southern states and Texas. The late Albert Einstein once stated: "What is important is that there is a prejudice against people who have been misused and abused. The Negroes [African Americans] were brought here [to the United States] by greediness. And people see in them the wrong they have done to them. There is a general trend in human nature that people hate most those to whom they have done wrong."[76]

Economic arguments are consistently used by anti-immigration advocates seeking to limit and/or prohibit immigration by tightening naturalization and citizenship processes, punishing businesses for hiring illegal immigrants, and denying social service programs to immigrants.

Separation Theory

Another manifestation of racism is the concept of **separation**. "The minute society separates people from each other by color and class it sets in motion diverse economic, psychological, and cultural processes. Society builds two antithetical cultures side by side. They can be different economies and different cultures separated by a railroad track or a picket fence, and one can then put one culture against the other and make each group hate and misunderstand the other."[77] Once races and other cultures have been separated from each other for generations, prejudice and racism are natural by-products. It is so easy for one group to hate and mistrust another group when they do not associate or understand each other. In early Texas, the Tejano settlements were located from the Rio Grande to San Antonio while the majority of the Anglo-American settlements were miles away in the eastern portion of the territory. They rarely, if at all, mingled or associated with each other. Their separation definitely contributed to the heightened racial suspicions and prejudices each group held for each other.

People of all races, colors, and nationalities have indirect prejudices against each other. These acquired behavioral patterns are as much a part of our roots and traditions as patriotism and nationalism. Not every Anglo person is a racist, nor is every member of a minority group a victim of racial discrimination. Regardless of their individual prejudices, the vast majority of the American people have learned to overcome these tendencies by coming to terms with them. However, there are some individuals who hold intense contempt, disrespect, and hatred towards others. The increase in the number of racially motivated criminal activities across the nation has introduced a new term to the annals of criminology—**hate crimes**. In 2017, there were 7,175 reported incidences involving 8,828 victims nationwide of criminal activities committed on the basis of hatred towards a person based on his race, religion, sexual orientation, ethnicity, disability, gender and gender identity.[78] Texas law enforcement reported 192 hate crimes in 2017 with 117 of them based on the race, ethnicity and ancestry of the victims.[79] A rise in crimes motivated by hate is usually directly tied to a highly charged issue such as immigration reform. The Anti-Defamation League reports "groups linking the Ku Klux Klan, skinheads and neo-Nazis grew more significantly active, holding more rallies, distributing more leaflets and increasing their presence on the Internet—much of it focused on stirring anti-immigrant sentiment. Extremist groups are good at seizing on whatever the hot bottom issue of the day and twisting the message to get new members. . . . Today many white supremacists blame immigrants, particularly Hispanics, for crime, struggling schools or unemployment."[80] The increase in crimes motivated by hatred has moved lawmakers across the country to press for legislation calling for stiffer penalties against any person convicted of a hate-based crime.

A common practice among law enforcement agencies is to develop a stereotypical profile of those most likely to commit crimes. This practice is based upon the assumption that criminals and would-be offenders possess certain common traits and characteristics that separate them from law-abiding citizens. This tool has been successful in apprehending criminals. However, when the profile is used to harass, search and, oftentimes, detain minorities over Anglos, law enforcement is practicing their own brand of racial discrimination known as **racial profiling**. Along the border region, the agents of the United States Border Patrol and the Texas Rangers have been detaining primarily Hispanics driving to and from the border areas. Border agents rationalized their actions by indicating that Hispanics, more so than Anglos, fit the profile of drug dealers and smugglers of illegal aliens into the United States. The 9th United States Circuit Court of Appeals ruled that the border patrol's actions constituted racial profiling, thus

infringing upon the rights of Hispanic citizens. The justices defended their decision by emphasizing that "stops based on race or ethnic appearance send the underlying message to all our citizens that those who are not white [Anglo] enjoy a lesser degree of constitutional protection—that they are in effect assumed to be potential criminals first and individuals second."[81] On July 29, 2010, a federal judge blocked the implementation of Arizona's controversial anti-immigration bill that would have mandated that state and local law enforcement agencies arrest and deport illegal residents.   Most troubling was the video and training manual instructing police and state troopers that when trying to determine who is legal and who is not, they should "consider that someone doesn't speak English well, is wearing several layers of clothing in a hot climate or is hanging out in an area where unauthorized immigrants are known to work . . . a person doesn't have identification, tried to run away, is traveling in an overcrowded vehicle or seems out of place and unfamiliar with the area."[82] The judge saw this as a clear case of racial profiling. The 2001 Texas Legislature passed a bill prohibiting law enforcement from using racial profiling. The measure also mandates that all patrol cars be equipped with video and audio equipment to ensure that officers are not participating in racial profiling or any discriminatory or criminal actions against those stopped for minor traffic violations or arrested for suspicion of committing a crime.

The Hispanic Community

Particularly after Texas won its independence from Mexico, the historically fragile relationship between the Hispanic or Tejano community and Anglo-Americans eroded into verbal and sometimes physical confrontations. Hispanics "often faced the wrath of Anglos, who considered them a conquered people and an alien race, and who persecuted them with impunity."[83] The traditional explanation attributes the tensions to just a clash of cultures. "On the one side was the Anglo-American immigrant, blunt, independent, efficient, a rebel against authority, a supreme individualist. On the other side was the Latin American, direct in his ways, by training and temperament, a worshiper of tradition and a creature of authority."[84] This simplistic explanation ignores the deep-rooted economic, social, and political issues that deeply divided the Hispanic and Anglo-American communities.

Initially, Tejanos and Anglo-Americans had very little contact with each other. "Within Texas, itself, relations between Mexicans from Texas and the Anglo-American newcomers were generally amicable. A few Anglo Americans had settled in the Mexican communities of San

Antonio and Goliad, where they became assimilated. In the main, however, the two groups lived essentially apart, separated by considerable distance. Most Anglo Americans lived in East Texas and most Mexicans in the area of San Antonio and Goliad. As a result, Anglo Americans enjoyed a good deal of autonomy."[85] In many respects, both Anglo Americans and Tejanos needed each other. Anglo Americans needed Tejanos to teach them how to survive the rigors of the Texas frontier. Tejanos, especially business-owners, saw the potential economic profitability of Anglo-American immigration into Texas. It could have been for both a win-win situation.

Both Tejanos and Anglo Americans expressed their concerns over the inability of the Spanish government to effectively govern and colonize Texas. As early as 1813, Anglo Americans joined by several prominent Tejanos drafted a declaration of independence from Spain, citing a lengthy laundry list of shortfalls including the lack of Spanish soldiers to protect settlers from hostile Indian attacks and the government's inability to provide everything from schools to hospitals and roads. Although there were some Tejanos loyal to the Spanish government, the majority sided with the Anglo Americans in support of Mexico's revolution against Spain. After winning its independence in 1821, Mexico began the difficult task of establishing its own governing institutions. Although initially supportive of the Mexican government, Anglo Americans soon began to criticize this government for the same ineptness and shortcomings they leveled against the Spanish government. Texans sent delegates to the Convention of 1833 to list their grievances against the Mexican government. However, Anglo Americans in Texas overlooked the fact that Mexico basically was creating a government from scratch. It would take more than just twelve years to form an effectively functioning government. Throughout its 300 years of control over Mexico, Spain ruled with an iron hand.

There were also four major and numerous minor revolutions in Mexico just between 1829 and 1835. Political instability was the norm, not the exception. Impatience on the part of Anglo Americans hastened the deterioration of Texas's relationship with both Mexico, and, unfortunately, Tejanos.

Historians have perpetuated the "clash of cultures" by insinuating that the Texas Revolution was an Anglo American versus Tejano clash with every Tejano siding with the Mexican government. "The lore surrounding the battle of the Alamo provides the clearest examples of how the Texas rebellion, like so many major events, has been romanticized to take on means that transcend the event itself and its principal characters reduced to caricature-heroes and villains. In certain kinds of history, and in American popular culture, the Texas fight for independence has come to represent a triumph of Protestantism over Catholicism, of democracy over despotism, of a superior white [Anglo-American] race over a degenerate people of mixed blood, of the future over the past, of good over evil. Heroes of the Texas revolt are portrayed as committed republicans fighting for the noblest of motives."[86] Once again, the myth hides the truth and helps to perpetuate the "clash of cultures." For Tejanos, the decision to support their own government or the cause of the Anglo American was extremely difficult.

> No matter how much mutual interests might tie them together, however, once the fighting began it must have been agonizing for Tejanos to decide whether to remain loyal to Mexico or to join forces with Americans and take up arms against fellow Mexicans. . . . Anglo Americans who vastly outnumbered Tejanos by the early 1830s, would surely dominate the state and tejanos would become, to paraphrase Juan Seguín, "foreigners in their native land." When, however, Coahuila fell into anarchy in the mid-1830s and Santa Anna's centralist dictatorship replaced Mexico's federalist Republic, Tejano leaders must have wrung their hands over their unhappy alternative—domination by Anglo Americans or domination by the centralist dictatorship.[87]

Oftentimes revolution divides rather than unites as individual family members choose to support "the other side" of the conflict. Once close neighborhood bonds are destroyed as fear and resentment replaces trust and friendship. The same agonizing choices faced by the Tejano community would resurface in the 1860s as families across the United States had to decide whether to support the Union or the Confederacy.

The casualty lists of the Texas Revolution include both Anglo Americans and Tejanos. Among the dead at the Alamo were Toribio Losoya, Gregorio Esparza and five other Tejanos who fought side by side with Davy Crockett and James Bowie. Esparza's wife and children were in the Alamo during the battle. A plaque near the Long Barrack Museum at the Alamo lists the women and children who survived the battle and were released by Santa Anna. The only Anglo survivors were Susan Dickerson and her daughter. James Bowie's slave was also released. There were at least six women of Mexican descent and their children that were in the Alamo during the battle and survived the carnage. Colonel of the Second Company of Texas Volunteers, Juan Seguín left the Alamo on a voluntary "suicide mission" to bring back reinforcements from Fannin's army held up in Goliad. Seguín's company would later distinguish themselves at the Battle of San Jacinto. Several men of Mexican/Spanish descent were at the Consultation in San Felipe and affixed their signatures to the conditional declaration of independence from Mexico. The official Texas Declaration of Independence from Mexico was signed by José Antonio Navarro and José Francisco Ruiz. It was Adina de Zavala, the granddaughter of Lorenzo de Zavala, a former governor of the state and one-time Mexican minister of France, who in the early 1900s formed San Antonio's Chapter of the Daughters of the Texas Republic to help preserve the Alamo and its surrounding grounds.

The contributions and sacrifices of the Tejano/Mexican community were quickly overlooked as the victorious Anglo community exerted its dominance over the region. Under the protective rule of the Spanish and then Mexican government, aristocratic Spanish/Mexican families owned vast acreage of prime lands given to them through royal land grant decrees. As an independent country, the Republic of Texas basically declared these land grants invalid, opening the door for Anglo settlers to take over lands owned for generations by Spanish/Mexican families. Verbal hostility towards people of Mexican descent soon erupted into mob violence.

Signed in 1848, the Treaty of Guadalupe Hidalgo not only officially ended the war between Mexico and the United States it permanently divided Texas from Mexico, leaving Mexican nationals and Tejanos in a precarious situation. With a stroke of a pen, approximately 75,000 to 100,000 Spanish-Mexican-Indians were now living in the United States. "As individuals, they had the right either to retain the title and rights of Mexican citizens, or acquire those of citizens of the United States. Those who did not declare their intention to remain Mexicans automatically became citizens of the United States after one year."[88] To retain Mexican citizenship, the individual or family on the wrong side of the Rio Grande would have to give up their land, homes, and livelihoods and relocate to the other side of the river. Unlike other immigrants who had a choice, "the creation generation of Mexican Americans had not decided to leave their native land and go to the United States. They simply discovered one day that by a mutual agreement of the United States and Mexico, the places where they lived were no longer in Mexico."[89]

Unfortunately for the Tejano community, the prediction of Juan Seguín became a reality. "Retaliation against Tejanos came swiftly in the form of forceful banishment by Anglos who saw nothing wrong in displacing a people with generational ties to their homes and regions. It appeared also in the form of violent depredations by lawless men who assumed the right to harassment just because Tejanos were Mexicans."[90] In Victoria, ranches, farms and city properties owned by Tejanos for generations were vandalized and even seized. "In the 1850s, several counties in Texas expelled Mexicans, and in 1854, the city of Austin ordered every Mexican to leave unless vouched for by Anglos."[91]

In Goliad, members of the Texas army destroyed property and stole livestock from ranches owned by Tejanos. "Lynching, as a form of retaliatory violence, also surfaced during the antebellum period, though not with the same fervor and vindictiveness as after the Civil War. When the first Tejano fell victim to extra-legal execution is unknown, but by the 1850s lynch law was being applied in the Central Texas areas."[92] Playing a role in retaliatory actions against Tejanos, the Texas Rangers were far too often guilty of "shooting first and asking questions later." The Rangers were supposed to capture, arrest, and hold for trial persons accused of committing a crime. Proper arrest procedures were systematically ignored. Between 1911 and 1920, "almost every lower-class ethnic Mexican [Hispanic] alive in those years carried a violent, superstitious fear of Rangers, and the folk-hatred had permeated so deeply into all Mexicans [Hispanics] that even third- and fourth-generation citizens, who had never actually seen a Ranger, reacted with an instinctive phobia toward the name."[93] By 1920, the number of Hispanics killed by the Texas Rangers and lynched numbered in "thousands of men, women and children of Mexican descent from the mid-19th century until well into the 20th century. . . Other mobs hanged, whipped or shot Mexicans, many of whom were U.S. citizens, sometimes drawing crowds in the thousands."[94]

Beginning at the onset with the arrival of the Spanish in Mexico, the superior/inferior concept of racism was gradually overshadowed by the economic theory of racism as Hispanics sought better educational and training opportunities as a mean of achieving economic viability. White fear is the feeling "of becoming a member of a new minority as the existing minority becomes a majority within the social community."[95] Since the Anglo majority could do little to offset a growing Hispanic population, Anglos decided to create a repressive system of political and economic tactics designed to offset the potential encroachment of the Hispanic community into those economic, social and political arenas normally preserved for Anglo Texans. Consequently, the job market for Hispanics was restricted to low paying manual, agricultural, manufacturing, and housekeeping employment opportunities. The political clout of the Hispanic community gained ground in 1929 with the founding of the **League of United Latin American Citizens (LULAC)** in Corpus Christi. LULAC leaders encouraged the development of over 151 LULAC councils throughout Texas. From its very beginning, this organization became "a tremendous force for advancing the education, employment, housing, health and political empowerment of Hispanic Americans."[96]

Economically oppressed Hispanic workers soon realized that the collective voice of unionized workers was far more effective in fighting for better working conditions and wage treatment than their individual voices.

Particularly in the 1930s, Hispanics began to organize and protest against low wages and poor working conditions. Since the door to the political arena was closed to them, they decided to join organized labor movements. In 1930, spinach workers in Crystal City joined the Catholic Workers Union to fight for better working conditions and a ban on child labor. The United Cannery, Agricultural, Packing and Allied Workers of America organized farm laborers in the Rio Grande Valley while the Texas Fruit and Vegetable Worker's Union attempted to organize citrus and vegetable pickers. In 1938, 12,000 pecan shellers employed by the Southern Pecan Shelling Company in San Antonio under the leadership of **Emma Tenayuca**, staged a walkout in protest over poor working conditions. "The pecan shellers worked under dismal conditions in crowded, poorly ventilated and lit rooms. Indoor toilets and running water often were not provided. The fine brown dust that hung in the air was said to be at least partly to blame for the city's high tuberculosis rate. Often whole families worked shelling nuts. In 1934, in the depths of the Depression, a pecan sheller's average wage for a 54-hour week was about $2."[97] For Tenayuca, the fight of the Hispanic community was:

1. Against economic discrimination—extra low wages; expropriation of small land holders; discrimination in the right to work in all trades and crafts, particularly skilled trades; discrimination against professional and white collar workers; discrimination in relief and right to employment in W.P.A. [Works Progress Administration]

2. For educational and cultural equality—equal educational facilities for the Mexican population; no discrimination against children of Mexican parentage; a special system of schooling to meet the needs of migratory families; the study of the Spanish language and *the use of Spanish as well as English in public schools and universities* in communities where Mexicans are a majority; the granting of equal status to the Spanish language, as has been done in New Mexico and in those counties and states where the Mexican people form a large part of the total population.

3. Against social oppression—for laws making illegal the various forms of Jim Crowism, segregation in living quarters, schools, parks, hotels, restaurants, etc. This struggle must be linked with that of the Negro [African-American] people.

4 Against political repression. The struggle for the right to vote is divided into two phases: a) The majority of the Mexicans are American-born. The problem is, therefore, one of enforcing their citizenship right. This means demanding that all legal and extra-legal restrictions to the free exercise of the ballot be removed. These include residence qualifications, difficult for semi-migratory workers to meet; and in Texas, the elimination of the poll tax. b) Those who are foreign born must join with all of the immigrant groups in the United States to secure the democratization of the federal regulations pertaining to length of time, cost and language conditions required for citizenship; the aim being to simplify the process whereby all who intend to remain permanent residents in the United States— and this includes nearly all the Mexicans—and who express a desire for naturalization, can become citizens."[98]

The 37-day long strike at the pecan factory ended in reaching a compromise "that called for workers to continue to receive wages of 5 to 6 centers a pound until June 1, when a ½ cent per pound per cent increase would take effect. The agreement expired Nov. 1."[99] Their pay "increase" was short-lived since the federal government enacted the Fair Labor Standards Act mandating a set minimum wage of 25 cents an hour. The managers of the pecan shelling business opted to lay off the majority of the shellers rather than pay them the new minimum wage.

Today, the Hispanic community is still fighting against economic discrimination and for educational and cultural equality. Once again, a lawsuit has been filed challenging the state's funding of its public school systems that has created rich versus poor schools with the majority of the state's minority school-age population attending the "poor" schools. The English-only movement is alive once again as the Hispanic community contends that the state does not have enough English-as-a-Second Language (ESOL) programs. And the debate continues about whether to allow illegal immigrants who have been in this country for decades, a fast-track to citizenship.

The story of the farm laborer or **campesino** in Texas is a microcosm of the plight and struggles Hispanic Texans have and still face. At the turn of the century, the majority of Hispanic Texans lived in rural areas, employed as farm workers, ranch hands and tenant farmers. Tenant farmers worked for the landowners in exchange for low wages and a very modest home on a small plot of land located on the owner's property. The future of the tenant farmer rested totally with the landowner who could at any time relocate and remove their tenants from their property or raise the rent. The farm worker of today toils in the fields in the same bent-over position as his or her parents and grandparents did for so many years. In the mid-1960s, the late César Chávez organized the **United Farm Workers Union**, bringing national awareness to the working and living conditions of farm workers particularly in Texas and California. Initially, he met with little success:

In the 1970s, they [the campesinos] still faced lamentable working conditions. Most fields lacked restrooms, and since modesty compelled women to delay their bodily functions for hours, they suffered from disproportionally high levels of kidney infections. Wages remained as low as $2 or $3 for a typical day of field labor. Diseases such as typhoid, typhus, dysentery, and leprosy afflicted farm workers to a degree unknown to other Texans. Infant mortality rates among the campensinos in South Texas were among the highest in the United States at the time, and the life expectancy for field hands hovered around forty-nine.[100]

Corrective legislation has improved the lifestyle of the farm worker. Workers can now apply for worker's compensation and unemployment benefits. Their children are required to attend school with schedules that accommodate children that must spend a part of their day in the fields. State health laws mandate that growers provide clean drinking water and field restrooms. Laborers must be informed of the pesticides used on the fruits and vegetables. The wage scale has increased. However, farm workers still do not have collective bargaining rights, health care programs, and employer provided benefits such as life insurance and pension plans. Despite the passage of the **Migrant and Seasonal Worker Protection Act**, work-related issues continue to pit migrant and seasonal workers against their employers.

Today, the majority of the state's Hispanic community resides in urban communities. Although there is a growing Hispanic middle class, far too many of the state's Hispanics live in low-income and depressed Hispanic neighborhoods known as the **barrios**, which were created by de facto discrimination as more affluent Anglos left older intercity areas for the "nicer" suburbs. Traditionally, the Hispanic, as well as the African-American sections of the state's major cities were routinely bypassed for service improvements. An obvious pattern developed whereby "diverted funds went to build drainage systems in the new parts of town; the issue came down to who would get the money, new or old, and it became clear that city politics, intentionally or not, favored the new. The consequences were obvious: people wanted to live where the drainage was, where the money was spent."[101] A barrio resident commented that "we had no drainage, no sidewalks, no curbs, no parks, we were cut in half by an expressway, we didn't have enough water pressure to water the yard and draw bath water at the same time."[102]

It took community-based associations such as San Antonio's **Communities Organized for Public Service (COPS)** to lobby and vocally protest at City Hall to bring service improvements to these areas. Although infrastructure improvements have been made, these neighborhoods are still economically depressed due to shrinking property values, lack of business development, and low tax revenues. The rapidly developing middle-class Hispanic Texans have joined the migration to those "nice" neighborhoods, leaving barrio problems behind. As lawmakers in Austin continue to argue over whether the federal government should build a fence separating Mexico from the United States and if the state should continue to patrol the border with the Texas National Guard, Hispanics across the nation are sharply divided over immigration reform. Surveys reveal that many United States born and middle class Hispanics agree with conservative Republicans about policing the border, halting illegal immigration, and building a fence separating Mexico from the United States. Recent immigrants and first generation Hispanics see things differently. They argue that illegal immigrants are just seasonal workers who come to the states to take at- or below minimum wage jobs that most American workers shun. While the majority of those who cross the border illegally are migrant and lower-skilled workers, the typical stereotype of an immigrant from Mexico is changing as quickly as public opinion on the other side of the Rio Grande. "Just as the U.S. Latin population isn't a homogenous group, neither is the profile of Mexicans considering migrating to the United States. The typical image of the poor and undereducated migrant may have been accurate decades ago, but no longer. More than a third of college graduates [in Mexico] polled said they'd move north [to the United States] if they could—13 percent said they'd consider doing it illegally."[103]

The so-called caravans of migrants seeking entrance to the United States are from Central American countries such as Nicaragua and Honduras. Fear of uncontrolled gang violence against inept governments have pushed whole families to head to the United States through Mexico. The Mexican government is providing as much assistance as possible as migrants huddle in make-shift camps awaiting their turn to seek political asylum in the United States.

Ultimately the key to Hispanic empowerment rests not only in the political but in the economic and social arenas. In a 1973 interview, the late César Chávez commented:

> But political power alone is not enough. Although I've been at it for some twenty years, all the time and the money and effort haven't brought about any significant change whatsoever. Effective political power is never going to come, particularly to minority groups unless they have economic power. And, however poor they are, even the poor people can organize economic power. Political power by itself, as we've tried to fathom it and to fashion it, is like having a car that doesn't have any motor in it. It is like striking a match that goes out. Economic power is like having a generator to keep that bulb burning all the time. So we have to develop economic power to assure a continuation of political power. . . As a continuation of our struggle, I think we can develop economic power and put it into the hands of the people so they can have more control over their own lives, and then begin to change the system. Nothing short of radical change is going to have an impact on our lives or our problems. **We want sufficient power to control our own destinies. This is our struggle. It is a lifetime job. The work for social change and against social injustice is never ending**.[104] (Emphasis added by author.)

Native American Texans

No racial group has suffered more abuse and humiliation from the "white man" or received less for their efforts than the American Indian. Native Americans have fought harder and longer for their civil rights than any other group. Although numerous tribes lived in Texas for

hundreds of years before the Spanish landed, few public school students can name one tribe or a tribal leader other than Geronimo. Nor do most Texans know that Native American tribes from other parts of the United States also migrated into Texas. In the 1780s, the Alabama and Coushatta Indians relocated to Louisiana and gradually moved into Texas territory. Primarily headquartered in North Carolina, Tennessee and Georgia, the Cherokees were forced to leave their lands and move west into the present day states of Arkansas and Oklahoma. A few of them also settled in Texas. "During the winter of 1820-1821, about sixty Cherokee families led by Chief Bowl, also known as Duwali, settled near the three forks of the Trinity River in the vicinity of modern Dallas. . . . By 1822, at least three hundred Cherokees lived in Texas."[105] Following the Delawares and the Shawnees, the Kickapoos left the ancestral lands along the Great Lakes region and resettled in Texas along the upper Sabine and Trinity Rivers. By the early 1820s, "Indians particularly the Alabamas, Coushattas, Caddos, Cherokees, Delawares, Shawnees, and Kickapoos, likely outnumbered settlers of European origin."[106] An honorary member of the Cherokee nation, Sam Houston was interview by Frenchman Alexis de Tocqueville author of the well-renowned *Democracy in America* about his feelings toward Native Americans. Houston replied that "the Indian is born free; he makes use of this freedom from his first steps in life. Surrounded by the dangers, pressed by necessities, and unable to count on anyone, his mind must be ever active to find means to ward off troubles and to maintain his existence. This necessity imposed on the Indian gives his intelligence a degree of development and ingenuity which are often wonderful."[107] However, Houston's viewpoints were in the minority. What happened to the Native American tribes in Texas patterns what occurred throughout the United States.

"The facts of history are plain: Most Texas Indians were exterminated or brought to the brink of oblivion by Spaniards, Mexicans, Texans, and Americans who often had no more regard for the life of an Indian than they had for that of a dog, sometimes less."[108] By 1859, the Tonkawa population had dwindled to only a few hundred. The Lipan Apaches gradually relocated to areas south of the Rio Grande.

The American Indian became the target of intense hatred because he possessed what American settlers desired the most —land. In Texas, the quest for the ancestral tribal lands of Native Americans began with the encroachment of the Spanish. The pace accelerated when Spanish and Mexican governments opened the

Texas territory to Anglo-American settlement. Guided by the spirit of **Manifest Destiny**, Anglo-American settlers used the rational of the superior/inferior and economic theories of racism to justify seizing Indian lands. In turn, Native Americans rightfully viewed the encroachment of the Anglo-American settler as a viable threat to their culture, livelihood and survival. They believed that their only option was to fight with whatever they had to keep what belonged to them.

Stereotyping Indians as savages, killers and vermin gave justification for the brutal attacks and discriminatory actions of both federal and state governments. For Texas residents, the unknown fate of Cynthia Ann Parker was a constant reminder of the potential brutality of Indian warriors. On May 19, 1836, nine-year-old Cynthia Ann and her brother were abducted by a small band of Comanche Indians who attacked and killed members of her family at their trading post called Fort Parker. Her brother was eventually traded to the Kiowa Apaches, but Cynthia Ann remained with her captors. She adopted the Comanche way of life, married the chief's eldest son, and bore him two sons and a daughter. In 1860, Cynthia Ann was "rescued" and, along with her infant daughter, returned to her "white" family. The belief was that after years of living in captivity in primitive harsh conditions, Cynthia Ann would be grateful for her rescue and anxious to resume her former lifestyle. However, Cynthia Ann felt differently. She longed for her sons and made several attempts to run away. She lost her will to live when her infant daughter, Prairie Flower, died. "In the end, the most idealized Texas woman of her time couldn't fit in. The Texans couldn't get through to her, couldn't make her realize how much better off she was. In bitter irony, they became her captors."[109]

Immediately after Texas won its independence from Mexico, the Texas Rangers were called into action with the orders that "the only good Indian is a dead one."[110] Those Indians who were not killed by bullets, starvation, or disease were finally subdued. After the Civil War, Texas lawmakers decided that "the Indians and the Indian problem were federal matters, but the land belonged to the state. If the citizens of the state proposed to occupy the lands, and if the Indians objected, it was the duty of the United States either to remove the Indians or keep them from harassing the settlers. . . . The Indians were troublesome, said the Texans, and the federal forces ought to make war on them; they shed the blood of helpless women and children, and should be punished; they were in the way of expansion, and should be pushed back; they had no right to remain in Texas."[111] In 1862, the United

States army was given its marching orders to begin the extermination of the Mescalero Apaches in Arizona and Texas. Approximately 400 of their tribal members were relocated to a reservation at Bosque Redondo, a remote area in the New Mexico territory. "Well over half of the estimated 12,000 Navajos eventually were rounded up. They first went to Fort Canby, near present-day Window Rock, Arizona, where many died of exposure and dysentery. Survivors were sent off in groups to march 300 miles to Bosque Redondo. . . Some who could not keep up the pace, including the elderly, children and pregnant women, were shot by the soldiers . . . In all, 3,000 Navajos died at Bosque Redondo."[112] Well known for their horsemanship, the Comanches during the 1870s successfully controlled an area from the western edge of San Antonio to the Texas Panhandle. The United States Calvary under the leadership of Col. Ranald Slidell Mackenzie initially confronted the Comanches now under the tribal leadership of Quanah Parker, the son of Cynthia Ann Parker, at the Battle of Blanco Canyon. The Comanches won the day and launched a full-scale attack on settlers and ranchers. Eventually, the fierce fighting took its toll for the "Indians' food, supplies, and most important, horses were gone. They had no way to hunt and steal back these basic necessities. They were, in a word, defeated."[113] After losing the Battle of Palo Duro Canyon in 1874, the Comanches were finally rounded up and sent to reservations in Oklahoma.

An alternative to extermination was the obnoxious policy of **assimilation**. The federal government launched the program with the passage of the **Allotment Act**, commonly known as the **Dawes Act** in 1887. The legislation allocated a section of land to each member of a tribe. Any leftover land would then be sold with the profits held in trust to the Indians by the United States Treasury. The interest earned from the fund would be used "to support activities to move the tribes toward Anglo conformity. If, after a 25-year trial period, an individual allottee proved to be capable of managing his or her own affairs, that person could receive a 'certificate of competency,' a title to his or her land, and citizenship."[114] Basically, Indians were to become "civilized" and part of the white (Anglo) man's society. "Bureau of Indian Affairs agents, who supervised the reservations, tried to root out native American ways and replace them with dress and hairstyles, the English language, and the Christian religion."[115] However, the assimilation policy was fought by state legislative houses across the country as they enacted means to prevent Indians from social, economic and political viability with their Anglo counterparts. For example, in 1924, the Virginia state legislature passed the Racial Integrity Act prohibiting marriages between Anglos and non-whites including Native Americans. "The act, an effort by Virginia's southern aristocracy to maintain white [Anglo] supremacy made it a crime for people to identify themselves as Indian."[116] Although the federal government reversed the assimilation policy with the passage of the 1934 **Indian Reorganization Act** urging a return to tribal identities, the damage was done as Native Americans did not know who they were or where they belonged in society.

The road to full equality has been an uphill battle. Native Americans did not become United States citizens until 1920 while voting privileges were granted in 1924. In 1953, the United States Congress finally freed Native Americans from the control of the federal government with the passage of **House Concurrent Resolution 108**. The United States Census has added a new column to their population breakdowns—Native American. However, determining who is actually a Native American and what tribe they belong to is a difficult process. Consequently, the federal government adopted a **blood quantum** formula, meaning that the degree of Native American blood a person claims determines their percentage of Native American heritage. "If both parents were 'pure' Indian, the blood quantum of their children was 100 percent. The children of racially mixed marriages were presumed to have calculable fraction of 'Indian blood,' such as three-fourths, one-half, or one eighth . . . A one-fourth blood quantum is the minimal requirement for receiving some government services such as medical care on the reservations. A large number of tribal governments use one-sixteenth to one-half blood quantum criteria for determining tribal membership."[117] The Smithsonian Institute recently opened a museum in Washington dedicated to Native Americans whereby each tribe is given equal recognition and floor space for their artifacts. Although Native Americans are occasionally winning court battles over treaty violations, the majority of "reservation Indians" are grossly undereducated and unskilled and have persistently the highest rates of unemployment, substance abuse, and suicides of any minority group in the country.

African-American Texans

The economic prosperity of early Texas was made to a large extent by the back-breaking labors of African-American slaves who toiled in the fields from sunup to sundown, either bent over picking cotton, wielding a machete cutting sugar cane, or standing in ankle-deep water planting and harvesting rice. The economic success of any large-acre southern plantation was dependent upon slave labor. Justifications for the use of slave labor were just as hideous and obnoxious as the system itself. On March 1, 1856, the editor of the *Texas Star Gazette* wrote, "Indeed we would urge the importation of Negroes [African Americans] from Africa for it would not only improve their physical condition but add to their happiness, while at the same time, serving the purpose of civilization in our own country."[118] It was the "system" that controlled the destiny of the slave. Slaves were part of their owner's belonging just like the house, the fields, and the furniture. Citizenship, voting privileges, property ownership, and education were denied to African Americans, even for those born on American soil. Frederick Douglass, himself a former slave, once wrote that "whatever of comfort is necessary for him [the slave] for his body or soul is inconsistent with his being property, is carefully wrested from him, not only by public opinion but by the laws of the country. . . . He is deprived of education. God gave him an intellect; the slaveholder declares it shall not be cultivated."[119] Although the Mexican government frowned on slavery, Anglo Americans continued to bring slaves initially into the eastern region of Texas. "The large-scale introduction of slaves accelerated still more after Texas joined the Union, and by the time of the Civil War nearly 200,000 blacks [African Americans], forming almost one-third of the total population, lived in the state."[120]

Across the nation the anti-slavery movement was gaining steam particularly through the writings and speeches of William Lloyd Garrison, Frederick Douglass, David Walker and Harriet Beecher Stowe, public demonstrations, and Harriet Tubman's **underground railroad**, a trail of safe houses and havens run by anti-slavery advocates to help slaves escape "the system." However in 1857, the United States Supreme Court dealt a near-fatal blow to the emerging anti-slavery movement with its ruling in *Dred Scott v Sanford*. Scott claimed that since his new master had moved from a slave state to a free state, Scott was no longer a slave. The Court took a different view. First, the jurists invalidated the Missouri Compromise of 1820 limiting the spread of slavery in the territories, as an unconstitutional intrusion into state affairs. Second, the Court ruled that Scott did not have the right to sue in the first place since he was not a citizen. Scott's slave status remained intact, since the Court declared slaves were the property of their owners and, consequently, could only be freed by their owners.

The slave system was guided by the superior/inferior concept of racism. The man who is hailed by the African-American community as their liberator, echoed superior/

inferior sentiments in a speech he delivered in 1858 at a Republican Party function. Abraham Lincoln stated:

> I will say then that I am not, nor ever have been in favor of bringing about in any way the social and political equality of the white [Anglo] and black [African American] races, [applause]—that I am not nor ever have been in favor of making voters or jurors of negroes [African Americans], nor of qualifying them to hold office, nor to intermarry with white [Anglo] people, and I will say in addition to this that there is a physical difference between black [African American] and white [Anglo] races which I believe will forever forbid the two races living together on terms of social and political equality. And inasmuch as they cannot so live, while they do remain together there must be the position of superior and inferior, and I as much as any other man, am in favor of having the superior position assigned to the white [Anglo] race."[121]

The "system" that for so long denied African Americans in this state political, social, and economic freedoms ended on June 19, 1865, when Major General Gordon Granger of the United States Army arrived in Galveston and declared the emancipation of slaves in Texas:

> The people are informed that, in accordance with a proclamation from the Executive of the United States, all slaves are free. This involves an absolute equality of personal rights and rights of property, between former masters and slaves, and the connection heretofore existing between them, becomes that between employer and hired labor. The Freedmen are advised to remain at their present homes, and work for wages. They are informed that they will not be allowed to collect at military posts; and that they will not be supported in idleness either there or elsewhere.[122]

June nineteenth is celebrated by the African-American community as the day of liberation, freedom, and independence.

However, few of the now-freed slaves knew what freedom meant. Once the celebrations stopped, they realized just how ill-prepared they were to make the necessary adjustment to live in a free society. "But the glee faded as most blacks [African Americans] realized that, essentially, they were still enslaved. Abolitionist Frederick Douglass wrote that his people were free but 'without roofs to cover them, or bread to eat, or land to cultivate."[123] Few achieved economic viability. Only a handful could read or write. The only life they knew was on a plantation, isolated from the outside world. During the final months of the Civil War, General William Sherman tried to entice African Americans into joining the Union's cause by promising them that after the war, their military service to the Union would guarantee them forty-acres of prime farmland in Georgia and South Carolina. Yet, "only 40,000 blacks [African Americans] were resettled on land seized or confiscated in the Confederacy, but many more than that got nothing."[124] The United States Congress created the **Freedman's Bureau** to provide some assistance to former slaves including the redistribution of approximately 850,000 acres seized by the federal government after the war. Faced with a hostile Congress, President Andrew Johnson quickly stopped land redistribution plans by ensuring that former Confederates could quickly reclaim their properties.

In 1865, Congress officially outlawed slavery with the passage of the **Thirteenth Amendment**. Former slaves were granted citizenship with the passage of the **Fourteenth Amendment**, and voting privileges were granted with the **Fifteenth Amendment**. The Radical Republican-controlled Congress passed the **Civil Rights Act of 1866**, which gave former slaves rights to own property, sue in court, and make contractual agreements. "Yet despite these enactments, despite the mandates of Amendment Fourteen, and despite the language of the Fifteenth Amendment of 1870 which on its face seemed to assure to blacks [African Americans] the privilege of the ballot, neither the myth of white supremacy nor the fact of color prejudice was wiped out."[125] A series of Jim Crow laws, white-only primaries, poll taxes, literacy tests, and the grandfather clause prevented the majority of African Americans from exercising their freedom of full political participation. National lawmakers soon realized "that you cannot change the mores of a people by law, and since the social segregation of the races is the most deep-seated and pervasive of the Southern mores, it is evident that he who attempts to change it by law runs risks of incalculable gravity."[126]

Former slaves were also kept economically depressed under the cash-rent or **sharecropping system** whereby they would spend the majority of the working day plowing, tilling, and harvesting someone else's crop in return for a less than modest wage, a place to live, and small plot to grow their own vegetables. The relationship between the landowner and the "cropper" was sealed through the sharecropping contract. Signed in 1886 between A. T.

Mial (the landowner) and Fenner X. Powell (former slave, now sharecropper), the contract specified:

> that Said Fenner Powell agrees to work faithfully and diligently without any innecessary [sic] loss of time, to do all manner of work on Said farm as may be directed by Said Mial. And to be respectful in manners and deportment to Said Mial. And the Said Mial agrees on his part to furnish mule and feed for the same and all plantation tools and Seed to plant the crop free of charge, and to give the Said Powell one half of all crops raised and housed by Said Powell on Said land except the cotton seed. The Said Mial agrees to advance as provisions to Said Powell fifty pounds of bacon and two sacks of meal pr month and occasionally Some flour to be paid out of his the Said Powell's part of the crop or from any other advance that may be made to Said Powell by Said Mial.[127]

In urban areas, undereducated former slaves had to settle for the "undesirable jobs" as house servants, maids and porters. "These economic conditions drove black [African Americans] Texans into dismal living standards. Although many blacks [African Americans] expressed the desire to acquire their own land and build their own dwellings, most found shelter in one-or two-room shanties with dirt floors. Illnesses such as smallpox and cholera ravaged black [African-American] communities, food scarcities lingered, and segregation forced many former slaves into districts lacking portable water. And, without access to proper medical attention, blacks [African Americans] faced high rates of mortality, especially infants."[128]

Separation of the races in South Africa was called **apartheid**. In the southern states, segregation was called an equally obnoxious term: "**separate but equal**." "There was nothing particularly secretive about either public or private discrimination; and it was simply an accepted way of life."[129] Jim Crow laws socially separated Anglo from African American. The United States Supreme Court gave its blessing to separate but equal in its 1896 decision in *Plessy v Ferguson*. In 1890, the Louisiana state legislature passed the **Separate Car Act** mandating that any railroad line passing through Louisiana had to have separate accommodations for Anglo and African-American passengers. "Under its terms any railway company that did not provide separate coaches for blacks [African Americans] and whites [Anglos] could be fined $500. Except for nurses attending children of the other race, individual whites [Anglos] and blacks [African Americans] would be forbidden to ride together or risk a $25 fine or

20 days in jail."[130] Railroad owners were incensed. Civil rights groups were equally angry over the law. Both groups joined forces to test the constitutionality of the act by purposely selecting Homer Plessy, who was one-eighth African American to ride in the "white" passenger car rather than the "black" car on a train headed from New Orleans to Covington. Railroad owners and civil rights groups truly believed that the uproar over Plessy's arrest would convince both the courts and the legislature that this law was unconstitutional. Indeed, when ordered to give up his seat, Plessy was arrested. His legal team hired primarily by the railroads, sued on the grounds that Plessy's constitutional rights under both the Thirteenth and Fourteenth Amendments had been violated. The United States Supreme Court thought otherwise and ruled 7-0 against Plessy. The majority opinion of the Court stressed that "a statute that made a legal distinction between the races on the basis of color did not destroy the legal equality of the races or create a condition of slavery; it merely reflected the social distinctions based on color that existed in society. Furthermore, while the object of the Fourteenth Amendment was to enforce the absolute legal and political equality of the two races, it was not intended to abolish distinctions based upon color or enforce social equality and the commingling of the two races upon terms unsatisfactory to either."[131] The ruling gave the state carte blanche approval to continue to pass laws separating the races as long as the accommodations were basically, in principle, equal. In another ruling, the Court also struck down the **Civil Rights Act of 1875** prohibiting private discrimination in accommodations, transportation, and public places of amusement. The Court felt that the Fourteenth Amendment applied to state and public actions, not private ones.

Consequently, African Americans were "kept in their place" through the legal arm of the courts and the intimidation of the Ku Klux Klan. Remaining a strong presence in southern politics until the late 1920s, Klan members garbed in white robes and hoods used a variety of scare tactics against defiant African Americans and their Anglo sympathizers. Burning crosses, public tar-and-featherings, floggings, and lynching were used throughout the southern states to vividly remind African Americans of their inferior position in society. A preeminent civil rights attorney who would became the nation's first African-American Supreme Court justice, Thurgood Marshall, once commented that "even in Mississippi a Negro [African American] will get a trial longer than 42 minutes, if he is fortunate enough to be brought to trial."[132] Throughout the South including Texas, African

Americans could be arrested for not "giving way" to an Anglo pedestrian walking on the same sidewalk. Far too often, southern justice was a lynch mob. Frederick Douglass once wrote that "an abandoned [White] woman has only to start to cry that she has been insulted by a black [African-American] man, to have him arrested and summarily murdered by the mob. . . . When a white [Anglo] man steals, robs or murders, his crime is visited upon his own head alone. . . . When a black [African-American] man commits a crime the whole race is made to suffer."[133] "In the last two decades of the nineteenth century, more than 2,500 blacks [African Americans] were lynched in the South. Another thousand or so were murdered in this way in the first decade and a half of the new century."[134] In 1892, Ida B. Wells, the first woman editor of a major newspaper, launched her campaign against lynching. In particular, Wells blamed the federal government for not affording protection to the African-American community:

> The government which made the Negro [African American] a citizen found itself unable to protect him. It gave him the right to vote, but denied him the protection which should have maintained that right. Scourged from his home; hunted through the swamps; hung by midnight riders and openly murdered in the light of the day, the Negro [African American] clung to his right of franchise with a

heroism which would have wrung admiration from the hearts of savages. He believed that in that small white ballot there was a subtle something which stood for manhood as well as citizenship, and thousands of brave black [African-American] men went to their graves, exemplifying the one by dying for the other.[135]

The last reporting lynching in Texas occurred in 1945. Acts of violence against African Americans erupted periodically in Beaumont, Sherman, Port Arthur, Houston and Brownsville.

In 1910 and 1911, the Texas Legislature embraced separate but equal by passing laws requiring railroad stations to have separate waiting rooms. Public facilities had separate drinking fountains, restrooms, swimming pools and even parks. African Americans were prohibited from moving into Anglo neighborhoods through the **restrictive covenant**, a provision in a mortgage contract forbidding the buyer from subsequently selling the house to a minority. If such a sale occurred, the property would revert back to the originating party of the agreement. Another ploy was to increase or decrease the sale price of the property based upon the potential buyer's race. **Steering** was showing properties to minorities located only in predominately minority residential areas, thus keeping them away from Anglo neighborhoods. **Redlining** was the tactic of denying money to those individuals desiring to buy residential properties in a racially

Martin Luther King, Jr. talks with President Lyndon B. Johnson in the Oval Office, White House. December 3, 1963 by Yoichi R. Okamoto. Photo credit: LBJ Library Photo

changing neighborhood. The Virginia State Legislature passed a 1912 law mandating segregated districts. The law made it "unlawful for any colored [African-American] person to move into a white [Anglo] district. This act [did] not preclude persons of either race employed as servants by persons of the other race from residing on the premises of the employer."[136] Throughout the South:

> they [African Americans] were either excluded from railway cars, omnibuses, stagecoaches, and steamboats or assigned to special "Jim Crow" sections; they sat, when permitted, in secluded and remote corners of hotels, restaurants, and resorts, except as servants; they prayed in "Negro pews" in the white [Anglo] churches, and if partaking of the sacrament of the Lord's supper, they waited until the whites [Anglos] had been served the bread and wine. Moreover, they were often educated in segregated schools, punished in segregated prisons, nursed in segregated hospitals, and buried in segregated cemeteries.[137]

The tide began to turn as African-American organizations became more vocal about acts of violence and discrimination. Founded nationally in 1909 by African-American scholar W.E.B. DuBois, the **National Association for the Advancement of Colored People (NAACP)** had thirty chapters in Texas by 1930. The **Association of Southern Women for the Prevention of Lynching** gained the public endorsement of local newspapers to stop lynchings. Groups leading the charge for equal treatment included nationally based organizations such as the **Congress of Racial Equality (CORE)** and the **Southern Christian Leadership Conference (SCLC)** founded by the late Dr. Martin L. King, Jr., in 1956. The modern civil rights movement brought national attention to the plight of African Americans: Mrs. Rosa Parks was arrested for refusing to give up her seat on a Montgomery, Alabama bus to an Anglo person; four African-American students at North Carolina Agricultural and Technical College sat peacefully at a lunch counter at Woolworth's for hours while employees refused to serve them and bystanders hurled racial insults; and Dr. King led protesters in peaceful non-violent demonstrations throughout the South. The 1960s Civil Rights Movement gave birth to a new term—**integration**. "One cannot be close to the problem very long without hearing that word. Integration is what the Negro [African American] has not got. He is on the outside, and he wants to be on the inside. He is not allowed to play or live or work as others. He occupies a negative position, and desires the positive. The principle

of integration (and its opposite, non-integration) cuts a pattern through the nation just as widespread but far more complex than the transportation system over which the trains roll, planes fly, farm wagons crawl, and people walk."[138] One by one the repressive practices of Jim Crow began to be challenged and successfully overturned by the federal courts.

The first major civil rights bill since Reconstruction, the **Civil Rights Act of 1957** created the United States Commission on Civil Rights, and the Civil Rights Section of the United States Justice Department. The federal government was empowered to obtain injunctions against illegal voting activities. The **Civil Rights Act of 1960** authorized federally-appointed voting referees to conduct voter registration drives and monitor federal elections in areas with historical patterns of voter-related problems. The **Civil Rights Act of 1964** prohibited discrimination in public accommodations and employment practices. Facing strong opposition from his own party membership, President Lyndon Johnson used the political skills he acquired as Senate Majority Leader to win approval of this sweeping civil rights legislation. With a stroke of a pen, "a southern president—a product of that cruel and unjust system and long a political captive of it—had helped to dismantle Jim Crow."[139] Discriminatory housing practices were outlawed with the passage of the **Civil Rights Act of 1968**.

Of course, the Texas school system was segregated, from public schools to colleges and universities. Herman Sweatt, an African-American mail carrier wanted to attend the University of Texas Law School. He was denied admission because of his race. His remaining option was to attend the Texas State University for Negroes, an inferior law school when compared to UT. In *Sweatt v Painter* (1950), the United States Supreme Court ruled that Sweatt should not be forced to attend a racially separated inferior school. A similar ruling was made that same year in *McLaurin v Oklahoma State Regents*. The University of Oklahoma did not have a separate graduate school for African Americans. Consequently, the university would admit African Americans on a segregated basis, meaning that they sat in totally segregated classrooms and facilities from Anglo students. The Court ruled in favor of McLaurin by declaring that the university's policy was an unconstitutional violation of the student's civil rights.

In its 1954 decision in ***Brown v. Board of Education of Topeka, Kansas,*** the United States Supreme Court shattered the "separate but equal" policies prevalent primarily throughout the southern states. The *Brown* case represented several other families where their children were attending poorly equipped, understaffed, and inadequately funded but segregated public schools. The question was whether the Fourteenth Amendment's equal protection clause extended to public facilities such as public schools. The Court ruled unanimously with Brown, concluding that "in the field of public education the doctrine of 'separate but equal' has no place. Separate educational facilities are inherently unequal. . . . The plaintiffs and others similarly situated for whom the actions have been brought are by reason of segregation complained of, deprived of the equal protection of the laws guaranteed by the Fourteenth Amendment."[140] This ruling dismantled the philosophical basis for both Jim Crow and separate but equal. Despite the ruling, lawmakers realized by 1970 that voluntary desegregation was not working and opted instead to use involuntary measures such as court mandated busing and federal threats of denying federal funds for any public school participating in discriminatory practices. Subsequent court decisions and legislative acts have mandated desegregation of all public facilities.

African-American Texans are still confronted with a vast array of chronic impediments that threaten their economic, social and political standing. High dropout rates from high schools equate to high unemployment and poverty. Many are employed in low-paying jobs without opportunities for advancement. The discrimination and intimidation African Americans faced in Vidor and Jasper is tragically indicative of the treatment they receive in far too many communities across this state. When the Vidors and Jaspers of this nation become merely historical references in a textbook, perhaps African-American Texans will have finally gained their rightful place at the table.

Women in Texas

In 2020 women will be celebrating the 100th anniversary of the passage of the **Nineteenth Amendment**, granting them the right to vote. The right to the ballot box as well as to own property, get an education, earn a decent wage, and even serve on a jury should have been guaranteed to all American citizens, male and female, when the Constitution and the Bill of Rights were written. Joined by their British counterparts, American women entered into a prolonged social, political and economic struggle to secure those rights and privileges. Gender-based discrimination disguised under a paternalistic attitude has kept women in a subservient role for centuries.

> The case of women, though seldom expounded in explicit detail, was based on the analogous connections of assumption and achievement, and in both instances, biological structure, genetics, and the chemistry of the body were to yield definitive

explanations of the differences. . . . It was not until the twentieth century that more than the merest handful of skeptics or malcontents declined to draw what seemed the common sense conclusion from the fact that there were female saints, but no female theologians, that there was female intuition, but no female philosopher, female musicians but few female composers, no female Rembrandts but innumerable nineteenth century lady colourists.[141]

Under Spanish rule, women in Texas had far more legal rights than women in the American colonies. Established by Alfonso X, the king of Castile and Leon (1252-1284) as part of the Las Siete Partidas or Seven Parts, "a woman could sell any separate property she had owned before marrying. Property purchased or inherited during marriage belonged to both spouses. Before selling any property that belonged to both of them, the wife had to give her consent. . . . Women inherited equally with men and daughters equally with sons."[142] All that dramatically changed when Texas gained its independence! Frontier women in Texas worked side by side their male counterparts to create this state with the realization that they "could not vote, hold office, control their property, write a will, or expect custody of their children."[143]

The **paternalistic attitude** of male superiority over women is supported by the myth that women are just too fragile mentally and physically to survive the rigors of life on their own. Women needed "a knight in shining armor" to protect them from harm and shield them from unpleasantness. In 1873, Supreme Court Justice Joseph Bradley reinforced the concepts of the separate spheres ideology and the Devine ordinance in his majority opinion in *Bradwell v Illinois*:

> Civil law, as well as nature herself, has always recognized a wide difference in the respective spheres and destinies of man and woman. Man is, or should be, woman's protector and defender. The natural and proper timidity and delicacy which belongs to the female sex evidently unfits it for many of the occupations of civil life. The constitution of the family organization, which is founded in the Devine ordinance, as well as in the nature of things, indicates the domestic sphere as that which properly belongs to the domain and functions of womanhood. The harmony, not to say identity, of interests and views which belong, or should belong, to the family institution is repugnant to the idea of a woman adopting a distinct and independent career from that of her husband. So firmly fixed was this

sentiment in the founders of common law that it became a maxim of that system of jurisprudence that a woman had not legal existence apart from her husband, who was regarded as her head and representative in the social state.[144]

The concept of paternalism has its roots in the British Victorian social system. Basically, "the ideal Victorian woman was passive, childlike, unreflective, self-sacrificing, and dependent. Whereas men were to be self-possessed, women were to submit to the control of others, principally to their husbands, fathers and brothers. Above all, women were to be adaptable, able to mold themselves to their husband's expectations and desires. In a Victorian marriage, potential conflict was removed through constant wifely adjustment, and thus submission sometimes included accompanying husbands to remote frontier regions such as Texas regardless of the wives' personal inclinations."[145] In Texas the Spanish tradition of a "woman's role" joined forces with the southern plantation lifestyle that placed women on pedestals. Frail and fragile like fine bone china, women were objects of worship requiring the constant protection of gentlemen. A mere mention of voting rights for women would ignite the traditional argument that women were too mentally frail to even discuss politics, much less to make a decision in a voting booth. Voting would introduce women to the ugly side of politics with its wheeling and dealing, a place where delicate females did not belong.

The **Suffrage Movement** in the United States involved a complex array of social, political, and economic issues apart from just obtaining the right to put a ballot into a box. Women were scorned, publically and socially humiliated, arrested, and killed in their quest to break the stranglehold of paternalism. Suffrage, or the right to vote, became a national issue in 1848 when pioneer feminist Elizabeth Cady Stanton addressed the issue in the *Declaration of Sentiments and Resolutions* delivered at the Seneca Falls Convention on women's rights. Stanton listed numerous grievances against men:

> The history of mankind is a history of repeated injuries and usurpations on the part of man toward woman, having in direct object the establishment of an absolute tyranny over her. . . . He has never permitted her to exercise her inalienable right to the elective franchise. He has compelled her to submit to laws, in the formation of which she had no voice. He has withheld from her rights which are given to the most ignorant and degraded men—both natives and foreigners. . . . He has made her, if married in the eye of the law, civilly dead.[146]

Inauguration of Ann Richards, January 15, 1991.
Photo credit: UTSA's Institute of Texas Cultures

Commonly known as suffragettes, supporters of "the vote" received sharp recriminations from those women wanting to uphold the traditional roles of wife and mother. Author of *Uncle Tom's Cabin*, Harriet Beecher Stowe was a leading spokeswoman against giving women the right to vote. In 1869, she wrote:

> Let us suppose that our friends [women] have gained the ballot and the powers of office: are there any real beneficent measures for our sex, which they would enforce by law and penalties, that fathers, brothers, and husbands would not grant to a united petition of our sex, or even to a majority of the wise and good? Would these not confer what the wives, mothers, sisters deemed best for themselves and the children they are to train, very much sooner than they would give power and office to our sex to enforce these advantages by law? Would it not be a wiser thing to ask for what we need, before trying so circuitous and dangerous a method? God has given to man the physical power, so that all women may gain, either by petitions or by ballot, will be the gift of life or of duty: and the ballot never will be accorded till benevolent and conscientious men

are the majority—a millennial point far beyond our present kin.[147]

In 1872, Susan B. Anthony, Stanton's partner in the suffrage movement, and thirteen other women were arrested for illegally voting in a Rochester, New York election.

While the women's movement was gaining ground in the North, it ran into the brick wall of southern paternalism below the Mason Dixon line. "The fierce opposition of most white southerners to the women's suffrage movement resulted from several interrelated cultural, political and economic factors. The southern suffrage movement took place in a period, from 1890 to 1920, in which white southerners were passionately devoted to the preservation of a distinct and, they believed superior 'Southern Civilization.' A key element of this Southern Civilization they wished to preserve was a dualistic conception of the natures and responsibilities of the sexes that precluded the participation of women in politics and cast 'the Southern Lady' in the role of guardian and symbol of southern virtue. Charged with transmitting southern culture to future generations, as well as inspiring current statesmen to serve as their noble defenders, southern womanhood had a vital role to play in preserving the values of 'the lost cause.'"[148]

In Texas, a woman could not sell or borrow against her own private property without her husband's permission. Women could not enter into contracts, apply for credit, or witness a will. With the rare exception of divorce, women could not sue. The Texas suffrage movement began at a constitutional convention in 1868 when delegates soundly defeated a proposal to grant voting rights to women. An organized suffrage effort was launched with the **Women's Christian Temperance Union**. The **State Equal Suffrage Association** was founded in Dallas in 1893. Annette Finnegan and her sister founded the **Women's Suffrage League** in Houston. The Mother of the Texas Woman's Suffrage Movement was Eleanor Brackenridge, sister of rancher George W. Brackenridge who founded the Men's League for Woman's Suffrage in Texas headquartered in San Antonio. Born in Indiana in 1837, she became active in the movement in 1898 and founded the Woman's Club in San Antonio to encourage women to become involved in social causes such as education, health, and prison reform. In 1918, she was the first woman in Bexar County to register to vote. She was also the first woman in the country to serve on the board of directors of two financial institutions. In 1912, eight socially prominent women in San Antonio including Ida Kampmann, Rena Maverick, and Brackenridge formed the Equal Franchise Society of San Antonio. Since they held their meetings at the Menger Hotel, they were known as the Menger Eight.

Senator Kay Bailey Hutchison
Photo credit: Sen. Hutchison's website,
http://www.hutchison.senate.gov/

Houstonian Annette Finnegan approached the Texas Legislature in 1914 to introduce legislation giving women the vote. The daughter of a millionaire owner of a meat-packing and hide business, she ran the business in her father's absence. As a freshman at Wellesley, she met suffrage pioneer Lucy Stone and became an ardent advocate for women's rights. Gaining the backing of the Texas Women's Press Association and the Texas Federation of Labor, women's groups led by Finnegan and Minnie Fisher Cunningham finally convinced the Texas Legislature in 1918 to pass a bill amending the state constitution giving women the right to vote in primary elections. On June 28, 1919, Texas became the ninth state nationally and the first state in the South to ratify the Nineteenth Amendment to the United States Constitution. Finnigan would become the president of the Texas Woman Suffrage Association. The first women in Texas to pass the bar exam, Hortense Ward authored the legislation granting married women the right to own property. An **Equal Rights Amendment** to the state constitution was passed on March 30, 1972.

Once women obtained access to the policy process through the vote, paternalistic barriers began to slowly crumble, opening the doors to employment, education, and financial independence. It was an arduous, oftentimes, snail-paced effort to gain equality. Women were prohibited from serving on juries until the 1970s. Employment opportunities were limited to a few low paying positions usually open to single women only. In most states, female public school teachers had to resign their positions when they married. Although women made gains in the workforce in the 1920s, the Depression era had an adverse effect since women were deliberately fired to open slots for unemployed men. World War II gave women their chance to prove themselves as productive and viable workers as they replaced men in industrial and manufacturing positions.

The economic necessity of the two-household income has substantially increased the number of women in the Texas workforce. In 2017, the state's civilian employed labor force included 5,788,000 women over the sixteen years of age.[149] Women are still confronted by a multiplicity of job-related discriminatory practices. The **pay equity** issue addresses the fact that women earn less than their male counterparts in comparable positions. Among the nation's high school graduates, it is estimated that in 2016, women employed in comparable positions with their male counterparts made an average of $16,292 less per year. A woman with a bachelor's degree employed in a comparable position to her male counterpart with the same level of education, earned only $52,461 in comparison to his $82,089. In the professional categories the gap widens considerably with women earning an average yearly salary of $90,487, which men in comparable positions earn an average of $151,019.[150] Women as a whole earn less since they hold the majority of the **pink collar** jobs such as clerical and secretarial positions. Opportunities for promotion and job mobility for women have increased substantially. However, women are still victims of the **glass ceiling**, which usually prohibits them from becoming the CEO or president of the firm.

The women's movement in Texas continues through the efforts of women's organizations. Affiliated with a national organization, the League of Women Voters at both the state and local levels remains a powerful non-partisan group promoting a broad-based agenda from voting rights to juvenile justice and water issues. It was the national organization that launched an intense campaign to push through Congress the Motor Voter Bill. The **National Organization for Women (NOW)** has chapters at both the state and local levels of all fifty states. The major issues of NOW concern gender-based discrimination and sexual harassment primarily in the workplace. The push for women to take an active role in the political process resulted in the founding of the Texas Women's Political Caucus (TWPC) in 1971. Guided by its national organization, TWPC actively recruits, promotes, and campaigns for women who support Caucus issues. Women in Texas have learned that they must lobby their issues before legislative houses and also become elected officials to preserve and promote their rights and issues. Barriers to elective office in Texas have been broken. Ann Richards (D) won an exceptionally tough campaign for the governor's seat, becoming the state's first free-standing female governor. Rose Spector (D) became the first female member of the State Supreme Court. In 2002, Alma Lopez (D) became the first female and Hispanic to serve as Chief Justice of the Texas 4th Court of Criminal Appeals. And for the first time in its history, Texans elected its first female United States Senator—Republican Kay Bailey Hutchison.

Where Do We Go From Here?

The public policy process has responded to the needs of minority population groups and women by removing many of the political, economic and social barriers, thus opening the doors that were locked for so long. However, the doors are only slightly cracked open, not wide open to the vast majority of the state's poor women and minority population groups. The punitive direction of the state's social service programs are demeaning, discriminatory in application, and ineffective in raising individuals out of poverty. Education is hailed as the answer to ending poverty, yet many low-income women and minorities in this state receive, at best, a second-rate education delivered from poorly funded public school districts. The job market leaves so many out of the market, as high-tech degreed positions become the exclusive property of the highly educated.

Far too often, the plight of the poor is often neglected by the very organizations that claim to represent all members of their groups. In essence, minority groups and women won rights for some members but left so many behind. A growing middle-class of women and minorities often fight for "their" issues, disregarding the obstacles and problems confronting their entire minority or gender group. The **separate sisters** are "women in minority groups; women in 'traditional' women's jobs; women who stay at home to raise children; and elderly, rural, some poor and younger women who acknowledge their debt to feminism's early battles. But they charge that the feminist movement has failed to broaden its base and remains made up large of white [Anglo], highly educated women who have not adequately addressed the issues that matter to them: child care rather than lesbian and abortion rights, economic survival rather than political equality, the sticky floor rather than the glass ceiling."[157] The NAACP is also wrestling with this problem as members from lower economic groups have threatened to drop their ties with the organization. Equality before the law and society itself will not become a reality as long as some groups and individuals are treated unequally.

Corrective legislation is part of the solution. However, women and minorities must fulfill their obligations by actively participating as cohesive members of the political system. Lawmakers favorable to minority and women's issues cannot continue to promote legislation in hostile political environments without the support of the groups they are trying to help. Particularly in Texas, low voter turnout among minority and female population groups feeds right into the hands of those seeking to hold the line and, in some instances, turn back the clock on civil rights and liberties for minorities and women.

Chapter Notes

[1]Bruce J. Schulman, *Lyndon B. Johnson and American Liberalism: A Brief Biography with Documents*, 2nd ed., (Boston, Massachusetts: Bedford/St. Martins, 2007), 216.

[2]Sarah Van Bonen and Anne Belli Gesalman, "A Fatal Ride in the Night," *Newsweek*, June 22, 1998, 33.

[3]Laura Tolley, "Klan, Panthers Descend on Jasper," *San Antonio Express-News*, (Sunday, June 28, 1998), 33.

[4]Helen Thompson, "State Wide: Race Wrangling," *Texas Monthly*, March, 1993, 70.

[5]"Troopers Posed in "KKK" Hoods," *San Antonio Express-News*, (Thursday, January 6, 2000), 3B.

[6]Patricia Berstein, "Past Tense," *Texas Monthly*, April, 1999, 24.

[7]Alan Barth, *The Rights of Free Men: An Essential Guide to Civil Liberties*, James E. Clayton, ed., (New York, N.Y.: Alfred A. Knopf, 1987), 111-112.

[8]Leon W. Blevins, *Texas Government in National Perspective*, (New Jersey: Prentice-Hall, 1987), 221.

[9]John C. Domino, *Civil Rights and Liberties: Toward the 21st Century*, (New York, New York: HarperCollins, 1994), 1.

[10]Ibid., 2.

[11]Barth, 112.

[12]Paul Brest, "The Intentions of the Adopters in the Eyes of the Beholder," *The Bill of Rights: Original Meaning and Current Understanding*, Eugene W. Hickok, Jr., ed., (Charlottesville, Virginia: University Press of Virginia, 1991), 23.

[13]Henry J. Abraham and Barbara A. Perry, *Freedom and the Court: Civil Rights and Liberties in the United States*, 8th ed., (Lawrence, Kansas: University Press of Kansas, 2003), 4.

[14]Lucius J. Barker and Twiley W. Barker, Jr., *Civil Liberties and the Constitution*, 6th ed., (Englewood Cliffs, New Jersey: Prentice-Hall, 1990), 13.

[15]Ibid.

[16]Thomas R. Hensley, Christopher E. Smith and Joyce E. Baugh, *The Changing Supreme Court: Constitutional Rights and Liberties*, (St. Paul, Minnesota: West Publishing Co., 1997), 132.

[17]Ibid., 141.

[18]Domino, 113.

[19]Hensley, Smith and Baugh, 139-140.

[20]Gary Martin, "High Court Oks School Vouchers," *San Antonio Express-News*, (Friday, June 28, 2002), 12A.

[21]Jodie Wilgaren, "Judge Rips Vouchers for Parochial Schools," *San Antonio Express-News*, (Tuesday, December 21, 1999), 10A.

[22]Gary Martin, "High Court Oks School Vouchers," 1A.

[23]Ibid., 12A.

[24]Abraham and Perry, 310.

[25]Hensley, Smith and Baugh, 162.

[26]Ibid., 163.

[27]J. Michael Parker and Cecilia Balli, "Justices to Tackle Football Prayers," *San Antonio Express-News*, (Tuesday, Nov. 16, 1999), 1A.

[28]Hensley, Smith and Baugh, 164.

[29]Jenny Lacoste-Caputo, "Law on Religion in School Spurs Fear," *San Antonio Express-News*, (Wednesday, July 25, 2007), 1B and 8B.

[30]David Kravets, "One Nation Under God," *San Antonio Express-News*, (Thursday, June 27, 2002), 1A.

[31]http://www.wsws.org

[32]Susan Welch, John Gruhl, Michael Steinman, John Comer and Susan M. Rigdon, *American Government*, 5th ed., (St. Paul, Minnesota: West, 1994), 450.

[33]Abraham and Perry, 178.

[34]Welch, Gruhl, Steinman, Comar and Rigdon, 454.

[35]Domino, 47.

[36]Ralph A. Rossum and G.Alan Tarr, *American Constitutional Law: Cases and Interpretations*, (New York, New York: St. Martin's Press, 1983), 383.

[37]Hensley, Smith, and Baugh, 381.

[38]Domino, 67.

[39]Rossum and Tarr, 418.

[40]Ibid., 397.

[41]Ibid., 398.

[42]Ibid., 410.

[43]Aaron Epstein, "Anti-Gang Loitering Ordinance Rejected," *San Antonio Express-News*, (Friday, June 11, 1999), 1A.

[44]Ibid., 1A and 20A.

[45]Gary Martin, "Bush Hails New Terror Law," *San Antonio Express-News*, (Saturday, October 27, 2001), 4A.

[46]Marc Robbins, "Are Civil Liberties at Risk?," 9A.

[47]"Guns in America: What Must Be Done?" *Newsweek*, Aug. 1999, 24.

[48]Ibid.

[49]Alexis de Tocqueville, *Democracy in America*, J. P. Mayer, ed., (Garden City, New York: Double Day and Co., 1969), 638-639.

[50]Abraham and Perry, 373.

[51]Blevins, 254.

[52]Domino, 2.

[53]Abraham and Perry, 109.

[54]Ibid.

[55]Ibid., 110.

[56]Catherine Marfin, "Gun Bills Face Legislators' Concern," *San Antonio Express News*, (Sunday, December 23, 2018), A3.

[57]Ibid.

[58]Ibid.

[59]Ibid., 367-368.

[60]Blevins, 255-256.

[61]S. Dale McLemore and Harriet D. Romo, *Racial and Ethnic Relations in America*, 7th ed., (New York, New York: Pearson Education Inc., 2005), 24.

[62]J. R. Poole, *The Pursuits of Equality in American History*, (Los Angeles, California: University of California Press, 1978), 6-7.

[63]Arnoldo De Leon, *The Tejano Community, 1836-1900*, (Dallas, Texas: Southern Methodist University Press, 1997), 10-11.

[64]De Tocqueville, 317.

[65]McLemore and Romo, 114.

[66]Robert Wernick, "The Rise and Fall of a Fervid Third Party," *Smithsonian*, November, 1996, 152.

[67]Arnoldo De Leon, "Early Anglo Settlers View Mexicans With Hostility," *Major Problems in Texas History*, Sam W. Haynes and Cary D. Wintz, ed., (New York, N.Y.: Houghton Mifflin Company, 2002), 99.

[68]George H. Sabine, *The History of Political Thought*, 3rd ed., (New York, New York: Holt, Reinholt and Winston, 1961), 906.

[69]McLemore and Romo, 117-118.

[70]Joseph E. Harris, *Africans and Their History*, 2nd ed., (New York, New York: Meridian, 1998), 7.

[71]Ibid., 8.

[72]Ibid., 9.

[73]"The Ritual of A Secret Society: June 4, 1868," *Documents of Texas History*, Ernest Wallace, David M. Vigness and George B. Ward, eds., 2nd ed., (Austin, Texas: State House Press, 1994), 208.

[74]Earl Conrad, *Jim Crow America*, 2nd ed., (New York, New York: Duell, Sloan and Pearce, 1947), 27.

[75]Ibid., 27-28.

[76]Ibid., 63.

[77]Conrad, 94.

[78]2017 Hate Crime Statistics, (Washington, D.C.: Department of Justice- Federal Bureau of Investigation, 2017), Table 1, http://ucr.fbi.gov/hate-crime/2017

[79]Ibid.

[80]Erin Texeira, "Hate Groups' Revival Tied to Immigration," *San Antonio Express-News*, (Tuesday, February, 6, 2007), 4A.

[81]Henry Weinstein, "Court Bars Racial Profiling On Border," *San Antonio Express-News*, (Wednesday, April 12, 2000), 19A.

[82]Jonathan J. Cooper, "Video Tells How Arizona Policy May Use the Law," *San Antonio Express-News*, (Friday, July 2, 2010), 6A.

[83]Arnoldo De Leon, "Los Tejanos: An Overview of Their History," *The Texas Heritage*, Ben Proctor and Archie P. McDonald, eds., 1st ed., (Illinois: Forum 1980), 134.

[84]Eurene Barker, "Mexico and Texas: A Collision of Two Cultures," *Major Problems in Texas History*, Sam W. Haynes and Cary D. Wintz, eds., (New York, New York: Houghton Mifflin Company, 2002), 131.

[85]David J. Weber, "Refighting the Alamo: Mythmaking and the Texas Revolution," *Major Problems in Texas History*, Sam W. Haynes and Cary D. Wintz, eds., (New York, New York: Houghton Mifflin Company, 2002), 135-136.

[86]David J. Weber, "Mythmaking and the Texas Revolution," *Major Problems in Mexican American History*, Zaragosa Vargas, ed., (New York, New York: Houghton Mifflin Company, 1990), 108.

[87]Weber, "Refighting the Alamo: Mythmaking and the Texas Revolution," 137.

[88]McLemore ande Romo, 231.

[89]Ibid.

[90]Arnoldo De Leon, *They Called Them Greasers: Anglo Attitudes Towards Mexicans in Texas: 1821-1900*, (Austin, Texas: The University of Texas Press, 1983), 77.

[91]Simon Romero, "Latinos Push for Recognition of Lynchings," *San Antonio Express News*, (Sunday, March 3, 2019), A8.

[92]Ibid., 80.

[93]T. R. Fehrenbach, *Lone Star: A History of Texas and Texans*, (New York, New York: McMillan, 1991), 693.

[94]Romero, "Latinos Push for Recognition of Lynchings," A8.

[95]Blevins, 259.

[96]Paula Allen, "LULAC's Royalty History Dates to Late '40s," *San Antonio Express News*, (Sunday, May 21, 2017), A4.

[97]Mariana Pisano, "Organizer Remembered for Passion, Controversy," *San Antonio Express-News*, (Saturday, July 24, 1999), 1A.

[98]"Emma Tenayuca and Homer Brooks, Officers of the Texas Communist Party, Outline Their Vision for Mexican Unification, 1939," *Major Problems in Texas History*, Sam W. Haynes and Cary D. Wintz, eds., (New York, New York: Houghton Mifflin Company, 2002), 380.

[99]"Activist Empowered Pecan Shellers," *San Antonio Express News*, (Thursday, August 30, 2018), A8.

[100]Arnoldo De Leon, *Mexican Americans in Texas: A Brief History*, (Arlington Heights, Illinois: Harlan Davidson, 1993), 134.

[101]Paul Burke, "The Second Battle of the Alamo," *Texas Monthly's Political Reader*, December, 1997, 11.

[102]Ibid., 9.

[103]Herman Rosemberg, "Not All U.S. Hispanics Embrace Immigrants," *San Antonio Express-News*, (Wednesday, Aug. 17, 2005), 9A.

[104]"An Interview," *Voices of Diversity: Perspectives on American Political Ideals and Institutions*, Pat Andrews, ed., (Guilford, Connecticut: The Dushkin Publishing Group, 1995), 164-165.

[105]Randolph B. Campbell, *Gone to Texas: A History of the Lone Star State*, (New York, New York: Oxford University Press, 2003), 98.

[106]Ibid., 99.

[107]Peter Carlson, "Sam Houston Meets Alexis de Tocqueville," *American History*, Vol. 45, No. 4, October, 2010, 17.

[108]W. W. Newcomb, Jr., *The Indians of Texas from Prehistoric to Modern Times*, 11th ed., (Austin, Texas: The University of Texas Press, 1995), 334.

[109]Jan Reid, "The Warrior's Bride," *Texas Monthly*, February 2003, 142.

[110]Blevins, 256.

[111]Newcomb, 354.

[112]Anthony Delafora, "Center May Preserve Story of Long Walk," *The Dallas Morning News*, (March 8, 1998), 45A.

[113]Richard A. Marini, "Comanches Halted Expansion West," *San Antonio Express News*, (Thursday, April 13, 2017), A8.

[114]McLemore and Romo, 298.

[115]Welch, Gruhl, Steinman, Corner and Rigdon, 505.

[116]Bill Baskerville, "Indians Say 'No Thanks,'" *San Antonio Express-News*, (Thursday, November 23, 2000), 3AA.

[117]McLemore and Romo, 311.

[118]Blevins, 259.

[119]C. VanWoodward, *The Strange Case of Jim Crow*, 3rd ed., (New York, New York: Oxford Unviersity Press, 1974), 11.

[120]Terry G. Jordaon, "A Century and a Half of Ethnic Change in Texas, 1836-1986," *Texas Vistas: Selections from the Southwestern Historical Quarterly*, Ralph A. Wooster and Robert A. Calvert, eds., (Austin, Texas: University at Austin, 1987), 336.

[121]Van Woodward, 21.

[122]"General Gordon Granger Frees All Texas Slaves, June 19, 1865," *Major Problems in Texas History*, Sam W. Haynes and Cary D. Wintz, eds., (New York, New York: Houghton Mifflin Company, 2002), 240.

[123]Anne Dingus, "Independence Day," *Texas Monthly*, June, 2001, 64.

[124]"As Blacks Celebrate Juneteenth, Initiative for Apology Is Revisited," *San Antonio Express-News*, (Tuesday, June 20, 2000), 5A.

[125]Abraham and Perry, 374.

[126]Van Woodward, 104.

[127]"A Sharecropping Contract, 1886," *Major Problems in the History of the American South*, Vol. 2: The New South, Paul D. Escott, David R. Goldfield, Sally G. McMillen and Elizabeth Hayes Turnner, eds., 2nd. ed., (New York, New York: Houghton Mifflin, 1999), 59.

[128]Robert A. Calvert, Arnoldo De Leon and Greg Cantrell, *The History of Texas*, 3rd ed., (Wheeling, Illinois: Harlan Davidson, Inc., 2002), 166.

[129]Abraham and Perry, 375.

[130]Keith Weldon Medley, "The Sad Story of How 'Separate But Equal' Was Born,' *Smithsonian*, February, 1994, 108-109.

[131]Domino, 226.

[132]David Uhler, "Jim Crow Was A Loser In Korean War," *San Antonio Express-News*, (Sunday, June 4, 2000), 1A.

[133]Richard Conniff, "Frederick Douglass Always Knew He Was Meant To Be Free," *Smithsonian*, February, 1995, 126-127.

[134]Paul Finkleman, "Race and the Constitution," *By and For the People: Constitutional Rights in American History*, Kermit L. Hall, ed., (Arlington Heights, Illinois: Harlan Davidson, 1991), 155.

[135]"Ida B. Wells Reports on the Horrors of Lynching in the South, 1892," *Major Problems in the History of the American South, Vol. 2, The New South*, Paul D. Escott, David R. Goldfield, Sally G. McMillen and Elizabeth Hayes Turner, (New York, New York: Houghton Mifflin Company, 1999), 157.

[136]Conrad, 98.

[137]Van Woodward, 18-19.

[138]Conrad, 156.

[139]Schulman, 78.

[140]Abraham and Perry, 396.

[141]Poole, 296.

[142]Carmina Danini, "Women's Rights Ahead of the Times," *San Antonio Express News*, (Wednesday, May 17, 2017), A10.

[143]Ibid.

[144]Lynne E. Ford, *Women and Politics: The Pursuit of Equality*, 2nd ed., (New York, New York: Houghton Mifflin Company, 2006), 13-14.

[145]Ann Patton Malone, "Victoria Womanhood on the Texas Frontier," *Major Problems in Texas History*, Sam Haynes and Cary D. Wintz, eds., (New York, New York: Houghton Mifflin Company, 2002), 200-201.

[146]"The 'Declaration of Sentiments' of the Seneca Falls Convention, 1848," *Major Problems in American Women's History*, 2nd ed., Mary Beth Norton and Ruth M. Alexander, eds., (Lexington, Massachusetts: D. C. Heath and Company, 1996), 167.

[147]"Catherine Beecher and Harriet Beecher Stowe on Why Women Should Not Seek the Vote, 1869," *Major Problems in American Women's History*, 2nd ed., Mary Beth Norton and Ruth M. Alexander, eds., (Lexington, Massachusetts: D. C. Heath and Company, 1996), 169.

[148]Majorie Sprull Wheeler, "The Woman's Suffrage Movement in the Inhospitable South," *Major Problems in the History of the American South: Vol. 2: The New South*, Paul D. Escott, David R. Goldfield, Sally G. McMillen and Elizabeth Hayes Turner, (New York, New York: Houghton Mifflin Company, 1999), 278.

[149]ProQuest, *ProQuest Statistical Abstract of the United States: 2019*, 7th ed., (Bethesda, Maryland, 2018), Table 618, 396.

[150]Ibid., Table 256, 169.

[151]"Separating the Sisters," *U.S. News & World Report*, March 28, 1994, 49.

Chapter 12

Social Service Public Policy Issues

**Signing of the Health Research Facilities Amendments
National Institute of Health, Bethesda, Maryland, August 9, 1965
Credit: LBJ Library**

Welfare is an issue that is not popular in Texas. Poverty. The Dole. Dependency. All appear to fly in the face of reality and the myth which is Texas. Texas is a state that champions success, whose people display their wealth conspicuously. Timber, cattle, cotton, water, oil, and high-tech are the concerns that have shaped Texas politics for the last fifty years. In Texas, poverty has been a side issue, a problem to be solved by further expansion of the economy. It has not been a matter of central concern to either policy makers or the public as a whole. Yet poverty is a problem in Texas, a problem that has haunted the state as it has been transformed from a rural backwater dependent upon outside economic interests into a dynamic urban economy in its own right. The Texas success story has not solved the problem of poverty in the Lone Star State. Indeed, the state has barely begun to address it.[1]

Since the 1980 election of Ronald Reagan to the White House, politicians and lawmakers from both political parties have been consumed with reforming the welfare system created during the New Deal administration of Franklin Roosevelt and health care. Reagan, in particular, used the perceived failure of the welfare system to justify his contention that government in general is too big, too intrusive, too expensive, and too narrow-minded to see that the nation's welfare system simply was not working. According to Reagan, far too many of the nation's impoverished had become totally dependent upon welfare as their sole source of income. Welfare had changed from an initial intention of temporary assistance to a permanent entitlement. Something had to be done to change the cycle of poverty with its dependency on the dole. Despite the rhetoric, the Reagan administration did not offer any unique approaches to welfare reform. The Clinton administration did attempt a reform package with the passage of the **Personal Responsibility and Work Opportunity Reconciliation Act**; however, their effort to reform health care failed. Although he bragged about his welfare reform efforts in Texas, the Bush White House did not initiate any meaningful efforts towards revamping welfare, opting instead to back prescription medication reform of Part D of Medicare. The Obama administration passed a major health-care reform package. Off to a slow start, Obamacare has provided millions with affordable or, if eligible, free heath care. Yet, there are still millions of Americans without any medical coverage whatsoever. Additionally, states with Republican governors including Texas have decided not to promote Obama's health care initiative, opting instead to file a federal lawsuit challenging the constitutionality of the entire program while Republican members of Congress continued unsuccessfully to either appeal it or unfund it.

Although it appears that the nation's economy is recovering, many state governors are still confronted with too many problems and too little money to address them particularly when it comes to the poverty stricken and chronically unemployed residents of their states. It appears that the economy is indeed recovering from the recent recession. Unemployment is at an all-time low. It appears on the surface that Americans are returning to work, earning more money, buying more goods and services, and stimulating economic growth across the nation. However, the benefits of a recovering economy have failed to trickle down fast enough to all Americans. Many are still faced with loss of jobs, prolonged periods of unemployment, and uncertainty about any future extensions of unemployment benefits. Far too many of the nation's middle- and lower-income workers are living pay check to pay check, wondering whether they will be next to receive "the pink slip" and eventually join the ranks of those statistically living below the poverty level. One wonders how can a nation endowed with so much wealth and know-how be so unable to adequately address the needs of its most needy citizens.

Unfortunately, the answers are embedded in an extremely complex and oftentimes painfully difficult reexamination of the American social conscious as well as the capitalistic free-market economic system. The Framers realized the responsibility government had to its citizens by charging it with the task of promoting the general welfare for **all** of its citizens, regardless of social class or economic position. While liberals and conservatives argue over philosophical positions and congressional and state legislative Democrats and Republicans continue to hurl insults and point fingers at each other, the sad reality is that the poor are becoming more numerous and poorer each day as the gap between the rich and poor widens. Reality reveals that millions of Americans are living below the poverty level with the majority toiling away at minimum-wage jobs without employer provided benefits or health-care coverage for themselves or their family members.

By the end of 2016, 44,269,000 Americans representing 14.0 percent of the nation's population were living below the poverty level.[2] However, the 2016 poverty rate for Texas was 15.6 percent for individuals and 12.0 percent for families, placing 4,261,000 individuals and 795,000 families in poverty. Among her sister states and the District of Columbia, Texas ranked 12th highest in the number of individuals and 2nd highest in the number of families living below the poverty level.[3] By the end of 2017, 6,982,000 or 4.4 percent of the nation's total civilian workforce were unemployed.[4] The Texas unemployment rate in 2017 at 4.3 percent is barely under the national rate. Basically, 578,000 Texans were unemployed of which 147,000 are also uninsured.[5] In 2017, the nation's civilian labor force totaled 160,320,000 but only 42.4 percent were employed in full time positions.[6] Although the nation's economy is slowing recovering from its 2008 recession, the trend still holds that businesses are reluctant to hire to the full-time levels they had before 2008. From 2016 to 2017, the average annual wage for American workers rose by 3.3 percent, but in Texas, it averaged only 2.7 percent.[7] Although the cost of living has been steadily rising, the size of the average worker's paycheck simply cannot keep up with rising costs. One's income does vary according to where one lives and works. In the northeast, one's median family income is $81,502 in 2016 compared to the south, which includes Texas, whereby the median family income is only $66,505.[8] Furthermore, the U.S. Department of House and Urban Development (HUD) reports that "on a single night in 2016, 549,928 people were experiencing homelessness in the United States . . .

with over one-fifth of people experiencing homelessness were children."[9] There is much truth to the adage that the rich are getting richer and poor are becoming poorer. Table 12.1 illustrates the share of the nation's aggregated income for 2016. Nationwide, the highest fifth or 20 percent of the nation's households have 51.1 percent of the nation's total income with the top 5 percent holding 22.6 percent of that wealth. The other four fifths or 80 percent of the nation's households collectively have only 48.5% of aggregate income. The lowest fifth possesses only 3.1 percent or $24,002 per household. Statistics alone do not adequately portray the depth of this nation's poverty. Every number or percentage on a chart, bar-graph, flip chart or bell-curve represents a man, woman or child who, with few exceptions, found themselves impoverished and struggling for survival through no direct fault of their own. America has a serious poverty problem that cannot be cured overnight with the stroke of a president's or a governor's pen.

In Texas, the myth of the economically successful rugged self-reliant individual has blinded many Texans from the stark reality that this state has a severe poverty problem. For too many years, the myth of potentially unlimited wealth for everyone who lives south of the Red River has hidden the truth of the state's poverty situation from outsiders and, unfortunately, ourselves. In reality, Texas is a rich state for the privileged few and a poor state for the many. Several border counties are so mired in impoverished conditions that living conditions are closely akin to third-world poverty. Sadly, most Americans believe that all poverty-stricken individuals are receiving benefits

---

Table 12.1 Share of Aggregate Income Received by Each Fifth and Top 5 Percent of Households – 2016

Total Number of Households as of 2016 – 126,224,000

Fifth	Upper Limit of Each Fifth	Percent Distribution of Aggregate Income
Lowest Fifth	$ 24,002	3.1%
Second Fifth	45,600	8.3
Third Fifth	74,869	14.2
Fourth Fifth	121,018	22.9
Highest Fifth		51.5
Top 5%, Lower Limit	$225,251	22.6%

Source: ProQuest LLC. *ProQuest Statistical Abstract of the United States, 2019*, (7th ed.), Bethesda, Maryland, 2018, Table 722, page 472.

through the welfare system. In reality, only a percentage of the state's impoverished qualify for cash support services and programs. The services themselves particularly in Texas are not ample enough to truly sustain qualifying poverty-stricken individuals.

This chapter examines the reality of poverty in Texas. While state lawmakers boast of the amount of money the state gives to the "less fortunate," reality shows that the majority of the state's money goes to public education and highways while the state's contributions to social service programs are constitutionally restricted to just 1 percent of the state's budget. Texas consistently ranks in the bottom forty-five among her sister states in its commitment to social service policy programs. "In the best of times, Texas has followed reluctantly the lead of other states in trying to meet the needs of poor people. In the worst, Texas has had to be compelled by either the courts or the federal government to meet what many considered to be a minimal level of subsistence."[10] This noticeable lack of enthusiasm for social service public policy initiatives on the part of both the state's legislative and executive branches is no sheer accident or minor oversight. This chapter delves into the impact that traditional anti-tax, anti-welfare, and pro-self-sufficiency attitudes have had on every discussion on poverty-related problems within this state. Basically, "sympathy for the downtrodden isn't a part of our history; within Texas, people have had to fend for themselves under harsh circumstances, and there has not been much dissatisfaction with the results."[11] Consequently, all state programs are marginally funded and aimed primarily at assisting the "truly" deserving poor who are subjected to stiff eligibility requirements. "A tragic fact is that the Texas economic system ill serves millions of Texans. Texas poverty is a poverty of cheap labor and inadequate services."[12]

The Reality of Poverty

Poverty is "the state of condition of being poor by lacking the means of providing material needs or comfort."[13] Determining the actual number of people living in poverty is totally dependent upon both the measurement tool used to define economic deprivation and the method of applying that tool. The primary source of information is the Census conducted every ten years by the federal government. Accurate data is essential since states receive federal funding for social service programs based on both the number of poverty-stricken residents and their income levels. Currently policy makers use a loose definition of the **poverty level** provided by the federal government to determine both the statistical database of the number of people living in poverty and their benefit eligibility based on a two-step approach: "first, the monetary cost of a nutritionally sound minimum diet is determined. Second, the cost of the minimum diet is multiplied by three to allow for expenditures on all other goods and services. The multiplier value of three was chosen because the cost of food represented about one-third of the average family's after-tax money income."[14] The level is adjusted annually for inflation. Table 12.2 lists the weighted average poverty thresholds for 1980 through 2016. In 2016, the poverty levels were $11,511 for an individual over the age of 65, $19,105 for a family of three, and $24,563 for a family of four. The highest range is $49,721 for a family of nine or more persons. Each year the income levels are only marginally increased. For example, the poverty level for one person (unrelated individual) increased by only $1,091 from 2010 to 2016. Usually the benefit eligibility income level for social service programs is set at 125 percent to as high as 200 percent above the poverty level.

In measuring poverty, one can apply either an elastic or inelastic approach. Currently, the federal government's approach uses **absolute poverty**, defined as the minimum amount of income needed to survive without deprivation. This is an inelastic measurement with marginal adjustments made only for yearly increases in inflation. On the other hand, **relative poverty** is determined by comparing an individual's income against society's overall standard of living. This is an elastic approach to measuring poverty. As standard living costs increase, the gap between rich and poor widens, resulting in an increase in the number of individuals living in poverty. The adverse situation would occur with a decline in the standard of living. The controversy over defining the poverty level sharply divides liberals and conservatives. "Conservative critics of the official definition point out that it is based on cash income and does not count family assets or in-kind (non-cash) benefits from government, such as food stamps, medical care, and public housing. If poverty rate calculations include these factors, the net poverty rate is lower than the official rate; fewer people are considered poor."[15] Liberals, on the other hand, believe that "taxes, work expenses, child care costs, and medical expenses paid by consumers from their own pockets should be deducted from cash income."[15] If poverty rate calculations included these costs the net poverty rate would be higher. Despite their concerns, Congress continues to use the current standard developed over forty years ago.

Within the ranks of the poverty-stricken, a distinction can be made between several subcategories. The **working**

Table 12.2   Weighted Average Poverty Thresholds: 1980 to 2016

Size of Unit	1980	1990	2000	20	2016
One Person (Unrelated Individual)	$4,190	$6,652	$8,794	$11,137	$12,228
Under 65	4,290	6,800	8,959	11,344	12,468
65 Years and Older	3,949	6,268	8,259	11,354	11,511
Two Persons	5,363	8,509	11,235	14,216	15,569
Householder Under 65 Years of Age	5,537	8,794	11,589	15,589	16,151
Householder 65 Years of Age and Older	4,983	7,905	10,418	13,194	14,522
Three Persons	6,585	10,419	13,740	17,373	19,105
Four Persons	8,414	13,359	17,604	22,315	24,563
Five Persons	9,966	15,792	20,815	26,442	29,111
Six Persons	11,269	17,839	23,533	29,904	32,928
Seven Persons	12,761	20,241	26,750	34,019	37,458
Eight Persons	14,199	22,582	29,701	37,953	41,781
Nine or More Persons	16,896	26,848	35,150	45,224	49,721

Source: ProQuest LLC. *ProQuest Statistical Abstract of the United States, 2019*, (7th ed.), Bethesda, Maryland, 2018, Table 736, page 480.

poor are generally undereducated high school dropouts either employed full time or part-time at minimum or below minimum wage salary levels. The nation's first minimum wage was set in 1940 at 25 cents per hour. Nationwide there has been a shift from a predominately full time workforce to part-time. Approximately 7,545,000 Americans hold two or more part time jobs.[16] The largest chunk of a company's expenses goes towards employee salaries and benefits. In 2009, the federal minimum wage was raised to $7.25 an hour. For a full time worker, 80 hours of work per week means $290 per pay check before deductions for a yearly total of $15,080. States do have the option to pay a **living wage,** a rate above the federal minimum to adjust for increases in living costs. As of 2019, twenty-eight states have set a minimum wage above $7.25 an hour. Employees in the District of Columbia earn $14 per hour while Washington state, California, and Massachusetts pay $12 per hour, the highest minimum wage among the states.[17] Texas opts just to pay the federal minimum wage. Standard deductions include Social Security, withholding taxes, and insurance and health-care premiums. Usually, health care is offered at 100 percent employer paid or a percentage of employer-paid for only full time employees. The employee must pay 100 percent of dependent care. Part-time workers fare worse. According to federal labor laws, employers are not required to offer health-care benefits to part-time wage earners working less than 37.5 hours per week. Health care and, if offered to full time employees, pension benefits are mandatory only if employees work over 37.5 hours per week for a total of 2,080 hours per year. Whether one is paid a living or minimum wage, "the reality for a minimum wage worker is that every penny makes a difference, because low-wage workers make the choice between putting food on the table and paying for electricity or buying clothes for their children."[18]

The **hyperpoor** are those individuals whose annual incomes amount to less than half of official poverty level. Nationwide in 2016, 7,1243,000 men and 3,102 women age fifteen and older earned less than $5,000 per year.[19] Nonworking poor include individuals currently receiving unemployment benefits, the totally disabled/mentally ill, the elderly whose incomes fall below the poverty level, and the homeless.

Estimating the actual number of homeless individuals depends on how one defines homelessness. HUD defines homeless as "a person who lacks a fixed, regular, and adequate nighttime residence." The agency differentiates sheltered homeless as individuals "who are staying in emergency shelters, transitional housing programs or safe havens" from the chronically homeless individual or people in families who are individuals or a family member "with a disability who has been continuously homeless for one year or more or has experienced at least four episodes of homelessness in the last three years where the combined length of time homeless in those occasions is at least twelve months."[20] According to HUD, of 549,928 people experiencing homelessness in 2016, "68 percent were staying in emergency shelters, transitional housing programs, or safe havens and 32 percent were in unsheltered locations. Furthermore, in 2016:

- Approximately 22 percent of the nation's homeless are children with 69 percent over the age of 24, and 9 percent between the ages of 18 and 24.
- 355,212 or 65 percent of the homeless are individuals with 89 percent over the age of 24, 10 percent between 18 and 24, and 1 percent under the age of 18.
- 194,716 people in families with children experienced homelessness of which 60 percent of the children were under the age of 18, 32 percent were over 24 and 8 percent were between the ages of 18 and 24.
- 35,686 of the homeless were unaccompanied youth with the majority (89 percent) between the ages of 18 and 24.
- 77,000 individuals were reported as chronically homeless. Two-thirds were living on the streets rather than staying in sheltered locations. This is the only population group whereby the number of unsheltered is greater than the number staying in sheltered facilities.
- Although strides have been made to address the housing needs for veterans, nearly 40,000 veterans are still experiencing homelessness, and 33 percent were on the street.[21]

A state by state analysis shows that the homeless population in Texas declined 2.4 percent from 2015 estimates. Yet, the 2016 homeless population in Texas is composed of:

- 15,959 homeless individuals
- 7,163 people in families with children
- 1,309 unaccompanied youth
- 1,768 veterans
- 3,534 chronically homeless individuals.[22]

Although many of the homeless do qualify for food stamps, they simply cannot use them effectively. Without permanent shelter, they cannot carry or store a large amount of perishable food items or can goods, and most shelters do not have cooking areas for public use. Only a handful of restaurants and fast-food chains will accept food stamps. These figures are not truly representative of the entire nation's homeless population. Many Americans are at-risk of becoming homeless due to a multiplicity of reasons such as unemployment, foreclosure, bankruptcy, and lack of affordable housing. For too many Americans, 50 percent or more of their monthly paycheck goes to rent or a mortgage payment. According to the National Alliance to End Homelessness, the number of households facing a severe housing burden reached 6,902, 600 in 2016, a 3.1 percent decrease over 2015 figures. However, the 6.9 million Americans facing a housing burden is 30 percent higher than 2007 figures. For many Americans, the monthly rent is just unaffordable. To avoid homelessness, 4,609,826 individuals in 2016 alone opt to move in or 'double up' with relatives or friends. Nationwide, this represents a 30 percent increase over 2007 figures. In Texas, the number of individuals doubling up increased in 2016 by 5 percent over 2015 figures.[23] Several major cities across the state have changed their approach to homelessness by building homeless campuses such as San Antonio's Haven for Hope. This facility provides a comprehensive approach to homelessness by providing separate housing for single persons and families as well as protected outdoor sleeping areas for those who simply are too uncomfortable sleeping in a confined place. Also, the facility provides medical, dental, psychological, and drug rehabilitation services as well as job training programs and job placement services. Day care services are provided for families with small children. School-age children are placed into local school districts. The aim is to provide the homeless with the tools they need to hopefully never be homeless again.

The **feminization of poverty** is a term used to recognize the increase of single-parent families headed by a female whose income falls below the poverty level. Since the 1960s, there has been a dramatic and steady increase in the number of female-headed households. The rise in matriarchal families is attributed to the increase in the number of divorces, separations and out-of-wedlock pregnancies as well as independent living styles. Usually these women are too undereducated and under-skilled for the higher salary paying job market. Consequently they are employed at the lowest ranking positions at minimum wage or slightly lower without meaningful opportunities for promotion or advancement. Women in and at-risk of poverty are also confronted with the widening pay gap issue. In 2016, the earnings of full-time year-round workers with a high school diploma was $50,557 for men, and only $35,613 for women, a difference of $14,944 per year.[24] Financially, these women are confronted with an inadequate child support system that simply does not cover the rising costs for day care, health care, education and other necessary children-related expenses. In 2016, the median income of a female householder, no husband present, was $41,027 while for a married couple, the median family income was $87,057, and for a male householder, no wife present, $58,051.25

Another category of poverty is the permanent or persistently poor versus the marginal or temporarily poor. The determination is based on the individual's income level over a ten-year span. An individual is categorized as **permanent** or **persistently poor** when his/her income level has been below the poverty level for eight years or longer within a ten-year period. Individuals whose incomes are below the poverty level for less than two years within a ten-year span are **temporarily** or **marginally poor**. Of course, each group has a different set of needs required to overcome their financial hardships. The persistently poor require long-term housing, food, and financial assistance as well as extensive job training and education programs. The temporarily poor need short-term assistance including unemployment compensation, rent subsidies, health-care benefits, and perhaps food stamps while seeking employment. However, most social service programs on both the federal and state level tend to be "one-size-fits-all" plans that do not meet the unique needs of both groups. Unfortunately, statistics from both the federal government and private groups do not adequately account for the millions of vulnerable Americans whose income levels are so close to the poverty level that any depreciable dip in income will plunge them into poverty. Living pay-check-to-pay-check, these are the American workers who do not accumulate savings, have few assets other than their homes or, as in most instances, do not own a home and are the hardest hit in the pocketbook when they get fired, laid off, widowed, or face a medical or financial crisis. There are few if any public policy initiatives that address these concerns.

One of the most prevalent myths about poverty is that it is primarily a minority problem. Statistics indicate otherwise. The percentage of Anglo families and individuals whose incomes place them below the poverty level is less than the figures for Hispanic and African-American families and individuals. However, the numbers reveal a different picture. In 2016, approximately 40,616,000 individuals accounting for 12.7 percent of the nation's population had incomes falling below the poverty level.[26] Traditionally, the percentage of poverty stricken Anglos (Whites) has been consistently lower than the rate for Hispanics and blacks (African Americans). However,

the total number of Anglo (White) individuals living below the poverty level continues to be higher than the combined totals for blacks (African Americans) and Hispanics. In 2016, nationwide 27,113,000 Anglo (White) individuals representing 11.0 percent of all Anglos (Whites) earned wages below the poverty level compared to 9,234,000 or 22.0 percent blacks (African Americans), 11,137,000 or 19.4 percent Hispanics and 1,908,000 or 10.1 percent Asians.[27] The same trend holds for families below the poverty level. In 2016, 8,081,000 or 9.8 percent of all families had incomes below the poverty level. The family poverty rate for Anglo (White) families is 8.3 percent, considerably lower percent-wise than black (African-American) families with a rate of 19.0 percent and 17.3 percent for Hispanic families but numerically, 5,433,000 Anglo (White) families live in poverty compared to 1,893,000 Black (African American) and 2,253,000 Hispanic families.[28] Nationwide, 12,803,000 or 17.6 percent of the nation's children under the age of eighteen are living in poverty. The percentages for black (African American) and Hispanic children living in poverty continue to be alarming. In 2016, 3,382,000 or 30.6 percent Black (African American) and 4,764,000 or 26.3 percent Hispanic children lived in poverty conditions.[29]

Profile of Texas Poverty

The 2000 Census and subsequent reports paint a bleak picture of Texas's poverty that clearly shoots holes into the myth of an abundantly rich state. In 2017, the per capita income for Texans was $46,942, ranking her as 26th in the nation among her sister states and the District of Columbia.[30] Since 2010, the state's per capita income increased by $9,046, moving the state's ranking from 28th to 26th. Table 12.3 indicates the per capita incomes for the state's fifteen highest and lowest ranking counties. Of its 254 counties, only 63 reported per capita incomes above the 2015 national figure of $48,112. Overall, these figures underscore that Texas has a very serious poverty problem. It is also a disproportionate problem for the majority of these counties listed in the lowest fifteen either directly share the international border with Mexico or are contiguous to those counties. Disposal income is "total personal income minus personal current taxes."[31] While the nation's average disposal income in 2017 was $44,107, overall disposal income in Texas was only $42,156, $1,951 below national figures.[32]

For the state's poor, it is a vicious cycle of the lack of education leading to a minimum wage or better job with no opportunity for promotion into a higher salaried

Table 12.3 – Ranking of Texas Counties by Per Capita Income – 2015

United States Average 2015 Per Capital Income - $48,112

Texas Statewide Average 2015 Per Capita Income - $46,947

The Top Fifteen in Per Capita Income—2015

Ranking	County	2011 Per Capita Income
1	Shackelford	$132,989
2	McMullen	107,627
3	Midland	106,588
4	Hemphill	88,255
5	Hansford	86,619
6	Sherman	81,876
7	Glasscock	78,529
8	King	78,216
9	Kendall	75,638
10	Ochitree	72,785
11	Hartley	71,581
12	Terrell	70192
13	Irion	69,555
14	Dallam	69,427
15	Kenedy	67,830

The Lowest Fifteen In Per Capita Income—2015

Ranking	County	2011 Per Capita Income
240	Jones	$29,819
241	Webb	29,778
242	Hudspeth	28,621
243	Bee	28,423
244	Willacy	28,078
245	Jim Hogg	27,961
246	Zapata	27,625
247	Childress	27,471
248	Maverick	26,982
249	Zavala	26,855
250	Cameron	26,826
251	Waller	26,061
252	Hidalgo	24,579
253	Starr	24,540
254	Concho	22,008

Source: *Texas Almanac 2018-2019*, Denton, Texas: Texas State Historical Association, page 627-629.

position. They only hope is to return to school for further education or job training. However, most companies do not provide cash incentives or tuition reimbursement programs for their workers. Far too many of the state's poor work more than the standard forty-hour work week, leaving little time for schooling or family responsibilities. Low paying jobs also equate to a lack of disposal income for decent housing, clothing, food, and particularly health care.

Studies prepared by the United States Department of Housing and Urban Development (HUD) point to the nation's lack of affordable housing for those who incomes are in the lowest brackets. Across the nation, the recent collapse of the home mortgage industry offset with a rise in foreclosures impacted primarily middle- and upper income groups. Nationally, there has always been a lack of affordable housing for lower-income families. These families can barely afford rental properties, much less the mortgage payment on a modestly priced home. In 1974, the federal government launched a rent subsidy program called **Section 8** with the passage of the **Housing and Community Development Act**. Local housing authorities can provide rent assistance to qualifying applicants whose total family income is less than 80

percent of the median family income of their individual city's family income levels. HUD pays up to 70 percent of the monthly payment. HUD uses a Fair Market Rent figure calculated for every state and city as their guide for establishing eligibility for federal rent subsidy programs. Currently, HUD estimates that approximately 843,060 or 23 percent of Texans are renters rather than homeowners simply because their incomes are too low to afford a mortgage payment. Furthermore, HUD estimates that 74 percent of extremely low-income renter households have a severe cost burden to even pay the rent. The annual household income needed to afford a two-bedroom rental home at HUD's Fair Market Rent in Texas is $40,185. Consequently, statewide Texas is short 594,631 affordable rental homes for extremely low-income renters.[33] Across the state, there are plenty of existing homes for those in the middle- and- upper- income brackets. However, there is not enough low-cost housing to go around. Even those who qualify for HUD assistance are placed on a three-month to three-year long waiting list.

Table 12.4 indicates how Texas ranks among her sister states. According to 2016 figures, Texas has the highest rating in the total number of persons in correctional facilities, and as of 2016, Texas ranked 12th in the total

---

Table 12.4   Poverty-Related Statistics: Texas Versus Her Sister States

Factor	Statewide Statistics	Ranking Among The States[1]
Personal Per Capita Income (2017)	$ 46,942	26th
Individuals Below the Poverty Level (2016)_	4,425,000	12th
Families Below the Poverty Level (2016)	639,000	2nd
Total Number of Persons in Correctional Facilities (2016)	172,506	2nd
Total Number of Families Receiving TANF3 (2017)	970,000	3rd
Total Number of Individuals Receiving TANF (2017)	61,600	6th
State Expenditures for TANF (2016)	$843,000,000	7th
Persons Receiving SNAP Benefits4 (2017)	3,921,000	2nd
Children Enrolled in CHIP5 (2017)	1,137,899	2nd
State Expenditures for CHIP (2017)	$93,700,000	3rd
Persons Without Health Insurance (2016)	4,545,000	1st
Children Without Health Insurance (2016)	671,000	1st
Number of Unemployed (2017)	583,000	2nd
Average Weekly Unemployment Benefits (2016)	$ 403	9th

[1]Ranking puts the worst state at number 1.
2Texas is tied with Georgia and Tennessee.
3TANF – Temporary Assistance for Needy Families
4SNAP- Supplemental Nutrition Assistance Program (Food Stamps)
5CHIP – Children's Health Insurance Program

Source: ProQuest LLC. *ProQuest Statistical Abstract of the United States, 2019,* (7th ed.), Bethesda, Maryland, 2018, Tables 156, 162, 380, 580, 586, 588, 618, 706, 735, pages 109, 113, 240, 375, 378, 379, 390, 460, 479.

number of families living in poverty. In 2017, Texas ranked 8th in the total number of families and 6th in the total number of individuals receiving Temporary Assistance for Needy Families (TANF) benefits. In 2016, the state had approximately 4,261,000 persons living in poverty, the 12th highest poverty rate among the fifty states. With approximately 583,000 unemployed Texans, the state gives qualifying jobless Texans an average benefit of only $403 per week. Unfortunately, these current statistics are merely a continuation of the state's dismal track record in addressing the needs of its neediest residents.

Table 12.5 is a summary of key indicators obtained from an annual survey conducted by the Annie B. Casey Foundation, a privately funded organization. In its 2018 report, Texas ranked 35th in providing for the economic well-being of the state's children; 32nd in education accomplishments, 41st in health-related concerns, and 47th in its provision of programs and benefits to assist family and community concerns. Overall, Texas garnered a ranking of 43rd among her sister states. The state was accessed the worst rating of first in the category of teens not in school and not working, the 5th highest in the number of 4th graders not proficient in reading, and highest in the nation of teen births per 1,000.

Education is and always will be the key to one's ability to leave poverty behind them. However, high dropout rates coupled with low high school and college graduation rates is a national problem with no clear-cut solution in sight. Nationally by 2009, 3,185,000, representing 7.0 percent of the nation's youth, dropped out of high school. The dropout rates for minorities continue to be alarming. In 2009, 125,000 or 4.1 percent of Hispanic students ages 16 to 17 and 548,000 or 17.8 percent of Hispanics between 18 and 21 did not complete their high school education. In total, 14.7 percent of all Hispanic youths between the ages of 16 to 24 did not earn a high school diploma. Approximately 66,000 black (African-American) youths between the ages of 16 to 17, and 330,000 between the ages of 18 and 21, and 175,000 between the ages of 22 and 24 dropped out of high school. Consequently, 8.2 percent of all black (African-American) youths between the ages of 16 to 24 did not graduate from high school. Although the percentages for Anglo (White) youths in the same age brackets are lower than the percentages for Hispanics and blacks (African Americans), approximately 2,421,000 Anglo (White) youths did not receive a high school diploma in 2009.[33]

Hunger and poverty go hand and hand. Nutritionists stress that hunger has a direct impact on a child's ability to retain knowledge. "Hungry children are more than four times as likely as other children to suffer from fatigue and twice as likely to suffer from frequent colds, ear infections, and headaches. Hungry children miss school because of sickness more often, and they go to the doctor almost twice as often."[36] These at-risk children far too often will become tomorrow's high school dropouts saddled with the same dismal employment and income cycles that keep their parents mired in poverty. Many children born in poverty do not live to adulthood. "Poor diet is closely related to low birth weight, which is a factor in the deaths of infants during their first twelve months. Twenty-three other developed nations have lower infant-mortality rates than the United States."[37] Unfortunately, children in poverty have been the forgotten victims for far too many years.

As the budget cutters in the Texas Legislature devise means to offset the state's deficit, senior citizens across the state are growing anxious as talks in legislative chambers focus on proposing deep cuts to social service programs, many geared towards the state's senior citizens. In 2017, approximately 15.6 percent of the nation's population was 65 years or older. In Texas, there are 2,089,000 individuals between the ages of 65 and 74, 988,000 between the ages of 75 and 84 years or age, and 395,000 over 85. Nationwide in 2016, 4,568,000 or 9.3 percent of the nation's total population over the age of 65 had incomes below the poverty level despite the fact that they were either employed or were receiving some form of government sponsored assistance.[38]

Poverty Along the Border and South Texas

Stretching along the Rio Grande from El Paso to Brownsville, the border counties are among the poorest in the nation. Fifteen of the state's 254 counties are the poorest in the state in per capital income with the remaining counties in the border region ranking just slightly above them. For over twenty years, Starr County has had the dubious distinction of being the nation's poorest county only to be replaced in 2015 by Concho County. The majority of the state's Hispanic population base is located in the Rio Grande Valley. The counties directly along the shared border with Mexico are heavily engaged in tourism and service-sector employment opportunities. The economic viability of these counties is directly tied to the state of Mexico's economy and, most recently, its rising drug-cartel violence. The survival of the American side of the border is just as dependent upon the Mexican tourist as the Mexican side depends upon the American bargain hunter. Also counties located in the interior of the border region are predominantly agricultural-based, dependent

Table 12.5   Kids Count 2018 Survey—Texas Report
Nationally Texas ranks 43rd about her sister states with New Mexico ranking the worst at 50.

Note: A number one ranking in bold means that the state has the highest ranking among her sister states. For example, New Hampshire has the highest overall ranking, making it the best state in the group in child-well being rankings A number one ranking in non-bold means that the state has the highest number of individuals in that category. For example, California ranks number one in the total number of children living in poverty.

Indicator	Findings
Economic Well-Being:	**35th**
Total Number of Children Living in Poverty – 1,619,000 (2016)	2nd
Total Number of Children Whose Parents Lack Secure Employment – 1,979,000 (2016)	2nd
Total Number of Children Living in Households with a High Housing Cost Burden - 2,287,000 (2016)	2nd
Teens Not in School and Not Working – 127,000 (2016)	1st
Education Rank:	**32nd**
Young Children (ages 3 &4) Not in School – 463,000 (2016)	1st
Fourth Graders Not Proficient in Reading – 71% (2017)	5th
Eighth Graders Not Proficient in Math – 67% (2017)	18th
Health Rank:	**41st**
Low Birth-Weight Babies – 33,445 (2016)	2nd
Children Without Health Insurance – 671,000 (2016)	2nd
Child and Teen Deaths per 100,000 – 2,027 (2016)	2nd
Teens Who Abuse Alcohol or Drugs 109,000 (2016)	2nd
Family and Community Rank:	**47th**
Children in Single Parent Families – 2,464,000 (2016)	2nd
Children in Families where the Household Head Lacks a High School Diploma – 1,1467,000 (2016)	2nd
Children Living in High Poverty Areas – 1,198,000 (2016)	2nd
Teen Births Per 1,000 – 29,765 (2016)	1st

Source: The Annie B. Casey Foundation, *2018 Kids Count Data Book: State Trends in Child Well-Being*, http://datacenter.kidscount.org/data

upon the prospects of a bumper citrus and vegetable crop. The majority of the region's inhabitants are employed as agricultural workers at minimum or below minimum wage. Consequently, higher paying job opportunities throughout the border region are extremely limited.

The majority of the border region counties experience poverty rates well above the state average. Basically, one-fourth to one-third of residents in each of these counties does not earn enough to keep them above the poverty level. Those not actually below the poverty level are hugging onto the edge, barely earning enough to keep them statistically above the poverty line. The unemployment rate is directly tied to the poverty rate. One's ability to climb up that corporate ladder is directly tied to one's level of education. The "American Dream" underscores that the key to economic success is directly linked to advanced education and job training skills. Unfortunately all of the counties in the border region are mired in high dropout rates in the public schools coupled with low completion and graduation rates from the area's colleges and universities. Although bilingualism should be encouraged, the reality of the higher paying job market is that employees must be able to speak and write English. In 2000, one-third of families in the border counties indicated that the primary language spoken in their home was a language other than English. In many of the counties in the border region, Spanish, not English, is the primary and the only language spoken in the home. For these individuals, the inability to adequately comprehend the English language means that they simply cannot apply for those non-manual labor higher paying jobs. Lacking one or two of these factors does not necessarily mean that an individual could not earn enough income to provide for themselves and their family members and still keep above the poverty level. For example, in Starr County, 96.3 percent of its population is Hispanic. In 96.4 percent of the households Spanish, not English is the primary language. Only 48.8 percent of its 64,454 residents twenty-five years and older have a high school diploma. Only 9.7 percent of the county's residents have a bachelor degree or higher. Approximately 32 percent have incomes below the poverty level since the 2017 median household income is only $27,133 and per capita income is only $23,167. Health insurance is a major issue since 28.2 percent of Starr residents under the age of 65 have no health coverage.[39] However, an individual who is vise gripped by the majority of these factors will be in and will probably remain in poverty until meaningful lifestyle adjustments are made. This is the reality of poverty.

The region's poverty is compounded by the living conditions, particularly in the **colonias**. Although colonias exist along the shared border with Mexico in California, New Mexico and Arizona, Texas has the largest number of these substandard housing developments. "The Mexican Americans [Hispanics] who inhabit these odd little rural settlements along the border, which now number 1,500 and are home to over 400,000 citizens (most of them, contrary to popular belief, legal), are poor and undereducated and work in agricultural industries or in low-wage service-industry jobs. They wind up here because they want to own their own home but can't afford anything more than a plot of raw land in unzoned regions of border counties. Here, they can put a few dollars down and then pay on average $225 a month to a developer for the privilege of either building their homes with discarded or stolen construction materials or buying a used trailer."[40] Regardless of its distance from a city's limits, the typical suburb consist of paved roads, street lights, sidewalks, twice- or at least weekly garbage collection, sewer systems, indoor plumbing, running water, hot water heaters, electricity, public transportation, and fire and police substations. A colonia is no typical suburb! There are very few colonia residents that have indoor plumbing, running water, a sewer system or even one paved street. They do not have police and fire substations. There are no fire hydrants because there is no water source powerful enough to even attach a fire hose to. There is no emergency medical service or a hospital nearby. To the typical colonia resident, the usual customary amenities associated with the "good life" in the suburbs are precious luxuries that they may not see during their lifetime. The drinking water is seriously contaminated. Colonia residents suffer from chronic tuberculosis, hepatitis A, gastroenteritis, amoebic dysentery, skin disease and cancer. The majority of colonia residents do not have health insurance. In the border counties, there are too many patients for the two medical facilities. Life in these small cinder-block and wooden structure homes is akin to third- and fourth-world poverty. How did this happen?

In the early twentieth century, land developers began to subdivide their unproductive acreage into small plots. Located in rural and unincorporated areas, any structures built on the land did not have to comply with the usual city building, sewer, plumbing and electrical codes. Poor migrant farm workers could not afford upscale housing. Offered at very cheap prices, the colonias proved to be the solution to their housing problems. The land developer served as the buyer's lender, since the majority of the potential buyers did not qualify for a traditional bank or mortgage loan. Once the dotted line was signed, the property owner could not resell that property until the total loan had been paid off. "Developers typically sold lots for 10 percent down, with monthly payments of $10 and $100 over a ten-year period."[41] The costs of installing adequate plumbing and sewer lines and other "upgrades" were the buyer's responsibility.

Since 1967, valley residents have fought an up-hill battle against land developers and the Texas Legislature to bring water and sewer lines to the colonias. In 1989, Governor Bill Clements actually signed the first colonias water bill. The estimated cost of the total funding required to solve the colonias' water and wastewater problems alone in 1992 was $696 million.[42] By 1997, the Texas Legislature realized that it was approximately $194 million short of what was needed "to bring water and wastewater services to rural subdivisions, meaning some 90,000 mostly Hispanic colonia residents will continue to dwell in unsanitary conditions will into the twenty-first century."[43] The fate of the colonias attracted national attention during the 2000 presidential campaign. In his first campaign for the governorship, George W. Bush was very critical of Governor Richards' efforts to improve conditions in the colonias. In his bid for the White House, Governor Bush countered opposition claims that he neglected the area by pointing out that "ours is the first administration to aggressively pursue hookups for the colonias. We'll have thousands of people [connected] who heretofore had no water or sewer at their homes by the time my administration is over."[44] However, his administration's track record in improving conditions in the colonias proved to be a mixed bag of successes and half-hearted promises. It was during Ann Richards's administration that the state was able to obtain $600 million in bonds to purchase and install water mains and sewer lines in some of the colonias. However, "the program stalled because residents could not afford to pay for the final few feet of ¾-inch pipe that would connect their homes to the water-delivery system."[45] The Bush administration did obtain additional federal grant money and, more importantly, an agreement with the North American Development Bank to help low-income colonias residents pay $1,200 each for that ¾-inch pipe connection. The full credit, however, belongs to the previous occupants of the governor's mansion.

Bush's successor Rick Perry took on the challenge of the colonias as one of his foremost objectives of his administration. Fifty state lawmakers introduced at the start of the 2001 legislative session, "the Texas Border Marshall Plan 2001," a comprehensive approach to improving the living conditions in the south Texas border region. The plan called for "new state spending needs of more than $1 billion through 2002-2003 and more than $4 billion through August, 2007."[46] The plan, however, was shelved as the Texas Legislature was confronted with cutting the budget to offset a substantial decrease in the projected budget surplus as well as forecasts of anticipated revenue shortfalls. State lawmakers have not been very successful in tapping the federal government for large cash outlays for colonia infrastructure. "Despite years of talk, Washington hasn't done much to help fix that system [water and sewage]. The Environmental Protection Agency provided $320 million over 10 years to the border states to improve wastewater treatment facilities, many of them in the colonias. But when HUD finally rolled out its Colonias Gateway Initiative, it asked for just $16 million."[47] The estimated cost of establishing just one independent water district is approximately $198 million. It will take billions, not a mere $16 million, to just fix the wastewater problems in the colonias. Gradually, the pipes are being installed; the indoor plumbing hookups are in place; clean water is flowing; the lights are coming on; and the roads are being paved—one colonia at a time. After waiting six years, the final water hookup was installed in Panorama Village, a colonia near El Paso. As the water began to flow from the pipe into their kitchen sinks, the residents decided to celebrate. "Neighbors roasted a pig, hired a mariachi band and invited politicians and the media. . . But on the day of the party, it rained. Water rushed across the desert, turning Panorama Villege's unpaved streets into muddy trenches. The TV trucks wouldn't turn off the main road to get to the hamlet."[48] Unfortunately, change and progress come so slowly to the oftentimes forgotten people of the colonias.

The Philosophy and Politics of Poverty

The impetus to reconfigure the welfare system has enjoyed widespread bipartisan support. Beginning in the 80s, both political parties made welfare reform a major campaign issue. However, both parties have traditionally taken different philosophical positions over the methodical approach, policy decisions, and, subsequently, the extent of the national government's monetary commitments to the nation's poor. Despite the tone of independence so often espoused in the Texas Legislature, this state as well as her sister states, has been and will continue to be directly impacted by the actions of decision makers on Capitol Hill. The debate is not just between Democrats and Republicans. The medical community is keenly interested in the course of both health-care and welfare reform.

Agriculture continues to lobby both sides of the aisle in Congress against any moves to slash federal allocations for SNAP (food stamp program), and school breakfast and lunch programs. These programs are money makers for farmers, ranchers, and dairy farmers. Far too often law makers from both political parties have been verbally demeaning to the recipients of public assistance programs. The recipients themselves have a vested interest in the outcome of the budget battles in Washington and Austin. The poverty-stricken, elderly, disabled, veterans, and every other group receiving some form of public assistance are seeing their benefits severely questioned, cut, or possibly eliminated. Public opinion has always vacillated about the appropriate role government at any level should play in addressing poverty-related issues. Opinion poll after poll shows that most Americans are "more sympathetic to programs that provide goods and services (such as food and health care) to the poor rather than giving them cash. . . . Public approval for programs that promote work is much stronger than for programs that don't. The public opposes the idea of 'welfare' but supports programs that help the poor help themselves."[49] Every segment of this nation's society is a partner in the debate over welfare and the direction of this nation's social consciousness.

Advanced by the Republican Party, the traditional conservative position is that poverty is a self-inflicted result of one's individual failures and, in some instances, laziness to avail oneself of economic viability and mobility. Holding to the belief that the free market system or capitalism creates unlimited opportunities for advancement, conservatives stress that "The American Dream" of economic success is the brass ring that is readily available to anyone *willing* to grab it. However, reality tells us that the capitalist system through its competitive nature, denies the brass ring to the majority while extending it to only a few. Conservatives justify the struggle between the haves and the have nots as inevitable but not an impossible situation. Their position is strengthen by their firm belief in Charles Darwin's concept of the survival of the fittest. Conservatives also draw a distinction between the deserving and undeserving poor. The **deserving poor** are those such as the elderly, the mentally ill, and the physically handicapped, who through no fault of their own became impoverished. Conversely, those individuals who failed to avail themselves of the opportunities to improve their lot created their own poverty and, thus, are **undeserving** of government assistance. Extreme conservatives believe that welfare programs have failed miserably because the poor are too culturally and intellectually deficient in the first place to take advantage of the programs' benefits to lift

themselves out of poverty. The **culture of poverty** concept as an inwardly or genetically acquired trait was outlined by Edward C. Banfield in *The Unheavenly City*:

> Extreme present-orientedness, not lack of income or wealth, is the principal cause of poverty in the sense of "the culture of poverty." Most of those caught up in this culture are unable or unwilling to plan for the future, to sacrifice immediate gratifications in favor of future ones, or to accept the disciplines that are required in order to get and to spend. Their inabilities are probably culturally given in most cases—"multi-problem" families being normal representatives of a class culture that is itself abnormal. No doubt there are people whose present orientedness is rationally adaptive rather than cultural, but these probably comprise only a small part of the "hard-core" poor.[50]

A strong advocate of the free-market and laissez-faire features of capitalism, Ronald Reagan decried welfare for creating dependency while robbing an individual of his/her dignity and self-reliance. "At the heart of President Reagan's opposition to federal welfare initiatives lies the suspicion that the poor are morally different from the non-poor—that they do not share the values and aspirations of working Americans, that they do not respond to the incentives and opportunities of the market in the same way as the prosperous do."[51] The 104th Congress led by Republican majorities in both Houses used traditional conservative positions as their justification for slashing federal budgetary dollars for social service programs in their efforts to dismantle the welfare system originally created by the **Social Security Act** and subsequent legislative acts.

The liberal camp has a cadre of their own champions advocating for the nation's poor. In the early 1970s, William P. Hobby headed a special committee studying welfare issues in Texas. In his final report, the future lieutenant governor of Texas underscored his belief in the liberal philosophy of poverty:

> Texas must realize that this is no longer a landed frontier where survival and well-being are products of individual faith, will, and effort alone. It will take resources and ingenuity to make this truly a land of opportunity. Those who are living in poverty have not individually crafted their poverty any more than those who are prosperous have individually produced their wealth. The fine line between success and failure represents one of the

most sensitive and complex unsolved phenomena of this era of space, conglomerates, and megalopolises. The future of the state and this nation may rest upon the effectiveness with which the political and economic leadership recognizes and provides for the needs of the less fortunate.[52]

Liberals firmly believe that poverty is not a self-inflicted generational condition but rather an unfortunate byproduct of the competitiveness of the free-market concept of capitalism. Liberals hold that when the Framers charged the newly created national government with the task of promoting the general welfare, it was their intent including providing government-sponsored assistance for those trapped in the web of poverty.

The Democratic Party became the banner carrier for the liberal philosophy with the election of Woodrow Wilson to the presidency. Liberals based their position on three major premises. First, they point to a tragically consistent historical pattern of economic prosperity followed by periods of dismal recession, high inflation, and even depression. In prosperous times, the average American worker sees only marginal improvements in his/her wages. However, economic downturns can mean economic ruin for those who live paycheck to paycheck. Second, hard-working Americans with limited opportunities are losing ground to the more affluent. Liberals believe government can play a key role. Liberals stress that without the intervention of the federal government, the "gap between rich and poor would tend to widen in an advanced economy, generating unacceptable disparities and straining the fabric of an open, free, and democratic society."[53] Federal programs were designed to narrow the gap by providing individuals with the tools to ultimately achieve economic stability. Third, liberals uphold that the economic, social, and political principles inherent in a democracy are achievable only by providing equality of opportunity to all regardless of their backgrounds and short-comings. Fourth, liberals stress that the **safety net** was created to provide economic security for all its citizens. The programs designed primarily under Democratic leadership "not only seek to prevent extreme deprivation among the most disadvantaged, but also attempt to cushion the impact of economic misfortune and uncertainty on the more advantaged and affluent members of society. The resulting safety net has been remarkably successful in shielding diverse segments of the population from the full brunt of the vagaries and hardships implicit in a free market economy."[54]

The Development of the Welfare System in Texas

"Many feel that without the inducement from the federal government and the major infusion of federal dollars, Texas would have no viable medical care, financial support, or social services for its neediest citizens. As it is, Texas has moved slowly and cautiously in the development of its limited welfare system."[55] Prior to the Great Depression, Texas followed the lead of her sister states by charging county and local governments, in cooperation with private charities, with the task of providing public relief. Article XVI, Section 8 of the Texas Constitution of 1876 stated that "each county must provide in such manner as may be prescribed by law, a manual labor poorhouse and farm, for taking care of, managing, employing and supplying the wants of its indigent and poor inhabitants."[56] Since the American Revolution, the answer to indigent housing was the **almshouse** or the **poorhouse**. Local private and religious-based charities offered housing to the poor, the mentally ill, and, in some instances, released inmates with the understanding that "institution life would not only protect the individual from corrupting influences but also allow the individual to reform."[57] "Residents" earned their keep by being farmed out as day laborers or to the wealthy as house servants. Reports of abuse and corruption led to what seemed to be a more benevolent means of addressing the needs of the poor—the **settlement house**. Patterned after the facilities in London, England, settlement houses were initially located in the slum areas of New York City, Boston, etc., and gradually moved across the United States. Many were organized along the lines of Jane Addams's Hull House established in 1889 in Chicago, Illinois. The settlement house movement was based on the belief that people could be schooled out of their poverty. A social conservative, Simon Newcomb, expressed in 1886, the extreme belief held by some social conservatives that "if children of the degraded classes could be taken in infancy, before their bad habits have had time to form, and trained to earn a livelihood, a certain proportion of them would be redeemed [from the poverty of their parents]."[58] Settlement houses were more like community centers where participants would attend classes during the days and return to their own residences. The majority of the facilities were staffed with groups of well-educated upper- and upper-middle class women. "The settlement house movement unabashedly promoted bourgeois values and habits instructing the poor in everything from art appreciation and home economics to the importance of establishing savings accounts. To children in poverty, it offered recreation, books, clubs, as well as a sense of history of American democratic institutions. It approached thousands of the urban poor, particularly children and teenagers, with a message of inclusion in the larger world beyond the slums."[59] Texas used a combination of poorhouses, settlement houses and orphanages. For example, the Southwest Mental Health Center located in San Antonio actually began as an orphanage. Conditions in both the poorhouses and orphanages were deplorable. The state legislature provided no mechanism for periodic inspections nor did they establish licensing standards for these facilities. To offset operationing costs, orphans and other residents of the poorhouses were used as manual laborers for farmers, ranchers, and businesses, and as servants for private residences. Stipends or welfare grants were provided only to Confederate veterans and their widows. The Texas Legislature eventually appropriated state funds to build the Terrell State Hospital (1883) and the San Antonio State Hospital (1899) for the mentally ill, as well as the State Orphans School (1887) and the Texas Blind, Deaf and Orphan School for Negroes [African Americans](1887). In 1917, the Texas Legislature extended benefits to mothers with dependent children. However, the program was offered to county governments on a voluntary basis with no funding from the state government, resulting in extremely low benefits for the needy.

The massive personal deprivation created by the Great Depression placed Texas and her sister states at the mercy of the federal government since the states were simply unable to provide assistance to the destitute. New Deal legislation resulted in the passage of the Civilian Conservation Corps, the Works Progress Administration, the Emergency Relief Administration and the National Youth Corps. These federal programs were designed to put the unemployed back to work. The states were required to share the costs. Without federal assistance, Texas would have been too financial strapped to provide any meaningful assistance to its needy. Even with federal money, Texas lagged behind her sister states by providing Depression benefits to only "7.1 percent of the state's population, far below the national average of 10.3 percent."[60]

The modern welfare system was initially launched when the United States Congress passed the **Social Security Act** in 1935. This landmark piece of legislation established two major insurance programs, one designed to provide the elderly and retired with safety net protection from poverty and the other to assist the unemployed. The **Old Age Insurance** program created a self-funded insurance plan providing pensions and benefits for the elderly and disabled; whereas, the **Unemployment Insurance** program provided cash payments to workers temporarily laid off from their jobs. The Social Security Act also created several public assistance programs including **Aid to Dependent Children** (later changed to **Aid to Families with Dependent Children** or **AFDC**), **Old Age Assistance**, and **Aid to the Blind**. Between 1945 and 1965, in Texas "state AFDC expenditures rose slowly from $1,495 million to $3,899 million and federal expenditures in the state rose from $1,242 million to $16,594 million."[61]

The nation's next major assault on poverty occurred in the 1960s when President Lyndon Johnson unveiled his **War on Poverty** plan. Johnson laid out his policy initiative in a speech delivered at the University of Michigan on May 22, 1964:

> The Great Society rests in abundance and liberty for all. It demands an end to poverty and racial injustice to which we are totally committed in our time. But this is just the beginning. The Great Society is a place where every child can find knowledge to enrich his mind and to enlarge his talents. It is a place where leisure is a welcome chance to build and reflect, not a feared cause of boredom and restlessness. It is a place where the city of man serves not only the needs of the body and the demands of commerce, but the desire for beauty and the hunger for community. It is a place where man can renew contact with nature. It is a place which honors creation for its own sake and for what it adds to the understanding of the race. It is a place where men are more concerned with the quality of their goals than the quantity of their goods. But most of all, the Great Society is not a safe harbor, a resting place, a final objective, a finished work. It is a challenge constantly renewed beckoning us toward a destiny where the meaning of our lives matches the marvelous products of our labor.[62]

While retaining many of the New Deal public assistance programs, the Johnson administration opted for a curative approach to solving poverty. It was believed that poverty could be actually eliminated by providing the poor with the tools to lift themselves out of their economic deprivation. The emphasis was placed on job training programs and expanded financial assistance for education. The **Economic Opportunity Act of 1965** established the Office of Economic Opportunity designed to coordinate all federal poverty-related initiatives. The

**NYA Project: Men working on metal bridge project in
Texas, 1936
Photo credits: FDR Presidential Library**

War on Poverty also attempted to enhance the quality of
life for the needy through programs such as **Model Cities**.
The nation also introduced a limited form of national
health insurance through the creation of Medicare for
the elderly and disabled, and the Medicaid program for
the economically disadvantaged. In 1964, the national
government adopted the Food Stamp program as a means of
providing nutritional food to the poor. "In Texas, between
1967 and 1973, participation rates and expenditures for
welfare support program surged. The number of families
on AFDC in Texas increased fourfold from 23,509 to
120,254. The number of children receiving benefits rose
from 79,914 in 1967 to 325,244 in 1973. Total state and
federal expenditures on AFDC, meanwhile escalated more
than five-fold from $31 million in 1967 to $163.5 million
in 1973."[63]

Of course, Johnson's dream of ending poverty did not
become a reality. However, the programs designed by his
administration did produce some tangible results. Years
after leaving the White House, Johnson evaluated the
effectiveness of his efforts:

We started something in motion with the attack
on poverty. Its effects were felt in education,
law, medicine, and social welfare, in business and
industry, in civil and philanthropic life, and in
religion. . . . Of course, we had not lifted everyone
out of poverty. There would be setbacks and
frustrations and disappointments ahead. But no
one would ever again be able to ignore the poverty
in our midst, and I believe that is enough to assure
the final outcome to change the way of life for
millions of our fellow human beings.[64]

Johnson's Great Society did re-establish the traditional
pattern future programs would follow. First, the federal
government would create the program targeting a specific
group for coverage or benefits. Second, the states would
receive federal funding for the program if they met
the minimal requirements established by the federal
government and created a state agency charged with
implementation and administration tasks. Third, the
federal government would allow the states to establish
their own benefit eligibility standards and benefit amounts
above the federally-mandated minimums. The rationale
for state involvement rested upon the traditional argument
that the states and not the federal government were more
capable of truly assessing the needs of their residents.
Fourth, program funding would be either totally provided
by the federal government or equally shared by state and
national governments. In reality, the federal government
has traditionally shouldered the bulk of the funding tasks.
Fifth, the states became dependent upon the national
government to assume the burden for the nation's needy.
Few state lawmakers since have initiated innovative plans
for public assistance needs independent of the national
government.

Entitlements: Social Security and Unemployment Compensation

Entitlements are "benefits provided by government to
which recipients have a legally enforceable right."[65] The
major entitlement programs totally or partially funded by
the federal government include Social Security, Medicare,
Medicaid, veteran's benefits and military retirement
plans. Bearing the bulk of the funding responsibilities,
the federal government is spending almost 50 percent
of its annual budget on entitlement programs. Initially
marketed as temporary programs, both Social Security
and unemployment compensation are considered as
absolute guaranteed benefits for the American worker.

Millions of retired citizens believe that they "toiled for years to send Uncle Sam a mountain of dollar bills. These taxes went into individual accounts with their names and Social Security numbers emblazoned on them; now seniors are simply withdrawing what is rightfully their own."[66] Social Security has become a sacred cow that politicians and lawmakers alike are fearful of attacking. However, Social Security was never envisioned to be the definitive retirement plan guaranteeing a pot of gold to totally fund one's golden years. The United States Supreme Court entered into the fray of whether Social Security is an absolute guaranteed right in its 1960s ruling in *Fleming v Nestor*. Justice John Harlan wrote that Social Security was "designed to function into the indefinite future, and its specific provisions rests on the predictions as to expected economic conditions, which must inevitably prove less than wholly accurate, and on judgments and preference as to the proper allocation of the nation's resources which evolving economic and social conditions will of necessity in some cases modify."[67] Basically, the federal government's guarantee of entitlement programs is valid as long as the funds are available to pay for them.

Social Security is funded through payroll taxes paid by both employees and employers. Workers are eligible for benefits as early as age fifty-five if they are deemed permanently disabled to work. Usually the bulk of retirees file for benefits at age sixty-five. The benefit amount is based on the individual's work history to include the length of employment and one's salary history. If Social Security were a true pension program, retirees would only receive benefits equal to what was paid into the plan on their behalf. Instead benefits are guaranteed throughout the life of the retired worker. Consequently, there is a point where Social Security ceases to be a pension and becomes an entitlement or public assistance payment. For the average American retired worker, the monthly benefits are simply not enough to maintain a comfortable lifestyle. Many elderly receive just enough in benefits to put them into the safety net, one perilous step away from poverty. In 2017, 4,126,000 Texans were beneficiaries of Social Security benefits with an average monthly benefit of $1,375 for retired workers, $1,179 for disabled workers, and $1,296 for nondisabled widows and widowers.[68] The initial intent of Social Security was to provide a government funded allotment to the nation's senior citizens who simply could not afford to establish their own retirement nest eggs. It was believed that all workers would contribute to the fund but that only those in need of assistance would receive it. However, every worker who contributes is eligible to receive some benefit for the duration of his/her life, regardless of their own personal wealth. The CEO retiring with a multi-million dollar pension is just as eligible for benefits as the dishwasher who toiled for years earning at or below minimum wages. Consequently, the bulk of Social Security spending goes to middle- and upper-income Americans. The fastest growing segment of the nation's poor is elderly widowed women. The surviving spouse receives only 50 percent of her late husband's Social Security benefits. Housewives do not qualify for benefits. Former Senator Kay B. Hutchison-(R) repeatedly but unsuccessfully introduced legislation granting partial Social Security earnings credit to housewives to address this issue.

Obviously, the survival of Social Security has lawmakers concerned and searching for remedies to keep the program intact. The major problem is the nation's aging population where in the near future, there will be more retirees taking money out of Social Security and less workers putting money into it. Several proposals have been discussed including making Social Security a quasi-private pension program whereby the worker could commit a portion of his/her payroll withholding deductions to stock market investments. In addition, Congress has eliminated the mandatory retirement age and a penalty against retirees working while at the same time collecting benefits.

Unemployment compensation was designed as a temporary entitlement benefit for those displaced from the job market. Although the program is mandated by the national government, the states determine the eligibility requirements, benefit allocations, and time frames. Not every unemployed worker receives benefits in Texas. An individual who has been involuntary separated from his/her employment through no fault of his/her own initiative will receive full benefits. Voluntary separations and terminations by employee-generated actions will result in reduced payments or no benefits at all. While receiving benefits, recipients must continuously search and document their efforts to find a job, cannot refuse suitable work, and must follow up on job referrals. Benefits are usually extended for twenty-six weeks. However, Congress can extend the benefit period during tough economic times. In 2016, the average weekly unemployment benefit for unemployed Texans was $403 for approximately 17 weeks of payments.[69]

Public Assistance Programs

The majority of both state and federal public assistance programs are mean-tested plans providing either in-kind services or cash transfer benefits. **Means-tested eligibility** is based upon an applicant's demonstrated inability to provide for him/or herself the desired benefit due to the individual's depressed income level and assets. Temporary Assistance to Needy Families (TANF) and Supplemental Social Security are two cash transfer programs available to the state's poor. **Cash transfers** provide direct payments to qualified recipients. An **in-kind program** such as subsidized public housing, day care, Medicaid, WIC, Food Stamps, and, in some cases, legal services provides direct payment to the provider of the service, not to the recipient.

A federally funded program, **Supplemental Security Income (SSI)** was designed to provide cash payments to low income elderly persons as well as to blind and disabled adults and children. Disability includes mental and physical conditions. As of 2017, 61,600 Texans received TANF benefits.[70] For nearly seventy years, when most Americans talked about the welfare system and being on the dole, they were referring to the Aid to Families with Dependent Children (AFDC) assistance program. Initially awarding benefits to only single-parent female householders with dependent children, the federal government mandated through the passage of the **Family Support Act** of 1988 that benefits be extended to qualifying two-parent families for at least six months out of a year if the principal wage earner was unemployed. One of the adults had to seek employment to continue receiving benefits. AFDC was highly criticized as producing welfare dependency leading to the "culture of poverty" whereby recipients would rather continue to receive welfare than work. Texas was well known for its stiff eligibility requirements and meager benefits. During the 1998-99 biennium, the Texas Legislature replaced AFDC with the **Temporary Assistant to Needy Families (TANF),** the new program created by the welfare reform act signed into law in 1996 by President Clinton. The program is available to Texans who have a child or children under the age of nineteen. To qualify, Texans must not have assets worth over $1,000 and have incomes greater than 12 percent of the federal poverty level. For example, a person with an income of no more $188 per month would receive $275 in TANF benefits. The federal limit for benefits is 48 months but Texas extends TANF benefits for 60 months.

The **Food Stamp Program** was developed in 1964 as part of President Johnson's War on Poverty legislation. The program was designed to provide an in-kind exchange of food coupons for food to offset nutritional deficiencies and hunger among America's needy. Administered by the Department of Agriculture through state and county public assistance agencies, the program itself is totally funded by the federal government including footing 2/3's of state and county administration costs. Food stamps are supposed to be used to purchase staple products, not cigarettes, alcoholic beverages or items that cannot be eaten such as paper products and household cleaners. The Census Bureau draws a distinction between food secure and food insecure households. **Food secure** is "a household [that] had access at all times to enough food for an active healthy life for all household members, with no need for recourse to socially unacceptable food sources or extraordinary coping behaviors to meet their basic food needs. **Food insecure** households with hunger were those with one or more household members who were hungry at least some time during the period due to inadequate resources for food."[72] Food stamps have become a household necessity for the nation's impoverished and low-income wage earners simply because their paychecks cannot be stretched far enough to cover usual living expenses such as rent, day care, utilities, medical costs and the monthly grocery bill. Reported incidences of fraud and abuse moved the Texas Legislature to abandon using coupon books and replaced them with the Lone Star Card, a plastic card similar to a credit card. The individual coupon books enabled an individual to purchase an item of higher value than the face value of the coupon. The cashier would then have to give cash back for the difference, enabling the individual to use the cash to purchase unacceptable items such as cigarettes. With the plastic card, the recipient is given a monthly line-of-credit in food stamp value that can be used at any time during that month to purchase approved items. Based upon a person's income, food stamp eligibility in Texas is set at 130 percent above the poverty level. The income range is a monthly income of no more than $1,287 for a single person up $4,430 per month for nine family members. Benefits are extended to immigrants who have a child under the age of eighteen as long as they are currently receiving federal benefits and living in the United States for at least five years. To continue benefits, recipients must be registered to work, have not refused any job offer and must be enrolled in a technological or vocational program. Unfortunately, for many food insecure households, the monthly allocation of food stamps simply is not enough to keep three meals a day on the table for the entire month. Especially at the end of the month, local food banks experience long lines and emptying shelves. Food insecure families with children are very dependent upon the federal government's free breakfast and lunch programs at the public schools. However, when school is out for the summer, these parents must once again, turn to the local food bank to provide meals for their children.

The Special Supplemental Program for Women, Infants and Children, commonly known as **WIC** was created twenty years ago to provide nutritional food staples to pregnant women, breastfeeding mothers up to six months after giving birth, and children under the age of five. The program is funded by the federal government and administered by the Food and Nutrition Service of the Department of Agriculture, with assistance from state and county public agencies. Recipients receive vouchers for a number of food items such as milk, iron-fortified infant formula, cheese, eggs, fruit juice, peanut butter, and beans. The WIC program also provides for free, or for a minimal fee, immunizations and prenatal care. The WIC program has proven to be successful in reducing health care costs for infants, particularly those with low birth weight.

Welfare Reform: Is It Working?

Welfare reform in Texas took a two-step approach. First, the Texas Legislature jump started the process by enacting its own version of reform measures in 1995, one year before Congress and the White House agreed on federal welfare reform legislation. The Texas version included the following provisions:

- Time limits on benefits ranging from one to three years. The employability of the recipient determines the extent of the benefits. Exceptions are allowed for medical reasons and for parents with children under four. Although adults lose their benefits once the time limit has expired, their dependent children continue to receive benefits.
- Recipients must wait five years before they can reapply for benefits.
- If the non-custodial parent is delinquent in child support payments, they will face loss of their driver's license and any professional certificates, i.e., teaching certificate for example.
- For TNAF, applicants must sign an agreement pledging to remain drug free, to actively participate in educational and job training programs, and to ensure that their children are immunized and attending school.
- To prevent fraud, all applications are fingerprinted.

In 1996, the federal government began implementation of the Personal Responsibility and Work Opportunity Act. This round of welfare reform called for the following:

- A five year lifetime limit on all benefits.

- Requires head of household to find work within a two year period or their family will lose its benefits.
- Mandating that at least 50 percent of all single parents below the poverty level in any state be employed or involved in school or job training programs. States in non-compliance lose a portion of their federal block grant money. Women with children under the age of six cannot be penalized for not working.
- Limitation of benefits for childless adults between 18 and 50 years of age to only three months of food stamps during a three-year period. If they become unemployed, they can apply for an additional three months of food stamps during a three-year period.
- Requiring unwed teenage mothers receiving benefits to live with their parents and attend school.
- Prohibits cash aid and food stamps to anyone convicted of felony drug charges. Pregnant women and adults in drug programs are exempt.
- Prohibits future legal immigrants from receiving Medicaid benefits during the first five years of their residency in this country.

The object of both welfare reform packages was to permanently remove low-income individuals from the dole to economic viability via the job market. Initially, the number of Americans on welfare began to decrease dramatically. Advocates enthusiastically pointed to the declining number of welfare recipients as the definitive sign that welfare reform was indeed moving people from dependency to self-efficiency. What welfare reform advocates overlooked was that the initial success of their reform packages was directly tied to a very healthy economy responsible for generating thousands of new jobs primarily in service-sector employment, which is the primary source of jobs for the marginally skilled and undereducated worker paid at minimum or below minimum wage. Business profits were soaring. However, investor confidence began to sour in 2001 as the corporate scandals of falsified profit margins began to generate federal indictments, bankruptcies, profit losses, retirees losing their pensions, and millions of Americans losing their jobs. Beginning in 2001, several states began to see an increase in the number of individuals requesting income support. By 2006, the housing market was on the skids as property values declined, mortgage loans were in default, and credit lines began to dry up. As previously pointed out, 2010 saw a steady rise in the poverty rate to the point that it surpassed the 1960 rate, which was at that time the highest since the Great Depression. The number of people on some form of government-backed assistance increased dramatically and will remain high until the job market can create the same number of jobs at or above the salaries originally offered. Creating more minimum wage jobs at part time hours will not put welfare reform's main goal back on track. Another promise of welfare reform is that once a person leaves the welfare dole he/she will never seek assistance again. Studies point out, however, that "about one in five was back on welfare; one in 10 had left welfare but wasn't working."[73]

The Texas Welfare Report Card

The development and subsequent implementation of Texas's welfare system has been molded by several factors. First, Texans as a whole have never been champions of public assistance programs. "The myths of the frontier, the idealization of the individual entrepreneur, the belief in self-help, and the idea that the government that governs the least is the government that governs best all are well and alive in Texas."[74] The state's political rhetoric is predominately anti-welfare, tinged with the desire to stop welfare cheats and abusers. Few pieces of legislation on the state level actually attempt to address the causal factors of poverty. Second, every public assistance program adheres to the punitive policy option. The Texas Legislature's usual practice is to simply tighten the eligibility requirements to guarantee that only the truly deserving are given assistance, coupled with stiffer penalties for abuse and fraud. Far too often applicants are treated suspiciously as potential abusers rather than as residents honestly seeking assistance. The punitive policy option pervades the Texas welfare system. Third, Texas has an embarrassing historical track record of offering the lowest benefits possible. Regardless of the program, Texas's per-individual benefit allocations and service provisions place her in the bottom forty among her sister states. The so-call "welfare queens" so often mentioned by anti-welfare advocates definitely do not lead a regal lifestyle in Texas. Low benefits are a by-product of the fourth characteristic—a low tax base. The over-reliance upon regressive tax programs does not generate enough tax revenues to adequately cover all of the state's expenses particularly for public assistance and social services.

The low-tax environment, however, has been traditionally supported by those seeking to enhance the state's purported favorable business climate. "In competing with other states for new businesses, Texas' economic and political leaders have stressed two features of the Texas economy: low taxes and traditionally, a low wage base. Not surprisingly, neither of these is particularly compatible with a liberal welfare program. Indeed many business leaders would argue that the barebones welfare programs found in Texas are in and of themselves a positive feature of the Texas economy."[75] Barebones funded welfare programs may be good for a positive business climate, but they are not adequately meeting the needs of the state's poor citizens. Fifth, anti-welfare advocates and benefit recipients are equally critical about the administration of the state's public assistance efforts. The bulk of the programs are handled through the **Department of Human Services (DHS)**. The department receives its policy directives from the gubernatorially appointed Texas Board of Human Services. The DHS is composed of three major program divisions: Health-Care Services, Client Self-Support Services, and Long-term Care Services. The state is divided into ten administrative regions, each under the direction of a regional administrator. State, county and local public assistance agencies are dogged by anti-welfare politicians for their wastefulness and inefficiency. Clientele groups criticize agencies for their insensitivity and slowness in responding to their needs. Are these charges of inefficiency, wastefulness and insensitivity fair?

Probably not. At all levels of government, public assistance agencies even before this current budget crisis have been traditionally underfunded, understaffed, and ill-equipped to satisfy either the needs of their clients or agency critics. Usually, the budget ax always chops appropriations for public assistance and social service programs before any other budget items are even mentioned. State, city and county agencies are always faced with too few social workers, case workers, and clerks to handle the ever-increasing number of Texans seeking some form of public assistance. In this state, there has never been enough money or manpower to properly address the needs of the poor, disabled and elderly. These trends are seen in every single public assistance program offered in this state.

Health Care Issues

Vowing to revamp the nation's health-care system, presidential candidate Barack Obama told millions of Americans about his personal experience with the existing health-care system as he watched his terminally ill mother suffer through the last stages of breast cancer while at the same time battling with insurance companies, doctors, and hospitals over whether certain procedures were covered, and working through the mounds of forms, bureaucratic red tape, and the ever-growing pile of unpaid medical and drug bills. On March 23, 2010, President Obama signed into law a highly partisan and very controversial sweeping health-care package aimed to meet his goals of a) providing insurance to the nation's uninsured; b) reducing rising health-care costs; c) shifting the emphasis of health care from reactionary to preventive; and d) correcting deficiencies in the prescription drug legislation passed during the Bush administration. Obamacare was one of the hottest issues in the 2012 presidential race. The package included the following:

- a rebate to offset the doughnut hole gap in Part D of the prescription drug bill passed during the Bush administration.
- a mandate that insurers cannot exclude children with pre-existing conditions from coverage.
- coverage for adult children up to their 26th birthday who remain on their parent's health insurance plans.
- removal of set lifetime limits on the amount of benefits paid.
- coverage for preventive services such as cancer screenings with no out-of-pocket charges to the patient.
- elimination of all pre-existing conditions clauses from health insurance policies.

The key element to the plan was that if one already has health insurance provided by their employer, then they do not need to sign up for health care coverage under Obama's plan. However, those who did not have insurance had to apply through the federal government's website and select a plan from the numerous plans offered through health exchange programs. The cost of the selected plan was either paid totally by the individual or if one's income falls below a certain level, then the federal government would pay either a percentage or the total amount of the coverage. The goal was to provide health care coverage for every American citizen.

Was this plan a step in the right direction and was it really necessary? While Democrats and Republicans were arguing over the merits of Obamacare, 27,304,000 Americans representing 8.6 percent of the nation's total population have no health insurance whatsoever. Among those 27.3 million are 3,277,000 children. For many Americans their primary care physician is an emergency room doctor. As of 2016, 4,545,000 Texans are uninsured of which 671,000 are children.[76] In addition to Obamacare, three basic publicly funded programs are Medicaid, Medicare and the Children's Health Insurance Program. A jointly funded federal and state program, **Medicaid**, was created n 1965 as part of the War on Poverty. Medicaid was designed as a preventive health-care system whereby a child with a cold would receive the medication necessary to prevent that cold from developing into a potentially life-threatening illness mandating more costly health-care services. Medicaid is an in-kind program with the payment given directly to the provider of the service. Medicaid spending consists of direct payments issued for outpatient and inpatient care services, hospital care, nursing home services, and long-term care facilities. Since the patients receive no direct cash payments, charges of fraud, overpricing and unnecessary medical treatments must be rightfully levied at health-care providers. Initially, the program provided benefits to only those receiving AFDC or SSI benefits. Congress extended Medicaid coverage in 1972 by adding benefits for nursing home and intermediate care facilities for the treatment of the mentally ill. Coverage for prenatal, obstetrics, and follow up medical care for one year for pregnant women was added in 1986. By 1988, states were required to extend Medicaid coverage for one year after families became ineligible for AFDC benefits to allow time for personal economic recoveries. Congress also lowered the original eligibility requirements to include children up to age six. In 1990, Congress extended coverage including children up to age eighteen.

With the Medicaid program, the costs are shared between the federal and state governments. To help states ease their Medicaid burden, President George W. Bush signed into law in 2008 a Medicaid reform package that enabled the states to charge recipients premiums and higher co-payments for doctor's visits, hospital care and prescription medications. The legislation also gave the states the latitude to drop coverage for those who opted not to pay the additional fees. States can opt not to participate in Medicaid, but the cost to the states to bear the total cost of providing health care for their needy would be staggering. Eligibility for Medicaid is dependent upon one's income. In Texas, a single individual qualifies if their annual income is less than $23,552. The graduated income scale is based on the number of qualified members in the family. For each additional member, $8,237 is added to the family's annual income. For example, the qualifying income for three persons is $39,917, four $48,144, seven $72,725 and $80,962 for eight qualifying family members. Besides basic health care services, the program offers managed care coverage. In 2015, 3,533,000 Texans were provided managed care services.[77]

Although Medicaid provides insurance coverage to the nation's poor, it does not cover children raised in families whose incomes are too high to qualify for Medicaid coverage but are still too low to afford the premiums for dependent care coverage. In 1997, Congress enacted the **Children's Health Insurance Program (CHIP),** also called the State Children's Health Insurance Program or SCHIP), to provide free low-cost health insurance to the nation's uninsured children. The program is funded by the federal government but implemented by state governments. In 2017, 1,137,899 children in Texas were enrolled in CHIP at a cost of $1,334,900,000 of which $1,241,100,000 was paid for by the federal government and $93,700,000 by the state of Texas.[78]

Medicare was supposed to be the nation's health-care plan extending coverage to all Americans. The ensuing battle between conservatives against the plan and the liberal camp promoting it resulted in a program that basically provides coverage only to the nation's elderly. Liberals originally hoped that over time, coverage would be expanded in a incremental fashion with children first, followed by pregnant women and other groups until the goal of universal coverage was achieved. "All Medicare enthusiasts took for granted that the rhetoric of enactment should emphasize the expansion of access, not the regulation and overhaul of United States medicine. The clear aim was to reduce the risks of financial disaster for the elderly and their families, and the clear understanding was that Congress would demand a largely hands-off posture towards doctors and hospitals providing the care that Medicare would provide."[79] Coverage is automatically granted to all persons over 65 who had paid Social Security taxes during their working lives and to their spouses. Funded totally by the federal government, the Medicare plan is administered by the Social Security Administration. The program provides two plans of health coverage. Part A, commonly known as HI, provides mandatory hospitalization coverage. Part B permits participants to purchase through beneficiary premiums and general tax revenues coverage for doctor's fees and other medical expenses to include prescription drugs. Basically, a program that started out as a universal health-care plan has become a very limited plan geared primarily for retired workers over sixty-five. Not all of the nation's seniors receive coverage.

The Bush administration launched its health-care reform package by focusing on Plan B of the original Medicare legislation. Passed in 2003, the **Medicare Prescription Drug Improvement and Modernization Act** was hailed as "the most sweeping change to Medicare since its founding in 1965," with the primary purpose of bringing "the accelerating costs of prescription drugs under control."[80] Major provisions of the legislation included

increasing the premium of the Part B Medicare Plan on a sliding scale whereby those with incomes over $200,000 would pay 80 percent of their premiums; raising the deductible to $110 and providing a tax shelter for those individuals with high-deductible health insurance. The plan, however, still maintained that the private sector and not the public sector would provide the insurance plans and coverage options to participants.

The most controversial section of the legislation dealt with prescription drugs. On paper, the new approach seemed to be simple. The drug portion of Medicare is known as Plan D. "In addition to a monthly premium, seniors must pay for the first $250 in annual costs for covered drugs, the standard deductible. When the year's drug costs reach $251, plan participants start paying out-of-pocket 25 percent of the cost [of the medications] until their contributions hit $2,250. Then comes the infamous **'doughnut hole'** in which Part D enrollees are responsible for the entire cost of drugs between $2,251 and $5,100. Above that, catastrophic coverage must kick in, whereby seniors shell out just a small portion (5 percent of the cost or a co-pay of a few dollars) of their annual drug costs."[81] One of the problems is that the cycle begins anew every January 1. Seniors can opt to stay with their current Medicare managed plan, their company retirement plan or opt for a private insurance carrier that offers a medical plan with prescription drug coverage. Regardless of the plan picked, seniors found out quickly that their annual drug costs fell into the doughnut hole when they went to the pharmacy to pick up their medications thinking they only had to pay a co-pay but instead had to pay the full amount. Unable to pay the full costs of the prescriptions, seniors are once again facing the choice that this reform package was supposed to fix. They are counting the number of pills they can afford, regardless of the medical necessity of taking the full amount of pills for the prescribed period of time. This situation basically leaves the elderly with only two choices. First, they can purchase **medigap insurance** to supplement their Medicare coverage. Supplemental insurance usually pays 80 percent or better of the costs not covered by Medicare once the policyholder's expenses exceed the standard deductible amounts. Second, those unable to purchase medigap plans must just limit their health-care options to what they can afford with Medicare. The Obama health-care law partially fixes the doughnut problem with an initial $150 rebate and by 2011, provided a 50 percent discount on prescriptions purchased in the doughnut hole range.

Supporters of the Obama health-care reform effort point out that this is the first time the federal government

President Lyndon B. Johnson, Former President Harry S Truman and others walk through the Truman Library after the Medicare Bill signing. In the background is a mural painted by Thomas Hart Benton "Independence and the Opening of the West." July 30, 1965   Credit: LBJ Library

has developed a comprehensive approach to addressing this nation's health-care issues. Since the New Deal legislation, health care has been reformed in an incremental fashion. The Johnson administration implemented Medicare for the qualifying elderly and Medicaid for the poor. In 1996, the Clinton administration supported the passage of legislation allowing already covered workers to obtain immediate health-care coverage after a change of jobs even if they had a pre-existing illness. It also mandated that new employees had to receive health-care coverage within twelve months of hire. Furthermore, the measure included tax-deductible medical savings accounts primarily for the self-employed and those employed by small companies unable to offer group plans.

Conclusions

Whether conducted by the federal government's Census Bureau or private agencies, Texas has a decades-old track record of its demonstrated inability to address the social needs of its poorest residents. For years, Texas has ranked last among her sister states in providing health-care coverage and mental health services to its children. Too many of this state's children are homeless, food insecure, and suffer from illnesses tied directly to obesity. Border-area counties are among the poorest in the nation. While legislative leaders in Austin slash state allocations for public and higher education, more students are dropping out of high school and of those who do graduate and attend college, the number of students receiving a four-year college degree is declining. Perhaps the only ray of light for the state's homeless has been the success of Haven for Hope, a comprehensive facility for San Antonio's homeless residents. While the Texas Legislature guided by the no new taxes pledge of Governor Abbott continues to cut money from social service programs, it is incumbent for us to understand that "if Texas fails to reverse current trends, the state is on course to pay a high price for inaction. Higher welfare and incarceration costs and lower levels of educational attainment and prosperity are what lie ahead in the forecast today for Texas, if we fail to close the gaps facing different groups of Texas children."[82]

Chapter Notes

[1]Edward J. Harpham, "Welfare Reform in Perspective," *Texas at the Crossroads: People, Politics and Policy*, Anthony Champagne and Edward J. Harpham, eds., (College Station, Texas: Texas A & M University Press, 1987), 262.

[2]ProQuest, *ProQuest Statistical Abstract of the United States: 2019*, 7th ed., (Bethesda, Maryland: 2018), Table 735, 479.

[3]Ibid.

[4]Ibid., Table 654, 420.

[5]Ibid.

[6]Ibid., Tables 618 and 627, 396, 401.

[7]Ibid., Table 668, 433.

[8]Ibid., Table 726, 474.

[9]*The 2016 Annual Homeless Assessment Report (AHR) To Congress: November, 2016*, (Washington, D.C.,:U.S. Department of Housing and Urban Development, 2016) 1.

[10]Harpham, "Welfare Reform in Perspective," 262.

[11]Nicholas Lemman, "Power and Wealth," *Texas Myths*, Robert F. O'Connor, ed., (College Station, Texas: Texas A & M University Press, 1986), 163.

[12]Randall W. Bland, Alfred B. Sullivan, Robert E. Biles, Charles P. Elloitt, Jr., and Beryl E. Pettus, *Texas Government Today*, 5th ed., (Pacific Grove, California: Brooks/Cole, 1992), 431.

[13]*The American Heritage Dictionary of the English Language: New College Edition*, (Boston, Massachusetts: Houghton Mifflin Co., 1982), 1027.

[14]Ansel M. Sharp, Charles A. Register and Paul W. Grimes, *Economics of Social Issues*, 16th ed., (Boston, Massachusetts: McGraw Hill/Irwin, 2004), 167-168.

[15]Bland, Sullivan, et al., 431.

[16]*ProQuest Statistical Abstract of the United States: 2019*, 7th ed., (Bethesda, Maryland, 2018), Table 632, 403.

[17]*https://www.minimum-wage.org*

[18]Jesse J. Holland, "Minimum Wage Raise Won't Be A Big Help," *San Antonio Express-News*, (Sunday, July 22, 2007), 5A.

[19]*ProQuest Statistical Abstract of the United States: 2019*, 7th ed, (Bethesda, Maryland, 2018), Table 730, 476.

[20]*Annual Homeless Assessment Report (AHR) to Congress: November, 2016*, 2.

[21]Ibid., 1-4.

[22]Ibid., 90.

[23]*National Alliance to End Homelessness*, (*https://endhomelessness.org*)

[24]*ProQuest Statistical Abstract of the United States: 2019*, 7th ed., Table 731, 477.

[25]Ibid., Table 720, 471.

[26]Ibid., Table 737, 480.

[27]Ibid.

[28]Ibid., Table 742, 483.

[29]Table 738, 481.

[30]Ibid., Table 706, 460.

[31]Ibid.

[32]Ibid., Table 707, 461.

[33]*https://nlihc.org/housing-needs-by-state/texas*

[34]*ProQuest Statistical Abstract of the United States: 2019*, 7th ed., Table 287, 190.

[35]Ibid., Table 257, 170.

[36]"Portrait of a Poor City," *San Antonio Light*, (Sunday, August 18, 1991), 6A.

[37]Ibid.

[38]*ProQuest Statistical Abstract of the United States: 2019*, 7th ed, Tables 17, 739, 20, 481.

[39]Quick Facts, (https://www/census/gov.quickfacts)

[40]Jim Atkinson, "Curing the Colonias," *Texas Monthly*, (April, 2001), 70.

[41]Robert H. Wilson and Peter Menzies, "The Colonias Water Bill: Communities Demanding Change," *Public Policy and Community Activism and Governance in Texas*, Robert H. Wilson, ed., (Austin, Texas: The University of Texas Press, 1997), 231.

[42]Ibid., 261.

[43]Thaddeus Herrick, "Utilities Finally Come to Colonia Residents," *Houston Chronicle*, (Sunday, February 2, 1997), 24.

[44]Russell Gold and Peggy Fikas, "Border Poverty Begs Bush to Answer to Colonia Question," *San Antonio Express-News*, (Sunday, August 6, 2000), 14A.

[45]Ibid.

[46]W. Gardner Selby, "Caucuses Seek 'Marshall Plan' for Border," *San Antonio Express-News*, (Thursday, February 22, 2001), 9A.

[47]Michael Schaffer, "American Dreamers," *U.S. News & World Report*, (August 26;September 2, 2002), 14.

[48]Ibid.

[49]Mark Carl Rom, "Transforming State Health and Welfare Programs," *Politics in the American States: A Comparative Analysis*, Virginia Gray and Russell L. Hanson, eds., 4th ed., (Washington, D.C.: CQ Press, 2004), 326.

[50]Edward C. Banfield, *The Unheavenly City*, 2nd ed., (Boston, Massachusetts: Little Brown, 1970), 125-126.

[51]Sar A. Levitan, "How the Welfare System Promotes Economic Security," *Political Science Quarterly*, (New York, New York: The Academy of Political Science), Vol. 26, No. 3, Fall, 1985, 449.

[52]Harpham, "Welfare Reform in Perspective," 283.

[53]Levitan, "How the Welfare System Promotes Economic Security," 453.

[54]Ibid., 447-448.

[55]Bland, Sullivan, et al., 434.

[56]Harpham,"Welfare Reform in Perspective," 270.

[57]Joel F. Handler, *The Poverty of Welfare Reform*, (New Haven: Connecticut: Yale University Press, 1995), 4.

[58]Banfield, 210.

[59]Howard Hysock, "Fighting Poverty the Old-Fashioned Way," *The Wilson Quarterly*, Vol. XIV, No. 2, Spring, 1990, 80.

[60]Harpham, "Welfare Reform in Perspective," 271.

[61]Ibid.

[62]Bruce J. Schulman, *Lyndon Johnson and American Liberalism: A Brief Biography with Documents*, 2nd ed., (Boston, Massachusetts: Bedford/St. Martins, 2007), 193.

[63]Harpham, "Welfare Reform in Perspective," 239.

[64]Schulman, 106.

[65]Jack C. Plano and Milton Greenberg, *The American Political Dictionary*, 10th ed., (Orlando, Florida: Harcourt Brace Janovich, 1993), 489.

[66]Susan Dentzer, "You're Not as Entitled As You Think," *U.S. News & World Report*, (March 20, 1995), 67.

[67]Michael Barone, "Future Shock," *U.S. News & World Report*, (June 13, 2005), 38.

[68]ProQuest Statistical Abstract of the United States: 2019, 7th ed, Table 569, 370.

[69]Ibid., Table 580, 375.

[70]Ibid., Table 584, 337.

[71]Ibid., Table 586, 378.

[72]Statistical Abstract of the United States: 2012, 131st ed., Table 209, 135.

[73]Jeanne Russell, "Leaving Welfare A Job Well Done," *San Antonio Express-News*, Monday, August 29, 2001), 4A.

[74]Harpham, "Welfare Reform in Perspective," 270.

[75]Ibid., 267.

[76]*ProQuest Statistical Abstract of the United States: 2019*, 7th ed., Table 162, 113.

[77]Ibid., Table 159, 112.

[78]Ibid., Table 157, 110.

[79]Ted Marmar and Julie Beglin, "Medicare and It Grew . . . and Grew . . . and Grew . . .," *San Antonio Express-News*, (June 25, 1995), 21.

[80]Travis E. Poling and Gary Martin, "Medicare Rewrite Is Not A Cure-All," *San Antonio Express-News*, (Friday, December 26, 2003), 1A.

[81]Katherne Hobson, "How the Plan Works," *U.S. News & World Report*, (November 7, 2005), 74.

[82]Melissa Fletcher Stoetje, "Texas Kids Rank Last in Health, Welfare Study," *San Antonio Express-News*, (Wednesday, January 26, 2011), 3B.

Chapter 13

Urban Governance and Public Policy Issues

San Antonio, Texas

From its origins onward, indeed, the city may be described as a structure specially equipped to store and transmit the goods of civilization, sufficiently condensed to afford the maximum space, but also capable of structural enlargement to enable it to find a place for the changing needs and the more complex forms of a growing society and its cumulative social heritage.[1]

Since its evolution centuries ago, the city has served as a powerful magnet drawing people from diverse cultures into its protective fold with its anticipated promises of commercial and economic viability, social enrichments, and protection from the fear and ravishes of war, invasion, and famine. The city has been an integral factor in understanding the evolution of humankind and its civilizations. By studying the ruins of ancient cities, archeologists can unravel the mysteries of a civilization's lifestyle from the basic execution of daily tasks to elaborate religious ceremonies. Each city or urban center has left is mark through its architecture, art, literature, street and sewer designs, housing structures, and cultural, religious and educational institutions. However, ancient cities were not pristine urban centers free of the problems associated with the present-day modern city. Yes, even the ancient Romans complained about traffic snarls and congestion, poor street maintenance, high taxes, crime, and overcrowding! The problems confronting today's mayors are the same issues faced by city leaders centuries ago.

The complexity of managing a modern-day city through its economic upheavals and population spurts and declines poses very difficult public policy issues for city leaders. Like their ancient counterparts,

> American cities may be described by the proverbial "good news-bad news" adage. The good news is that they embody the best of our accomplishments in institutional and commercial developments, the arts, architecture and culture. They are the focal point of most American lives: even if we do not live in cities, we work and play in them. The bad news is that American cities house the worst of our excesses as evidenced by congestion, deterioration, pollution, crime and poverty. Not unexpectedly, therefore, public programs for cities are mixed. Some are aimed at city growth and development, while others deal with deteriorating conditions and the increasing number of city poor.[2]

Unfortunately, Texas's cities are not exempt from the problems housed in the urban mega-cities of New York, Chicago, and Los Angeles. While Houston, San Antonio, Austin and the Dallas/Fort Worth metroplex have enjoyed the benefits associated with population growth and economic development, their leadership has and will continue to wrestle with the negative factors of the three S's—**spreading, sprawling** and **spawning**. The spreading of a major metropolitan area's city limits is gradually overtaking the Texas frontier lifestyle as more and more family farms and ranches are transformed into tract and small-acre housing developments. The sprawling of the population growth patterns has been erratic with disproportionate growth on one side of the city offset with little or no growth on the other sides. Sprawling puts pressure on city leaders to provide more public services. Every new resident to a city brings one more demand for fire, police, and emergency medical assistance services; one more automobile adds more stress to already crowded roadways and bridges; and one more student in a public school classroom costs the school district more money.

On the one hand, city leaders in Houston celebrate when a new petrochemical plant picks Houston as its location site, a move that means hundreds of new well-paying job opportunities for Houstonians. On the other hand, the celebration is tainted with the realization that this new plant will only add to the city's serious pollution problems. And while that petrochemical plant flourishes and provides the city with those new job opportunities, city leaders must still deal with crime, urban-centered poverty, decaying older neighborhoods and central business districts, and a shrinking property tax base.

In *"Cities As Partners In The Federal System,"* Robert D. Thomas develops a two-prong public policy agenda for city leaders.[3] The **corporate side** of a city is the pursuit of economic viability; whereas, the **reservation side** is the development of policies focusing on quality-of-life issues for city residents. This chapter explores the quest of city leadership to keep their urban centers economically viable in a changing world economy. Today, cities openly complete with each other over everything from business relocations and convention venues to sporting activities. In San Antonio, city leadership jubilantly announced that it had beat out a city in Arkansas for the location of a new Toyota manufacturing plant. The competition between the two cities was tough. In the end, it took a coordinated effort on the part of national, state, county, and city officials, as well as lucrative economic concessions and tax abatements, to convince Toyota executives that San Antonio was the perfect site. Yet, cities simply cannot ignore the needs of their citizens. A declining quality of city life will eventually destroy a city's corporate image. Although these philosophies are diametrically opposite of each other, they are inevitably dependent upon each other for survival. This chapter focuses on this unique relationship.

Balancing this unique relationship are our state's mayors and county commissioners. While most view the presidency and Congress as the most important arms of government, the one arm that has the most impact on our daily lives and routines is housed in city halls and commissioners courts. It is our local governing bodies that determine the quality and quantity of the police; the fire and emergency medical services we receive; when the garbage is going to be collected; when the streets with their usual potholes are going to get fixed; where to put the traffic lights; how to maintain the local parks and libraries; how to allow for population growth while at the same time protect the environment, and so forth. To say the least, it is not an easy task. The fate of an entire city rests upon the shoulders on who must be up to the job—the mayor. "The greatest powers of the office [of mayor] are available only to those Mayors who understand its full political dimensions. They must possess . . . a high sophistication about the nature and uses of political power, and a strong appetite for exercising such power themselves . . . For lesser men [and women] the Office of Mayor is not an office of weaknesses. Average men as President are more fortunate; the office reinforces the man. But the mayoralty is the highest vulnerable symbol of all defects in the city and its government. It is within reach of its critics. And against these demands, an ordinary mayor can bring only limited resources to bear."[4] This chapter discusses the structure and governing authority of both city and county governments in Texas.

City leaders are confronted by an increasing array of city problems coupled with shrinking city budgets and the continuing threats of federal aid cuts. City and county leaders must also keep a watchful eye on the Texas Legislature. One of the key issues of his campaign, Lt. Governor Da Patrick has been advocating sweeping property tax reform. If he finally wins the day on this issue, any reduction of property tax rates of the percentage of property eligible for taxation does not hurt the state coffers but it seriously would adversely impact the budgets of city and county governments. The state of Texas does not rely upon revenue from property taxes, but local governments surely do since this tax is their primary source of revenue. While federal and state officials do play a role in urban-related policy issues, the responsibility and, ultimately, accountability falls directly upon the shoulders of county and city leaders. For example, a host of federal and state officials visited flood ravaged San Antonio after nearly 25 inches of rain wrecked havoc with the city on October 15, 1998. Each group sympathized, promised funding and assistance, and left. The individual ultimately responsible for cleaning up the mess and repairing broken lives was the mayor of San Antonio. He could not leave and go home because this city is his home. Mayors and county judges along the coast are still dealing with the damage caused by Hurricanes Harvey (2017) and unfortunately Rita (2005) and other major storms that have hit the Texas Gulf Coast area. Once again, federal officials have promised federal assistance to help rebuild destroyed businesses and homes. But, it will take years of patience on the part of city/county leadership to deal with the frustrations of a federal government that makes glowing promises to the America public that they are charging ahead with the provision of all of the resources needed to assist in the speedy recovery from damages caused by a natural disaster, a chemical fire, wildfire, or an off-shore oil spill. Once the cameras have left the press conference and perhaps after filming the visit of either the vice president or the president to personally access the severity of the damage, reality sets in. Yes, the federal government will provide federal funds and manpower, but as seen in far too many disaster situations, the recovery period and a "return to normal" is anything but speedy. This chapter delves into the problems of urban life, with a special emphasis on the alternatives and options available to city leaders to address and hopefully reverse the crippling effects of crime, high unemployment, deteriorating neighborhoods, depleting budgetary dollars, and crumbling infrastructures on the future of the Texas city.

The Development of Texas's Cities

Initially, people relied on a self-sufficient nomadic lifestyle whereby the individual was totally responsible for his/her own survival against the rages of nature and the encroachment of others. The gradual realization that the collective efforts of the many through the community environment could lessen the hardships of survival convinced nomadic hunters to form societies. Ideally the modern city of today is a true melting pot of people from diverse nationalities and backgrounds who have joined forces to preserve collectively their quality of life. Subsequently, "the city is not so much a mass of structures as a complex of inter-related and constantly interacting functions—not alone a concentration of power, but polarization of culture."[5]

Gradually, the isolation of the Texas frontier lifestyle guided with the firm belief in self-sufficiency gave way to the collective embracing lure of the urban environment simply because the city offered what the frontier could not guarantee. First, the city served as a citadel or fortress offering protection from hostile and life-threatening forces. Particularly in Spanish/Mexican Texas, it was the presidio that provided protection from hostile Indian raids and the adverse conditions of frontier life. Second, cities and towns became social centers whereby isolated farmers and ranchers would come to town in their Sunday best to attend church and social functions. "Interest in cultural entertainment was creditable. Most towns had amateur theatrical organizations. As early as 1838 San Augustine had its 'Thespian Corps' . . . San Antonio, with its large German population, was a center for artists. The German Casino Association owned a fine building there that was used for theatrical performances, concerts, lectures, exhibits, and dramatic readings. In almost every community, literary societies sponsored debates on ponderous subjects; there were many lectures, both pay and free; vocal and band concerts could be heard; and professional troupes appeared in all of the larger towns."[6] Third, towns and cities developed into trade centers whereby farmers and ranchers could market their wares. The creation of an intercity market place has played a fundamental role in the historical development of urban centers. It is symbolic of the successfulness of individual efforts that new technologies enabled them to produce more than they needed to feed, clothe and shelter themselves and their immediate family members. The accumulation of wealth within the city began to draw merchants from beyond the city's limits. "What gives the market a permanent place in the city is a population big enough to offer a handsome living to merchants with distant connections and costly commodities, and sufficient local productivity to enable the surplus of urban workshops to be offered for general sale."[7]

Even at the earliest stages of industrialization, city leaders realized that the viability of their economic future was directly tied to their transportation system. Cities near large rivers could move their products to distant markets far faster than those who were dependent upon land routes. Urban centers such as Houston grew because

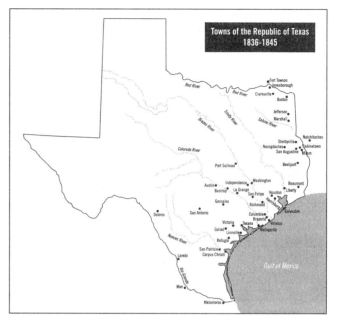

"people live in the city primarily because it offers better facilities for trade and industry . . . and secondarily, because it provides better opportunities for enjoying the amenities of life. Trade and industry are dependent mainly upon a market and facilities for communication with the market. Therefore, the cities which have grown most rapidly are those with the largest tributary areas and the most efficient means of transportation, where possible utilizing both water and rail."[8] It was the wealth accumulation of the market place that gradually brought the luxuries produced east of the Mississippi River to the Texas frontier cities. "By 1860, one could purchase in the larger Texas towns almost any article to be made in the stores and warehouses in the East. Advertisements indicate that merchants kept in stock all kinds of farm machinery, carriages, wagons, building supplies, furniture, kitchen supplies, many kinds of cloth and clothing, jewelry, gold and silver plate, a large assortment of processed foods, ice, quantities of drugs and cosmetics and liquors-indeed, an almost endless list of items."[9] Fourth, urban areas became centers of business and employment opportunities for everyone from the moneyed entrepreneur to the displaced farmer. "Businessmen, lawyers, and doctors walked alongside blacksmiths, gunsmiths, wheelwrights, tanners and saddlers, tailors, and carpenters."[10]

Life on the frontier encouraged the development of small towns, not large metropolitan cities. The permanency of a town was dependent on how long the town could continue to provide what the settlers needed. For example, the discovery of gold in the American west resulted in the founding of hundreds of small towns clustered around the mining fields. The miners came to find gold. The towns supplied the goods and services for the miners and their families. However, once the mines and the ore veins played out, the miners left in search of new gold veins, leaving the town to gradually deteriorate into a "ghost town." Towns in early Texas oftentimes faced the same fate. The town of Harrisburg, for example, has "its name from Mr. Harris, the owner of a steam saw-mill at this place. There are now [in 1836] steam saw-mills belonging to the Harrisburg Saw Mill Company; and large quantities of lumber are constantly made and disposed of. Vessels are frequently loaded at these mills with lumber, destined for the Mexican Ports of the Gulf. . . The situation is, probably rather unhealthy, and the importance of the village can be sustained only by its valuable mills, which furnish more lumber than all the others in Texas."[11] By 1853, Harrisburg was the starting point for the Buffalo, Bayou, Brazos, Colorado Railroad (later named the Galveston, Harrisburg, San Antonio Railway). However, the rail yard was destroyed by fire. The owners of the railroad decided to rebuild in Houston, bypassing Harrisburg. Eventually, the population of Harrisburg dwindled with the loss of the railroad and the opening of the Houston Ship Channel. The once thriving community of Harrisburg virtually vanished, and in 1926, the area was annexed into the thriving city of Houston.

In 1836, a visitor to Texas noted "that towns in Texas, are of mushroom growth; they spring up in a day, and decay as soon, being abandoned for some more alluring spot, which is the charm of novelty for a roving and unsettled emigrant."[12] In 1850, Melinda Rankin, a missionary, commented that "a person coming into Texas, direct from the Northern States, might, perhaps, be surprised upon seeing many places called towns in Texas. He would, probably, as had been frequently the case, inquire, 'where is the town?'"[13] Towns in Texas were hardly the congested metropolises of New York City or Chicago. In 1850, "Galveston, with 4,177 inhabitants, was the largest. San Antonio, Houston, New Braunfels, and Marshall followed in the order named. No other towns had populations of as many as a thousand."[14]

Although sparsely populated, Texas's cities began to form their own unique identifies. Founded in 1824 by Stephen F. Austin and Baron de Bastrop, the original name for Austin was San Felipe de Austin. By 1836, "the state and municipal officers of the jurisdiction hold their offices here; and this was the capitol designation for Texas, when its separation from Coahuila and its reception as an independent State of the Mexican confederacy, should take place. Here, likewise, all the land and judicial business of the colony is transacted. It contains several stores, and

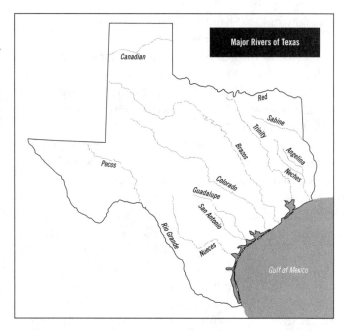

presents altogether the appearance of a busy and pleasant little village."[15] Located thirty miles from the mouth of the Brazos River, the city of Brazoria "will always be important as the first stopping place for emigrants . . . Here may be found those necessaries which the newly arrived, and those wishing to penetrate into the interior, have need of."[16] Located along the banks of the San Antonio River, the city of San Antonio began as a military outpost for the Spanish government in 1718. By 1731, the Spanish government was able to bring several families from the Canary Islands to settle there. By 1836, the city's population was "two thousand five hundred inhabitants, all native Mexicans, with the exception of a very few American families who have settled there."[17] San Antonio acquired a European cosmopolitan look as European immigrants blended their culture with Spanish-Mexican traditions. "The pride of San Antonio was the Menger Hotel on Alamo Plaza, which was opened in 1859. The building of fine-cut stone, two and one-half stories high, together with its carpets, decorations, and beautiful furniture cost $16,000."[18]

Located on the Texas Gulf Coast, Galveston prospered in the 1870s and, for a brief time, was the largest city in Texas. Visitors were amazed at the beauty of this remote port city. It was "briefly beautiful, with six public squares, two parks, two miles of esplanade, street railways drawn by horses, thirteen hotels, three concert halls, and an opera house."[19] The modern-day headquarters for Aggie Land, Bastrop or Mina was "laid out in 1830 by the Empresario General Austin, in his contract of 1827, and is already a considerable place, and continues to grow rapidly. It is a favorite spot for new settlers, and is quite the rage at present [1836]."[20] The city of Houston was founded by two brothers, Augustus C. and John K. Allen. The brothers wanted property between the Brazos and Trinity Rivers whose soils were suitable for cotton and timber production, and its rivers large enough for ultimately shipping those products to foreign markets. "Having located the spot at the confluence of Buffalo and White Oak Bayous, the founders of Houston energetically laid out the streets and reserved plots for a school, churches, a courthouse, and even the nation's capitol [the Republic of Texas]."[21] By 1839, however, Austin was chosen as the site for the state capitol.

The Texas landscape was dotted with a considerable number of small towns. For example, the town of Velasco was located in Austin's colony at the mouth of the Brazos River. In 1836, it was well-renowned for "its salt works which are very notable. . . . Velasco is the resort in summer of great numbers of visitors from the north of the colony, who come to enjoy the delightful sea-breezes, sea bathing, and the comforts with which they are everywhere surrounded. Excellent accommodations can always be obtained at boarding houses, which, among other attractions, are always furnished with supplies of oysters and fish of the first quality. Musqutoe [sic] bars are not often needed here, and altogether, it is one of the most delightful places in the country. . . "[22] After the Civil War, immigrants from European countries settled in Texas, forming their own culturally unique cities. A large contingent of German immigrants began coming to Texas in the 1840s. By 1860, over 20,000 German residents formed the "German Belt," "stretching across the south-central part of the State from Galveston and Houston to Kerrville and Mason in the Hill Country."[23] Texas soon became the Western catalyst for European immigration particularly from France, Czechoslovakia, Poland, Sweden and Norway. Founded in 1855 by Victor Considerant, the French established a short-lived colony called La Reunion. In addition to Cat Spring, other Czech-founded communities included "New Ulm, New Bremen, Hostyn, and Fayetteville. From Poland, came several hundred families in the 1850s to an area south of San Antonio, where they founded the town of Panna Maria in Karnes County. A small Norwegian settlement was planted in Henderson County in 1845."[24] Other hamlets included San Patrick, a community founded by Irish immigrants, Marion or Bell's Landing, Cox's Point, Quintana, Powhatan, Tuscasito, Aransaso, Copano, Lynchburg, and Bevil's Settlement.

As Texas's cities entered into the twentieth century, they had acquired their own unique economic, social, cultural, and demographic patterns that distinguished them from each other. "San Antonio retained its military installations and historic sites and sustained a steady growth rate but a somewhat leisurely atmosphere. Dallas became a financial and mercantile center, widely known for its cultural achievements and aspirations. Fort Worth, generally regarded as a city of the west, developed an extensive livestock market and packing facilities, as well as the sobriquet 'Cowtown.' Houston perhaps because of its more varied economy and sprawling explosive growth, could not be given only one label."[25] The population growth of Texas's major cities indicates marginal but steady growth until the boom years of the twentieth century. Dallas, Fort Worth, Houston, and San Antonio did not reach the 100,000 population mark until the 1920s. Houston exceeded the one million population milestone in 1970. Table 13.1 indicates population figures for the ten largest cities in Texas for years 1990 through 2017. Today, Texas has three of the nation's ten largest cities with Houston ranking 4th, San Antonio 7th and Dallas 9th.

Rural vs. Urban vs. Suburban Growth

Texas began as a predominately frontier region dominated with family-owned plantations, farms and ranches. The 1850 Census indicates that 96.4 percent of the state's 212,592 residents lived in rural areas. However, the appeal of the urban lifestyle gradually eroded the traditional hold to the rural/frontier homestead. Table 13.2 illustrates the gradual but steady decline of rural population, offset with increases in urban population. In 2000, 82.5 percent of Texans resided in urban environments, whereas only 17.5 percent opted for the rural lifestyle. The number of privately held farms has drastically decreased from a total of "420,000 in 1940 to 241,500 in 2016, with an average size of 537 acres. The number of small farms is increasing, but part time farmers operate them."[26] The harshness of rural life is a contributing factor to the decline of the family-owned farm and ranch. At the start of the twentieth century, "work patterns had changed little from pioneer days. The rural family was a relatively tight, cohesive unit, with every family member sharing the workload. Daylight to dark was the schedule, with some planting, plowing and cultivating, while others chopped weeds and tended the livestock. Harvest season demanded the efforts of everyone; many youngsters could not attend school until the crop was at the gin."[27] The fate of agriculture has always been irreversibly tied to the fickleness of the weather cycle and the ups and downs of the economy. Severe dry spells offset with harsh freezing winters and devastating floods place the livelihoods of both the farmers and the ranchers at the mercy of Mother Nature. Despite

Table 13.1 Population of Texas's Major Cities 1990-2017
(Population in thousands – 158 represents 158,000)

City	1990 Total	2000 Total	2010 Total	2017 Total	2017 Rank in Size Nationwide
Amarillo	158	174	191	200	117
Arlington	262	333	365	396	48
Austin	466	657	802	951	11
Brownsville	114	140	175	183	135
Corpus Christi	258	277	305	326	59
Dallas	1,008	1,189	1,198	1,341	9
El Paso	515	564	648	684	22
Fort Worth	448	535	745	874	15
Garland	181	216	227	238	95
Grand Prairie	100	127	175	194	125
Houston	1,631	1,954	2,094	2,313	4
Irving	155	192	216	240	93
Laredo	12	177	236	261	80
Lubbock	186	200	230	254	83
Plano	128	222	260	286	69
San Antonio	935	1,145	1,327	1,512	7

Sources: *ProQuest LLC. ProQuest Statistical Abstract of the United States, 2019*, (7th ed.), Bethesda, Maryland, 2018, Table 24, page 30.

the backbreaking efforts of the farmer and his/her family, an economic decline, no matter how slight, can depress the cost of the harvested crop to the point of economic ruin.

In sharp contrast, the urban environment offers an abundance of services and basic conveniences usually unavailable in rural areas. The appeal of public educational facilities, hospitals, libraries, reliable water and electrical sources, fire and police protection, coupled with a sense of job security that agriculture simply cannot guarantee over the long term, historically drove people to abandon the frontier for city life. It became clearly and painfully evident that the city could offer a far better quality of life under less strenuous and stressful conditions. After all, as Aristotle once stated that "men come together in the city to live; they remain there in order to live the good life."[28] The steady exodus from rural environments to urban centers completely changed the direction of the population growth in this state by 1950, as urban population finally and permanently exceeded rural population figures.

However, the zeal of living within the confines of city boundary lines began to lose its appeal as Texas's cities finally faced the problems so often see in major cities in the north and northeastern sections of the nation. In the 1960s and 70s, city leaders began to realize that population density had negative side effects such as rising incidences of crime, pollution, overcrowded residential areas, and lack of available land within city limits for future commercial and residential construction. City life also stifled that strong strain of individual freedom so often associated with the "native" Texan. Life outside the city limits appeared to be the answer. "Though the retreat from the city had manifest advantages for health and family life, it was equally an attempt to achieve liberation from the sometimes dreary conventions and compulsions of an urban society; an effort, given the necessary financial means, to have life on one's own terms, even if it meant having it alone."[29] Consequently, Texans began to feel the urge to leave the confines of the city for a new Mecca—the suburbs. Located only a few miles outside of city limits the suburbs were extremely appealing. One could have the freedom of a semi-rural lifestyle with the modern conveniences and, oftentimes, the services offered in an urban environment without the constraints and congestion of city life:

To sum it up: the early romantic suburb was a middle-class effort to find a private solution for the depression and disorder of the befouled metropolis: an effusion of romantic taste but an evasion of civic responsibility and municipal foresight. The instincts that promoted this exodus were valid: caught in the new urban wreckage, the old cry, "women and children first," was a sound one. Life was actually in danger in this new urban milieu of industrialization and commercialism, flee-flee with all one's goods, as Lot and his household had fled from the sultry hell of Sodom and Gomorrah.[30]

Table 13.2 – Rural/Urban Population Trends

Census Year	State Population	Urban Population	Rural Population	Percent of Total Urban	Rural
2010	25,146,000	21,298,000	3,848,000	84.7%	15.3%
2000	20,852,000	17,204,000	3,648,000	82.5	17.5
1990	16,986,510	13,634,517	3,351,000	80.3	19.7
1980	14,119,191	11,333,017	2,896,174	79.6	20.4
1970	11,196,730	8,920,946	2,275,784	79.7	20.3
1960	9,579,677	6,963,114	2,616,563	72.7	27.3
1950	7,711,194	4,612,666	3,098,528	59.8	40.2
1940	6,414,824	2,911,389	3,503,435	45.4	54.6
1930	5,824,715	2,389,348	3,435,367	41.0	59.0
1920	4,663,228	1,512,689	3,150,539	32.4	67.6
1910	3,896,542	938,104	2,958,438	24.1	75.9
1900	3,048,710	520,759	2,527,951	17.1	82.9
1890	2,235,527	349,511	1,886,016	15.6	84.4
1880	1,591,749	146,795	1,444,954	9.2	90.8
1870	818,579	54,521	764,058	6.7	93.3
1860	604,215	26,615	577,600	4.4	95.6
1850	212,592	7,665	204,927	3.6	96.4

Sources: U.S. Censuses.

Land developers enticed city dwellers to the tract-housing of the suburbs with the lofty promises of a life free from the ills of congested city life with the understanding that all of the usual and customary public services provided within city limits would be provided to them without the burden of city taxes. The race for the suburbs reminded one of the Oklahoma land rush days, as people with the economic means to relocate, impatiently waited for their tract houses to be built. The decline of the family farm is also directly linked to the increase in the number of sporadic suburban areas surrounding the state's major cities. It is extremely difficult for a rancher or a farmer to raise cattle and plow fields when their land is completely surrounded by suburban housing developments.

The Perils of the Three S's

Unfortunately, those Texans who left the city limits "moved to the suburbs largely for privacy, mobility, security, and ownership. Increasingly they now have isolation, congestion, rising crime, and overwhelming costs. . . . The resulting sprawl has left in its wake a chronic rot, eroding our region from inside out. Now even the suburbs grapple with its ill effects."[31] Suburbanites must face the reality that the problems they thought they left behind merely followed them.

Inevitably today's new suburbs will eventually become older suburbs as newer housing developments are built. Older suburbs will, if not closely monitored and maintained, acquire the same social ills that initially drove city-dwellers from the interior of the city. Homeowners are faced with two alternatives. First, they can individually and collectively strive to maintain the value of their properties and preserve their quality of life. Ideally, each homeowner should want to maintain his/her property. However, many opt not to fix the fence, maintain the yard, and so on. In newer subdivisions, the trend has been for residents to bond together and form their own governing bodies known as **homeowners associations** (HOAs). Each association's charter outlines the parameters for homeowners on a wide array of issues from properly maintaining a yard to the acceptable number of pets for each household. Elected officers usually serve as the approving authority whenever a homeowner decides to change the outside appearance of the property including structural additions, changing the original paint color, installing a swimming pool or replacing a fence. To force compliance with the rules and to ensure that residents pay their annual dues, HOAs have the right to assess fines and, as a last resort, foreclose on the homeowner's property. As detailed in their charter, HOA deed restrictions or **restrictive covenants** are usually set by the original developer of the subdivision. Supporters of HOAs point out that "when houses are built so close together, 5 and 10 feet from the next house, it's not just what you want to do, it's how your house impacts the sale of my house."[32] On the surface, HOAs appear to be an essential tool to preserving the beauty of a neighborhood. Yet beginning with the 1999 session, the Texas Legislature continues to hear a wide variety of angry complaints about the severity of the rules and the propensity for HOAs to see foreclosure as the only compliance option. Citing over 1,000 foreclosures in just one year, Houston HOAs have "banned political signs, children and spouses under a certain age, pets above a certain weight, day care centers, the use of backdoors, pickup trucks and even goodnight kisses on the front steps."[33] A homeowner in San Antonio was hauled before her HOA board because she repainted her house purple, a color viewed as demeaning to the quality of the neighborhood. Each subsequent legislative session has seen unsuccessful attempts to curtail HOA legislative restrictions and rights to foreclosure. Advocates believe that restrictions would put their associations out of business because "without foreclosure, we have no way to ensure people will follow deed restrictions and pay their fees. And if enough people don't pay their assessments, then physical facilities like swimming pools and tennis courts could not be maintained."[34]

Second, homeowners can simply continue to sprawl out by moving to newer subdivision.

Yes, buyers flock to affordable houses outside cities, but many of them hate the sprawl that spreads around them. The most vociferous opponents of sprawl, in fact, are the homeowners who realize that they will soon have to live surrounded by it. They love their freestanding house, its interior spaces, and best of all, the surrounding natural landscape. But, as others seek the same things and sprawl creeps out around them, they grow irate. Similarly, consumers love the prices and inventory inside a Wal-Mart, but they hate the environment it creates outside the store. It's the public realm that leaves them wishing they were someplace else. Indeed, as sprawl matures and ages poorly, people flee it, only to build more sprawl further down the road.[35]

Traditionally the vestiges of frontier spirit keep driving urban Texans to continue to spawn, sprawl and spread. Once it was a common practice for a person to purchase only one home during his/her lifetime, opting to perform customary maintenance and occasionally a major "make over." Today, the urge to move to a better home in a better neighborhood with better schools is directly tied to the ups and downs of the real estate market. Before the latest economic upheaval, the real estate market was strong as mortgage rates declined and

a homeowner could sell his/her property at a premium price, more than enough for a down payment on a new home. In 2009, the real estate market began to hit the skids, and property values declined. A person seeking to sell their existing home saw that home on the market for at least a year or more. Declining property values mean that the seller will sell for less, leaving less than needed for a down payment in a newer home or, at worst, upside down on the existing mortgage. Those who do make that leap to a newer suburb are oftentimes at the mercy of land developers. Homes built outside of the city limits do not have to be built under the same restrictive building code standards used for inner-city construction. For example, several subdivisions in San Antonio were built in the 1960s with plastic sewer and plumbing pipes. City of San Antonio building codes require clay pipes, a more expensive but long-lasting alternative. Clay pipes, unlike the cheaper plastic pipes, expand and contract with changing weather conditions, causing less breakages and leaks. The summer heat in Texas can cause plastic pipes to crack and leak. Even though these subdivisions could be eventually annexed by the city, San Antonio authorities are not required to pay for the replacement of pipes on the private homeowners property since they are responsible for only the pipes under public domain. Therefore, it is the responsibility of the homeowner to bear the cost of replacing those pipes running from the interior of his/her home to curb where the "public" line begins.

"Henry Ford was reported to have said, 'We shall solve the city problem by leaving the city.'"[36] However, the city that the former residents left behind could well become a part of their city once again. The **Municipal Annexation Act of 1963** grants Texas's cities an **extraterritorial jurisdiction (ETJ)** from 0.5 to 1.5 miles on all sides beyond their current city boundary lines. The ETJ is automatically extended whenever a city annexes new territories.   The term **annexation** denotes "the addition by a city of land adjacent to it as an aggressive policy of growth or to meet the problems of metropolitan expansion."[37] While most states require permission from outlying suburban areas, Texas's cities do not need prior approval of suburbanites to annex. The annexation option allows cities to expand their city limits and increase their revenues by bringing new (presumably) well-developed subdivisions, and industrial and commercial properties into the controlling embrace and pocketbook of municipal government. The good news for suburbanites is that they will eventually receive the same quality and quantity of city public services already provided to city residents. The bad news is now the newly annexed residents will have to pay city property taxes for these services even though they may not have them within the immediate future.

Although quick to approve annexation plans, metropolitan city councils across the state were very slow in providing the promised city services. State laws allowed city governments to take as long as 4½ years to provide annexed suburbs with fire, police, ambulance services, street lights, sidewalks, comparable drainage systems, libraries, etc. Consequently, the residents of their newly annexed territories were being billed for years for services they were simply not receiving. The Texas Legislature finally passed laws mandating that capital improvements must be completed and traditional city services provided to annexed areas within 2½ years or the original annexation agreement could be in jeopardy. Passed in the 2001 legislative session, Senate Bill 89 requires city governments to give a three-year advanced notice to areas slated for annexation. Once areas are annexed, the city's ETJ is automatically extended to the mandated 0.5 to 1.5 miles radius.

Suburban areas can successfully avoid annexation by **incorporation**, seeking permission from the legislature to become a municipality under the laws of the state. In order to apply for incorporation, the area must have at least two hundred residents, and be outside the jurisdiction of an existing municipality or if inside an existing municipality, receive permission from that city government to form its own city. A petition seeking incorporation is presented to the county judge with the signatures of at least 10 percent of the area's registered voters. If the results of an area-wide election are positive, then the area is now an incorporated city. Residents will now vote on a city charter, which under state guidelines details the structure of the government, the powers and responsibilities of the government, and so forth. These bedroom cities operate under their own taxing authority to assess and collect property and a piggy-back option for sales taxes and user fees. However, a major problem confronting these smaller incorporated cities and towns centers on the quality and quantity of traditional public services. Since these communities cannot afford the type of services offered by major metropolitan cities, bedroom cities usually have a volunteer police, fire and emergency medical service units and contract out for other essential public services.

The Future of the Small Town

The desire of the residents of Boerne, San Marcos, and New Braunfels to preserve the uniqueness of their small town environment is indicative of the thousands of small communities across this state that are now being overshadowed and, in some instances, gobbled up by their larger neighboring metropolitan cities. The encroachment of suburban living has placed many of these small towns on the endangered list. For example, the I-35 corridor between San Antonio and Austin has witnessed a population explosion since the 1980s. "Sprawl has reached out of San Antonio and Austin and cluttered once rural towns such as Boerne and Dripping Springs with billboards, strip malls and low-density development. Population pressure has threatened the watersheds, congested highways, and raised land prices to such exorbitant levels that many ranchers—struggling with the tax burden and shaky livestock market—are selling out to developers."[38] The small communities of New Braunfels and San Marcos are in the middle of Austin's southern expansion and San Antonio's northern suburban growth. For decades the only major cities in Comal and Hays counties were the small German communities of New Braunfels and San Marcos. Their county officials are facing the reality that the quest for a "life in the country" has placed the future of their communities in jeopardy. With the opening of the Toyota plant in San Antonio, land developers are eyeing rural properties south of the city's boundary lines. Nestled in Wilson County, the small community of Floresville is best known for its annual peanut festival and as the birthplace of former governor John Connally. Once predominately rural, Floresville is rapidly transforming itself into an urban community. "This county [Wilson] of almost 34,000 residents southeast of San Antonio saw its population rise 43 percent from 1990 to 2000. . . . The northern third of the county has just exploded. . . the boom is centered in the top one-third to one-half of the county—the northwestern portion that borders Bexar County and extends through La Vernia and south to Floresville, the county seat."[39] Developers have big plans for Wilson County. On the plus side, Wilson County continues to attract new businesses, which means over time, more tax revenues for infrastructure improvements. On the negative side, county officials and school board members are scrambling just to keep up with the demands of rapid population growth.

Initially settled by German immigrants, the Hill Country includes the counties of Edwards, Kimble, Real, Uvalde, Medina, Bandera, Kerry, Mason, Gillespie, Kendall, Llano, Bexar, Blanco, Burnet, Comal, Hays, Travis, and Williamson. The Hill County was once a sparsely populated area with numerous small communities. There were more deer than people. Today, the Hill Country is experiencing rapid population growth coupled with an expanding tourist trade that has brought resorts, hotels, golf courses, bed-and-breakfasts, and, of course, millions of tourists and seasonal "snow birds." The peach capitol of the nation, Fredericksburg in Gillespie County, was founded by German immigrants in the 1850s. "An enduringly German community built on the old virtues of hard work and thriftiness, has become in the past decade or so, one of the most popular tourist destinations in Texas."[40] The once quiet isolated community is no more. "Every day of the week, and particularly on weekends, the sidewalks along Main Street fill with visitors from across Texas and elsewhere, 30,000 on a big weekend, 1.3 million a year, according to the local Convention and Visitors Bureau. Six hundred tour buses rumble into Fredericksburg every month."[41] The family-owned pharmacies, grocery stores, feed stores, and general stores have been replaced with antique shops, gift stores and the usual assortment of tourist-attracting businesses. "Along a couple of the busier blocks of Main Street, where not too many years ago the odors of farm life and farm animals were an everyday familiarity, the cloying smells of potpourri and scented candles have taken over."[42] The city of New Braunfels is caught in the same quandary. The business faction wants to build convention facilities, more hotels and restaurants while others want to preserve what's left of the city's small town charm. Their dilemma is the same faced by so many small town city residents. They want to be able to preserve their individually unique cultures, histories, and small town environments while at the same time, keep their cities alive by courting economic growth and development.

Governing the Urban Metropolis

Legal Status of Sub-government Units

Under the federal system, national and state governments operate under shared governance with the United States Constitution establishing the guidelines for this relationship. However, the relationship between state governments and their local governing units follows a unitary format whereby local units serve at the discretion of their respective state governments. The Framers of the United States Constitution never intended for any governing body to be created by or to operate independently of the principles embodied in that document. As emphasized by the United States Supreme Court in its 1819 ruling in **Dartmouth College v Woodward**, "the American legal system does not recognize any right of the inhabitants of an urban area to create a municipal government and perform

functions generally associated with local government on their own volition."[43] In 1868, Chief Justice of the Iowa Supreme Court John F. Dillon reinforced the Dartmouth ruling by basically stating that state governments had the legal right to exercise total control over all local governing units. According to the **Dillon Rule**:

> Municipal corporations owe their origin to, and derive their powers and rights wholly from, the legislature. It breathes into them the breath of life, without which they cannot exist. As it creates, so it may destroy. If it may destroy, it may abridge and control. Unless there is some constitutional limitation on the right, the legislature might, by a single act, if we can suppose it capable of so great a folly and so great a wrong, sweep from existence all the municipal corporations in the State, and the corporation could not prevent it. We know of no limitation on the right so far as the corporations themselves are concerned. They are also, so to phrase it, the mere tenants at *will* of the legislature.[44]

While the general public believes that their mayors and county commissioners can act independently of the Texas Legislature, in reality, these governing bodies were created by, are regulated by, and can be dismantled by the state's legislative branch. Article 9, Section 1 of the Texas Constitution states that "the Legislature shall have the power to create counties for the convenience of the people" and Article II, Section 1 recognizes county and municipal corporations (city and special district governments) as "legal subdivisions of the state."

There are four basic units of local government in Texas: municipal or city, county, independent school districts and special districts. One would think that the units would be legislatively charged with coordinating with each other in the execution of their governing responsibilities. In reality, each unit acts independently of each other, coming together only by necessity such as a natural disaster or for mutual benefit. This lack of coordination leads to decentralized or fragmented government. The Texas Constitution of 1876 created this "system" of local government and the Texas Legislature, either by design or oversight, has been unwilling to change it. Currently, Texas has 5,147 local governing bodies of which 254 are county, 1,214 municipal or city governments, 1,079 public school districts, and 2,600 special districts overseeing natural resources, fire protection and housing.[45]

City Governments

The Texas Legislature provided limited self-governing rights to its cities in 1913 with the passage of the **Home Rule Enabling Act**. Essentially this legislation divided Texas's cities into two major governing categories with placement based on each city's population. Cities with less than 5,000 are **general law cities** basically governed by the Texas Legislature. "Under this plan the state legislature adopts a single charter of incorporation to be granted to all urban areas seeking incorporation. This practice emphasizes uniformity, since each new city would have identical powers, be subject to the same limitations, and operate under the same type of governmental institutions as existing cities."[46] **Home rule** status was granted to cities with populations over 5,000. Within guidelines established by the Texas Legislature and the state constitution, home rule cities can determine their own form of government through a voter-approved **city charter**, a document that specifies the powers and duties of elected city leadership to include candidate qualifications, terms of office, election cycles, salaries, as well as the organizational structure of city administration, types of public services provided to residents, and so forth. Home rule cities govern its residents through **ordinances**, which have the force of the law but must be in compliance with state and national laws. Changing from general law to home rule is not automatically triggered by reaching the 5,000 benchmark in population since municipalities must apply for and receive approval from the Texas Legislature to become home rule cities.

At the local level, citizens can directly participate in the governing process through the initiative process, referendum and, if necessary, recall elections. For example, perhaps city dwellers want to change the process used by the city council to determine garbage collection cycles. If council opts not to initiate the change on their own, then concerned citizens can present council with an **initiative petition**, an official document detailing the requested change signed by a pre-determined number of registered voters. Usually, this action drives the council to call for a referendum election, which presents the measure before the entire population for its approval or disapproval. When all else fails, disgruntled city dwellers can use the initiative process to drive a **recall election**, which allows city dwellers to remove their elected mayor or council members from office and place new candidates up for election.

Another avenue for citizen participation is appointment as a member of an official board, commission or committee of city government. Usually these are non-salaried positions with the city picking up the costs for general expenses to include parking, luncheons, etc. Acting in an advisory capacity, board and commission members recommend everything from initiation of a new program, improvements for service provisions, and to policy changes. Service on a city board or commission is a win-win situation for both the city government and the citizen. For the citizen, it gives an individual the opportunity to contribute to his/her community while at the same time gaining a valuable insight into the internal operations of city government. Oftentimes, this gives a person the opportunity to "get their feet wet" in city politics and may actually lead that individual to run for a council or mayoral position in a subsequent election. For the city leadership, it gives them the opportunity to use the expertise of its citizenry that can foster a meaningful connection between the governing and the governed. For example, citizens in San Antonio complained about the inaccessibility to and the acceptance from their individual council members and the mayor whenever citizens before a council session wanted to voice a concern. Then Mayor Ed Garza created a special committee composed of city leaders in education, business, and community organizations. Whereas the average citizen felt uncomfortable in addressing the council, they were not shy about voicing their concerns to committee members. The end result was a change in attitude at City Hall.

In selecting a governing format, home rule city dwellers can opt for either a mayor-council or, rarely used, commission format. In the **mayor-council arrangement,** the mayor is elected in a city-wide or at-large election with council members elected either from single- or a combination of single- and multi-member districts. Regardless of the authority given to a mayor in a mayor-council format and even the council-manager scheme, he/she serves as both the chief of state and chief executive officer of city government. "To most city residents and to visitors to the city the mayor personifies the city, and he/she is expected to represent the city at all major ceremonial occasions. Because of the public image of the office as the personification of the city, all kinds of private and public organizations seek to use the prestige of the office to promote their causes."[47] Whether it be a businessman seeking a site to relocate his business, a visiting head of state, the state's governor or the president of the United States, it is the mayor they seek out, not a delegation of city council members. The community wants to see their mayor at the ribbon cutting ceremonies, riding in their parades, delivering the commencement address at the local college and university, and so forth. And, of course, it is the mayor and not individual council members that gets the credit when things go right and bears the blame when things go wrong. In the wake of Katrina, it was the mayor of New Orleans who carried the weight of the criticism for the city's inability to evacuate residents and address the needs of those left behind. No newspaper article or television commentary mentioned the name of a single councilperson. As the city's chief executive officer:

- The mayor in his /her relations with those who carry on the day-to-day work of the city can set the tone or determine the style of administrative personnel. . . .
- The mayor may act as the spokesperson for administrative employees of the city by pleading their cause for more adequate salaries and working conditions in public discussion and before city councils or their committees.
- The mayor may make a strong impact on the enforcement of ordinances by executive decrees, orders, and directives which are necessary to clarify language in ordinances or to determine conditions under which ordinances become effective.
- He/she may achieve a greater coordination of effort of various administrative agencies by meeting with responsible administrators and working out plans which clarify the areas in which each agency is to function and which establish specific means for setting any jurisdictional problems that arise in practice.
- He/she may stimulate long-range planning by departments through cabinet [council] meetings where innovations and new ideas are encouraged. . .
- He/she may select certain problems which face the city for special treatment and through his [her] contacts with administrators secure a concentrated effort toward their solution even though other problems may have to be shelved for a time.[48]

The power structure of city government really depends on how much authority city residents want to give to their mayor. In the **strong-mayor council format**, the mayor serves as both the executive and administrative head of city government. The mayor has the authority to appoint and remove all department heads and city workers with or without council approval as specified in the city charter. Under guidelines established by city council, the mayor is charged with the preparation and execution of the city budget. The mayor usually has veto authority, which, as specified by the charter, can be either absolute or overridden by council action. Houston is the only major city in Texas using the strong-mayor format. The **weak-mayor council format** strips the mayor of any independent governing authority and actually considers this position to be on the same level as the city council members. The majority of the state's cities have opted for a combination of the two formats under the **council-manager format**. The duties and functions of the mayor follows the weak-mayor format with the day-to-day operations of the city handled by a professional city manager. Depending upon the city charter, city managers can hire, fire and direct city staff with or without prior approval of the council, prepare and execute the budget, and basically run the city. Basically, the mayor serves as the chief of state carrying out the ceremonial duties of the office while the city manager is the chief executive officer. The successfulness of a council-manager format is very dependent upon the mayor and the city manager having a close working relationship and being "on the same page." Both the day-to-day operation of the city and the city's overall image is seriously damaged when a city manager is at loggerheads with the mayor. The salary and tenure of the city manager was put to a charter referendum election in San Antonio in 2018. Voters approved the measure that term limits of the city manager to eight years and limits the salary to "no more than ten times the annual salary furnished to the lowest paid full-time city employee, and to require a supermajority vote of City Council to appoint the city manager."[49]

Originally initiated in Galveston after the 1900 hurricane destroyed the city, the **commission format** operates without a mayor. Basically, the legislative and administrative powers usually assigned to a mayor are vested in several elected commissioners. Collectively, they develop the city budget, pass ordinances, etc. The day-to-day management of the city is divided among the commissioners. For example, one commissioner will oversee the police and fire department, another the city public works, etc. Once hailed as the "way to go," the commission form is rarely used since it developed into commissioners establishing their own "empires" and instead of instilling the spirit of cooperation, basically pitted commissioners against each other, rendering the city ungovernable.

Unfortunately, each city determines whether they wish to compensate mayors and councilpersons for their service to the community. Usually, strong-mayor formats offer a salary to the mayor and, if warranted, to city council members. For example, the mayor of New York City receives a generous salary and compensation package including a mayoral residence. However, mayors and councilpersons in Texas are not given such consideration. In cities with a city manager-council format, the city manager is contractually awarded a salary. Traditionally the mayor and the city council members in San Antonio were paid a minimum stipend for attending the council meetings plus reimbursement for pertinent expenses and city-required travel. At the end of the fiscal year, the mayor's total 'salary' was only $4,040 and a council member earned only $1,040. In comparison, the mayor Austin had a yearly salary of $81,344 and the mayor of Dallas $80,000. There was much to the saying that in order to be a member of San Antonio's city government, one had to have a good paying day job or be independently wealthy. In 2015, city leadership decided to put it to the voters to approve a viable salary package for both its mayor and city council members. The charter amendment passed. Now the mayor of San Antonio has a base yearly salary of $61,725 plus expenses and each council member receives a yearly base salary of $45,722.[50] City-related expenses are reimbursed. Staffers working for the mayor and councilpersons are hired as city employees and receive salaries and benefits.

Regardless of the format, the majority of these positions are filled in non-partisan elections with the mayor running at-large or citywide and individual council members running from single member districts. The primary issue confronting city government is term limits for their mayors and council members. The state constitution states that mayor and council members can serve either two- or four year terms of office, but does not specify the number of terms an individual can serve. Several cities have opted to limit the number of terms an individual can hold as a council person and mayor. Although voters recently approved a charter change from two two-year terms to two four-year terms, San Antonio still uses a life-time ban on individuals seeking to return to elective city positions. A person can serve two four-year terms as a council person and then be elected to two four-year terms as mayor. There are pluses and minuses to term limits. On the positive side, it prevents an individual from seeing a seat on council as a permanent job. It removes the potentiality of "empire building" along with the taint of corruption, cronyism, and favoritism that has been associated with city government. It also removes the political barriers of a newcomer from running against an established incumbent. On the downside, term limits automatically remove talented well-intentioned individuals from continuing to serve their local communities. A term-limited council person may not work as hard for his/her constituents knowing that

their efforts will not be recognized at the ballot box. Also, the constant turnover in city hall means that the policy process is oftentimes bogged down with "reinventing the wheel." It becomes a question of who actually runs city hall, the council members who will be in office for a relatively short period of time or city staffers who are long term employees.

County Government

Whereas city governments have limited autonomy, the state's 254 county governments serve as directed by the Texas Legislature and the state constitution. The primary function of county government is to serve as an administrative arm of the state government. Their constitutionally mandated responsibilities are to 1) conduct elections including voter registration, maintenance of voter lists, counting election ballots, etc.; 2) record and store vital records including birth, death, land titles, marriage certificates, divorce records, wills, etc., 3) maintain and build roads; 4) preserve law and order including maintaining the county jail and providing support to the county courts; 5) issue marriage licenses, automobile license plates, hunting and fishing permits, etc., and supporting the county court system; and 6) protect the public health and the general welfare of their state residents including indigent care. Although they are paid only an administrative fee, county governments collect the state's sale tax revenues. County governments are also responsible for provision of customary services to residents outside of the city limits that cities usually provide such as emergency medical services, fire protection, parks and recreation, libraries, and cultural needs. Unlike home rule cities, county governments do not have ordinance making capabilities of their own. Any changes to county governments must be through the state legislature in the form of a state law or a constitutional amendment.

Overseeing the day to day operations of county government is the **commissioners' court**. Elected to four-year unlimited terms of office, the "court" is composed of a county judge and four commissioners. The county judge runs at-large while commissioners are elected from single member districts in staggered election cycles with two seats up for election every two years. These are salaried positions. Whereas city leaders get to hire and fire their administrative chiefs, the majority of a county's administrative officials are elected by the voters to staggered four-year terms of office. Consequently, the commissioners' courts do not have the right to fire ineffective administrators. The key positions are:

The San Antonio Riverwalk, or Paseo Del Rio,
is a 2 1/2 mile stretch of landscaped waterfront in the
heart of the city. Spanish explorers used the waterway to
supply water to their missions. The Riverwalk was
refurbished in the 1960s.
3/17/2005
Credit: Library of Congress

- **County** or **District Attorney**—the legal official of county government representing the state in all criminal cases arising in his/her county
- **Justices of the Peace**—the lowest rung of judicial proceedings, hears small claims civil suits and misdemeanor offenses
- **County Sheriff**—the chief law enforcement officer whose duties include management of the county jail and supervision of all county law enforcement employees
- **Constables**—serve as the county's process servers for legal issues arising in the county
- **County Clerk**—the county's official record keeper of vital records and statistics; files legal documents for the county courts and commissioners' courts; certifies candidates for elective office on the general election ballot and if the county does not have an elections administrator, prepares the election ballots
- **District Clerk**—provides staff support for the district courts within his/her county

- **Tax Assessor Collector**—chief tax collector for a county, additional duties include issuing certificates of title and collecting license fees for motor vehicles
- **County Treasurer**—chief financial officer of county government, primary duties are to manage the county's money, issue monthly financial reports, etc.
- **County Auditor**—the Texas Legislature mandates that counties with a population of over 10,000 must have a county auditor who is appointed by the district court judge or judges having jurisdiction in the county.

City/County Consolidation

As previously pointed out, the Texas Legislature through the State Constitution created city and county governments as separate bodies, independent of each other. Each body maintains its own police force, fire and emergency medical units, road maintenance departments, and so on. Historically, these two bodies have not fully cooperated with each other. This is a decades old problem. "Perhaps the best example of the need for city-county mutual agreement happened on February 26, 1971, when a $9 million Volkswagon plant at Interstate 35 and O'Connor Road caught fire, [near] the San Antonio City limit at that time. A San Antonio Fire Department unit responded to the first call but returned when it determined that the plant was not within the city limits. More than 200 volunteer firefighters from 14 departments fought the blaze."[51] The slow response time coupled with the out-of-date equipment of the volunteer fire departments could not save the building. The majority of the plant burnt to the ground. Volkswagon decided not to rebuild, closed the plant, and San Antonio lost a major employer. Afterwards officials from both the city and county governments reached a mutual agreement, a pact of cooperation and sharing of manpower and equipment so another plant would not burn to the ground while firefighters stood by and watched. City and county governments do oftentimes successfully work with each other on projects that benefit both. For example, the AT&T Center in San Antonio, home of the Spurs, was built on county property with city backing. Both the mayor's office and the Bexar County Commissioners Court joined forces in promoting a series of special elections to expand the Riverwalk to the north and south, one day connecting water-borne tourists to art museums and the missions. Bringing Toyota to Texas was a joint effort between city and county leaders. While not mandated by the state constitution, city and county governments can and do work with each other.

The Texas Legislature entertained legislation introduced in 1995, 1997, 1999 and reintroduced into the 2011 session to move towards city/county consolidation. Supporters believe that the duplication of public services is just too costly for both governing bodies and too confusing for city/county residents. The duplication of services reminds one of Noah's Ark—two of everything from police and fire to refuse collection and street repairs. Because of funding issues, city governments have the ability to offer better salaries and frequently upgraded equipment while county governments simply do not have these options. Consequently, service quality provided by county governments is a serious concern. Opponents believe **consolidation** would cost cities more money since county services would have to be enhanced considerably just to equal the quantity and quality of city-offered services. One of the primary concerns is which governing body would be in charge: city councils, commissioners' court, or a combination of the two into one body. Of course, voters would have to approve the plan, which is a major stumbling block. City residents can vote because their councils have the ordinance making authority to put the issue before the voters. County governments do not have ordinance making powers so county residents would not be able to voice their approval or disapproval. Until counties are given ordinance making powers, the question of city/county consolidation will remain a item for discussion, not action.

Special Districts

A **special** district is "a unit of local government typically performing a single function and overlapping traditional political boundaries."[52] The most visible special district government in Texas is the elected public school board and community college board of trustees. These two governing bodies are discussed in the chapter on Education in Texas. However, the state does have a wide range of special government bodies including those overseeing mass transportation systems, water, sewage, parks, housing, historical preservation, medical facilities, and flood protection. The membership is usually appointed but a few such as the Edwards Aquifer Authority in San Antonio are elective positions. Either through the state legislature or city government, special districts can be allocated a percentage of property tax revenues and have the authority to charge fees and issue bonds.

Problems Confronting the Metropolitan Areas

The Decline of the Central Business District

Traditionally the primary organ of the urban environment was the center of the city, commonly known as the downtown area or the **central business district (CBD)**. "The CBD was the heart of the city; often it was the entire city. These central districts housed the major industries, shopping outlets, and local government. The CBD dominated the urban focus, being the place of work, and concomitantly, the face-to-face contact necessary for business dealings and a sense of community."[53] The initial designs for cities placed the business sector at the center or hub since the survival of the entire community was totally dependent upon the economic capability of the business community. Due to a lack of rapid transportation, the workforce lived relatively close to the business area, thus forming a "downtown" urban environment.

The invention of the automobile at the turn of the twentieth century, coupled with the popularity of the developing suburbs following World War II, spelled disaster for the CBD. The migration began in a logical sequence. First, middle- and upper-income residents moved from the older residential areas located in the downtown area. They were followed by retail and service-sector businesses such as the drug store, grocery store, cleaners, the family physician, and so on. Finally, primary business establishments moved beyond the city limits because major employers could not find affordable land within the city limits for expansion of their plants and corporate headquarters. In the aftermath, the once-thriving core of urban life was a crumbling mess of deteriorating neighborhoods, block after block of boarded-up businesses, and a decaying infrastructure. The trek to the suburbs meant a disastrous depletion of property and sales tax revenues from city coffers. City leaders were left pondering how they could revamp and revitalize their cities. After all, it is extremely difficult to market an economically depressed and aesthetically depleted city to a major Fortune 500 company seeking to relocate to a more favorable environment.

Deteriorating CBD Housing

The exodus to the suburbs appealed to the upper- and middle income Texan who had the disposable income or existing residential property to purchase a more expensive home. The rapid drop in mortgage interest rates allowed apartment dwellers and renters to become first-time home buyers. The thrill of owning your own home also gave the property owner equity, an investment source for the future. A homeowner can use the selling price of the house and the equity to purchase another home. However, inner city life for low-income residents is a vicious and often frustrating cycle. For lower-income workers and the elderly living on fixed incomes, a monthly mortgage payment is cost prohibitive. Lower-income residents usually opt for rental properties or lower-valued single-family properties located in the CBD. Renters do not accumulate equity from their monthly payments. While there is an abundance of residential properties for middle- and upper-income individuals, the availability of affordable low-income housing for both multi- and single family units is rapidly declining.

Another problem with rental property is the customary upkeep and maintenance tasks. The renter, whether in upper- or lower income brackets, bears little or no responsibility for repairs. It is the responsibility of the landlord to ensure that the housing unit does not fall into a state of irreversible disrepair: severe structural defects, sinking foundations, inadequate plumbing, and wiring problems. Although city governments have building code restrictions, it is extremely difficult for them to keep the so-called slum landlords from taking advantage of their tenants. With the nationwide lack of affordable lower-end housing, for many life in rundown buildings is the only alternative available to them. They are basically at the mercy of their landlords. In cities across the state, "landlords skirt the law in other ways, promising tenants to renovate after they move in, opening boarded-up houses and re-renting them or offering to sell a rental at '**contract for deed**' where the owner keeps the title, charges a high interest rate and can take back the property if the buyer falls behind on the payments."[54] In the major cities in the north and northeastern sections of the country, neighborhoods with substandard housing are called ghettos; in Texas, they are called the slums for private building units, and "the projects" for government-sponsored multi-family units.

The federal government ventured into the public housing market as a result of the Great Depression. Prior to the collapse of the stock market, most homeowners financed their dream house through a **balloon mortgage** whereby the buyer was required to make a substantial down payment ranging from 35 to 40 percent of the cost of the house with the understanding that the monthly mortgage payment was interest only for ten to fifteen years with the balance of the principal due in a lump sum when

the loan matured. The Great Depression put millions of Americans on the unemployment line, and homeowners without the ability to pay off their balloon mortgages. The federal government came to the rescue with the passage of the **Housing Act of 1937**. The legislation called for the federal government to provide local communities with the money needed to build affordable housing for middle- and lower-income individuals. In turn, local communities would create a local housing authority that would be in charge of the initial construction, property management, and continuing maintenance of the housing units. With the end of the Depression, the majority of the nation's unemployed returned to work, enabling those in the upper- and middle-income brackets to regain enough economic viability to purchase their own homes. Consequently, the nation's poor became the primary residents of public housing units. For a variety of reasons, the majority of the local housing authorities failed to provide the required usual upkeep and maintenance.

One of the nation's first housing projects, the Victoria Courts, was built in 1941 in downtown San Antonio. Home to approximately 660 low-income families, the "courts" suffered the all too familiar fate of government housing. After years of neglect, the property became too expensive to renovate. The residents were evicted and relocated around the city to other publically-financed housing. The "courts" were demolished to make way for a newly opened complex of upscale homes, townhouses, apartments and shops with a minimal number of affordable units for low-income families. Another adventure has not fared well either. Located on the west side of San Antonio, the Mirasol Homes subdivision was funded by the federal government and managed by the San Antonio Housing Authority (SAHA). In 1995, the Department of Housing and Urban Development (HUD) gave the housing authority $48.3 million to revitalize the area by either renovation of existing properties or the construction of new units.[55] The contract was awarded and building began in 2000. The project was in trouble from the very beginning. "The San Antonio Housing Authority 'discovered' a landfill on Mirasol property just before construction began in 1999, even though records in its own files since 1951 showed the landfill was there."[56] Also to save money, the contractor readily admitted using substandard building materials. Records indicate that the SAHA "saved between $5,340 and $8,000 per house, or about $1.3 million to $2 million for the project by lowering quality . . . SAHA allowed [the builder] to use roofing shingles with a 20-year warranty instead of 30 years and substitute 7/16 inch oriented strand board (OSB) roof decking for 5/8-inch plywood. The builder also substituted 2X4 trusses for 2X6 inch joists, eliminated front and side screen doors, didn't use noise-reducing wall insulation in the bathrooms and installed less efficient air conditions, resulting in higher utility bills for low-income residents."[57] The complaints from homeowners began in 2001 as they noticed cracks in the walls caused by sinking and cracking foundations.

Of course, not all landlords or property management firms are greedy, insensitive misers bent on profit at the expense of human dignity. Some property owners do desire to repair their properties. However, major property improvement lending institutions have turned down rehabilitation loans through the use of **redlining**, the practice of drawing an arbitrary red line around deteriorating neighborhoods, marking them as too high of a risk for a loan. Consequently, discouraged property owners have allowed time and neglect to take their toll.

Segregated Neighborhoods

Urban areas, particularly the inner-city zone, are victims of both de jure and de facto discriminatory trends. Non-purposeful or de facto discrimination occurs through normal growth patterns and population shifts. Occurring over the years, **white flight** to the suburbs resulted in a steady stream of Anglos leaving the inner-city neighborhoods. The development of more affluent suburbs has left lower- and lower-middle-income Anglos behind in older suburban areas and lower-income minority population groups closer to the downtown area. The CBD is, unfortunately, the center of several often lopsided concentric circles. Each new ring separates itself from the other rings on the basis of wealth and race. The circle furthest from the core is usually the wealthiest. "The growing gap between suburbs, together with the continuing flight of the middle and working classes from the city, is producing a nation in which people of different incomes live in ever greater isolation from each other. . . As a result, the suburbs of most American cities can be divided into sectors that roughly correspond to the paths different income and occupational groups took out of the city."[58] De jure discrimination is encouraged by creative zoning practices on the part of city leaders that legally prevent certain groups from buying or renting residential properties in certain areas. **Exclusionary zoning** occurs when the original land developer or the original buyers in a suburb initiate restrictive covenants and building standards such as a mandated lot size, two or three car garages, paved driveways, mandated minimum square footage

for homes, townhomes rather than apartments, etc., that are designed to attract only a certain type of buyer and, more importantly, to exclude those who lack the financial resources to meet the building code requirements.

The latest trend in wealthier exclusive housing subdivisions is to put fences around them with a huge iron gate as a means of keeping "undesirables" out of one's suburban paradise. Gated communities with the security guard in his small hut or standing by the gate, requires residents and non-residents to show identification items and if they are non-residents, to tell the guard the reasons why they need to enter the property. If a guard is not present, then the resident must enter in a code for the gate to open. To the 'outsider', a gated community is a clear sign of segregated housing. A recent study reveals that the "Austin-Round Rock metro area is the most economically segregated metro area in the country. The metro areas of San Antonio, Houston, and Dallas-Fort Worth are also in the top ten."[59] As the residents of Victoria Courts in San Antonio learned that their low-income housing development was going to be demolished and that they would be relocated throughout the city, the residents of the Courts were upset and scared. In the Courts, they lived with each other under the common bond of poverty. They were dependent upon each other for assistance and support. For them, the residents of the Courts were their extended family who accepted them for who they were. They knew all too well what others had already faced that "any attempts to expand affordable housing opportunities into wealthier areas face fierce opposition from residents and elected officials in those areas. And even court intervention has been necessary to introduce housing opportunities for lower-income families in places such as Sunnyvale in Dallas County."[60] A court order or a city mandated relocation does not guarantee to the relocated low-income person that his/her new middle- or upper-income neighbors will accept them and allow them to become part of the neighborhood and their "family."

Segregated neighborhoods based on race or income place inordinate demands upon city leaders to avoid perceived favoritism of one area over another. When the south side of the city, which happens to house upper-income groups, receives a new road, library or park, the remaining sectors cry "foul" and claim discrimination. When the eastern, western, northern and southern parts of a city are jealously pitted against one another, city hall becomes a political battleground leading to policy impasses. Divided neighborhoods defeat the process of cultural assimilation by polarizing subcultural groups, eventually pitting one group against another with fear and suspicion. Particularly among the inner city poor, life in segregated non-diversified neighborhoods breeds distrust and frustration that oftentimes spills over into violence. For example, the frustration of chronic unemployment, deep poverty and racism in the predominately African-American neighborhood of Watts in Los Angeles came to a very violent and deadly breaking point when a predominately all-Anglo jury acquitted several police officers of the near-deadly beating of African-American, Rodney King. Angry mobs overturned cars and burned local businesses owned primarily by Koreans who opted not to hire residents of the local community to work in their establishments.

The Dependent Underclass

In particular, the inner city has produced an economic class distinction of its own, commonly known as the **underclass**. Poorly educated and lacking employable job skills, these are the men, women and children who live on the streets, sleep in the parks, and eat at charitable soup kitchens. Some work as day laborers for small contractors or work at below-minimum wage service-sector jobs. Many of these individuals have entered into the United States illegally in search of better jobs and more money. The city has always been the last hope for the displaced and the unwanted. Unfortunately, cities cannot pick and choose who can live within their boundaries. It is the responsibility of a compassionate and caring society to welcome all into its fold. The problem confronting Texas's city leaders is: how can they afford to meet the service needs of individuals who contribute little or nothing to the cost of those services? As budget dollars continue to shrink, city leaders must begin to debate whether to provide services and assistance to the inner city underclass.

Particularly in the states that border Mexico, city and state leaders have been confronted with the problem of illegal immigration from Mexico and Central and South America. Public opinion over illegal immigration is directly tied to the health of the economy. During "good times," few Americans complain about the flow of illegal workers into this country. A healthy economy produces an overabundance of job opportunities. However, a recession shrinks the job market as businesses down-size through lay-offs and plant closings. A depressed job market coupled with high unemployment and inflation rates brings out anti-legal and –illegal immigrant sentiments. The latest economic upheaval has moved lawmakers at both the state and national levels to introduce measures to close the shared border between Mexico and the United States, round up and deport those who are working and living illegally in

the United States, and to even change the Constitution's guarantee that those born on American soil are naturalized citizens of the United States. In December 2010, the United States Senate defeated the Dream Act that would have granted a fast-track to full citizenship for those illegal individuals who came to this country as infants but who demonstrated their commitment to be "good" citizens by either attending and graduating from college or serving in the military.

An equally complex problem is homelessness. The majority of the nation's homeless call the streets and alleys of the inner city their home. The problem is compounded with the realization that a large percentage of the homeless have severe mental, physical, and substance abuse problems. The plight of the homeless reaches crisis levels during severe winters and heat-burdened summers. Cities have responded by joining forces with private agencies to provide shelters and meal programs; however, these programs cannot keep up with the demand for assistance. Citizens were once very tolerant of the homeless, but the homeless have worn out their welcome in cities across the country. Residents have demanded that the homeless not use the public parks and expressway underpasses as their homesteads. City leaders realize that the homeless will not just disappear from the city streets since they are now part of the metropolitan scene.

Congestion and Smog

Overcrowding in Texas's major cities has created problems of growth so often associated with the major metropolitan cities of the north and northeast. Spending more and more hours commuting to work, Texans pile into their personal cars and tune into the morning traffic reports for advanced warnings of wrecks and traffic snarls. Cities across the state have installed an electronic computer highway warning system on its major freeway systems that through a series of monitors and lane arrows, inform motorists of traffic problems. Particularly in Texas, the private automobile and the pickup truck have become, and will probably remain, the preferred mode of transportation over the bus, train or subway. However, Texans have paid a price for their love of the roadways. "By allowing mass transportation to deteriorate and by building expressways out of the city and parking garages within, our highway engineers and city planners have helped to destroy the living tissue of the city and to limit the possibilities of creating a larger organism on a regional scale."[61] The lack of parking in the inner city has hurt economic development as shoppers remember the nightmarish traffic jams driving into downtown coupled with the equally frustrating search for a precious parking space. Shoppers now think twice about making another downtown adventure.

Of course, congestion has created environmental concerns for Texas's major urban centers. Usually rated as one of the nation's worst polluted cities, Houston's problems have been and continue to be created by the growth of the petrochemical industry and the pollution caused by gasoline-driven vehicles. In the state's major cities, an "ozone action alert" informs residents not to put gas into their cars or mow their lawns on particular days because the rate of ozone pollutants has already reached unacceptable EPA levels. Residents with lung problems, allergies, or breathing-related illnesses are becoming prisoners in their own homes thanks to pollution, smog and ozone damage.

Shrinking Job Market

The inner city is plagued with a lack of above minimum wage jobs. When the major employers left the CBD, they abandoned their facilities and the majority of their employees. Historically, Texas is infamous for its blatant disregard for the benefits of mass transportation systems; as a consequence, too often the transportation needs of inner city residents are overlooked by the mentality that every Texan is born to own a car. Many inner city residents lack reliable personal transportation that would enable them to get that higher paying job outside of their immediate area. Bus routes are far too often unreliable and time consuming due to frequent transfers from bus to bus. Trapped in a economically deteriorating CBD, inner city residents must settle for lower paying service sector employment opportunities. The lack of viable employment in some instances leads to a rise in criminal activity. However, inner city residents have been unfairly blamed for crime; statistics indicated that all areas, rich and poor, have reported incidences of criminal activity. With high unemployment, the inner city seems to be the perceived focal point for crime, drugs, and gang violence. Once again, it is very difficult for city leaders to court economic development with the promise of new jobs at high salary levels to an inner city area targeted as a haven for criminals.

The City's Budget Woes

The ability of city leaders to provide city services to their residents is totally dependent upon a city's revenue generating capabilities. Cities cannot deny basic essential services to its residents since garbage collection is essential for health reasons and fire, police and medical assistance is essential to the survival of both the city and its residents. However, these services require large yearly expenditures that severely drain a city's limited resources. The traditional income source for cities is the property tax. City governments can surely depend upon an ample flow of revenue when the majority of their residents live in well-maintained neighborhoods with high property values. Yet, white flight to the suburbs beyond the reach of the city limits coupled with deteriorating property values in the inner city, severely decreases revenue streams from property taxes. The Texas Legislature does provide an additional source of revenue for cities through the state sales tax. Cities can piggyback the state's base sales tax rate by adding up to 1 percent above the state's rate. However, cities only receive the revenue from the piggyback percentage since the bulk of the tax revenue collected belongs to the state. Normally, sales and property tax revenues are used for operating expenses and minor capital expenditures.

Major capital expenditures are traditionally funded by federal grant programs and the sale of **municipal bonds**. Federal grants have been used to build major infrastructure projects such as roadways, drainage and sewer systems, airports, parks, and so on. Cities rely upon the sale of municipal bonds for a wide variety of projects ranging from street maintenance to major arena and convention construction projects. Bonds are politically safe since they are not a tax program, and citizens are not required to purchase them. Municipal bonds are sold at interest rates higher than traditional savings bonds. When the bond reaches maturity, the purchaser will receive the face value of the bond plus accrued interest. On the positive side, municipal bonds provide cities with large sums of money within a relatively short period of time. The negative side is that cities must be able to complete the project in enough time to allow cities to recapture enough money to pay the bondholders. A city can rapidly lose its favorable bond rating by failing to reimburse bondholders.

City and county governments use a wide variety of user fees charged to residents for use of public services and facilities. Usually residential user fees for water consumption offset the operating costs for the operation and maintenance of water and sewer systems. The cost of trash collection and disposal is paid through a garbage fee charged to city dwellers. Additional user fees are charged for the maintenance and daily operations of parking lots and garages, zoos, golf courses, museums, stadiums, city-own tennis courts and sports facilities, historical sites, and so on. San Antonio charges a restaurant and hotel/motel tax to hospitality concerns operating on the San Antonio River Walk and the surrounding downtown area. Tax revenues are used to offset costs for the upkeep of the River Walk as well as to supplement the budget for the San Antonio Convention and Visitors Bureau. Some metropolitan areas charge an impact fee to land developers to offset infrastructure costs for parks, sewer systems, streets, sidewalks, fire and police protection, and street lighting treatment for new residential, industrial and commercial developments. County governments charge a flood tax, county road and bridge tax and so forth, to fund road maintenance and improvement projects.

The expense side of a typical city's budget demonstrates the desire of city leaders to provide a wide variety of city services to its residents without demanding tax increases. City dwellers want the best of both worlds by demanding a wide range of top quality services provided at the cheapest costs possible, often an unrealistic and even impossible task for city budget makers. Usually crime and public safety issues are the primary focus for city leaders as poll after poll reveals crime to be the number one concern of Texans across the state. Sanitation issues revolving around trash collection and disposal capture the second largest piece of the budgetary pie, followed by health department expenditures, culture and recreation, street repair and construction. Most Texas cities allocate only a marginal budget consideration for welfare and environmental programs, relying instead upon federal payments and grants to cover these expense items.

Service Delivery Options

Despite the strong belief in rugged individualism, city dwellers have become totally dependent upon city services. The average Texan is confronted by the reality that the "modern urban is born in a publically financed hospital, receives his education in a publicly supported school and university, spends a good deal of his time traveling on publicly built transportation facilities, communicates through the post office or the quasi-public telephone system, drinks his public drinking water, disposes of his garbage through the public removal system, reads his public library books, picnics in his public parks, is protected by the public police, fire, and health systems; eventually he dies, again in a hospital, and may be buried in a public cemetery."[62] These essential public services must be provided to secure the well-being of the citizenry. The question before city leaders is how to distribute these services effectively in an equitable manner without bankrupting the city treasury.

Service delivery options are limited, leaving city leaders to make extremely tough decision.

City services are public rather than private goods. **Private goods** are "those products or services that can be individually packaged, sold or used."[63] Only the buyer and the seller are involved in the transaction, while government plays an indirect, oftentimes, regulatory role. Streets, traffic signals, sewer/drainage systems, and public libraries are **public goods** that can be used by all residents when needed. Counties, for example, charge all of its citizens a road-and-bridge tax based on the premise that all citizens may eventually have a need to use those roads and bridges in the near future. **Non-renewable goods** such as water and oil are **common pool goods** "that can be individually packaged, bartered and used, but their use by one person decreases the availability of the good for others."[64] These goods pose a totally different array of service delivery problems. Water is essential to survival; however, it is not an unlimited resource, particularly in areas hard hit by seasonal droughts. The quandary is how much to charge users to encourage conservation without making the item cost prohibitive to those in economic need. The denial of common pool goods to those who cannot afford to pay for them creates moral considerations that society as a whole will not allow city leaders to ignore. The denial of heat in freezing weather or electricity to cool a room during a heat wave simply because a person cannot pay the bill is an intolerable situation. Consequently, the pricing of common pool goods must be affordable to all residents while at the same time be punishing to those who waste these precious non-replenishable resources.

The distribution of public services impacts all parties including those not currently utilizing them. An **externality** is "an impact on a third party, one who is not directly involved as either the buyer or seller in a private transaction but who still either enjoys some benefit or suffers some negative consequence from the private exchange."[65] Public transportation is an essential public service for those without private transportation. However, buses do emit obnoxious fumes. The person walking on the street is directly impacted by those fumes, even though this individual does not ride the bus. Second-hand smoke is an externality. Recognizing the adverse impact of cigarette smoke on nonsmokers, city leaders have passed ordinances prohibiting smoking in public areas including most restaurants.

In allocating public goods, city leaders must consider six basic factors. First, the **demand** for the service will increase or decrease as the population grows or declines. When the population of a city explodes, once ample parkland soon becomes overcrowded and inaccessible to many weekend picnickers. A city experiencing a sudden rapid population spurt suddenly discovers that there is not enough of any public service to meet the demands of its residents. Second, the principle of **elasticity** must apply to city service budgets. As demand increases, the revenue side of the budget must increase enough to cover anticipated costs. Third, **quality** and **quantity** of services are directly tied to resources. City leaders cannot guarantee twenty-four hour police patrols if they do not have enough officers, cars, and equipment. Unfortunately, resources are budget-driven. Fourth, the quality of the service is directly related to the **availability of resources**. For example, cities promise fire and police protection to all of their residents. Annexation increases city revenues while at the same time increases the service area. If the resources and the budget are not aligned, the quality of service delivery will suffer and the complaints to city hall will flood the switchboards. These services will not be available to the entire targeted audience unless the city has the monetary resources to hire, train, and equip the manpower needed to meet the demand. Fifth, city leaders must determine in advance of delivery the intended purpose and **expected results** of the service program. City budgetary restraints may compel city leaders to narrow the purpose of a traditionally multi-purpose service. For example, some city leaders may view the primary purpose of law enforcement as a reactionary role through the apprehension of law breakers. The expected result would be a noticeable drop in the crime rate. All available resources would be concentrated on achieving this primary purpose to the detriment of other functions associated with law enforcement such as crime prevention and traffic control. What is the proper role for the Parks and Recreation Department? It is to provide city-sponsored entertainment for city residents or is it to provide park rangers to protect citizens from the criminal element roaming the parks? Finally, the delivery of public services must consider the issue of **equity**. City services should be allocated in a fair, just, and equitable manner. Regardless of the public service program, "every service delivery decision involves a standard of equity whether or not it is expressed."[66]

There are several service delivery options available to city decision makers. For example, the city of Boxwood (a fictitious city) is trying the decide how to provide police and refuse collection services to its residents. Perhaps the easiest method to achieve equity is to divide the services **equally** among the residents. One police officer would be assigned to an equal number of residents. One garbage truck and crew would be assigned to an equal number

of structures. Equally dividing the services of police and garbage collection does overlook the fact that not all areas of the city have an equal crime problem or refuse collection need. In particular, police protection should be placed where it can be most effective, primarily in high crime areas just as some areas of the city need more frequent garbage collection services. City leaders could opt to distribute services solely on the **need** for the service. High crime areas need more police officers and substations while areas with little or no crime would need less police coverage. More densely populated areas would need more garbage trucks and more frequent refuse collections over those areas that are sparsely populated. City leaders using this option must determine what each area's needs are and weigh the intensity of that need against the need for that service in the other sectors of the city. Public services can be distributed in response to citizen's **demands**. Statewide polls indicate that crime is the foremost concern of most Texans. Responding to the demands of their residents, the Boxwood City Council could divert funds from other service budget items to supplement the budget for police. However, merely reacting to demands can cause major problems for city leaders. First, failure to produce immediate results can cause severe political repercussions from irate voters. Second, diverting funds from other service programs will jeopardize the effectiveness of these services in both quality and quantity. A highly uneven distribution of public services results when the **preferences** of the residents guide the hands of city leadership. Far too often, "differences in service preferences are closely associated with differences in personal incomes."[67] The less affluent sectors of Boxwood prefer increasing services for police protection, streets, drainage, refuse collection, recreation and so on. On the other hand, the more affluent areas who already have nice streets, adequate drainage, and convenient refuse collection schedules want increased city funding for the cultural arts, libraries, bicycle trails, etc. Should not all of the city's residents enjoy the full benefits of the urban lifestyle?

Allocated services based on the **willingness and ability to pay** is the most cost-effective option but potentially the least normally palatable choice. Under this option, the city leaders of Boxwood could offer police protection and refuse collection to only those citizens willing to pay a monthly fee for these services. While this option does save the city money, the moral dilemma is whether a public servant or even an innocent bystander can just watch and do nothing to assist a person who is being assaulted before their very eyes. Some cities do charge a hefty fee for the use of public services after the service is rendered.

For example, police and fire personnel will respond to rescue a stranded motorist who opted to go around the high water barricades during a flood. Obviously, it would be inhumane for officers just to stand by and watch the person drown. But, the rescued person is given a citation and billed afterwards for the cost of the rescue. Finally, **co-production** is another viable option whereby a partnership is formed by the public sector with the private sector either through the business community or private citizens. The residents of Boxwood could offset the cost of city-sponsored refuse collection by cleaning up vacant lots, recycling and collecting old newspapers and used plastic products, and cutting down unwanted trees and brush. Police protection can be selectively shared through neighborhood watch patrols who report criminal activities to the police. Co-production makes citizens more aware of the complexity in the provision of public services. The downside is that co-production is dependent upon a volunteer effort from the private sector. Often volunteers provide a short-term commitment for a long-term problem.

City leaders, whether they be from Boxwood or Dallas, use a combination of all of these options to provide services to their citizens. Cities cannot function without the basic services of fire, police, medical assistance, streets, sewers, drainage, refuse collection, and so on. However, city leaders are constantly stretching every tax dollar to assure a constant flow of a reliable quantity and quality of public service programs.

A City's Key to Survival

While much has been said about the residential side of the city, cities still must be able to project a positive corporate side. To accomplish this, cities must operate as a business. A healthy viable business thrives on capital investments, job creation, plant expansion, and business development. Like a business, cities must be able to enhance their economic viability by attracting new businesses while at the same time encouraging existing businesses to expand their operations. It's a simple formula. "Residential, commercial and industrial developments provide jobs, capital accumulation, and generate revenue for governmental services."[68] The opportunities, however, are limited. Cities must aggressively compete with each other and offer lucrative deals including **tax abatements** to lure top corporations into their city limits. For example, Quaker State Oil Company relocated its entire corporate headquarters to Dallas. This relocation generated new high-paying jobs, increased demand for residential housing, and increased tax revenues. The southern sector

of Bexar County is experiencing both commercial and residential development due to the Toyota plant, the primary manufacturing plant for the Tundra pickup truck. In competition with a city in Arkansas, city and county officials successfully offered an incentive laden package promising $22 million in tax abatements; $9.1 million to extend a major roadway leading to the plant site; $45 million in tax discounts from the Southwest Independent School district, although Toyota will pay the district up to $34 million to offset losses in state funding relating to the abatement; $15 million in state funds for building a rail line that links the plant to the Burlington Northern-Santa Fe Railroad; $26 million in state funding for area highway and road expansion; $16.9 million in city financing to purchase the 2,600 acre plant site; an additional $10 million in city funding for the site preparation; $3 million in city funding for a training center; $13 million in fee waivers including the extension of fresh and recycled water and sewer services; and $10 million to extend natural gas and electric power service and build a power station on the plant's property.[69] In addition, county officials agreed "to finance $17.8 million to widen Zarzamora Street and Applewhite Road in the vicinity of the project."[70]

Economic development takes careful planning to ensure the best options for the city's future growth. Business development should not jeopardize the quality of life for a city's residents. Hopefully, Texas's city leaders have benefited from the painful lessons learned from the unchecked industrial and commercial development of the older industrial cities of the northern and northeastern sections of the nation. "While factories were usually set near the rivers, no authority was exercised to concentrate factories in a particular area, to segregate the more noxious or noisy industries that should be placed far from human habitations, or to insulate for domestic purposes for the appropriate adjacent areas. 'Free competition' alone determined location, without the thought of the possibility of functional planning and the jumbling together of industrial, commercial, and domestic functions went on steadily in industrial cities."[71] The price of irresponsible industrial development is extensive environmental damage that places the residential side of a city into peril. Years of uncontrolled petrochemical and oil-and-gas-related industrial development in Houston have contributed to the city's continuous ranking as one of the nation's most polluted cities. Known as refinery row, a ten-mile corridor of six major petrochemical refineries in Corpus Christi may be the city's economic backbone, but collectively these businesses have severely jeopardized the environmental quality of the entire community. Carte blanch industrial

Two tall buildings—one modern and one historic stand tall next to each other in the heart of San Antonio, Texas. 3/17/2005 Credit: Library of Congress

development may enhance a city's corporate image and bring additional tax dollars to the city's treasury, but at the same time, unless it is a well-planned effort guided by prudent respect for the environment, this type of development could well render the city uninhabitable.

Cities should be a place where people can live peacefully surrounded by a pleasing reasonable quality of life, the **reservation** side. An urban area's ability to provide a quality infrastructure capable of meeting its resident's needs is just as important to the corporate side of the city. Reservation infrastructure includes greenbelts or inner-city parks, environmentally sound mass transportation systems, shopping centers and markets, playgrounds, gardens, medical facilities, public and higher instructions of education, and so on. People should desire to live in their central downtown area, not be forced to because of personal economic conditions. It is possible for city leaders to create an urban environment combining economic development with the needs of its residents that ultimately will avoid the dismal deterioration seen so often in America's downtown areas. In *The City in History: Its Origins, Its Transformation, and Its Prospects*, Lewis Munford believed

that a city's mission is "to put the highest concern of man at the center of all his activities: to unite the scattered fragments of the human personality, turning artificially dismembered men—bureaucrats, specialists, 'experts,' depersonalized agents—into complete human beings, repairing the damage that has been done by vocational separation, by social segregation, by over-cultivation of a favored function, by tribalisms and nationalisms, by the absence of organic partnerships and ideal purposes."[72] Texas's cities may never achieve the lofty expectations of Munford's ideal city. However, a city can strike a balance between the corporate pursuit of its business image and the preservation of its cultural and historical integrity of its past and future, guaranteeing a palatable quality of life for its residents. In 1913, city leaders in Houston realized the need to merge the corporate and reservation functions of their city:

> With the growth of cities there has come a great increase in the mutual interdependence of their inhabitants. Whether we believe in socialistic doctrines or not, we all recognize the value of commercial activity in a great variety of directions, such as preserving law and order, safety from fire, provision for pavements, sewerage, and the other usual municipal departments. But it is only recently that any thought has been given toward correlating these activities and planning on broad lines in advance to secure the greatest public good, as would be done by a private corporation.[73]

Preserving the Past While Planning for the Future

Cities across the nation are confronted with the task of preserving historical buildings and monuments while at the same time, bending to the cries for a skyline of high rise hotels, and luxury apartments and condominiums all with a breath-taking view of the city along with state-of-the art convention facilities, cultural venues, restaurants, retail shops, etc. For many city councils, the decision comes down to whether or not to preserve a crumbling century-old vacant building constructed of limestone bricks that once housed the city's first hotel or to tear it down and replace it with a multi-purpose modern building of glass and steel. The necessity of preserving the past is essential to the longevity and vitality of today's "modern" city for the city is the repository of its past and is itself, a museum.

> But if the big city is largely responsible for the invention and public extension of the museum,

there is a sense in which one of its own principal functions is to serve as a museum: in its own right, the historical city retains, by reason of its amplitude and its long past, a large and more various collection of cultural specimens than can be found elsewhere. Every variety of human function, every experiment in human association, every technological process, every mode of architecture and planning, can be found somewhere within its crowded area. . . . If all the materials of our culture were too widely scattered, if the relevant data and artifacts were not capable of being assembled in one place, assorted, made available for redistribution, they would exercise only a small fraction of the influence. . . . The great city is the best organ of memory man has yet created.[74]

Today's tourist attraction is a piece of yesterday's past!

Currently, a special committee of business leaders, historians, and community leaders are reevaluating Alamo Plaza in San Antonio. The "Cradle of Texas Liberty" commonly known as the Alamo, is located in the middle of downtown San Antonio. The mission of the committee is to see how the city of San Antonio can preserve the historical significance of the mission while at the same time, provide the types of businesses that attract tourism and convention attendees to the downtown area. Of course, returning the Alamo and its property to its original acreage is impossible since it would mean tearing down a major sector of the downtown area including a major shopping mall, numerous restaurants and shops, and demolishing several major hotels. The question is how to accommodate both the historical importance and reverence the Alamo demands while at the same time, ensuring the economic development and revitalization of the downtown area.

The fate of the Alamo, or as it is officially known as Mission San Antonio de Valero, has always been in limbo. Today, tourists visit only a small portion of the mission property, primarily the church and the Long Barrack. After the fall of the Alamo, Santa Anna assigned Colonel Juan Jose Andrade with the task of repairing the damaged compound and occupying it until the Mexican army withdrew in May 1836. Santa Anna's final order was to destroy what was left of the Alamo compound to prevent the Texan forces from occupying it. Mexican troops tore down the outer walls including the long wall known as Crockett's Palisade. During the Republic years, the Alamo was periodically occupied by Texas troops who also pillaged the grounds for souvenirs. After Texas joined the Union, the U.S. army turned the abandoned mission into a regional quartermaster depot and converted the Long Barrack into a warehouse. "Despite legal battles with the Catholic Archdiocese, which proved its claim of ownership to the old mission property, the U.S. Army would have nearly a thirty year-long presence at the Alamo. In 1850, when quartermaster operations expanded to the old Alamo church, the Catholic Church received $150 a month in rent from the Army."[75] The fate of the Alamo grounds changed once again when Texas joined the Confederacy. The U.S. army withdrew from the property only to return once again after the Civil War ended. By 1876, the U.S. army abandoned the Alamo and moved its military operations to the newly opened Fort Sam Houston military base.

With the army's departure, parcels of the Alamo grounds were sold while the Catholic Church maintained ownership of the church. By 1871, the Catholic Church sold a portion of the property to the City of San Antonio who subsequently demolished a few buildings to make way for Alamo Plaza, the bricked-in park located in front of the church. In 1877, the U.S. military sold the Long Barrack to Honore Grenet, a French businessman, who refurbished it into a museum and general store. The Catholic Church rented the church to Grenet to use as a warehouse. With the death of Grenet and the approaching 50th anniversary of the Battle of the Alamo, State Senator Temple Houston, a son of Sam Houston, introduced legislation in 1883 authorizing the state of Texas to purchase the church for a mere $20,000.

The legislature then turned the church over to the city of San Antonio who in 1890 used a portion of the church as a police station. Meanwhile, the Long Barrack became a grocery and dry goods store owned by Hugo & Schmelzer. The straw that broke the camel's back was a 1903 proposal to sell a large portion of the property including some of the remaining buildings to a land developer eyeing the construction of a new modern hotel.

The saviors of the Alamo are two women from different backgrounds. Clara Driscoll was the daughter of a veteran of the Battle of San Jacinto and wealthy cattle rancher. Adina de Zavala was a schoolteacher whose passion was saving San Antonio's historical landmarks. She was the granddaughter of Lorenzo De Zavala, the first vice president of the Republic of Texas. In 1902, she met with Driscoll at the Menger Hotel to plot their plan to save the Alamo. A founder of the Daughters of the Republic of Texas (DRT), de Zavala encouraged Driscoll to join the organization. In 1903, a $75,000 counter offer by Gustav Schmelzer was accepted by the DRT and "over the next five years, Driscoll paid almost the entire amount herself, but De Zavala was able to shame the Texas legislature into reimbursing her friend's generosity."[76] In 1905, the two

Alamo buildings (the church and Long Barrack) were assigned to the DRT by the Texas Legislature. A rift developed between the two friends over the fate of the Long Barrack. De Zavala wanted to save it for she believed that was where the majority of the Alamo defenders died. Driscoll, on the other hand, saw it as an eyesore that needed to be demolished. The animosity between the two split the DRT into two warring factions.

In 1908, the fight over the survival of the Long Barrack made national news as De Zavala locked herself in the Alamo for three days. Like Travis in 1836, De Zavala drew her own line in the sand defending her disparate fight to save the Alamo and of course, the Long Barrack:

> My immortal forefathers suffered every privation to defend the freedom of Texas. I, like them, am willing to die for what I believe to be right . . . The officers cannot starve me into submission.[77]

Not wanting to arrest her, Bexar County Sheriff Don Tobin left her behind without food, water or even electricity. However, De Zavala's siege was a successful one as Texas Governor Thomas Campbell put the Alamo and all of its associated buildings under state control with the guarantee that none would be demolished. In 1968, the Long Barrack was turned into museum by the DRT. A third battle of the Alamo pitted the DRT against the Texas Legislature as maverick members of the DRT claimed that the "old guard" of the organization was mismanaging it and allowing the property to deteriorate. Consequently, in 2011 the Texas Legislature gave overall control of the Alamo to the Texas General Land Office who, in turn, created a non-profit Alamo Endowment to raise funds for the preservation of the "Cradle of Texas Liberty."

The four missions in San Antonio have suffered similar fates. For nearly 150 years missions Concepcion, San Jose, San Juan and Espada were basically abandoned. Interest in re-establishing and restoring Mission San Jose was initiated by Benedictine monks from Pennsylvania in 1859. Also, the Brothers of the Society of Mary from France came to San Antonio around the 1860s and founded the St. Mary's Institute, a school located in the downtown area which would eventually be relocated and renamed as St. Mary's University. The brothers focused their efforts on Mission Concepcion. In 1858, French priest Father Francis Bouchu moved into Mission Espada and helped to restore Espada and Mission San Juan. Founded in 1924, the San Antonio Conservation Society purchased the granary at Mission San Jose. In 1978, the four missions along the San Antonio River were designated

as a national park under the supervision of the National Park Service. The Archdiocese of San Antonio oversees the churches at each of the missions. With the expansion of the River Walk along the San Antonio River, the prospects of new commercial and residential development along with increased tourism to the Mission Trail area has perked increased interest into the historical significance of the missions.

Another area that was once doomed to demolition was La Villita, one of San Antonio's original settlements. Initially, it was just a series of primitive huts used by Spanish soldiers garrisoned for the protection of the Alamo. After a tragic flood in 1819, the huts were replaced by small houses built of brick, stone and adobe. During the siege of the Alamo, Santa Anna used the area to set up his cannon line. In the 19th Century, European immigrants primarily from Germany and France moved into the area. But by 1939, the beauty and historical significance of La Villita was lost as the area declined into a slum and dump site. In 1939, San Antonio's mayor Maury Maverick commissioned a group of civic leaders and historians to study the area and recommend its fate. Restoring the "little village" back to its original configuration was assigned to the National Youth Administration, a federally funded program designed to address youth unemployment. The first task was to relocate families living in the deteriorating houses. The second task was to clean up the area. In *La Villita: Progress Report*, it was noted that "these young men had finished all of the preliminary clearance—demolition-grading work. For the city's trucks to haul away, they loaded 325 trucks of scrap lumber to be used for kindling in the public parks; they loaded 162 truckfuls [sic] of junk-filthy refuse, old tires, abandoned automobile bodies, dilapidated baby carriages, bottles, tin cans, broken pottery—all bespeaking of broken lives that had been living in these ruins of ancient buildings. . . . They fumigated, cleaned, stripped, sustained and made safe and ready for restoration five of the seven adobe and caliche houses in the plot."[78] The final task was to restore structurally sound buildings. The La Villita of today definitely does not look anything like the La Villita of 1939. Today, it is a cultural center with small arts and crafts shops housed in the originally restored adobe and caliche houses.

Master Planning

Today, all major cities across this nation have a planning function that plots the short- and long-term growth patterns for both the CBD and the outlying areas. The planning function can be handled internally through a city department or contracted out to the private sector. The end result is the **master plan**. This planning document details economic and cosmetic improvements ranging from sewer and drainage to museums and concert halls, for ten- or twenty-year periods. It also includes estimated costs and anticipated sources of revenue to fund future projects. The primary goals of a master plan are:

1. Improvements of the physical environment of the community as a setting for human activities— to make it more functional, beautiful, decent, healthful, interesting and efficient—especially with respect to their transportation and sanitation services.
2. Promotion of the public interest, the interest of the community at large rather than the interest of individuals or special groups within the community.
3. Facilitation of the democratic determination and implementation of community policies relating to the physical development of the city.
4. Inclusion of long-range considerations of short-range actions so that the cumulative effect of individual decisions may not have the effect of blunting or undermining long-range goals.[79]

A well crafted master plan serves as a futuristic blueprint for city planners. "This, then is city planning— to study and determine in advance the physical needs of the growing city, and lay out a scheme of development in such a way that each improvement will dovetail into the next, thus gradually forming an organically related whole. The complex activities of a city demand an equally complex plan for development, so that each of its functions may be fulfilled without undue interference with each other."[80]

The implementation of a master plan is accomplished in part, through careful orchestration of land use management. **Zoning** is the "division of a city into districts and the regulation of the types of buildings and activities permitted within districts."[81] Usually city property is zoned as either commercial or residential. The privacy and integrity of residential areas is preserved by zoning out commercial development. For example, a family residence cannot become a business without first securing a city business permit. Zoning can artfully segregate certain types of commercial development from the CBD and residential areas. Usually light commercial activity is permitted around residential areas including service-sector businesses, i.e., restaurants, grocery stores, etc. Because of the toxic substances involved, gasoline stations or a dry

cleaners is permissible only under strict environmental and construction controls. Medium and heavy commercial and industrial activities are allowed away from residential areas into primarily industrial parks or industry zones. In San Antonio, zoning ordinances have been used to restrict both residential and, in particular, commercial development over the Edwards Underground Recharge Zone, an aquifer system that supplies the majority of the water for Bexar and surrounding counties. Unrestricted and unchecked commercial growth can ruin residential areas by placing potentially hazardous businesses and industries too close to neighborhoods. The last major city in the United States without a comprehensive zoning and land management plan, Houston finally ended its no-holds-barred approach to business and industrial development by passing a zoning ordinance plan in 1991.

City leaders are successfully luring business development and former and new residents back to the CBD through redevelopment and revitalization plans. The National Trust for Historical Preservation developed the **Main Street Project** as a means of encouraging city leaders of communities under 50,000 residents to revamp their downtown areas. Low-cost loans augmented with federal and private grants and funding is helping these communities preserve their historical and cultural assets while, at the same time, modernizing the CBD. Old building left to rot may be historically significant and worthy of revitalization into store-fronts for retail stores, business offices or even residential units. Throughout the nation's major cities, any effort to revamp or demolish a building designed as "historical property" must win the approval of the city's historical preservation department or committee. For example, San Antonio's Historic and Design Review Commission, a 15-member panel of appointees of the city council, acts as the city's review board over historical buildings. Created in 1992, the Commission "reviews plans to build, remodel, or demolish any buildings in the city's 16 historical districts or plans affecting any of the 1,200 designated landmarks not in historic districts. It also decides if projects qualify for historic-property tax incentives. The panel's responsibilities also include overseeing all development on the River Walk, the main visitor attraction in Texas."[82] Once-deteriorating older neighborhoods located in downtown areas became valued properties as low-cost improvement incentives encouraged citizens to purchase an older residence at a lower cost and revitalize it to its original form.

Across the nation, city leaders are focusing on **gentrification** efforts designed to bring upper- and middle-income new comers and former residents back to the CBD by offering them the same conveniences that initially compelled them to leave the city for the suburbs. It involves more than just converting a former multi-story department store into upscale condominiums and apartments.

Across the nation, city planners are looking at a new concept of CBD development based on the layout of older towns in Northern Europe. The **New Urbanism** movement calls for the "reconfiguration of sprawling suburbs into communities of real neighborhoods and diverse districts, the conservation of natural environments . . . buildings are close to the street, defining sidewalks and parks are usable civic spaces. Streets are narrow and form distinct city blocks. Most parking is hidden from view. Residential and commercial uses coexist next to and on top of each other."[83] This new planning concept has been used in Austin, Dallas, and Port Aransas. Although not a new concept, city planners are now trying to convert concrete into green space. In 1870, Frederick Law Olmsted lamented about the ill-effects of city life in New York City. He urged city leaders to set aside land for a park—Central Park:

We want a ground to which people may easily go after their day's work is done, and where they may stroll for an hour, seeing, hearing, and feeling nothing of the bustle and jar of the streets. . . Practically, what we most want is simple, broad, open space of clean greensward . . , as a central feature. We want depth of wood enough about it . . . to completely shut out the city from our landscapes. . . The park should, as far as possible, complement the town. Openness is the one thing you cannot get in buildings. Picturequeness you can get. Let your buildings be as picturesque as your artists can make them. This is the beauty of a town. Consequently, the beauty of the parks should be the other. It should be the beauty of the fields, the meadow, the prairie, of the green pastures, and the still waters. What we want to gain is tranquility and rest to the mind.[84]

Of course, few cities in Texas can afford to duplicate the splendor of New York City's Central Park.

Conclusions

Traditionally the city has served as the mecca or savior of society by bringing peoples of diverse cultures and beliefs under one roof. It has offered protection to those confronted by ravishing invaders and the cruelty of Mother Nature. It has become the center for culture, fine arts, and educational facilities. The "ancients" and the "moderns" view their cities as shining tributes of their accomplishments and contributions to the development of civilization. However, the boastfulness of city leaders from the ancient Greeks to modern-day Texans could not then or now successfully hide the problems associated with urban life. Overcrowding has led to traffic and pedestrian congestion, crowded housing, lack of parks and recreational facilities, and so on. The flight away from the madness of city life left behind a dependent underclass far too often the victims of poor housing, chronic crime, low-paying jobs and unemployment along with a deteriorating infrastructure desperately in need of repair.

Yet, cities are like the phoenix. The fabulous bird dies only to regenerate itself into a far more beautiful creature than before. The regeneration process of Texas's cities rests on the shoulders of their city leaders. Faced with shrinking tax bases and budgets, urban leaders must develop innovative schemes to rescue their urban environments from the deterioration seen so often in the older industrial cities across the globe. Although a seemingly insurmountable task, it can be accomplished by a long-term dedicated effort to chart effectively the growth of both residential and business developments through master plans, land-use commissions, zoning regulations, and innovative revitalization programs.

Chapter Notes

[1]Lewis Mumford, *The City in History: Its Origins, Its Transformation, and Its Prospects*, (New York, New York: Harcourt, Brace and World, 1961), 30.

[2]Robert D. Thomas, "Cities as Partners in the Federal System." *Political Science Quarterly*, The Academy of Political Science, Vol. 101, No 1, 1986, 49.

[3]Ibid., 49-64.

[4]Carl A. McCandless, *Urban Government and Politics*, (New York, New York: McGraw-Hill Book Company, 1970), 225.

[5]Mumford, 85.

[6]Rupert N. Richardson, Adrian Anderson, Cary D. Wintz and Ernest Wallace, *Texas: The Lone Star State*, 9th ed., (Upper Saddle River: New Jersey: Prentice-Hall, 2005), 180-181.

[7]Mumford, 71.

[8]"Boston City Planner Arthur Comey Presents a Plan for the Development of Houston, 1913," *Major Problems in Texas History*, Sam W. Haynes and Cary D. Wintz, eds., (New York, New York: Houghton Mifflin Company, 2002), 342-343.

[9]Ibid., 176.

[10]Robert A. Calvert, Arnoldo De Leon and Gregg Cantrell, *The History of Texas*, 3rd ed., (Wheeling, Illinois: Harlan Davidson, Inc., 2002), 96.

[11]"A Description of Towns in Texas: 1836," *Documents of Texas History*, Ernest Wallace, David M. Vigness and George B. Ward, eds., 2nd ed., (Austin, Texas: State House Press, 1994), 122.

[12]Ibid., 123.

[13]Richardson, et al., 175.

[14]Ibid., 191.

[15]"A Description of Towns in Texas: 1836," *Documents of Texas History*, 120.

[16]Ibid.

[17]Ibid.

[18]Richardson, et al., 175.

[19]T. R. Fehrenbach, *Lone Star: A History of Texas and the Texans*, (New York, New York: Random House, 1968), 601.

[20]"A Description of Towns in Texas: 1836," *Documents of Texas History*, 121.

[21]Calvert, etc., 95.

[22]"A Description of Towns in Texas: 1836," *Documents in Texas History*, 122.

[23]Randolph Campbell, *Gone to Texas: A History of the Lone Star State*, (New York, New York: Oxford University Press, 2003), 208.

[24]Richardson, et al., 155.

[25]Ibid., 349-350.

[26]*Texas Almanac 2014-2015*, (Denton, Texas: Texas State Historical Society, 2014), 682.

[27]Richardson, et al., 357.

[28]Mumford, 111.

[29]Ibid., 485.

[30]Ibid., 492.

[31]Richard Moe and Carter Wilkie, "The Ideal City," *Preservation, National Trust for Historical Preservation*, Vol. 49, No. 6, November/December, 1997,34.

[32]Linda Byrne, "Covenants Ensure Value, Experts Say," *San Antonio Express-News*, (Wednesday, January 13, 1999), 6H.

[33]"Legislators Targeting Homeowners' Groups," *San Antonio Express-News*, (Monday, December 21, 1998) 16A.

[34]Chuck McCullough, "Debate Heats Up in Legislature," *San Antonio Express-News*, (Wednesday, March 10, 1999), 4H.

[35]Moe and Wilkie, "The Ideal City," *Preservation*, 36-37.

[36]Ibid., 38.

[37]Jack C. Plano and Milton Greenburg, The American Political Dictionary, 10th ed., (New York, New York: Harcourt Brace, 1997), 605.

[38]Joe Holley, "Finding a Solution for Growing Pains," *San Antonio Express-News*, (Sunday, October 1, 2000), 14A.

[39]Kate Hunger, "Wilson County Beckons," *San Antonio Express-News*, (Sunday, August 4, 2002), 16A.

[40]Joe HIlley, "Saving the Soul of Fredericksburg," *San Antonio Express-News*, (Sunday, September 17, 2000), 1AA.

[41]Ibid.

[42]Ibid.

[43]McCandless, 50.

[44]Ibid., 51.

[45]ProQuest, *ProQuest Statistical Abstract of the United States: 2019*, 7th ed., (Bethesda, Maryland, 2018), Table 465, 294.

[46]McCandless, 55.

[47]Ibid., 217.

[48]Ibid., 218.

[49]Josh Baugh, "Charter Changes Topic of Town Hall," *San Antonio Express News*, (Thursday, September 20, 2018), A2.

[50]*https://ballotpedia.org/city-of-san-antonio-council-and-mayor-salaries*

[51]Chuck McCullough, "County Firefighting Pact Drafted," *San Antonio Express-News*, (Wednesday, December 23, 1998), 2H.

[52]*The HarperCollins Dictionary of American Government and Politics*, Jay M. Shafriz, ed., (New York, New York: HarperCollins Publishers, 1992), 533.

[53]Gerry Riposa and James D. Slack, "Texas Urban Revitalization: The Main Street Project," *Texas Public Policy*, Gerry Riposa, ed., (Dubuque, Iowa: Kendall/Hunt, 1987), 70.

[54]Jeanne Russell, "Not Up to Code," *San Antonio Express-News*, (Sunday, February 4, 2001), 12A.

[55]Ron Wilson, "American Dream Now Homeowner's Nightmare," *San Antonio Express-News*, (Sunday, August 21, 2005), 12A.

[56]Ibid.

[57]Ibid.

[58]"A Tale of Two Suburbs," *U.S. News & World Report*, (November 9, 1992), 33.

[59]Heather Way, "Segregated Housing Set Back Texas," *San Antonio Express News*, (Sunday, April 12, 2015), F1-F3.

[60]Ibid.

[61]Mumford, 510.

[62]Kenneth R. Mladenka and Kim Quaile Hill, *Texas Government: Politics and Economics*, 2nd ed., (Pacific Grove, California: Cole, 1989), 247.

[63]Gerry Riposa and Nelson Dometrius, "Studying Public Policy," *Texas Public Policy*, Gerry Riposa, ed., (Dubuque, Iowa: Kendall/Hunt, 1987), 4-5.

[64]Ibid., 5.

[65]Ibid., 6.

[66]Mladenka and Hill, 251.

[67]Ibid.

[68]Thomas, "Cities as Partners in the Federal System," *Political Science Quarterly*, 52.

[69]Tom Bower, "Toyota Incentive Gets County's OK," *San Antonio Express-News*, (Wednesday, May 21, 2003), 4B.

[70]Ibid.

[71]Mumford, 460.

[72]Ibid., 575.

[73]"Boston City Planner Arthur Comey Presents a Plan for the Development of Houston, 1913," *Major Problems in Texas History*, 343.

[74]Mumford, 562.

[75]www.thealamo.org

[76]Andres Carroll, "Holding the Fort in San Antonio," *American History*, vol. 46, No. 6, February, 2015, 28.

[77]Ibid.

[78]*La Villita: Progress Report*, (San Antonio, Texas: The National Youth Administration, 1939)

[79]Neal J. Pearson, "Managing the Growth and Amenities of City Life: The Role of Planning and Zoning," *Texas Public Policy*, Gerry Riposa, ed., (Dubuque, Iowa: Kendall/Hunt, 1987), 85.

[80]"Boston City Planner Arthur Comey Presents a Plan for the Development of Houston, 1913," *Major Problems in Texas History*, 343.

[81]Randall W. Bland, Alfred B. Sullivan, Robert E. Biles, Charles B. Elliot, Jr., and Beryl E. Pettus, *Texas Government Today*, 5th ed., (Pacific Grove, California: Brooks/Cole, 1992), 312.

[82]David Anthony Richeliu, "History Panel Wields Big Stick," *San Antonio Express-News*, (Monday, August 28, 2000), 4A.

[83]Mike Greenburg, "New Urbanism: A Shift from Earlier Codes," *San Antonio Express-News*, (Sunday, May 18, 2003), 4B.

[84]"Frederick Law Olsted Advocates Parks as Cures for Urban Malaise, 1870," *Major Problems In Urban History*, (Lexington, Massachusetts: D. C. Heath and Company, 1994), 98.

Chapter 14

Texas Transportation

The Atchison, Topeka, and Santa Fe Railroad, Amarillo, Texas
March 1943 Credit: Library of Congress

Far from supplementing public rail transportation, the private motor car became largely a clumsy substitute for it. Instead of maintaining a complex transportation system, offering alternative choices of route and speed to fit the occasion, the new suburban sprawl has become abjectly dependent upon a single form, the private motor car, whose extension has devoured the only commodity the suburb could rightly boast: space. Instead of buildings set in a park, we now have buildings set in a parking lot. . . . To ensure the continuous flow of traffic, even in rural areas, immense clover leaves and job-handles are designed, demolishing still more open space. And instead of freight yards and marshalling yards at the far terminals of a railroad system, the very dispersion of motor traffic demands similar facilities around every individual building where people congregate. Thus, each new factory or office, each new department store or shopping center, established in the midst of the open country, demands parking lots so ample that those who park on the rim have a far longer walk to the shop than they would have in a densely crowded city after leaving their bus or their subway train, though they still obstinately retain the illusionist image of the motor car taking them from 'door to door.'"[1]

The promise of rich free land brought thousands of settlers to the frontier areas of the United States. Like most rugged unsettled regions, Texas could offer rich land at cheap prices. The problem was getting across those vast stretches of rough terrain without a decent transportation system of roads and waterways. The "system" barely existed in Texas. Crudely hewn out paths, laughingly called roads, quickly turned to quagmires when a shower drenched the area. Having experienced this frontier nightmare, early Texas leaders vowed to bring a transportation system to their state that all Texans could be proud of and that would leave other states green with jealousy.

It took nearly one hundred years of legislative wheeling and dealing, plus billions of dollars, to create a massive system of highways, railroads, airports, and ports that Texans can claim with pride. Texans love to travel over their approximately 300,000 miles of mostly well-maintained municipal streets, highways, and interstate roadways. Today, Texans drive "more than 24 million vehicles . . . on over 300,000 miles of roadways, including city- and county-maintained roads."[2] The automobile has replaced the horse as the Texan's symbol of personal independence! However, the creation and maintenance of this vast transportation system has cost Texans dearly. Highway construction and customary maintenance is expensive and takes precious budget dollars away from other policy considerations such as education and social services. The state's commitment to highways remains very strong, since highway funds are one of the few state dedicated budgetary items. The state budget, however, cannot bear the burden alone. Consequently, the state has become heavily dependent upon billions of dollars in federal highway funding.

In Texas, transportation policies are dominated by the cultural and historical image of rugged individualism. The lion's share of the budget is spent on highways to meet *private* transportation needs to the detriment of *public* or mass transportation systems. To the poor, handicapped and elderly, life without a car can be difficult in this state. Texas lags far behind other states in its commitment to public transportation. In this chapter, a detailed discussion of both public and private transportation systems will be presented with an emphasis on future trends and developments.

Politics is a key component of transportation public policy. Interest group rivalry is evident from the site selection of the highway to the letting of the construction and maintenance contracts. Highways are big business for construction and energy firms. The oil and gas business pays close attention to the politics of highways. The automobile mentality and the promise of additional road construction plays into the profit motivations of the oil industry. It is a high stakes game involving key actors vying for lucrative contracts. It is an ongoing battle for environmentalists and property owners who desire to uphold the delicate relationship between the balance of nature and the rights of private property owners. Almost like David and Goliath, the well-financed and politically connected highway lobby flexes its big muscles over the demands of the poor, the elderly, the handicapped, property owners, and environmentalists. Highway policies in Texas involve more than just deciding where to build the road. It is a complex process encompassing construction guidelines, signage requirements, and even protection of the state's wildflowers. This chapter explores the historical, political, and future course of transportation public policy initiatives in Texas.

The Creation of the Transportation System

The absence of viable roadways made colonizing Texas a monumental challenge for both the Spanish and Mexican governments. In the 1800s, roadways were merely well trodden paths just wide enough for a wagon. The most famous of the paths was the Camino Real de los Tejas. Initially, the path into Texas was a series of "2,500 trials that span from Mexico City diagonally through Texas, to Natchitoches, Louisiana, were footpaths of the ancient Caddo nation, or those of dozens of other Native American tribes, which were later adopted by European travelers."[3] Known as the King's Highway or the San Antonio Road, "There were four main trails . . . El Camino Real itself runs more or less southwest to northeast from Guerrero, Mexico to Natchitoches. The Lower Road loops south of El Camino Real both west of San Antonio and east of San Antonio, reaching Cuero. The Laredo Road dips further south still, connecting San Antonio, Cuero, and Goliad and Laredo and Villa de Dolores to the south. Finally, the Old San Antonio Road trails southwest of El Camino, running through Bastrop before meeting up with the other caminos near Bryan and then heading east into Louisiana."[4] Initially settling in East Texas, Anglo-American settlers began to establish their own pathways into the interior. "The chief roads, or routes of travel that were called roads, were the Old Military Road, from the Red River through Dallas, Waco, and Austin; the old San Antonio-Nacogdoches Road, passing through Bastrop and Crockett; the road from Indianola to San Antonio; and a road from Dallas and vicinity southward to Houston."[5] Travel was difficult even under the best of weather conditions. For example, the roadway from Victoria to Lavaca was described as "a mere collection of straggling wagon ruts, extending far more than a quarter of a mile in width, from outside to outside, it being desirable in this part of the country, rather to avoid the road that follow it."[6]

Freight and an occasional passenger were either transported on boats or hauled overland on heavy-duty wagons pulled by teams of mules and horses. In 1857, the San Antonio-San Diego Mail Route was established, making the Aue's Settlement Inn at Leon Springs in San Antonio the first stop of the **Jackass Line**. Stretching approximately 1,476 miles, it took fifty-three days to complete the trip to San Diego.[7] Stage coaches carried mail and an occasional passenger. The mail run was "a twice-monthly transcontinental enterprise from 1857 to 1860 under a four-year Post Office Department contract held by James Birch, a wealthy California stage line owner, in partnership with George Henry Giddings, owner of the San Antonio & San Diego." For passengers, the trip was long and costly—$200 for a one-way ticket![8] Route managers ensured that passengers were well prepared and equipped

for their journey. "Each passenger had to carry a good rifle, 100 cartridges, a revolver, two pounds of balls, and a sharp Bowie knife. Ability and willingness to use the weapons were a must. Specifics for clothing and toiletries were as follows: thick boots, woolen pants, 6 pairs of woolen socks, six undershirts, three woolen overshirts, two pairs of woolen longjohns, gauntlet gloves, a sack coat, a greatcoat, a rubber poncho, two blankets, [and] a wide-awake hat (soft felt halt, broad brim and low crown). As far as toiletries, four towels, a sponge, hairbrush, comb and soap needed to be packed in a oil-silk (oilskin or oilcloth) bag.[9] The coach and the ride were uncomfortable with passengers sitting on wooden planks without benefit of upholstery. "The dangers of the road included dust storms, brackish waters, torrential thunderstorms, fiery sands, hellish heat, and frigid nights. Where the roadbed was too sandy or steep, the mail road in comfort and the passengers walked behind. If an axle broke, the mail continued on horseback, and the passengers waited with the coach until it was repaired."[10] Fortunately, the expansion of the railroad west of the Mississippi River eventually replaced the stage coach as the preferred method of traveling across the western frontier.

The pathetic state of Texas's transportation system became painfully evident as the state began its economic recovery from the Civil War and Reconstruction. The economic viability of the state was severely threatened by the lack of adequate roadways, railroads, and water routes needed to deliver goods and services across the state. There was absolutely no assurance that the goods would ever reach their destination. For state lawmakers, the answer to the state's transportation woes began with enticing railroad companies to lay track in Texas. The railroad was a blessing in disguise because it could guarantee swift and reliable delivery of settlers, goods, and services to remote areas. Rail appeared in the state as early as 1836 as the newly formed Republic of Texas sponsored the ill-fated Texas Railroad Navigation and Banking Company. Four years later a railroad project on the Buffalo Bayou near Houston was abandoned due to lack of funding. In 1850, the now state of Texas pledged a portion of its ten million dollar settlement with the United States government over the acquisition of its upper northwest territory (a part of present-day Oklahoma) to building railroads. The Buffalo Bayou, Brazos and Colorado (BBB&C) did successfully complete twenty miles of track between Harrisburg and Stafford's Point. Despite offering sixteen sections of free land for every mile of track laid, Texas had only 407 miles of working rail located primarily in the eastern part of the state at the start of the Civil War. Passenger service was extremely difficult and, far too often, a life threatening experience:

After riding the BBB&C in 1863, the British traveler A.S. Fremantle noted in his journal that the train gave a tremendous jolt when it started in motion. "Every passenger," he continued, "is allowed to use his own discretion about breaking his arm, neck, or leg without interference by the railroad officials." Passengers were even more startled by the manner in which the train crossed the Brazos at Richmond. A steep inclined plane led to a low, rickety trestle bridge. A similar plane was cut into the opposite bank. Four floating spans, totaling 200 feet in length, formed the center of the bridge. These were pushed against the bank when a steamboat needed to pass . . . Noted Fremantle, "Even in Texas, this method of crossing a river is considered rather unsafe."[11]

After the Civil War, Texas joined her former Confederate sister states in the realization that the railroad had the magical powers to transform states into industrial giants, small towns into thriving metropolises, and, unfortunately, small towns into ghost towns when the railroad did not come their way. The Texas Legislature launched an all out effort to bring the railroad to this state. The competition was keen as railroads pitted one bidder against the other. In 1876, the Texas Legislature passed the **Land Grant Law**, which gave "sixteen sections of land to railroad companies for every mile of main-line track they completed."[12] Before the Land Grant Law was repealed, the state handed over to forty-one railroad companies "32,150,000 acres of the state's public domain, an area the size of the state of Alabama."[13] Railroad companies began competing with each other for freight and passenger business. The larger rail carriers drove the smaller ones out of business. Unfortunately, several bankrupt and severely cash-strapped railroads sold their gifted parcels of land to settlers for a fraction of their actual worth. The state lost millions of dollars in potential land revenue sales by just giving large tracts of land to the railroad companies. The Radical Republican administration of E. J. Davis faced bribery charges when it gave "Southern Pacific and the Southern Transcontinental Railway Companies provisional grants in bonds aggregating $6,000,000."[14]

Gifts, land, and money, however, began to pay off as mile after mile of track was laid across the state. "In 1872, Texas ranked twenty-eighth among the states in total railroad mileage; by 1880, it had jumped to twelfth; by 1890, it ranked third; and by 1904, it had over 10,000 miles of track, more than any other state in the nation.[15] Railroad fever brought economic prosperity to the state as farmers and ranchers expanded their markets. The remote areas of West Texas were opened for settlement as the railroad brought more settlers and goods into the area. All because of the railroad and its miles of shining track, towns became cities, and cities became thriving business centers.

However, the honeymoon was short-lived. The railroads began to participate in price fixing schemes designed to maximize their own profits at the expense of farmers and ranchers. "Critics asserted that railroads discriminated between shippers often charged more for short than for long hauls, granted free passes to political friends, gave rebates to preferred customers, signed pooling and monopolistic agreements, frequently gave poor or inadequate service, and used their considerable economic and political resources to prevent any legislation that

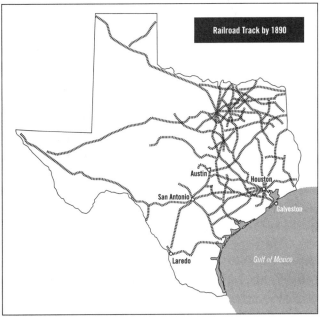

would attempt to stop their abusive practices."[16] Anger over these abusive practices was clearly articulated by the delegates to the 1876 state constitutional convention representing rural interests. Using the battle cry of "stop the banks and the railroads," they wrote a document that placed severe restrictions on both the banking and railroad industries aiming at preventing further damage to the farming and ranching industry. It took the election of James Hogg as the state's attorney general and eventually to the governorship that finally broke the railroad's price fixing organization known as the Texas Traffic Association by empowering a new regulatory body called the **Texas Railroad Commission** to oversee shipping rates and railroad practices. Despite the underhanded greedy tactics of a few, it was the railroads that finally united the entire state from east to west and north to south, enabling farmers, ranchers, and businessmen to get their wares to new markets in a much faster and safer conveyance, particularly in the 1900s with the invention of the refrigerated boxcar. "The Missouri, Kansas and Texas (Katy) Railroad reached Denison [Texas] in 1872, and the next year, through Houston, and the Texas Central linked the Gulf Coast to North Texas. Now farmers received goods quickly from the Gulf Coast, and after the Texas and Pacific (T&P) Railroad entered the state, they could ship their cotton through St. Louis [Missouri] and on to the East Coast. . . . By 1881, Southern Pacific tracks linked El Paso to Galveston to Fort Worth, and eventually to the Panhandle. Finally, by 1900, the Great Northern Railroad linked Laredo to Marshall [Texas]."[17]

The invention of the automobile revived the interest in roads. "The first automobiles were seen in Texas about 1900, and the success of these machines was apparent within a short time. Houston was the home of 80 automobiles by 1905, and had already experienced a fatal automobile accident. The state recognized the automobile in 1907 with the adoption of an 18-mile-per-hour speed limit."[18] The automobile was a blessing in disguise for city-dwellers. "The arrival of the automobile got rid of all the horses, mules and oxen . . . the blight of manure on the streets, the disease and the flies went away. . . The automobile helped accelerate the development of suburbs, the wealthy suburbs, and the less-wealthy suburbs. It also allowed for zoning with heavy industry, warehousing and manufacturing moving from the city center. Before trucks, these businesses had to be downtown because that's where the railroads were. So automobiles made the city cleaner."[19] Politically and economically, the automobile permanently connected the oil and gas businesses with the state's highway policy makers. The increased mobility

offered by the personal ownership of an automobile contrasted sharply with the restrictive and, oftentimes, undependable railroad. The automobile gave workers the independence to move away from their jobs in the central business district. The worker no longer had to live near his/her place of employment. Cities began to experience urban sprawl. However, automobiles needed gasoline to fuel their engines. The oil and gas business seized upon the "horseless vehicle" as their ticket to profitability. The mode of transportation had shifted from the company owned public railroads to the privately individually owned automobile. Joining forces, the oil and gas business and automobile manufacturers became the dominate actors in creating Texas's massive network of federal, state, county, and city roadways. A major problem for city leaders was the realization that automobiles with their rubber tires simply could not navigate smoothly on uneven dirt roads that turned into a muddy mess whenever it rained. New industries were introduced to accommodate the unique needs of the automobile—road/highway construction firms and paving contractors. Cities across the nation used everything from wooden bricks made by cedar, mesquite and pine to bricks. However, bricks and wood do not hold up well when confronted with periodic flooding, the intense heat of the usual Texas summer, and, most importantly, the constant pressure of and from the wear and tear caused by vehicles. Repairing potholes with wood and bricks became a very expense undertaking. Today, the primary road surface is asphalt composed of crushed rock glued together with tar. Less expensive than brick, asphalt has caused headaches of its own for city and state leaders as they try to figure out how to minimize potholes and deal with the increasingly expensive but necessary periodic resurfacing of their roads and highways.

The Development of Highway Public Policies

Government at all levels is involved in the development and maintenance of this nation's highways and road systems. This nation's economy would come to a standstill if all the nation's roads were inaccessible to the millions of workers commuting to their job sites and to the thousands of truckers transporting goods and services. Although the levels of responsibility for government are clearly delineated, the goal is collectively shared. Federal, state, county, and city officials share the task of providing this nation with the best possible system of roadways that money can buy. In fiscal year 2018, the Texas Department of Transportation spent $5,765,685,951 on highway construction and

$616,340,623 on the purchase of right-of-way property acquisitions. In total, $6,381,670,144 was spent on highway construction.[20] The figures do not include the salaries, benefits, and expenses associated with maintaining the highways, operating the Department of Transportation, or money spent on roads by city and county governments. The role each level of government plays is essential to understanding the complexity of transportation-oriented public policy initiatives. Other key actors are the various construction-related interest groups who are collectively known as the powerful **highway lobby**. This section explores the responsibility and the role each plays in the development and implementation of roadway policies in Texas.

The Federal Government's Role

Initially, roads were the sole responsibility of state governments. However, the transition from the railroad and stagecoach to the automobile motivated the federal government to take notice of the lack of and the condition of existing roads and ultimately to determine that the national government needed to become an active participant in the quest to build an extensive national highway system. The **interstate commerce clause** of Article I of the United States Constitution gives the federal government the power to regulate **interstate** commerce, leaving state governments responsible for **intrastate** commerce. Consequently, the partnership between the federal and state governments was formalized. The federal government demonstrated its intentions to build a nationwide federal highway system with the passage of the **Federal Road Act** in 1916. This legislation provided dollar for dollar federal matching funds to any state that in compliance with the law's specifications including the creation of state controlled departments overseeing highway and road construction activities. In turn, these state departments would submit for prior federal approval all construction designs, road site locations, and cost estimates. The federal government created the **Bureau of Public Roads** to ensure that individual state roadways connected to each other at their shared boundary lines.

Desiring to put the unemployed back to work, the Roosevelt administration enacted the **National Industrial Recovery Act** allocating at "least one-fourth of the federal-aid highway funds for extensions of roads through incorporated municipalities and permitted the use of another 25 percent for secondary or feeder roads."[21] The **Works Progress Administration** also put Depression-era unemployed Americans to work fixing the nation's transportation system. The **Highway Act of 1944** solidified

the federal government's commitment to construct approximately 42,500 miles of interstate highways. Passed in 1956, both the **Federal Aid Highway Act** and the **Highway Revenue Act** mandated a four-cent-per-gallon gasoline tax to fund a newly created federal highway trust fund and offered states a 90-10 percent matching formula whereby participating states would receive $90 million for every $10 million their legislative houses dedicated for highway construction. In 1966, Congress created the **Department of Transportation,** a cabinet level agency. The Secretary of Transportation is directly responsible for the United States Coast Guard, Federal Aviation Agency, Federal Highway Administration, National Highway Safety Bureau, Federal Railroad Administration, Urban Mass Transportation Administration, and the St. Lawrence Seaway Development Corporation. The Department of Transportation has the responsibility of overseeing all of the nation's transportation needs and deals directly with state agencies to ensure conformity to national guidelines and compliance with transportation-related federal laws.

For the short term, the Highway Trust Fund provided ample money for transportation and highway systems. However, gradually the revenues generated by federal and state gasoline taxes decreased sharply during the oil shortage crisis in the 1970s, once again in the 1980s with the cutting of crude oil prices by OPEC, and in the 2000s with the rising cost of gasoline at the pump causing many to drive less. In 1982, the Reagan administration attempted to address fund shortfalls with the passage of the **Surface Transportation Assistance Act**. This legislation increased the federal gasoline tax from five to nine cents per gallon with four cents earmarked for the repair, maintenance, and construction of interstate roadways and an additional one cent allocated for mass transportation. Currently, the tax is fourteen cents per gallon. In 1988, Congress passed the **Transportation Equity Act for the 21st Century,** which allocated an additional $216 billion in federal highway money to "help states improve transportation systems worn down by increase commerce due to the passage of the North American Free Trade Agreement or NAFTA."[22] Mayors of Texas border towns voiced concerns about the traffic snarls caused by trucks entering into the United States through Mexico. They emphasized that from 1998 to 1993 more than 2 million trucks entered through these border cities. They wanted $60.35 million as a partial payment for the estimated $219 million needed to complete ten major highway construction projects.[23] The bulk of the money was targeted for highway expansion projects for I-35 in Comal County and I-35 in Hays County. Over the years the federal government has been

President Lyndon B. Johnson signing the Highway Beautification Act as others, including Lady Bird Johnson, look on. October 22, 1965. White House Photo Office.

very generous in giving federal highway money to Texas for the expansion and maintenance of its highway system. In August 2005, President George W. Bush signed a $286.4 billion transportation bill into law. Approximately $754.4 million was allocated to Texas for nearly 231 projects.[24] In 2007, the federal government's cash contribution to the Highway Trust Fund for Texas was $1,887,000,000.[25] Federal money continues to flow into the state. For example, in 2009 the Texas Department of Transportation received $2,715,159,247 and another $2,700,037,782 from the federal government.[26] In 2014, the federal government's annual allocation of highway money to Texas amounted to $3,383,800,362.[27] The flow of federal funding for the state's highway system continues for in 2015, the federal allocation was $3,113,916,162, in 2016, $3,961,224,209, in 2017, $4,150,529,667, and in 2018, $3,875,223,749.[28]

Although Texans readily accept federal highway money, they decry the federal mandates, ranging from environmental requirements to signage restrictions. For example, the federal government responded to the oil crisis of the 1970s by encouraging gasoline conservation. Experts believed that lowering the speed limit to 55mph on all major roads including highways would conserve energy and prevent accidents.   Initially, few states voluntarily lowered their speed limits to 55mph. Therefore, the federal government responded by attaching the compliance to the new speed limit as a qualification for receiving federal

highway money. States resisting the speed limit (by avoiding active enforcement) would lose their federal monies. Texas complied with the mandate.   A federal transportation bill passed in 1987 allowed states to increase the speed limit to 65 mph on rural roads and interstate highways outside of metropolitan areas. The Untied States Congress finally ended the federal speed mandates by allowing state legislative houses to set their own speed limits.

The individual freedom and personal choice of the citizen definitely conflicts with federal mandates requiring that drivers use seat belts, and most vehicles now have air bags. Once again, these measures are aimed at decreasing serious personal injuries in vehicle accidents. The Texas Legislature took further steps by requiring canvas covers for dump trucks. A bill passed in 1999 prohibits children from riding in the bed of a pickup truck. Seat belt laws have been strengthened to require all passengers to "buckle up"; and children under a certain height must be restrained in a car seat. The Reagan administration tackled the issue of drinking and driving by enacting the **National Minimum Drinking Age Act**. The minimum age requirement was raised from eighteen to twenty-one.   "In cases where state law failed to comply, the federal government could withhold 5 percent of a state's highway trust fund after the first year and could slap a 10 percent delinquency penalty on the state in the second year."[29] Additional federal requirements include highway signage and outdoor advertising guidelines. The **Highway Beautification Act** passed during the Johnson administration places stiff guidelines on the use of highway signage. The interstates could no longer display sign after sign of advertisements of everything from hamburgers to shaving cream. The law also included the creative hiding of junkyards and other eyesores from travelers on interstate highways and provided for the protection of plants, trees, and wildflowers on interstate roadways. As part of his stimulus package, President Obama decided to put the unemployed to work by providing the states with a portion of the money they needed to fix existing and, hopefully, build more roads and bridge. Signed into law on February 17, 2009, the **American Recovery and Reinvestment Act** provided $26.6 billion for more than 12,000 road, highway and bridge projects across the nation. All of the money was allocated by March 2010. During the 2016 presidential election, candidates from both parties advocated the need for federal infrastructure funding to fix the nation's deteriorating roads and bridges. Although congressional committees in both houses of Congress have introduced infrastructure legislation, none of these bills have made it to the president's desk for signature.

The State's Role

The Texas Legislature created the **Highway Department** in 1917 in order to receive federal funding under the Federal Road Act of 1916. In 1991, the Texas Legislature merged the Department of Highways and Public Transportation with several smaller agencies into the **Department of Transportation Commission**. A policy making body, the commission is composed of three-members appointed by the governor with Senate confirmation for six-year overlapping terms. The governor selects the chairperson from the three commissioners. In turn, the commissioners select the state **engineer-director** who serves as the chief administrator of the department. The department is separated into fourteen different divisions with seven as administrative arms involved in finance, insurance, and personnel. The remaining seven are charged with operations including highway design, construction, and maintenance. Approximately seventy thousand miles of state highways carrying 70 percent of the state's traffic fall under the supervision of the Department of Transportation or **TxDOT**. Nearly two-thirds of the department's entire budget is targeted for construction. All highway construction projects are awarded to private contractors. Maintenance of existing state roads, the second largest highway expenditure, is handled by state employees or contracted out to the private sector. The operation side of the department is charged with other responsibilities including regulation of outdoor advertisements, signage, and junkyards, operating tourist information centers, and overseeing vehicle license and title services. Since the state is so large, the department is geographically divided into twenty-five semiautonomous districts. Each district, headed by a district engineer, has considerable latitude in daily operations and, at times, each acts independently of the state agency. The fragmentation and independent style of management among the subunits makes the Department of Transportation an easy target for highway- and transportation-oriented interest groups.

County and City Road Responsibilities

Unfortunately, the state of Texas and the federal government do not have direct responsibility for the entire road system. "Three-fourths of Texas roads remain the responsibility of counties and municipalities and thus an entirely different set of highway finance issues emerges."[30] County governments rely upon property taxes as their sole source of revenue. As cities annex more of county properties, the county's tax base continues to shrink. Consequently, there is not enough funding to maintain existing county roads much less to build new ones. In cash-strapped counties, one can noticeably see the difference in the quality of their roads versus well-financed and maintained state roads. An additional roadblock is the dividing of county road funds into four separate parts, distributed equally to each one of the four commissioners' districts within that county. Individual commissioners tend to become territorial with their budget dollars and often do not give their surplus money to other commissioners whose districts need more money for road construction and repair.

City or municipal roads face the same fate as county roads. City coffers are funded by property and, if applicable, a portion of the state's sales tax revenues. City budgets are strained with an ever increasing demand for city services pitted against shrinking tax bases. Most cities focus on pothole repairs and maintenance with scant attention afforded to new road construction. Although some federal and state monies are available to counties and cities, both governing bodies depend upon the sale of bonds to fund road improvements.

The Highway Lobby

In the late 1960s, the city of San Antonio faced a highway crisis. The city had two highways, Interstate 35 and Loop

410, independently "looping" around the city with no major roadway connecting the loops to each other. A driver could not directly go from one loop to the other via a highway. The downtown section of the city was in the middle of both loops. The answer was to construct a segment of Highway 281, now known as McAllister Freeway, from the airport located just outside of Loop 410, which would connect the two loops or freeways and provide direct highway access from the airport to the central business district. It looked simple on paper. However, this relatively short segment of a freeway took nearly fifteen years of law suits, court injunctions, name-calling, and hundreds of millions of dollars before the ribbon was finally cut. The now functioning US 281 segment cuts across some of the richest residential properties in San Antonio, slices in two the property belonging to the Sisters of Charity of the Incarnate Word, cuts off Trinity University from its athletic facilities, and winds its way around the major parkland in San Antonio as well as the city zoo. However, it still did not directly connect with Loop 410. This problem was finally solved indirectly with a series of interconnecting ramps and overpasses.

Even before the construction contract was awarded, the battle lines were drawn. The city council and the highway contractors joined with the business community, particularly the tourist and convention interests, in favor of the highway segment. Angry and wealthy property owners garnered the support of the San Antonio Conservation Society, animal rights groups, environmentalists, and the Sisters of Charity in fighting the proposed expressway expansion. The war was won with the property owners securing attractive soundproofed walls hiding the expressway from their properties. The Sisters of Charity were compensated for their land, and a bridge was built over the freeway to allow access to the divided property. Trinity University received a large cash settlement. The Conservation Society, animal rights groups, and the environmentalists were quieted with the construction of walls around the zoo and parkland that contain special anti-noise and anti-pollution devices to protect the animals, plants, and park atmosphere. The segment was finally built. What happened in San Antonio is not an isolated incident but just one example of the hostilities highway advocates face whenever new construction plans are announced. Everyone wants a quicker way to get from one place to another; however, few want the road to cut through their property. Highway business is high stakes politics at its best and worst. Unfortunately, the highway that benefits some segments of the population is built at the expense of others.

The supporters of perpetual highway construction and maintenance are automobile manufacturers, oil and gas interests, the trucking and commercial busing community, businesses involved in automobile support (including parts and repairs), highway construction firms, hotels, motels, and restaurants. All of these supporters have vested interests and profitability in mind. The auto industry wants miles and miles of highways to encourage individuals to purchase vehicles. Of course, the longer one drives the vehicle, the more frequently the owner will need maintenance on the vehicle and replacement parts. There are lucrative highway contracts for road maintenance and repair. Attractive well-maintained roads encourage more driving miles and, subsequently, more sales at the gas pump and the car lots.

The leading supporter of highways in Texas is the powerful **Texas Good Roads Association**. Founded in 1911, the initial charge of the organization was basically to educate Texans about the necessity of building and maintaining a modern roadway system and to apply pressure upon state lawmakers and the governor to provide the guidance and, most importantly, the funding for this venture. The group's founding fathers represented highway contractors, oil companies and bus line interests. Today, the association continues to play an extremely aggressive role in promoting highway issues to the Texas Legislature. In addition, this organization works closely with the Texas Department of Transportation. This cozy relationship is so evident that it clearly resembles a subgovernment or iron triangle association.

Highway politics seem to enjoy bipartisan support among Republicans and conservative Democrats. While the budget ax is always chopping at social service support programs, transportation programs, particularly highways, usually escape without undo punishment. Liberal Democrats, on the other hand, seem to favor public or mass transportation over the private automobile-highway mentality. The big push to build extensive state-funded roadways came when moderate Democrats and recently Republicans controlled both the governor's mansion and the Texas Senate and House. Members of the highway lobby are well-financed, politically connected, and active contributors to political candidates favorable to pro-highway policies. However, anti-highway forces claim their share of victories. Highways are not always economic pots of gold; they destroy property, uproot property owners, stifle business development in those areas bypassed by expressway exit ramps and cut off by the highway itself, increase traffic congestion, upset the delicate balance of nature by destroying breeding grounds and habitats for plants and animals, and contribute to increased levels of air and noise pollution. The anti-highway lobby is composed of those groups that see roadways as a threat to their quality of life. It is a diverse mixture of environmentalists, conservationists, property owners, taxpayers, minority groups and concerned citizens. The anti-highway group uses public protests, federal environmental laws, political pressure, and the courts to block unwanted highway construction.

The Highway Budget

The third largest budgetary expense, the state highway system is maintained by a vast array of regressive tax programs. Like most states, Texas dedicates budget dollars specifically for highways. Once dedicated, this money cannot be transferred to another budgetary category. While dedicating ensures budget dollars for a specified functional area, it also has its drawbacks. "The practice of earmarking funds (from state motor fuel taxes, automobile registration fees and road user fees) for highways puts the agencies' state financial support beyond the control of governors and legislators."[31] The Texas Department of Transportation's budgetary independence leaves the door wide open to interest groups and construction-related businesses to exert influence and pressure. The dedicated state **Highway Fund** was the brainstorm of the Texas Good Roads Association to guarantee a permanent state commitment to building and maintaining a "good" road system. Passed in 1946, the amendment to the state constitution dedicates "three-fourths of the sales tax on gasoline and oil and 82 percent of motor vehicle registration fees to highways."[32] As of 2016, the state motor fuel tax was 20 cents per gallon, generating $3,490,000,000 in revenue.[33] Over the years the Texas Legislature has added other revenue sources to the highway fund including highway beautification fees, land sale revenues, fees from special vehicle permits, revenues from toll roads, oil and gas leases and rental fees, tax revenues generated by the sale of vehicles, boats and aircraft, revenue from fees collected on dormitory, cafeteria and merchandise sales, and motor vehicle registration fees. However, the bulk of the money comes from the federal government's transportation programs amounting to $3,828,212,673 just in 2017 alone. With the start of the 2017-2018 budget cycle, the State Highway Fund had a starting cash balance of $3,828,212,673. The balance of the fund increased over the year with the addition of $42,568,120 from revenue generated by the motor fuel lubricants sales tax, $1,518,490,101 from motor vehicle registration

fees, $122,951,092 from special vehicle permits, and in addition to other funding sources, $10,852,027 from the fees or rentals paid by businesses to post highway signs indicating their logos, major shopping centers and the usual tourist-oriented signs. By the end of the fiscal year, the ending revenue balance as $14,022,355,467. On the expense side of that budget, $5,723,977,020 was spent on highway construction. The funds ending cash balance on August 31, 2018, was $3,653,798,955.[34]

The future of the dedicated fund was jeopardized in the 1970s as oil prices increased and Texans began to buy smaller more fuel efficient vehicles. Although the price of gas increased, revenue from the gas tax did not since it was legislatively fixed at five cents per gallon. In 1977, the Texas Legislature passed a bill rescuing the plunging Dedicated Fund. This legislation mandates that whenever the balance in this fund falls below $750 million, money is automatically transferred from the general revenue fund into the state highway fund. The amount of revenue collected from the motor fuels tax is tied directly to two factors that the state really has little or no control over. First, the price of gasoline is driven by the tactics of the oil producing countries to control supply and demand. In the early 2000s, gasoline prices at the pump rose dramatically to nearly $5 per gallon. In 2014, the price of gasoline drastically decreased to below $2 per gallon for regular gasoline. The other factor is the fickleness of the consumer. When gas prices are high, one rethinks their use of their personal vehicles. Motorists will use their vehicles less often opting instead to either limit their personal errands and daily travels or use mass transportation. Bus ridership increases when the price of gas increases. An increase in gas prices means a decrease in state revenue because people are buying less gasoline. However, when the price of gas is "cheap," motorists fill up whenever they can. Of course, a decrease in gas prices means an increase in state revenue.

A high percentage of the highway budget revenues are collected from user fees including using gasoline. This concept is usually referred to as the **pay-as-you-go** policy option. The individuals who use the vehicles, the required gasoline products, and subsequently the roads, pay for the maintenance and construction of those roads. Since tourism is a major industry in this state, a large portion of the user tax is paid by non-Texans who come to see the state's attractions or to attend a convention.

The Status of the State's Roads

A status report on the nation's highways and bridges is prepared yearly by the Federal Highway Administration.

Basically, the state's existing system is in need of major repairs and, in some instances, existing roads must be totally replaced. After pouring billions of dollars into highway project after project and suffering through perpetual construction, frustrated taxpayers and motorists alike may well wonder how did the state's lawmakers allow this to happen?

First, highways, like anything else, will deteriorate. Under perfect conditions, roads have only a forty-year life span. The key to a road's survival is constant maintenance. Second, the state's roads and highways suffer from adverse weather conditions. Severe droughts and heat waves cause asphalt to crack and crumble. Standing water creates pot holes. Raging flood waters will completely destroy even the best built highway. Third, the state must have enough money to adequately repair and maintain these road systems including bridges and overpasses. Nationwide, there are as of 2017, 615,002 bridges of which 54,560 or 8.9 percent are structurally deficient.[36] The Federal Highway Administration defines a **structurally deficient bridge** as one that has been "restricted to light vehicles [and] requires immediate rehabilitation to remain open, or closed."[35] Furthermore, the Federal Highway Administration issues grades for bridges ranging from good to poor. A **good bridge** is one where the "pavement and bridge infrastructure is free of significant defects, and has a condition that does not adversely affect its performance"; a **fair bridge** is one in which "pavement and bridge infrastructure has isolated surface defects or functional deficiencies on pavements or minor deterioration of bridge elements" and one deemed as a **poor bridge** has "pavement and bridge infrastructure that is exhibiting advanced deterioration and conditions that impact structural capacity."[37] The 2017 report indicates that Texas has a total of 53,869 bridges of which 847 or 1.6 percent are structurally deficient. Across the state, 52.4 percent are rated as good, 46.4 percent as fair and only 1.2 percent as poor.[38] Oftentimes, Mother Nature wrecks havoc with the state's roadways. The Great Flood in 1998 flooded South Texas twice and brought 25 inches of rain to San Antonio in a two-day period. The estimated damage to public property was $71.2 million including $42.3 million in damage to paved roads and $6.5 million to the city's bridges. The incorporated cities and unincorporated portion of Bexar County estimated another $31.4 million in private and public property damage."[39] The city's budget did not include funds for flood-related damage. Any city along the Texas coast is a target for major damage during hurricane season while other areas are prone to destructive tornados and floods. Texas is not the only state facing aging highways and

deteriorating bridges. The nation's entire federal interstate highway system is itself over forty years old. Texas's roads have fared far better than other states because the Texas Legislature has traditionally placed a high priority on highway construction and maintenance. Overall, Texas has the second best roads and highways in the nation.

The Problems with Highways

While the highway can bring economic benefits and conveniences of travel, highways and the politics associated with the construction and maintenance of these systems creates several major problems for the state of Texas. Charges of corruption and patronage are heard every time a lucrative construction contract is awarded. State construction contracts are very specific in detailing every aspect of construction, from the depth of the base and asphalt materials to the machinery required to build the roads. Each phase of construction is inspected by TxDOT engineers before the next phase can begin. The bidding process is highly competitive and favors large highway construction firms over smaller ones. The major construction companies benefit from the attachment Texans have to their highways. Contracts are usually awarded to those construction companies affiliated with the Texas Good Roads Association and the pro-highway lobby.

When and where to build new roads or expand existing roadways is directly tied to the fickleness of population growth. It would seem logical that as a city's population increases and its boundary lines expand through annexation of new suburban areas, city and state planning staffs would adequately plan for the expansion of city streets and state highway systems to meet anticipated growth. Unfortunately, few voters will support a major expenditure to build a new road in an undeveloped area simply because a demographer predicts a potential population explosion. Major population spurts automatically lead to new residential construction in under- or non-developed areas where for decades a one-lane country road was all that was needed. Now, acres of tract housing have rendered that one-lane picturesque country road a commuter's nightmare as one spends hours stuck in traffic that moves at a snail's pace. Government justifies new freeway systems as the definitive answer to traffic congestion. However, regardless of the number of expressways with their multiple lanes, traffic congestion simply increases rather than decreases. Traffic snarls have resulted in "frustration and a loss in time to the average commuter of from forty to seventy days a year. Because of congestion, traffic in some cities moves at a pace of twelve miles per hour—the same rate it did a hundred years ago when horse-drawn carriages were used."[40]   Of course, traffic congestion adds to the state's air pollution problems. Traffic snarls have caused cities to hire additional law enforcement officers just to direct traffic and respond to motor vehicle accidents. States, county and city leaders are plagued with traffic-related problems. Every commuter wants to be able to get to work in a reasonable amount of time. A minor accident on an expressway can cause mile upon mile of parked cars waiting in line for hours just to move a few inches every minute or so. Traffic is a mess.

Several of the state's cities have implemented programs designed to alleviate traffic snarls. For example, San Antonio updated its 25-year transportation plan with the realization that the city will have to "explore new technology or keep widening its highways and adding huge asphalt parking lots that alter the city's drainage pattern."[41] Instead of expanding the existing expressway horizontally by adding more lanes, San Antonio's solution follows Austin's trend of building expansive flyover bridges over existing expressways. Houston and Dallas have built light-rail systems. A **busway** or bus lane is "a roadway or highway lane reserved exclusively for buses."[42] The **high occupancy vehicle lane** or HOV is "a lane on a street or highway that is reserved for buses and vehicles with at least two to three occupants."[43] Houston currently has 75 miles of highway HOV lanes. TxDOT has installed a computerized warning system known as Transguide. Monitors are placed at intervals over segments of major expressways to warn motorists of traffic snarls, stalled vehicles, and accidents. Special boxes hang over expressway lanes to warn motorists in advance whether the lanes are free of a traffic-related problem. This early-warning system has been helpful in preventing serious rear-end accidents and traffic snarls.

This drive for more freeways, highways and city streets robs both citizens and the government of a precious commodity—land. Few freeways are scenic works of art. It is disturbing to note that "about one third of all land in an average American city is occupied by streets and parking facilities. More than 60 percent of the land in central business districts is devoted to the moving and storage of automobiles."[44] Despite improvements, traffic is still moving at a snail's pace. Nationwide, automobile commuters spent an average of 26.6 minutes each morning driving from home to work and an additional 26.6 miles in the evening from work to home, meaning that Americans spent approximately 6.65 hours per week just getting to and from work.[45] Yet, Americans by and large still prefer their personal automobiles over carpooling and public transportation. For Texans, the commute is just as time consuming. In the Dallas/Forth Worth area, commuters spend 186,535,000 hours per year for an average of 53 hours per auto commuter stuck in traffic congestion wasting an average of 22 gallons of gasoline while in the Houston area, its 203,173,000 hours per year for an average of 61 hours per automobile commuter per year with a waste of 29 gallons of gasoline, and in San Antonio, its 64,328,000 hours per year with a waste of 20 gallons of gasoline.[46] While Texans may boast that they are safe drivers, statistics tell us otherwise. In 2016, Texas ranked first among her sister states with a record of 3,776 traffic-related fatalities.[47]

Mass Transportation

Regardless if the conveyance is a airplane or railroad car, Texans have rarely culturally or historically embraced mass transportation. The average Texan will cling to his/her individual vehicle regardless of what fuel alternative is available after the gasoline pumps run dry. Mass transportation can became an equal partner with the highway system if both the national and state governments would properly fund and promote the concept. In Europe, few own a personal vehicle for several valid reasons. First, the cost of gasoline is almost cost prohibitive. Second, their cities are much older than American cities. These urban centers are laden with very narrow streets that simply will not accommodate a two- much less a four-lane street. Third, European cities are compact since people live near where they work. The usual modes of transportation are trains and bicycles. It is amazing that the United States, now the second largest industrial country in the world, does not have a sophisticated national network of commuter trains. To the average Texan, mass transportation is the bus. While Houston and Dallas have a light-rail system, the majority of the state's cities simply do not have the commuter railroads and subways associated with the northern and northeastern sections of the nation.

Mass transportation is a prime example of redistributive public policy. The working poor and the elderly are the primary users of mass transportation systems. Unfortunately, the fares paid by the riders are simply not enough to totally fund a mass transportation system. Subsequently, it is the taxpayers who actually either directly or indirectly pay for the bus fleets, the drivers, the construction of tracks for railroads and commuter trains, and the maintenance upkeep whether they will ever use these modes of transportation.

The Federal Government's Role in Mass Transportation

Until the 1960s, the federal government did not take serious note of the need for mass transportation programs. Passed in 1961, the **Housing and Urban Development Act** provided emergency loans for commuter railroads and modest cash outlays for pilot mass transportation projects. The **Federal Aid Highway Act** (1963) granted highway funding to those metropolitan areas promoting both private highway systems and public transit programs. The federal government provided federal grants for public transit planning as part of the **Urban Mass Transportation Act** passed in 1964. Federal funding to cover construction and operating costs became a reality in 1970 when the federal government allocated approximately $3.1 billion spread over a five-year period for these initiatives. Support for mass transportation gained momentum with the passage in 1974 of the **Urban Mass Transit Act**. Once again, the federal government vowed to pour billions into the development of mass transportation initiatives. A portion of the federal gasoline tax was allocated for public transportation with the passage of the **Surface Transportation Assistance Act** passed in 1982.

State Shifts Burden to Cities

Unfortunately the state of Texas did not develop a statewide mass transportation plan nor did it apply for federal funding for proposed federal projects. The current state budget does not include a specific expense item for mass transportation initiatives such as buses and commuter trains. Consequently, the burden for mass transportation services falls upon cities and metropolitan areas. Only the major cities in Texas have transit systems. There have been noticeable service improvements in Dallas, Austin, Houston, and San Antonio. Some cities have opted to privatize their transit systems. For example, the former San Antonio Transit Authority was converted to private ownership called VIA with the VIA Metropolitan Transit Board serving as its policymaking body. Membership consists of both city and county appointees. However, once appointed, the board members act independently of both the city and county officials in both policymaking and day-to-day operations.

Technological innovations have enabled city governments to improve as well as to expand their service options. Traditionally, riding the bus to work has not always been easy or convenient for the commuter. A person dependent upon bus transportation still has to wait for the bus to arrive, hopefully on time. Buses usually do not follow a personal direct route from one's home to one's place of employment. Consequently, riders must transfer from one bus to another at least one time during the commute. Bus schedules are oftentimes complicated and difficult to follow, particularly for the mentally challenged rider. In the majority of the nation's cities, buses do not run their routes twenty-four hours a day. This adversely impacts those who work graveyard shifts from sun down to sun up. Oftentimes, city-owned, or even in the case of VIA, bus routes only extend to the city limits. If a person has a job outside of the city's limits, then that individual must seek additional transportation or walk to their place of employment. In addition, incorporated cities within a major city have the option of whether or not to pay for bus service in their communities. In particular, San Antonio's bus routes are not direct routes from point A to point B simply because several incorporated cities have opted not to carry bus service, forcing the bus lines to go around that area. These meandering bus routes are frustrating to the commuter who could take direct routes and arrive at their destination faster if they owned or used their personal vehicles. Bus service has not always been user-friendly to the state's elderly or handicapped. Consequently the task for city leaders is to reverse the negativity of bus ridership in order to encourage the average worker to use mass transit rather than his/her personal mode of transportation.

City leaders have responded with enacting several new initiatives. To address time delays, many cities have designated special lanes on their city streets and freeways for buses only. While larger buses handle the majority of the commuters, smaller-sized buses are being used to meet the needs of the handicapped and elderly. For a monthly fee, some cities provide **para transit fleets** of small vans that provide group personalized door-to-door services or **dial-a-ride** for individual transport similar to taxi cabs. For tourist- or convention-dependent cities such as San Antonio, Houston and Dallas, mini-buses or stop-and-ride buses or gasoline or electric powered street cars are used to provide shuttle services between hotels and convention centers or to the general public for major entertainment or sports events. San Antonio has special park-and-ride fees for all of its major events held in the downtown area. One takes their personal vehicle and parks it at an outlying VIA station and boards the bus for both the incoming and outgoing trip for a fee. This saves the hassle of driving into the downtown area and searching for a parking spot. With the passage of the **Americans with Disabilities Act (ADA)**, all public transportation services must provide services for the handicapped. Initially, cities opted for smaller more personalized handicapped-fitted buses that caused scheduling, service-delivery and convenience problems for their customers. Consequently, newer larger buses are being equipped with ramps and special seating to accommodate the needs of the handicapped. However, regardless of whether the private or public sector manages the system, reliance upon a bus system as a city's only means of mass transportation simply does not meet the needs of growing urban communities.

Light rail systems are also viable alternatives to the automobile mentality. In 1996, Dallas launched its adventure into light rail with the opening of the Dallas Area Rapid Transit or DART system. Initially, DART consisted of a 21-mile route of track dedicated to two main routes. The route of the Red Line ran north to Park Lane and the south through the downtown area to Westmoreland Road. The route of the Blue Line ran from the downtown area south to Ledbetter Road. The cost of those DART lines was "42 million per mile, including $122 million for a 3.2 mile tunnel under the Central Expressway to Mockingbird Station near Southern Methodist University."[48] The light rail system joined the traditional bus lines as the city's two major sources of mass transportation. Despite a shaky start, DART has proved to be a very successful venture. Well known for its traffic congestion, Houston launched a light rail system in January 2003, initially with a 7.5 mile line of track running through the downtown area south to Reliant Stadium.

To Whom the Toll Tolls—Perhaps

Governor Rick Perry appeared to be trying to please both the highway-construction mentality of transportation interest groups and those commuters weary of wading through traffic jams. During the 2003 legislative session, Perry once again advocated the adoption of his Trans Texas Corridor plan, a fifty-year construction project of approximately 4,000 miles of highways and rail corridors with an conservative estimated price tag of $183 billion. His plan was basically a super multi-purpose freeway system with each corridor or roadway consisting of separate lanes for passenger-only vehicles, trucks only, light-rail or railroad cars carrying passengers and freight, alongside specially designed utility lanes for the transportation of water, natural gas, petroleum, electric and fiber-optics. This was not just a passing whim on the part of the governor. Experts believed that this was the only viable option for fixing the segment of IH-35 running from the border through San Antonio, Austin and Dallas. The

Trans Texas Corridor plan successfully passed both houses, and Governor Perry signed HB 3588 into law.

However, the project ran into insurmountable problems ranging from lack of funding to potential environmental clashes with the EPA. First, the price tag for the project was just beyond what the state could fund through the Highway Trust Fund and the state gasoline tax. Perry's solution was toll roads. He wanted to toll all existing and future highways. Additional money was supposed to come from federal low-cost loans, municipal and state bonds, and other private investments. Second, land acquisition was a delicate topic. According to the plan, the first two sections of the system would be to reconfigure the existing IH-35 and build a new Interstate 69 corridor from the Rio Grande Valley to Northeast Texas. Third, environmentalists joined forces with the Texas Farm Bureau and the Texas Wildlife Association in voicing their opposition to the corridor based on the preliminary environmental impact study that pointed out not only the potential loss of prime farm and ranchland, agricultural production, and displacement of landowners and homeowners, but the potential harm to the environment since the system would, according to the plan, be built over nine aquifers, destroying miles of established parks, resulting in draining miles of valuable wetlands, potentially destroying approximately 50 or more listed endangered or threatened species of plants, wildlife, etc., and threaten national historical sites. Lastly, commuters were very opposed to toll roads. Across the state, motorists felt that since they were already paying for the construction and maintenance of state roads through the motor fuel tax, why should they be subjected to paying another fee or tax to drive on the roads that they had already paid for? In Houston, voters soundly rejected a proposal to toll one of their main freeways. In San Antonio, members of the Aquifer Guardians in Urban Areas and the People for Efficient Transportation, Inc., filed for a federal injunction to block the tolling of US 281. In addition, established businesses along the proposed route voiced their opposition since their business properties would be condemned under eminent domain, forcing them to relocate or close down completely. The 2007 legislative session ended with members from both sides of the political fence putting the brakes on the corridor project, particularly toll roads. In 2007, the Texas Legislature did authorize the construction of state highway 130, a toll road named after former United States Congressman J. J. "Jake" Pickle. Opening in 2012, the highway runs from Interstate 35 in San Antonio along Interstate 410, then north as a toll road from Interstate 35 North of Georgetown. The route was intended to relieve the nightmarish traffic on IH35, the San Antonio-Austin corridor. The good news is that the speed limit is 80 miles mph (miles per hour). The bad news for TxDOT is that very few motorists use it!

Is There a Future for Mass Transportation in Texas?

Despite the costs, mass transportation does have its supporters. "Public transit is a necessity for poor workers whose income hardly warrants the car per worker minimum seemingly required by an auto-dependent society; for senior citizens whose driving abilities have deteriorated and who might otherwise be immobilized were public transit unavailable; and for the young, who can experience urban society beyond the confines of their immediate neighborhoods."[49]   Environmentalists see mass transportation as a means to reduce air and noise pollution. The rate of carbon monoxide fumes in the air decreases when the use of the private automobile decreases. Public transportation saves valuable fossil fuels and helps to eliminated traffic jams and congestion.

The primary opponents to mass transit are the members of the highway lobby. Their message to the public points out that public transportation is unreliable, too complicated with frequent transfers from bus to bus, too noisy, too uncomfortable, and unsafe. Their fear of mass transit is also self-serving. If more people rode the bus or the train, there would be a decrease in automobile and vehicle sales, gasoline consumption, auto repairs, replacement parts, and automobile insurance policies. While many American workers actively carpool and use public transportation as their means of commuting to work, carpooling in Texas seems to become popular only when the price of gasoline goes up. Once the price of gas becomes more appealing to the pocketbook, carpooling becomes distasteful. The average Texan is extremely reluctant to take the bus to work or to any destination. The bus is the last and least pleasing transportation option next to walking. Mass transportation plans are vigorously opposed by rural communities and small towns. These areas do not benefit from mass transportation proposals; consequently, citizens in rural communities fear their tax dollars will pay for a transportation system that they will not be able to use.

Cases in Point—The Bullet Train and San Antonio's Light Rail Defeat

Any new alternative challenging the highway dependent mentality ruffles the feathers of the highway lobby. In 1991, a proposal was introduced to the Texas Legislature to build a French-designed and French-engineered TGV train (*train a' grande vitesse* or train of great speed) to connect San Antonio, Austin, Houston and Dallas. The so-called bullet train would travel 200 miles per hour. A passenger could travel between Houston and Dallas in ninety minutes. The environmentalists were thrilled because these trains are well known to use less energy and create less air pollution. The interests of the average frequent traveler were aroused. Here was a public transportation system proven to be faster than air travel that would save travelers wear and tear on their personal vehicles and save money on gasoline. Promoters of the train estimated that the project would create "25,000 jobs during construction and 9,000 permanent jobs when the train starts rolling."[50] The price tag was approximately a $6.8 billion joint venture of federal, state and private money.

The opposition to the train included the usual members of the highway lobby joined by rural and small town interests and major air carriers such as Southwest Airlines. They formed DERAIL (Demanding Ethics, Responsibility and Accountability in Legislation). They criticized Texas TGV for "overstating its ridership projections, for understating its costs, for seeking public subsidies after promising it would not, for missing a deadline to raise $167 million in equity, and for failing to address the fears of Texans along the proposed routes that the fenced railroad right-of-way would amount to a Berlin Wall through rural Texas."[51] The Texas Legislature bowed to the opposition by introducing legislation abolishing the Texas High-Speed Rail Authority who was initially charged with overseeing the project and by setting unreasonable deadlines for Texas TGV to provide the equity payment. The payment was not made, and the project died.

In 2000, the city council of San Antonio proposed a light-rail system that would augment the traditional bus service. In 1977, voters approved a half-cent increase in the sales tax to create the current VIA bus system. Although VIA had increased its ridership, the bus system simply could not keep pace with the city's population growth. A light-rail system similar to DART in Dallas seemed to be a simple solution. The city council decided to fund the project through a "permanent ¼ cent tax estimated to generate $1.5 billion over 25 years, to fund 53 miles of light rail."[52] City staffers drew up the proposed routes with lines going north to south and east to west. The campaign was intense with the City of San Antonio launching a costly media blitz. The battle lines, however, were quickly drawn. Supporters joined city staffers in stressing that "the light rail system is the key to the city's growth and quality of life. They say the city must provide alternatives to auto travel, as a way both to ease traffic and to improve air quality."[53] The opposition forces launched their own media campaign by pointing out that the proposal was a waste of money and would not reduce pollution or traffic.

From the beginning the proposal ran into problems. First, the design of the routes awakened the tensions between the economically prosperous growing north side of San Antonio against the economically depressed primarily minority populated south side. The map clearly supported the fears of southsiders. Although the routes extended east to west in both directions from the city, the northern routes were longer in distance reaching out to the farthest suburbs than those proposed for the southern sector. And, the balloting process was complicated. Nineteen various suburbs and bedroom cities were to participate in the election. If one suburb defeated the project, then a route that included that area would have to be redrawn to exclude it. However, the residents of San Antonio had to approve the measure regardless of the outcome in the other areas. Held on May 6, 2000, the election was the victim of extremely low voter turnout. Despite the efforts of city leaders and their media blitz, the measure was soundly defeated.

Not to be deterred, the city of San Antonio joined forces with VIA Metropolitan Transit to promote an ambitious plan of streetcars running through the downtown area. Costing an estimated $280 million, the streetcar projected was hailed as the perfect solution to providing intercity transportation for tourists and convention attendees who usually leave their personal vehicles at home. The Convention and Visitors Bureau pointed out that the convenience of riding on a streetcar rather than walking to important downtown historical sites would be a plus in attracting more visitors to the Alamo City. The usual cadre of opponents lined up to fight the project. Through a series of petition drives, they successfully stopped the project and moved the city council to put the plight of future streetcars or other modes of mass transportation up to the voters. At the bottom of the May 2015 city council/ mayoral ballot was a charter amendment mandating that any future streetcar and light rail projects must go before the voters for approval. The measure passed.

Flying the Texas Skies

The major cities of Fort Worth, Dallas, Houston, and San Antonio are very dependent upon the revenues generated from the tourism and convention industries. Major sports teams in Dallas, Houston and San Antonio attract fans from the opposing teams to see the games. Hosting the NACCA Final Four Basketball Tournament in San Antonio generated in just one weekend millions of dollars in additional revenue. An NBA playoff berth or hosting the Super Bowl draws thousands to these cities. However, convention attendees and sports fans alike want to be able to arrive at the airport within hours of the start of the event and leave as soon as possible. To accommodate their needs, the state's major airports must be able to provide a consistently convenient and customer friendly experience for our state's visitors. A bad experience for one person can be detrimental for any city actively marketing its convention facilities, hotel accommodations, quality of restaurants, etc. When seeking a convention site, transportation is a major concern. It is no accident that the sites for the national Democrat and Republican conventions are held in major cities that have multiple transportation options from highways to airports. Unfortunately, Texas has only five of its airports making the 2016 list of the nation's top forty—Dallas/Fort Worth International, Houston Intercontinental, Dallas Love Field, Austin-Bergstrom International and William B. Hobby in Houston.[54]

As early as the 1970s, San Antonio's city leadership tasked a special committee through its Greater San Antonio Chamber of Commerce to devise a long-term plan to expand the runways and add more terminals at the San Antonio Airport. Accomplishing this posed serious problems. First, the airport is landlocked. Beginning in the 1950s, subdivisions spouted up so close to the airport that residents still complain of the noise from outgoing and incoming flights. If an airport cannot lengthen its runways to accommodate bigger planes, then those planes will take off and land elsewhere. Second, the city has several major military bases that have security-controlled airspace that commercial flights cannot fly into on a regular basis. The committee's recommendation was to seek a deal with Austin to build a regional airport located between the two cities. Unfortunately, no deal was made. Meanwhile, Austin's Municipal Airport was simply too small to accommodate its growing population. The federal base closing committee did Austin a tremendous favor when it decided to close Bergstrom Air Force Base. When Bergstrom officially closed, Austin's city leadership quickly claimed the base and its long runways as the home for its new municipal airport.

The Future of Mass Transportation

The fate of the bullet train is just one example of the strength of the highway lobby in Texas. The dependence upon the automobile is tied directly to the cultural and historical development of this state. The frontier experience taught Texans the lessons of self-reliance and independence. The automobile symbolizes independence of movement, and the highway provides the route. This marriage of automobile, highway, and freedom of movement plays right into the hands of the highway construction companies, oil and gasoline firms, and the automobile industry. After all, Toyota chose to locate its plant in San Antonio not just because of the land but for the connection Texans have to what Toyota produces in that plant—the Tundra truck. The future of these economic entities is tied directly to the continuation of these traditions.

However, the highway lobby is faced with serious problems. These miles upon miles of asphalt and concrete roadways are deteriorating and need immediate repair. The cost of maintaining this elaborate system is overwhelming. The state has become too dependent upon federal highway funding and too lax in devising alternative funding options. The construction business is a major employer in this state. Lack of funding means more than denial of a multi-million dollar contract. It means potential unemployment.

Other means of transportation face maintenance and future construction woes also. Airport runways need resurfacing. Airspace is becoming extremely limited. The airports at Houston, Dallas, and San Antonio have airplanes lined up behind each other waiting for takeoff like cars stacked up behind each other waiting for the traffic light to change. Arriving aircraft must circle around the airports waiting for landing space. If Texas is to compete with other states for major international markets, additional airports must be built to meet air traffic needs. The railroad that once dominated the Texas frontier has been given a secondary seat to the automobile-highway mentality. If rail is to become a major player in the transportation game, major repairs must be made to railroad tracks and railcars. Amtrak is not the answers either. Railroad tracks in Texas are deteriorating. Some rural areas still lack modern railroad crossing signals. The state of Texas cannot be blamed for the condition of its railroads for the federal government and the railroad industry itself bears the burden.

Eventually the highway lobby must secure an equal footing for mass transportation. As the second most populous state in the United States, Texas cannot afford to overlook the transportation needs of its elderly, poor and handicapped citizens. If Texas wants to be considered as a major player in the world economy, it must be able to offer a high-tech transportation system. The automobile-highway format is not the sole answer. There can be a workable relationship between public and private

transportation, and the state needs both in order to meet the social and economic needs of its citizens.

Chapter Notes

[1]Lewis Munford, *The City In History: Its Origins, Its Transformations, and Its Prospects*, (New York, New York: Harcourt, Brace and World, 1961), 506-507.

[2.]*Texas Almanac: 2019*, (Denton, Texas: Texas State Historical Association, 2018), 677.

[3]Allison Boerger, "El Camino Real Here Long Before S.A.," *San Antonio Express News*, (Wednesday, December 6, 2017), A14.

[4]Ibid.

[5]Rupert N. Richardson, Adrian Anderson, Cary D. Wintz, and Ernest Wallace, *Texas: The Lone Star State*, 9th ed., (Upper Saddle River, New Jersey: Prentice-Hall, 2005), 178.

[6]Ibid., 202.

[7]Kit Myers, "Aboard the Jackass Line," *San Antonio Express-News*, (August 3, 1999), 3M.

[8]_____, "1.476-Mile Route Put Texas On the Map," *San Antonio Express News*, (Monday, July 9, 2018), A7.

[9]Kit Myers, "Abroad the Jackass Line," *San Antonio Express News*, (August 3, 1999), 3M.

[10]Ibid.

[11]Robert A. Griffin, "Antebellum Texas: Railroad Fever in a New State," *The Texas Heritage*, Ben Procter and Archie P. McDonald, eds., 1st ed., (Arlington Heights, Illinois: Forum Press, 1980), 78.

[12]Calvert and De Leon, 206.

[13]Joe B. Frantz, *Texas: A History*, 2nd ed., (New York, New York: W. W. Norton, 1984, 144.

[14]Ibid., 120.

[15]Calvert and De Leon, 207.

[16]Ibid., 209.

[17]Ibid., 208.

[18]Rupert N. Richardson, Adrian Anderson, Cary D. Wintz, and Ernest Wallace, *Texas: The Lone Star State*, 9th ed., (Upper Saddle River, New Jersey: Pearson Prentice Hall, 2005), 307.

[19]_____, "Big Changes for S. A. As Autos Arrived," *San Antonio Express News* (Sunday, October 21, 2018, A8.

[20]*State of Texas Annual Cash Report 2018: Revenue and Expenditures of State Funds for the Year Ended August 31, 2018*, (Austin, Texas: Comptroller of Public Accounts, 2018), 15.

[21]Robert S. Friedman, "The Politics of Transportation," *Politics in the American States: A Comparative Analysis*, Virginia Gray, Herbert Jacob and Robert B. Albritton, eds., 5th ed., (New York, New York: Harper Collins, 1990), 552.

[22]Gary Martin, "State Requests Funds for 33 Road Projects," *San Antonio Express-News*, (Thursday, February 4, 1999), 1A+.

[23]Ibid., 7A.

[24]Bob Dart, "Bush Signs Highway Bill, But Is Not the Road to Happiness for All," *San Antonio Express-News*, (Thursday, August 11, 2005), 3A.

[25]U. S. Bureau of the Census, *Statistical Abstract of the United States: 2010, 129th ed.,* (Washington, D.C.: 2009), Table 1056, 668.

[26]*State of Texas Annual Cash Report 2010: Revenues and Expenditures of State Funds for the Year Ended August 31, 2010,* 39.

[27]*State of Texas Annual Cash Report 2014: Revenues and Expenditures of State Funds for Year Ended August 31, 2014,* 939.

[28]*State of Texas Annual Cash Report 2018: Revenue and Expenditures of State Funds for the Year Ended August 31, 2018,* 15.

[29]Friedman, "The Politics of Transportation," 555.

[30]Glenn A. Robinson, "Highway Policy," *Texas at the Crossroads: People, Politics and Policy,* Anthony Champagne and Edward J. Harpham eds., (College Station, Texas: A & M University Press, 1987, 216.

[31]David R. Berman, *State and Local Politics,* 7th ed., (Dubuque, Iowa: Brown and Benchmark, 1994), 396.

[32]Randall W. Bland, Alfred B. Sullivan, Robert E. Biles, Charles P. Elliott, Jr., and Beryle E. Pettus, *Texas Government Today,* 5th ed., (Pacific Grove, California: Brooks/Cole Publishing Company, 1992), 423.

[33]ProQuest, *ProQuest Statistical Abstract of the United States: 2019,* 7th ed., (Bethesda, Maryland, 2018), Table 1112, 702.

[34]*State of Texas Annual Cash Report 2018: Revenue and Expenditures of State Funds for the Year Ended August 31, 2018,* 131-133.

[35]*Statistical Abstract of the United States: 2012,* Table 1093, 686.

[36]*ProQuest Statistical Abstract of the United States: 2019,* Table 1110, 701.

[37]Ibid.

[38]Ibid.

[39]Jacque Crouse and Christopher Anderson, "Damage Estimates Still Rising," *San Antonio Express-News,* (October 29, 1998), 1A+.

[40]Berman, 394.

[41]Scott Huddleston, "Public to Shape Future of Transit," *San Antonio Express-News,* (Sunday, November 29, 1998), 1B+.

[42]Ibid.

[43]Ibid.

[44]Berman, 394.

[45]*ProQuest Statistical Abstract of the United States: 2019,* Table 1136, 716.

[46]Ibid., Table 1135, 715.

[47]Ibid., Table 1123, 708.

[48]David Anthony Richelieu, "Dallas Light Rail On A Roll Against the Odds," *San Antonio Express-News,* (Tuesday, April 18, 2000), 6A.

[49]Robinson, "Highway Policy," 219.

[50]Stephanie Scott, "Bullet Train Sees Route Plan," *San Antonio Express-News,* (Friday, April 16, 1993), 2E.

[51]Paul Burka, "The Little Engine That Might," *Texas Monthly,* (April 16, 1993), 135.

[52]Scott Huddleston, "Phoenix Mirrors SA Transit Fight," *San Antonio Express-News,* (Thursday, April 20, 2000), 9A.

[53]Cindy Tumiel, "Saturday's Light-Rail Vote To Be Complex," *San Antonio Express-News,* (Sunday, April 30, 2000), 16A.

[54]ProQuest Statistical Abstract of the United States: 2019, Table 1092, 692.

Education in Texas

A&M Consolidated School, Agricultural and Mechanical College, Texas, between 1900 and 1920.

Public education under the rules prescribed by the government and under the magistrates put in place by the sovereign, is therefore one of the fundamental maxims of popular or legitimate government. If children are raised in common and in the bosom of equality, if they are imbued with the laws of the state and the maxims of the general will, if they are instructed to respect them above all things, if they are surrounded by examples of objects that constantly speak to them of the tender mother who nourishes them, of the love she bears for them, of the inestimable benefits they receive from her, and in turn of the debt they owe her, doubtlessly they thus will learn to cherish one another as brothers, never to want anything but what the society wants, never to substitute the actions of men and of citizens for the sterile and vain babbling of sophists, and to become one day the defenders and the fathers of the country whose children they will have been for so long.

Jean Jacques Rousseau, *Discourse on the Political Economy*[1]

In his special message to Congress delivered on January 28, 1957, President Dwight D. Eisenhower emphasized that "in a nation which holds sacred the dignity and worth of the individual, education is first and foremost an instrument for serving the aspirations of each person. It is not only the means for earning a living, but for enlarging life, for maintaining and improving liberty of the mind, for exercising both the rights and obligations of freedom, for understanding the world in which we live. Collectively, the educational equipment of the whole population contributes to our national character—our freedom as a nation, our national security, our expanding economy, our cultural attainments, our unremitting efforts for a durable peace."[2] Eisenhower's words mirror those sentiments expressed by the first settlers to Texas who dreamed of a top-notch public and higher education system for their children. The failure of the Mexican government to fulfill its obligation to provide settlers with a viable public school system was one of the reasons given by Texans in severing their colonial relationship with Mexico. Although it was always on the brink of bankruptcy, the leadership of the struggling Republic of Texas stressed the need for education by setting "aside of four *sitios* [approximately 4,428 acres per *sitio*] of land in each county for the support of public schools and fifty *sitios* for the endowment of two universities or colleges."[3] Since becoming a state, both Democrat and Republican governors have boldly announced that improving the state's public and higher education system would be a cornerstone of their administrations. Each legislative session has attempted to leave its mark on the direction of the state's educational system. As a presidential candidate, Governor George W. Bush hailed the educational reforms passed under his tenure as the model for the nation's troubled school systems. President Bush and his fellow Republicans in Congress passed into law a national mandate that all public schools implement his "No Child Left Behind"

program. Governor Rick Perry has also made education one of his top issues since he ran for the governorship. After fourteen years in office, Perry's education initiatives had very little impact on improving the state's education system. As a candidate, Greg Abbott vowed that he would make Texas's public schools the best in the nation, indeed a daunting task! As he begins his second term, Governor Abbott reemphasized his commitment to improving the state's public school system. In *State of the State* message, he challenged the Texas Legislature to reform the state's public and higher education formulas, increase state allocations for education, and give every public school teacher at least a $1,000 raise per year. Texas like so many of her sister states are wrestling over the direction of their education systems. Where once the "buzz words" at the state capitol were the "three R's," today's rhetoric has been replaced with two new "buzz words"—accountability and student success.

Despite the commitment from both the governor and the Texas Legislature, the report card on the state's public and higher educational system is a dismal one. Issued by the Editorial Projects in Education Research Center, the 2006 *Chance for Success Report* evaluates the state's public school systems on several factors. According to their assessment, Texas overall received a grade of C, ranking it as 41st in the nation among her sister states and the District of Columbia. This is an improvement since the agency's 2016 report ranked Texas as 48th! The yearly analysis is based on thirteen indicators that span a person's life from cradle to career. Those indicators fall into three sub-sections: early foundations, school years, and adult outcomes."[4] The findings for Texas are:

a) For early foundations, which examines factors that help children get off to a good start, Texas earns a C and ranks 48th.

b) Texas receives a C for the school years, a sub-category focusing on metrics related to Pre-K enrollment through postsecondary participation. It finishes 36th in the nation in this area.

c) In the area of adult outcomes, based on postsecondary educational attainment and work-force indicators, Texas's grade is a C. It ranks 34th in the nation.[5]

The failure of the state's education system to train and educate all of its youth properly continues to frustrate lawmakers, parents, educators, the business community, and, of course, the students. The cost of financing an extensive system of public schools, community colleges, and state-supported universities and colleges is staggering. "Texas' second largest expenditure function was for education, totaling $36.8 billion in fiscal 2018, an increase of $1.3 billion or 3.6 percent more than in fiscal 2017."[6] Legislative session after session has failed to adequately fund the state's public school systems. Members of the 2019 legislative session are toying with different funding options as they face the reality that for the seventh time a judge has ruled that the state's funding system is unconstitutional. Each legislative has the same results of legislators putting "a Band-Aid on a Band-Aid on a Band-Aid. We have a constitutionally and fundamentally broken system and it's time that it be repaired and be repaired on a non-Band-Aid approach."[7]

This chapter examines the historical relationship Texans have with its fickle education system. An in-depth analysis of the problems confronting both public and higher education reveals a system in desperate need of innovative and radical changes. The traditional reform measures offered by legislative session after session shows lawmakers trying to use traditional and conservative policy options that are, quite simply, out of date and not in tune with the times.

The Historical Development of the Public School System

The Role of the National Government

Initially, the responsibility for the establishment and administration of the nation's public school system rested with the states and local communities with the national government providing land grants and money for the development of public and higher educational institutions. This trend began with the passage of the **Northwest Ordinance of 1785**, whereby one section of land in each township in the Northwest Territory was reserved for the endowment of schools. The 1862 **Morrill Act** provided grants in the form of land for the establishment of college-level agricultural and mechanical arts programs. The **Smith Hughes Act** (1917) provided federal grants for vocational college programs. The United States Congress provided education assistance to World War II veterans with the passage of the **Servicemen's Readjustment Act** in 1944, commonly known as the **GI Bill of Rights**. Federally funded free lunch and milk programs for impoverished children enrolled in private and public schools were approved in 1946. Congress enacted legislation creating both the **National Science Foundation** and the **National Endowment for the Arts and Humanities** to encourage scientific research and to stimulate programs in the arts and humanities. Federal grants for college loans, graduate fellowships and technological equipment were provided through the **National Defense Education Act** (1958).

The national government's traditional passive role in education was changed dramatically with the surprisingly successful launching of *Sputnik* in 1957. Lawmakers, educators, and the American public were shocked that those supposed 'intellectually backward" Russians beat the Americans in the race to become the first nation to have an orbiting satellite in outer space. The National Defense Education Act provided federal funding to public schools for the development of additional courses in science, mathematics, and foreign languages. In 1960, newly elected President John Kennedy vowed that the United States would be the first nation to place a man on the moon. *Sputnik* was an educational crisis ripe for a reform movement. Federal money was doled out to public and higher educational institutions to strengthen math and science curricula.

The most sweeping piece of national legislation for public schools was the **Elementary and Secondary Education Act** of 1965. President Lyndon Johnson signed the bill into law sitting at his teacher's desk in his old Johnson City one-room schoolhouse. "As a former teacher," he declared, "I have great expectations of what this law will mean for all of our young people. As President of the United States, I believe no law I have signed or will ever sign means more to the future of America."[8] Title I provides federal funds for compensatory education programs for children living within designated poverty levels. Federal money is allocated under Title II for the purchase of library books and instructional materials. Other titles provide federal grants for innovative learning programs, education resource centers, programs for the mentally retarded and physically handicapped, and so on. The **Civil Rights Act of 1964** provides the national government the avenue to punish schools for noncompliance of federal civil rights laws. Public and private schools that openly practice segregated admissions policies and encourage discriminatory practices could lose their federal funding. The United States Congress provided an additional $2 billion through the **Elementary School Act** (1972) to eliminate minority group segregation and discriminatory practices in elementary and secondary schools. In 1972, the federal government established a federal assistance program for college students under the **Basic Educational Opportunity Grant**, commonly known as the **Pell Grant**.

Another educational crisis erupted in 1983 when the National Commission on Excellence in Education issued its assessment of the nation's education system. Titled *A Nation at Risk*, the commission's findings revealed several serious problems:

- Students in most other leading industrial nations scored better than American students on a variety of standardized tests.
- American students attend school about 180 days per year, compared to 240 for German and Japanese students.
- About 13 percent of the nation's seventeen-year-olds were functionally illiterate.
- Students spent about four hours per week on homework; they watched television about twenty-four hours per week.
- SAT scores for high school seniors declined steadily from 1963 to 1980.
- Average starting salaries of public school teachers in 1988 were $19,400 compared to $23,500 for an average liberal arts graduate employed in another profession.[9]

This report painfully indicated the problems within the American educational system at all levels of the spectrum. All of the federal money poured into the system for nearly 200 years still could not guarantee that all of the nation's Johnnies could read! The commission concluded that "the schools must spend $24 billion per year to make minimally necessary improvements in education."[10]

However, the 1980s saw the national economy take a dive as budget managers sought cuts rather than increases in all categories of the federal budget. For example, the **Educational Consolidation and Improvement Act** of 1981 consolidated half of the federal government's education programs into one large block grant, while Congress slashed the federal budget for elementary, secondary, and vocational programs by 25 percent.

Signing of the Elementary and Secondary Education Bill by President Lyndon B. Johnson seated beside his first schoolteacher, Kate Deadrich Loney. Grounds of former Junction Elementary School, Johnson City, Texas. April 11, 1965. Credit: LBJ Library photo.

President George H.W. Bush broke the mold by advocating an expanded role for the national government in public education. Bush believed that national standards for testing and school efficiency backed by federal mandates for noncompliance would be the incentive for school districts to reverse dismal trends. His philosophy fell upon deaf Republican ears as both the Republican-controlled House and Senate argued over how much to cut from education budgets while agreeing to give states more local control and responsibilities for educating the nation's students. Under the watchful eye of Bush's Secretary of Education, many state legislative houses did pass education reform bills aimed at improving student achievement. Student-oriented legislative packages included the establishment of statewide core course requirements for graduation from high school; state-mandated exit tests for assessing students' acknowledge; statewide assessment testing at the elementary and secondary grade levels; adding more rigorous courses to the core curriculum; and requiring kindergarten for all pre-school age children. Reform legislative packages required teachers take and pass subject matter competency tests, established rigorous teacher qualifications, and provided financial tuition assistance programs to teachers wanting to teach high-priority subject areas such as reading, English, math and science.

Beginning in the 1990s, the focus of national education initiatives shifted to assessment of student learning outcomes. State legislative reform packages emphasized the need to identify what students needed to know at each level of their educational development as well as the means for accessing their achievement levels for those identified skills. The primary assessment tool became "the test," a series of standardized testing instruments that students must take and pass to either be promoted to the next highest grade level or to graduate. In some school districts, a graduating senior who fails "the test" does not get to participate in graduation ceremonies. President Bill Clinton envisioned a more active role for the federal government. Initially, he "promised to seek budget funds and send Congress a bill to ensure that: schools stop promoting students who are failing; teachers are qualified to teach subjects they are assigned; states fix or shut down low-performing schools; parents get annual report cards on schools' performance; and schools maintain disciplined classrooms."[11] His proposals, however, met with the criticism that the federal government would become too intrusive into an area traditionally reserved for the states and local communities.

President George W. Bush proposed many of the same reforms and initiatives that his father and President Clinton endorsed during their terms in the White House. On January 2, 2002, Bush announced his "**No Child Left Behind**" program by signing into law a sweeping national education reform package. Bush defended his plan by pointing out that the American taxpayer has "spent billions of dollars with lousy results. Now it's time to spend billions of dollars and get good results. We do not want children trapped in schools that will not change and will not teach."[12] The legislation:

• Authorized $26.5 billion alone for the 2002 budget year, approximately $8 billion more than spent the previous year.
• Required annual state tests in reading and math for every child in grades three through eight beginning with the 2005-2006 school year. Schools that failed to improve their scores two years in a row would receive more federal aid to reverse poor test results.
• Required that all schools raise their reading and math proficiency levels within two years.
• Required schools to close the "test results" gap between wealthy and poor students as well as Anglo and minority students.
• Allowed churches and religious groups to provide tutoring and after-school programs.
• Required schools to ensure that within four years, all teachers are qualified to teach in their subject areas. If a teacher was not qualified in that subject field, then the schools would be required to send a letter notifying the parents. Allowed school districts to spend federal teacher-quality funds for other purposes, such as training and increasing salaries.
• Required schools to develop periodic report cards showing parents their child's standardized test scores.
• Provided $5 billion per year over five years to improve reading, with a goal to make sure that every student could read by the third grade.
• Required schools to test students with limited English skills after three consecutive years of attending school.[13]

The ultimate goals of his program were to hold schools more accountable to student performance and decrease dropout rates while encouraging students to complete their programs and "walk the stage" with a diploma in hand. To drive home the point, No Child Left Behind included several punitive sanctions that would be levied on failing schools. If a school failed to have acceptable test scores, they would be placed on notice. If the following year the school produced the same results, the school would be subjected to Stage One sanctions, mandating that the school would have to develop an improvement plan. The school was also required to notify parents of the school's failing test scores. Parents had the option to send their children to a "better" school with the offending public school district paying for the child's transportation. Continuing failing test scores would place that school at Stage Two. The sanctions would be the same as those at Stage One with the exception that the school would have to provide tutors to failing and low-income students. At Stage Three, the school was required to replace the entire school staff, extend the school day, and strip the principal of his/her authority. The most punitive sanctions were saved for Stage Four. At this juncture, the school had to replace the entire school staff from janitors to principals and if improvements still were not made, the management of the school would be turned over to a private company or to the state.

In 2003, the Bush administration gained congressional passage of a law mandating that all of the nation's public schools must declare that "they allow prayer wherever and however the Constitution permits" or the schools could lose their share of approximately $32 billion in federal money earmarked for elementary and secondary schools.[14] According to guidelines released by the United States Department of Education:

1. Students may say grace before meals, pray with fellow students during recess and generally take part in religious expression outside of class instruction.

2. Students may organize prayer groups to the same extent as other extracurricular activities. Schools may disclaim sponsorship, but only in ways that do not favor or disfavor the religious group.

3. Teachers may neither encourage nor discourage students from praying during moments of silence.

4. Students may express religious beliefs in schoolwork. Teachers should judge such work on ordinary standards of substance.

5. Teachers may not participate in prayer with students. But teachers can take part in religious activities such as prayer meetings, as long as they make clear they are not doing so in their official capacities.

6. Schools may not organize prayer at graduations or choose speakers in a way that favors religious speech. However, speakers cannot be restricted from religious or anti-religious expression.[15]

The provisions of the law clearly mirror the decisions rendered by the United States Supreme Court over separation of church and state issues involving prayer in the public schools. The Court has always upheld that voluntary prayer is constitutional, whereas, involuntary prayer or any government sponsored prayer is unconstitutional.

On the campaign trail, Barack Obama pledged that if elected, he would end the No Child Left Behind program. He stressed that it failed to meet its objectives and tied school districts to just teaching to the test and not much more during the course of the school year. Pledging quality educational opportunities from "cradle through career," President Obama included many of his education reform proposals into the **American Recovery and Reinvestment Act** signed by the president in February 2009. The law

provided approximately $5 billion for early learning programs including Head Start, Early Head Start, child care, and programs for special needs children. Approximately $77 billion was pledged to strengthen elementary and secondary education. The reform package itself echoes reform efforts of the past: make improvements in teacher effectiveness, hire only high-quality teachers, ensure students are prepared for college, improve achievement in historically low-performing schools, and provide more financial assistance to college students to offset costs.

Traditionally, governing of the nation's schools rests at the local level through the guidance of each state's legislature. Whether the occupant of the White House is a Democrat or a Republican, toying with local governance of the public school system has been and will continue to be met with sharp criticism. Outright resistance is difficult since cash-strapped school districts are very dependent upon receiving federal funding to cover the costs for almost everything from buildings to buses and equipment. Once again, a federal "one-size fits all approach" program does not meet the different specific needs of the nation's children. According to James Watt of the Southern Regional Education Board's research group, "there should not be a common prescription for all 50 states any more than a state should have a common prescription for all of its districts. Federal support can make a difference. But states can do the diagnoses and decide for themselves how to use those resources."[16] However, the dilemma confronting all involved in education is how far should the federal government extend its influence into an issue that has traditionally been the privy of state governments? Are state governments capable of shouldering the responsibility of educating the state's children with little or no assistance from the federal government?

The Texas Story

In declaring its independence from Mexico, among their numerous complaints against the Mexican government, Texans claimed that the government had failed to provide a public or even a private school system for the settlers. However, the Mexican government was not totally at fault. The frontier lifestyle did not include a formal education. The skills of farming, ranching, hunting, and basic survival techniques were far more essential to Texans than the three R's—reading, writing and arithmetic. Most individuals learned from home schooling to read and write enough to get by.

The 1836 State Constitution of the Republic of Texas provided public funding and land grants for the establishment of both private and public schools. "The Congress of the Republic granted four leagues (17,712 acres) to each county to support public schools and provide for a school board to administer these lands and the schools that they paid for, but virtually nothing came of this legislation."[17] Not regulated by a state agency, schools usually held elementary and secondary levels of instruction in one-room schools called institutes, academies, colleges and even universities. Usually, one teacher taught all subjects at all grade levels. The 1845 State Constitution officially mandated the establishment of a system of schools. The document also specified that one-tenth of the state's annual revenue from taxation had to be set aside for educational purposes.

Sentiments toward public education changed radically by 1854, when the Texas Legislature dedicated $2 million in United States Indemnity Bonds for schools. State funds were now available for any child to attend a school. Any group or individual could establish a school, or children could be sent to private church schools and receive reimbursement. However, "the share for each child was pitifully small: only .62 cents in 1854 and $1.50 the following year."[18] The first known public school in Texas opened its doors in 1853 in San Antonio. As the state gradually changed from a predominately rural to a more urban population, the development of educational facilities became more of a necessity rather than a luxury. "From annexation to the beginning of the Civil War the [Texas] [L]egislature granted charters to 117 schools and incorporated in addition 9 educational associations. There were 40 academics, 30 colleges, 27 institutes, 7 universities, 5 schools, 3 high schools, 2 seminaries, 1 college institute, 1 orphan asylum, and 1 medical college."[19] Since the state did not actually fund educational facilities, only those children whose parents could pay the tuition could attend school. The more costly academics were able to offer advanced curriculum beyond the basic three Rs. "For example, students at the Marshall Grove Academy in Harrison County could take Latin, Greek, Hebrew, Higher Mathematics, Natural Philosophy, Metaphysics, Declamation, and Composition. All such schools generally admitted boys and girls, although some separated them into male and female departments."[20] For antebellum Texas, education was dogged by issues of quality, cost and accessibility. Education was simply not available for far too many children in Texas. "A five-month session typically cost from $15 per student in the primary department up to $30 for senior-level instruction. 'Ornamental' courses such as instrumental music bore an additional cost. Books and supplies were an additional expense, and students who

boarded had to pay for a room and food. Considering that in most part of antebellum Texas an acre of land cost less than $50, it is clear that relatively few families could afford education for their children."[21] The quality of one's educational experience was severely hampered by the lack of a state-mandated curriculum coupled with the propensity of hiring unqualified teachers. Although Texas did not have a law prohibiting slaves from receiving an education, the majority had no formal or informal education at all and remained illiterate.

The 1869 Constitution was more generous to the state's evolving education system. The profits from the sale of public lands were added to the permanent school fund, with the available school fund set aside for the education of all children, regardless of race, between the ages of six and eighteen. The school financing system saw increased revenues from the poll tax and one-fourth of the annual state tax. This constitution created a free public school system with compulsory attendance requirements. However, the administration of Governor E. J. Davis placed the state in charge of education. The writers of the 1876 Constitution returned control back to the local communities as part of their effort to reverse the control the Davis administration had in the governor's office. The movement to divorce education from state control was evident in a 1884 law that completely reorganized the public school system in Texas by providing for an elected state superintendent with limited authority over school district operations. County schools were placed under the supervision of county judges; teachers were required to be state certified in teaching; and schools were required to maintain attendance and grade records. Counties were subsequently subdivided into school districts with local taxing authority.

Between 1880 and 1920, the public school system was divided into two types of districts—common and independent. **Common schools** were one building schools located in rural areas. The school's trustees oversaw the administration of the school, collected taxes, and hired the teachers. **Independent districts** were located in urban areas. "Between 1890 and 1920 the number of pupils in public schools grew by 120 percent. About 73 percent of school-age children attended some public school in 1920, with a correspondent drop in illiteracy to 8.3 percent of the population, the lowest in the South."[22] However, the inequities in per-student expenditures between the various independent districts and common schools were evident from the inception of separate local based taxing authorities. "Primarily because of conditions in rural schools, as the new century [1900] began, Texas ranked near the bottom among the states of the nation in terms of the adequacy of its school system. In 1900, towns and cities spent $8.35 per student for education, while country [rural] schools spent only $4.67; students in cities and towns averaged 162 days per year in the classroom, while their rural counterparts averaged only 98 days."[23] The low tax base of rural areas could not generate enough money to properly fund the schools. The Progressive Era in Texas ushered in a term often associated with education funding issues: **consolidation**. A series of state legislative acts enabled rural or common schools to consolidate among themselves and/or with independent urban-centered school districts. "By 1929, more than 1,500 consolidations had been accomplished."[24]

Additional legislation included a constitutional amendment passed in 1918 mandating state-issued free textbooks in all public schools. The Texas Legislative passed a bill in 1915 requiring that all children between ages six and eighteen attend at least a sixty-day term (expanded to 100 days two years later). Through a constitutional amendment passed in 1920, school districts were granted expanded flexibility to independently raise their tax rates. In 1929, the State Department of Education was replaced by the State Board of Education. Appointed by the governor, this nine-member board oversaw the distribution of state funds to school districts, selection of textbooks, and so on.

Teacher qualifications and salary issues were also addressed by the Texas Legislature in the 1920s. "As of late 1920, 48 percent of common school teachers in Texas had not graduated from a high school. Only 16 percent had graduated from a normal school, and 5 percent from a college or university. In the case of independent districts, teacher qualifications were considerably better, with 92 percent holding at least a high school certificate, and with over 50 percent having graduated from a normal school, college or university. But all teachers tended to be transient, with most staying on the job under two years."[25] To address this problem, the Texas Legislature encouraged the development of teachers' colleges with specialized curriculum in education. Of course, a highly trained teacher would demand a higher salary. Bearing in mind that African-American and rural teachers were paid substantially less than Anglo urban teachers, "in 1920, the average annual salary for a Texas teacher was $615, or about 55 percent of that of the average Texas wage earner. . . . By 1929, Texas teachers' salaries averaged $924 per year, as compared to the national mark of $1,420."[26] Teachers did receive salary increases, but historically, the amounts were not sufficient enough to meet national average salary scales.

The next attempt at education reform occurred in 1949 with the passage of the **Gilmer-Aiken School Laws**. These laws completely reorganized the state's public school system by creating a Central Education Agency "composed of the State Board of Education, the State Board for Vocational Education, the State Commissioner of Education, and the State Department of Education. It shall carry out such educational functions as may be assigned to it by the Legislature . . . The Central Education Agency shall be the sole agency of the State of Texas empowered to enter into agreements respecting educational undertakings, including the providing of school lunches and the construction of school buildings . . ."[27] The name of the Central Education Agency has been changed to the Texas Education Agency (TEA). In addition, the law established a statewide elected State Board of Education and a governor-appointed commissioner to oversee the TEA. It also called for a nine-month school year. The package addressed teacher qualifications and salary. "Beginning with the school year 1949-1950, the Board of Trustees of each and every school district in the State of Texas shall pay their teachers, both whites [Anglos] and negroes [African-Americans], upon a salary schedule providing a minimum beginning base salary plus increments above the minimum for additional experience in teaching as hereinafter prescribed. The salaries fixed herein shall be regarded as minimum salaries only and each district may supplement such salaries . . . All teachers and administrators shall have a valid Texas certificate. Salary increments for college training shall be based upon training received at a college recognized by the State Commissioner of Education for the preparation of teachers."[28] The legislation specified salary minimum levels for teachers. For example, a teacher with a bachelor's degree would earn a base pay of $267 per month with $6 per month added for each year of teaching experience, not to exceed $72.[29] Other features of the legislation included guidelines for the financing of the Foundation School Program, establishment of a statewide textbook committee, and reaffirming the state's commitment to provide free textbooks to the state's public school students. Gilmer-Aiken gave the state more control over the internal operations of school districts, as more schools opted for consolidation. The positive results were the end of the one-room schoolhouse and increased student enrollments across the state. The negative effects were a direct result of the traditional approach to education reform in Texas, with its emphasis on too much rhetoric and too little money. For example, "although Texas teachers' salaries rose from an average of $3,231 in 1955 to $5,421 ten years later, as late as 1960, the state ranked twenty-seventh for public school instructors. State per-pupil expense followed a similar pattern. Although state appropriations had more than tripled, the state ranking of thirty-two in 1955 had dropped to thirty-nine in 1965."[30]

In 1982 gubernatorial candidate Mark White promised that if elected, he would finally put education on the right track. The resulting **Select Committee for Public Education** or **SCOPE** was formed in 1983, with H. Ross Perot as its chairperson. It should be noted that "the reforms that came in the 1980s did not originate within the education community, nor did they involve much input from educators. There were no teachers on the Select Committee for Public Education from which HB 72 originated, nor were educators directly involved once the school finance issues went to the courts. Legislators, judges, and a billionaire businessman from Dallas were the ones deciding what would happen to, and in, Texas's public schools."[31] The "back to basics" approach of the committee produced a wide range of legislative reforms including:

1. Raising the passing grade for courses from 60 to 70
2. Raising the minimum pay for teachers and establishing a career ladder for progression
3. Mandatory testing for current teachers and those entering schools of education and the teaching profession
4. Reducing maximum class size
5. Providing more aid to poorer school districts
6. Establishing the "no pass-no play" rules for students participating in extra-curricular activities
7. Establishing stricter standards for absences and grade level promotions.[32]

The plan also called for tougher accreditation standards for public school districts implemented through the Texas Education Agency. All Texas public school students were to take the TEAMS competency tests in reading, writing, and mathematics. Teachers were required to pass a literacy test, or lose their state teaching certificates, and submit to yearly classroom observations. HB 72 created a new state agency called the **Legislative Education Board (LEB)** just to implement HB 72 provisions. With HB 72, "the state had considerable control over curriculum, textbooks, accountability measures, administrative decisions, and education spending."[33]

Perot's recommendations were credited for their innovative and tough approach to improving the quality of education in Texas. However, a closer examination reveals that Perot's plan was short on innovative ideas, short on funding, and lacking in widespread support within the education and teaching professions. "In the end, three of the state's four teacher's groups withdrew support for the reforms because of the small salary increase and teacher opposition to such measures as competence testing of certified teachers, and the merit system imposed under the guise of 'career ladder.'"[34] In addition, the Texas Legislature did not adequately fund the reform package. The majority of the state's teachers received no salary increases. Poorer school districts received additional state funds, but the state did not provide enough money to ward off a series of law suits and court battles filed by several property-poor school districts. The reduction of teacher/student ratios never happened since the Texas Legislature did not give the school districts additional funding to hire new teachers or to build additional classrooms. Stricter accreditation guidelines were marginally followed since the only strong muscle the TEA had was to close school districts for noncompliance, a politically unwise move. Unfortunately, in 1984,

Texas ranked third in total state population, and in school age population, and in total personal income. However it ranked 32nd in state and local expenditures per capita for schools, 45th in estimated current per-pupil expenditures based upon average daily attendance; and 49th in percentage of total personal income set aside for public elementary and secondary schools. During the 1982-83 school year, the average per-pupil expenditure in Texas was $2,557, while in Alaska, it was $6,301 and in New York it was $4,303.[35]

Perot's hard efforts produced just another reform effect without substantial positive results. The political future of Governor White was directly linked to HB 72. "Although it [HB 72] was perhaps a historic achievement, education reform was not what his supporters had signed on for. When the governor's term expired, Texas teachers remembered his promises. Without their support, and facing economic conditions far worse than when his term began (a condition he and Perot had hoped education reform would help to avoid), Mark White failed to win re-election."[36] Instead it was Bill Clements, the first Republican elected to the governorship since Reconstruction that moved into the governor's mansion.

Governors Bill Clements, Ann Richards (D) and George W. Bush (R) attempted to address the on-going controversy over state funding for public education. This problem will be discussed in detail in another section of this chapter. Governor Rick Perry and the Texas

Legislature were confronted with the same sobering statistics of increased illiteracy, failing test scores, teacher dissatisfaction, and rising dropout rates. The 2011 Texas legislative session began on a dismal note as lawmakers had to drastically reduce spending in all categories just to balance the budget. The governor's mandate was that the budget would be balanced without increasing taxes and without dipping too far into the state's "rainy day" fund. Democrats felt that it was definitely a rainy season for education. However, the governor's wishes prevailed. At the start of the 2011 school year, public school districts in Texas had far less in state funding to fill their coffers and, with declining property values, not enough tax dollars coming in to offset the decreases in state funding. They too have had to slash their budgets, meaning drastic reductions in instructional and support staff, and those reductions in maximum class sizes that were the cornerstone of Perot's reforms are a thing of the past. The state mandate is 24 to 25 students in every classroom regardless of the grade level. As the nation began to recover from the recession, increased revenue from state sales and other revenue streams deposited into the general fund allowed the Texas Legislature to spend approximately $33.7 billion in fiscal year 2012 for education, an increase of $145 million or 0.4 percent over fiscal 2011.[37] The trend of adding more money into the education budget has continued and with the beginning of the 84th Texas Legislature, the initial plan called for an increasing state school funding by $1,000 per student for an estimated total of $6.4 billion.[38]

The 85th Legislative Session ended with the passage of several bills out of each chamber's respective education committees that successfully passed the other house and garnered the governor's signature. SB1 reduced the allocations to the Texas Higher Education Coordination Board (THECB) by $1.25 million by slashing $208,000 from the College Readiness and Success Division, $237,000 from the academic Quality and Workforce Division, and $358,000 from the Strategic Planning and Funding Division. The Central Administration office's budget was cut by $446,130. Meanwhile, HB 264 mandates that school districts provide information to parents and students about career and college readiness components and the curriculum required to enter college. This bill also requires that the messaging be delivered in English, Spanish and Vietnamese.[39] The most controversial piece of legislation was the "bathroom bill" that failed to pass in both the regular and special sessions. Budget wise, all was not doom and gloom. For fiscal year 2018-2019, the legislature allocated $20 million for higher education, an increase of 1.2 percent from the previous fiscal year. Money

was allocated for the addition of two new medical schools at the University of Texas in Austin and the University of Texas Rio Grande Valley. The state's community colleges got additional $18.0 million in General Revenue Funds for "core operations" and $10.8 million for success points. The state's contract hour reimbursement was increased to $2.70, one cent higher than the 2016-17 rate.[40]

The 86th Legislative Session began with trying to fulfill the governor's and many state legislative candidates' campaign pledges to reform the state's public school financing formulas with the objective of finally ending the "Robin Hood" plan and replacing it with an equitable funding program eliminating the divide between "rich" and "poor" school districts. Also, the governor pledged in his *State of the State* address that he wanted to give all teachers a salary increase. Appreciative of the governor's acknowledgement that teachers are underpaid, the teachers then demanded that any pay increase in the state's public school system had to include everyone, including the janitors, cafeteria workers, bus drivers, etc. Legislators and the governor agreed!

The State of the State's Education "System"

Public School Enrollment Trends

"Enrollment in Texas public schools reached a peak of 5,284,306 students in the 2015-2016 school year."[41] In 2017, total enrollment in the state's public schools was 5,399,682.[42] These figures do not include school age children attending private or parochial schools, charter schools, or home schooling programs. By 2023, it is estimated that the total public elementary and secondary school enrollment will reach 6,669,000.[43] While enrollments may be increasing, the Census Bureau reported that in 2016, only 82.9 percent of Texans over the age of 25 are high school graduates, an increase of 2.2 percent over 2010 census tallies. Furthermore, of the state's high school graduates, only 28.9 percent hold either a bachelor's degree or more college hours, and only 10.0 percent have an advanced degree beyond the bachelors.[44] Once again, these figures do not include students who completed their high school education through private or parochial schools, charter schools or home schooling. While growth in enrollment is impressive, slight increases in high school completion rates are not. While the increased number of high school graduates enrolling in higher education programs is a welcomed sign, the number actually completing their degree programs is not. Obviously, overall the public school system in this state is not doing a stellar job of ensuring that yesterday's kindergarten children will successfully walk today's stage with a high school diploma in hand nor is the "community" providing the proper incentives for young Texans enrolled in higher education institutions to actually graduate with a four-year or higher degree.

Governance of Public Schools

The Texas Legislature is responsible for establishing the roles and policies governing the state's supported public and higher education systems. At the public school level, there are two separate agencies administering everything from textbook selection to school board conduct. Established in 1949, the **Texas Education Agency (TEA)** is the primary agency overseen by its policy-making body the **State Board of Education (SBOE)**.

The TEA is a powerful actor in the state public school system since it provides basic support for school districts. The agency's primary functions are to ensure that schools comply with state laws and to distribute state funding to the various school districts. Those schools meeting state standards are granted accreditation by the TEA, meaning that students attending schools in those districts will receive credit for their course work in other school districts and higher education institutions. Schools are inspected on a regular basis and graded on their performances. A school dropping from "accredited" to "accredited advised" has potentially serious problems that must be addressed within a TEA-specified time period or the school may face loss of accreditation. The TEA has the option to assign a TEA monitor to observe the daily operations of a school, its district and even its board, or in extreme cases a master will be tasked with veto powers over any action taken by that district's board. The evaluation process includes factors such as the length of the school term, proper record keeping, teaching effectiveness, salary treatment, maintenance of appropriate student-teacher classroom ratios, quality of special education and handicapped programs, appropriate curriculum selections for each grade level and subject, the certification and evaluation process of staff, teachers, counselors, appropriate bus routes, and school board-superintendent relations. Legislation passed in 1990 allowed the TEA to compare a school district's performance against performances of their sister districts. Schools given an "exemplary" status receive special privileges and additional state funding. However, schools with less-than-satisfactory ratings face sanctions, takeovers

from TEA management teams, or consolidation with another school district.

The SBOE is composed of fifteen members elected from single-member districts for four-year staggered terms of office. The only qualifications to run for a seat on the SBOE are residency and age, no prior education experience either as an education professional or school board member is required. Recently, there was a candidate who ran for a SBOE seat who truly believed that if elected, he would now be an employee of the State of Texas with a salary and medical benefits. What he should have known was that SBOE members only receive reimbursement for travel and lodging costs for attending meetings! Appointed by the governor with Senate confirmation, the **Commissioner of Education** is selected from the membership of the board for a two-year term. Responsibilities of the SBOE include establishing the standards for school accreditation and the certification process for teachers and other processional staff, overseeing the investments of the Permanent School Fund, approving textbook selections, and implementing state and federally mandated education laws.

In Texas, the public school system is composed of common and independent school districts. **Common districts** are governed by county-wide elected superintendents and trustees; whereas, **independent school districts** are directly supervised by the TEA. In Texas, there are 1,024 independent and common school districts and 183 charter schools.[45] The Texas Legislature authorizes four types of **charter schools**: the home-rule district charter, the campus or campus-program, the open-enrollment model and the university-sponsored charter. Usually granted for a five-year period, charter school agreements are issued by the State Board of Education. In independent school districts, governing authority rests with an elected school board held accountable by both the voters and the TEA. Most school boards are composed of seven members, while larger districts may have as many as nine. Board members are elected through an at-large, single-member, or combination thereof. The rationale for an elected board stems from the Jeffersonian concept of democracy whereby communities exercise control over their schools rather than a higher governing authority. While Jefferson saw the importance of citizen involvement, Texans simply do not turn out in large numbers for school board elections. The duties assigned to school boards include the hiring and firing of school administrators, approving the district budget, determining the tax rate within state mandated parameters, setting salary schedules within state mandated parameters, approving contracts for new construction and maintenance of schools and facilities, selecting textbooks from state approved adoption lists, establishing district policies for conduct and dress of both students and staff, and establishing the overall philosophy and mission of the district. Under ideal conditions, school boards are policy making organizations, leaving the day-to-day management of the district to the superintendent.

However, school board members in Texas have the tendency to overly micromanage and meddle into the day-to-day operations of the schools. Rarely professional educators themselves, school board members have the tendency to focus less on the broader scope of policy making and educational policies and more on issues and concerns that are the responsibilities of the superintendents and their principals. Unfortunately, infighting among board members is the norm rather than the exception. Under extreme cases, the TEA has warned and/or dismissed school board members and even threatened to strip the accreditation of the district itself for mismanagement by school board members. For example, in January 2002, the TEA issued a stern warning to the South San Antonio Independent School District board that they had six months to address serious concerns about the board's conduct or a special master would be assigned to oversee the management of the district. The TEA found that several of the board members:

1. improperly got involved with daily activities at the schools;
2. improperly bypassed the superintendent and contacted staff members directly;
3. improperly took hiring recommendations from people other than the superintendent; and
4. abused their authority by taking work that belongs to the superintendent.[46]

The TEA further recommended other remedies including special state-sponsored training on the proper duties and responsibilities of school board members.

The Political Environment of Education

Unfortunately, education policies are not immune from the influence of political and special interest group wheeling and dealing. Politicians and lawmakers represent the full ideological spectrum of liberal and conservative views. Oftentimes, they lock horns with the demands of the business community to educate the state's future workforce by providing them with the technical skills they need while at the same time, addressing the concerns of parents and educational professionals who want to see the state's children intellectually prepared for adulthood.

While oftentimes in conflict with each other, these two objectives influence at every step of the decision making process from textbook and curriculum selections to financing and taxing decisions. Few can deny that the American educational system is an essential component in molding the future of this nation.

> Perhaps no single word better describes the American attitude toward education than *reverence*. Education has been the means to realize the American Dream. Not only does the school provide the knowledge necessary for success, but it teaches discipline, the value of hard work, and patriotism—all values intimately related to The Dream. Moreover, the public school provides these things in equal measure for all. It not only transmits the democratic creed but also is a product of that creed. The public school system is widely regarded as the prime exemplar and the chief defender of democracy.[47]

It is the public school system that in many respects prepares our children for adulthood by shaping their moral, ethical, and social roles. Obviously, the philosophical foundation of this teaching process must be artfully molded, guided, and monitored by various interested parties. Far too often, school board decisions are politically motivated actions based upon the presentation of conflicting social and moral views that are outside of education itself but do ultimately become an integral part of foundation of educational policies.

The conservative philosophy shared by many Texans views public schools as laboratories producing a well-trained workforce driven to achieve economic success. Curriculum should be based on what is needed to achieve economic viability, that is, the basics of reading, writing and arithmetic. They advocate a back-to-basics philosophy that de-emphasizes the necessity for liberal and fine arts and, lately, physical education in the classroom. Creative thinking should be replaced with rote learning skills. Conservatives believe that the Texas education system has failed to properly prepare young Texans for the workforce because of lax discipline in the classrooms and a curriculum that abandons basic skills. They also adhere to the belief that the high school dropout rate among minority population groups is due mostly to individual failures, broken families, and, once again, the culture of poverty. Traditionally, the conservative voices in Texas politics prefer a limited role for both state and national government in education by returning more authority back to the school districts themselves. In the 1960's and

70's, they were adamantly opposed to forced integration by busing. Conservatives openly support home-schooling and a voucher system whereby parents can use vouchers to pay the tuition and transportation costs to send their children to the school of their choice.

In the late 1980's and early 90's, the radical right of the conservative wing of the Republican Party entered into the education picture by actively recruiting and running candidates for local school board positions. Also known as the Christian Coalition, the agenda of the radical right included the reinstitution of mandatory school prayer in the classroom, the teaching of basic family values, and an emphasis on sexual abstinence and prolife positions. Some radical right school board members have voiced the desire to purge the public school library shelves of books using profanity, sexually explicit and suggestive language and illustrations, anti-religious themes, and permissive behavior. In 1997, the in-fighting between the six social conservative Republicans and the moderate Republican and Democrat members of the SBOE made national headlines. It was reported that "disagreements have taken an ugly turn, with monthly meetings deteriorating into name-calling and finger pointing. Some members of the public have fallen victim to the testiness, being subjected to rude and brusque comments from board members of all political persuasions."[48] The arguments this time centered on issues of multiculturalism, national testing, and achievement standards.

Liberals share the conservative viewpoint that the education system should adequately prepare Texas's youth for adulthood. However, liberals embrace the philosophy of John Stuart Mill that man's creativity must be encouraged, not suppressed. Rote learning of the basics restricts the creative nature. Liberals support both the basic curriculum and the inclusion of creative liberal arts courses taught through innovative teaching styles that broaden one's perspective. They support more openness in the classroom, academic freedom for teachers, special instructional programs for the mentally and physically challenged learners, desegregation, and decentralization and increased community involvement in the educational process. Usually affiliated with the Democratic Party, liberals believed that no one should be denied a quality education. They support an expansive network of government- and private-sponsored financial aid packages and learning assistance programs to meet students' needs.

The business community is keenly and often painfully aware that their potential workforce is a product of the state's public school system. America's ability to keep its competitive edge over its international economic competition rests with a highly trained competent force of engineers, technicians, scientists, and researchers capable of meeting the demands of high-tech industries. At the opposite end of the spectrum, low-tech jobs in the service sector require employees capable of working long hours at repetitive tasks. Concerned with increasing illiteracy and dropout rates, the business community supports education reforms measures closely akin to traditional conservative viewpoints.

Traditionally, teachers bear the brunt of the blame for student failures. However, teachers are voters who can deliver a fatal blow at the polls. Former Governor Mark White discovered the negative wallop teachers can deliver when their vote coupled with their very vocal opposition spoiled White's re-election bid in 1986. In 1984, White promised all teachers salary increases, career-ladder promotions, reduced student/teacher ratios in the classroom, and more academic freedom. Unfortunately, only less than one-half of one percent of the state's teachers received the promised salary raises since the increase applied only to the state's mandated minimum starting salary level. Salaries above that level were not subject to the increase. Having failed to deliver on the other promises, White subjected teachers to a degrading state-mandated test called the Texas Examination of Current Administrators and Teachers or TECAT. Furthermore, teachers were told that if they failed the test, they would lose their jobs and their state teaching licenses. Few teachers failed this simple English test. After supporting him solidly in 1982, they completely abandoned White in 1986. Also, teachers rose to the occasion again in 1999 when the Texas Legislature seriously considered passing a school voucher program. Representatives from teachers' unions, education professional organizations, parent/teacher groups, and public school districts from across the state successfully fought the issue. During the 2011 legislative session, proposals to slash education by multi-billions of dollars were met with very vocal public protests from teachers, students and parents. Although budget cuts were inevitable, the legislature retreated by cutting approximately $4 billion rather than a double digit figure from the education budget.

Parents and their children are far often the forgotten "consumers" of the public education system. Parents pay the property taxes that finance the lion's share of the public school system. Like any other consumer, they want to purchase a product that works, not one that repeatedly breaks down, requiring expensive and constant repair. After sending their children off to public schools for twelve years, parents should have a reasonable expectation that their children will be academically prepared for adulthood, college, and the job market. Year after year of having dismal performance reports followed with requests for more money, parents are frustrated about the entire public school system's failures. Their anger is vented at the polls as incumbent school board members are defeated along with referendums for tax increases and multi-billion dollar bond elections for new school construction projects. The consumers want results, not promises.

The Politics of Textbooks

Prior to 1918, only a handful of school districts provided all of their students with a new up-to-date textbook at the start of the school year. For the majority of the state's public school students, a textbook was an out-of-date book with a worn or torn cover and dog-eared pages that was shared by two or more students. Consequently, the state's children were receiving a mediocre education. The Texas Legislature responded by enacting a 1918 law authorizing the state of Texas to purchase and provide free of charge, up-to-date textbooks in every subject for every student attending a state-funded public school. The state of Texas was now in the textbook business! The process of selecting the *appropriate* text fell upon the Textbook Selection Committee, which was created under the 1949 Gilmer-Aiken School Laws. The process seemed so simple on paper. A committee reviews the textbooks submitted by the various publishers and then selects two to three books for each subject area. The committee's official adoption list is provided to all of the public schools for their selections. In turn, the state purchases the books for the school districts. The logic also appears to be reasonable. The state actually saves money by purchasing a large number of texts at discounted bulk rates. The school districts do not have to set aside money for textbook purchases; the state foots the bill. Parents do not have to bear the financial responsibility of buying books for their children. More importantly, the Textbook Selection Committee guarantees that every child in the Texas public school system will receive the same information. Today, only California and Texas provide free textbooks for public school attendees.

Unfortunately, for the state's public school students, the selection of their textbooks has become a political nightmare pitting liberals against conservatives, and, eventually, textbook publishers against the members of the Textbook Selection Committee. Historically, the committee's political philosophy has dominated the selection process by excluding texts that are deemed to be "politically and socially incorrect." "In an effort to cut down on the eternal squabbling over textbooks, the [Texas] Legislature adopted a law in 1995 limiting the board to rejecting textbooks solely on their basis of errors, not ideology. But sometimes the line between the two can be blurred."[49] Publishers far too often are willing to cave into the wishes of the committee since "Texas accounts for a hefty 8 percent of America's $4.5 billion textbook market."[50] Of course, waiting on the side lines are the ones most directly impacted by the selections made by the committee—educators, classroom teachers, parents, and the students whose opinions are rarely sought.

A controversy that made national headlines involved the rewrite of the state's history curriculum. Individual board members and interested parties invited to participate carefully examined over two hundred proposed texts. "Each side of the controversy had its pet peeves. Traditionalists want democracy and free enterprise presented more favorably, while progressives lobby for more representation for minorities and women. Meanwhile, creationists object to passages referring to glaciers sculpting the Earth millions of years ago."[51] From the very beginning of the discussion, key civil rights groups including the GI Forum, LULAC, and the NAACP vocally complained about the proposed changes. Despite heated arguments the conservative members of the Textbook Selection Committee won the day, at least temporarily. Of course, this was the same committee that on the last go round on the history texts approved a text that had over 200 factual errors including the Battle of the Alamo as occurring in 1936, not 1836. Democrats and liberals were incensed but so were numerous Republicans. A conservative-leaning education organization, the Thomas B. Fordham Institute, issued its own highly critical review of the history text. For example, they noted that in the text "there is no mention of the Black codes, the Ku Klux Klan or sharecropping; the term 'Jim Crow' never appears, incredibly, racial segregation is only mentioned in a passing reference to the 1948 integration of the armed forces."[52] They basically declared the new social studies curriculum as riddled with "misrepresentations at every turn."[53]

In 2016, the Textbook Committee made headlines once again. This time it involved the selection of a text for the newly created Mexican-American Studies program for high school students offered as elective courses. The same groups that protested the American history text were quick to gather forces against the adoption of this textbook. Several passages in the book are highly critical and basically discriminatory towards the Mexican American community. One critic pointed to a page in the text that read:

Industrialists were very driven, competitive men who were always on the clock and continually concerned about efficiency. They were used to their workers putting in a full day's work, quietly and obediently, and respecting rules, authority and property. In contrast, Mexican laborers were not reared to put in a full day's work so vigorously. There was a cultural attitude of "manna" or "tomorrow" when it came to high-gear production.[54]

Oddly, this was the only text up for consideration. The publisher, Momentum Instruction is owed by a former member of the Textbook Committee. The racist-tone of this text created such a fire storm of protests that the State Board of Education stepped and rejected it.

Particularly with the Textbook Committee, representatives of both the liberal and conservative camps are supported by a number of heavy hitting interest groups. The leading conservative group is the Texas Public Policy Foundation founded by James Leininger. Other conservative groups include the Texas Eagle Forum and Citizens for a Sound Economy. The preeminent spokesperson for the liberal camp is the Texas Freedom Network, an organization advocating ideology-free but factual laden textbooks. What will become of the Textbook Selection Committee may be more budget driven rather than ideological. Since the 2003 legislative session, proposals to shift the burden of textbook purchases from the state to the individual school districts have been made as a means of saving the state money. Although these proposals have failed to win much support, a bill introduced in the 2011 session to eliminate the textbook committee had considerable but unsuccessful support.

Special Education Programs

One of the most difficult issues confronting the nation's public schools is the provision of appropriate accommodations for special needs children. Initially, these children were not allowed to attend public schools. When they were admitted, special needs children in most instances, were separated from 'normal' children. They sat in separate classrooms from the first bell to the last bell of the day from first grade to twelfth grade, involved in activities that had very little to do with learning the 3Rs. Few schools had ramps or even elevators for physically handicapped and blind students. Blind students were oftentimes paired with sighted students to help them navigate up and down the stairs. Schools did not have sign-language teachers for the deaf or a testing center to accommodate those students with a learning disability who needed extended testing time, a reader, etc. With the passage of the Elementary and Secondary Education Act, the Americans with Disabilities Act and a Congress willing to use the carrot and stick approach with federal funding, public schools had to accommodate the learning needs of their special education students or face losing their federal funding.

In 2016, House Speaker Joe Straus was apprised that the Texas Education Agency (TEA) issued a directive in 2004 for the public schools across the state to reduce its special needs populations to 8.5 percent of the student body. In the Laredo Independent School District, TEA officials told them in 2007 "to remove as many kids as possible. . . . The staffers . . . purged their rolls, discharging nearly a third of its special education students. . . More than 700 children were forced out of special education and moved back into regular education."[55] In 2012 "Texas reduced its special education budget by $33 million, so the federal government withheld $33 million as a penalty."[56] Believing that they were in the right, the TEA along with the support of the state's attorney general, decided to challenge the Department of Education's actions through the courts. While the state's fight against the federal government was going through the courts, the TEA continued to enforce its policy. Consequently, "over the past 12 years, the percentage of Texas students receiving special ed[ucation] has dropped from 12 percent to exactly 8.5 percent, the lowest rate of any state in America. Houston and Dallas, the state's two largest school systems, are even lower, at 7.4 percent and 6.9 percent, respectively."[57] Laying the blame on the TEA, Straus "expressed outrage at the target, saying it has deprived tens of thousands of disabled children an adequate education. . . . The monitoring system was [designed to prevent schools from identifying students for special education when it isn't necessary. However, he stressed the importance of providing services to all students who need them while continuing top make sure students are not improperly identified for special education."[58] Finally, in 2018, the 5th United States Circuit Court of Appeals ruled that the state of Texas was in violation of the federal rule. It is now up to the Texas Legislature to direct the TEA to address the educational needs of Texans, especially the state's special needs children and, of course, pay the $33 million penalty.

Curriculum Issues and Illiteracy

Although the United States prides itself on its ability to provide a top notch education for its citizens, statistical data shows a very different picture. A study completed by the Programme for International Students is conducted every three years to measure competencies in reading, math, and science literacy for fifteen-year-olds in both developed and developing countries. The latest results from the round of tests administered in 2015, reveal that the "math achievement of American high school students in 2015 fell for the second time in a row . . . pushing the United States down to the bottom half of seventy-two nations and regions around the world who participate in the international test."[59] For reading and science, the results placed the United States near the international average test scores. Particularly in math, "students are often good at answering the first layer of a problem in the United States, but as soon as student have to go deeper and answer the more complex parts of a problem, they have difficulties."[60] Basically, students enrolled in mathematics courses in Singapore, China, Japan, Estonia, Canada, Poland, Norway, Vietnam, Russia, France, Great Britain, Iceland, Malta, to name a few, scored higher than students from the United States.[61] In its 2018 report to the Texas Legislature, the TEA noted that "for the class of 2017, 53 percent of [high school] graduates were considered college ready in reading, and 423 percent were considered college ready in mathematics. Overall for the class of 2017, 38 percent were considered college ready for both subjects."[62] The reality is that unless this nation as a whole bridges the education gap, the nation's economic posture in the international community will be severely threatened. Some educators fear that iniquities in the quality of education will eventually lead to the demise of the middle class, leaving only a two class society with the well educated holding the higher paying jobs alongside the severely undereducated minimum wage or below laborer. As both governor and president, George W. Bush's "No Child Left Behind" program was supposed to reverse this trend. However, recent studies indicate that the number of illiterate Americans is increasing, not decreasing.

A literate population is absolutely essential to Texas as it strives to continue to be a key player in the high-tech job market. The majority of functionally illiterate Texans are gainfully employed in low-paying minimum wage positions. Texas can only marginally court high-tech industries since a large percentage of its workforce cannot even read and comprehend a college-level work manual. There is a direct link between literacy, dropouts, and poverty. An illiterate student will quickly fall behind his/her more literate counterparts, leading to frustration and failure in school performance, and, ultimately, dropping out of school. An illiterate worker is doomed to a lifetime

of minimum wage or lower paying job opportunities as job mobility and promotional chances pass him/her by. As governor, Bush's education plan called for third graders to pass a reading proficiency test before they could be promoted to the fourth grade, thus ending "social promotion." At various internals, students are tested for proficiency in math, reading and writing. During the 2005-2006 legislative session, lawmakers strengthened the high school core curriculum by mandating four rather than three years of both science and mathematics courses. Beginning with the 2007 school term, students are required to take geometry, algebra I and II, and an additional course either in pre-calculus, advance placement statistics or calculus. The four credits in science include biology I and II and either chemistry, physics, and principles of technology. While mandating the additional courses, the Texas Legislature once again failed to provide the additional money to hire teachers and equip science laboratories.

The Texas Legislature also proposed accountability standards for bilingual education programs. The conservative wing of the Republican Party has always been in favor of eliminating all bilingual courses. However, these programs are essential to developing a literate workforce. It is estimated that approximately 700,000 of the state's youths have limited English proficiency. While educators do support more accountability in their programs, they also have repeatedly requested additional funding from the state for more bilingual instructors, high-tech language program equipment, and in- and after school tutoring programs. Unfortunately, the Texas Legislature has only marginally funded their requests. Educators also stress that there is a direct connection between classroom performance and the home learning environment, particularly for students with limited English proficiency. For low-income families across the state, there is simply not enough family income to purchase a computer, the language-specific software or the outside of the classroom reading materials that would help these children to make the transition to English proficiency. Consequently, bringing technology to the classroom is key, especially for language-specific programs. When Al Gore ran for president, he was laughingly dubbed the "internet candidate." What Gore was saying was true. Just putting a computer in a classroom in an older school building does not bring the technology to the school. For example, brand-new donated computers were slated to be installed in four community centers in Webb County including the small community of El Cenzio and a colonia located south of Laredo. They received the computers but their federal grant money did not cover the costs to access the internet service, hook up the equipment, or purchase the computer desks. The key to bridge the gap between the classroom and the home environment is more than just acquiring computer equipment and reading materials. Also, non-English proficient parents need to become English proficient so they can help their children. The partnership between teachers and parents needs to be strengthened in order for bilingual programs to be truly effective in reversing illiteracy trends.

The Quest for Better Test Scores

All of the nation's state legislative houses have been wrestling with the problem of tying funding allocations for public education to state-mandated pupil performance levels in their public school systems. The 1990s introduced a new concept in public school funding—accountability. In other words, legislators wanted solid evidence that their state's money and, more importantly, the tax payers' dollars are actually achieving the goals of educating their children. The rationale was that public money should be used only to fund successful programs. A public school district that shows a clear pattern of increasing student achievement, should be rewarded for its efforts while districts not producing the intended results should be punished by seeing reduced state funding allocations until improvements are made. However, at the onset of this adventure, the state did not have an objective measurement tool to assess students' performance levels. Prompted by Governor Ann Richards, the Texas Legislature in 1991 mandated that all public schools use the Texas Assessment of Academic Skills (TAAS) test as the primary tool for determining reading, writing, and mathematics proficiencies. The tests were administered to all students in grades 3, 5, 7, 9, and 11. Initially, the accountability standards included TAAS scores, student attendance records, and dropout rates. "The state's goals with TAAS wasn't to play Big Brother, but to prod schools where children weren't mastering key subjects."[63] Based on the scores, schools were graded as either low performing, acceptable, recognized or exemplary. The 1991 law mandated that no public high school student could graduate without successfully passing this test.

Despite the fact that for two consecutive years more than 37,000 third-graders failed the TAAS test, state legislators decided to up the ante by mandating a new series of more academically challenging tests collectively known as the Texas Assessment of Knowledge and Skills or TAKS. Full scale administration of the series of tests began with the 2003 school term. Students are tested by either the standard TAKS, the TAKS (Accommodated)

designed for students in special education programs, the TAKS (Modified) for those students whereby the TAKS is not the appropriate assessment tool, TAKS (Alternative) for students with significant cognitive disabilities, and the Texas English Language Proficiency Assessment System (TELPAS) for those students with limited English proficiency. Regardless of the test used, the results fall into three categories:

- **Commended performance**. This category indicates high academic achievement. Students in this category performed at a level that was considerably above the state passing standard.
- **Met the standard**. This category indicates satisfactory academic achievement. Students in this category performed at a level that was at, or somewhat above, the state passing standard.
- **Did not meet the standard**. This category indicates unsatisfactory academic achievement. Students in this category performed at a level that was below the state passing standard.[64]

In 2012, the TAKS test was replaced with the State of Texas Assessments of Academic Readiness or STAAR, annual assessments for reading and mathematics for grades 3-8, writing for grades 4 and 7, science for grades 5 and 8, social studies for grade 8, and end-of-course assessment tests for English I, English II, Algebra I, biology and U.S. history. In 2016, Algebra II and English II were added to the testing list.

While testing is probably the proper measurement tool to determine student academic proficiency, tying the test score results to the amount of money a school district will receive has put undue pressures upon teachers, administrators, parents, and, most importantly, the students. Administrators know that in order to continue to maintain their current funding levels, they must produce high test scores. Several public school districts have resorted to unfair tactics in their quest to achieve high enough test scores to merit an "exemplary" rating for their schools. Students complain that several weeks of the school year are dedicated specifically to preparing for just taking the test. They may well pass the test but many students feel that they are not receiving a well-rounded educational experience that adequately prepares them for college and university level work.

Dropouts and At-Risk Students

Despite the billions poured into public education year

after year, Texas does have a significant problem with its increasing dropout rate particularly with at-risk students, and its offsetting decreasing retention rates. According to the National Center for Education Statistics (NCES), a **dropout** is "a student who is enrolled in public school in Grades 7-12, does not return to finish school the following fall, is not expelled, and does not graduate, receive a GED, continued school outside the public school system, begin college, or die."[65] The Texas Education Agency (TEA) findings indicate that:

a) Of the 2,376,528 students who attended Grades 7-12 in Texas public schools during the 2016-2017 school year, 1.4 percent were reported to have dropped out, unchanged from the previous year. The number of dropouts in Grades 7-12 decreased to 33,050, a 1.2 percent decrease from the 33,466 students who dropped out in 2015-16.

b) A total of 21,171 students in the class of 2017 dropped out over a four-year span. In each year after the first year of high school, a majority of students who dropped out were one or more grade behind the grade expected for the class.

c) In 2016-2017, a total of 2,754 students dropped out of Grades 7-8, and 30,296 dropped out of Grades 9-12. The Grades 7-8 and Grades dropout rates were 0.3 percent and 1.9 percent respectively.

d) Across the first largest racial/ethnic groups in 2016-2017, the grades 7-12 dropout rate was highest for African-American students (2.1%), followed by Hispanic (1.7%), multiracial (1.0%), White (0.8%), and Asian (0.4%).

e) The Grades 7-122 dropout rate for males (1.6%) was higher than the rates for females (1.1%) in 2016-2017.

f) In 2016-2017, the Grades 7-12 dropout rate for students identified as economically disadvantaged was 1.7 percent. By contrast, the rate for students not identified as economically disadvantaged was 1.0 percent. Economically disadvantaged students accounted for 69.0 percent of Grades 7-12 dropouts.[66]

Conversely, the TEA measures **completion rates** defined as "the percentage of students from a class of beginning seventh or ninth graders who graduate, receive General Educational Development (GED) certificates, or are still enrolled in the fall after the class graduates."[67] Traditionally, dropouts missing only a few courses away from high school graduation could complete their high school programs through a General Education Development (GED) Certificate. In 2018, the TEA announced TxCHSE, a new program that gives these individuals three avenues to complete their high school programs: the traditional GED, the High School Equivalency Test (hiSET), and the Test Assessing Secondary Completion (TACS).

There are several reasons why students just drop out of school. First, an academically underprepared student will soon fall behind in his/her studies, become frustrated, and eventually leave school. Second, many students from low-income families must work to supplement the family income. The appeal of a full time minimum-wage job is sometimes overpowering to a young teenager trying to balance school work with a part-time job. Third, the alarming rise in teen pregnancies has led to an increase in the feminization of poverty, as young mothers fail to return to public school after giving birth. Their limited education and work skills place them on the welfare rolls. Fourth, although educators do not want to admit it, a rote uninspiring school curriculum will "turn off" some students who see no value whatsoever to an education.

These trends can be reserved through, once again, innovative reforms that truly meet the needs of the student and not the needs of the school districts or the Texas Legislature. The academically underprepared student can benefit from small-sized classes that provide more one-on-one quality time with the teacher. There are also pilot programs that actually teach parents how to help their children with their homework assignments. These students need positive reinforcement to overcome their defeatism and lack of self-esteem.

The Texas Legislature did take steps to prevent school districts from just expelling disruptive students. In the past, school administrators could permanently expel a student but still receive state reimbursement money for that student. In 1995, the Texas Legislature mandated that disciplinary problem children had to be sent to alternative schools in order for the school district to continue to receive funding for those students. At the alternative school, students are supposed to receive behavior-related counseling as well as the opportunity to continue with their academic programs. It is hoped that eventually these students will be able to return to their original schools.

To meet the needs of working students, the public school system could offer night classes, weekend schooling, and part-time school programs. There should be no magic timetable demanding that students must successfully graduate from high school at eighteen. A five- or six-year high school program may be the answer for the working teen. Few high schools in Texas offer night or weekend school programs or internet course offerings. Also, few schools offer parenting skills classes or provide on-campus day care services for teenage mothers. In many respects, the traditional approach to education punishes rather than assists these young mothers desiring to complete their educations. Returning meaningful academic freedom back to the teachers would provide the flexibility for instructors to tailor their teaching approach to meet the needs of the audience—the students. Experimental teaching styles might prevent students from seeing school as a "waste of time." These policy recommendations will not totally eliminate the state's dropout problems; however, a substantial reversal of the trend could be accomplished if both legislators and school board members would actually address the needs of these at-risk students.

The Teaching Profession

The quest for better schools, higher student test scores, and higher graduation/completion rates offset with declining dropout rates rests primarily on the shoulders of a highly professionally trained, positively motivated, and dedicate cadre of teachers, principals, librarians, and support staff. However, Texas is seeing this valuable pool of resources dwindle every year as more and more veteran teachers and other educational professions leave the field. Across the state, teachers share the same complaints of low salaries, stress, job burnout, too much paperwork, poor working conditions, and lack of support from their school administrators and board members. Nationwide even when the economy is booming, "a third of people who enter teaching leave the profession within three years. After five years, 46 percent of those teachers are gone."[68] Despite the increase in the number of college graduates with teaching certificates, it is estimated that in Texas alone "350,000 certified teachers aren't teaching," opting for higher paying but less stressful positions in the business sector.[69] Why?

Basically, teachers are tired of being the scapegoat for every failure within the public school system. They feel that they are underpaid professionals treated as second-class citizens subjected to rules made by legislators and bureaucrats without their input. Perpetually denied an active role in school management and curriculum decisions, teachers are being blamed for the disappointing results of poorly conceived and implemented policies that they did not create in the first place. A 1997 article in the *Dallas Morning News* summed it up: "put another way, low pay, poor benefits and inferior working conditions are driving good people out of the teaching profession in Texas

in alarming rates."[70] Unfortunately, little has changed. In particular, the salary situation is critical as many teachers often work part-time jobs just to make ends meet. With the exception of the 2011 legislative session, teachers have been given a marginal pay increase or a cost of living adjustment of 2 to 3 percent. However, every tangible increase has been applied to just the minimum starting salary levels. In other words, a Texas teacher's salary has been increased just enough to keep up with the increases in prices. Teachers are not gaining financially. Over the years, the Texas Legislature has raised only the minimum starting salary, leaning the rest of the state's teachers at the mercy of their individual school district board members to grant them any pay increase. At best, seasoned teachers received the customary yearly costs of living increase between 2 and 3 percent. Ranking 13th among her sister states, the average starting salary for a teacher in the Texas public schools is $40,725 for a nine-month contract. The average salary of all Texas public school teachers is $52,575, ranking the state 25th highest among her sister states. "The national average starting salary is $38,617, while the average teacher salary in America (non-starting) is $58,950."[71]

The Battle of School Vouchers

Since 1997, the Texas Legislature has been battling over the most controversial issue of its education legislative concerns—vouchers. However, the measure died in a House subcommittee. A **voucher system** is "a government program that issues redeemable coupons to eligible citizens to purchase services on the open market."[72] The conservative wing of the Republican Party adopted the position that parents should be able to choose whether their children attend public or private schools. To ease the financial costs of private tuition, parents could apply for a state-funded voucher. Supporters of the voucher movement gained powerful voices in Austin with George W. Bush and Rick Perry. As lieutenant. governor, Perry commented that "those parents should be free to send their children to other public, private or religious schools. That freedom—that choice—will give those children a chance to get the education they need to achieve their dreams. And that freedom—that choice—will provide our low-performing schools with another enticement to improve."[73] The voucher plan continues to be advocated by the Coalition for School Choice, the Texas Cities for a Sound Economy, and the San Antonio-based Children's Educational Opportunity Foundation whose members include two conservative groups backed by Dr. James

Leininger, namely, the Texas Justice Foundation and the Texas Public Policy Foundation. Those opposing school voucher programs include the National Education Association (NEA), San Antonio's Edgewood Independent School District, the Texas Freedom Network, the Texas Association of School Boards, and the Coalition for Equity and Excellence in Public Education. They believe that the voucher system takes state funding away from property-poor school districts. They contend that low-performing schools located in property-poor districts will be unable to afford the very tools they need to reverse dismal student performance levels.

The United States Supreme Court entered in the fray when it upheld the use of public tax dollars to provide vouchers to children to attend both public and private or parochial schools. This ruling has left the door wide open for the Texas Legislature to adopt its own state-funded voucher program.

The Sage of Public School Financing in Texas

Regardless of the state's economic viability, the most serious and chronic problem confronting the state's public school system is the funding inequity between property-rich and property-poor districts. The root of the problem rests with how the Texas Legislature funds its public schools. The burden is really shared between the Texas Legislature and the individual local school districts. The federal government has increased its financial role by giving in-kind money to school districts to service the educational needs of underprivileged and physically and mentally challenged students. Funding approximately 65 percent of the total public school budget, the state's share of the funding comes from the general revenue fund. The bulk of the money in the fund comes from general sales and motor fuel taxes, and the interest on investments from the **Permanent School Fund (PSF)** and the **Foundation School Program (FSP)**. At the beginning of the 2017-2018 fiscal year, the beginning cash balance of the Permanent School Fund was $3,450,773,207. The August 31, 2018, ending balance after deducting yearly expenditures was $4,295,156,274.[74] A dedicated fund established in 1854, the PSF consists of revenues from the lease and sale of state lands, royalties received for oil, gas, and natural resources, and the state's offshore oil deposits known as the Tidelands. The money available to Texas public schools is given through the **Available School Fund (ASF)** consisting of income earned from investments from the PSF. ASF money is allocated on a standard per-student basis. Consequently, school districts with larger enrollments receive more state funding than those with smaller enrollments. Since 1949, the Texas Legislature has augmented the FSP to enable property-poor districts to make up their income differences. These additional funds are allocated based upon the difference between a district's per-student expenditure level and the state-mandated per-student expenditure level.

Individual school districts raise money through property taxes. A minimum-maximum scale is established by the Texas Legislature allowing districts to set their own rates within this range. All school districts must spend a set amount for each child enrolled in their schools; however, school districts can keep those dollars above the state mandated level. Known as **enrichment money**, these revenues can be used at the district's discretion. The inequity in funding occurs because property-poor districts can barely meet state per capita expenditure levels by charging the maximum percentage of tax at 100 percent of the assessed value of the property. There is no enrichment money for the property-poor districts. They could definitely use additional revenue for building renovations, construction, purchase of technological instructional equipment, and salary increases.

School districts are constitutionally restricted to using property taxes as their sole source of revenue outside of state and federal funding. There are several problems associated with property taxes. First, property appraisals in Texas must be based on **ad valorem**, that is, the fair market value of the property. The quality of the surrounding neighborhood affects the fair market value of a residential property. A well-kept house nestled in a deteriorating area will be assessed at less than its actual value than if it were sitting in a "nice" neighborhood, resulting in a loss of tax revenues. Second, the taxing authority determines the percentage of the property subjected to taxation. An assessment ratio set at less than 50 percent of the market value in a property-rich area will still generate more revenue than a house assessed at a ratio of 100 percent in a property-poor area. Third, property taxes are regressive tax programs that place a disproportionate burden on middle- and lower-income groups. Fourth, school districts are tied directly to the ups and downs of the housing market, particularly in resale values. When property values are high, schools will gain revenue. When property values are down, schools loose revenue. Fifth, property taxes have become a hot bed issues for Republican candidates. Lt. Governor Dan Patrick introduce in the last session an unsuccessful attempt to legislatively mandate that city, county, and school districts lower their property rates. He also wanted to set a minimum to maximum tax rate range that if a governing body wants to exceed the range, it would require voter approval. He introduced similar legislation in the 2019 Legislative Session. The two sources of revenue for school districts are property taxes and state funding. Patrick's proposal just cuts the property tax revenues but does not include any provision for the state to compensate school districts for the lost in property tax revenues they would be facing if his proposal passes.

The creation of property-poor school districts is directly tied to white flight and business relocations. The more affluent Anglo and upper mobile minorities left their "older" neighborhoods behind for the "newer" or "nicer" suburbs. Subsequently, businesses moved along with their clientele—the more affluent. Economically depressed school districts must recapture the wealth by fixing up the neighborhoods, cleaning up the presumed image that their neighborhood is riddled with crime, and courting businesses back. It is, in most instances, a hopeless situation. Confronted with the realization that property-poor school districts would never be able to catch up led a group of parents to take action. The battle lines over equitable funding were drawn in 1969 when Demetrio Rodriguez on behalf of fifteen parents in the San Antonio's Edgewood Independent School District filed a lawsuit challenging the state's funding system as a violation of the United States Constitution's Fourteenth Amendment's equal protection clause. The Rodriguez case centered on the argument that the inequities in property values within each district's boundary lines naturally lead to the creation of property-rich and property-poor districts. The litigants charged that it was up to the state to address the inequities by providing property-poor districts with the additional money to even the playing field. The first Edgewood case was titled *San Antonio Independent School District v Rodriguez*. In 1971, a lower federal court ruled that indeed the state's funding method was unconstitutional. This ruling was overturned by a federal appellate court. This decision was appealed to the United States Supreme Court. The two primary questions before the Court were whether poverty was a suspected class deserving special protection under the Civil Rights Act, and whether education was a fundamental right under the Fourteenth Amendment to the Constitution. On March 21, 1973, the Court overturned the lower appellate court's ruling by claiming that the funding system in Texas, although not fair, was definitely constitutional. In writing for the majority, Justice Powell tackled the two major issues:

First, in support of their charge that the system discriminates against the "poor," appellees have made no effort to demonstrate that it operates to the peculiar disadvantage of any class fairly definable as indigent, or as composed of persons whose incomes are beneath any designed poverty level. Indeed, there is reason to believe that the poorest families are not necessarily clustered in the poorest property districts. . . . Second, . . . lack of personal resources has not occasioned an absolute deprivation of the desired benefit [education]. The argument here is not that the children in districts having relatively low assessable property values are receiving no public education; rather in that they are receiving a poorer quality education than that available to children that have more assessable wealth . . . At least where wealth is involved the Equal Protection Clause does not required absolute equality or precisely equal advantage.[75]

Property-poor districts lost the first round. Round two begins in 1984 when the Edgewood Independent School District in San Antonio in conjunction with twelve of the state's poorest school districts sued the State of Texas through the Commissioner of the State Board of Education, William Kirby, on the grounds that the current public school financing plan was an unconstitutional violation of the Texas Constitution. Article VII of the current state constitution guarantees an equal educational opportunity to every resident of the state. *Edgewood v Kirby* renewed the see-saw battle in the courts and the Texas Legislature over fiscal disparities between property-poor and property-rich school districts. The Edgewood attorneys interpreted the term "equal" includes funding. In 1987, State District Judge Harley Clark ruled that the method used to fund the state's public school system was indeed unconstitutional. However, the Third Court of Appeals overruled Clark by ruling that the system was indeed unfair to the property-poor districts but constitutional. On October 2, 1989, the Texas Supreme Court unanimously ruled the funding process unconstitutional. The Court gave the Texas Legislature until May 1990, to devise an equitable plan.

Governor Clements called a special session of the Texas Legislature to avoid court sanctions. The Texas Legislature decided to provide an additional $528 million for school financing. The money was allocated primarily to property-poor districts. However, State District Judge F. Scott McCown declared this fix unacceptable and unconstitutional. In January 1991, the Texas Supreme Court gave the Texas Legislature until April 1 (later extended to April 15) to design a suitable plan. On April 11, 1991, the Texas Legislature announced a "**Robin**

Hood" approach whereby millions of dollars in enrichment money from the wealthy districts would be shifted to the poorer school districts. The expected happened as two wealthy school districts in Dallas joined forces with the Alamo Heights Independent School District in San Antonio and filed their own law suit, claiming that the new funding plan created in essence a state property tax. After hearing this round of arguments, the Texas Supreme Court ruled 7 to 2 in 1992 that this latest financial reform package was unconstitutional. A frustrated Court set a date for June 1, 1993, for the Texas Legislature to draft a suitable constitutional option, or they would seek to close down the public school system.

State leaders, however, opted to put the Robin Hood concept on the ballot by declaring a special election. The voters soundly rejected it. On May 31, 1993, Governor Ann Richards signed Senate Bill 7, which mandated that the property-rich districts share their wealth with the property-poor districts. This legislation was "a complex plan that included two tiers of funding, and required districts whose property wealth was above a certain level to choose from among five options to help spread the wealth around. If a district didn't pick one of the five options, it would be consolidated by force" with another district.[76] The state courts ruled this plan constitutional. However, round three was a challenge to the plan filed by the West Orange-Cove Consolidated and Port Neches-Grove school districts in Southeast Texas, Coppell School District in Dallas County and La Porte School District near Houston. Three dozen school districts filed documents in support of the challenge. The suit did not deny that property-poor school districts needed additional money. The property-rich districts involved in the law suit felt that they should not continue to be forced to shoulder the state's responsibility to ensure proper funding of all of the state's public schools. The state court ruled against the property-rich districts.

Round four began with Governor Rick Perry calling a special session of the Texas Legislature in April 2004, to hopefully pass House Bill 1. This legislation would have provided approximately $18 billion for education from an increase in the state sales tax, a employer-paid employee tax, and new taxes on boats, Internet services and home repairs. Another House bill would have used revenue from legalized slot machines to fund schools. Both measures failed. In September 2004, 300 school districts representing both sides of the funding issue filed a lawsuit against the State of Texas. A state judge ruled in November 2004, that the current funding system was, once again, unconstitutional. The judge gave the Texas Legislature a new deadline, October 2005, to fix it or he would order all of the schools to close their doors. While the State Attorney General was filing an appeal to the Texas Supreme Court, Governor Perry was opening the 2005 session of the Texas Legislature with the warning that fixing the school funding mess had to be the number one priority. Coming up empty handed, Perry called the legislature into special session. The session ended with an agreement that property taxes should no longer be the primary source of revenue but lawmakers failed to come up with a replacement revenue source. Called into a second special session, the Texas Legislature toyed with just plugging the loopholes in the state's franchise tax program. This too failed to win approval. Meanwhile, Perry appointed former Comptroller John Sharp to head a special committee to find an alternative funding source. The Texas Supreme Court issued its ruling in the pending lawsuit. The Court sided with the various school districts that the current funding plan was an unconstitutional state property tax and gave the Legislature a June 1, 2006, deadline or else. Perry called another special session with the sole agenda being to find a legal alternative. Lawmakers did pass a proposal to drop property tax rates while at the same time, provide additional funding to the schools by imposing a new business tax, using a portion of the motor vehicle sales tax, and upping the taxes on a pack of cigarettes to $1. Perry used an executive order to mandate that all public schools dedicate approximately 65 percent of their own tax revenues for classroom expenses including instructional salaries, textbooks, supplies, and equipment.

Round five saw the Texas Legislature in 2011 slashing public education budgets to address an anticipated deficit in the state's budget. As predicted, The Texas Taxpayer & Student Fairness Coalition composed of approximately 600 public school districts, taxpayers, and parents filed a lawsuit against the state claiming "the state's public school finance system is unconstitutional because it does not treat Texas taxpayers and school children fairly."[77] The sixth major lawsuit challenging the state's funding of its public school is unique in that for once, the property-rich and property-poor school districts were on the same side. They point out "per student funding in Texas now ranges from less than $5,000 per child in some school districts to more than $10,000 in others."[78] On February 4, 2013, State District Judge John Dietz ruled that once again, the state's method of funding its public schools is unconstitutional. In his opinion, Dietz pointed out "the state's school finance system is unconstitutional not only because of inadequate funding and flaws in the way it distributes money to districts, but also because it imposes a de facto state property tax."[79] Dietz, however, decided to see if the Texas Legislature could fix the funding problem and "ordered a new trial four months later, after the Texas Legislature restored $3.0 billion of the $5.4 billion of the biennial public education budget the lawmakers cut in the 2011 session when they tackled a $27 billion shortfall."[80] While the plaintiffs were pleased, then Texas Attorney General Greg Abbott was not. He charged that the "school districts sued because their leaders were unhappy about being required to do more for less."[81] Meanwhile, he tried unsuccessfully to have Judge Dietz removed from the case on the grounds that Dietz was biased in favor of the school districts. In September 2014, Abbott filed an appeal. In January 2015, the Texas Legislature was in session discussing various public school finance proposals as the two warring parties were back in court. Once again, the lawyers for the plaintiffs argued "the Legislature failed to bridge funding gaps between wealthy and poor school districts despite partial restoration of cuts."[82] The state's attorneys countered by emphasizing "the state has addressed plaintiffs' concerns by injecting more money into the system, revamping graduation standards and reducing the number of end-of-course assessments from fifteen to five."[83] In May 2016, the Texas Supreme Court ruled in favor of the state's public school funding system. However, the Court did strongly suggest, but did not mandate, that the Texas Legislature should seriously devise the appropriate reform measures to address it funding options.

Whether it be round one or round six, property-poor districts have a legitimate claim that poor funding does lead to poorly prepared students. Upgraded equipment, textbooks, modern classroom facilities, and highly qualified teachers cost money. These property-poor districts make do with what they have. Unfortunately, it is the children in these districts who suffer because they are not provided with the same quality of tools as their peers from wealthier districts. Imagine that a potentially brilliant pianist will never develop his/her talent to the fullest if they are unfortunate enough to attend a property-poor school district that can only provide him/her with an out-of-date poorly tuned broken piano or, worse yet, a xeroxed copy of a piano keyboard! The job market demands word processing skills for secretaries that cannot be learned on a manual typewriter. Yes, Texas does provide an equal access to an education for all of its children. No, they do not have equal access to the quality tools needed for a good education.

Higher Education

The first public college established in Texas, Texas Agricultural and Mechanical College, now known as Texas A & M University (A&M), opened its doors in 1876. Originally chartered in 1839, the University of Texas (UT) launched its academic programs in 1883. The number of students enrolling in the state's institutions of higher learning is impressive.

> Enrollment in Texas public independent, career and private colleges and universities in Fall, 2016 totaled 1,521,216 students, an increase of 33,070 from 1,488,146 in Fall, 2015. Enrollment in Fall, 2016 in the 39 public universities was 636,750, an increase over 619,175 in Fall, 2015. Health-related institutions had enrollment in 2016 of 27,353, an increase over 26,363 in Fall, 2015. The state's public community college districts, Lamar State Colleges and Texas Technical College System, which offers two-year degree programs, reported Fall, 2016 enrollment totaling 732,877 students, an increase over 719,176 reported in Fall, 2015. Enrollments for Fall, 2016 at independent colleges and universities increased to 124,236 students, up from 123,432 students from Fall, 2015.[84]

Enrollments are rising every year as more and more young Texans realize that their economic and social success is dependent upon a college degree, not just a high school diploma.

The University of Texas and Texas A&M systems are among the wealthiest state-support universities in the nation. The Republic of Texas initially reserved fifty leagues, or 211,540 acres of land, for these two schools. The Constitution of 1876 went a step further by setting aside an additional million acres alone for UT and its branch campuses. In the 1930s, the Santa Rita Well, now located on the UT campus, hit a lucrative pool of liquid gold. Two-thirds of the revenues went to UT with the remaining third allocated to A&M. "By 1976 the University of Texas endowment ran second only to Harvard, somewhere in the neighborhood of $1,000,000,000, enabling its regents to build a magnificent and sometimes extravagant plant, and lifting the school out of the class of its sister state universities in nearby states."[85] The UT and A&M systems continue to receive the bulk of the state's budget for higher education while leaving the state's other colleges and community colleges to battle over their small share of the budgetary pie.

Higher education funding for the state's colleges and universities is a combination of state appropriations and investment earnings from the **Permanent University Fund (PUF)** held in the **Available University Fund (AUF)**. The PUF was established through the 1876 Texas Constitution as a dedicated fund for UT and Texas A & M. The fund consists of state land, the sale and lease of the properties, and royalties derived from the land's natural resources. At the end of the 2017-2018 fiscal year, the PUF earned $1,033,805,140 from its investments and other revenue streams.[86] The earnings from the PUF investments are distributed from the AUF with two-thirds earmarked for UT and one-third for A&M. Schools within the UT and A&M systems receive their money in turn from the Austin and College Station campuses with the main campuses keeping the bulk of the money. In addition, all colleges and universities including UT and A&M receive state appropriations allocated on a per-student rate. Schools with higher enrollments receive more state money. Colleges and universities can receive additional revenue from federal grants, private donations, and, of course, student tuition and fees plus revenues from their athletic programs. In the case of community colleges, their funding from the state is augmented from property tax revenues and student tuition and fees. The Texas Legislature recognized the inequities in its higher education funding by creating the **Higher Education Assistance Fund (HEAF)** to fund building repairs and construction for those facilities not funded by the PUF.

The state's fifty-four community college districts received $1,035,663,324 from the state in 2018.[87] The Texas Legislature always allocates less to community colleges since they are special district governing units with their own taxing authority, a right not granted to state-supported colleges and universities. Community colleges are funded by state appropriations based on enrollment, district assessed property taxes, student tuition and fees, and federal grant programs.

Higher Education Governance

The **Texas Higher Education Coordinating Board (THECB)** oversees the operation of the state's four- and two-year colleges and universities. The Board is composed of eighteen members appointed by the governor with Senate approval for six-year staggered terms. Although day to day governance rests with the individual campuses, the THECB's primary duties are to determine the function of each institution, faculty workloads, compensation and benefits packages, use of campus facilities and resources,

curriculum design, and degree plans. Accreditation issues are the privy of the **Southern Association of Colleges and Schools (SACS)** headquartered in Atlanta, Georgia. A SACS review is conducted periodically to ensure that institutions of higher learning are fulfilling their obligations and responsibilities to the educational process.

Public universities and colleges are governed by their own **board of regents**. These nine-member boards are staffed by gubernatorial appointments with Senate confirmation for six-year staggered terms. On the other hand, community colleges are governed by popularly elected **boards of trustees**. Board members are elected from single-member districts for usually six-year staggered terms. Both boards are supposed to leave the day-to-day operations to the chancellors of the college districts and university systems and, subsequently, to the presidents of the individual campuses within each system. However, some board members whether appointed or elected, do possess the same micromanagement techniques often observed in local school board activities.

Problems in Higher Education

Student Enrollment

Although enrollments in both four- and two-year universities and colleges continue to increase, the number of students actually completing their degree requirements at one of the state's higher education institutions follows the national trend—decreasing numbers of individuals crossing the stage with a bachelor's degree in hand. While there are more men actually enrolling into college than women, more women are graduating from college than men. In 2016, nationwide, 1,920,718 bachelors degrees were awarded with 1,099 awarded to women and 822 to men   The usual assumption is that college students will complete their bachelor's program of study within four years. Yet, national and state trends indicate otherwise. In Texas, only 27.6 percent of students enrolled in the state's public colleges and universities completed their degree programs in four years while it took another 51.7 percent six years to earn their bachelor's degrees. The national average among four-year public colleges and universities is 33.3 percent in four years and 57.6 percent in six or more years.[89]

Of course, part of the problem rests with the lack of financial resources. Texans used to brag about how low tuition costs were for attending the state's public universities and colleges. Tuition was kept low because the Texas Legislature set a ceiling on tuition rates. With the state gradually decreasing its state per-student funding allocations, the campuses made up their budget shortfalls by dramatically charging more each semester for parking, fees for science laboratories and libraries, dorm and food costs, etc. During the 2003 legislative session, state legislators passed a measure permitting the governing bodies of all state-funded colleges and universities to set their own tuition rates subject to review by a legislative oversight committee. The rationale was to shift a portion of the state's financial obligations unto the backs of the colleges and universities. However, instead of the state increasing its contribution to higher education, the burden is placed upon the student body. There was a "gentleman's agreement" that once the cap was lifted, college and university administrators would gradually and prudently raise tuition. The agreement fell by the way side as tuition has dramatically increased by approximately 62 percent since 2003. An unsuccessful legislative effort would have restored the cap but at the current tuition levels. As long as financial aid packages were adjusted every semester to match tuition increases, students were able to still afford to attend college. The 2011 Texas Legislative session's budget cuts sliced a huge chunk from the state's student loan program. Also, the federal government while increasing the dollar amount of Pell grant awards has attached more punitive sanctions on those students with poor academic performance who need financial aid to continue their education. Of course, students and parents alike are concerned about the rising costs of a college education.

The civil rights movement of the 1960s also impacted university admission programs and financial aid assistance packages. Many campuses across the nation adopted minority-based scholarship programs designed to encourage Hispanics and African Americans to seek college degrees. All of these programs were dealt a near fatal blow when the 5th United States Circuit Court of Appeals ruled in **Hopwood v Texas** that these programs were unconstitutional. In Texas, then Attorney General Dan Morales cautioned state-funded public colleges and universities to omit minority admissions programs from their recruitment plans. Consequently, minority enrollment declined considerably due to the lack of scholarship opportunities. The United States Supreme Court partially reversed the *Hopwood* decision in its 2003 ruling involving the minority admissions standards established by the University of Michigan. Consequently, Texas colleges and universities made the appropriate adjustments and re-established their minority recruitment programs. Absolutely, scholarships, grants and financial

aid loans are necessary for low-income students to have an opportunity to attend college.

Faculty-related Issues

Higher education suffers from some of the same problems associated with the public schools. Faculty members are underpaid and subject to the same marginal salary increases granted to public school teachers. The higher education field is very competitive. Obviously, UT and Texas A&M can offer more lucrative salary treatment than other four-year private and public colleges and universities. College-level faculty members enjoy two privileges not extended to public school teachers in Texas: academic freedom and tenure. Academic freedom, however, is not absolute; faculty members feel the added pressure of being "politically correct" in their classroom presentations. Boards of Regents are well known for dismissing professors whose views conflict with the philosophy of the institution. Moreover, tenure is not automatically granted to all faculty members. Many higher education institutions will retain faculty in a "tenure-track" status and release them as soon as they are eligible for tenure. Consequently, low salaries, increased committee activities, increased classroom sizes, more pressure to teach more classes per semester, and the threat of denying tenure are costing Texas's colleges and universities dearly, as excellent, highly qualified faculty members are leaving the field for private sector employment opportunities.

Researchers or Classroom Instructors

Four-year colleges and universities are often turned into laboratories and research facilities for business and industry. The business sector donates millions of dollars to fund academic programs complementary to their business fields. The major oil companies only promote engineering, petroleum, geological and business degree programs, while the pharmaceutical companies turn to university labs to research new medical breakthroughs. Both sides win. A major "discovery" brings additional money and name recognition to the universities, while businesses reap the benefits of marketing a new product. Universities often serve as employment agencies for those businesses that donate heavily to endowment, scholarship, or building programs. If a university is rated as a Tier I research institution, millions of dollars pour into key science, mathematics, engineering, and biomedical programs. If a university is rated as one of the leading law schools in the state or the country, that recognition helps to market the university's law program to potential students since big-name firms will hire its graduates. Tenure is often granted more on how often a professor publishes and conducts research rather than on classroom teaching performance. The Select Committee on Higher Education even recommended to the Texas Legislature in 1987 a two-tier university system with community colleges teaching freshman and sophomore courses, while colleges and some universities teaching just junior and senior level programs, while main campuses such as UT in Austin and A&M in College Station would focus on graduate level work and research.

The recommendation of the Select Committee did not pass the legislature's scrutiny in 1987 and fell upon deaf ears in 2011. The Texas Legislature wanted to take the professor out of the lab and back into the classroom. The downfall to focusing one's senior faculty members on research and development is that traditional courses are taught by TAs or teaching assistants. Students do not receive a discount on their tuition because the professor that they thought was going to teach their class turns out to be a doctorate student hired as a teaching assistant. Several legislators believe that budget dollars are wasted when the professor is not in the classroom. Consequently, they wanted the professor to do both—teach a full load and research at the same time. During the 2011 Texas Legislative session, legislation was introduced to eliminate Tier I status. The measure died simply because the four-year institutions rightfully asked that if they were to be denied the opportunity to bring millions to their campuses with one research grant or proposal, would the state provide them with enough money so they would not have to go elsewhere for their funding? The answer was no.

Community College Issues

Community colleges are constantly trying to overcome the unfounded notation that they are second-rate institutions of higher learning. These two-year colleges provide a valuable service to the community through their open-door policies that provide a first-rate education at very affordable costs to a segment of the population that probably could not afford a full four-year degree program at a public institution much less a private college or university. Community colleges also service the educational needs of nontraditional students: working parents, older students, the economically disadvantaged, non-college bound individuals seeking occupational and work skills training, and the academically underprepared.

The transition from the high school environment to a two- or four-year college and university can be unsettling even for the most academically prepared student. However, large segments of the nation's entering college freshmen do not even meet the skills levels required to successfully pass college-level mathematics or writing and reading intensive courses. To help these students to "catch up," state governments like Texas mandate that colleges and universities enroll these students into non-college credit remediation courses. The four-year schools basically shifted the remediation programs onto the community colleges without, of course, additional money to hire faculty and counselors for remediation programs. The state, however, did grant contact hour reimbursement for these courses to the community colleges. The remediation programs have helped to identify academically underprepared students and provide them with the skills they need to eventually pass college-level courses. The problem is that many students have to repeat these courses two to three times before they acquire acceptable proficiency levels. Across the nation, legislators facing huge deficits are reevaluating the need for remediation and ESOL (English As A Second Language) courses. These programs have become a political hot potato for conservatives.

Conclusions: The Challenges Ahead

Although the 2011 special session of the Texas Legislature did cut nearly $4 billion in funding for the state's public schools and institutions of higher learning, the 2013, 2015, and 2017 legislative sessions have seen some of the funding restored with legislation introduced increasing budgetary dollars to education. The Texas Legislature has stressed the need for both public schools and higher education institutions to address dropout rates, non-completion rates, and student success. Funding is allocated at the beginning of the school term with the anticipation that every student registered in August will, as in the case of the public schools, still be in school in May. The sentiment is that tax dollars are being wasted with every public school student who drops out or is removed from the school due to disciplinary problems. Should not the state reimburse the schools at the end of the school year on a per-student basis of completers? The same argument is used for state-supported colleges and universities. So the dilemma for both public and higher education is how to keep students in the classroom so they can "walk the stage" with a diploma. The Texas Legislature has tried to speed up the journey to a four-year degree by encouraging high schools to offer dual credit courses whereby high school students take college-level courses on the high school campus for both public school and college credit. The Texas Legislature also introduced the early college program whereby qualified high school students from freshman to seniors can attend college courses taught on a college campus. At the community colleges, qualifying high school students can earn an associates degree with sixty college credit hours in the same year they earn their high school diploma. Both dual credit and early college programs are offered either free of charge or at a reduce tuition rate, saving parents the money they would have spent if their son or daughter had taken the traditional route to college of finishing high school then entering a four-year college program as a freshman. Legislation also included the three-peat rule whereby a student taking a college-level course for the third time would pay out-of-district or out-of-state-tuition for that course. The thought was that if students knew they would have to pay about three times as much for one course, they would not drop their courses so frequently. The task of financing the state's public school systems, as well as its institutions of higher learning, is a never ending budget concern. However, in the case of public education, it should not take a lawsuit to prompt the Texas Legislature to take the appropriate steps to ensure that every public school student in this state has an equal educational opportunity. What is woefully obvious is that members of the Texas Legislature are very good at articulating their concerns but fall short of initiating the appropriate corrective legislation to address those concerns.

Chapter Notes

[1]George Klosko, *History of Political Theory: An Introduction*, Vol. 2, Modern Political Theory, (New York, New York: Thomson/Wadsworth, 1995), 247.

[2]*Treasury of Presidential Quotations*, Caroline Thomas Harnsberger, ed., (Chicago, Illinois: Follet Publishing, 1964), 77-78.

[3]"The Establishment of the Texas School System-January 31, 1854," *Documents of Texas History*, Ernest Wallace, David M. Vigness and George B. Ward, eds., (Austin, Texas: State House Press, 1994), 181.

[4]*https://www.edweek.org*

[5]Ibid.

[6]*State of Texas Annual Cash Report 2018: Revenues and Expenditures of State Funds for the Year Ended August 31, 2018*, (Austin, Texas: Comptroller of Public Accounts, 2018), 17.

[7]Joshua Fechter, "School-Fund Solution Blasted," *San Antonio Express-News*, (Sunday, March 2, 2015), A3.

[8]*Lyndon Johnson and American Liberalism: A Brief Biography with Documents*, Bruce J. Schulman, ed., 2nd ed., (Boston, Massachusetts: Bedford/St. Martins: 2007), 95.

[9]Steven A. Peterson and Thomas H. Rasmussen, *State and Local Politics*, (New York, New York: McGraw-Hill, 1994), 296.

[10]Ibid.

[11]Anjetta McQueen, "States Are Unsure How Clinton's Education Package Will Fly," *San Antonio Express-News*, (Sunday, January 31, 1999), 26A.

[12]Ron Fournier, "Bush Signs $26 Billion Education Reform Bill," *San Antonio Express-News*, (Wednesday, January 9, 2002), 1A.

[13]Ibid.

[14]Ben Feller, "With Funds at Stake, Schools Assure Feds They Allow Prayer," *San Antonio Express-News*, (Tuesday, May 13, 2003), 4A.

[15]Ibid.

[16]McQueen, "States Are Unsure How Clinton's Education Package Will Fly," 26A.

[17]Randolph Campbell, *Gone to Texas: A History of the Lone Star State*, (New York, New York: Oxford University Press, 2003), 228.

[18]Rupert Richardson, Ernest Wallace and Adrian Anderson, *Texas: The Lone Star State*, 4th ed., (Englewood Cliffs, New Jersey: Prentice-Hall, 1981), 207.

[19]Ibid.

[20]Campbell, 229.

[21]Ibid., 230.

[22]Robert A. Calvert, Arnoldo De Leon and Gregg Cantrell, *The History of Texas*, 3rd ed., (Wheeling, Illinois: Harlan Davidson, Inc., 2002), 288.

[23]Rupert Richardson, Adrian Anderson, Cary D. Wintz and Ernest Wallace, *Texas: The Lone Star State*, 9th ed., (Upper Saddle River, New Jersey: Pearson Education Inc., 2005), 314.

[24]Calvert and De Leon, 289.

[25]Ibid., 320.

[26]Ibid.

[27]"The Gilmer-Aiken School Laws: June 1 and 8, 1949," *Documents of Texas History*, Ernest Wallace, David M. Vigness and George B. Ward, eds., 2nd ed., (Austin, Texas: State House Press, 1994), 277.

[28]Ibid., 279.

[29]Ibid.

[30]Calvert and De Leon, 368.

[31]Clark D. Thomas, "Education Reform in Texas," *Texas Politics: A Reader*, Anthony Champagne and Edward J. Harpham, eds, 2nd ed., (New York, New York: W. W. Norton & Co., 1998), 230.

[32]Nelson C. Dometrius, "Education Policy," *Texas Public Policy*,

Gerry Riposa, ed., (Dubuque, Iowa: Kendall/Hunt, 1987), 47.

[33]Thomas, "Education Reform in Texas," 230.

[34]Randall W. Bland, Alfred B. Sullivan, Robert E. Biles, Charles P. Elliott, Jr., and Beryl E. Pettus, *Texas Government Today*, 5th ed., (Pacific Grove, California: Brooks/Cole, 1992), 408.

[35]Leon W. Blevins, *Texas Government in National Perspective*, (Englewood Cliffs, New Jersey: Prentice-Hall, 1987), 366.

[36]Thomas, "Education Reform in Texas," 225.

[37]*State of Texas Annual Cash Report: Revenue and Expenditures of State Funds for Year Ended, August 31, 2012*, (Austin, Texas: Comptroller of Public Accounts, 2012) 51.

[38]Peggy Fikas, "Legislatures Expected to Push for Tax Relief in '15," *San Antonio Express-News*, (Sunday, December 7, 2014), A3.

[39]*Texas Almanac: 2018-2019*, (Denton, Texas: Texas State Historical Association, 2018), 616.

[40]Ibid.

[41]Ibid. 608.

[42]Ibid. 81.

[43]Fikac, "Legislatures Expected to Push for Tax Relief in '15", A3.

[44]ProQuest, *ProQuest Statistical Abstract of the United States: 2019*, 7th ed., (Bethesda, Maryland, 2018), Table 257, 170.

[45]*Texas Almanac: 2018-2019*, 610.

[46]Edward S. Tijerina, "South San Gets TEA Reprimand," *San Antonio Express-News*, (Tuesday, January 15, 2002), 1A.

[47]Richard D. Bingham and David Hedge, *State and Local Government in a Changing Society*, 2nd ed., (New York, New York: McGraw-Hill, 1991), 304.

[48]Kathy Walt, "Infighting Escalates in State Board of Education," *Houston Chronicle*, (Sunday, March 2, 1997), 1A.

[49]Patricia Kilday Hart, "Right Makes Might," *Texas Monthly*, May, 2002, 70.

[50]Mary Lord, "Remaking History," *U.S. News & World Report*, (November 25, 2002), 46.

[51]Ibid.

[52]Gary Scharrer, "GOP Leaders in Austin Rap History Curriculum," *San Antonio Express-News*, (Wednesday, March 16, 2011), 9A.

[53]Ibid.

[54]Alia Malik, "Group Opposes Textbook on Mexican-Americans," *San Antonio Express News*, (Friday, September 9, 2016), A4.

[55]Brien M. Rosenthal, "Schools Purge Kids from Special Ed," *San Antonio Express News*, (Sunday, October 23, 2016), A1 and A10.

[56]Alejandra Matos, "Court: Texas Broke Special Ed Rule," *San Antonio Express News*, Friday, November 9, 2018), A1-A13.

[57]Brien M. Rosenthal, "Straus Posts Concerns Over Access to Special Ed," *San Antonio Express News* , (Friday, September 16, 2016), A4.

[58]Ibid.

[59]https://hechingerreport.org

[60]Ibid.

[61]Ibid.

[62]Texas Education Agency, *2018 Comprehensive Biennial Report on Texas Public Schools*, (Austin, Texas: Texas Education Agency, 2019), 2.

[63]Jeanne Russell, "TAAS Measures Education Miracle, But Is The Yardstick Flawed," *San Antonio Express-News*, (Sunday, August 15, 1999), 17A.

[64]*Texas Education Agency, 2010 Comprehensive Biennial Report on Texas Public Schools*, (Austin, Texas, 2010), 26.

[65]Department of Assessment and Accountability and Data Quality, *Secondary School Completion and Dropouts in Texas Public Schools: 2007-2008*, (Austin, Texas: Texas Education Agency, July, 2009), 9.

[66]Texas Education Agency, *Secondary School Completion and Dropouts in Texas Public Schools 2016-17*, (Austin, Texas: Texas Education Agency, September, 2018), xii-xiii.

[67]Sharon K. Hughes, "Training, Support Blamed for Teacher Burnout," *San Antonio Express-News*, (Thursday, January 30, 2003), 11A.

[68]Ibid.

[69]John C. Cole, "Teacher Crisis: Poor Pay Drives Away Many Qualified People," *Dallas Morning News*, (Sunday, June 1, 1997), 6J.

[70]http://www.txcharterschools.org

[71]https://www.niche.com

[72]*The Harper Collins Dictionary of American Government and Politics*, Jay M. Shafritz, ed., (New York, New York: HarperCollins Publishers, 1992), 603.

[73]Laura Trolley, "Pro-Voucher Group Rallies at Capitol," *San Antonio Express-News*, (Wednesday, February 17, 1999), 1B.

[74]*State of Texas Annual Cash Report Revenue and Expenditures of State Funds for the Year Ended August 31, 2018*, 142-144.

[75]Ralph A. Rossum and G. Alan Tarr, *American Constitutional Law: Cases and Interpretations*, (New York, New York: St. Martin's Press, 1983), 693-694.

[76]Diana R. Fuentes and Stephanie Scott, "Texas School Finance Law Upheld," *San Antonio Express-News*, (Tuesday, January 31, 1995), 4A.

[77]Gary Scharrer, "Lawsuit Challenged Texas Public School Funding, *The Houston Chronicle*, (October, 11, 2011).

[78]Ibid.

[79]http://www.texastribune.org

[80]Enrique Rangel, "Ruling in Texas School Funding Lawsuit May Come Down on Thursday, *Lubbock Avalanche-Journal*, (August 27, 2014), http://lubbockonline.com

[81]Ibid.

[82]Fechter, A3.

[83]Ibid.

[84]*Texas Almanac: 2018-2019*, 616.

[85]Joe B. Frantz, *Texas: History*, 2nd ed., (New York, New York: W. W. Norton & Company, 1984), 172.

[86]*State of Texas Annual Cash Report: Revenue and Expenditures of State Funds for the Year Ended August 2018*, 144.

[87]Ibid., 20.

[88]*ProQuest Statistical Abstract of the United States: 2019*, Tables 319 and 320, 206 and 207.

[89]http://collegecompletion.chronicle.com

Texans and Their Environment

Oil refinery next to the Gulf of Mexico near Houston, Texas

From the beginning, Americans had a lively awareness of the land and the wilderness. The Jeffersonian faith in the independent farmer laid the foundation for American democracy; and the ever-beckoning, ever-receding frontier left an indelible imprint on American society and the American character. . . . Yet, at the same time that Americans saluted the noble bounty of nature, they also abused and abandoned it. For the first century after independence, we regarded the national environment as indestructible-and proceeded vigorously to destroy it. Not till the time of [George Perkins] Marsh and [Carl] Schurz and [John Wesley] Powell did we begin to understand that our resources were not inexhaustible. Only in the twentieth century have we acted in a systematic way to defend and enrich our natural heritage.[1]

President John Kennedy, 1963

The deteriorating quality of Texas's precious environment is perhaps the most hotly debated issue confronting Texans today. The quest to maintain a delicate balance between the constitutionally protected rights of property owners and the preservation of the environment evokes strong historically and culturally based sentiments that sharply divide public opinion. On the one hand, property owners should be able to use their property in whatever manner they choose. On the other hand, the desire to preserve society depends upon maintaining an ecosystem free of pollution and contamination whereby plant life and wildlife can successfully coexist with people. In every legislative house in this country and in the chambers of the United States Congress there is a yearly battle between environmentalists and property owners with virtually no hope in the future for a peaceful resolution. This chapter explores the complexity of environmental issues in Texas.

Few Texans will deny that irreversible waste and damage has been done to the state's environment. Few regions of our planet have been blessed with the quality and abundance of resources found in Texas.

When Columbus landed in the New World 499 years ago, the land that would become Texas was hardwood forests in the East along the Sabine and other rivers. It was blackland prairie, thick with grass, in a dark slash seemingly drawn with a huge pallet knife from northeast to southwest across the North Central Texas. It was mucky bottom lands, marshes and dunes across a slowly descending plain; windy, trackless tall grass prairie over the high plateau of the Panhandle; strong oak and cedar thickets in the High Country; a moonscape junkyard for giant rocks in the Big Bend; a thorn forest along the Rio Grande.[2]

However, Texans discovered that the state was resource rich and the extraction of these resources would be a vital key to its economic viability. For example, the discovery of vast oil deposits propelled this state into the oil and gas business that consistently pumps billions of dollars into the state's treasury. The state's vast acreage of rich grasslands feed the millions of head of cattle that make Texas the leader in the cattle and ranching industry. The Texas coastline originally served as a port of entry for the region's immigrants and as the center for the flow of exports and imports. The state's lucrative tourist industry has benefited from the beautiful, once pristine coastal areas that are havens for native species of plants, birds, and wildlife.

The late 1960s and 70s awakened this nation's consciousness and urged Americans to take a realistic look at the condition of their country's environment. Texans, like most Americans, became painfully aware that their historical track record of wasteful and wantonly abusive habits had resulted in an extensive list of severe incidents of environmental damage. To varying degrees, the state's rivers are polluted with runoffs from pesticides and fertilizers and had become dumping grounds for industrial and municipal wastes. In various rural areas, residents must boil their drinking water to avoid ingesting harmful substances. The once clear blue skies hang heavily laden with pollution and smog over the state's major industrial areas. The victim of infrequent but severely damaging oil spills, the Texas coast is further victimized by the tourists who, while admiring the beauty of the natural surroundings, scatter their trash across the sand dunes. Forest and wetlands have been the targets of progress's bulldozers, as precious plants and wildlife are pushed to the brink of extinction. This chapter explores the extent of the damage to the state's environment—air, water, coastal areas, the wetlands, and problems associated with the disposal of hazardous and solid wastes.

This chapter takes a balanced approach by emphasizing the role that government at all levels has played in attempting to reverse the rate of environmental damage. Federal and state legislative houses have passed numerous laws with stiff sanctions to be levied against the violators. However, the punitive rhetoric of the law has not always been arduously enforced upon violators. Traditionally, business and industry have fought against environmental legislation.   Joined by irate property owners, anti-environmental interest groups are currently attempting to reverse existing laws and to substantially decrease dreaded regulations, fines, and penalties.   Environmentalists vowing to protect our environment at all costs had a field day in the 1970s and 80s as the majority of the environmental protection laws were passed. Their mission is a noble one: safeguard the delicate balance between man and nature. This chapter focuses on another important delicate balance: the one among environmentalists, anti-environmental forces, and legislative houses.

A Report Card on the State's Environment

The extent of the damage is alarming. Houston is continuously listed as one of the nation's most polluted cities. San Antonio and several other cities and counties across the state have made the EPA's dirty air list because their levels of ozone, smog and haze have exceeded federally mandated compliance levels. Big Bend National Park is now listed as endangered parkland. Farmers and ranchers along the Rio Grande are challenging the United States State Department to level economic sanctions against Mexico for its violation of the 1949 treaty mandating the sharing of water in the Rio Grande between the United States and Mexico. More and more of the state's animals, fishes, birds, and plants are being placed on the federal endangered and threaten species lists. The closing of military bases across the state has uncovered the depth of the United States Department of Defense's polluting ways. The oil and gas businesses are fighting with the Texas Railroad Commission over who should bear the costs of plugging the industry's abandoned wells.

The Texas Legislature has not been generous in allocating state funds for environmental programs. For fiscal year 2018, the various environmental state agencies lumped under the budget category of "natural resources/recreational services" spent approximately $1,747,406,652, an increase of 34.0 percent from the funds spent during the previous fiscal year.[3] Traditionally, state per capita expenditure for environmental programs places her at the bottom of the scale in comparison to the money spent by her sister states. While highways are managed totally by the Texas Department of Transportation, environmental management and oversight responsibilities are parceled out to a myriad of state agencies including the General Land Office, the Railroad Commission, Department of Agriculture, Texas Animal Health Commission, Texas Water Development Board, Texas Commission on Environmental Quality, Soil and Water Conservation Board, and the Parks and Wildlife Department.

Compelled by the muscle of the federal government, the Texas Legislature has passed laws addressing the most serious threats to the environment. However, the pattern of implementation bears close scrutiny.   The text of each legislative act addressing everything from air pollution to the disposal of hazardous waste materials, specifically stresses that accused violators will be subjected to an investigation that could lead to litigation and the assessment of hefty fines and penalties. Yet, there is a clear distinction between the written intent and the actual application of the law. To put it simply, Texas has an exceptionally poor record in investigating, prosecuting, and fining violators of environmental laws. Each key environmental topic discussed in this chapter is covered by at least one legislative act placing the implementation and investigative functions with at least one or two state agencies. The problem rests with a severely fragmented state bureaucracy mired in duplication of functions without the guiding hand of a state department specifically charged with coordinating all of the state's environmental legislation. "The point is that by charge; no one actually takes responsibility. Moreover, there is no coordination; much slips through the cracks."[4] This pattern of passing laws with supposedly strong language followed by a sad record of "strong teeth" in enforcement is seen in every policy initiative in Texas pertaining to the environment.

The Federal and State Role in Environmental Policies

In accordance with the Tenth Amendment to the United States Constitution, environmental concerns were the sole responsibility of state and local governments, with the national government playing only a marginal role. Until the twentieth century, state and local governments as well as private charities bore total responsibility for the damages caused by severe weather, droughts, floods, tornados, hurricanes, environmental damage and so on. The federal government supplied absolutely no federal disaster relief nor were there punitive federal legislative acts addressing pollution and the protection of the environment. For example, the Johnstown Flood of 1889 awakened sympathy across the nation as over 2,200 residents of several small Pennsylvanian towns were swept away by a deluge of water released by the collapse of a man-made earthen dam that was defiantly and sloppily built to challenge the whims of Mother Nature. However, no major legislation was passed by Congress nor was any punitive action taken against the individuals responsible for the construction and oversight of the dam.

One of the original environmental groups, the American Forestry Association, was founded shortly after the publication of George Perkins Marsh's 1864 novel entitled *Man and Nature*, a story about mankind's destruction of the world's forests. Arguing "that humans had changed the world on a geological scale, Marsh documented the ways that civilizations had turned humid regions into arid deserts by removing tree cover and how they had caused erosion, sending silt down mountainsides to build up rivers and harbors. Since people could change the earth, said Marsh, they had a moral responsibility to manage it."[5] John Muir took a more romantic approach to the environment. Based upon his visit to Yosemite Park, Muir wrote in *My First Summer in the Sierra*:

> No pain here, no dull empty hours, no fear of the past, no fear of the future. These blessed mountains are so completely filled with God's beauty, no petty personal hope or experience has room to be. Drinking this champagne water is pure pleasure, so is breathing the living air, and very movement of limbs is pleasure, while the whole body seems to feel beauty when exposed to it as it feels the camp fire or sunshine, entering not by the eyes alone, but equally through all one's flesh like radiant heat, making a passionate ecstatic pleasure glow not explainable.[6]

In 1892, Muir founded the **Sierra Club** with the belief that if more individuals learned to appreciate the beauty of the environment they would become more protective of it.

The first two notable items of federal environmental legislation was the General Revision Act and the Refuse Act. Passed in 1891, the **General Revision Act** gave authority to the president to set aside forest lands for parks and natural preserves. The 1899 **Refuse Act** mandated that any business seeking to dump waste into navigable rivers had to first obtain a permit from the Army Corps of Engineers. The first president to embrace environmental issues, Teddy Roosevelt, established **Pelican Island** as the nation's first wildlife sanctuary. In 1905, he founded the **United States Forestry Service**. In 1906, Roosevelt signed into law the **Antiquities Act**, which empowered the president to set aside for federal protection any monument, historical site, or forest considered to be precious or threatened of destruction. This is the same law that both Presidents Clinton and Obama used to protect millions of acres of land across the nation from any kind of development. The

John Muir

nation's first national park was **Yellowstone**. By 1916, the nation had a mere thirteen national parks. Unfortunately the end of Teddy Roosevelt's tenure in the White House also curtailed enthusiasm for environmental protection. With the exception of Franklin Roosevelt's Civilian Conservation Corps in the 1930s, environmental issues were not top priority concerns.

By the end of the 1960s, it became painfully obvious that the individual states had not taken or were not likely to take the initiative to address environmental issues. "They [the states] could not afford to develop the technical expertise on pollution issues; they had no jurisdiction over pollution generated in neighboring states upstream or upwind, and polluting industries could threaten to move their operations elsewhere to escape compliance with strict environmental rules."[7] Once again, the states demonstrated their inability to handle a problem properly, leaving the door wide open for the federal government to fill the policy void. Meanwhile, public support for protection of the environment grew rapidly after Rachel Carson published *Silent Spring* in 1962. In Carson's words:

> The history of life on earth has been a history of interaction between living things and their surroundings. To a large extent, the physical form and the habits of the earth's vegetation and its animal life have been molded by the environment. Considering the whole span of earthly time, the

opposite defect, in which life actually modifies its surroundings, has been relatively slight. Only within the moment of time represented by the present century has one species—man—acquired significant power to alter the nature of his world.

During the past quarter century this power has not only increased to one disturbing magnitude but it has changed in character. The most alarming of all man's assaults upon the environment is the contamination of air, earth, rivers, and sea with dangerous and even lethal materials. This pollution is for the most part irrecoverable; the chain of evil it initiates not only in the world that must support life but in living tissues is for the most part, irreversible. In this now universal contamination of the environment, chemicals are the sinister and little-recognized partners of radiation in changing the very nature of the world—the very nature of its life. All has been risked—for what?[8]

Her publication was an indictment against the wasteful and fatal destruction of the earth as people, animals, and plants gradually succumbed to the adverse effects of pesticides. *Silent Spring* launched the modern environmental effort in the same manner as *The Jungle* motivated a shocked President Teddy Roosevelt to push for the passage of the Pure Food and Drug Act. National leaders began to publically acknowledge the deterioration of the nation's environment.

With the passage of the **Clean Air Act** in 1963, the federal government assumed a powerful and potentially permanent role over state and local governments in implementing environmental public policy initiatives. In her role as First Lady, Lady Bird Johnson became the White House spokeswoman for environmental concerns. Speaking at the White House Conference on Natural Beauty, she challenged Americans to join her efforts to protect the environment:

All of our national history proves that a committed citizenry is a mighty force it bends itself to a determined effort. There is a growing feeling in this land today that ugliness has been allowed too long, that it is time to say, "Enough," and to act. The beauty of our land is a natural resource. Its preservation is linked to the inner prosperity of the human spirit. The tradition of our past is equal to today's threat to that beauty. Our land will be attractive tomorrow only if we organize for action and rebuild and reclaim the beauty we

inherited. Our stewardship will be judged by the foresight with which we carry out these programs. We must rescue our cities and countryside from blight with the same purpose and vigor with which, in other areas, we moved to save the forests and the soil. . .[9]

In addition to the **Wilderness Act** of 1964, President Lyndon Johnson enacted "major federal initiatives restricting water and air pollution, . . . a national highway beautification program and added more land to the national wildlife refuges, wilderness, and national park systems than any president of the postwar era."[10] During the 1968 presidential election, both Democratic presidential candidate Edmund Muskie and his Republican counterpart Richard Nixon campaigned for rapid and strict federal responses geared towards cleaning up existing environmental damage and preventing further erosion of our natural resources. Although an advocate of less government regulation, it was President Nixon who signed into law the most sweeping environmental law of the twentieth century—the **Environmental Protection Act (EPA).**

The conservative Republican agenda of the Reagan administration was based on the Jeffersonian philosophy that the government that governs best governs the least. Reagan's economic program was centered on a balanced federal budget whereby costs equaled anticipated revenues. The federal government was simply spending too much money. In his acceptance speech for the 1980 Republican presidential nomination, Reagan set out his plan to weaken the federal grip over state and local governments while at the same time, reducing the federal deficit. Consequently, the Environmental Protection Agency (EPA) joined the ranks of many federal agencies that saw their budgets severely cut, jobs eliminated, and regulatory responsibilities shifted back to state governments. The George W. Bush administration's pro-business posture on environmental issues clearly placed him at odds with environmentalists, Democrats, and even members of the Republican Party. Immediately after taking the oath of office, Bush reversed his campaign promise of stricter EPA implementation and enforcement over carbon emissions from power plants. President Bush also reversed his initial position of supporting legislation passed during the Clinton administration mandating lower acceptable levels of arsenic in drinking water by claiming that the new levels would mean at "least $200 million in new costs to local communities."[11] The outcry from environmentalists plus the release of a medical study linking higher arsenic levels in drinking water to cancer caused the Bush administration to, once again, reverse its position. EPA Administrator Christie Whitman announced that Bush would indeed enforce the standards established by the Clinton administration. Of course, environmentalists joined the ranks of Democrats angered over Bush's selection of New Jersey Governor Whitman to head the EPA. Already a heavily polluted industrial state, the state of New Jersey's environment declined rather than improved during Whitman's term of office. Democrats, environmentalists, and especially moderate Republicans were concerned about Bush's plan to shift more of the responsibility for environmental oversight and enforcement from the federal government to the states. Historically, all fifty states "have failed to report violations of federal pollution laws, allowed major industrial polluters to operate without permits, and failed to conduct basic emissions tests of industry smokestacks."[12] Eventually Whitman resigned her EPA assignment citing pressing family matters. The international environmental community was also not pleased with Bush's environmental positions. Withdrawing the United States from the Kyoto Agreement, every time Bush attended an international environmental conference, he encountered well-organized loud protests from pro-environmental groups. Throughout his two terms of office, Bush effectively crafted a national energy policy advocating increased oil and gas drilling to include the Arctic National Wildlife Refuge and relaxation of regulatory policies over water quality, clean air, and energy efficiency standards. In contrast, Barack Obama ran his presidential campaign on the promise to promote alternative energy sources that would gradually eliminate the nation's dependency on fossil fuels. In 2015, Obama joined leaders from 200 other countries in signing the Paris Climate Agreement, designed to fight climate change and global warming. The agreement pledged the signees to enact measures within their own countries to collectively reduce greenhouse gas emissions. The Trump administration, however, took a pro-business posture by withdrawing the United States from the agreement.

Table 16.1 lists the major environmental packages enacted at the national government level as well as subsequent Texas legislative responses. Like most legislation, current environmental laws at both the national and state levels have a ten- or twenty-year life cycle whereby Congress or state legislative houses must decide whether to extend the legislation for another life cycle.

The Role of the EPA

The primary federal agency overseeing the implementation and enforcement for the majority of the nation's environmental laws is the **Environmental Protection Agency (EPA)** created with the passage of the **Environmental Protection Act** in 1970. Initially charged with air and water pollution control tasks, the EPA also establishes **national ambient air quality standards,** or **NAAQS,** for carbon monoxide, sulfur dioxide, ozone, lead, nitrogen dioxide, and particulate matter. If an entity meets federal standards, it is designated as **attainment.** However, those failing to meet federal standards are rated as **nonattainment** and the governing unit (state, city or county) or the business cited for the pollution is subjected to daily fines until attainment status is reached. The EPA now has regulatory control over hazardous wastes, noise pollution, pesticides, and endangered species. The EPA requires that all federal agencies file an environmental impact statement for every federal program or federally-sponsored initiative. The statement or report must include any existing and/or potential harm the project will pose to the environment, proposed solutions to avoid an adverse impact, and the project's on-going future plans to enhance the productivity of the environment. Federally-sponsored projects can include everything from a municipal sewer system to the expansion and maintenance of the federal highway system. The EPA can determine the future of any project simply from the **impact statement**. If the environment will be irreversibly harmed, the EPA has the authority to cancel the project. Usually the EPA will attach additional specifications to the project to address existing or potential environmental damage. The cost of these additional requirements alone may cancel the project. The EPA also reserves the right to inspect all aspects of the project's construction to ensure compliance with EPA standards.

The EPA is the enemy to a wide variety of interest groups in Texas. Construction firms, land developers, and property owners have few kind words for the EPA and its environmental impact statements and regulations. First, critics point out that the EPA's standards are just too universal to meet specific regional needs. They believe that the EPA is "excessively rigid and insensitive to geographical and technical differences and for being inefficient."[13] Sparsely populated rural areas are subjected to many of the same standards imposed on heavily populated urban centers.

Second, new environmental standards, like most laws, are applicable for future violators but cannot be applied to pollution and environmental damage caused prior to the new regulations. The United States Constitution prohibits ex post facto laws. For example, while both state and federal legislation mandates that any underground

Table 16.1

Selective List of Federal Environmental Laws

Air Pollution Control Act (1955) - provides federal funding for air-pollution control research projects.

Air Quality Act (1967) - created nationwide federal air quality regions and set acceptable pollution levels for each region. Required that all state and local governments develop their own standards for air-quality or follow federal mandates.

Antiquities Act (1906) – authorizes the President of the United States to set aside by proclamation sites including national monuments and parcels of land that are objects of historical and scientific interests.

Atomic Energy Acts (1946 and 1954) – created the nation's civilian nuclear energy programs.

Clean Air Act (1955) – mandates the establishment of national air quality standards for air pollutants deemed dangerous to public health.

Clean Air Act (1963) - provided federal funding and assistance to local and state governments in their efforts to establish air pollution control programs.

Clean Air Act Amendments (1965) - set federal pollution standards for automobile exhaust emissions.

Clean Air Act Amendments (1970) - empowers the Environmental Protection Agency to establish national air pollution standards; restricted the discharge of major pollutants into the lower atmosphere; mandated that automobile manufacturers reduce emissions of nitrogen oxide, hydrocarbon, and carbon monoxide by 90 percent.

Clean Air Act Amendments (1990) - established formulas for the development of anti-polluting gasoline fuels for use in the nation's smoggiest cities; mandated further emissions reductions of carbon monoxide and exhaust emissions by year 2003; placed additional restrictions on toxic pollutants.

Clean Water Act (1974) (known as the Safe Water Drinking Act) - set federal safe drinking water standards for all water suppliers servicing more than 25 people.

Clear Water Act (1966) – allocates federal funding for the construction of wastewater treatment plants.

Clean Water Act Amendments (1972) – also known as the Water Pollution Control Act, a series of amendments establishing water quality standards for the nation's major rivers and lakes; mandates discharge permits for private and public facilities.

Clean Water Act Amendments (1990) - establishes guidelines for addressing the hazards of oil spills.

Coastal Barrier Resources Act (1982) - sanctions the Secretary of the Interior to establish a nationwide coastal barrier resource system.

Coastal Zone Management Act (1972) – created the Office of Ocean and Coastal Resource Management to give federal grants to states for the development of their plans to preserve coastal areas and estuarine sanctuaries.

Coastal Zone Act Reauthorization Amendments (1990) – authorizes federal environmental agents to work in conjunction with state authorities to develop plans for the prevention of polluted runoffs.

Comprehensive Environmental Response, Compensation, and Liability Act (1980) - established the federal-level Superfund to clean up toxic waste sites.

Community Right-to-Know-More Act (1991) – requires businesses to notify communities within their immediate area about the kinds of hazardous substances they use and how these products are being stored, used, and disposed.

Emergency Planning and Community Right-to-Know Act (1986) – requires businesses to notify communities within their immediate area about the kinds of hazardous substances they use and how these products are stored, used and disposed of including substances released into the air or water.

Endangered Species Act (1973) - empowers the Departments of Interior and Commerce to purchase land and water for the sole purpose of protecting, restoring, and propagating endangered species; established an identification and listing system for endangered and threatened species.

Farm Bill (1985) - mandates federal sanctions against farmers who convert wetlands to croplands.

Farm Bill (1990) – creates a cost-share program to encourage private landowners to protect wetlands and wildlife located on their properties.

Farm Bill (1996) - allocates federal funds to ranchers and farmers for the improvement of wildlife habitats for birds, mammals and reptiles.

Federal Environmental Pesticide Control Act (1972) – mandates that all pesticides used in any interstate commerce activities be officially approved and certified as harmless to humans, animal life, and so on.

Federal Food, Drug and Cosmetic Act (1938) - empowers the Federal Food and Drug Administration to regulate all contaminants in food including pesticides.

Federal Insecticide, Fungicide and Rodenticide Act (1972) - requires the registration and regulation of pesticides and agricultural chemicals.

Food Quality Protection Act (1996) – ensures that all levels of pesticides in food meet federal standards; overhauls the Federal Food, Drug and Cosmetic Act and the Federal Insecticide, Fungicide and Rodenticide Act; protects infants and children from pesticides in food and water and from indoor exposure to pesticides; prohibits the addition of any cancer causing or related chemicals to processed food.

Federal Forest Incentive Act (1973) - creates a federally funded cost-share incentive program for landowners participating in reforestation efforts.

Federal Hazardous Liquid Pipeline Safety Act (1979) - sets federal guidelines for the transportation of hazardous liquids by pipelines.

Federal Land Policy and Management Act (1976) – empowers the Bureau of Land Management to oversee the leasing of federally held lands for livestock grazing.

Federal Natural Gas Pipeline Safety Act - sets federal guidelines for the transportation of natural and other gases by pipelines.

Federal Solid Waste Disposal Act (1965) – grants federal assistance to state and local governments for the establishment of guidelines for solid waste disposal activities.

Federal Water Pollution Control Act (1948) - establishes federal standards for the treatment of municipal wastes prior to discharge. (Revised in 1965 and 1967)

Federal Water Pollution Control Act Amendments (1972) - mandates national water quality standards and goals for the rehabilitation of polluted waters into safe water sources for recreational and fishing purposes.

Fish and Wildlife Coordination Act (1958) – establishes the criteria for the determination of adverse impacts on wildlife as a result of water resource development projects.

Fish Conservation and Management Act (1976) - restricts foreign fishing in U. S. territorial waters; establishes healthy levels of fish stocks; prevents overharvesting.

General Revision Act (1891) – authorizes the President of the United States to establish forest reserves on public land.

Lacey Act (1900) - outlaws interstate exportation or importation of wildlife harvested or possessed in violation of federal laws.

Marine Mammal Protection Act (1972) - prohibits the killing and importation of whales and nearly all marine mammals.

Migratory Bird Conservation Act (1929) - empowers the federal government to purchase land for waterfowl refuges.

Migratory Bird Hunting Stamp Act (1934) - requires hunters over age 16 to purchase a stamp or license before hunting migratory waterfowl.

Migratory Bird Treaty Act (1918) - prohibits the hunting or injury of wild birds migrating between the United States, Britain, and Mexico.

Multiple Use Act (1960) – enables the National Forest Service to oversee all nationally designated forests used as wildlife habitats, recreational facilities and watersheds as well as those lands used for livestock grazing and timber extraction.

National Environmental Policy Act (1969) - mandates the establishment of the Council for Environmental Quality, and the Environmental Protection Agency.

National Park Act (1916) – states that the purpose of national parks are to guarantee public enjoyment and public use without impairment. This legislation established the National Park Service.

Occupational Safety and Health Act (OSHA) (1970) – establishes strict standards to protect workers from on-the-job exposure to hazardous chemicals, materials, and so on.

Oil Pollution Act (1990) – passed immediately after the Exxon *Valdez* oil spill; requires all oil companies to create and submit oil spill contingency plans and to train their employees on containment efforts.

Park Protection Act (1894) – prohibits hunting in national parks.

Pelican Island National Refuge Act (1903) – created the nation's first federally protected habitat known as the Pelican Island National Refuge.

Pittman-Robertson Act (1937) - allocated revenue for state wildlife conservation efforts from the collection of excise taxes on rifles, shotguns, ammunition, and archery equipment.

Pollution Prevention Act (1990) – establishes guidelines for the reporting of any amount of waste materials recycled and the quantity of waste not produced due to the use of antipollution devises.

Public Health Service Act (1902) – provides guidelines for allowable contaminants association with communicable diseases.

Refuse Act (1899) - mandates issuance of a permit for dumping of refuse into any navigable waterway.

Resource Conservation and Recovery Act (1976) - grants federal control over hazardous wastes; prohibits the creation of new dumping sites without prior permission; mandates the upgrade of existing open dumps to sanitary landfills or face closure.

Rivers and Harbors Act (1899) – requires any buildings of piers, docks and wharfs to obtain a permit for construction from the Army Corps of Engineers.

Solid Waste Disposal Act (1965) - provides federal assistance to state and local governments for the establishment of guidelines for solid waste disposal activities.

Surface Mining Control and Reclamation Act (1977) – places strict guidelines for strip mining projects including the restoration of areas subject to strip mining.

Surface Transportation Act (1991) – provided $151 billion over a six-year period to participating state and local governments for highway and public transportation projects.

Toxic Substances Control Act (1976) – empowers the EPA to identify, register, evaluate and regulate all commercially used chemicals that posed an "unreasonable risk."

Water Quality Act (1965) - sets federal standards for the discharge of harmful substances into water sources.

Weeks Laws (1911) – provides federal funding to state governments for the development of wildlife control programs.

Wild and Scenic Rivers Act (1968) - enables the Department of the Interior to designate any water source as a scenic, recreational or of habitat value.

Wilderness Act (1964) – authorizes a "hands-off" protection for special areas carved out of the national forest, national parks and Bureau of Land Management lands.

Selective List of State Laws

Act to Preserve and Protect Wild Game, Wild Birds, and Wild Fowl (1903) – mandates a five-year closed season for the hunting of antelope, mountain sheep and pheasants; prohibits the commerce of wild animal meat, skins, and plumage.

Agricultural Hazard Communication Act – requires proper notification and information of potential dangers to agricultural workers and other persons working with chemicals.

Clean River Act (1977) – allows the Texas National Resource Conservation Commission (TNRCC) to use the 'water shed' approach to water pollution management.

Coastal Coordination Act (1977) – mandates that the General Land Office develop a long-range plan for the management of all coastal areas.

Comprehensive Municipal Solid Waste Management, Resource Recovery and Conservation Act (1983) – establishes the Municipal Solid Waste Management and Resource Recovery Advisory Council to local agencies in the development of regional solid waste management programs.

County Solid Waste Control Act – grants licensing authority to counties and in their unincorporated areas for solid waste activities to ensure compliance with state and federal laws.

Dune Protection Act (1973) – mandates that all coastal counties develope long-range efforts for the protection of dunes located within their jurisdictions.

Endangered Species Act (1973) - enables the Texas Parks and Wildlife Department to establish lists of plants, fish and wildlife threatened or endangered of extinction.

Special Non-Game and Endangered Species Fund (1983) – provides state money for research and management of facilities protecting endangered species.

Omnibus Recycling Act (1991) – establishes a statewide recycling program for municipal solid waste; empowers the General Land Office, the Railroad Commission, the Texas Department of Commerce, and TRNCC to develop and implement comprehensive marketing plans for the sale and use of recycled goods.

Open Beaches Act (1959) – guarantees free and unrestricted areas to all coastal areas designated as public beaches.

Sanitation and Health Protection Act – prohibits unsanitary drinking water; sets guidelines for the protection of public water supplies; complies with the Federal Safe Drinking Water Act.

Solid Waste Resource Recovery Financing Act – grants permission to certain political subdivisions to own, sell, lease, and contract for water resource recovery systems and to issue bonds to finance such projects.

State Injection Well Act - gives the TNRCC authority over the construction and use of injection wells used for the disposal of industrial/municipal wastes, extraction of minerals, and injection of fluids; sets guidelines for permits.

Texas Clean Air Act (1971) - empowers the Texas Air Control Board to issue permits for the release of contaminants into the atmosphere; implements the Federal Clean Air Act; allows for the issuance of bonds by political subdivisions to address air-pollution concerns.

Texas Hazardous Communication Act – implements the Federal Emergency Planning and Community Right-to-Know Act; distributes information about hazardous chemical substances.

Texas Hazardous Liquid Pipeline Safety Act – passed to enforce federal legislation enacted in 1979; requires immediate notification by telephone or other devices of any accidents; calls for the filing of inspection and maintenance plans, annual reports, and pre-construction reports.

Texas Hazardous Substance Spill Prevention and Control Act – establishes regulations for spills or discharges of hazardous substances into the state's waters.

Texas Herbicide Law – authorizes the Texas Department of Agriculture to regulate the sale, use and transportation of specified herbicides, derivations, and formulations of such substances.

Texas Pesticide Control Act – authorizes the Texas Department of Agriculture to regulate the collection, reporting, handling, storage, sale, transportation, and labeling of pesticides to ensure compliance with federal pesticide rules and regulations.

Texas Radiation Control Act – regulates mining, disposal facilities and industrial testing sites; sets licensing requirements for these activities.

Texas Solid Waste Disposal Act (1969) – empowers the Texas Department of Public Health to oversee the design, construction, and eventual operation of all municipal solid waste facilities.

Texas Surface Coal Mining and Reclamation Act - grants the Texas Railroad Commission authority to enforce federal laws regarding all surface and underground coal exploration and mining operations.

Texas Water Well Drillers Act – authorizes the TNRCC to establish standards and implementation procedures for plugging abandoned and tapped out water wells.

Waste Reduction Policy Act (1991) – mandates that all industries generating more than 100 kilograms a month of hazardous wastes or releasing toxic chemicals to develop a waste minimization and reduction plan and subsequently, release the report for public viewing.

Water Bill (1997) – provides low-interest loans through the Federal Safe Drinking Water Revolving Fund to small cities and communities for the development of regional water use planning, drought management, and conservation plans and programs for the emergency authorization of water transfers during droughts.

injection well must be plugged upon completion of extraction activities, these laws do not mandate the plugging of wells created *before* the regulations were enacted.

Third, the EPA provides businesses and industries no incentives to exceed federally mandated levels or requirements. A factory might be able to reduce its emissions by 70 percent rather than the required 50 percent at little additional cost, but the factory most likely will not do the additional cleanup—its goal is to minimize the cost of the product, not to provide a cleaner environment for society.[14]

Fourth, EPA enforcement is sporadic, and far too often falls heavily upon small businesses, which simply cannot afford expensive litigation costs to fight the federal government. Larger firms can afford to pay the daily fines and keep the EPA in court for years as they continue their environmentally harmful polluting ways. Basically, the EPA is "reluctant to enforce standards against large companies with political clout or small profit margins, especially industries crucial to the nation's economic health. To take action against a large industry requires significant political will all the way up to the White House."[15] Like the United States Justice Department and civil rights federal agencies, the EPA has become dependent upon court litigation to force compliance and punish violators. Once again, the EPA armed with a cadre of legal experts is seen as the enemy. Far too often, environmental rules and regulations are "based on collected evidence marshaled by contending sides and interpreted according to specific procedures that are open to appeals and legal challenges at all stages. The rule making is typically long and contentious, often ending in litigation."[16] Charged with the actual protection of the environment, the EPA's likely ally would be environmentalists and related interest groups. Both should be working together, side by side against those accused of violating the environment. However, the litigation pattern indicates otherwise. "Environmentalists constantly sue the regulatory agencies to secure stricter regulation, while business groups sue to get standards relaxed. The two principal adversaries seldom meet in the same courtroom. Environmentalists have tended to concentrate on challenging regulations with national applicability, while businesses have tended to focus instead on source-specific regulations. In individual enforcement cases, district court judges have decided on compliance schedules and sanctions by balancing society's interests in a clean environment against the industries' claims of hardship. The results of this system have been lengthy litigation, lenient schedules, and few fines."[17] Far too often the EPA speaks with a loud voice but carries a weak stick.

Fifth, the EPA was designed to stop and actually prevent pollution and other forms of environmental damage from occurring in the first place. However, this agency relies heavily upon alleviative and punitive actions. The punitive nature of the EPA is a major bone of contention to businesses, industry, farmers, ranchers and other property owners. Particularly with the EPA "the implementation process in the United States is for the most part formalized, rule-oriented, and adversarial—in a word—confrontational."[18] Critics see the EPA as not a friendly partner promoting a cleaner environment but as a sinister rule-laden bureaucratic monster, bent on destroying the livelihood of business and industry. "Interestingly, the government of the United States, whose political and legal culture is the most protective of private property rights, takes the most confrontational position toward private polluters of any nation. . . It's laws are the strictest, giving administrators the least discretion in their dealings with industry. But the strictness of laws and procedures in the United States has not necessarily produced better results than in other countries that take a more conciliatory stance toward industry."[19]

Sixth, a shift in the political balance between Democrats and Republicans in Washington either in a presidential term of office or in the halls of Congress wrecks havoc with the effectiveness of all federal agencies. In particular, the EPA is very vulnerable to a shift in political power. Under Democratic presidents, the EPA has been granted more authority and, of course, more money. On the average, Democratic presidents have been supportive of the EPA taking a more aggressive role against polluters by supporting stronger regulations and increasing the EPA's budget. On the other hand, Republican presidents guided by the philosophical position of less government are inclined to support deregulation of federal agencies. Subsequently, the enforcement muscle of the more visible federal agencies, such as the EPA, are weakened considerably.

Seventh, the fragmentation and duplication of functions at the federal level harms the effectiveness of the EPA. The agency shares its authority with approximately seventeen other federal agencies including the Corps of Engineers, the Fish and Wildlife Service, the Bureau of Land Management, and the Nuclear Regulatory Commission. In addition, Texas has its own problem with fragmentation and duplication of functions and responsibilities. It is this bureaucratic nightmare that frequently pits a single business against an army of government regulators who issue regulations and rulings that often conflict with each other. A project can be tied up for years as agencies at both the federal and state levels argue amongst themselves. Meanwhile, the business community and property owners are wondering just who is in charge and, most importantly, which rules do they follow. The EPA would be more effective if it was the sole federal environmental agency. In addition, the actions of the states add to the confusion and inconsistency of federal environmental regulations. "Generally, the states are not precluded from enforcing criteria more stringent than those required by the federal laws, and are given considerable leeway to follow enforcement interpretations which may not be fully consistent with those applied at the federal level."[20] Consequently state governments have the latitude to enact their own environmental laws that may be more strident in scope, investigation, and penalties than federal enactments. There is, of course, the other side of the coin. Although the federal government threatens to revoke federal money and projects to states with lax enforcement policies, it is very reluctant to carry out its threats. This weakness leaves ample opportunity for states like Texas to use a minimalist approach to federal regulations and mandates.

Texas's Search for Precious Clean Water

Throughout the development of civilization, the quest for viable long-lasting water sources has been an ever-ending quest. Beginning with prehistoric peoples, mankind realized that their survival was dependent upon their nearness to a water source. As they were exploring Texas, the Spanish explorers and eventually the colonizers realized that Texas was a vast landmass with preciously scattered major water sources. As they were building missions, presidios, and villas, the Spanish introduced "the first acequias—water canals, carefully engineered with technology developed in the Middle East to provide above-ground supplies of fresh water—were built in Texas, starting with use by missionaries near El Paso."[21] The same concerns expressed by the Spanish in the 1600s are the same issues confronted by all Texans in the 21st Century. On paper, Texas appears to be a water-rich state: Nine major and twenty-one minor underground aquifer systems that naturally purify water for urban and agricultural areas; 11,247 named streams and 14 major rivers with a combined length of nearly 80,000 miles; 188 major water supply reservoirs (normal capacity of 5,000 acre-feet or larger); and 21 major non-water supply reservoirs (those who do not have a supply function). There are 6,976 reservoirs in Texas with a normal storage capacity of 10 acre-feet or larger. Texas collectively has 5,607 square miles of inland water, ranking it first among the contiguous states.[22] Despite the impressive statistics, Texas is a state confronted with potentially devastating water shortages, a lack of consistent rainfall coupled with severe hot dry summers, and absolutely no statewide comprehensive plan detailing water usage, regional sharing, and conservation measures. Despite over forty years of proposing plan after plan, the Texas Legislature has come up just as dry as a Texas rainless summer heat wave.

The need for a statewide water plan is crucial for several reasons. First, underground and surface water sources are not equally distributed across the state. East Texas has an abundant supply of water, whereas the Plains region of West Texas and the border region experience annual water shortages. Second, there is an equally alarming historical pattern of disproportionate rainfall that ranges from "an annual average of fifty-six inches in Southeast Texas to eight inches in West Texas to fourteen inches in the northwest."[23] Third, the demands of rapid urban growth have taken their toll on the state's water resources. It is estimated that from 1990 to 2040, Texas's cities will increase their consumption demands by 74 percent, while manufacturers and power plants will increase their water needs by 118 percent.[24] Fourth, the water needs of this state's agricultural industry cannot be overlooked. Once accused as being the primary water wasters, farmers are using more efficient but costly irrigation systems. The

agricultural community, particularly in the Plains area of West Texas, is totally dependent upon irrigated farming. The High Plains region, or the Panhandle, produces one-fourth of the nation's cotton and is the primary site of the state's beef cattle industry. A drought can prove to be extremely expensive. For example, the 2000 drought resulted in "$1.1 billion damage on the state's economy. West Texas was hit especially hard. Only 54 percent of the Texas summer cotton crop and 48 percent of the summer peanut crop survived."[25]

The frustration of the Texas Legislature to develop a successful comprehensive statewide water plan is a sad saga of overly ambitious ideas, poor timing, and unconvinced voters. In 1969 the Texas Legislature culminated a four-year effort by sending to the voters a constitutional amendment establishing a water plan. The provisions were very ambitious and creative. With a price tag of $9 billion, the plan envisioned "the delivery of 7.6 million acre-feet [of water] to West Texas for irrigation, 1.2 million acre-feet for municipal and industrial use in North Central Texas, and 1.5 million acre-feet to eastern New Mexico, in addition to meeting all other water needs for all uses in Texas to the year 2020."[26] The hitch was that approximately $3.5 billion in bonds had to be sold to purchase the water from the Mississippi River that would be carried through 800 miles of pipelines and concrete canals generated by a sophisticated system of pumps and locks fueled by electricity. The measure failed to win over the skeptical Texas voter. This defeat was followed by two more failed attempts to pass constitutional amendments to fund statewide water plans. In 1973, Governor Dolph Briscoe decided to tackle the state's water problems by creating the Water Resource and Conservation and Development Task Force. The committee's recommendations included a proposed constitutional amendment to increase funding for the development fund. This amendment was soundly defeated by the voters in 1976. The Sierra Club, one of the nation's most influential environmental organizations, entered the picture by issuing a very critical evaluation of the Texas Water Development Board and introduced their own plan calling for severe residential, industrial and agricultural conservation efforts. The plan was not well received.

An unusual budget surplus in 1981 moved Speaker of the Texas House Bill Clayton to get the House members to approve a proposed constitutional amendment dedicating one-half of the budget surplus for the water project trust fund. Once again, voters rejected the amendment. In 1983 a series of water bills passed in the Texas Senate but failed to win approval from the House. In 1985, the Texas

Legislature finally hit pay dirt by passing a plan regulating the use of ground water and requiring cities requesting state funding for water projects to develop their own water conservation plans. According to the amendment, "water construction projects would receive $980 million, $200 million loans to farmers who purchase water-saving equipment, and a $250 million state insurance fund would be set up to guarantee water bonds issued by cities."[27] Although voters approved the amendment, the bonds did not sell as anticipated due to a national and statewide economic recession.

Meanwhile, West and Southwest Texas began to experience water shortages due to several consecutive years of drought and severe heat waves. Cities such as San Antonio were casting an envious eye upon smaller urban areas that had ample water sources. Could San Antonio arbitrarily take water from another city without their consent or without just compensation? The Texas Legislature responded with an unqualified "no" by passing Senate Bill 1 in 1997. The legislation did sanction inter-basin transfers, but it "stipulated they would be 'junior' or secondary to all other existing water rights, meaning imported water could be reduced or cut off in times of drought because the holder would have the 'senior' right."[28] Inter-basin transfers are essential to a statewide water plan since sharing of resources is crucial in areas that face severe droughts year after year while other areas of the state simply have too much water. For example, an inter-basin transfer to Valley farmers who are watching their crops burn up and die could well save the family farm from bankruptcy and foreclosure if a pre-approved alternative water source was readily available to them. Senate Bill 1 clearly underscored the number one obstacle to a statewide water conservation plan—**rule of capture**—"a long-standing law-approved by the State Supreme Court in 1904 that says all 'percolating' groundwater, such as a spring, belongs to the owners of the land where it is found."[29] For nearly 200 years, property owners in this state have upheld their absolute right to do whatever they want to do with their property including the groundwater setting on it. "Under the rule of capture, property owners may pump unlimited amounts of groundwater, regardless of whether neighbors' wells and springs dry up."[30] Obviously this rule is in direct conflict with the Texas Legislature's on-going desire to collectively pool water resources and redistribute water to areas experiencing severe water shortages.

During the 1997 legislative session, the Texas Legislature basically abandoned the concept of cooperative sharing of water by passing a measure that divided the state into sixteen regional planning districts. Each separate district was required to develop its own study on how future population trends and projected commercial and residential developments would impact their area's water resources. It was now the responsibility of each district to devise their own plans to predict water use, encourage water conservation, and seek new water sources. It is this lack of a comprehensive statewide plan and a single state agency dedicated to overseeing its implementation and enforcement that has left this state with a multiplicity of state laws and local ordinances that fail miserably to solve this state's water problems. The fragmented governmental response has left the door wide open for interest groups, business and industrial interests, construction interests, environmental groups, and property owners to wage a continuous piecemeal battle over who owns the water, who controls its use, and how much can be safely used on a daily basis. The ordinary citizen usually remains a silent bystander until he or she hears the words "water rationing" and "individual sacrifices must be made." Then citizens become vocal. Unfortunately, local communities plan on the short-term year after year whenever a drought is upon them. Urban areas pumping water from the Edwards Aquifer developed their own five-stage drought plan with each stage tied to a designed level of the aquifer. (See Table 16.2) Sadly, the solution (or in this case, the lack of a solution), is "grounded in the way the state as a whole allocates and manages both the quantity and quality of its water resources."[31]

The War with Mexico over the Rio Grande's Water

Although heavily polluted, the water in the Rio Grande has led to an international dispute over pumping rights between Mexico and the United States. "Under a 1944 treaty, Mexico and the United States share water in reservoirs on the Rio Grande; Mexico must provide an annual average of 350,000 acre-feet of water from its six main tributaries into the Rio Grande. The treaty also requires that the United States provide Mexico with 1.5 million acre-feet of water a year from the Colorado River. . . . The treaty allows withholding of water in cases of 'extraordinary drought.'"[32] The six tributaries are the Rio Conchos, Rio Salado, Rio San Diego, Rio San Regrigo, Rio Escondido and the Arroyo de las Vacas. The United States has continued to fulfill its treaty obligations to Mexico. However, Mexico has not fulfilled its obligations opting to sparingly and sporadically attempt to "catch up" on its outstanding millions of acre-feet of water. Confronted with costly droughts, South Texas farmers believe that Mexico is purposely violating the treaty as

Table 16.2 – San Antonio Water Restrictions Based on the Level of the Aquifer

Year-Round Rules: Water waste is prohibited at all times such as lawn watering overspray and runoff. Restaurants may serve water only on request. Charity car washes allowed only at commercial car wash facilities.

For All Stages: Days of watering is based on the last digit of the address:

Last Digit	Watering Days
0 or 1	Monday
2 or 3	Tuesday
4 or 5	Wednesday
6 or 7	Thursday
8 or 9	Friday

No Watering on Weekends.

Stage	Aquifer Level	Restrictions
1	660 feet	Watering with an irrigation system, sprinkler or soaker hose allowed only once a week before 11 a.m. or after 7 p.m. on designated watering day. Water waste such as water running off into a gutter, ditch, or drain or failing to repair a controllable leak is prohibited. Overnight watering is not allowed. Non-public swimming pools must have a minimum of 25% of the surface area covered with evaporation screens. Watering with hand-held hose, drip irrigation, bucket or watering can is permitted any time and any day. Washing impervious cover such as parking lots, driveways, streets or sidewalks is prohibited. Residential car washing allowed during drought once per week on Saturday or Sunday as long as there is no water waste. Use of commercial car wash facilities is allowed any day. Operators of golf courses, athletic fields and parks must submit a conservation plan to the San Antonio Water System but watering may not occur between the hours of 11 a.m. and 7 p.m. Landscape areas of golf courses not directly "in play" are required to follow one-day-per-week watering based on address.
2	650 feet	All restrictions from Stage 1 remain in effect along with Stage 2 restrictions: Landscape watering with irrigation system, sprinkler or soaker hose only once a week from 7-11 a.m., and 7-11 p.m. on designated day. Hotels, motels, and other lodging must offer and clearly notify guests of a linen/towel change by request only. The use of treated wastewater or recycled water is allowed -without waste- any day during the restricted hours if the customer has posted signage approved by the San Antonio Water System.
3	640 feet	All restrictions from Stage 1 and Stage 2 remain in effect along with Stage 3 restrictions: Landscape watering allowed only every other week with an irrigation system, sprinkler or soaker hose from 7-11 a.m. and 7-11 p.m. on the designated watering day. Watering with hand-held hose is allowed any time on any day. Operators of golf courses, athletic fields or parks must reduce watering per city ordinance. Hotels, motels and other lodging must limit linen/towel changes to once every three nights, except for health and safety.
4		This stage is declared if the total supply of water from the Edwards Aquifer and other sources have been declared as insufficient to meet customer demand. This stage can be declared by the City Manager upon completion of a 30-day monitoring of Stage 3 restrictions. For Stage 4, all restrictions under Stage 3 would remain in effect. Additional restrictions can be mandated by the City Council.

a means of enhancing the quality and quantity of their own produce and agricultural crops. NAFTA allows for the duty-free shipment of Mexican-grown fruits and vegetables into United States markets. Growers in the Rio Grande Valley are contending that Mexico is "using our water to irrigate crops in Mexico and then selling them to us here in the United States."[33] The need for Mexico to use more water from the Rio Grande is further complicated by the **maquiladoras**, a series of American- and foreign-owned factories located near the shared international border. Wanting to bring both industry and higher paying jobs to its country, the Mexican government enacted the Border Industrialization Program in 1965. With over 700 maquiladora plants, the Mexican government still is not "fully equipped to cope with the environmental or public and water health implications of the rapid industrial development at its northern border—an area far-removed from the center of regulatory authority in Mexico City."[34] Also provisions in the original NAFTA package of 1992 touches upon environmentally-related maquiladora issues including "problems in tracking and accounting for hazardous waste generated at maquiladora plants; concerns about industrial air and water pollution associated with maquiladora plants and other border industry; and concerns about whether worker health protections were being adequately implemented especially in assembly plants with high solvent usage."[35] The Mexican government does admit that it is withholding water. However, they cite the treaty provision that Mexico can keep the water if they themselves are experiencing drought conditions. Since the inception of the treaty, the Mexican government has persistently claimed that the northern sections of Mexico are indeed victims of a continuously severe drought. Mexico's inability to meet its treaty obligations translates for Texans a lack of much needed water as well as both economic losses on crops and agricultural-related jobs. Unsympathetic South and West Texas farmers believe that the United States government should "shut the border or severely limit importation of certain water-intensive products—such as sugar, citrus and vegetables."[36] Others suggest that the United States should retaliate by withholding Mexico's share of water from the Colorado River. Governor Perry even went as far as to request that President George W. Bush consider a declaration of war with Mexico!

Federal Water Legislation

The **Water Pollution Control Act** of 1972 (also known as the **Clean Water Act**) establishes the framework for overseeing water pollution standards across the nation. The main emphasis of the legislation was to set 1985 as the deadline for elimination of discharging pollutants in all navigable rivers and to hopefully deem the waters as fishable and swimmable by 1983. Basically, **pollution** is defined as "human additions of undesirable substances into the environment."[37] The federal legislation also drew a distinction between point-source and non-point source pollution. The key to litigation and assessment of penalties is to identify the guilty party. **Point-source pollution** is "a pollution source that has a precise, identifiable location such as a pipe or a smokestack" whereas; **non-point source pollution** is diffused with no clear cut indication as to its origination.[38] In conjunction with the federal legislation, the Texas Water Code defines point source pollution as "any discernible, confined and discrete conveyance, including but not limited to any pipe, ditch, channel, tunnel, conduit, well, discrete fissure, container, rolling stock, concentrated animal feeding operation, or vessel or other floating craft, from which pollutants or wastes are or may be discharged into or adjacent to any water in the state."[39] It is a far simpler task to determine what caused the pollution of a waterway if only one factory along its banks is dumping hazardous substances into the water than it is when there are several factories located along the same river. Federal legislation also established the **National Pollution Discharge Elimination System (NPDES)**, which requires all businesses and industries to file a permit to discharge or dump any effluents into a waterway. Discharges exceeding established federal standards are to be denied a permit to dump. The Water Pollution Control Act also requires municipal sewer systems to install water treatment units. The EPA is charged with administering the provisions of the federal legislation. The Clean Water Act has been successfully renewed every ten years since 1977. The **Safe Drinking Water Act** was passed in 1974. This legislation set acceptable standards for drinking water suppliers serving more than twenty-five people. Once again, the EPA was charged with setting the acceptable standards while the states were responsible for the implementation and enforcement tasks. It is questionable whether the Safe Water Drinking Act has been effective simply because far too many rural areas must deal with small water companies that charge residents for tap water that is safe to drink only after being boiled. Dirty yellowish-brown water from the kitchen tap is not what lawmakers define as clean water.

In addition to the EPA, the **Corps of Engineers** and the **Bureau of Reclamation** are actively overseeing the implementation of federal environmental laws. The Corps of Engineers is charged with ensuring viable navigational and flood control plans throughout the nation. The Corps conducts the initial feasibility study for the selection and construction of everything from hydroelectric dams to levees. A Corps analysis can determine whether a municipal flood plan will qualify for federal funding. The Bureau of Reclamation's primary task is to provide irrigation water for areas in the Western states. The **Soil Conservation Service** of the Department of Agriculture works closely with rural and small towns to provide flood retardation structures. These three federal agencies are often viewed as unwanted visitors. Texans are frustrated with the red tape and the duplication of responsibilities as these three agencies argue among themselves over which one has priority over the other two.

State Water Governance

The Texas Legislature took a serious look at the state's water pollution problems when it passed its own version of the **Water Pollution Control Act** in 1961. According to the Texas Water Code, **water pollution** is "the alteration of the physical, thermal, chemical, or biological quality of, or the contamination of, any water in the state that renders the water harmful, detrimental, or injurious to humans, animal life, vegetation, or property or to public health, safety, or welfare, or impairs the usefulness or the public enjoyment of the water for any lawful or reasonable purpose.[40] This measure created the Water Pollution Control Board, which was renamed the **Texas Water Quality Control Board** in 1967. The agency was eventually absorbed into the Department of Water Resources. In 1985, this department was separated into agencies: **Texas Water Development Board (TWDB)** and the **Texas Water Commission (TWC)**. In 1991, the TWC was merged with other agencies under the banner of the **Texas Natural Resources Conservation Commission (TNRCC)**, which is now known as the **Texas Commission on Environmental Quality (TCEQ)**. The enforcement of state water pollution and conservation efforts is still a fragmented frustrating maze of duplicated agencies with overlapping jurisdictions. The TCEQ's primary responsibility is to oversee the state's water resources and solid and hazardous waste programs. The agency's jurisdiction over surface water programs includes water rights disputes, water quality, oil and hazardous spill response efforts, certification and monitoring of waste water treatment facilities, regulation of water wells, and general supervision of special water. The board determines water quality and acceptable pollution levels based upon a daily limit of **biochemical oxygen demands (BOD)**.

One of the several standards used to measure water pollution, the BOD is "the amount of oxygen required for decomposition of a given amount of waste."[41] The agency has quasi-judicial and legislative functions. However, the TCEQ does share enforcement duties with several other state agencies. The **Texas Railroad Commission (TRC)** is involved in water and water pollution since the Texas Water Code charges it with protecting state waters from contamination caused by the oil and gas industry. The **Texas Parks and Wildlife Department (PWD)** enforces all state laws concerning game, fish, oysters, and marine life and manages recreational and historical sites. Recreational areas include surface water reservoirs, dams, lakes, streams and rivers. The **Health and Human Services Commission** is responsible for the management of municipal solid and radioactive wastes and all public drinking water supplies and systems. The **Texas Department of Agriculture (TDA)** oversees the use of pesticides and herbicides present in the water system due to runoffs from rain and irrigation systems. The **General Land Office (GLO)** is also involved in water issues, particularly in tidelands or offshore oil exploration, wetlands, coastal areas, and dune protection. In addition, numerous political subdivisions at the county and municipal government levels oversee flood control, local road and dam construction, water conservation, and so on.

Empowering the TCEQ with the authority to set water quality standards for all water within the state, the Texas Water Code defines **water** or **water-in-the-state** as "groundwater, percolating or otherwise, lakes, bays, ponds, impounding reservoirs, springs, rivers, streams, creeks, estuaries, wetlands, marshes, inlets, canals, the Gulf of Mexico, inside the territorial limits of the state, and all other bodies of surface water, natural or artificial, inland or coastal, fresh or salt, navigable or non-navigable, and including the beds and banks of all watercourses and bodies of surface water, that are wholly or partially inside or bordering the state or inside the jurisdiction of the state."[42] Consequently, all water as defined above falls under the water-quality standards established by the TCEQ as detailed in the federal Clean Water Act and subsequent state statutes. All water sources are tested periodically for aesthetic quality (taste, odor, presence of floating debris, etc.), nutrient parameters (acceptable levels of nitrogen and phosphorus), radiological parameters (i.e., presence of radioactive or potentially radioactive chemicals), toxic parameters, temperature levels, and so forth. Any agent releasing discharges and other sources of contamination into water is required to obtain a permit for dumping and to comply with the ongoing permit review process. The

Texas Water Code also defines **waste** as "sewage, industrial waste, municipal waste, recreational waste, agricultural waste or other waste."[43] The permit process is supposed to allow the TCEQ the opportunity to determine whether levels of requested discharge comply with federal and state laws. Under normal circumstances, discharge permits are issued for periods not to exceed ten years.

Although the Texas Water Code provides detailed procedures, enforcement of water pollution laws is haphazard. First, all state agencies involved with water and discharge issues have their own enforcement programs. Second, the process of penalizing a violator is a costly time-consuming process. For example, the TCEQ can institute a civil suit and seek an injunction to halt further damage or request that the state attorney general handle the investigation to determine civil action, or the TCEQ can use an internal administrative process. Third, while the fines appear to be steep on paper, in reality they are not punitive enough to convince a multi-billion dollar industry, which continues to dump hazardous levels of contamination and waste into the state's waters, to stop its polluting habits. Consequently, despite the efforts of the various agencies, water pollution is an ongoing serious problem. The EPA conducts pollution-level tests for all of the nation's rivers, streams, and lakes. Similar to the endangered species lists, waterways can be listed as **threatened**, meaning that if the pollution levels are not reduced, the body of water is uninhabitable for plants, wildlife, marine life, and people. Waterways can also be declared as **impaired** meaning that they cannot support aquatic life or are deemed to be unsafe for fishing and swimming. The leading cases of impairment are unacceptable levels of pathogens, sediment, nutrients, organic enrichment (fertilizers), and habitat alterations.

Can Texans Have Safe Drinking Water?

Every resident of this state should be assured that the water from their kitchen tap is safe for human consumption. Despite the federal government's Safe Drinking Water Act and state laws, far too many Texans are consuming water tainted with unacceptable levels of in-organics, nitrates, fluorides, and organics. State and federal laws specifically set standards for acceptable drinking water. Once again, the enforcement mechanisms are not arduously followed by state agencies. Regulated primarily by the Health and Human Services Commission (HHSC), **drinking water** as defined by the state's **Sanitation and Health Protection Act,** is "water distributed by an individual or public or private agency for human consumption, for use in preparing food or beverages, or for use in

cleaning a utensil or article used in preparing food or beverages, for, or consuming food or beverages by, human beings. The term includes water supplied for human consumption or used by an institution catering to the public."[44] Compliance standards established by HHSC conform to the requirements set by both the federal Safe Drinking Act and the EPA. To ensure a safe supply of drinking water, the HHSC is empowered to review any plan for the construction of a drinking water system for public use, conduct periodical sampling and analysis, and mandate that the production, processing, distribution, and treatment of drinking water for public consumption be supervised by a water works operator certified by HHSC. The agency also requires that all public facilities provide adequate and safe supplies of drinking water. Violators may be subject to both civil and criminal penalties. However, the expediency of enforcement is for all practical purposes nonexistent. Rural residents dependent upon a sole water provider must wait months or even years before their cries of contaminated water are actually heard and addressed.

The quality of the drinking water in Starr, Hidalgo and Cameron counties is directly tied to its primary source—the Rio Grande. The residents along the shared border with Mexico were warned that their drinking water was "laced with high levels of trihalomethanes, chemicals that are a product of the water chlorination process."[45] High levels of these chemicals are linked to increased incidents of cancer, liver and kidney diseases, central nervous system related problems, miscarriages and birth defects caused "when a sheath of embryonic cells fails to close completely to form the spinal cord and brain during the first month of pregnancy."[46] Initially, medical experts connected the increase in birth defects to the usual suspects such as improper pre-natal care, lack of proper diet, and so on. Experts determined that the high level of the chemicals in the water were indeed the primary cause. Today, residents fearful of potential health-related risks drink only bottled water or boil the water from their kitchen taps.

The Battle Royal over the Edwards

Since its inception, the city of San Antonio has relied upon the purified waters flowing forth from the Edwards Aquifer as its sole source of water for everything from irrigation to human consumption. The Texas Water Code defines **Edwards** as "that portion of an arcuate belt of porous, water-bearing limestone composed of the Comanche Peak, Edwards, and Georgetown formations trending from west to east to northeast through Kinney, Uvalde, Medina, Bexar, Kendall, Comal, and Hays counties, respectively."[47]

Usually, San Antonians periodically realize the value of this water source when the area is threatened by a drought. Mention water rationing and San Antonians are glued to their television sets as nightly newscasts report the depth of the aquifer level. One of the seven major underground water sources in Texas, the Edwards Aquifer begins in the Edwards Plateau located in Kenney County and flows through a series of porous limestone layers, known as the **Recharge Zone.** The Edwards replenishes itself with runoffs from rainfall. The cavernous depth of Edwards is home to dozens of species of plants, wildlife, and fish, including the endangered fountain darter and blind catfish as well as endangered crustaceans. It is estimated that the Edwards "holds more water than all the surface reservoirs in the state—between 20 million and 50 million acre feet of water."[48] One would imagine that 20 to 50 million acre feet of water replenished annually by rainfall would provide an ample source of water for generations to come. However, rapid urban growth increases the demand for water. San Antonio, like so many cities in this state, is subjected to heavy rainy seasons followed by prolonged heat waves and droughts. Rainfall alone cannot replenish the loss of an estimated 60 billion gallons of water per year used by San Antonio and surrounding communities. The public policy dilemma is to devise a meaningful and enforceable year-round conservation plan while seeking alternative water sources.

The battle over the management of and the future use of the Edwards Aquifer is a classic tale of federalism at its worst, as both federal and state judges are still debating whether the aquifer is actually an underground river under federal EPA guidelines or just a pool of underground standing water that legally is governed by the state. Meanwhile, city, county, state, and federal agencies and commissions as well as environmental groups rage bloody war over who controls it and subsequently determines the water supply for the nation's seventh largest city. While environmentalists seek to halt all future business and residential development over the Recharge Zone, land developers approach property owners over the Recharge Zone with lucrative cash offers. Political careers have ebbed and flowed with the changing depths of the aquifer's water levels. Businesses dependent upon water anxiously watch the ruckus and express their concerns. Tourism, one of the city's key industries centers on the beauty of the San Antonio River Walk with its barges winding up and down the river. While it may boost the city's tourist business, depending solely upon the Edwards Aquifer system to supply all of the water needs is foolhardy.

Although the controversy over Edwards has been brewing since the 1900s, a major confrontation began in the mid 1960s particularly with Hemisfair, an international event held in San Antonio in 1968. Although not as successful as hoped, Hemisfair did prompt land developers to seek permits to build in the north central sector of Bexar County, the home of the Recharge Zone, as city leaders pondered whether to purchase the acreage for themselves and put the area under permanent protection, banning any further development. Unfortunately, the City Council opted not to purchase the land. Also city leaders looked to purchasing water from Canyon Lake as a means of providing an additional source of water. The Canyon Lake deal fell through as the City Council opted to construct a surface-water reservoir known as Applewhite. Located in the southern sector of Bexar County on the Medina River, Applewhite was marketed as the definitive answer to San Antonio's water woes. However, conflicts soon arose as political opposition composed of taxpayer watchdog groups, the Sierra Club, environmentalists, and disgruntled citizens on the Southside joined forces to defeat the project.

Originally supportive of the plan, Uvalde and Medina counties became muddled in political and territorial squabbles and withdrew their support. In 1991, the San Antonio City Council opted to defy opposition forces by actually signing the contracts and initiating land acquisition, clearance, and even construction of Applewhite. Vocal opposition forces compelled city leaders to put the fate of the project into the hands of the voters. Despite an all-out public relations effort on the part of city leaders, the Applewhite project was soundly defeated in two special elections. Besides the cost of the project, the major bone of contention was how the water was to be distributed. City leaders told the residents of the southern sector of the city that they would be the primary users of Applewhite water, which initially would be sewer treated water while the northern sector would be the exclusive users of water from Edwards, hailed as almost 100 percent pure water. The cancellation of the project proved to be very expensive since the city of San Antonio defaulted on the existing construction contracts.

Meanwhile, the lack of a comprehensive water plan for the aquifer left the door wide open for both the Sierra Club and the then Texas Water Commission (TWC) to assume a major role. In 1992, the TWC seized control of the Edwards Aquifer, claiming it to be a river rather than an underground reservoir. The Sierra Club filed its own lawsuit requesting that the United States Department of the Interior through the Fish and Wildlife Commission manage Edwards. United States Senior Judge Lucis D.

Bunton III ruled in favor of the Sierra Club, ordering pumping limits while his appointed monitor was supposed to bring the warring factions together to create a comprehensive regional water plan, which lead to the creation of the **Edwards Aquifer Authority (EAA)**. Subsequently, the board determined that only 450,000 acre feet of water should be extracted from the Edwards on an annual basis. An **acre foot** is "325,851 gallons, enough to supply the needs of two families of four for a year."[49] The EAA set an interim pumping limit whereby users could "take out up to the maximum they withdrew in any one year between 1972 and 1993."[50] However in October 1995, a Hondo judge negated the initial charge of the EAA since it would have limited pumping of aquifer water in six counties. His ruling was based on a Texas property right older than the state itself—the **rule of capture**. In 1998, the owner of a commercial catfish farm and a group of Uvalde irrigation farmers sued the EAA. Judge Joseph Hart of the 126 District Court invalidated EAA's pumping limits by upholding the rule of capture. However, his ruling did leave room for the EAA to limit pumping during drought conditions.

Another important player in the water issue, the San Antonio Water Systems (SAWS) board decided to surcharge its residents for using too much water particularly for landscapes. SAWS developed a 50-year water plan that called for an immediate effort to limit pumping from the Edwards as well as the development of a waste water recycling plan to meet agricultural and industrial needs, and a concerted effort to acquire additional surface water. "For the years 2010 to 2030, the plan anticipates continued water conservation and development of the recycled water program; purchase of existing surface water; and delving into non-Edwards groundwater, most likely in the Carrizo-Wilson Aquifer in Southern Bexar County, where excess water also might be stored for later recovery. For 2030 and beyond, the report projects the need for new surface supplies, most probably from construction of new reservoirs by regional partnerships."[51] SAWS joined the San Antonio River Authority (SARA) in negotiating a deal with the Guadalupe-Blanco River Authority (GBRA) to purchase approximately 22.8 billion gallons of raw water to be delivered within five to ten years from the mouth of the Guadalupe River via a 132-mile pipeline.[52] SAWS also developed the Aquifer Storage and Recovery Project. Excess water from the Edwards or other sources is stored for future use in the Carrizo-Wilcox Aquifer, a massive underground water system that stretches from Northern Mexico through Texas to Canada.

As previously discussed in Chapter 13, every city must reconcile its corporate side by bringing new business development into its area while at the same time ensuring that its reservation side provides a more than decent quality of life for its residents. City leaders in San Antonio certainly had their work cut out for them when the corporate and reservation sides butted heads over the building of a Professional Golfers Association (PGA) sanctioned golf course, resort club and a multi-functional hotel over a portion of the Edwards Aquifer Recharge Zone. Lumberman's Investment Corporation headquartered in Austin purchased a 2,855 acre tract of land located in the north central portion of Bexar County. The land had been undeveloped for years since it sits right over the Recharge Zone. Initially Lumberman's deal with the PGA included three golf courses, 1,500 single family homes, 2,000 condominiums and apartments, 500 time-share units and two hotels.[53] The environmental community was aghast. Members of the League of Women Voters, Sierra Club, COPS, Metro Alliance and north side community and neighborhood associations formed the Smart Growth Coalition in hopes of blocking the PGA deal. They voiced concerns "over the golf resort's huge demand for water, as well as what runoff tainted with fertilizers and chemicals could do to pollute the aquifer."[54] Supporters of the project included the Greater San Antonio Chamber of Commerce, the North San Antonio Chamber of Commerce, the Hispanic Chamber of Commerce and, surprisingly, the EAA whose "board members voted 9-3 to approve a letter to city officials that states the golf resort development is 'superior' from an environmental standpoint to any alternative uses of the land."[55] Lumberman basically threatened the city by vowing to build as many as nine to ten thousand single family homes on the property. While the Smart Growth Coalition was launching a citywide petition to put the issue to a popular vote, the City Council negotiated a deal to build the original golf course resort plan with an agreement that the PGA would use "only organic pesticides and fertilizers and that Lumberman's will pay the San Antonio Water System $100,000 a year for monitoring, well testing, and soil sampling."[56] In return, Lumberman received tax abatements worth potentially $60 million over fifteen years.[57] The project has been completed and to date, there have been no complaints of environmental damage!

Other Municipalities Seek Water Sources

Located in Guadalupe County, the two cities of Schertz and Seguin form the Schertz/Seguin Local Government Corp. and successfully "purchased or leased more than 6,000 acres of land in Gonzales County. Six wells were drilled on this land which lies over the heart of the Carrizo-Wilcox Aquifer."[58] A rapidly growing community in the

Texas Hill Country, Blanco was hard hit by the 2000 drought that nearly caused their sole source of water, the Blanco River, to dry up. The community had been drilling for new water sources without luck since 1996. The rapid residential growth in the area coupled with the lack of rain placed an unreasonable burden upon the Blanco River. In addition, the Blanco feeds into the Trinity Aquifer System. Blanco residents purchased water from Canyon Lake and moved it through a pipeline system. Bandera, Blanco, Comal, Gillespie, Hays, Kendall, Kerr, and Travis counties developed their own organization called the Hill Country Priority Groundwater Management Area. They too, like SAWS, developed a fifty-year water conservation plan, which includes the search for new water sources.

The Fate of the Texas Coast and Wetlands

Padre Island and Mustang Island are traditional vacation destinations for spring-breakers and summer tourists. Fifty years ago there were more cattle than people on the islands. Today, the area is eyed by land developers seeking to add more tourist-oriented businesses into the area. The Texas Coast and the Gulf of Mexico are far more vital to the economic viability of this state than just providing a place to get a good tan. Consider these facts:

- It [the Gulf of Mexico] covers nearly 700,000 square miles. That is about seven times larger than the Great Lakes.
- More fish, shrimp, and shellfish are caught annually in the Gulf than in the entire U.S. Atlantic coast, including Chesapeake Bay.
- About 75 percent of waterfowl that transverse the United States pass through the Gulf region.
- About 90 percent of all U.S. offshore oil and gas comes from the Gulf.
- Gulf ports handle about 45 percent of all U.S. imports and exports. Seventy percent of all hydrocarbons shipped in and out of the nation pass through the Gulf.[59]

The Texas coastal areas are also the home and breeding grounds for numerous endangered plants, birds, fish, wildlife, and the endangered whooping crane. The **Aransas National Wildlife Refuge** eagerly awaits the annual arrival of these beautiful cranes as environmentalists count them and watch their daily routines. "More than four hundred bird species have been spotted here, along with bobcats, coyotes, alligators, white-tail deer and javelinas."[60] 0However, these precious birds and other species of plant

and wildlife have became caught in the middle of human progress as precious stretches of wetland areas are seen as prized land developments and industrial sites. The economic boost from tourism coupled with the desire to live by the "sea" has resulted in unprecedented population growth. Perhaps the most alarming and damaging threat to the Coast and its human and animal residents, is the increased incidences of pollution and environmental damage. What steps are federal and state governments taking to stop the abuse of the state's coastal areas?

In 1937 the federal government purchased 54,829 acres of Texas coastline for the creation of the Aransas National Wildlife Refuge. The General Land Office under the direction of the statewide elected land commissioner has the authority under several state environmental laws to safeguard certain sand dunes and wetland areas. In 1973 the Texas Legislature passed a law creating a dune protection program whereby counties could voluntarily participate in a state-sponsored effort to supervise commercial and land development in coastal areas. Initially, only Nueces and Brazoria counties joined the program. Alarmed by the rapid development in the South Padre Island area, Willacy and Cameron counties joined in 1991. The program has been expanded since including more counties along the coastal area. In March 2002, the Nature Conservancy of Texas announced its purchase of "24,532 acres on South Padre Island—an estimated one-third of all remaining underdevelopment property on the popular barrier island—and plans to preserve it forever as a wild and scenic place."[61] This area is home to several of the state's endangered and threatened species including the peregrine falcon, loggerhead sea turtle, Kemp's Ridley sea turtle, and the reddish egret. Located in the Aransas Pass area, Redfish Bay has been designated as a scientific area by the Texas Parks and Wildlife Commission (TPWC). Despite protests from fisherman and boating enthusiasts, the TPWC wanted to preserve the area's valuable grass beds from further commercial and residential development. "Sea grasses are critical to the coastal ecosystem, because they trap nutrients, prevent erosion, serve as food to sea turtles and provide habitat to juvenile crabs, shrimp and game fish that are at the center of a multi-billion dollar state fishery."[62]

In 1972, the federal government enacted the **Coastal Zone Management Act** defining a **coastal zone** as "the coastal waters (including the lands therein and thereunder), and the adjacent shorelands (including the waters therein and thereunder), strongly influenced by each other and in proximity to the shorelines of the several coastal states, and includes islands, transitional and intertidal areas, salt marshes, wetlands and beaches."[63] Subsequent state legislation extended protection to the state's **wetlands** defined as "areas that are inundated or saturated by surface or groundwater at a frequency and duration sufficient to support, and that under normal circumstances do support, a prevalence of vegetation typically adapted for life in saturated soil conditions."[64] Officially recognized as "waters-of-the-state" in 1991 under the Texas Water Quality Standards, the Texas Legislature has given more authority to the Texas Land Commissioner to oversee wetland areas and establish a coastal zone management plan encompassing a wide variety of issues ranging from erosion control to recreational and beach access. The fifty-five miles of the Padre Island National Seashore has been joined by the Matagorda Island as a joint federal-state wildlife area. Approved by both the EPA and the Texas Legislature, the 1995 Galveston Bay Plan restored 30,000 acres of wetlands and aimed at "controlling storm waterborne pollution to build on past progress toward reducing contaminants that are discharged directly from industries and sewer systems."[65] Designed by former Land Commissioner Garry Mauro, the adopt-a-beach-program has successfully integrated the community into assisting the state to clean up the coastal areas, while at the same time educating citizens about the ecological importance of protecting coastal and wetland properties.

On a Positive Note: Mitchell Lake and Other Revitalization Projects

A primary example of how successfully federal, state, county and city governments can work with environmentalists is the rehabilitation of Mitchell Lake, a former dumping site for untreated sewage located in San Antonio. Identified on maps dating to 1764, "the lake, reportedly once referred to as Espada Lake, was known by the late 1800s as Mitchell Lake, after Asa Mitchell a businessman who came to Texas in 1821 as one of Stephen F. Austin's original 'Old 300' colonists and fought at San Jacinto."[66] Known as a hunting and fishing site, the city of San Antonio purchased the property in 1901. "The city began dumping untreated sewage in the area in the early 1900s. Even after the San Antonio City Council designated Mitchell Lake a wildlife refuge in 1973, the city council continued to pour refuse into the area for more than another decade."[67] By 1987, city leaders stopped dumping sewage into the lake, opting instead to join forces with environmentalists to launch an extensive cleanup effort to turn the once smelly dump site into a 1,300-acre wildlife refuge offering protection for the area's wildlife and bird populations. Well-known

as a key resting and nesting area for birds, Mitchell Lake is now known as home to "owls, flycatchers, roadrunners, sandpipers, black-crowned night herons, crested caracaras (or Mexican eagles), red tailed hawks, northern harriers, egrets, vultures, mockingbirds, white faced ibises, white pelicans, blackneck stilts, herons, and even whopping cranes, an endangered species. Other wildlife at the lake that contribute to its ecosystem include muskrats and nutria-rodents hunted by hawks and other birds of prey-and everything from butterflies and other insects to lizards, tortoises, raccoons, possums, bobcats and coyotes."[68] Additional improvements included repairs of the dikes, the construction of roads and bridges, and the relocation of a historically significant building known as the Leeper House from the McNay Art Institute that serves as the Lake's information center.

The World Birding Center is located in the Rio Grande Valley near the cities of Brownsville and Weslaco around Laguna Madre. Despite the encroachment of residential and industrial developments, "the Valley has the best bird viewing in the country, paralleled only by southwest Arizona. About 485 bird species regularly fly through the region, including 35 species found only in the unique terrain at the Gulf Coast and lower Rio Grande."[69] A popular tourist attraction, the birding center adds nearly $100 million per year to the local economy.[70] In 2003, the Nature Conservancy purchased 137 square miles of pristine property along the banks of Devils River in West Texas. "Fed by the springs emanating from the Edwards-Trinity Aquifer the crystal-clear waters of the Devils River run through steep cliffs, limestone mesas and sculpted canyons for 60 miles before emptying into Lake Amistad."[71]

The State's Endangered and Threatened Species

The federal government took action to protect the nation's animal, marine, bird and plant life with the passage of the **Endangered Species Act (ESA)** in 1973. This legislation places any species listed as endangered or threatened under federal protection until the species can recoup its losses and survive on its own. "Once the listing takes effect, any intentional act that results in harm to any of the species can be punishable by a fine up to $100,000 or a year in jail."[72] The ESA defines **endangered species** "as one in danger of becoming extinct throughout all or a significant part of its natural range"; whereas, a **threatened species** is "one likely to become endangered in the foreseeable future."[73] Currently, Texas has 97 species on the list of which 78 are endangered and 19 are threatened. Of the 97, 67 are animals and 30 are plant species.[74] The ESA has had some success stories such as the American Bald Eagle. Our national symbol was on the brink of extinction. An accomplished hunter, the Bald Eagle was the enemy of the nation's ranchers who retaliated by shooting, trapping, and poisoning the birds as well as destroying their nesting areas. Under the protective arm of the ESA, the dwindling number of Bald Eagles could no longer be hunted nor their nesting areas destroyed. Gradually, the number of eagles increased to the point that the ESA removed them from its protection. Existing for only 10 million years, the number of sea turtles have diminished to the point that basically all of their species are listed as endangered. The Kemp Ridley sea turtle's future became questionable when "cattle trucks began shuttling onto the beaches of Tamaulipas in northeast Mexico and hauling off their eggs by the thousands to be sold as aphrodisiacs. The population was depleted even further by the nets and hooks of commercial shrimpers and fisherman, who killed many as an unintended consequence of their harvesting efforts."[75] In 1978, both the Mexican and United States governments launched efforts to save the turtles. After over thirty years of conservation efforts, environmentalists believe that this specie has reached sustainable population levels.

Despite its successes, the ESA is the focal point of ranchers, property owners, mining operators, and the timber industry who feel that their livelihoods are threatened and imperiled by the federal government's desire to protect a bird, fish, plant, or animal from extinction. Environmentalists defend the ESA's efforts by pointing out that the intent of the law is to find a balance between protecting the environment including all of its creatures and plants while at the same time, allowing for the development people need for survival. Federal and state guidelines "allow some damage to habitat as long as it does not jeopardize one or more of the endangered species or allows the property owner to move forward with his plans so long as the other lands harboring endangered species are protected instead."[76]

The Quality of the Air We Breathe

Our survival is dependent upon the quality of the air we breathe. **Air** is "a mixture of nitrogen (78.084 percent), oxygen (20.948 percent), argon (0.934 percent), carbon dioxide (0.0322 percent), and traces of neon, helium, krypton, hydrogen, xenon, methane, and vitreous oxide."[77] The survival of plant and animal life is dependent upon nitrogen, oxygen, and carbon dioxide. Oxygen is essential for higher life (human). Carbon dioxide plays a key role in photosynthesis and food production. Ozone, a byproduct of oxygen, protects us from the sun's dangerous ultraviolet light. The slightest degree of contamination to any of these elements seriously jeopardizes the quality of the air we breathe.

Conversely, **air pollution** is defined "as a group of chemical compounds that are in the wrong place or in the wrong concentration at the wrong time."[78] The primary cause of air pollution is the release of **suspended particulates** such as ash, smoke, dust, soot, and liquid droplets through the burning of fuels and the use of pesticides. Particularly harmful, sulfur dioxide (SO_2) is a substance released by the burning of sulfur-based fuels such as oil and coal, and carbon monoxide (CO) released when fuels such as gasoline are not completely burned. Air pollution also contains the toxic air pollutants released into the air through the manufacturing processes used in refineries, chemical plants, dry cleaners, and so on. The combination of all of these substances into the air usually forms smog, haze or acid rain. **Smog** occurs when "nitrogen oxides (N_2O) produced by burning fuel and volatile organic compounds (VOCs) escape into the atmosphere."[79] Smog appears as a hazy brown cloud. **Ozone** is a primary ingredient of smog. Texas's major cities now have ozone action alert days whereby residents are asked not to fuel their cars or mow the lawn during alert hours. Individuals with respiratory ailments and allergies are advised to remain indoors. Ozone is not friendly to the agricultural community. It is believed that ozone alone can "reduce potential crop yields in the United States by 5 to 10 percent."[80] **Haze** is "wide-scale, low-level pollution that obstructs visibility."[81] In the 1980s Americans realized that they were contributing to the nation's air pollution problems with their use of products containing **chlorofluorocarbons** or **CFCs**. The term CFC refers to "a family of inert, non-toxic and easily-liquefied chemicals used in refrigeration, air conditioning, packaging, and insulation or as solvents or aerosol propellants."[82] Federal legislation bans the use of CFCs in vehicle air conditioners. Another term associated with air pollution is **acid rain**, a "complex chemical and atmospheric phenomenon that occurs when emissions of sulfur and nitrogen compounds and other substances are transformed by chemical processes in the atmosphere, often far from the original source, and then deposited on earth in either wet or dry form. The wet form, properly called 'acid rain,' can fall as rain, snow or fog. The dry forms are acidic gases and particulates."[83]

The federal government began its assault on air pollution in 1955 with the passage of the **Air Pollution**

Control Act. However, this law limited the federal government's role to just providing federal funding to state and local governments for only research activities. The **Clean Air Act** of 1963 created a $95 million grant-in-aid program to assist states in establishing air quality standards. Congress established emissions standards for motor vehicles in 1965. The 1967 **Air Quality Act** created 247 air-quality control regions across the country for the monitoring of air pollution levels. The Clean Air Act of 1970 required all states to develop state implementation plans for meeting federally established air quality standards. A series of amendments to the Clean Air Act passed in 1977 required the states to attack air pollution problems arduously or face losing federal highway and sewage treatment funds. Although the Reagan administration sought to weaken the Clean Air Act, the George H. Bush administration did pass amendments to the Clean Air Act in 1989. This package included the mandatory phase-out of the

President Bush signs the Clean Air Act as William Reilly and Secretary Watkins look on in the Rose Garden of the White House. July 21, 1989.
Photo credit: George Bush Presidential Library

production of chlorofluorocarbons, carbon tetrachloride, methyl chloroform and hydro-chlorofluorocarbons. These chemicals are major contributors to ozone damage. The 1990 amendments further reduced auto emissions by requiring manufacturers to improve emission control devices and required gasoline companies to produce cleaner burning fuels. These new laws also grappled with acid rain by demanding reduction of emission levels of sulfur dioxide and nitrate oxide. Over 250 categories of hazardous pollutants were identified for pollution control and reduction of their emissions by 90 percent by 2003. A 1993 law added diesel-engine trucks to the list of motor vehicles subjected to emission control requirements. As the primary federal agency overseeing air pollution-related problems, the EPA can declare urban areas as either **attainment** or **non-attainment** in meeting established **national ambient air quality standards (NAAQS)**, predetermined acceptable levels of total suspended particulates, sulfur dioxide, nitrogen oxide, carbon monoxide, ozone, lead, and fine particulate materials.

State and local communities are charged with the eventual implementation and enforcement of federal air pollution laws. The **Texas Clean Air Act** went beyond federal requirements by placing stiffer air pollution control standards on businesses, industries, and urban areas. The TNRCC is responsible for enforcing state and federal air and anti-pollution laws. The Texas Clean Air Act empowers the TNRCC to investigate and search any properties suspected of polluting as well as to issue to businesses and industries emission permits to release harmful substances as long as the permit recipient releases them at acceptable levels. Permits are issued for specified time periods with the holders subjected to inspection and reporting requirements. The TNRCC works with local governments to bring both civil and criminal charges against violators. In addition, the TNRCC can assess administrative penalties up to $10,000 for each violation of the Texas Clean Air Act or a TNRCC rule. A suspected violator is usually issued a notice of violation with the understanding that compliance must be accomplished with 180 days. Civil lawsuits can involve penalties ranging from $40 to $25,000 for each day the violation occurs.

Few can deny that Texas has considerable air pollution problems. For nearly three decades, Houston has been in the top ten of the nation's most polluted cities. One of the contributing factors to her air pollution problem is the number of oil refineries located in the area. The nation's largest refinery in terms of crude oil production, the ExxonMobil Baytown Refinery, was singled out for numerous pollution-related problems from 1984 to 2000.

The Sustainable Energy and Economic Development Coalition, an environmental advocacy group, cited the Baytown facility with "repeated and persistent accidental releases of air pollutants, known as upset emissions; failure to properly maintain emissions monitors; and possible violations of federal law on reporting and modifications" and cited the TNRCC for "failure to issue notices of violations, failure to pursue reporting discrepancies or violations and failure to conduct independent review of emissions and other reporting."[84] On March 19, 2019, a major explosion and fire erupted at the Intercontinental Terminals Company in Deer Park, about 15 miles from Houston. The fire engulfed several large storage tanks containing components of gasoline and by-products used in nail polish removers, glue and paint thinners. Although no injuries were reported, firefighters could not put the fire out, but opted to let it burn out by itself over a two-day period. A few days later, the fire reignited and spread rapidly to other filled storage tanks, damaging eleven storage tanks. The huge thick plume of black smoke carrying hazardous substances such as benzene into the air, caused city leaders to close the schools and eventually evacuate the entire community. With its concentration of oil refineries and storage facilities, the Houston-area has been the scene of major fires and storage tank explosions. For example, the Shell Deer Park refinery was built in 1929. The refinery is a joint business venture between Shell Oil and Penmax, the national oil company of Mexico. In 1979, several workers at this facility were critically injured when a tanker exploded at the plant. In 2010, a major fire broke out, injuring several including firefighters, followed by another one in 2014.

One of the state's most polluted areas is a 10-mile corridor of oil refineries in Corpus Christi known as Refinery Row. The petro-chemical business in Corpus is the city's leading industry employing over 2,300 just at these sites with thousands more employed at businesses that supply equipment and product support. Corpus zoning laws allowed residential areas to be built near Refinery Row, causing residential property values over the years to dramatically decline as the incidences of refinery-related pollution increased. It is extremely difficult to sell a home when it is located next to an oil refinery! "While refineries stoke the fires of economic progress, pockets of low-income residents reap the downsides: blighted neighborhoods, sickening odors, and the risk of catastrophe."[85] Residents complain that "there are days when the pungent smell of rotten-eggs, caused by the hydrogen sulfide, wafts over neighborhoods. On some occasions when the flares burn, inky black smoke spreads across the sky drifting wherever the wind takes it. Residents wake up on some mornings to find their vehicles coated with ash."[86] The potential for a major disaster looms over the area. The EPA has indicated that the refineries repeatedly release unacceptable levels of benzene into the air.

Hazardous and Solid Wastes

The proper disposal of solid and hazardous wastes is a problem confronting all levels of government. For example, in the late 1980s the City of San Antonio wanted to build an ultramodern convention and dome stadium facility in the downtown area. Desiring to relocate for plant expansion purposes, an iron works firm offered its prime downtown location at a more-than-reasonable price to the city. Subsequently, the Alamo Dome was built on the land vacated by the Alamo Iron Works Company. However, city leaders soon learned that their prized site for a dome stadium was sitting on tons of contaminated dirt. Decades of melting scrap iron and other metals at the iron works factory had resulted in the company dumping toxic substances on their property. Of course, this was a perfectly acceptable practice before federal legislation declared these by-products as hazardous and harmful to humans, animals, and plant life. The problem confronting city leaders was the proper identification and the disposal of the hazardous dirt. After nine years of litigation and $5 million in costs, the City of San Antonio and the two primary Alamo Dome contractors agreed to pay an additional $2.6 million whereby the approximate seven hundred residents near the dome site would receive payment to settle their personal-injury claims ranging from a few hundred dollars to more than $10,000 each.[87] The removal and subsequent disposal of the dirt nearly cost more than it did to build the Alamo Dome. Dallas was confronted with a similar problem. The site of the city's newest basketball and hockey arena was contaminated with approximately 40,000 tons of oily dirt. The source of the contamination was a nearby rail yard owned by Union Pacific who, once again, dumped hazardous substances prior to the passage of laws prohibiting the wanton dumping of hazardous wastes. Of course, San Antonio and Dallas will not be the only cities confronted with this problem.

The federal government set the stage for state legislative acts by passing a series of laws focusing on the identification, monitoring, and disposal of solid and industrial waste products. Passed in 1976, the **Toxic Substance Control Act** required the EPA to establish testing procedures for new chemical substances before they are sold, authorized the EPA to ban harmful substances, and prohibited the sale of toxic polychlorinated biphenyls (PCB) not contained in enclosed systems. The federal government's Superfund was created in 1980 for the sole purpose of providing financial support for the cleanup of hazardous waste sites. The **Resource Conservation and Recovery Act (RCRA)** of 1976 established the process for the disposal of hazardous waste products. The **Texas Solid Waste Disposal Act** and the **Injection Well Act** are two primary pieces of state legislation regulating hazardous and solid wastes. In adherence with federal laws, the state's guidance for the storage and disposal of industrial wastes covers a wide spectrum from landfill site selections to dumping substances in ponds and lagoons. Identical to the RCRA definition, the Texas Administration Code defines **solid waste** as "any garbage, rubbish, sludge from a waste treatment plant, water supply, treatment plant or air pollution control facility and other discarded materials, including solid, liquid, semisolid or contained gaseous material resulting from industrial, municipal, commercial, mining and agricultural operations, and from community and institutional activities."[88] The definition purposely excludes "all waste materials which result from activities associated with the exploration, development, or production of oil or gas or geothermal resources, any other substance or material regulated by the Railroad Commission of Texas."[89] The TNRCC prohibits the storage and/or disposal of any hazardous waste that will adversely impact any water source and endanger public health or welfare. Both federal and state laws prohibit the transportation of hazardous materials through municipal areas. Redirecting vehicles and rail carriers to rural areas does minimize the risk of a major disaster in loss of life and property; however, the risk of a major derailment or accident resulting in the release of harmful substances into rivers, streams, soil and the air is still a tragic reality. Proper notification of impending storage or disposal of hazardous substances must be followed with the recording of the site with the County Deed Records office as well as the filing of monthly and yearly reports. Violators may be liable for fines ranging from $100 to $25,000 per day, per violation.

Unfortunately, it oftentimes takes a very tragic accident to remind us of the volatility of chemical substances such as ammonium nitrate. On a sunny day in April 2013, the small semi-rural community of West, Texas, was nearly flattened by an explosion at the West Fertilizer Co., the city's largest employer. A fertilizer producing plant, the company stored an inordinate amount of ammonium nitrate, an essential ingredient of fertilizer. The explosion rocked the community, killed fifteen people, injured over 160 others, and destroyed a nearby nursing home, the city's school, and countless number of homes. This tragic explosion drove home the point that the state lacked the legislative teeth that would have mandated that the TNRCC conduct more than a cursory annual inspection to ensure compliance with both state and federal laws overseeing the storage of hazardous substances. The West Fertilizer Co., is not the only fertilizer firm in Texas lacking sound environmental oversight. "Two-thirds of the ammonium storage facilities—about 62—in Texas are in jurisdictions with no local fire code. State law prohibits areas with a population under 250,000 [such as West] from developing a code, and no statewide code exists. Previous legislative attempts to require such a code, or place more stringent standards on ammonium nitrate facilities, have been unsuccessful."[90]

Municipal solid waste is defined as "solid waste resulting from or incidental to municipal, community, commercial, institutional, and recreational activities including garbage, rubbish, ashes, street cleanings, dead animals, abandoned automobiles, and all other solid waste other than industrial waste."[91] The primary problem confronting city and county governments is refuse disposal. Both state and federal regulations over landfills are extremely strict. Trash can be piled only to a certain height in a landfill before a variance to pile it higher must be obtained from the EPA. Cities with limited landfill space are confronted with the ongoing problem of too much garbage and too little space for dumping it. With growths in population, city leaders are faced with the task of finding additional landfill space or developing alternative means to deal with its trash. Recycling programs for aluminum cans, plastic and glass products and paper has had limited success. The cost of recycling the items into re-useable products is costly. Consumers do not wish to pay higher prices for paper that has been recycled, no matter how environmentally conscious they are. Energy conservationists, however, point to the potential silver lining of garbage and its decomposition process. As landfill waste begins to decompose, it releases gases including methane or natural gas and carbon dioxide. It is estimated that "one million tons of landfill gases can generate enough energy to power 700 homes for a year."[92] As a source of energy, landfill gas would augment the nation's supply of natural gas. In addition, harvesting landfill gas will be good for the environment. Experts point out that "using landfill gas energy from 1 million tons of waste has the same effect as planting 8,300 acres of trees or removing 6,100 cars from the road for a year."[93] Austin has been using landfill gases from its Sunset Farms dump site. Obviously, the search for a viable environmentally safe and cost-effective waste disposal plan is a continuing process.

Environmental Politics

The evidence clearly and tragically shows that Texas, as well as the entire nation, has serious environmental concerns. Despite the numerous legislative acts supporting protection of the environment, incidents of environmental damage continue to increase in numbers and severity of (often irreversible) damage. Public sympathy leans towards the crises of environmental groups particularly after a devastating major oil spill with the images of oozing thick oil spoiling beaches and killing plants and marine life. It would seem reasonable to assume that if public opinion was so supportive of protecting the environment, lawmakers and environmentalist could easily solve this public policy issue. However, fickle public opinion too often joins and supports the voices of business and industry when the words "sacrifice," "cost" and "accountability" enter into the picture. Former Vice President Al Gore's movie an "Inconvenient Truth" about global warming did not attract a large attentive audience until he won an Academy Award!

Leading environmental groups continue to assail lawmakers at all levels to enact corrective legislation. The preeminent groups are the Sierra Club, Wildlife Federation, Environmental Defense Fund, Natural Resources Defense Council, and Greenpeace. Their message is clearly evident by the alarming incidents of irreversible environmental damage. However, the doomsday predictions and tactics often label them as extremists who are willing to sacrifice the economic viability of this country and this state in order to protect the environment and wildlife from the inevitable advancement of people. "Environmentalists' penchant for doom-saying is coming back to haunt them. By overstating evidence, by presenting hypotheses as certainties and predictions as facts to create a sense of urgency, scientist-activists have jeopardized their own credibility."[94] In particular, the Sierra Club has used its doomsday message time and time again in its quest to take the Edwards Recharge Zone away from state/local control. These environmental groups have valid concerns; however, threatening self-sufficient Texans already hostile to any kind of government regulation over their sacred property rights is not always the wisest course of action to take.

In addition, environmental groups, like most interest groups, attract their advocates from upper- and middle-income individuals. These individuals view the issue of the environment differently from low-income groups. "The economically secure are more willing to close down polluting factories. They are more willing to ban logging operations in order to preserve wilderness areas . . . to pay extra for canned goods in order to reduce the cannery's waste emissions into a river."[95] The more affluent can afford to make these sacrifices without seriously jeopardizing their economic and social viability. However, the poor do not have the luxury of making these personal sacrifices just to preserve the environment. To them, environmental regulations equate to factory closings and loss of jobs. To the oil field worker, the machinist, and the farm worker, "their jobs depend on exploiting environmental resources; their first priority is to maintain a healthy growing economy and keep factories operating even if emissions pollute the air; feeding one's family and paying the rent are of primary importance; an unpleasant smell in the air is of relatively little concern. Smoke means jobs."[96] Widespread support for environmental protection and regulations cannot be achieved until the economic viability of those individuals dependent upon the jobs generated by polluting industries and businesses can be protected. This may be an impossible task.

Political reality also has a bearing on the development of environmental policy issues. The cause of environmentalists has been a platform issue of both the state and national Democratic Party organizations. However, the political reality in Texas favors the politician who modifies pro-environmental position statements. Particularly in this state, "politicians attempt to please the voting public by jumping onto the 'ecological bandwagon' while not alienating the business interests so essential to their political successes."[97] The Republican Party has been well known for its opposition to environmental regulations. Their cries that big government has no business whatsoever meddling into the affairs of private property owners wins advocates among Texans traditionally fearful of the encroachment of government at any level. Despite the damage caused by the explosion at the West Fertilizer Co., and the extent of the loss of lives and property, a bill introduced in the Texas Legislature has drawn criticism from Republican lawmakers. One commented that "we don't want to do damage to the industry."[98] Another tried to downplay it as just a tragic isolated incident that will soon fade into an obscure memory. "We had that crisis a couple of years ago. But this is all faded from the public memory, and, on the other hand, the companies that are likely to be regulated are still around. Their lobbyists are still there and they're going to do their best to make sure nothing comes of this."[99]

The business community has been painted as the evil monster bent on destroying the environment. An economy driven on a free market philosophy is opposed to any form of costly government-sponsored regulation. However, not every business in Texas participates in the wanton destruction of the environment nor openly defies environmental laws. Environmental cleanups are extremely expensive and time consuming. Polluters should be held accountable for their actions. However, environmentalists could win more supporters within the business community by actively recognizing the efforts of these businesses and industries that have taken the proper steps to ensure that they are producing products made in an environmentally safe process.

Conclusions

Although some progress has been made, dismal reports provide alarming statistical documentation of serious environmental damage to this state's air, water supply, lakes, rivers, forests, coastline, wetlands, and wildlife. Environmentalists are not all left-wing extremists using unsubstantiated doomsday predictions. The damage is real. If left unchecked, we will continue to destroy our once abundant natural resources. Unfortunately, the current array of federal and state laws is strong in verbiage and intent but exceptionally weak in implementation and enforcement. The TNRCC has been criticized by lawmakers and citizens alike for its lax enforcement and close ties to the industries it is supposed to be regulating. The parceling out of implementation tasks to several state agencies severely weakens the strength of the law. Lengthy court battles deplete state funds that could be used to actually cleanup existing problems and educate both the public and business community on how to avoid future damage. The violators are rarely punished with the severity intended by the legislation. Culturally and historically, public sentiment in this state rests with property owners who are seen as the Davids trying to overcome the Goliaths of big government.

Barack Obama came to the White House with the intent of moving Americans away from their dependency on fossil fuels by encouraging automobile manufacturers to build more gas efficient vehicles, while at the same time, scientists and engineers would develop alternative non-polluting fuels. The oil and gas industry continued to seek new oil deposits, particularly in deep water offshore untapped deposits. However, on April 20, 2010, a massive oil rig known as the "Deepwater Horizon," owned by Transocean and leased to BP (British Petroleum) Oil

exploded. Killing and seriously injuring many of the rig workers, the explosion ruptured the main pipeline and for nearly four months poured millions of gallons of crude oil into the Gulf of Mexico. Although the oil primarily fouled the Louisiana coast, Texans were worried that the liquid gold would destroy the precious Texas Gulf Coast. President Obama issued a moratorium on all deep-water and off shore drilling projects. The ban has since been lifted. The political turmoil in the Middle East, particularly in Libya, has pushed gasoline prices at the pumps to all time lows. The Obama administration wanted also to explore nuclear power as a viable alternative energy source. On March 6, 2011, a major 8.9 earthquake and a massive tsunami hit the Japanese coastal area causing untold misery in loss of life and property. In particular, the nuclear power plant Fukushiama Daiichi with its numerous reactors was seriously damaged. The real potential threat of a nuclear reactor meltdown reminds one of the potential deadly damage of nuclear generated power, leaving one to wonder if there is a much safer nonpolluting source of energy yet to be discovered.

Short of a crystal ball, perhaps the solution rests with a collective realization among all parties involved that environmental damage will not disappear or abate on its own by simply wishing it would disappear. The community as a whole—industrialists, workers, consumers, and yes, property owners—have created this mess. Governments can pass mounds of punitive legislation. However, the legislation is meaningless unless those same industrialists, workers, consumers and property owners collectively and equally bear the responsibility of making the needed sacrifices to prevent further environmental damage. Unfortunately, it will take more than just adopting a stretch of a highway or a sand dune to preserve this state's environment.

Chapter Notes

[1]"President John F. Kennedy Assesses the Environment, 1963," *Major Problems in American Environmental History*, Carolyn Merchant, ed., (Lexington, Massachusetts: D. C. Heath and Company, 1993), 497.

[2]Randy Lee Loftis, "Texas Environment: State of Neglect," *The Dallas Morning News*, (Sunday, November 24, 1991), 3N.

[3]*State of Texas Annual Cash Report 2018: Revenues and Expenditures of State Funds for the Year Ended August 31, 2018*, (Austin, Texas: Comptroller of Public Accounts, 2018), 56.

[4]Randall W. Bland, Alfred B. Sullivan, Robert E. Biles, Charles P. Elloitt, Jr., and Beryl E. Pettus, *Texas Government Today*, 5th ed., (Pacific Grove, California: Brooks/Cole, 1992), 458.

[5]*U.S. Environmentalism Since 1945: A Brief History with Documents*, Steven Stoll, ed., (Boston, Massachusetts: Bedford/St. Martins, 2007), 9.

[6]Ibid., 8.

[7]Steven A. Peterson and Thomas H. Rasmussen, *State and Local Politics*, (New York, New York: McGraw Hill, 1994), 251.

[8]"Rachel Carson Warns of a Silent Spring, 1962," *Major Problems in American Environmental History*, Carolyn Merchant, ed., (Lexington, Massachusetts: D. C. Heath and Company, 1993), 494 and 496.

[9]"Lady Bird Johnson: Remarks before the General Session, 1965," *U.S. Environmentalism Since 1945: A Brief History with Documents*, Steven Stoff, ed., (Boston, Massachusetts: Bedford/St. Martins, 2007), 128.

[10]*Lyndon Johnson and American Liberalism: A Brief Biography with Documents*, Bruce J. Schulman, ed., 2nd ed., (Boston, Massachusetts: Bedford/St. Martins, 2007), 99.

[11]John Heilprin, "Bush to Adopt Stricter Arsenic Standard," *San Antonio Express-News*, (Thursday, November 1, 2001), 16A.

[12]Eric Pianin, "Bush Eyes Giving EPA Role to States," *San Antonio Express-News*, (Sunday, July 22, 201), 7A.

[13]Gary C. Bryner, *Blue Skies, Green Politics: The Clean Air Act of 1990*, 1st ed., (Washington, D.C.: CQ Press, 1993), 20.

[14]Peterson and Rasmussen, 251.

[15]Susan Welch, John Gruhl, Michael Steinman, John Comer, and Susan M. Ridgon, *American Government*, 5th ed., (Minneapolis, Minnesota: West Publishing Co., 1994), 614.

[16]Arnold Heidenheimer, Hugh Helco, and Carolyn Teich Adams, *Comparative Public Policy: The Politics of Social Choice in American, Europe and Japan*, 3rd ed., (New York, New York: St. Martins Press, 1990), 323.

[17]Heidenheimer, etal., 324.

[18]Ibid., 323.

[19]Ibid., 310.

[20]J. Gordon Arbuckle, *Environmental Law Handbook*, 11th ed., (Rockville, Maryland: Government Institutes, Inc., 1991) 8.

[21]Scott Huddleston, "Pioneering Spanish Influences Abound," *San Antonio Express News*, Thursday, April 6, 2017), A8.

[22]*Texas Almanac: 2018-2019*, (Denton, Texas: Texas State Historical Association, 2018), 89 & 99.

[23]Joe G. Moore, Jr., "Water for Texas," *Texas at the Crossroads: People, Politics and Policy*, Anthony Champagne and Edward J. Harpham, eds., (College Station, Texas: Texas A & M University Press, 1987), 111.

[24]"Many Regions Face Prospect of Worsening Water Deficits," *The Dallas Morning News*, (Sunday, November 24, 1991), 11N.

[25]Jerry Needham, "This Parched Land," *San Antonio Express-News*, (Sunday, January 16, 2000), 16A)

[26]Moore, "Water for Texas," 118.

[27]Ibid., 128.

[28]Laura Trolley, "Rep. Puente Backs Water Transfer Bill," *San Antonio Express-News*, (Thursday, January 7, 1999), 9A.

[29]Nicole Foy, "Landowners Challenging Water Law in High Court," *San Antonio Express-News*, (Friday, November 20, 1998), 11A.

[30]Ibid.

[31]Moore, "Water for Texas," 123.

[32]Dan McGraw, "A Boiling Tex-Mex Water War," *U.S. News and World Report*, (May 1, 2000), 24.

[33]Alison Gregor, "Valley Farmers Say Mexico Owes Water," *San Antonio Express-News*, (Friday, February 18, 2000), 10A.

[34]*The Texas Environmental Almanac*, compiled by Mary Sanger and Cyrus Reed, 2nd ed., (Austin, Texas: Texas Center for Public Studies, 2000), 35.

[35]Ibid.

[36]Gregor, "Valley Farmers Say Mexico Owes Water," 10A.

[37]Susan L. Cutter and William H. Renwick, *Exploitation, Conservation and Preservation: A Geographic Perspective on Natural Resource Use*, 4th ed., (Hoboken, New Jersey: John Wiley & Sons, Inc., 2004), 377.

[38]Ibid.

[39]*Texas Water Code, Title 2: Water Administration*, Subtitle D, Chapter 2, 4. http://www.statutes.legis.state.tx.us/Docs/WA/htm/WA.26.htm

[40]Ibid., 3

[41]Wilbourn E. Benton, *Texas Politics: Constraints and Opportunities*, 5th ed., (Chicago, Illinois: Nelson-Hall, 1984), 374-375.

[42]Texas Water Code, 1.

[43]Ibid.

[44]Texas Health and Safety Code, Section 341.001. Definitions, http://law,onecle.com/texas/health/341.001.html

[45]Alison Gregor, "Chemical Tainting Valley Towns' Water," *San Antonio Express-News*, (Saturday, September 8, 2001), 1A.

[46]Ibid.

[47]Texas Water Code, 47.

[48]Tom Bower, "State Takeover Shakes View of Aquifer as Endless Pool," *San Antonio Express-News*, (Sunday, May 17, 1992), 6L.

[49]Jerry Needham, "Judge Axes Pumping Limits Adopted by Aquifer Authority," *San Antonio Express-News*, (Monday, December 2, 1998), 8A.

[50]Ibid.

[51]Jerry Needham, "SAWS 50-Year Plan Praised for Inclusiveness," *San Antonio Express-News*, (Sunday, October 18, 1998), 5B.

[52]Jerry Needham, "SAWS Set to Join SARA in Guadalupe Water Deal," *San Antonio Express-News*, (Monday, January 15, 2001), 1A.

[53]John McCormack, "Coalition Threatens PGA Petition," *San Antonio Express-News*, (Monday, January 14, 2002), 1B.

[54]Christopher Anderson, "PGA Project On Fragile Land," *San Antonio Express-News*, (November 4, 2001), 1B.

[55]Christopher Anderson and Jerry Needham, "Aquifer Authority Rankles City," *San Antonio Express-News*, (Saturday, March 9, 2002), 1B.

[56]Joe Nick Patoski, "Water Hazard," *Texas Monthly*, (November, 2002), 96.

[57]Cindy Tumiel, "PGA's Tax Break Would Be Huge," *San Antonio Express-News*, (Saturday, February 23, 2002), 1A.

[58]Karen Adler, "Water Alliance Forming Between Schertz, Seguin," *San Antonio Express-News*, (Wednesday, March 7, 2001), 4H.

[59]"'America's Sea' Has Major Environmental Damage," *San Antonio Light*, (Sunday, April 12, 1991), D2.

[60]Suzy Banks, "Love Birds," *Texas Monthly*, (February, 2002), 102.

[61]Christopher Anderson, "Nature Conservancy Buys Third of Open Land on South Padre," *San Antonio Express News*, (Thursday, March 30, 2000), 1A.

[62]Christopher Anderson, "State Oks Redfish Bay Restriction," *San Antonio Express-News*, (Friday, June 2, 2000), 1A.

[63]Coastal Zone Management Act of 1972, as amended through Pub. L. No. 109-58, the Energy Policy of 2005, 16 U.S.C. 1453, Definitions, Section 304, 4.

[64]*Texas Environmental Almanac*, 92.

[65]Bill Dawson, "A Plan for the Future: Bay Rescue Depends on Consensus," *Houston Chronicle*, (Sunday, October 15, 1995), 1A and 30A.

[66]Scott Huddleston, "Mitchell Lake Is Vital for Birds," *San Antonio Express-News*, (Sunday, May 19, 2002), 2B.

[67]Elisa Schement, "Mitchell Lake's Rehabilitation, Refuge Plan In Motion," *San Antonio Express-News*, (Wednesday, April 25, 2001), 3H.

[68]Huddleston, "Mitchell Lake Is Vital for Birds," 2B.

[69]Alison Gregor, "Whose Haven?," *San Antonio Express-News*, (Monday, September 18, 2000), 1A.

[70]Ibid.

[71]Christopher Anderson, "Devils River Salvation," *San Antonio Express-News*, (Friday, July 11, 2003), 1A.

[72]Christopher Anderson, "Aquifer Land Set for List," *San Antonio Express-News*, (Friday, December 22, 2000), 6A.

[73]U. S. Bureau of the Census, *Statistical Abstract of the United States: 2010*, 129th ed., (Washington, D.C., 2009), Table 373, 227.

[74]*https://ballotpedia.org.endangered-species-in-Texas*

[75]Alison Gregor, "Hatching a Comeback," *San Antonio Express-News*, (Sunday, June 25, 2000), 1A.

[76]Anderson, "Aquifer Land Set for List," 6A.

[77]Bryner, 41.

[78]Ibid., 42.

[79]*The Information Please Environmental Handbook*, compiled by World Resource Institute, (New York, New York: Houghton Mifflin Co., 1993), 88.

[80]Ibid.

[81]Bryner, 42.

[82]Ibid., 188.

[83]Ibid., 187.

[84]Jerry Needham, "Groups Blast Baytown Refinery," *San Antonio Express-News*, (Thursday, May 3, 2001), 8B.

[85]John Tedesco, "Clearing the Air on Refinery Row," *San Antonio Express-News*, (Saturday, October 7, 2000), 8A.

[86]Ibid.

[87]Kate Hunger, "$2.6 Million Deal Ok'd in Dome Suit," *San Antonio Express-News*, (Sunday, July 20, 1998), 1A.

[88]*Texas Safety Health and Safety Code*, Section 363.004 Definitions.

[89]Ibid.

[90]Lauren McGaughty, "Stricter Regulation Is Sought of Ammonium Nitrate Storage," *San Antonio Express-News*, (Wednesday, July 2, 2014), A6.

[91]Ibid.

[92]Bob Richter, "Bill Pushes Garbage Power," *San Antonio Express-News*, (Saturday, April 14, 2001), 12A.

[93]Ibid.

[94]"The Doomsday Myths," *U.S. News & World Report*, (December 13, 1993), 81.

[95]Peterson and Rasmussen, 243.

[96]Ibid.

[97]Benton, 375.

[98]McGaughty, "Stricter Regulation Is Sought of Ammonium Nitrate Storage", A6.

[99]Ibid.

Glossary

1st Amendment to the U.S. Constitution – grants the freedoms of speech, religion, assembly, press, petition and redress of government, association, and religion

2nd Amendment to the U.S. Constitution – grants citizens the right to bear arms

4th Amendment to the U.S. Constitution – protects against unreasonable searches and seizures

6th Amendment to the U.S. Constitution – guarantees the right of legal representation and counsel

8th Amendment to the U.S. Constitution – prohibits cruel and unusual punishment

10th Amendment to the U.S. Constitution – grants the states their reserved powers

13th Amendment to the U.S. Constitution – abolishes slavery in the United States

14th Amendment to the U.S. Constitution - grants citizenship to former slaves and guarantees to all citizens due process of the law and equal protection before the law

15th Amendment to the U.S. Constitution – grants voting privileges to former African-American slaves

19th Amendment to the U.S. Constitution – grants women the right to vote

24th Amendment to the U.S. Constitution – prohibits the use of a poll tax for voting privileges

26th Amendment to the U.S. Constitution – changes the legal voting age from twenty-one to eighteen

Abington School District v Schempp (1963) - United States Supreme Court ruling that involuntary participation of public school students in reading Biblical passages in class was an unconstitutional violation of the First Amendment to the United States Constitution

Absentee Voting – a process enabling those qualified voters to cast their ballots in an election without going to the polls on election day

Absolute Poverty – the minimum amount of income needed to survive without deprivation

Access – the ability to gain the attention and to influence the decisions of key political agents

Acid Rain – complex chemical and atmospheric phenomenon that occurs when emissions of sulfur and nitrogen compounds and other substances are transformed by chemical possesses in the atmosphere, often far from the original source, and then deposited on earth in either wet or dry form

Acre foot – 325,851 gallons of water estimated to be enough to supply the needs of two families of four for a year

Act to Preserve and Protect Wild Game, Wild Birds, and Wild Fowl (1903) – state law mandating a five-year closed season for the hunting of antelope, mountain sheep and pheasants; prohibits the commerce of wild animal meat, skins and plumage

Ad Hoc Committee – short-term committee assigned a specific task that once completed, the committee is disbanded; also known as select committee

Ad Valorum – property appraisal based on the fair market value of the property

Address – the legislative process of removing a judge from his/her bench with a 2/3's vote in both houses

Administrative Law – that branch of law that creates administrative agencies, establishes their methods of procedure, and determines the scope of judicial review of agency practices and actions

Adversary System – an individual accused of a crime is innocent until proven guilty

Advocacy Groups - organizations created to seek benefits on behalf of groups or persons who are in some way incapacitated, otherwise unable to represent their own interests

Affective Orientations – feelings of attachment, involvement, rejection about political objects

Affirmative Action – the corrective steps taken on the part of government to address previous incidences of discrimination

Agricultural Hazard Communication Act – state legislation requiring proper notification and information to agricultural workers and others working with potentially dangerous chemicals

Aid to Families with Dependent Children – basic welfare program that provided cash transfer payments primarily to women living below the poverty level with dependent children; also known as Aid to Dependent Children

Aid to the Blind – program created through the Social Security Act of 1935 establishing federal assistance to sight-impaired individuals

Air – a mixture of nitrogen, oxygen, argon, carbon dioxide and traces of neon, helium, krypton, xenon, methane and vitreous oxide

Air Pollution – a group of chemical compounds that are in the wrong place or in the wrong concentration at the wrong time

Air Pollution Control Act (1955) – federal legislation establishing research activities for air pollution control

Air Quality Act (1967) – federal legislation establishing air quality regions and acceptable pollution levels for each region; mandates state and local governments to design and implement plans to set air quality standards in keeping with federal guidelines

Alamo (San Antonio de Valero) – Spanish mission built in 1718 on the banks of the San Antonio River

Alcalde – Spanish for mayor

Alleviative Public Policy Approach – policy designed to address current suffering caused by a policy-related problem or issue without actually attempting to solve the problem or issue itself

Almshouse – indigent housing program whereby local private and religious organizations offered housing to the poor, the mentally ill, and, in some instances, released inmates; also known as the poor house

American Recovery and Reinvestment Act (2009) – federal legislation providing $26.6 billion to fund more than 12,000 road, highway, and bridge projects across the nation

Americans with Disabilities Act – federal legislation requiring that all public transportation services be handicapped accessible

Anti-Federalists – those opposed to the ratification of the United States Constitution

Antiquities Act (1906) – federal legislation authorizing the President of the United States to set aside any national monuments or parcels of land considered to be objects of historical or scientific significance

Annexation – the addition by a city of land adjacent to it as an aggressive policy of growth or to meet the problems of metropolitan expansion

Apache – Nomadic Native American Indian tribe of the southern plains of central and northwest Texas

Apartheid – the former practice of separating whites and blacks in South Africa

Appellate Jurisdiction – the authority of a court to review decisions of an inferior court

Apportionment – the allocation of legislative seats

Appropriations Bill – legislation approving money to fund a program

Article I – section of the United States Constitution detailing the legislative branch of the national government

Article I, Section 8 – Section of the United States Constitution granting the national government the authority to enact legislation that is "necessary and proper" to operate the country as long as the legislation is not in conflict with the spirit and meaning of the United States Constitution; also known as the Necessary and Proper Clause or the Elastic Clause

Article I, Section 9 – Section of the United States Constitution placing restrictions upon both the national and state governments

Article I, Section 10 – Section of the United States Constitution placing restrictions upon the individual states

Article III – Section of the United States Constitution detailing the judicial branch of the national government

Article IV – Full faith and credit clause of the United States Constitution; see Full faith and credit clause

Article VI – Supremacy clause of the United States Constitution; see Supremacy Clause

Articles of Confederation – the nation's first constitution establishing a confederative form of government

Assimilation – the process of abandoning either voluntarily or involuntarily one's culture for another

Association of Southern Women for the Prevention of Lynching – women's organization dedicated to promoting legislation outlawing lynching

Attainment – status given by the EPA to a city or municipality in compliance with federal air quality standards

Austin, Stephen F. – one of the original empresarios in Texas; known as the Father of Texas

Australian Ballot – a secret ballot

Authorization Bill – a legislative act creating a program, specifying its general aims and how they are to be achieved, and unless open ended, puts a ceiling on monies that can be used to finance it

Available School Fund – state account consisting of income earned from investments of money from the Permanent School Fund

Bail – a cash payment for release from legal custody

Baker v Carr (1962) – the United States Supreme Court ruled that mal-apportioned districts are unconstitutional

Balanced Budget – a budget strategy whereby revenues equal expenses

Balloon Mortgage – financial agreement requiring a mortgage down payment of 35 to 40 percent with the balance of the loan payable in ten or fifteen years

Barron v Baltimore (1833) – the United States Supreme Court decision that the United States Constitution's Bill of Rights was enforceable only upon the national government

Basic Education Opportunity Grant – federal program that created the Pell Grant program for college students

Battle of San Jacinto – decisive battle of the Texas Revolution resulting in Texas's independence from Mexico

Bedroom Cities – a term used to describe incorporated cities within a metropolitan area

Bellwether Polling – a composition of a microcosm representing the entire population of a designated area

Benefit Principle System – a tax program whereby those who use the service more often than others are accessed a higher user fee or tax burden

Beyond a Reasonable Doubt – the criteria to establish guilt for a criminal offense

Bipartisan Campaign Reform Act (2002) – federal legislation limiting the use of soft-money contributions and placing restrictions on end-of-campaign advertisements; ruled unconstitutional by the United States Supreme Court

Bleeding Heart Conservatives – conservatives that support government-sponsored efforts to alleviate poverty and inadequate housing through conservative programs that empower people to help themselves as opposed to traditional government handouts

Blood Quantum Formula – the degree of Native American blood a person has determines their percentage of their Native American heritage

Biennial Budget – a two-year budgetary plan

Bill – a proposed law that either changes an existing one or creates a new one

Bill of Rights – the term applied to the first ten amendments to the United States Constitution

Biochemical Oxygen Demand (BOD) – the amount of oxygen required for decomposition of a given amount of waste

Blanket Primary – an open primary election allowing voters to participate in the nomination of candidates from multiple parties on the same day

Block Grants – federal grants given for a prescribed broad activity ranging from health care to public education

Blue Laws – a series of laws passed in Texas prohibiting the opening of businesses and purchases of certain items on Sundays

Boll Weevils – a long-used term for southern Democrats in the United States House of Representatives who support conservative policies

Bradwell v Illinois (1873) – case in which United States Supreme Court Justice Joseph Bradley wrote in his opinion that women must accept their traditional roles of mothers and wives

Brady Bill – federal legislation mandating a background check and a waiting period for individuals wanting to purchase a firearm

Brandenburg v Ohio (1969) – the United States Supreme Court ruled that Ohio's Syndicalism Act was an unconstitutional violation of the Fourteenth Amendment to the United States Constitution

Brown v Board of Education of Topeka, Kansas (1954) – United States Supreme Court decision overturning the concept of "separate but equal"

Buchanan v Warley (1917) – United States Supreme Court ruled municipal ordinances segregating housing unconstitutional

Buckley v Valeo (1976) – United States Supreme Court ruled that provisions of the 1974 Campaign and Finance bill as unconstitutional violations of freedom of speech as detailed in the First Amendment to the U.S. Constitution

Budget – an estimate of the receipts and expenditures needed by government to carry out its program in some future period usually a fiscal year

Bull Moose Party – a third political party movement founded by Theodore Roosevelt

Bureaucracy – the totality of government offices or bureaus that constitutes the permanent government of a state; that is, those people and functions that continue irrespective of changes in political leadership

Busway – a roadway or highway lane reserved exclusively for buses, also known as bus lane

Caddo – East Texas Indian tribe credited with naming the State as Texas or Tejas, meaning friendship

Camino Real – original road beginning from San Juan Bautista on the Rio Grande to the East Texas settlements, also known as the King's Highway or the San Antonio Road

Canon Law – ecclesiastical or church law

Common Law – judge-made law that originated in England from decisions shaped according to prevailing customs

Campesino – Spanish for farm laborer

Capital Expenses – multi-year or amortized costs such as a fleet of new police cars, computer systems, etc.

Carpetbaggers – southern term used to describe northern businessmen who came to the South

Casework – the services performed by legislatures and their staffs at the request of and on behalf of constituents

Cash Transfers – direct cash payments from income assistance programs to the recipient of the benefit

Casta – a person of mixed Spanish, Indian and African ancestry born in the New World

Categorical Grant – federal payment to a state or local government for a special purpose

Caucus – a meeting of party members in one of the houses of a legislative body for the purpose of making decisions on selections of party leaders and on legislative business

Censure – official discipline of a member for inappropriate behavior

Central Business District (CBD) - the downtown area of a city

Centrist – an individual or political group advocating a moderate approach to political decision making and to the solution of social problems

Change of Venue – moving a high-profile trial to an area unfamiliar with the case

Chávez, César – civil rights leader who founded the United Farm Workers Union

Checks and Balances – governmental system where power is distributed to prevent one branch of government from overpowering another branch or abusing power

Child Benefit Theory – an understanding that government or public tax dollars can be used to fund public and private education programs that benefit the child, not the school

Children's Health Insurance Program (CHIP) – a federally funded health-care plan for uninsured children whose parents' earnings do not qualify them for Medicaid and/or private health insurance

Chisholm Trail – the famous cattle drive trail beginning in south Texas through Austin, Lampassas, and Fort Worth to its final destination of Caldwell, Kansas

Chlorofluorocarbons (CFCs) – a family of inert, non-toxic and easily liquefied chemicals used in refrigeration, air conditioning, packaging, and insulation or as solvents or aerosol propellants

Church of Lukumi Babbalu Aye v Hialeah (1993) – the United States Supreme Court ruled that animal sacrifices used as part of a religious ceremony are constitutionally protected under the First Amendment's provision of freedom of religion

Citizen Groups – grassroots interest groups that originally develop at the community level to address unique locally based issues that do not fit under a national interest group umbrella

Citizens United v Federal Elections Commission (2010) – United States Supreme Court ruled that a provision in the Bipartisan Campaign Reform Act barring the airing of advertisements days before an election an as unconstitutional violation of the First Amendment

City Charter – a document specifying the powers and duties of elected city leadership to include candidate qualifications, terms of office, election cycles, salaries, as well as the organizational structure of city administration, types of public services provided to residents, etc.

City/County Consolidation – the movement to merge city with county government and consolidate basic services offered by both governments

City Manager – an individual hired by city council to perform administrative duties for the council to include budget creation and implementation, hiring and firing of personnel, and management of all city departments and functions

City of Rome v Mitchell (1980)– the United States Supreme Court ruled that the provision in the Voting Rights Act prohibiting any changes in voting practices that could have an unintentional discriminatory impact were unconstitutional

Civil Law – body of law dealing with disagreements between individuals

Civil Liberties – those inalienable rights that belong to individuals by the nature of humanity, which cannot be taken away without violating that humanity

Civil Rights – the acts of government intended to protect disadvantage classes of persons or minority groups from arbitrary, unreasonable, or discriminatory treatment

Civil Rights Act (1866) – federal legislation granting former slaves the right to own property, file law suits, and make contractual agreements; later ruled unconstitutional by the United States Supreme Court

Civil Rights Act (1875) - federal legislation prohibiting private discrimination in accommodations, transportation and public places of amusement; ruled unconstitutional by the United States Supreme Court

Civil Rights Act (1957) – federal legislation creating both the United States Commission on Civil Rights and the Civil Rights Section of the Justice Department; granted the federal government injunction authority to halt illegal voting activities

Civil Rights Act (1960) – federal legislation authorizing the appointment of federal voting referees to conduct voter registration drives and monitor federal elections in areas with historical patterns of illegal and discriminating voting practices

Civil Rights Act (1964) – federal legislation prohibiting discrimination in public accommodations and employment practices

Civil Rights Act (1968) – federal legislation prohibiting discriminatory housing practices

Civil Service Reform Act (1883) – established procedures for individuals seeking government employment to include comprehensive examinations; also known as the Pendleton Act

Clean Air Act (1955) – federal legislation establishing national air quality standards for air pollutants

Clean Air Act (1963) - federal legislation providing assistance to local and state governments in establishing air pollution control programs and related research activities

Clean Air Act (1965) - federal legislation establishing standards for automobile exhaust emissions

Clean Air Act Amendments (1970) – federal legislation authorizing the EPA to set national air pollution standards; limited discharge or major pollutants into the lower atmosphere; required automobile manufacturers to reduce by 90 percent nitrogen oxide, hydrocarbon, and carbon monoxide emissions

Clean Air Act Amendments (1990) – federal legislation setting formulas for development of new gasoline fuels to be used in smoggy cities; mandated further reduction of carbon monoxide and exhaust emissions for the year 2003; placed new restrictions on toxic pollutants

Clean River Act (1977) – state law allowing the Texas National Resource Conservation Commission to use the "watershed" approach to water pollution management

Clean Water Act (1966) – allocated federal funding for the construction of waste water treatment plants

Clean Water Amendments (1972) – a series of amendments to the Federal Water Pollution Control Act of 1948 establishing water quality standards for the nation's major rivers and lakes; mandated discharge permits for private and public facilities

Clean Water Act (1974) – federal legislation establishing standards to ensure safe water supplies for human consumption; also known as the Safe Water Drinking Act

Clear and Present Danger – a term applied to any portion of a speech that creates a danger to public safety. These actions are not constitutional and are not protected by the First Amendment to the United States Constitution.

Clientele Agency – a loose term for any government organization whose prime mission is to promote, serve, or represent the interest of a particular group

Closed Primary – the selection of a party's candidates in an election limited only to avowed party members

Cloture – a parliamentary technique used by a legislative body to end debate and bring the matter under consideration to a vote

Cluster Migration – settlement pattern resembling a hub of daughter colonies surrounding the mother colony

Coahiciltecan – band of inland Native American tribes in East Texas; a common language of the East Texas Indian tribes

Coastal Zone - the coastal waters to include the lands therein and thereunder, and the adjacent shorelines strongly influenced by each other and in proximity to the shorelines of the several coastal states, and includes islands, transitional intertidal areas, salt marshes, wetlands and beaches

Coates v Cincinnati (1971) – United States Supreme Court decision invalidating a city ordinance mandating the arrest of three or more individuals gathering in a public place who demonstrated annoying behavior as an unconstitutional violation of the freedoms of speech and assembly

Coattail Effect – tendency for a candidate heading a party ticket to attract or detract votes for other candidates of his or her political party on the ballot

Cognitive Orientations – knowledge, accurate or otherwise, of political objects

Cohen v California (1971) – United States Supreme Court ruled as constitutionally protected speech the wearing of a jacket with a four-letter word protesting the Vietnam War

Cohen v Virginia (1821) – the United States Supreme Court ruled that they have the authority to review state laws and, if need be, overturn them

Collective Bargaining – bargaining on behalf of a group of employees as opposed to individual bargaining, where each worker represents only himself or herself

Collective Benefits – one enjoys the benefits derived from an interest group's initiatives but that individual contributed nothing to the group that brought him/her those benefits

Colonias – underdeveloped rural properties in the border counties that have been leased or sold in small plots to primarily low-income Hispanics

Comanche – buffalo hunting Native American Indian tribe located in the Southern Plains of central and northwest Texas

Commission Format – form of city government composed of commissioners overseeing a particular functional area of city operations, i.e., police, fire, parks, public works, etc.

Committee of the Whole – a procedure used by a legislative body to expedite business by convening the official entire body of a house of the legislature into a committee for the consideration of bills and other matters

Common Pool Goods – goods that can be individually packaged, bartered and used, but their use by one person decreases its availability of the goods for others

Common Schools – public schools located in rural communities that are governed by county-wide elected superintendents and trustees

Communities Organized for Public Service (COPS) – San Antonio-based group located on the west side dedicated to bringing infrastructure improvements to their neighborhood through political participation and advocacy

Commutation – the reduction of a prison sentence

Compact Theory – belief that the relationship between the national and state governments is a binding contractual agreement

Concurrent Majority – John C. Calhoun's belief that the people should have a direct role in approving or disapproving of any legislative acts prior to their implementation

Concurrent Powers – governing authority shared by all levels of government to include taxation

Concurrent Resolution – a legislative act that must be approved by both houses of the Texas Legislature and signed by the governor in order to become law

Confederation System – a governing system composed of a loose collection of states in which principal power lies at the level of the individual states rather than with a central or national government

Conference Committee – an ad hoc committee composed of members from both houses to reconcile differences in similar bills passed by both houses in hopes of producing one bill

Conflictual Party System – a party system whereby the legislature is dominated by parties that are far apart on issues or highly antagonistic towards each other and the political system

Consensual Party System – a party system whereby the parties commanding most of the legislative seats are not too far apart on policies and have a reasonable amount of trust in each other and in the political system

Conservatism – the political outlook which springs from a desire to conserve existing things, held to be either good in themselves, are at least safe, familiar, and the objects of trust and affection

Consolidation – the merging of smaller independent school districts into one city- or county-wide district; the merging of city and county governments

Constable – warrant officer for the county's sheriff's office

Constitution – the fundamental or organic law that establishes the framework of government of a state, assigns the powers and duties of governmental agencies, and establishes the relationship between the people and their government

Constitutionalism – the political principle of limited government under a contract

Constrained Empathetic Federalism – combination of federal and non-federal resources to fund urban and rural empowerment zone objectives

Contract Clause – Article I, Section 10 of the United States Constitution guaranteeing citizens protection of their property

Contract for Deed – a property agreement whereby the owner keeps the title, charges a high interest rate and can take back the property if the buyer falls behind on the payments

Converting Election – a election whereby the majority party wins, but there are some noticeable basic changes in the distribution of the party membership and philosophical preferences

Cooperative Federalism – intergovernmental relationship where all levels of government share responsibilities and financing of government programs

Coproduction – the partnership between the private and public sectors to jointly provide residents with goods and services

Corporate Side – the economic/business sector of a city

Corrupt Practices Act – federal legislation limiting and regulating the amounts and sources of campaign contributions and expenditures, and barred contributions from labor organizations to any federal election campaign

Council Manager Format – city government structure whereby the city council acts as the policy making entity while the day-to-day operations of the city are entrusted to a council-hired city manager

Council of Governments (COGs) – regional organizations of rural and municipal government officials

County Attorney – serves as chief prosecuting official for a county; also known as District Attorney

County Auditor – serves as chief financial officer of county government to include accounting and budget creation and execution functions

County Clerk – official keeper of county records to include deeds, wills, birth and death certifications, marriage licenses, and so on, as well as serves as the county elections administrator in those counties without a separate office for elections administration

County Government – the administrative arm of state government

County Sheriff – the chief law enforcement officer of county governments; duties include management of the county jail and supervision of all law enforcement personnel

Cousins v Wigoda (1975) – the United States Supreme Court ruled that only the credentials committee of a national political party has the authority to settle credential disputes between rival state delegations

Court of Last Resort - the decision of the highest level of judicial authority

Creative Federalism – an intergovernmental relationship whereby political initiatives are created at the national level and then imposed on the states for implementation and enforcement

Creoles – landed aristocracy in Spanish Texas

Criminal Law – offenses against the state itself; actions that may be directed against a person but that are deemed to be offensive to society as a whole

Criollos – individuals of Spanish ancestry born in the New World

Critical Election – an election that heralds a new political alignment, that produces a new political majority, or that indicates a long-term shift in electoral behavior

Crosscutting Regulations – federal mandates of across-the-board requirements that affect all or most federal assistance programs such as environmental impact statements

Crossover – the technique used by both major political parties to enhance the chances of a victory for their candidates by casting a vote for the weakest candidate on the ballot

Crossover Sanctions – federal mandates whereby state and local governments will lose federal funding for non-compliance

Cultural Conservatism – political perspective based on support for Western Judeo-Christian values not just as a matter of comfort and faith, but out of a firm belief that the secular, the economic and the political success of the western world is rooted in this value

Culture of Poverty – concept developed by Edward Banfield in his book *The Unheavenly City* based on the belief that poverty is a culturally acquired trait

Curative Public Policy Approach – policy option that attempts to cure the cause(s) of an identified problem or issue

Dark Horse Candidate – a marginal candidate or non-candidate for public office who has little support and almost no chance of winning the election

Dartmouth College v Woodward (1819) – United States Supreme Court ruled that citizens cannot create a local government on their own volition

Dawes Act – federal legislation passed in 1887 allocating a section of land to each member of a Native American tribe; also known as the Allotment Act

De Coronado, Francisco Vásquez – Spanish explorer task to locate the Seven Cities of Cibola

De Facto Discrimination – an undeliberate action that adversely impacts one group or groups over another group or groups

De Jure Discrimination – a purposeful action that adversely impacts one group or groups over another group or groups

De Pineda, Alonso Álvarez – Spanish explorer who explored the Texas coastline in 1519

De Vaca, Álvar Núñez Cabeza – Spaniard survivor shipwrecked on the Texas coastal area in 1528; explored the interior of Texas

Decree – an administrative order having the force of the law

Dedicated Funding – purposely allocating money to a particular budget item with the understanding that the money cannot be used for any other purpose

Decision-making – a discrete choice from among two or more alternatives

Dedicated Revenues – budgetary allocations specifically and permanently assigned to a particular budget category

Defendant – the person accused of causing harm to the plaintiff

Deficit – budgetary situation whereby expenses or debits exceed income or credits

Democratic Ideology – political belief based on the concepts of individualism, liberty, equality, and fraternity

Democratic Party v LaFollette (1891) – the United States Supreme Court ruled that a state's party leadership could not force the Democratic National Party organization's credentials committee to accept a delegation that was selected in violation of DNC rules

DERAIL (Demanding Ethics, Responsibility and Accountability in Legislation) - interest group formed by members of the highway lobby, small town leadership, major air carriers and Southwest Airlines to fight the 1991 bullet train initiative

Deserving Poor – usually the elderly, the mentally-ill and physically handicapped individuals who through no fault of their own, became impoverished

Deviating Election – a new party wins, not because there has been a realignment in political party preferences but because the wining party just happened to have an attractive candidate or some other factor in its favor

Dial-Para Transit Fleets – small vans providing group personalized door-to-door services

Dillon Rule – a judicial ruling that municipal corporations, i.e., cities and counties, owe their origin to and derive their powers and rights wholly from the legislature

Direct Lobbying – interest group or lobbyist activities such as assisting a legislator in drafting legislation, working directly with legislative supporters in planning legislative strategy, making personal visits to legislative offices, etc.

Direct Order - a federal mandate embodied in a congressional law or regulation that must be enforced or state and local officials may be held accountable to civil and/or criminal penalties

Discharge Petition – a legislative procedure that forces a bill out of committee

Direct Primary – an intraparty election in which voters select candidates who will run on a party's ticket in the subsequent general election

Discrimination – an unfavorable action toward people because they are members of a particular racial or ethnic group

Disposable Income – income available to persons for spending or saving; income less personal tax and non-tax payments

Distributive Policies – governmental actions that convey tangible benefits to individuals, groups or corporations

District Attorney – chief prosecuting officer in counties that do not have a county attorney

District Clerks – county employees providing staff assistance for the district courts within the county

Doughnut Hole – the gap between covered and uncovered prescription drug costs under the Medicare plan

Dred Scott v Sandford (1857) – the United States Supreme Court ruling that invalidated the Missouri Compromise of 1820

and declared that slaves were not citizens, and subsequently did not have the right to sue the national government

Drinking Water – water distributed by an individual or public or private agency for human consumption, for use in preparing food or beverages, or for use in cleaning a utensil or article used in preparing food or beverages, or for consuming food or beverages by human beings

Dual Budgeting Concept – a budgetary strategy whereby both the executive and legislative branches submit their own budgets

Dual Federalism – intergovernmental relationship whereby autonomous national, subnational, and local governments all pursue their own interests independent of each other

DuBois, W.E.B. – founder of the National Association for the Advancement of Colored Persons

Due Process – an individual's protected right against arbitrary deprivation of life, liberty or property

Dye in the Wool – the most partisan of the partisans

Earmarking – budgetary practice of allocating a specific tax revenue stream for a specific purpose

Economic Opportunity Act (1965) – federal legislation establishing the Office of Economic Opportunity charged with the responsibility of coordinating all federal poverty-related initiatives

Economically Disadvantage Student – one who is eligible for free or reduced-priced meals under the National School Lunch and Children Nutrition Program

Edgewood v Kirby (1989) – United States Supreme Court ruled that the method of funding public schools in Texas is discriminatory towards property-poor districts

Educational Consolidation and Improvement Act (1981) – consolidated half of the federal government's education programs into one large block grant.

Elastic Tax – the most reliable and predictable tax revenue source since the revenue expands or contracts along with the economy

Elasticity – an economic criterion applied to a tax referring to its ability to generate increased revenue as economic growth increases or generates less when the economic growth decreases

Election – a process of selecting one person or more for an office, public or private, from a wider field of candidates

Election Precinct – the lowest level of a political party's organization; also known as precinct

Elementary and Secondary Education Act (1965) – federal legislation establishing a series of education reforms to include the free lunch program for low-income students

Elementary School Act (1972) – federal legislation eliminating segregation and discriminatory practices in elementary and secondary schools

Elitism – the view that political power and the ability to influence the most important policy decisions are held by a few individuals who derive power from their leadership positions in large institutions

Eminent Domain – the legal right of any government to take privately-held property for public use

Empowerment Zones – national urban development project using non-federal resources combined with modest federal cash outlays for business and redevelopment activities

Empresario System – land grant system developed by both the Spanish and Mexican governments to encourage the settlement of Texas. The land grant recipient was responsible for colonizing the area to include provisions for schools, hospitals, roads, and protection of the settlers

Endangered Species – one in danger of becoming extinct throughout all or a significant part of its natural range

Engle v Vitale (1962) - the landmark case heard by the United States Supreme Court challenging school sponsored mandatory prayer in the public schools. The Court ruled this practice of involuntary prayer as unconstitutional.

Enrichment Money – tax revenues collected by a school district that exceed the state-mandated per student expenditure

Entitlements – benefits provided by government to which recipients have a legally enforceable right

Enumerated Powers – those delegations of authority that are expressly written and granted to the national government through the United States Constitution

Environmental Protection Act (1969) – federal legislation creating the Environmental Protection Agency

Environmental Protection Agency – federal agency established to coordinate the implementation and enforcement of federal environmental laws

Equal Rights Amendment (1972) – state constitutional amendment giving women equal rights to those of their male counterparts

Equity Law – a remedy to a justifiable claim

Establishment – the elite members of the Democratic Party in Texas

Establishment Clause – the portion of the 1st Amendment to the United States Constitution stating that "Congress shall make no law respecting an establishment of religion, or prohibiting the free exercise thereof"

Estuary – a coastal area where fresh water from rivers and streams comes together with salt water from the ocean

Evaluative Orientations – judgments and opinions about political objects and events

Everson v Board of Education of the Township of Ewing (1947) – the United States Supreme Court ruled that the use of a sanctioned state board of education prayer for reciting in public school classrooms constituted involuntary prayer, which is not protected by the First Amendment's establishment clause

Excise Tax – a tax applied to a specific commodity such as motor fuels, utilities, telephones, hotels and motels, and so on

Exclusionary Rule – evidence which is otherwise admissible may not be used in a criminal trial if it is a product of illegal police conduct

Exclusionary Zoning – an ordinance requiring each resident to have expensive amenities such as a large lot, a garage, a paved driveway and other costly building code demands, plus prohibiting the construction of low-rent apartment buildings

Executive Clemency – an action by the governor that sets aside or reduces a convict's sentence

Executive Order – any rule or regulation issued by a chief administrative authority that, because of precedent and existing legislative authorization, has the effect of law

Executive Order 12612 – executive order enacted by President Ronald Reagan to eliminate and/or relax several federal regulations dealing with public service programs

Expressive Benefits – a benefit derived from one advancing a particular cause or ideology; also known as purposive benefits

Externality – an impact on a third person that is not directly involved as either the buyer or the seller in a private transaction but who still enjoys some benefit or suffers some negative consequences from the private exchange

Extraterritorial Jurisdiction – the extension of a city's jurisdiction ranging from 0.5 to 5 miles beyond its city limits

Faction – a political group or clique that functions within a larger group, such as a government, party or organization

Family Support Act – federal legislation extending AFDC benefits to two-parent families for at least six months out of a year if the principal wage earner is unemployed

Farmer's Alliance – an agrarian movement of small farmers advocating the issues addressed by Grange organizations

Federal Aid Highway Act (1956) - federal legislation in companion with the Highway Revenue Act (1956) establishing the Highway Trust Fund consisting of revenue collected from the federal gasoline tax

Federal Aid Highway Act (1963) – federal legislation providing funding to metropolitan areas promoting both private highway systems and public transit programs

Federal Elections Campaign Act (1974) – authorizes the formation of political action committees and provides public financing for presidential general elections

Federal Elections Commission – oversees the implementation and regulation of the Federal Elections Campaign Act

Federal Road Act (1916) - established the nation's first federal funding program for highway systems

Federal Voting Assistance Act (1955) – federal legislation allowing members of the military, their spouses and qualified dependents as well as others temporarily residing outside of the United States to vote in federal elections

Federalism – a form of governmental structure in which power is divided between a central government and lower-level governments

Felony – a serious crime punishable by death or imprisonment in a penitentiary for a year or more

Feminization of Poverty – a term used to describe single-parent families headed by women whose incomes are below the poverty level

Fighting Words – words that are not germane to the meaning of a speech but have the power to create a "clear and present danger" to others

Filibuster – an attempt to grab control of the Senate floor and literally talk the bill to death

Fiscal Policy - public policy concerning taxes, government spending, public debt, and management of government money

Fiscal Year – the budgetary cycle beginning in Texas on September 1 and ending August 31

Fleming v Nestor (1960)– the United States Supreme Court ruled that Social Security it not a guaranteed entitlement

Food Insecure – households whereby one or more family members were hungry at least sometime during the period due to inadequate resources for food

Food Secure – a household that has access at all times to enough food for an active healthy life for all household members with no need for recourse to socially unacceptable food sources or extraordinary coping behaviors to meet their basic food needs

Food Stamp Program – federal program developed in 1964 to provide an in-kind exchange of coupons for food items to qualifying individuals

Formula Grant – federal money allocated by Congress based on a formula of joint funding

Freedman's Bureau – agency established by the federal government after the Civil War to provide assistance to newly freed slaves

Freerider – an individual who does not belong to an organized group, such as a union or a political party, but who nevertheless benefits from its activities

Frontier Thesis - concept that the western frontier functioned as a great lever of persons and a blender of cultures

Franchise Tax – a tax levied on both domestic and foreign businesses operating in Texas

Full Faith and Credit Clause – Article IV of the United States Constitution mandating the acceptance of a state's public acts, records and judicial proceedings by every other state

Garcia v San Antonio Metropolitan Transit Authority (1985) – United States Supreme Court ruling applying the National Fair Labor Standards Act to employees of state and local governments

Gary v Sanders (1963)– United States Supreme Court ruled that each person's vote must be counted equally in statewide primary elections

General Election – voters regardless of party affiliation cast a vote to choose among the candidates to serve in an elective office

General Land Office – state executive agency responsible for implementation of water standards for off-shore oil exploration, wetlands, coastal areas and dune protection; manages all state-owned land

General Law Cities – cities of usually less than 5,000 persons who lack independent governing rights and must rely upon the state legislature for governing directives

General Revenue Fund – federal fund created in 1972 to provide money to qualifying state and local communities

General Revision Act (1891) – federal legislation granting authorization to the President of the United States to establish forest reserves on public lands

Gentrification – the efforts designed to bring upper- and middle-income newcomers and former residents back to the Central Business District by offering them the same conveniences that initially compelled them to leave the city for the suburbs

Gerrymandering – the drawing of legislative district boundary lines to obtain partisan or factional advantage

Ghost Voting – someone other than the lawmaker assigned to his/her legislative floor desk casting the vote

Gibbons v Ogden (1824) - United States Supreme Court ruling defining interstate commerce as every species of commercial intercourse which concerns more than one state

Gideon v Wainwright ((1963) – the United States Supreme Court ruled that indigent defendants charged with a felony offense must be provided legal counsel

Gilmer Aiken School Laws (1949) – major public school reform measure creating a Central Education Agency composed of the State Board of Education, State Board for Vocational Education, the State Commissioner of Education and the State Department of Education

Gitlow v New York (1935) – the United States Supreme Court ruled that the United States Constitution's Bill of Rights was enforceable on all levels of government, i.e., national, state, local, etc.

Glass Ceiling – the concept that women are prohibited from achieving top management positions within corporate America

Goal – the targeted end result of an action of activity

Gonzales, Texas – site of the first battle of the Texas Revolution

Government – the formal institutional structure and processes of a society by which policies are developed and implemented in the form of law binding on all

Grand Jury – a judicial body that reviews the evidence of a case gathered by the prosecution to determine whether or not the evidence is enough to merit a trial

Grandfather Clause – the requirement that individuals whose grandfathers could not vote before 1860 had to pass a literacy test to qualify to vote

Grange – an organization of small farmers and ranchers promoting increased railroad regulation, improvements in public education, reforms in land sale policies and prohibition

Grants-in-Aid – federal payment to a state or local government for some activity

Greenback Party – a third political party movement advocating the increase use of paper money

Gridlock – the freezing of action in an issue as a result of the sometimes overly effective operation of the separation of powers and the checks and balances system provided by the United States Constitution and the natural functioning of the two-party system

Gross Premium Tax – a tax applied to 2 percent of the gross premium receipts to life, health, and accident insurance carriers if they invest less than 90 percent of their revenues in other states

Gross Receipts Tax – a tax applied to the gross receipts of certain businesses to include telegraph and telephone companies, express companies, motor carriers, textbook publishers, collection agencies, and so on

Guinn v United States (1915)– the United States Supreme Court invalidated the grandfather clause

Hacienda – a Spanish unit of land consisting of five sitios

Hard Money Contributions – direct contributions to a political candidate or political party

Harper v Virginia State Board of Education (1966) – the United States Supreme Court ruled unconstitutional the use of a poll tax in any election

Hasinai Confederacies – confederate leagues formed among East Texas Indian tribes

Hatch Act (1939) – prohibited federal employees from participating in any political activities, forbade any political committee from spending more than $3 million in any campaign, and limited individual contributions to $5,000 per political committee; also known as the Political Activities Act

Hate Crimes – criminal acts motivated by hate

Haze – wide-scale, low-level pollution that obstructs visibility

Health Maintenance Organization (HMO) – prepaid health-care systems emphasizing preventive medical services as a means of avoiding costly serious illnesses

Help American Vote Act (2002) – federal legislation providing funds to states to upgrade their voting technology and to expand voting rights

High Occupancy Vehicle Lane (HOV) – a lane on a street or highway that is reserved for buses and vehicles with at least two to three occupants

Highway Act (1944) – federal legislation committing funds to construct an interstate highway system

Highway Beautification Act – federal legislation regulating the use of outdoor signage on federal highway systems

Highway Fund – a state budget fund dedicated to the construction, repair and maintenance of the state's highways and roadways

Highway Revenue Act (1956) – federal legislation in companion with the Federal Aid Highway Act (1956) establishing the Highway Trust Fund consisting of revenue from the federal gasoline tax

Highway Trust Fund – federal fund established by the Highway Revenue Act and the Federal Highway Act for the construction and maintenance of the nation's interstate highway system

Home Building and Loan Association v Blaisdell (1934) – United States Supreme Court decision upholding reasonable restrictions on property ownership

Home Rule Cities – cities with 5,000 or more persons granted governing authority independent of the legislature to include ordinance making and governance under a city charter approved by the residents

Home Rule Enabling Act (1913) – legislative act establishing home rule cities

Homeowners Associations (HOAs) – neighborhood or subdivision organizations empowered to maintain quality standards for homeowners

Homestead Provision – a provision in a constitution protecting one's personal property

Horizontal Federalism – interstate relations in accordance with Article IV (full faith and credit clause) of the United States Constitution

Host Culture – the initial cultural group in a given area or country

House Concurrent Resolution 108 (1953) – federal congressional action permitting the United States Census Bureau to officially add Native Americans to their data base

Housing Act (1937) - federal legislation providing to local communities funding to build affordable housing for middle- and lower-income individuals

Housing and Urban Development Act (1961) - federal legislation providing emergency loans for building commuter railroads and pilot mass transportation programs

Houston, Sam – commander of Texas forces during the Texas Revolution; served as U.S. Congressman from Tennessee, governor of both Texas and Tennessee, U.S. Senator from Texas, and President of the Texas Republic

Hopwood v Texas (1996) – the United States Supreme Court ruled that minority-based scholarship programs were unconstitutional

Hung Jury – a jury that cannot render a verdict

Human Rights – the right of individuals and groups to be treated in humane ways and with respect for human dignity and personal well-being

Hunt v Cromartie (2001) – the United States Supreme Court ruled that race could not be the primary factor in determining legislative district boundary lines

Hyper-poor – those individuals whose annual incomes amount to less than half of the official poverty level

Hyperpluralism – governing situation wherein so many groups so successfully compete for political power that power becomes decentralized and nothing much can get done

Ideologues – those who believe intensely in a certain system of political beliefs

Ideology – the way of life of a people reflected in their collectively held ideas and beliefs concerning the nature of the ideal political system, economic order, social goals and moral values

Illinois v Krull (1967) – United States Supreme Court ruled that the good faith exception did apply to warrantless searches

Impact Statement – federal contracting requirement indicating any existing and/or potential harm to the environment, proposed solutions to avoid an adverse environmental impact, and the project's potential efforts to maintain and/or enhance the productivity of the environment

Impaired River – a waterway that cannot support aquatic life or is deemed to be unsafe for fishing and swimming

Impeachment – a formal accusation, rendered by the lower house of a legislature that commits an accused civil official for trial in the upper house

Imperial Colonization Law (1823) – Mexico's law establishing an empresario land grant program

Implied Powers – authority given to the national government by inference from the powers specifically granted to it by the United States Constitution; see Article I, Section 8

Impoundment – the withholding by the executive branch of funds authorized and appropriated by law through the legislative branch

In-Kind Programs – programs such as subsidized housing, day care, Medicaid, etc., that provide payments to the provider of the service rather than to the recipient

Incorporation – the legal process whereby a suburban area establishes itself as a free standing governing entity with a city charter and a form of city government

Incremental Budgetary Process – a virtually automatic budgetary strategy whereby state agencies receive marginal budgetary increases or decreases with each new budgetary cycle

Incrementalism – a doctrine holding that change in a political system occurs only by small steps, each of which should be carefully evaluated before proceeding to the next step

Independent School Districts – school districts primarily located in rural areas under direct supervision of the Texas Education Agency (TEA)

Independents – individuals not committed to any political party

Indian Reorganization Act – federal legislation enabling Native Americans to officially affiliate with their individual tribes

Indictment – the formal accusation drawn up by the prosecutor and brought by a grand jury charging a person with the commission of a crime

Indirect Lobbying – influencing government decision makers through pressure usually in the form of letters, postcards, telegrams, and phone calls from a large number of constituents; also known as grassroots lobbying

Individual Liberty – the condition of being free from restrictions or constraints

Individualism – the political, economic and social concept that places primary emphasis on the worth, freedom and well-being of the individual rather than on the group, society or nation

Inelastic Taxes – a tax program that does not generate increased revenues in proportion to economic growth

Initiative Petition – the process of forcing an issue to a public vote

Injection Well Act – state legislation pertaining to the regulation of hazardous and solid wastes

Injunction – a court order that requires a person to take an action or to refrain from taking an action

Instructed Delegate View – a style of representation whereby the lawmaker seeks the opinion of his/her constituents prior to casting his/her vote on a legislative item

Integration – the practice of desegregating public schools, public accommodations, residential areas, etc.

Interest Aggregation – the process of bringing together the concerns of diverse groups into a workable program

Interest Group – an organized collection of individuals who are bound together in shared attitudes or concerns and who make demands on political institutions in order to realize goals which they are unable to achieve on their own

Interest Group Liberalism – concept based on the belief that interest groups expect to use government in a positive and expansive role

Interim Committee – a legislative committee that meets when the legislature is not in session

Interlocking Directorate – a relationship whereby two or more individuals representing different interests or businesses serve together either as board members or officers of key business and civic organizations

Interposition – a state's right theory advanced by John C. Calhoun placing the states as the protector of their people by preventing the enforcement of an unwanted national law upon the residents of their states

Interstate Commerce – the flow of goods, services and persons across state boundary lines

Interstate Commerce Act – passed in 1887, created the Interstate Commerce Commission to establish the national government's regulation of vital private sectors of the nation's economy

Interstate Commerce Clause – Article I of the United States Constitution empowering the federal government to regulate commerce between the states

Interstate Compact – agreement between two or more states requiring congressional approval

Intrastate Commerce – the flow of goods, services and persons within state boundary lines

Iron Law of Oligarchy – observation that in every organization, whether it be a political party, a professional union or any other association of the kind, the aristocratic tendency manifests itself very clearly

Iron Triangle – a pattern of stable relationships between an agency in the executive branch, a congressional or state legislative committee or subcommittee, and one or more organized groups or clients

Islenos – from the Canary Islands, the original settlers of San Antonio

Issue Network – an organization composed of various organizations, sympathetic lawmakers, and lobbyists bound to a common issue or concern

Jackass Line – stagecoach route beginning at Aue's Settlement Inn in Leon Springs in San Antonio to San Diego, California

James Byrd, Jr., Hate Crime Bill – state legislation mandating stiffer criminal penalties for crimes prompted by racial hatred or bias against race, religion, color, sex, disability, age, or national origin

Jim Crow Laws – a series of written and unwritten laws and ordinances that severely hampered the acquisition of personal, social and political freedoms for African Americans and other minority population groups; also known as the Black Codes

Joint Committee –a legislative committee composed of members from both houses

Joint Resolutions – a legislative act that must be approved by both houses of the Texas Legislature and requires the governor's signature

Joint Sessions – a scheduled meeting combining the entire membership of the Texas House and Senate

Judicial Review – the right of the United States Supreme Court to hold unconstitutional, and hence unenforceable, any law, any official action based upon a law, any other action by a public official found to be in conflict with the spirit and meaning of the United States Constitution

Judiciary Act (1789) – federal legislation establishing the federal court system and granting courts the power of judicial review

Jumanos – a Native American Indian tribe located in the Trans-Pecos area of Texas

Jurisdiction – the authority vested in a court to hear and decide a case

Jury – an impartial panel that sits in judgment on charges brought in either criminal or civil cases

Kadohadacho Confederacies – confederative leagues formed among East Texas Native American tribes

Karankawan – East Texas Native American tribe living along the Texas coastline

Kilgarlin v Martin (1965) – United States Supreme Court mandated that Texas adhere to the one-man, one-vote principle

Know-Nothing Party – third party movement that began in the late 1840s advocating restrictions on immigration, prohibiting both Catholics and the foreign-born from holding public office, and English as the nation's official language

La Salle (Cavelier, René Robert) – French explorer who founded Fort St. Louis in Texas in 1687 and declared French ownership of Texas

La Raza Unida – third party movement advocating issues of the Hispanic community

Labor – a Spanish unit of land consisting of one thousand varas on each side

Land Grant Law (1876) – allocated sixteen sections of land to railroad companies for every mile of main-line track they completed

Law – the rules of conduct that pertain to a given political order of society, rules that are backed by the organized force of the community

Law of April 6, 1830 – collectively a series of restrictive measures issued by the Mexican government against Texans

Layered Cake Federalism – a term used to describe dual federalism

League of United League American Citizens v Perry (2006) – United States Supreme Court ruled the United States Constitution only requires at least one revisit of district boundary lines after a census, meaning that states can redistrict as many times as they wish within that ten-year period

Lee v Weisman (1992) - the United States Supreme Court ruled that a prayer at a graduation ceremony was constitutional only if school officials instructed students to keep the prayer non-sectarian and non-proselytizing

League – a Spanish unit of land consisting of five thousand varas

Legislative Budget Board (LBB) – created in 1949, the dominating actor in the drafting of the Texas budget

Legislative Council –an interim committee that meets to explore and study state problems

Legislative Education Board (LEB) – implementation body for HB 72 provisions

Legislative Redistricting Board (LRB) – a special committee called to draft redistricting plans when the Texas Legislature fails to do so

Legislative Immunities – protection for in-session legislative members from lawsuits over individual statements or comments made during any official legislative activity

Lemon v Kurtzman (1971) – United States Supreme Court case resulting in the application of a three-part test to determine the extent of government involvement in religion or vice versa

Libel – defamation of character in print or by other visual presentations

Liberalism – a political doctrine that espouses freedom of the individual from interference by the state, toleration by the state in matters of morality and religion, laissez-faire economic policies, and a belief in natural rights that exist independent of government

Liberty – in a state, that is, in a society where there are laws, liberty can consist only in having the power to do what one should want to do and in no way being constrained to do what one should not want to do

License – a privilege granted by government to do something that it otherwise considers to be illegal

Line-Item Veto – veto authority allowing governors to veto or zero out specific budgetary items in an appropriations bill without vetoing the entire bill

Living Wage – salary level based upon a rate above the federally mandated minimum wage that adjusts for increased living costs

Lobbyist – a person usually acting as an agent for a pressure group, who seeks to bring about the passage or defeat of legislative bills or to influence their contents

Local Bill – the scope of the legislation is limited to a specified geographical area of a state or unit of local government such as a city, school district, precinct, etc.

Main Street Project - a program sponsored by the National Trust for Historical Preservation to encourage municipalities to redevelop their central business districts

Mainstream – the midpoint in the political spectrum

Maintaining Election – an election whereby the political loyalties in the last election remain stable with the majority party winning the election

Majority Vote – an election outcome of 50 percent plus one vote

Mandates – a requirement attached to a federal program whereby the recipient of the grant is punished for noncompliance

Manifest Destiny – the belief that it was the fate of the American people to settle all of the territory between the Atlantic and Pacific Oceans

Maquiladoras – series of American- and foreign-owned factories located near the shared border between the United States and Mexico

Marble Cake Federalism – term used to describe cooperative federalism

Martial Law – the temporary imposition of military presence ordered by a governor in case of an extreme emergency, riots or insurrections

Master Plan – a city's blueprint indicating future growth and development

Material Benefits – tangible awards that have monetary value

Mayor/Council Format – form of city government with an elected at-large mayor and a single- or multi-member district council members

McCullough v Maryland (1819) – United States Supreme Court decision establishing the national government's right to eminent domain

McLaurin v Oklahoma State Regents (1950) – United States Supreme Court ruling that the practice of the University of Oklahoma admitting African-American students into segregated graduate programs was discriminatory and unconstitutional

Means-Tested Eligibility – program assistance eligibility based upon the applicant's demonstrated inability to provide for him/herself the desired benefit due to the individual's depressed income level and assets

Medicaid – jointly funded state and federal program providing health-care benefits to individuals whose incomes are below the poverty level and who meet certain other qualifications

Medicare – federally funded health-care plan for the nation's elderly citizens over the age of 65

Medicare Prescription Drug Improvement and Modernization Act (2003) – reform legislation to the prescription drug provisions of the Medicare program

Medigap Insurance – additional health-care coverage used by citizens to cover expenses not paid through either Medicare or Medicaid

Mestizo – a person of mixed Spanish and Indian ancestry

Mexican – a person from Mexico or of Mexican ancestry living in Mexico

Migrant and Seasonal Worker Protection Act – federal legislation mandating appropriate working conditions for migrant farm workers

Miller v California (1973) - United States Supreme Court defined obscenity and established a three-part test for determining obscenity

Minority Vote Dilution – a districting scenario whereby the majority of a minority population is divided into several legislative districts therefore preventing the election of a minority candidate

Minority Vote Packing – a districting scenario whereby the majority of a minority population is confined to one legislative district, therefore, barring the election of more than one minority candidate

Misdemeanor – a minor criminal offense

Mission System – a combination of colonization and religious conversion program implemented in Texas

Mitchell v Helms (2000) – United States Supreme Court upheld the constitutionality of a Louisiana law providing public funds to both public and parochial schools for the purchase of instructional equipment

Moore v Dempsey (1923)– the United States Supreme Court ruled the exclusion of African Americans from juries as a unconstitutional violation of the 6th Amendment to the United States Constitution

Morrill Act (1862) – federal legislation providing grants in the form of land for the establishment of college-level agricultural and mechanical programs

Motor Fuels Tax – a regressive consumer tax program levied on gasoline, diesel and liquid petroleum gas

Motor Vehicle Sales Tax – tax accessed on the sale price of any motor vehicle

Multiparty System – an electoral system usually based on proportional representation that often requires a coalition of several parties to form a majority to run the government

Municipal Annexation Act (1963) – state law granting cities an extraterritorial jurisdiction from 0.5 miles to 5 miles beyond city limits

Municipal Bonds – the instruments used by sub-government units to borrow money for infrastructure improvements and debt payments

Municipal Elections – selection of city government officers; also known as local elections

Municipal Solid Waste – solid waste resulting from or incidental to municipal, community, commercial, institutional, and recreational activities including garbage, rubbish, ashes, street cleanings, dead animals, abandoned automobiles, and all other solid waste other than industrial waste

Nation-centered Federalism – an arrangement favoring a strong central government with expanded authority over the states

National Ambient Air Quality Standards (NAAQS) – established by the EPA to measure levels of carbon dioxide, sulfur dioxide, ozone, lead, nitrogen dioxide and particulate matter

National Association for the Advancement of Colored Persons (NAACP) – founded in 1909 by African-American scholar W.E.B. Dubois; the preeminent organization for the advancement of civil rights for the African-American community

National Civil League – founded in 1900 by the business community; advocates government regulation of business practices

National Defense Education Act (1958) – provided federal grants for college loans, graduate fellowships and technological equipment

National Industrial Recovery Act – national law allocating federal funds for highway and road construction

National Minimum Drinking Age Act – federal legislation changing the legal drinking age from 18 to 21

National Pollution Discharge Elimination System (NPDES) – enacted by the federal government; requires all businesses to file for a permit to discharge or dump any hazardous substances into the water

Nativism – a theory of racism based on the belief that those born on the soil of their native country should be the only ones to benefit from that birthright

Near v Minnesota (1931) - United States Supreme Court established the concept of "no prior restraint" between the print media and the government

Negligence – carelessness or the failure to use ordinary care under the particular circumstances revealed by the evidence in the law suit

Networking – the process of various interest groups meeting on a regular basis to exchange information with each other

New Federalism – intergovernmental relationship advocated by President Ronald Reagan to make states' rights the effective policy of the land by reducing the role of the national government in state and local affairs

New Left – the far-left political movement of the 1960s

New Urbanism – the re-configuration of sprawling suburbs into communities of real neighborhoods and diverse districts, the conservation of natural environments, and the preservation of an area's building legacy

New York Times v Sullivan (1964) - United States Supreme Court defined libel as the printing of known falsehoods with actual malice in mind

New York Times v United States (1971) – landmark United States Supreme Court ruling allowing the *New York Times* and the *Washington Post* to print excerpts from the *Pentagon Papers* regarding the government's initial involvement in Vietnam

No Bill – a judgment by a grand jury not to send a case to trial

No Child Left Behind – federal educational reform package initiated by President George W. Bush

No Prior Restraint – the concept that government cannot prevent the printing of sensitive information unless the publication of this information would create a serious and eminent threat to national security as outlined by the Court's ruling in *Near v Minnesota* (1931)

Non-Point Source Pollution – a pollution source with a diffused indication as to its origin

Nonattainment – status given by the EPA to any city or municipality that is not incompliance with federal air quality standards

Nonpartisan Election – an election whereby candidates run without a political party label

North American Free Trade Agreement (NAFTA) – trade agreement signed by the United States, Mexico and Canada guaranteeing the removal of all trade barriers between the three nations; created concept of seamless borders

Northwest Land Ordinance Act (1785) – federal legislation setting aside one section of land in each township in the Northwest Territory for the endowment of schools

Nullification – state's right position advocated by John C. Calhoun holding that the people have the absolute right to veto or nullify any congressional act and if necessary, separate their state from the national government

Obamacare – the name given to President Obama's health-care reform package

Obnoxious Acts – a series of unpopular laws passed during the Davis administration

Objective – strategy used to obtained desired goal

Office-Block Ballot – a ballot arrangement with the elective office listed across the top of the ballot with the candidates vying for the office listed below

Old Age Insurance – original program under the Social Security Act of 1935 establishing a self-funded insurance plan to provide pensions and benefits for the elderly and disabled; also known as the Social Security Program

Open Government Act (2007) – federal legislation amending the Lobbying Disclosure Act of 1995 clarifying who must register as a lobbyist and what activities they can legally participate in

Open Primary – a voting system that permits voters to choose the party primary of their choice without disclosing party affiliation or allegiance, if any; also known as the crossover primary

Operating Expenses – yearly costs needed to run government such as salaries, benefits, equipment, rent, utilities, supplies, etc.

Ordinance – a city or county directive that has the force of a law but must be in compliance with state and national laws

Original Jurisdiction – the authority of a court to hear a cause in the first instance

Ozone – the primary ingredient of smog

Palko v Connecticut (1937) – the United States Supreme Court tied the constitutional rights of the accused to the states

Pardon – an executive order granting a release of an individual from legal consequences of a criminal act

Parole – freedom granted to a convicted offender after he/she has served a period of confinement and so long as certain conditions of behavior are met

Partial Pre-Emption Mandate – a mandate applied by the federal government when a state or local government fails to establish its own requirements, allowing the federal government to assume partial or outright jurisdiction over the project

Partisan Election – an election whereby candidates run under a political party label

Party Column Ballot – a ballot arrangement with the candidates listed under their party affiliation

Party Purity Law – the requirement that voters declare their party affiliation three to six months prior to the primary election

Paternalism – the belief that women are too mentally and physically weak to survive for themselves without the protection of a male counterpart

Patronage – the process of an elected official offering a lucrative government job to those who contributed the most to his/her campaign coffers

Patriot Act – anti-terrorism bill passed by the United States Congress in the aftermath of September 11, 2001; created a cabinet-level position for the Department of Homeland Security; granted extra-ordinary surveillance powers to both the FBI and CIA

Pay-as-You-Go – policy option funded totally by user fees

Pay Equity - an issue with women's groups addressing the concern that women earn less than their male counterparts in comparable job positions

Payayas – ancient Native American Indian tribe who settled along the banks of the San Antonio River and the San Pedro Springs

Peak Association – an interest group that advocates for the entire board spectrum of its consistency

Pelican Island National Refuge Act (1903) – federal legislation creating the nation's first federally protected habitat known as the Pelican Island National Refuge

Peninsulars – Spanish-born nobility living in the New World

Persistently Poor – term used to describe the permanently poor or those individuals whose incomes have fallen below the poverty level for eight or more years over a ten-year period; also known as permanently poor

Personal Responsibility and Work Opportunity Reconciliation Act – federal legislation enacted by the Clinton administration instituting welfare reform

Pigeonhole – a killed bill

Pink Collar – traditional clerical jobs held predominately by women

Planning Program Budgeting Concept (PPB) – budgetary strategy that sets out goals and objectives, develops and approves programs for reaching these goals and objectives, prices and allocates inputs required for each of these objectives and goals

Plaintiff – in a civil case, the person who initiates the law suit

Platform – a statement of principles and objectives espoused by a political party or a political candidate that is used during a campaign to win support from voters

Plea Bargaining – the process through which a defendant pleads guilty to a criminal charge with the expectation of receiving some consideration from the state

Plentz v United States (1997) – United States Supreme Court decision declaring the background check requirement of the Brady Bill as an unfunded mandate and thus an unconstitutional intrusion upon the states

Plessy v Ferguson (1896) – United States Supreme Court upheld the concept of separate but equal

Pluralism – the view that competition and the subsequent negotiation and bargaining among multiple centers of power is the key to understanding how decisions are made

Pluralist Theory – concept that assumes that within the public arena there will be countervailing centers of power within governmental institutions and among outsiders

Plurality Vote – an election outcome whereby the candidate that gets the most votes wins

Point Source Pollution – a pollution source that has a precise identifiable location such as a pipe or a smokestack

Political Culture – the pattern of individual attitudes and orientations towards politics among members of a political system

Political Efficacy – the belief that one's political participation has an effect on the course of political events

Political Party – an organization whose members are sufficiently homogeneous to band together for the purpose of winning elections, which entitles them to exercise governmental power in order to enjoy the influence, prerequisites, and advantages of authority

Political Socialization Process – the process of individuals acquiring their political culture and perspectives

Policy – purposive course of action followed by an actor or set of actors in dealing with a problem or matter of concern

Policy Outcomes – the unmeasureable consequences of a policy decision or directive

Policy Output – the action actually taken in pursuance of policy decisions and statements

Policymaking – flow and pattern of action that extends over time and includes many decisions, some routine and some not so routine

Politico – a view of representation combining the trustee and delegate models

Poll Sample – a selected representative portion of a large population for the purpose of determining through the views, actions or intentions of that population

Pollution – human additions of undesirable substances into the environment

Populism – political movement of the 1890s based on the need for government to defend the economically and politically weak, especially farmers from the powerful industrialists and the wealthy

Populist Party – nationwide third party movement articulating the concerns of small farmers, small businesses and organized labor to include government ownership of the railroads and an expanded use of paper currency

Pork Barrel Legislation – an appropriation made by a legislative body providing for expenditures of sums of public money on local projects not critically needed

Pork Barrel Politics – the use of political influence by members of Congress or a legislative body to secure government funds and projects for their constituents

Post-Adjournment Veto – governor's action of vetoing a bill after the legislature has officially adjourned

Poverty – the state or condition of being poor by lacking the means of providing material needs or comfort

Poverty Level – income measurement used to identify the poor based on three times the amount of income needed to eat according to a moderate food plan

Pragmatic Federalism – concept devised by President George W. Bush to return more regulatory and budgetary responsibilities back to the states

Preamble – an introductory paragraph of a constitution detailing the ideological and political framework of the government

Preferred Provider Organization (PPO) – managed healthcare plan allowing members to choose from a preapproved list of doctors providing medical services at predetermined fees

Prejudice – a feeling or act of any individual or group in which a prejudgment about someone else or another group is made on the basis of emotion rather than reason

Preponderance of the Evidence – the deciding factor in a civil case

Presidential Primaries – the process of political parties selecting their candidate for president

Presidio – the military garrison attached to Spanish colonial cities in Texas

Pressure Group – an organized group that seeks to influence the policies and practices of government

Preventive Public Policy Approach – policy action that recognizes the potential for future suffering by providing a safety net for those who could be adversely impacted by the problem or issue

Primary Election – an interparty election to select candidates for the general election

Private Goods – those products or services that can be individually packaged, sold or used

Private Purposive Incentive – individuals join groups to gain the satisfaction of contributing to what they regard as a worthy goal or purpose

Privatization – the general effort to relieve the disincentives toward efficiency in public organizations by subjecting them to the incentives of the private market

Pro Tempore – an appointed legislative member serving as the presiding officer when the Speaker of the House and/or the lieutenant governor is not present

Pro Warranto Proceedings – a process whereby the courts can remove a governor's appointee from office

Problem – a condition or situation that produces needs or dissatisfaction among people and for which relief or redress by governmental action is sought

Procedural Due Process – the manner in which a law, an ordinance, an administrative practice or a judicial task is carried out

Procedural Policies – pertains to how something is going to be done or who is going to take action

Procedural Standing Committees – legislative bodies dealing with the internal process or the flow of proposed legislation through the various steps leading to a final vote

Proclamations – official public announcements honoring a notable individual or recognizing an important event in Texas history

Progressive Tax – any tax in which the tax rates increase as the tax base increases

Project Grant Program – federal grant program whereby the federal government would appropriate a set amount of money to be used specifically for a nationally created program

Promulgation – a form of veto authority whereby if the governor does not agree with the legislation he could suspend the implementation of the law until the legislative body addresses the governor's concerns

Proportional Tax – a tax program that imposes equal tax burdens regardless of one's income level

Provisional Ballots – the method of allowing a voter to cast a ballot even though his/her name is not on the official registered voters' roster

Public Bill – a legislative act which applies to all affected parties; also known as a general bill

Public Goods – items that can be used by all residents when needed

Public Interest Group – organized pressure groups seeking to develop positions and to support national causes relating to a broader definition of the public good

Public Policy – an officially expressed intention backed by a sanction, which can be a reward or a punishment

Punitive Public Policy Approach – policy response that seeks to punish those deemed responsible for the creation of the problem in the first place as well as those adversely impacted by it who abuse the benefits received from the response

Pure Speech – speech without any conduct

Quasi-judicial Powers – authority of bureaucratic agencies to conduct several functions ordinarily performed by the courts to include investigative authority, power to adjudicate and to judge those guilty of a policy infraction

Quasi-legislative Powers – rule-making authority granted to bureaucratic agencies

Racial Profiling – the practice of stereotyping individuals based on certain characteristics

Radical Republicans – the term used to describe a faction within the Republican Party during Reconstruction

Reasonable Restrictions – the logical and rational curtailments enacted by government upon the absolute and unrestrained pursuit of inalienable rights

Recall Election – an election to remove an elected official

Recess Appointment – an appointment made by a governor when the legislature is not in session

Recidivism – a relapse into criminal behavior

Recognizance – the release of the accused due to ties to the community and no prior criminal record

Redistributive Policies – conscious attempts by the government to manipulate the allocation of wealth, property, rights, or some other value among broad classes or groups in society

Redistricting – the action of a state legislature or other body in redrawing legislative electoral district lines following a new population census

Redlining – the tactic of denying a mortgage or home improvement loan to individuals desiring to buy a house in a racially changing neighborhood

Reduction Veto – veto authority enabling the governor to reduce an appropriations item without actually eliminating it

Referendum Election – the process of the electorate approving or disapproving a proposed city ordinance, bond initiative or constitutional amendments

Refuse Act (1899) – federal legislation requiring a permit for the dumping of refuse into navigable waters

Regressive Tax – any tax in which the burden falls relatively more heavily upon low-income groups than upon wealthy taxpayers

Regular Sessions – In Texas, a biennial legislative session of 140 days in odd-numbered years

Regulation of Lobbying Act (1946) – federal legislation specifying the registration and reporting processes for lobbyists; also known as Title III of the Legislative Reorganization Act

Regulatory Policies – governmental actions that extend government control over a particular behavior of private individuals or businesses

Relacion – Álvar Núñez Cabeza De Vaca documentary of his travels in Texas

Relative Poverty – measure of poverty determined by comparing an individual's income against society's overall standard of living

Religious Right – political perspective seeing an extremely limited role for government in all policy areas to include the economy, welfare programs, the environment, etc.

Religious Viewpoints Anti-Discrimination Act – Texas law requiring that all public school districts to specifically allow for spontaneous religious expression by students

Remand – holding the accused in jail until trial

Remedy – a monetary settlement to an injured party, fine paid to courts, or, in some instances, a prison term and a fine

Representative Democracy – political philosophy that the people elect representatives to act as their agents in making and enforcing laws and decisions

Reservation Side – the need for cities to preserve a quality of life for its residents

Reserved Powers – governing authority granted to the states by the 10th Amendment to the United States Constitution to include policing authority, taxing authority, propriety powers and eminent domain

Resolutions – formal expressions of opinions or decisions that are offered by a member of either the House or Senate that are offered for approval by one or both houses of the legislature

Resource Conservation and Recovery Act (1976) – federal legislation placing hazardous wastes under the control of the federal government; prohibits the opening of new sites; mandates existing open dumps upgraded to sanitary landfill status or be closed

Restrictive Covenant – provision in a mortgage contract forbidding the buyer from subsequently selling the property to a member of a minority group and/or placing special restrictions on the property, i.e., certain type and height of fences, outside paint colors, two-car garages, etc.

Revenue Act (1971) – federal legislation allowing for income tax filers to approve $3 of federal money to fund the presidential elections

Revenue Sharing – a federal grant program that gave money to state and local communities with few strings attached; phased out by the Reagan administration

Reynolds v Sims (1964) – the United States Supreme Court ruled bicameral legislative houses must be apportioned on an equal population basis

Reynolds v United States (1862) - the United States Supreme Court ruled that the Mormon practice of polygamy was not a constitutionally protected practice of religious expression

Robertson Insurance Law – enacted in 1907, required insurance companies to keep 75 percent of their reserves in Texas or forfeit the right to issue policies in the state

Robin Hood Approach – federal funding distribution system whereby tax dollars are distributed to the neediest states first

Roth v United States (1957) – United States Supreme Court defined the difference between constitutionally and unconstitutionally protected creative expression

Rule of Capture – approved by the Texas Supreme Court in 1904, all percolating ground water, such as a spring, belongs to the owners of the land where it is found

Rules and Resolutions Committee – Texas House of Representative's committee that determines the rules under which legislation is debated, amended and given final consideration

Runaway Scrape – after the fall of the Alamo thousands fled to East Texas in anticipation of Santa Anna's advancing forces

Safe Drinking Water Act (1974) – federal legislation establishing acceptable quality standards for drinking water for suppliers serving more than twenty-five people

Safety Net – the term used to describe the use of federal assistance programs to prevent individuals' incomes from falling below the poverty level

Sales Tax – a tax levied on consumer goods and services

San Antonio Independent School District v Rodriguez (1971) – the United States Supreme Court ruled that although the states' system of funding public schools was unfair, it was still constitutional

San Francisco De Las Tejas – the first Spanish mission built in Texas constructed in 1690 in East Texas

Santa Anna (Antonio López de Santa Anna) - president of Mexico and commander of the Mexican Army during the Texas Revolution; led the final assault on the Alamo; later defeated and captured at the Battle of San Jacinto

Scalawags – derogatory term used to describe Southerners who aligned themselves with Northerners during the Reconstruction period

Schenek v United States (1917) – the United States Supreme Court ruled that any portion of a speech that creates a "clear and present danger" to others is unconstitutionally protected speech

Search Warrant – a written document, signed by a judge or magistrate, authorizing a law enforcement officer to conduct a search

Section 8 – federally funded rental/mortgage subsidy program created under the Housing and Urban Community Act to provide assistance to qualifying individuals and families

Select Committee for Public Education (SCOPE) (1982) – special ad hoc committee chaired by H. Ross Perot to propose public education reforms

Select Committee on Higher Education – ad hoc committee that recommended a two-tier system for higher education with community colleges offering freshman and sophomore courses and the four-year schools offering junior and senior level courses

Selective Benefits – awards, perks and benefits derived from joining an interest group

Selective Incorporation – the strategy used by the United States Supreme Court to selectively and gradually tie the states to the Bill of Rights

Senatorial Courtesy – the practice of a governor contacting the home senatorial district of an potential appointee prior to officially announcing the nomination

Seniority System – the practice of legislative leadership appointing those who have served the longest in a legislative house to the most prestigious or important committees

Separate But Equal – the concept of segregating Anglos from African Americans under the premise that accommodations and services could be offered separately as long as they were equal in quality and quantity

Separate Car Act (1890) – a Louisiana law mandating that all railroad trains passing through Louisiana had to have separate cars for Anglo and African-American passengers

Separation of Church and State Doctrine – the doctrine separating government from religious institutions and practices as detailed in Article I of the United States Constitution

Separation Theory – racist theory mandating the division of diverse cultures into separate ethnic clusters to the exclusion of all others

Serviceman's Readjustment Act – established the GI Bill of Rights and provided federal education assistance to World War II veterans

Settlement House – patterned after Jane Addams's Hull House and guided by the belief that people could be schooled out of their poverty

Severance Tax – a tax levied for the extraction of any natural resource from the earth to include off-shore oil drilling operations

Sharecropping System – agreement between a landowner and workers to share the burden of the labor in exchange for a percentage of the profit on the crop and living accommodations

Shelly v Kraemer (1948) – the United States Supreme Court ruled restrictive covenants unconstitutional

Sherman Anti-Trust Law – federal legislation designed to breakup monopolies to include Standard Oil Company

Sierra Club – environmental protection group founded by John Muir in 1892

Silent Spring – written by Rachel Carson in 1962, details the destruction of earth through the overuse of pesticides and hazardous chemicals

Simple Resolution – a measure adopted by one chamber of a legislative body that does not require approval by the other house or the governor

Sin Taxes – taxes charged on alcoholic beverages, bottled alcohol and tobacco products

Single Issue Groups – interest groups advocating issues pertinent only to their group's goals and objectives

Sitio – another Spanish word for a square

Slander – verbal malicious attacks against other person

Smith Act (1940) – a national law prohibiting anyone to organize or knowingly become a member of any organization advocating by force or violence the overthrow of any United States government agency or branch

Smith v Allwright (1944) – the United States Supreme Court ruled that the Texas Democratic Party was not a private club but an agent of the state and must adhere to both state and federally mandated rules and regulations for voting

Smith-Hughes Act (1917) – provided federal grants to establish vocational college programs

Smog – occurs when nitrogen oxides produced by burning fuel and volatile organic compounds escape into the atmosphere

Social Contract – political theory that people are absolutely free as individuals to come together as a community to form a governing body that will establish the rules for the exercise of basic fundamental rights with the understanding that if the government fails to meet its responsibilities, the people can abolish it and begin anew

Social Darwinism – the belief that an individual's economic and social success is directly a result of Charles Darwin's concept of the survival of the fittest

Social Security Act (1935) – federal legislation establishing the social security system as well as unemployment compensation and Aid to Dependent Children programs

Soft Money Contribution – indirect campaign donations given to a candidate to offset campaign costs such as providing the venue, the food, entertainment, etc.

Solid Waste – any garbage, rubbish, sludge from a waste treatment plant, water supply, treatment plant or air pollution control facility and other discarded materials, including solid, liquid, semisolid or contained gaseous material resulting from industrial, municipal, commercial, mining and agricultural operations, and from community and institutional activities

Solidary Benefits – socially derived, intangible rewards of association, i.e., camaraderie, fun and the status of prestige

South Carolina v Baker (1988) – United States Supreme Court ruling allowing Congress to tax the interest earned on savings accounts and state and local bonds

South Carolina v Katzenbach (1966) – the United States Supreme Court upheld the constitutionality of the Voting Rights Act

Southern Association of Colleges and Schools – accreditation agency for all of the state's two- and four-year colleges and universities

Special Bill – a legislative action providing an exception to a law for an individual rather than trying to change the entire bill

Special District – a unit of local government typically performing a single function and overlapping traditional political boundaries

Special Election – an election specifically scheduled to fill an office that has become vacant before the term of its expiration

Special Sessions – a specially called session of legislative houses usually called by governors

Special Supplemental Program for Women, Infants and Children – commonly known as WIC, provides nutritional food staples to pregnant women, breast feeding mothers, mothers up to six months after giving birth, and children under the age of five

Split Ticket Voting – a pattern of voting for candidates from different political parties

Square – a Spanish unit of land consisting of four leagues

Standing Committees – regular or permanent bodies that consider legislation within their particular subject areas

State of the State Message – the address delivered by the governor at the start of a legislative session

Statute of Limitations – a state or federal legislative act that establishes a time limit within which lawsuits may be brought, judgments endorsed, or crimes prosecuted

Statutes – laws enacted by a state legislative house

Steering – the showing of residential and business properties located only in minority areas thus keeping minorities from purchasing properties in predominately Anglo neighborhoods

Street v New York (1969) – the United States Supreme Court ruled that the burning of the American flag is a constitutionally protected form of protest

Straight Ticket Voting – the practice of voting for all of the candidates from a particular political party

Strong-Mayor Council Format – city governing format whereby the mayor has the authority to appoint and remove all department heads, prepares the city budget, and oversees the day-to-day operation of the city

Subsidies – government grants, cash, or other commodities used to offset potential hardships, i.e., food stamps, farm subsidies, etc.

Substantive Due Process – the content or subject matter of a law or ordinance

Substantive Policies – decisions involving what government is going to do to address an identified problem or situation

Substantive Standing Committees – legislative bodies focusing on the crafting of legislation

Suffrage – the right to vote

Sunset Act (1997) – established the Sunset Advisory Commission to periodically evaluate all state agencies to determine their status

Sunset Laws – legislative actions mandating an automatic expiration date for non-essential state agencies

Superior/Inferior Theory of Racism – concept that a chosen or inherently superior cultural group should rule over those considered to be inferior

Supplemental Security Income (SSI) – federally funded program providing cash payments to lower income elderly and disabled adults and children

Supremacy Clause – Article VI of the United States Constitution making the United States Constitution the supreme law of the land

Surface Transportation Act (1982) – federal legislation increasing the federal gasoline tax from five to nine cents per gallon; dedicating a portion of the tax revenue for public transportation

Surface Transportation Act (1991) – federal legislation providing $151 billion over a six-year period to state and local governments for highway and public transportation projects

Suspended Particulates – ash, smoke, dust, soot, and liquid droplets released through the burning of fuels and the use of pesticides

Sweatt v Painter (1950) – United States Supreme Court ruling that separate but not equal law schools are a violation of equal protection clause of the 14th Amendment to the United States Constitution

Symbolic Speech – the use of symbols, rather than words to convey ideas

Tacit Consent – an individual who enjoys some benefit from living in a particular country consents to obey the rules of that country, therefore, acknowledging its right to govern

Taft-Hartley Act (1947) – labor-related federal legislation mandating that states would opt to use section 14B of the measure commonly known as the right-to-work clause, meaning that non-union workers can work in union shops; also known as the Labor Management Act

Tax – a compulsory contribution for a public purpose rather than for the personal benefit of an individual

Tax Abatements – temporary tax relief programs granted by government as an incentive for future economic development and job growth

Tax Assessor/Collector –chief tax collector for county government

Tax Base Rate – the items subjected to taxation

Tax Deductions – a reduction or tax break for certain investments and expenditures

Tax Effort – measurement of whether a state is taxing above or below its capacity to raise revenue

Tax Equity – the fairness of assessing tax liabilities

Tax Visibility – the prominence of a tax program

Tax Yield - the amount of money generated by a tax

Tayshas – Caddo for allies or friends

Tejano – a person of Mexican ancestry living in Texas

Temporarily Poor – term used to describe those individuals whose incomes have been below the poverty level for less than two years during a ten-year period; also known as marginally poor

Temporary Assistance for Needy Families (TANF) – basic welfare program replacing Aid to Families with Dependent Children (AFDC)

Tenayuca, Emma – a member of the American Communist Party, led a strike of women pecan shellers against the Judson Candy Company in San Antonio in 1938

Terrell Election Law – state law establishing the primary election as the process for political parties to select candidates for general elections

Texas Air Control Board (TACB) – state agency responsible for enforcement of state and federal air and anti-pollution laws

Texas Clean Air Act – state legislation empowering the Texas Air Control Board to issue permits for the release of contaminants into the atmosphere; established implementation for the federal Clean Air Act

Texas Commission on Environmental Quality (TCEQ) – formally the Texas Natural Resource Conservation Commission

Texas Department of Agriculture (TDA) – state agency overseeing the use of pesticides and herbicides present in water systems due to runoffs from rain and irrigation systems

Texas Department of Health (TDH) – state agency responsible for the management of municipal solid and radioactive waste and all public drinking water supplies and systems

Texas Department of Transportation (TexDoT) – state agency responsible for the construction, repair, and maintenance of the state's roads and highways

Texas Education Agency (TEA) – established in 1949 to oversee all public school districts in Texas

Texas Election Code – created by Texas Legislature, the primary source of election laws

Texas Ethics Commission (TEC) – oversees the registration of lobbyists and monitors the activities of both interest groups and lobbyists

Texas Fair Defense Act – provides state funds for indigent legal defense

Texas Good Roads Association – founded in 1911, the primary organization promoting the state highway system

Texas Higher Education Coordinating Board (THECB) – oversees the operation of the state's two- and four-year colleges and universities

Texas Parks and Wildlife Department (P&WD) – state agency charged with implementing all state laws concerning game, fish, oysters and marine life; manages the state's recreational and historical sites

Texas Railroad Commission – created by James Hogg to oversee shipping rates and railroad practices; currently oversees oil production and leasing rights

Texas v White (1869) – United States Supreme Court declared state secession unconstitutional

The Establishment – a loosely knit plutocracy comprised mostly of Anglo businessmen, oilmen, bankers and lawyers

The Texas Two-Step – the process used by the Texas Democratic Party to determine the delegates pledged to the party's presidential candidate for the national party convention

The Village of Skokie v the National Socialist Party (1978) – United States Supreme Court ruled that the denial to issue a parade permit for the National Socialist Party (American Nazi Party) was unconstitutional since the presumption of violence is not a valid reason to deny the group to march

Third Party – a temporary political party that often arises during a presidential election year to affect the fortunes of the two major parties

Thornburg v Gingles (1986) – United States Supreme Court ruled that redistricting plans have to maximize minority representation in both national and state legislative redistricting efforts

Threatened Species – one likely to become endangered in the foreseeable future

Tidelands – offshore oil deposits located in the Gulf of Mexico belonging to Texas

Tinker v Des Moines School District (1969) – United States Supreme Court ruling declaring the wearing of black arm bands in high school classes as a silent protest against the Vietnam War was a constitutionally protected right

Tort Law – the law of civil wrongs

Toxic Substances Control Act – federal legislation requiring the EPA to establish testing procedures for new chemical substances before they are sold; empowers the EPA to ban harmful substances and the sale of toxic polychlorinated biphenyls (PCB) not contained in enclosed systems

Transportation, Department of – federal government cabinet office charged with overseeing all transportation needs for the nation

Transportation Equity Act for the 21st Century (1988) – federal legislation allocating $216 billion for the repair of existing and construction of new federal highway systems

Treaty of Guadalupe Hidalgo – signed on February 2, 1848, ended the war with Mexico; officially recognized the independence of Texas and acknowledged the Rio Grande as the international boundary between the United States and Mexico

Treaty of Velasco – initial treaty with Mexico ending the Texas Revolution; called for Mexico to give official recognition of a free Texas and guarantee the withdrawal of all Mexican troops to the South of the Rio Grande

True Bill – a judgment by a grand jury to send a case to trial

Trustee View of Representation – concept that lawmakers are empowered to vote according to what they consider to be in the best interests of the people they represent

Twin Sisters – the name given to the two major artillery pieces carried by Sam Houston at the Battle of San Jacinto

Uncontested Candidate – a candidate running without an opponent

Underclass – a term used to describe the working and non-working poor in the United States

Underground Railroad – a trail of safe houses and havens run by the anti-slavery advocates to help slaves escape the southern slave system

Undeserving Poor – a term used to describe those individuals who have failed to avail themselves of the opportunities to improve their financial situation and have thus created their own impoverishment

Unemployment Insurance – program established through the Social Security Act of 1935 to provide financial assistance to unemployed workers

Unfunded Mandate – one level of government requiring another to offer without compensation a program as a matter of law or as a prerequisite to partial or full funding for either the program in question or other programs

Unincorporated Areas – rural and suburban areas outside of the confines of municipal government

Unitary System – governing system in which principal power within the political system lies at the level of a national or central government with the lower-level units acting as implementors of national directives

United Farm Workers Union – organization founded by César Chávez in the mid-1960s for the improvement of working conditions for migrant farm workers

United States v Lopez ((1995) – United States Supreme Court ruling declaring a ban on the possession of handguns near public schools unconstitutional

United States v O'Brien (1968) – United States Supreme Court upheld a lower court's conviction of a person's actions of burning draft cards during a protest against the Vietnam War

Urban Mass Transportation Act (1964) – federal legislation providing funding for the construction and operation of mass transit systems in metropolitan areas

Urban Mass Transportation Act (1974) – federal legislation committing $2.2 billion per year in federal funds for mass transit development

User Fees – specific sums that consumers of a government service pay to receive that service

Vara – the Spanish unit of land consisting of three geometrical feet. A straight line of five thousand varas constituted one league

Vertical Federalism – distribution of power flowing from the national government to the states and from the states to the national government

Veto – the governor's action of disapproving a potential law passed by both legislative houses

Viceroy – the governor of a Spanish colonial possession in the New World

Voir dire – French for speaking the truth

Voting Rights Act (1965) – required all redistricting plans to receive a pre-clearance from the United States Justice Department; overturned by the United States Supreme Court

Voucher System – a government-sponsored program that issues redeemable coupons to eligible citizens to purchase services on the open market; used by state governments to allow parents to send their children to the schools of their choice

Wallace v Jaffree (1985) – the United States Supreme Court ruled that a 1981 Alabama law mandating a moment of silence or prayer in the public schools violated the First Amendment to the United States Constitution

War on Poverty Program – the collective term for President Lyndon Johnson's package of anti-poverty initiatives

Waste – sewage, industrial waste, municipal waste, recreational waste, agricultural waste or other waste

Water or **Water-in-the-State** – groundwater, percolating or otherwise, lakes, bays, ponds, impounding reservoirs, springs, rivers, streams, creeks, estuaries, wetlands, marshes, inlets, canals, the Gulf of Mexico, inside the territorial limits of the state, and all other bodies of surface water, natural or artificial, inland or coastal, fresh or salt, navigable or non-navigable, and including the beds and banks of all watercourses and bodies of surface water, that are wholly or partially inside or bordering the state or inside the jurisdiction of the state.

Water Pollution – as defined by the Texas Water Code – the alternation of the physical, thermal, chemical, or biological quality of, or the contamination of, any water in the state that renders the water harmful, detrimental, or injurious to humans, animal life, vegetation, or property to public health, safety or welfare, or impairs the usefulness or the public enjoyment of the water for any lawful or reasonable purpose

Water Pollution Control Act (1972) – federal legislation requiring permits to discharge or dump effluents into waterways; established the National Pollution Discharge Elimination System

Weak Mayor Council Format – city governing structure whereby the mayor has veto authority that can be overridden by council and has limited power over council actions

Wesberry v Sanders (1964) – the United States Supreme Court ruled that United States congressional districts must be as close as possible equal in population; introduced the concept of one-man, one vote

Wetlands – areas that are inundated or saturated by surface or groundwater at a frequency and duration sufficient to support, and that under normal circumstances do support, a prevalence of vegetation typically adapted for life in saturated soil conditions

White Fear – the feeling of becoming a member of a new minority as the existing minority becomes a majority within the social community

White Flight – relocation of Anglo population groups from racially mixed inner city neighborhoods to predominately all Anglo suburban areas

Wilderness – an area where the earth and its community of life are untrammeled by man, where man himself is a visitor who does not remain

Wilderness Act (1964) – federal legislation designating federally-owned lands as "protected" wilderness areas

Winner-Take-All – in the presidential primaries, the individual that wins the most votes gains the entire slate of delegates from that state

Working Poor – generally undereducated individuals either employed full time or part-time at minimum or below minimum wage salary levels

Works Project Administration (WPA) – federal work program created as part of the New Deal during the Great Depression

Writ of Certiorari – an order issued by a higher court to a lower court to send up the record of a case for review

Writ of Habeas Corpus – a direct order to the person detaining another commanding him/her to produce the body of the person or persons detained before a judge or magistrate

Yellow-Dog Democrat – the generational obligation to vote straight party Democrat, even if a yellow dog was on the ballot

Zero-Based Budgeting (ZBB) – based on the concept that the allocation of funds for any expenditures begins anew with each budgetary cycle

Zoning – the division of a city into districts and the regulation of the types of buildings and activities permitted within districts

Index